DIAGNOSTIC AND STATISTICAL MANUAL OF MENTAL DISORDERS

(THIRD EDITION - REVISED)

DSM-III-R

Published by the
American Psychiatric Association
Washington, DC
1987

The correct citation for this book is:
American Psychiatric Association: Diagnostic and Statistical Manual of Mental Disorders, Third Edition, Revised. Washington, DC, American Psychiatric Association, 1987.

Library of Congress Cataloging-in-Publication Data

Diagnostic and statistical manual of mental disorders.

   Prepared by the Work Group to Revise DSM-III of the American Psychiatric Association.
   Includes index.
   1. Mental illness—Classification. 2. Mental illness—Diagnosis. I. American Psychiatric Association. II. American Psychiatric Association. Work Group to Revise DSM-III.
[DNLM: 1. Mental Disorders—classification. 2. Psychiatry—nomenclature. WM 15 D536]
RC455.2.C4D54   1987   616.89'075   87-1458
ISBN 0-89042-018-1
ISBN 0-89042-019-X (soft)

First printing, 75,000, May 1987
Second printing, 80,000, June 1987
Third printing, 75,000, November 1987
Fourth printing, 50,000, May 1988
Fifth printing, 80,000, September 1988
Sixth printing, 50,000, April 1989
Seventh printing, 50,000, March 1990
Eighth printing, 50,000, November 1990

Contents

		Page
Introduction		xv
Cautionary Statement		xxix
CHAPTER 1	**DSM-III-R Classification: Axes I and II Categories and Codes**	1
CHAPTER 2	**Use of This Manual**	13
CHAPTER 3	**The Diagnostic Categories: Text and Criteria**	
	Disorders Usually First Evident in Infancy, Childhood, or Adolescence	27
	Organic Mental Syndromes and Disorders	97
	Psychoactive Substance Use Disorders	165
	Schizophrenia	187
	Delusional Disorder	199
	Psychotic Disorders Not Elsewhere Classified	205
	Mood Disorders	213
	Anxiety Disorders	235
	Somatoform Disorders	255
	Dissociative Disorders	269
	Sexual Disorders	279
	Sleep Disorders	297
	Factitious Disorders	315
	Impulse Control Disorders Not Elsewhere Classified	321
	Adjustment Disorder	329
	Psychological Factors Affecting Physical Condition	333
	Personality Disorders	335
	V Codes for Conditions Not Attributable to a Mental Disorder That are a Focus of Attention or Treatment	359
	Additional Codes	363
Appendix A	Proposed Diagnostic Categories Needing Further Study	365
Appendix B	Decision Trees for Differential Diagnosis	375
Appendix C	Glossary of Technical Terms	389
Appendix D	Annotated Comparative Listing of DSM-III and DSM-III-R	407
Appendix E	Historical Review, ICD-9 Glossary and Classification, and ICD-9-CM Classification	431
Appendix F	DSM-III-R Field Trial Participants	491
Appendix G	Alphabetic Listing of DSM-III-R Diagnoses and Codes	497
Appendix H	Numeric Listing of DSM-III-R Diagnoses and Codes	507
Symptom Index:	Index of Selected Symptoms Included in the Diagnostic Criteria	517
Diagnostic Index:	Index of DSM-III-R Diagnoses and Selected Diagnostic Terms	553

ACKNOWLEDGMENTS

This manual was prepared with the help of many people. Special thanks are given to the members of the Work Group to Revise DSM-III, the various Advisory Committees and the members of the Ad Hoc Committee to Review DSM-III of the Board of Trustees and Assembly of District Branches. In addition, the work of the participants in the field trials of certain DSM-III-R categories, who are listed in Appendix F, is gratefully appreciated.

A final word of thanks must be given to the many other participants in this effort who have not received formal recognition, but who provided critiques and suggestions that were helpful in the preparation of DSM-III-R.

Robert L. Spitzer, M.D.
Chair, Work Group to
Revise DSM-III

Janet B. W. Williams, D.S.W.
Text Editor

Subcommittee on Specific Developmental Disorders

Lorian Baker, Ph.D.
Michael Bender, Ed.D.
Dennis Cantwell, M.D.
Donald Cohen, M.D.
Anthony Costello, M.D.

James D. McKinney, Ph.D.
David Shaffer, M.D.
Margaret J. Shepherd, Ed.D.
Robert L. Spitzer, M.D.
Janet B. W. Williams, D.S.W.

Subcommittee on Disruptive Behavior Disorders

Thomas Achenbach, Ph.D.
Russell Barkley, Ph.D.
David J. Berndt, Ph.D.
Dennis Cantwell, M.D.
William Chambers, M.D.
Anthony Costello, M.D.
Felton Earls, M.D.
Harriet Hollander, Ph.D.
Rachel G. Klein, Ph.D.
Maria Kovacs, Ph.D.
Jan Loney, Ph.D.
William Mitchell, M.D., Ph.D.
Daniel Offer, M.D.

Eric Ostrov, Ph.D., J.D.
William E. Pelham, Jr., Ph.D.
Joaquim Puig-Antich, M.D.
Herbert C. Quay, Ph.D.
Judith L. Rapoport, M.D.
Lee Robins, Ph.D.
Bennett Shaywitz, M.D.
Robert L. Spitzer, M.D.
James Swanson, Ph.D.
A. Hussain Tuma, Ph.D.
Gabrielle Weiss, M.D.
Paul Wender, M.D.
Janet B. W. Williams, D.S.W.

Subcommittee on Eating Disorders

Katherine Halmi, M.D.
David B. Herzog, M.D.
James I. Hudson, M.D.
Harrison G. Pope, Jr., M.D.

Robert L. Spitzer, M.D.
B. Timothy Walsh, M.D.
Janet B. W. Williams, D.S.W.

Subcommittee on Gender Identity Disorders

Anke Ehrhardt, Ph.D.
David McWhirter, M.D.
Heino Meyer-Bahlburg, Dr.rer.nat.
John Money, Ph.D.

Ethel Person, M.D.
Robert L. Spitzer, M.D.
Janet B. W. Williams, D.S.W.
Kenneth J. Zucker, Ph.D.

Subcommittee on Tic Disorders

Ruth Bruun, M.D.
Eric Caine, M.D.
Dennis Cantwell, M.D.
Donald Cohen, M.D.
David E. Comings, M.D.
Gerald Golden, M.D.

James Leckman, M.D.
Arthur K. Shapiro, M.D.
Elaine Shapiro, Ph.D.
Robert L. Spitzer, M.D.
Janet B. W. Williams, D.S.W.

Subcommittee on Reactive Attachment Disorder of Infancy or Early Childhood

Robert N. Emde, M.D.
Stanley Greenspan, M.D.
Robert N. Harmon, M.D.
Reginald Lourie, M.D.
Klaus Minde, M.D.
Robert A. Nover, M.D.

Joy Osofsky, Ph.D.
Sally Provence, M.D.
Chaya H. Roth, Ph.D.
Albert Solnit, M.D.
Robert L. Spitzer, M.D.
Janet B. W. Williams, D.S.W.

ORGANIC MENTAL SYNDROMES AND DISORDERS (NON-SUBSTANCE-INDUCED), SOMATOFORM DISORDERS, AND PSYCHOLOGICAL FACTORS AFFECTING PHYSICAL CONDITION

Arthur Barsky, M.D.
Frank Benson, M.D.
Jack Burke, Jr., M.D., M.P.H.
Barbara J. Burns, Ph.D.
C. Robert Cloninger, M.D.
Jeffrey Houpt, M.D.
Stephen Jencks, M.D.
Robert Kellner, M.D.
Zbigniew J. Lipowski, M.D.
Richard Mayeux, M.D.

Nancy E. Miller, Ph.D.
Roger Peele, M.D.
Michael Popkin, M.D.
Peter Rabins, M.D.
Darrel Regier, M.D.
Benjamin Seltzer, M.D.
Steven Sharfstein, M.D.
Robert L. Spitzer, M.D.
Janet B. W. Williams, D.S.W.

PSYCHOACTIVE SUBSTANCE USE DISORDERS AND SUBSTANCE-INDUCED ORGANIC MENTAL DISORDERS

Henry David Abraham, M.D.
Thomas Babor, Ph.D., M.P.H.
Sheila Blume, M.D.
Thomas J. Crowley, M.D.
Jack Durrell, M.D.
Richard Frances, M.D.
Frank Gawin, M.D.
Donald W. Goodwin, M.D.
John E. Helzer, M.D.
John R. Hughes, M.D.
Jerome H. Jaffe, M.D.
David C. Lewis, M.D.
Thomas McLellan, Ph.D.

Robert Niven, M.D.
Charles O'Brien, M.D., Ph.D.
Eugene Oetting, Ph.D.
William Pollin, M.D.
Lee Robins, Ph.D.
Bruce Rounsaville, M.D.
Sidney H. Schnoll, M.D.
Edward Senay, M.D.
David E. Smith, M.D.
Robert L. Spitzer, M.D.
George Vaillant, M.D.
Arnold M. Washton, Ph.D.
Janet B. W. Williams, D.S.W.

PSYCHOTIC DISORDERS

Nancy C. Andreasen, M.D., Ph.D.
Jack D. Burke, Jr., M.D., M.P.H.
William T. Carpenter, Jr., M.D.
C. Robert Cloninger, M.D.
Samuel J. Keith, M.D.
Kenneth S. Kendler, M.D.
Herbert Y. Meltzer, M.D.

Alistair Munro, M.D.
Nina R. Schooler, Ph.D.
Andrew E. Skodol, M.D.
Robert L. Spitzer, M.D.
Janet B. W. Williams, D.S.W.
Lyman C. Wynne, M.D., Ph.D.

MOOD DISORDERS

Hagop Akiskal, M.D.
Nancy C. Andreasen, M.D., Ph.D.
Paula J. Clayton, M.D.
William Coryell, M.D.
Michael B. First, M.D.
Allen J. Frances, M.D.
Elliot Gershon, M.D.
Frederick K. Goodwin, M.D.
John F. Greden, M.D.
Robert M. A. Hirschfeld, M.D.
Martin Keller, M.D.
Kenneth S. Kendler, M.D.
Donald F. Klein, M.D.
Rachel G. Klein, Ph.D.
Gerald L. Klerman, M.D.

James H. Kocsis, M.D.
Maria Kovacs, Ph.D.
David Kupfer, M.D.
J. Craig Nelson, M.D.
Joaquim Puig-Antich, M.D.
Frederic Quitkin, M.D.
Richard Ries, M.D.
Norman Rosenthal, M.D.
A. John Rush, M.D.
Robert L. Spitzer, M.D.
Jonathan W. Stewart, M.D.
Myrna Weissman, Ph.D.
Janet B. W. Williams, D.S.W.
Mark Zimmerman

ANXIETY DISORDERS

James Ballenger, M.D.
Mitchell Balter, Ph.D.
David H. Barlow, Ph.D.
Jeffrey H. Boyd, M.D., M.P.H.
George Curtis, M.D.
Peter A. Di Nardo, Ph.D.
Edna B. Foa, Ph.D.
Allen J. Frances, M.D.
Abby Fyer, M.D.
Thomas Insel, M.D.
Donald F. Klein, M.D.
Gerald L. Klerman, M.D.
Michael Liebowitz, M.D.
Isaac Marks, M.D.
Jack Maser, Ph.D.
William Matuzas, M.D.

Russell Noyes, M.D.
John C. Pecknold, M.D.
Stanley J. Rachman, Ph.D.
Judith L. Rapoport, M.D.
Darrel A. Regier, M.D., M.P.H.
Arthur Rifkin, M.D.
Arthur K. Shapiro, M.D.
Elaine Shapiro, Ph.D.
Katherine Shear, M.D.
David Sheehan, M.D.
Robert L. Spitzer, M.D.
Richard P. Swinson, M.D.
Myrna Weissman, Ph.D.
Janet B. W. Williams, D.S.W.
Charlotte Zitrin, M.D.

Subcommittee on Post-Traumatic Stress Disorder

Margaret Allison, M.A.
Arthur Arnold, M.D.
Roland M. Atkinson, M.D.
Arthur S. Blank, Jr., M.D.
Ghislaine Boulanger, Ph.D.
Jeffrey Boyd, M.D., M.P.H.
Elizabeth A. Brett, Ph.D.
Allan Burstein, M.D.
George C. Curtis, M.D.
Nathan R. Denny, Ph.D.
Charles Figley, Ph.D.
Patricia Gongla, Ph.D.
Bonnie L. Green, Ph.D.
Carol Hartman, D.N.Sc.
Charles Kadushin, Ph.D.

Terence M. Keane, Ph.D.
Gerald L. Klerman, M.D.
Lawrence C. Kolb, M.D.
Richard A. Kulka, Ph.D.
Charles R. Marmar, M.D.
Frank Ochberg, M.D.
Walter E. Penk, Ph.D.
Robert Pynoos, M.D.
Lee Robins, Ph.D.
William E. Schlenger, Ph.D.
John R. Smith, M.A.
Robert L. Spitzer, M.D.
Lenore C. Terr, M.D.
Janet B. W. Williams, D.S.W.
John Wilson, Ph.D.

DISSOCIATIVE DISORDERS

Bennett G. Braun, M.D., M.S.
Philip Coons, M.D.
Richard P. Kluft, M.D.
Frank Putnam, M.D.

Robert L. Spitzer, M.D.
Marlene Steinberg, M.D.
Janet B. W. Williams, D.S.W.

SEXUAL DISORDERS

Subcommittee on Paraphilias

Gene Abel, M.D.
David Barlow, Ph.D.
Judith Becker, Ph.D.
Fred Berlin, M.D.
Park Elliott Dietz, M.D., Ph.D.

Raymond A. Knight, Ph.D.
Vernon Quinsey, Ph.D.
Robert L. Spitzer, M.D.
Janet B. W. Williams, D.S.W.

Subcommittee on Sexual Dysfunctions

Ellen Frank, Ph.D.
Helen Kaplan, M.D.
Sandra Leiblum, Ph.D.
Harold Lief, M.D.
Joseph LoPiccolo, Ph.D.

David McWhirter, M.D.
R. Taylor Segraves, M.D.
Robert L. Spitzer, M.D.
Janet B. W. Williams, D.S.W.

SLEEP DISORDERS

Peter Hauri, Ph.D.
Anthony Kales, M.D.
David Kupfer, M.D.
Quentin Regestein, M.D.
Charles Reynolds, M.D.

Howard Roffwarg, M.D.
Constantin Soldatos, M.D.
Robert L. Spitzer, M.D.
Michael Thorpy, M.D.
Janet B. W. Williams, D.S.W.

FACTITIOUS DISORDERS

Bernard Gert, Ph.D.
Steven Hyler, M.D.

Robert L. Spitzer, M.D.
Janet B. W. Williams, D.S.W.

IMPULSE CONTROL DISORDERS NOT ELSEWHERE CLASSIFIED

Robert Custer, M.D.
Park Elliott Dietz, M.D., Ph.D.
Jeffrey Geller, M.D.
Henry Lesieur, Ph.D.

John R. Lion, M.D.
Michael Popkin, M.D.
Robert L. Spitzer, M.D.
Janet B. W. Williams, D.S.W.

PERSONALITY DISORDERS

Martin Blum, M.D.
Paul Chodoff, M.D.
Karyl G. Cole, M.D.
Arnold M. Cooper, M.D.
Michael B. First, M.D.
Allen J. Frances, M.D.
John Gunderson, M.D.
Robert M. A. Hirschfeld, M.D.
Steven Hyler, M.D.
Karen John
Jeffrey Jonas, M.D.
Frederic Kass, M.D.
Kenneth Kendler, M.D.
Donald F. Klein, M.D.
Gerald L. Klerman, M.D.
W. John Livesley, M.D.
Armand Loranger, Ph.D.
Roger MacKinnon, M.D.
Jack Maser, Ph.D.

John Oldham, M.D.
J. Christopher Perry, M.D.
Ethel Person, M.D.
Bruce Pfohl, M.D.
Paul Pilkonis, Ph.D.
Harrison G. Pope, Jr., M.D.
James Reich, M.D.
Ronald Rieder, M.D.
Lee Robins, Ph.D.
Tracie Shea, Ph.D.
Larry Siever, M.D.
Richard C. Simons, M.D.
Andrew E. Skodol, M.D.
Robert L. Spitzer, M.D.
A. Hussain Tuma, Ph.D.
George Vaillant, M.D.
Thomas Widiger, Ph.D.
Janet B. W. Williams, D.S.W.
Jeffrey Young, Ph.D.

LATE LUTEAL PHASE DYSPHORIC DISORDER

Judith Abplanalp, Ph.D.
Susan Blumenthal, M.D.
Jean Endicott, Ph.D.
Ira Glick, M.D.
Jean Hamilton, M.D.
Wilma Harrison, M.D.
Roger Haskett, M.D.

Howard J. Osofsky, M.D., Ph.D.
Barbara Parry, M.D.
Harrison G. Pope, Jr., M.D.
David Rubinow, M.D.
Sally Severino, M.D.
Robert L. Spitzer, M.D.
Janet B. W. Williams, D.S.W.

OTHER ADVISORY COMMITTEES

DEFENSE MECHANISMS

David Barlow, Ph.D.
Michael Bond, M.D.
Allen J. Frances, M.D.
William A. Frosch, M.D.
J. Christopher Perry, M.D.

Andrew E. Skodol, M.D.
Robert L. Spitzer, M.D.
George Vaillant, M.D.
Janet B. W. Williams, D.S.W.
Jeffrey Young, Ph.D.

MULTIAXIAL SYSTEM

Dennis Cantwell, M.D.
Donald Cohen, M.D.
Richard Finn, M.D.
Richard Gordon, M.D.
Louis Linn, M.D.
Juan Mezzich, M.D., Ph.D.
Roger Peele, M.D.
Judith L. Rapoport, M.D.

Theodore Shapiro, M.D.
Steven Sharfstein, M.D.
Andrew E. Skodol, M.D.
Robert L. Spitzer, M.D.
John Strauss, M.D.
Janet B. W. Williams, D.S.W.
Lyman C. Wynne, M.D., Ph.D.

CROSS-CULTURAL ISSUES

Arthur J. Barsky, M.D.
C. Robert Cloninger, M.D.
Arthur Kleinman, M.D.
Raymond H. Prince, M.D.

Pedro Ruiz, M.D.
Robert L. Spitzer, M.D.
Janet B. W. Williams, D.S.W.

OTHER CONSULTANTS

Robert B. Aranow, M.D.
Mark Davies, M.P.H.
Martha Gay, M.D.

Miriam Gibbon, M.S.W.
Cynthia Last, Ph.D.
Ronald M. Winchel, M.D.

SUPPORT STAFF

Betty Appelbaum
Harriet Ayers
Thomas Borsay
Sandy Ferris, APA Liaison

Justine Gottlieb
Kate Josephson
Lenore Thomson

PRODUCTION

Richard E. Farkas

INTRODUCTION

Introduction

Robert L. Spitzer, M.D.
Chair, Work Group to Revise DSM-III

Janet B.W. Williams, D.S.W.
Text Editor

This is the revision of the third edition of the American Psychiatric Association's *Diagnostic and Statistical Manual of Mental Disorders*, better known as DSM-III-R. The last sentence of the Introduction to DSM-III, published in 1980, stated ". . . DSM-III is only one still frame in the ongoing process of attempting to better understand mental disorders." DSM-III-R represents another still frame.

In 1983 the American Psychiatric Association decided, for several reasons, to start work on revising DSM-III. For one, data were emerging from new studies that were inconsistent with some of the diagnostic criteria. In addition, despite extensive field testing of the DSM-III diagnostic criteria before their official adoption, experience with them since their publication had revealed, as expected, many instances in which the criteria were not entirely clear, were inconsistent across categories, or were even contradictory. Therefore, all of the diagnostic criteria, plus the systematic descriptions of the various disorders, needed to be reviewed for consistency, clarity, and conceptual accuracy, and revised when necessary.

Also in 1983, the American Psychiatric Association was asked to contribute to the development of the mental disorders chapter of the tenth revision of the International Classification of Diseases (ICD-10), which is expected to go into effect around 1992. In order for the American Psychiatric Association to provide its best recommendations, it was necessary to assemble committees of experts to review DSM-III and to make suggestions for updating it.

The publication of DSM-III coincided with that of ICD-9; the publication of DSM-IV was planned to coincide with that of ICD-10. Although by 1983 there had been only a few years of experience with DSM-III, it was clear that, with the burgeoning literature in the field, revisions would be needed long before the anticipated publication of DSM-IV in the 1990s.

In this Introduction to DSM-III-R, we discuss the following:

The Impact of DSM-III, p. xviii
Historical Background of the DSMs, p. xviii

The Process of Revising DSM-III, p. xix
Basic Features of DSM-III-R, p. xxii
Cautions in the Use of DSM-III-R, p. xxvi
The Future, p. xxvii

THE IMPACT OF DSM-III

The impact of DSM-III has been remarkable. Soon after its publication, it became widely accepted in the United States as the common language of mental health clinicians and researchers for communicating about the disorders for which they have professional responsibility. Recent major textbooks of psychiatry and other textbooks that discuss psychopathology have either made extensive reference to DSM-III or largely adopted its terminology and concepts. In the seven years since the publication of DSM-III, over two thousand articles that directly address some aspect of it have appeared in the scientific literature. In some of these articles, the results of research studies using the DSM-III diagnostic criteria to select samples have been reported; in others, the reliability or validity of DSM-III-defined disorders has been critically examined.

DSM-III was intended primarily for use in the United States, but it has had considerable influence internationally. As a result, the entire manual, or the Quick Reference to the Diagnostic Criteria ("Mini-D"), has been translated into Chinese, Danish, Dutch, Finnish, French, German, Greek, Italian, Japanese, Norwegian, Portuguese, Spanish, and Swedish. Many of the basic features of DSM-III, such as the inclusion of specified diagnostic criteria, have been adopted for inclusion in the mental disorders chapter of ICD-10.

HISTORICAL BACKGROUND OF THE DSMs

DSM-I. The first edition of the American Psychiatric Association's *Diagnostic and Statistical Manual of Mental Disorders* appeared in 1952. This was the first official manual of mental disorders to contain a glossary of descriptions of the diagnostic categories. The use of the term *reaction* throughout the classification reflected the influence of Adolf Meyer's psychobiologic view that mental disorders represented reactions of the personality to psychological, social, and biological factors.

DSM-II. In the development of the second edition, a decision was made to base the classification on the mental disorders section of the eighth revision of the *International Classification of Diseases*, for which representatives of the American Psychiatric Association had provided consultation. Both DSM-II and ICD-8 went into effect in 1968. The DSM-II classification did not use the term *reaction*, and except for the use of the term *neuroses*, used diagnostic terms that, by and large, did not imply a particular theoretical framework for understanding the nonorganic mental disorders.

DSM-III. In 1974 the American Psychiatric Association appointed a Task Force on Nomenclature and Statistics to begin work on the development of DSM-III, recognizing that ICD-9 was scheduled to go into effect in January 1979. By the time this new Task Force was constituted, the mental disorders section of ICD-9, which included its own glossary, was nearly completed.

Although representatives of the American Psychiatric Association had worked closely with the World Health Organization on the development of ICD-9, there was concern that the ICD-9 classification and glossary would not be suitable for use in the

United States. Most importantly, many specific areas of the classification did not seem sufficiently detailed for clinical and research use. For example, the ICD-9 classification contains only one category for "frigidity and impotence"—despite the substantial work in the area of psychosexual dysfunctions that has identified several specific types with different clinical pictures and treatment implications. In addition, the glossary of ICD-9 was believed by many to be less than optimal in that it had not made use of such recent major methodologic developments as specified diagnostic criteria and a multiaxial approach to evaluation.

For these reasons, the Task Force was directed to prepare a new classification and glossary that would, as much as possible, reflect the most current state of knowledge regarding mental disorders, yet maintain compatibility with ICD-9. Successive drafts of DSM-III were prepared by fourteen advisory committees composed of professionals with special expertise in each substantive area. In addition, a group of consultants provided advice and information on a variety of special subjects.

ICD-9-CM. Because of dissatisfaction with ICD-9 expressed by organizations representing subspecialties of medicine (not including the American Psychiatric Association), a decision was made to modify the ICD-9 for use in the United States by expanding the four-digit ICD-9 codes to five-digit ICD-9-CM (for Clinical Modification) codes whenever greater specificity was required. This modification was prepared for the United States National Center for Health Statistics by the Council on Clinical Classifications. The American Psychiatric Association, in December 1976, was invited to submit recommendations for alternate names and additional categories based on subdivisions of already existing ICD-9 categories. This made it possible for the developing DSM-III classification and virtually all of its diagnostic terms to be included in the ICD-9-CM classification, which in January 1979 became the official system in this country for recording all "diseases, injuries, impairments, symptoms, and causes of death." The ICD-9-CM codes and diagnostic terms for mental disorders are included in Appendix E.

THE PROCESS OF REVISING DSM-III

Work Group to Revise DSM-III. In May 1983, the Board of Trustees of the American Psychiatric Association approved the appointment of a Work Group to Revise DSM-III. The members of the Work Group were selected to ensure a broad representation of clinical and research perspectives. In addition, they were chosen to ensure expertise in major areas of DSM-III, such as disorders of childhood and adolescence, mood disorders, psychotic disorders, anxiety disorders, personality disorders, and multiaxial evaluation. From the beginning, the Work Group functioned, as did the DSM-III Task Force, as a steering committee to oversee the ongoing work. All of its members shared a commitment to the attainment in DSM-III-R of the same goals that had guided the development of DSM-III:

(1) clinical usefulness for making treatment and management decisions in varied clinical settings;
(2) reliability of the diagnostic categories;
(3) acceptability to clinicians and researchers of varying theoretical orientations;
(4) usefulness for educating health professionals;
(5) maintenance of compatibility with ICD-9-CM codes;
(6) avoidance of new terminology and concepts that break with tradition except when clearly needed;

(7) attempting to reach consensus on the meaning of necessary diagnostic terms that have been used inconsistently, and avoidance of terms that have outlived their usefulness;

(8) consistency with data from research studies bearing on the validity of diagnostic categories;

(9) suitability for describing subjects in research studies;

(10) responsiveness, during the development of DSM-III-R, to critiques by clinicians and researchers.

The major task of the Work Group members was threefold: to serve on advisory committees on subjects in which they had special expertise, to develop a process that would ensure that all proposals for revisions would be systematically reviewed by the appropriate advisory committees, and to resolve certain controversies that could not be resolved within the advisory committees.

Advisory Committees. Twenty-six advisory committees were formed with over two hundred members selected on the basis of their expertise in particular areas. Proposals for substantive revisions in the DSM-III classification and criteria were made and reviewed at a series of advisory committee meetings, several of which were co-sponsored by the National Institute of Mental Health. These were usually followed by smaller meetings of a few members to develop proposals further. Frequently, decisions made by an advisory committee had to be reconsidered when the details of the proposal were worked out by these smaller groups; in some cases, the advisory committee was reconvened to discuss a particular issue further. Most advisory committee decisions were the result of a consensus that emerged among committee members. However, several controversies, particularly in the areas of childhood, psychotic, anxiety, and sleep disorders, could be resolved only by actually polling committee members.

Most of the proposals for revisions came from advisory committee members; some came from other professionals with a particular area of expertise. Most of the proposals were based on clinical experience with the DSM-III criteria, which revealed the need for fine-tuning the criteria to improve their sensitivity and specificity. For example, the DSM-III criteria for Panic Disorder did not permit giving the diagnosis (as the Anxiety Disorders Advisory Committee agreed they should) to people who had only a single panic attack followed by agoraphobic avoidance.

Many proposals for revisions were based on experience using the DSM-III and the proposed DSM-III-R criteria in structured diagnostic interviews. For example, in the process of constructing questions to which responses would allow a clinician to evaluate the DSM-III criteria for Personality Disorders, it was found that many of those criteria were imprecise and in need of further specification. Some proposals were based on reconsideration of a DSM-III decision. For instance, a proposal to revise the DSM-III definition of Paranoid Disorder was based on the realization that a broader definition would be more consistent with historical and clinical concepts and with research findings. Finally, some of the proposals came directly from research studies that had evaluated DSM-III criteria. For example, a proposal to eliminate the DSM-III requirement that the onset of Schizophrenia be before age 45 came from a review of several studies in which that distinction was found to lack validity.

The advisory committees had the difficult task of balancing the potential advantages and disadvantages of each proposal. This often involved seeking informed answers to the following questions:

1. Was the proposal supported by data from empirical studies?

2. Was there a consensus among experts that the revision would significantly increase the utility (validity) of the category for making treatment and management decisions?

3. Would the presumed advantages of the proposal sufficiently offset the disadvantages to researchers of having to switch to new criteria when studies that had not yet been completed were still using the DSM-III criteria?

4. Was the proposed revision consistent with general approaches taken in the rest of the classification, for example, in restricting the use of diagnostic hierarchies to a limited number of situations (see discussion of diagnostic hierarchies below)?

5. Would the proposal interfere with compatibility between DSM-III-R and ICD-9-CM codes?

6. Could the proposal be operationalized in specified diagnostic criteria with the expectation of at least a fair degree of diagnostic reliability?

7. Did the proposal imply an underlying theory about the mechanism of the disorder that was not supported by data?

8. Was the proposal premature for consideration in DSM-III-R, and more properly within the scope of DSM-IV, e.g., a proposal for a new diagnostic class of disorders associated with psychosocial stress?

If the proposal involved dropping a category from the DSM-III classification (e.g., Ego-dystonic Homosexuality) or adding a new diagnosis to the classification (e.g., Late Luteal Phase Dysphoric Disorder), there were two additional considerations:

1. Does the proposed category meet the requirements of the DSM-III definition of mental disorder?

2. How compelling is the research or clinical need for the category?

In attempting to evaluate proposals for revisions in the classification and criteria, or for adding new categories, the greatest weight was given to the presence of empirical support from well-conducted research studies, though, for most proposals, data from empirical studies were lacking. Therefore, primary importance was usually given to some other consideration, such as: clinical experience; a judgment as to whether the proposal was likely to increase the reliability and validity of the diagnosis under consideration; or, in the case of a new diagnosis under consideration, the extent of the research support for the category as contrasted to its perceived potential for abuse.

It should be noted that in all of the discussions regarding the revision of the over two hundred DSM-III categories, the possible impact of a proposal on reimbursement for treatment was mentioned only with regard to three of the categories. Furthermore, that issue did not play a major role in the relevant decisions.

DSM-III-R in Development. During the process of developing DSM-III-R, two successive drafts (10/5/85 and 8/1/86) of the proposed revised diagnostic criteria were made available to interested professionals and widely distributed for critical review. Feedback from reviewers of these drafts was extremely helpful in identifying problems that needed further attention.

Field Trials of Proposed DSM-III-R Criteria. Three national field trials were conducted to help in the development of diagnostic criteria for the following diagnoses: Disruptive Behavior Disorders (Attention-deficit Hyperactivity Disorder, Oppositional Defiant Disorder, and Conduct Disorder); Pervasive Developmental Disorders (Autistic Disorder); and Generalized Anxiety Disorder and Agoraphobia without History of Panic Disorder. A brief description of each field trial and a list of its participants are given in

Appendix F. In addition, the diagnostic criteria for Self-defeating Personality Disorder were studied by examining the data from an anonymous questionnaire that was distributed to several thousand members of the American Psychiatric Association who had indicated a special interest in Personality Disorders.

Joint Ad Hoc Committee of the Board of Trustees and Assembly of District Branches to Review DSM-III-R. In September 1985, the Board of Trustees appointed a Joint Ad Hoc Committee with members from both the Board of Trustees and the Assembly of District Branches to review the progress being made by the Work Group, paying special attention to proposed revisions that were particularly controversial.

The Joint Ad Hoc Committee held several meetings with members of the Work Group in an effort to resolve controversies that surrounded the revision and its process. These two groups also met with representatives of the American Psychological Association and other people who had expressed specific concerns about the revision, in order to better understand objections that had been raised to advisory committee proposals and, if possible, to modify these proposals to make them more acceptable to all concerned. In addition, the Committee responded to various critiques of drafts of DSM-III-R, developed by members of the Assembly of District Branches and by several APA components, on a number of controversial and technical issues.

Final Approval. In November 1986, the Assembly of District Branches approved the final draft of DSM-III-R. In December it was approved by the Board of Trustees.

BASIC FEATURES OF DSM-III-R

Mental Disorder. Although this manual provides a classification of mental disorders, no definition adequately specifies precise boundaries for the concept "mental disorder" (this is also true for such concepts as physical disorder and mental and physical health). Nevertheless, it is useful to present a definition of mental disorder that has influenced the decision to include certain conditions in DSM-III and DSM-III-R as mental disorders and to exclude others.

In DSM-III-R each of the mental disorders is conceptualized as a clinically significant behavioral or psychological syndrome or pattern that occurs in a person and that is associated with present distress (a painful symptom) or disability (impairment in one or more important areas of functioning) or with a significantly increased risk of suffering death, pain, disability, or an important loss of freedom. In addition, this syndrome or pattern must not be merely an expectable response to a particular event, e.g., the death of a loved one. Whatever its original cause, it must currently be considered a manifestation of a behavioral, psychological, or biological dysfunction in the person. Neither deviant behavior, e.g., political, religious, or sexual, nor conflicts that are primarily between the individual and society are mental disorders unless the deviance or conflict is a symptom of a dysfunction in the person, as described above.

There is no assumption that each mental disorder is a discrete entity with sharp boundaries (discontinuity) between it and other mental disorders, or between it and no mental disorder. For example, there has been a continuing controversy concerning whether severe depressive disorder and mild depressive disorder differ from each other qualitatively (discontinuity between diagnostic entities) or quantitatively (a difference on a severity continuum). The inclusion of Major Depression and Dysthymia as separate categories in DSM-III-R is justified by the clinical usefulness of the distinction. This does not imply a resolution of the controversy concerning whether these conditions are in fact quantitatively or qualitatively different.

A common misconception is that a classification of mental disorders classifies people, when actually what are being classified are disorders that people have. For this reason, the text of DSM-III-R (as did the text of DSM-III) avoids the use of such expressions as "a schizophrenic" or "an alcoholic," and instead uses the more accurate, but admittedly more cumbersome, "a person with Schizophrenia" or "a person with Alcohol Dependence."

Another misconception is that all people described as having the same mental disorder are alike in all important ways. Although all the people described as having the same mental disorder have at least the defining features of the disorder, they may well differ in other important respects that may affect clinical management and outcome.

Conditions Not Attributable to a Mental Disorder (V Codes). A behavioral or psychological problem may appropriately be a focus of professional attention or treatment even though it is not attributable to a mental disorder. A limited listing of codes, taken from the V codes section of ICD-9-CM, is provided for noting such problems.

Descriptive Approach. For some of the mental disorders, the etiology or pathophysiologic processes are known. For example, in the Organic Mental Disorders, organic factors necessary for the development and maintenance of the disorders have been identified or are presumed. Another example is Adjustment Disorder, in which the disturbance, by definition, is a reaction to psychosocial stress.

For most of the DSM-III-R disorders, however, the etiology is unknown. Many theories have been advanced and buttressed by evidence—not always convincing—attempting to explain how these disorders come about. The approach taken in DSM-III-R is atheoretical with regard to etiology or pathophysiologic process, except with regard to disorders for which this is well established and therefore included in the definition of the disorder. Undoubtedly, over time, some of the disorders of unknown etiology will be found to have specific biological etiologies; others, to have specific psychological causes; and still others, to result mainly from an interplay of psychological, social, and biological factors.

The major justification for the generally atheoretical approach taken in DSM-III and DSM-III-R with regard to etiology is that the inclusion of etiologic theories would be an obstacle to use of the manual by clinicians of varying theoretical orientations, since it would not be possible to present all reasonable etiologic theories for each disorder. For example, Phobic Disorders are believed by many to represent a displacement of anxiety resulting from the breakdown of defense mechanisms that keep internal conflicts out of consciousness. Others explain phobias on the basis of learned avoidance responses to conditioned anxiety. Still others believe that certain phobias result from a dysregulation of basic biological systems mediating separation anxiety. In any case, clinicians and researchers can agree on the identification of mental disorders on the basis of their clinical manifestations without agreeing on how the disturbances come about.

DSM-III-R can be said to be "descriptive" in that the definitions of the disorders are generally limited to descriptions of the clinical features of the disorders. The characteristic features consist of easily identifiable behavioral signs or symptoms, such as disorientation, mood disturbance, or psychomotor agitation, which require a minimal amount of inference on the part of the observer. For some disorders, however, particularly the Personality Disorders, the criteria require much more inference on the part of the observer. An example of such a criterion in Borderline Personality Disorder is "marked and persistent identity disturbance manifested by uncertainty about at least two of the following: self-image, sexual orientation, long-term goals or career choice, type of friends desired, preferred values."

This descriptive approach is also used in the grouping of the mental disorders into diagnostic classes. All of the disorders without known etiology or pathophysiologic process are grouped into classes on the basis of shared clinical features. For this reason, in DSM-III and in DSM-III-R there is no diagnostic class of "neuroses," as there was in DSM-II.

The subdivision of each diagnostic class in DSM-III-R into specific disorders, even with further subtyping of some individual disorders, reflects the best judgment of the advisory committees that such subdivisions will be useful. In this regard, we have been guided by the judgments of the clinicians who will be making most use of each portion of the classification.

It should be noted that DSM-III-R's generally atheoretical approach to the classification and definition of mental disorders does not imply that theories about the etiology of the various mental disorders are unimportant in other contexts. In formulating treatment plans, many clinicians find it helpful to be guided by theories about etiology. Similarly, many research studies are designed to test various theories about the etiology of mental disorders.

Diagnostic Criteria. DSM-I, DSM-II, and ICD-9 did not contain explicit criteria, leaving the clinician using these manuals on his or her own in defining the content and boundaries of the diagnostic categories. In contrast, DSM-III and DSM-III-R provide specific diagnostic criteria as guides for making each diagnosis since such criteria enhance interjudge diagnostic reliability. It should be understood, however, that for most of the categories the diagnostic criteria are based on clinical judgment, and have not yet been fully validated by data about such important correlates as clinical course, outcome, family history, and treatment response. Undoubtedly, with further study the criteria will be further refined.

In several areas of the classification (Disruptive Behavior Disorders, Psychoactive Substance Use Disorders, and Personality Disorders), the diagnostic criteria have been revised to form an index of symptoms of which a certain number, but no single one, is required to make the diagnosis. This *polythetic* format, in contrast to a *monothetic* format in which *each* of several criteria must be present for the diagnosis to be made, is likely to enhance diagnostic reliability.

Diagnostic Hierarchies. In DSM-III, many of the diagnostic classes were hierarchically organized on the assumption that a more pervasive disorder high in the hierarchy (e.g., Affective Disorders) might present with symptoms found in less pervasive disorders lower in the hierarchy (e.g., Anxiety Disorders), but not the reverse. For example, according to DSM-III, a diagnosis of Panic Disorder is not given if the panic attacks occur only during the course of an episode of Major Depression; in such a case, the panic attacks are to be regarded merely as associated symptoms of the Depressive Disorder, and of no diagnostic significance. Studies have since shown that research and clinical practice would be improved by eliminating many of the diagnostic hierarchies that have prevented giving multiple diagnoses when different syndromes occur together in one episode of illness.

In DSM-III-R, diagnostic hierarchies are governed by two principles:

1. When an Organic Mental Disorder can account for the symptoms, it preempts

the diagnosis of any other disorder that could produce the same symptoms (e.g., Organic Anxiety Disorder preempts Panic Disorder).

2. When a more pervasive disorder, such as Schizophrenia, commonly has associated symptoms that are the defining symptoms of a less pervasive disorder such as Dysthymia, only the more pervasive disorder is diagnosed if both its defining symptoms *and* associated symptoms are present. For example, only Schizophrenia (not Schizophrenia and Dysthymia) should be diagnosed when the defining symptoms of Schizophrenia are present along with chronic mild depression (which is a common associated symptom of Schizophrenia).

Multiaxial Evaluation System. DSM-III-R has a multiaxial system for evaluation to ensure that certain information that may be of value in planning treatment and predicting outcome for each person is recorded on each of five axes. Axes I and II comprise the mental disorders; Axis III, physical disorders and conditions; and Axes IV and V, severity of psychosocial stressors and global assessment of functioning, respectively. In its entirety, the multiaxial system provides a biopsychosocial approach to assessment.

The Distinction between "Mental Disorder" and "Physical Disorder." Throughout this manual there is reference to the terms *mental disorder* and *physical disorder*. The term *mental disorder* is explained above. As used in this manual, it refers to the categories that are contained in the mental disorders chapter of the *International Classification of Diseases* (ICD). The term *physical disorder* is used merely as a shorthand way of referring to all those conditions and disorders that are listed outside the mental disorders section of the ICD. The use of these terms by no means implies that mental disorders are unrelated to physical or biological factors or processes.

Systematic Description. The text of DSM-III-R systematically describes each disorder in terms of current knowledge in the following areas: essential features, associated features, age at onset, course, impairment, complications, predisposing factors, prevalence, sex ratio, familial pattern, and differential diagnosis. Although descriptively comprehensive, DSM-III-R is not a textbook, since it does not include information about theories of etiology, management, and treatment. It should also be noted that the DSM-III-R classification of mental disorders does not attempt to classify disturbed dyadic, family, or other interpersonal relationships.

Compatibility with ICD-9-CM. While nearly all of the DSM-III codes were ICD-9-CM codes, a small number were non-ICD-9-CM codes, and caused some problems for record-keeping systems with responsibility for reporting to federal agencies. In contrast, all DSM-III-R codes are legitimate ICD-9-CM codes.

Appendix for Proposed Diagnostic Categories Needing Further Study. The Work Group to Revise DSM-III and the Joint Ad Hoc Committee were able to resolve numerous controversies that arose during the revision process. However, there were three categories whose proposed inclusion in DSM-III-R by the Work Group provoked strenuous objections, both within the profession and without. These categories were Late Luteal Phase Dysphoric Disorder, Self-defeating Personality Disorder, and Sadistic Personality Disorder. The advisory committees that had worked on the definitions of these disorders and the Work Group believed that there was sufficient research and clinical evidence regarding the validity of each of these categories to justify its inclusion in the revised manual. On the other hand, critics of each of these categories believed that not only was adequate evidence of the validity of these categories lacking but these categories had such a high potential for misuse, particularly against women, that they should not be included.

This controversy was resolved by the inclusion of these three categories in Appendix A: Proposed Diagnostic Categories Needing Further Study (see p. 367). They are not listed in the Classification of Mental Disorders, but are included in the manual to facilitate further systematic clinical study and research.

Decision Trees for Differential Diagnosis. Appendix B provides decision trees to aid clinicians in understanding the differential diagnosis of the major DSM-III-R disorders.

Glossary of Technical Terms. Technical terms used in the text for describing the disorders are defined in a glossary in Appendix C.

Annotated Comparative Listing of DSM-III and DSM-III-R. Included in Appendix D is a table containing an explanation for each major revision in DSM-III. This table can help the reader to make the transition from DSM-III to DSM-III-R and understand the reasons for the changes.

CAUTIONS IN THE USE OF DSM-III-R

DSM-III-R and Planning Treatment. Making a DSM-III-R diagnosis represents only an initial step in a comprehensive evaluation leading to the formulation of a treatment plan. Additional information about the person being evaluated beyond that required to make a DSM-III-R diagnosis will invariably be necessary.

Cautionary Statement. The reader is directed to a cautionary statement, appearing following this Introduction, that amplifies three points: the proper use of DSM-III-R requires specialized clinical training; conditions not included in the DSM-III-R classification may be legitimate subjects of treatment or research efforts; and the clinical and scientific considerations that were the basis of the DSM-III-R classification and diagnostic criteria may not be relevant to considerations in which DSM-III-R is used outside clinical or research settings, e.g., in legal determinations.

The Use of DSM-III-R in Different Cultures. When the DSM-III-R classification and diagnostic criteria are used to evaluate a person from an ethnic or cultural group different from that of the clinician's, and especially when diagnoses are made in a non-Western culture, caution should be exercised in the application of DSM-III-R diagnostic criteria to assure that their use is culturally valid. It is important that the clinician not employ DSM-III-R in a mechanical fashion, insensitive to differences in language, values, behavioral norms, and idiomatic expressions of distress. When applied in a non-Western-language community, DSM-III-R should be translated to provide equivalent meaning, not necessarily dictionary equivalence. The clinician working in such settings should apply DSM-III-R with open-mindedness to the presence of distinctive cultural patterns and sensitivity to the possibility of unintended bias because of such differences.

When an experience or behavior is entirely normative for a particular culture—e.g., the experience of hallucinating the voice of the deceased in the first few weeks of bereavement in various North American Indian groups, or trance and possession states occurring in culturally approved ritual contexts in much of the non-Western world—it should not be regarded as pathological. Culture-specific symptoms of distress, such as particular somatic symptoms associated with distress in members of different ethnic and cultural groups, may create difficulties in the use of DSM-III-R, because the psychopathology is unique to that culture or because the DSM-III-R categories are not based on extensive research with non-Western populations.

THE FUTURE

DSM-III and DSM-III-R reflect an increased commitment in our field to reliance on data as the basis for understanding mental disorders. The Work Group to Revise DSM-III and its advisory committees had far more data about the diagnostic categories than did the Task Force that developed DSM-III. The groups that develop DSM-IV should have even more data as the basis for their deliberations. Therefore, the prospects for the future, and for DSM-IV in particular, are bright.

CAUTIONARY STATEMENT

The specified diagnostic criteria for each mental disorder are offered as guidelines for making diagnoses, since it has been demonstrated that the use of such criteria enhances agreement among clinicians and investigators. The proper use of these criteria requires specialized clinical training that provides both a body of knowledge and clinical skills.

These diagnostic criteria and the DSM-III-R classification of mental disorders reflect a consensus of current formulations of evolving knowledge in our field but do not encompass all the conditions that may be legitimate objects of treatment or research efforts.

The purpose of DSM-III-R is to provide clear descriptions of diagnostic categories in order to enable clinicians and investigators to diagnose, communicate about, study, and treat the various mental disorders. It is to be understood that inclusion here, for clinical and research purposes, of a diagnostic category such as Pathological Gambling or Pedophilia does not imply that the condition meets legal or other nonmedical criteria for what constitutes mental disease, mental disorder, or mental disability. The clinical and scientific considerations involved in categorization of these conditions as mental disorders may not be wholly relevant to legal judgments, for example, that take into account such issues as individual responsibility, disability determination, and competency.

CHAPTER 1

THE DSM–III–R CLASSIFICATION

DSM-III-R Codes which have 4th and 5th digit zeros
not found in ICD-9-CM

DSM-III-R Code	TO	ICD-9-CM Code	DSM-III-R Code	TO	ICD-9-CM Code
290.00		290.0	302.60		302.6
290.30		290.3	302.90		302.9
291.00		291.0	307.00		307.0
291.10		291.1	307.10		307.1
291.20		291.2	307.30		307.3
291.30		291.3	307.60		307.6
291.40		291.4	307.70		307.7
291.80		291.8	309.00		309.0
292.00		292.0	309.30		309.3
292.90		292.9	309.40		309.4
293.00		293.0	309.90		309.9
294.00		294.0	310.10		310.1
294.10		294.1	311.00		311
294.80		294.8	312.90		312.9
296.70		296.7	313.00		313.0
297.10		297.1	315.10		315.1
297.30		297.3	315.40		315.4
298.80		298.8	315.90		315.9
298.90		298.9	316.00		316
300.30		300.3	317.00		317
300.40		300.4	318.00		318.0
300.60		300.6	318.10		318.1
300.70		300.7	318.20		318.2
300.90		300.9	319.00		319
301.00		301.0	799.90		799.9
301.40		301.4	v61.10		v61.1
301.60		301.6	v61.80		v61.8
301.70		301.7	v62.20		v62.2
302.20		302.2	v62.30		v62.3
302.30		302.3	v65.20		v65.2
302.40		302.4			

DSM-III-R Diagnoses which have different ICD-9-CM codes

DSM-III-R		ICD-9-CM
294.80	Organic mental disorder NOS	294.9
305.30	Hallucinogen hallucinosis	292.12
307.40	Parasomnia NOS	307.47
312.39	Impulse Control disorder NOS	312.30
780.50	Hypersomnia related to known organic factor	780.54
780.50	Insomnia related to known organic factor	780.52
780.54	Primary hypersomnia	307.44
v40.00	Borderline intellectual functioning	v62.89

DSM-III-R Classification: Axes I and II Categories and Codes

All official DSM-III-R codes are included in ICD-9-CM. Codes followed by a * are used for more than one DSM-III-R diagnosis or subtype in order to maintain compatibility with ICD-9-CM.

Numbers in parentheses are page numbers.

A long dash following a diagnostic term indicates the need for a fifth digit subtype or other qualifying term.

The term *specify* following the name of some diagnostic categories indicates qualifying terms that clinicians may wish to add in parentheses after the name of the disorder.

NOS = Not Otherwise Specified

The current severity of a disorder may be specified after the diagnosis as:

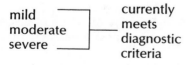

in partial remission
   (or residual state)
in complete remission

DISORDERS USUALLY FIRST EVIDENT IN INFANCY, CHILDHOOD, OR ADOLESCENCE

DEVELOPMENTAL DISORDERS
Note: These are coded on Axis II.

Mental Retardation (28)
317.00	Mild mental retardation
318.00	Moderate mental retardation
318.10	Severe mental retardation
318.20	Profound mental retardation
319.00	Unspecified mental retardation

Pervasive Developmental Disorders (33)
299.00	Autistic disorder (38) *Specify* if childhood onset
299.80	Pervasive developmental disorder NOS

Specific Developmental Disorders (39)
       Academic skills disorders
315.10	Developmental arithmetic disorder (41)
315.80	Developmental expressive writing disorder (42)
315.00	Developmental reading disorder (43)

3

Language and speech disorders

315.39 Developmental articulation disorder (44)
315.31* Developmental expressive language disorder (45)
315.31* Developmental receptive language disorder (47)

Motor skills disorder

315.40 Developmental coordination disorder (48)

315.90* Specific developmental disorder NOS

Other Developmental Disorders (49)

315.90* Developmental disorder NOS

Disruptive Behavior Disorders (49)

314.01 Attention-deficit hyperactivity disorder (50)

Conduct disorder, (53)
312.20 group type
312.00 solitary aggressive type
312.90 undifferentiated type
313.81 Oppositional defiant disorder (56)

Anxiety Disorders of Childhood or Adolescence (58)

309.21 Separation anxiety disorder (58)
313.21 Avoidant disorder of childhood or adolescence (61)
313.00 Overanxious disorder (63)

Eating Disorders (65)

307.10 Anorexia nervosa (65)
307.51 Bulimia nervosa (67)
307.52 Pica (69)
307.53 Rumination disorder of infancy (70)
307.50 Eating disorder NOS

Gender Identity Disorders (71)

302.60 Gender identity disorder of childhood (71)
302.50 Transsexualism (74)
      Specify sexual history: asexual, homosexual, heterosexual, unspecified

302.85* Gender identity disorder of adolescence or adulthood, nontranssexual type (76)
      Specify sexual history: asexual, homosexual, heterosexual, unspecified
302.85* Gender identity disorder NOS

Tic Disorders (78)

307.23 Tourette's disorder (79)
307.22 Chronic motor or vocal tic disorder (81)
307.21 Transient tic disorder (81)
      Specify: single episode or recurrent
307.20 Tic disorder NOS

Elimination Disorders (82)

307.70 Functional encopresis (82)
      Specify: primary or secondary type
307.60 Functional enuresis (84)
      Specify: primary or secondary type
      Specify: nocturnal only, diurnal only, nocturnal and diurnal

Speech Disorders Not Elsewhere Classified (85)

307.00* Cluttering (85)
307.00* Stuttering (86)

Other Disorders of Infancy, Childhood, or Adolescence (88)

313.23 Elective mutism (88)
313.82 Identity disorder (89)
313.89 Reactive attachment disorder of infancy or early childhood (91)
307.30 Stereotypy/habit disorder (93)
314.00 Undifferentiated attention-deficit disorder (95)

ORGANIC MENTAL DISORDERS (97)

Dementias Arising in the Senium and Presenium (119)

Primary degenerative dementia of the Alzheimer type, senile onset, (119)

290.30   with delirium
290.20   with delusions
290.21   with depression
290.00*   uncomplicated

(Note: code 331.00 Alzheimer's disease on Axis III)

Code in fifth digit:
1 = with delirium, 2 = with delusions,
3 = with depression, 0* = uncomplicated

290.1x   Primary degenerative dementia of the Alzheimer type, presenile onset, _____ (119)
(Note: code 331.00 Alzheimer's disease on Axis III)

290.4x   Multi-infarct dementia, _____ (121)

290.00*   Senile dementia NOS
Specify etiology on Axis III if known

290.10*   Presenile dementia NOS
Specify etiology on Axis III if known (e.g., Pick's disease, Jakob-Creutzfeldt disease)

Psychoactive Substance-Induced Organic Mental Disorders (123)

Alcohol
303.00   intoxication (127)
291.40   idiosyncratic intoxication (128)
291.80   Uncomplicated alcohol withdrawal (129)
291.00   withdrawal delirium (131)
291.30   hallucinosis (131)
291.10   amnestic disorder (133)
291.20   Dementia associated with alcoholism (133)

Amphetamine or similarly acting sympathomimetic
305.70*   intoxication (134)

292.00*   withdrawal (136)
292.81*   delirium (136)
292.11*   delusional disorder (137)

Caffeine
305.90*   intoxication (138)

Cannabis
305.20*   intoxication (139)
292.11*   delusional disorder (140)

Cocaine
305.60*   intoxication (141)
292.00*   withdrawal (142)
292.81*   delirium (143)
292.11*   delusional disorder (143)

Hallucinogen
305.30*   hallucinosis (144)
292.11*   delusional disorder (146)
292.84*   mood disorder (146)
292.89*   Posthallucinogen perception disorder (147)

Inhalant
305.90*   intoxication (148)

Nicotine
292.00*   withdrawal (150)

Opioid
305.50*   intoxication (151)
292.00*   withdrawal (152)

Phencyclidine (PCP) or similarly acting arylcyclohexylamine
305.90*   intoxication (154)
292.81*   delirium (155)
292.11*   delusional disorder (156)
292.84*   mood disorder (156)
292.90*   organic mental disorder NOS

Sedative, hypnotic, or anxiolytic
305.40*   intoxication (158)
292.00*   Uncomplicated sedative, hypnotic, or anxiolytic withdrawal (159)
292.00*   withdrawal delirium (160)
292.83*   amnestic disorder (161)

Other or unspecified psychoactive substance (162)
305.90*   intoxication

292.00*	withdrawal
292.81*	delirium
292.82*	dementia
292.83*	amnestic disorder
292.11*	delusional disorder
292.12	hallucinosis
292.84*	mood disorder
292.89*	anxiety disorder
292.89*	personality disorder
292.90*	organic mental disorder NOS

Organic Mental Disorders associated with Axis III physical disorders or conditions, or whose etiology is unknown. (162)

293.00	Delirium (100)
294.10	Dementia (103)
294.00	Amnestic disorder (108)
293.81	Organic delusional disorder (109)
293.82	Organic hallucinosis (110)
293.83	Organic mood disorder (111)
	Specify: manic, depressed, mixed
294.80*	Organic anxiety disorder (113)
310.10	Organic personality disorder (114)
	Specify if explosive type
294.80*	Organic mental disorder NOS

PSYCHOACTIVE SUBSTANCE USE DISORDERS (165)

	Alcohol (173)
303.90	dependence
305.00	abuse

	Amphetamine or similarly acting sympathomimetic (175)
304.40	dependence
305.70*	abuse

	Cannabis (176)
304.30	dependence
305.20*	abuse

	Cocaine (177)
304.20	dependence
305.60*	abuse

	Hallucinogen (179)
304.50*	dependence
305.30*	abuse

	Inhalant (180)
304.60	dependence
305.90*	abuse

	Nicotine (181)
305.10	dependence

	Opioid (182)
304.00	dependence
305.50*	abuse

	Phencyclidine (PCP) or similarly acting arylcyclohexylamine (183)
304.50*	dependence
305.90*	abuse

	Sedative, hypnotic, or anxiolytic (184)
304.10	dependence
305.40*	abuse

304.90*	Polysubstance dependence (185)
304.90*	Psychoactive substance dependence NOS
305.90*	Psychoactive substance abuse NOS

SCHIZOPHRENIA (187)
Code in fifth digit: 1 = subchronic, 2 = chronic, 3 = subchronic with acute exacerbation, 4 = chronic with acute exacerbation, 5 = in remission, 0 = unspecified.

	Schizophrenia,
295.2x	catatonic, _____
295.1x	disorganized, _____
295.3x	paranoid, _____
	Specify if stable type
295.9x	undifferentiated, _____
295.6x	residual, _____
	Specify if late onset

DELUSIONAL (PARANOID) DISORDER (199)

297.10	Delusional (Paranoid) disorder

Specify type: erotomanic
grandiose
jealous
persecutory
somatic
unspecified

PSYCHOTIC DISORDERS NOT ELSEWHERE CLASSIFIED (205)

298.80   Brief reactive psychosis (205)
295.40   Schizophreniform disorder
(207)
Specify: without good
prognostic features or with
good prognostic features
295.70   Schizoaffective disorder (208)
Specify: bipolar type or depressive type
297.30   Induced psychotic disorder
(210)
298.90   Psychotic disorder NOS
(Atypical psychosis) (211)

MOOD DISORDERS (213)

Code current state of Major Depression
and Bipolar Disorder in fifth digit:
1 = mild
2 = moderate
3 = severe, without psychotic
features
4 = with psychotic features (*specify*
mood-congruent or mood-
incongruent)
5 = in partial remission
6 = in full remission
0 = unspecified

For major depressive episodes, *specify*
if chronic and *specify* if melancholic
type.

For Bipolar Disorder, Bipolar Disorder
NOS, Recurrent Major Depression, and
Depressive Disorder NOS, *specify* if
seasonal pattern.

Bipolar Disorders

Bipolar disorder, (225)
296.6x   mixed, _____
296.4x   manic, _____
296.5x   depressed, _____
301.13   Cyclothymia (226)
296.70   Bipolar disorder NOS

Depressive Disorders

Major Depression, (228)
296.2x   single episode, _____
296.3x   recurrent, _____
300.40   Dysthymia (or Depressive
neurosis) (230)
Specify: primary or secondary type
Specify: early or late onset
311.00   Depressive disorder NOS

ANXIETY DISORDERS (or Anxiety and Phobic Neuroses) (235)

Panic disorder (235)
300.21   with agoraphobia
Specify current severity
of agoraphobic avoid-
ance
Specify current severity
of panic attacks
300.01   without agoraphobia
Specify current severity
of panic attacks
300.22   Agoraphobia without history
of panic disorder (240)
Specify with or without limited symptom attacks
300.23   Social phobia (241)
Specify if generalized type
300.29   Simple phobia (243)
300.30   Obsessive compulsive disorder (or Obsessive compulsive
neurosis) (245)
309.89   Post-traumatic stress disorder
(247)
Specify if delayed onset
300.02   Generalized anxiety disorder
(251)
300.00   Anxiety disorder NOS

SOMATOFORM DISORDERS (255)

300.70*   Body dysmorphic disorder
(255)
300.11   Conversion disorder (or
Hysterical neurosis, conversion type) (257)
Specify: single episode or
recurrent
300.70*   Hypochondriasis (or Hypochondriacal neurosis) (259)
300.81   Somatization disorder (261)

307.80   Somatoform pain disorder
          (264)
300.70*   Undifferentiated somatoform
          disorder (266)
300.70*   Somatoform disorder NOS
          (267)

DISSOCIATIVE DISORDERS (or Hysterical Neuroses, Dissociative Type) (269)

300.14   Multiple personality disorder
          (269)
300.13   Psychogenic fugue (272)
300.12   Psychogenic amnesia (273)
300.60   Depersonalization disorder
          (or Depersonalization neuro-
          sis) (275)
300.15   Dissociative disorder NOS

SEXUAL DISORDERS (279)

Paraphilias (279)
302.40   Exhibitionism (282)
302.81   Fetishism (282)
302.89   Frotteurism (283)
302.20   Pedophilia (284)
          Specify: same sex, opposite
          sex, same and opposite sex
          Specify if limited to incest
          Specify: exclusive type or
          nonexclusive type
302.83   Sexual masochism (286)
302.84   Sexual sadism (287)
302.30   Transvestic fetishism (288)
302.82   Voyeurism (289)
302.90*   Paraphilia NOS (290)

Sexual Dysfunctions (290)
Specify: psychogenic only, or psycho-
genic and biogenic (Note: If biogenic
only, code on Axis III)
Specify: lifelong or acquired
Specify: generalized or situational

          Sexual desire disorders (293)
302.71   Hypoactive sexual desire
          disorder
302.79   Sexual aversion disorder

          Sexual arousal disorders
          (294)
302.72*   Female sexual arousal
          disorder

302.72*   Male erectile disorder

          Orgasm disorders (294)
302.73   Inhibited female orgasm
302.74   Inhibited male orgasm
302.75   Premature ejaculation

          Sexual pain disorders (295)
302.76   Dyspareunia
306.51   Vaginismus

302.70   Sexual dysfunction NOS

Other Sexual Disorders
302.90*   Sexual disorder NOS

SLEEP DISORDERS (297)
Dyssomnias (298)
          Insomnia disorder
307.42*   related to another mental
          disorder (nonorganic) (300)
780.50*   related to known organic
          factor (300)
307.42*   Primary insomnia (301)
          Hypersomnia disorder
307.44   related to another mental
          disorder (nonorganic) (303)
780.50*   related to a known organic
          factor (303)
780.54   Primary hypersomnia (305)
307.45   Sleep-wake schedule
          disorder (305)
          Specify: advanced or de-
          layed phase type,
          disorganized type,
          frequently changing type
          Other dyssomnias
307.40*   Dyssomnia NOS

Parasomnias (308)
307.47   Dream anxiety disorder
          (Nightmare disorder) (308)
307.46*   Sleep terror disorder (310)
307.46*   Sleepwalking disorder (311)
307.40*   Parasomnia NOS (313)

FACTITIOUS DISORDERS (315)
          Factitious disorder
301.51   with physical symptoms
          (316)
300.16   with psychological
          symptoms (318)
300.19   Factitious disorder NOS (320)

IMPULSE CONTROL DISORDERS NOT ELSEWHERE CLASSIFIED (321)

312.34	Intermittent explosive disorder (321)
312.32	Kleptomania (322)
312.31	Pathological gambling (324)
312.33	Pyromania (325)
312.39*	Trichotillomania (326)
312.39*	Impulse control disorder NOS (328)

ADJUSTMENT DISORDER (329)

Adjustment disorder

309.24	with anxious mood
309.00	with depressed mood
309.30	with disturbance of conduct
309.40	with mixed disturbance of emotions and conduct
309.28	with mixed emotional features
309.82	with physical complaints
309.83	with withdrawal
309.23	with work (or academic) inhibition
309.90	Adjustment disorder NOS

PSYCHOLOGICAL FACTORS AFFECTING PHYSICAL CONDITION (333)

316.00	Psychological factors affecting physical condition *Specify* physical condition on Axis III

PERSONALITY DISORDERS (335)
Note: These are coded on Axis II.
Cluster A

301.00	Paranoid (337)
301.20	Schizoid (339)
301.22	Schizotypal (340)

Cluster B

301.70	Antisocial (342)
301.83	Borderline (346)
301.50	Histrionic (348)
301.81	Narcissistic (349)

Cluster C

301.82	Avoidant (351)
301.60	Dependent (353)
301.40	Obsessive compulsive (354)
301.84	Passive aggressive (356)
301.90	Personality disorder NOS

V CODES FOR CONDITIONS NOT ATTRIBUTABLE TO A MENTAL DISORDER THAT ARE A FOCUS OF ATTENTION OR TREATMENT (359)

V62.30	Academic problem
V71.01	Adult antisocial behavior

V40.00	Borderline intellectual functioning (Note: This is coded on Axis II.)

V71.02	Childhood or adolescent antisocial behavior
V65.20	Malingering
V61.10	Marital problem
V15.81	Noncompliance with medical treatment
V62.20	Occupational problem
V61.20	Parent–child problem
V62.81	Other interpersonal problem
V61.80	Other specified family circumstances
V62.89	Phase of life problem or other life circumstance problem
V62.82	Uncomplicated bereavement

ADDITIONAL CODES (363)

300.90	Unspecified mental disorder (nonpsychotic)
V71.09*	No diagnosis or condition on Axis I
799.90*	Diagnosis or condition deferred on Axis I

V71.09*	No diagnosis or condition on Axis II
799.90*	Diagnosis or condition deferred on Axis II

MULTIAXIAL SYSTEM

Axis I   Clinical Syndromes
          V Codes

Axis II   Developmental Disorders
          Personality Disorders

Axis III Physical Disorders and
          Conditions

Axis IV   Severity of Psychosocial
          Stressors

Axis V   Global Assessment of
          Functioning

Severity of Psychosocial Stressors Scale: Adults

See p. 18 for instructions on how to use this scale.

Code	Term	Examples of stressors	
		Acute events	**Enduring circumstances**
1	None	No acute events that may be relevant to the disorder	No enduring circumstances that may be relevant to the disorder
2	Mild	Broke up with boyfriend or girlfriend; started or graduated from school; child left home	Family arguments; job dissatisfaction; residence in high-crime neighborhood
3	Moderate	Marriage; marital separation; loss of job; retirement; miscarriage	Marital discord; serious financial problems; trouble with boss; being a single parent
4	Severe	Divorce; birth of first child	Unemployment; poverty
5	Extreme	Death of spouse; serious physical illness diagnosed; victim of rape	Serious chronic illness in self or child; ongoing physical or sexual abuse
6	Catastrophic	Death of child; suicide of spouse; devastating natural disaster	Captivity as hostage; concentration camp experience
0	Inadequate information, or no change in condition		

Severity of Psychosocial Stressors Scale: Children and Adolescents

See p. 18 for instructions on how to use this scale.

Code	Term	Examples of stressors	
		Acute events	**Enduring circumstances**
1	None	No acute events that may be relevant to the disorder	No enduring circumstances that may be relevant to the disorder
2	Mild	Broke up with boyfriend or girlfriend; change of school	Overcrowded living quarters; family arguments
3	Moderate	Expelled from school; birth of sibling	Chronic disabling illness in parent; chronic parental discord
4	Severe	Divorce of parents; unwanted pregnancy; arrest	Harsh or rejecting parents; chronic life-threatening illness in parent; multiple foster home placements
5	Extreme	Sexual or physical abuse; death of a parent	Recurrent sexual or physical abuse
6	Catastrophic	Death of both parents	Chronic life-threatening illness
0	Inadequate information, or no change in condition		

Global Assessment of Functioning Scale (GAF Scale)

Consider psychological, social, and occupational functioning on a hypothetical continuum of mental health-illness. Do not include impairment in functioning due to physical (or environmental) limitations. See p. 20 for instructions on how to use this scale.

Note: Use intermediate codes when appropriate, e.g., 45, 68, 72.

Code

90   **Absent or minimal symptoms** (e.g., mild anxiety before an exam), **good functioning in all areas, interested and involved in a wide range of activities, socially effective, generally satisfied with life, no more than everyday problems or concerns** (e.g., an
81   occasional argument with family members).

80   **If symptoms are present, they are transient and expectable reactions to psychosocial stressors** (e.g., difficulty concentrating after family argument); **no more than slight impairment in social, occupational, or school functioning** (e.g., temporarily falling
71   behind in school work).

70   **Some mild symptoms** (e.g., depressed mood and mild insomnia) **OR some difficulty in social, occupational, or school functioning** (e.g., occasional truancy, or theft within the household), **but generally functioning pretty well, has some meaningful interpersonal
61   relationships.**

60   **Moderate symptoms** (e.g., flat affect and circumstantial speech, occasional panic attacks) **OR moderate difficulty in social, occupational, or school functioning** (e.g., few
51   friends, conflicts with co-workers).

50   **Serious symptoms** (e.g., suicidal ideation, severe obsessional rituals, frequent shoplifting) **OR any serious impairment in social, occupational, or school functioning** (e.g., no
41   friends, unable to keep a job).

40   **Some impairment in reality testing or communication** (e.g., speech is at times illogical, obscure, or irrelevant) **OR major impairment in several areas, such as work or school, family relations, judgment, thinking, or mood** (e.g., depressed man avoids friends, neglects family, and is unable to work; child frequently beats up younger children, is
31   defiant at home, and is failing at school).

30   **Behavior is considerably influenced by delusions or hallucinations OR serious impairment in communication or judgment** (e.g., sometimes incoherent, acts grossly inappropriately, suicidal preoccupation) **OR inability to function in almost all areas** (e.g., stays
21   in bed all day; no job, home, or friends).

20   **Some danger of hurting self or others** (e.g., suicide attempts without clear expectation of death, frequently violent, manic excitement) **OR occasionally fails to maintain minimal personal hygiene** (e.g., smears feces) **OR gross impairment in communication**
11   (e.g., largely incoherent or mute).

10   **Persistent danger of severely hurting self or others** (e.g., recurrent violence) **OR persistent inability to maintain minimal personal hygiene OR serious suicidal act with clear
1   expectation of death.**

0   **Inadequate information.**

CHAPTER 2

USE OF THIS MANUAL

Use of This Manual

This chapter includes a discussion of the following:

MULTIAXIAL EVALUATION, p. 15
Axes I and II, p. 16
Multiple diagnoses within Axes I and II, p. 16
Axis II and description of personality features, p. 16
Principal diagnosis, p. 17
Provisional diagnosis, p. 17
Levels of diagnostic certainty, p. 17
Axis III, p. 18
Axis IV, p. 18
Axis V, p. 20
Examples of how to record the results of a multiaxial evaluation, p. 21
TYPES OF INFORMATION IN THE TEXT, p. 21
EXPLANATION OF COMMONLY USED TERMS AND PHRASES, p. 22
SPECIFYING CURRENT SEVERITY OF DISORDER, p. 23

MULTIAXIAL EVALUATION

A multiaxial evaluation requires that every case be assessed on several "axes," each of which refers to a different class of information. In order for the system to have maximal clinical usefulness, there must be a limited number of axes; there are five in the DSM-III-R multiaxial classification. The first three axes constitute the official diagnostic assessment.

Use of the DSM-III-R multiaxial system ensures that attention is give to certain types of disorders, aspects of the environment, and areas of functioning that might be overlooked if the focus were on assessing a single presenting problem.

Each person is evaluated on each of these axes:

Axis I   Clinical Syndromes and V Codes

Axis II   Developmental Disorders and Personality Disorders

Axis III Physical Disorders and Conditions

Axis IV   Severity of Psychosocial Stressors

Axis V   Global Assessment of Functioning

Axes IV and V are available for use in special clinical and research settings; they provide information that supplements the official DSM-III-R diagnoses (on Axes I, II, and III) and that may be useful for planning treatment and predicting outcome.

Axes I and II. Mental Disorders and V Codes

Axes I and II constitute the entire classification of mental disorders plus V Codes (Conditions Not Attributable to a Mental Disorder That Are a Focus of Attention or Treatment). The disorders listed on Axis II, Developmental Disorders and Personality Disorders, generally begin in childhood or adolescence and persist in a stable form (without periods of remission or exacerbation) into adult life. With only a few exceptions (e.g., the Gender Identity Disorders and Paraphilias), these features are not characteristic of the Axis I disorders. The separation between Axis I and Axis II ensures that in the evaluation of adults, consideration is given to the possible presence of Personality Disorders that may be overlooked when attention is directed to the usually more florid Axis I disorder. The Axis I–Axis II distinction in evaluating children emphasizes the need to consider disorders involving the development of cognitive, social, and motor skills.

In many instances there will be a disorder on both axes. For example, an adult may have Major Depression noted on Axis I and Obsessive Compulsive Personality Disorder on Axis II, or a child may have Conduct Disorder noted on Axis I and Developmental Language Disorder on Axis II. In other instances there may be no disorder on Axis I, the reason for seeking treatment being limited to a condition noted on Axis II. In this latter case, the clinician should write: *Axis I*: V71.09 No diagnosis or condition on Axis I, or one of the Conditions Not Attributable to a Mental Disorder should be recorded. On the other hand, if a disorder is noted on Axis I but there is no evidence of an Axis II disorder, the clinician should write: *Axis II*: V71.09 No diagnosis on Axis II.

Multiple diagnoses within Axes I and II

On both Axes I and II, multiple diagnoses should be made when necessary to describe the current condition. This applies particularly to Axis I, on which, for example, a person may have both a Psychoactive Substance Use Disorder and a Mood Disorder. It is also possible to have multiple diagnoses within the same class. For example, it is possible to have several Psychoactive Substance Use Disorders or, in the class of Mood Disorders, it is possible to have Major Depression superimposed on Dysthymia or Bipolar Disorder superimposed on Cyclothymia. In other classes, such as Schizophrenia, however, each of the types is mutually exclusive.

Within Axis II, the diagnosis of multiple Specific Developmental Disorders is common. For some adults the persistence of a Specific Developmental Disorder and the presence of a Personality Disorder may require that both be noted on Axis II. Usually, a single Personality Disorder will be noted; but when the person meets the criteria for more than one, all should be recorded.

Axis II and description of personality features

Axis II can be used to indicate specific personality traits or the habitual use of particular defense mechanisms (see Glossary for definitions). This can be done when no Personality Disorder exists or to supplement a Personality Disorder diagnosis. (Code numbers are not used when personality traits are noted, since a code number indicates a Personality Disorder.)

> *Examples:* Axis II: 301.40   Obsessive Compulsive Personality Disorder with paranoid traits
> Axis II: V71.09   No diagnosis on Axis II but massive denial of Axis III disorder (juvenile diabetes)

Principal diagnosis

When a person receives more than one diagnosis, the *principal* diagnosis is the condition that was chiefly responsible for occasioning the evaluation or admission to clinical care. In most cases this condition will be the main focus of attention or treatment. The principal diagnosis may be an Axis I or an Axis II diagnosis; but when an Axis II diagnosis is the principal diagnosis, the Axis II entry should be followed by the phrase "(Principal diagnosis)."

> *Example:* Axis I: 303.90   Alcohol Dependence
> Axis II: 301.70   Antisocial Personality Disorder (Principal diagnosis)

When a person has both an Axis I and an Axis II diagnosis, the principal diagnosis will be assumed to be on Axis I unless the Axis II diagnosis is followed by the qualifying phrase "(Principal diagnosis)."

When multiple diagnoses are made on either Axis I or Axis II, they should be listed within each axis in the order of focus of attention or treatment. For example, if a person with Schizophrenia, Paranoid Type, Chronic, comes to an emergency room for treatment of Alcohol Intoxication, the diagnosis should be listed:

> Axis I : 303.00   Alcohol Intoxication
> 295.32   Schizophrenia, Paranoid Type, Chronic

Provisional diagnosis

In some instances not enough information will be available to make a firm diagnosis. The clinician may wish to indicate a significant degree of diagnostic uncertainty by writing "(Provisional)" following the diagnosis—e.g., Schizophreniform Disorder (Provisional, rule out Organic Delusional Disorder).

Levels of diagnostic certainty

The following table indicates the various ways in which a clinician may indicate diagnostic uncertainty:

Term	Examples of clinical situations
V Codes (for Conditions Not Attributable to a Mental Disorder That Are a Focus of Attention or Treatment)	Insufficient information to know whether or not a presenting problem is attributable to a mental disorder, e.g., Academic Problem; Adult Antisocial Behavior.
799.90 Diagnosis or Condition Deferred on Axis I	Information inadequate to make any diagnostic judgment about an Axis I diagnosis or condition.

799.90 Diagnosis Deferred on Axis II	Same for an Axis II diagnosis.
300.90 Unspecified Mental Disorder (nonpsychotic)	Enough information available to rule out a psychotic disorder, but further specification is not possible.
298.90 Psychotic Disorder Not Otherwise Specified	Enough information available to determine the presence of a psychotic disorder, but further specification is not possible.
(Class of disorder) Not Otherwise Specified	Enough information available to indicate the class of disorder that is present, but further specification is not possible, because either there is not sufficient information to make a more specific diagnosis, or the clinical features of the disorder do not meet the criteria for any of the specific categories in that class, e.g., Depressive Disorder Not Otherwise Specified.
Specific diagnosis (Provisional)	Enough information available to make a "working" diagnosis, but the clinician wishes to indicate a significant degree of diagnostic uncertainty, e.g., Schizophreniform Disorder (Provisional).

Axis III. Physical Disorders or Conditions

Axis III permits the clinician to indicate any current physical disorder or condition that is potentially relevant to the understanding or management of the case. These are the conditions listed outside the mental disorders section of ICD-9-CM. In some instances the condition may be etiologically significant (e.g., a neurologic disorder associated with Dementia); in other instances the physical disorder may not be etiologic, but important in the overall management of the case (e.g., diabetes in a child with Conduct Disorder). In yet other instances, the clinician may wish to note significant associated physical findings, such as "soft neurologic signs." Multiple diagnoses are permitted.

Axis IV. Severity of Psychosocial Stressors

Axis IV provides a scale, the Severity of Psychosocial Stressors Scale (see p. 11) for coding the overall severity of a psychosocial stressor or multiple psychosocial stressors that have occurred in the year preceding the current evaluation and that may have contributed to any of the following:

(1) development of a new mental disorder
(2) recurrence of a prior mental disorder
(3) exacerbation of an already existing mental disorder (e.g., divorce occurring during a Major Depressive Episode, or during the course of chronic Schizophrenia)

(Note: Post-traumatic Stress Disorder is an exception to the requirement that the stressor has occurred within a year before the evaluation.) The current disorder that is related to the psychosocial stressor may be either a clinical syndrome, coded on Axis I, or an exacerbation of a Personality or Developmental Disorder, coded on Axis II. In some instances the stressor is anticipation of a future event, e.g., imminent retirement.

Although a stressor frequently plays a precipitating role in a disorder, it may also be a consequence of the person's psychopathology—e.g., Alcohol Dependence may lead to marital problems and divorce, which can then become stressors contributing to the development of a Major Depressive Episode.

Rating the severity of the stressor. The rating of the severity of the stressor should be based on the clinician's assessment of the stress an "average" person in similar circumstances and with similar sociocultural values would experience from the particular psychosocial stressor(s). This judgment involves consideration of the following: the amount of change in the person's life caused by the stressor, the degree to which the event is desired and under the person's control, and the number of stressors. For example, a planned pregnancy is usually less stressful than an unwanted pregnancy. Even though a specific stressor may have greater impact on a person who is especially vulnerable or has certain internal conflicts, the rating should be based on the severity of the stressor itself, not on the person's vulnerability to the particular stressor. If a vulnerability to stress exists, it will frequently be due to a mental disorder that is coded on Axis I or II.

The specific psychosocial stressor(s) should be noted and further specified as either:

predominantly acute events (duration less than six months)

predominantly enduring circumstances (duration greater than six months)

Examples of predominantly acute events are entering a new school or beginning a new job, having an accident, and death of a loved one. Examples of predominantly enduring circumstances are chronic marital or parental discord, and persistent and harsh parental discipline. The distinction between these two types of stressors may be important in formulating a treatment plan that includes attempts to remove the psychosocial stressor(s) or to help the person cope with it (them). Furthermore, there is evidence that predominantly enduring psychosocial stressors are more likely to predispose children to develop mental disorders than predominantly acute events.

In evaluating the stressors that may have contributed to the development of the current episode of illness, more than one may be judged to be relevant, but rarely should more than the four most severe be recorded. When more than one stressor is present, the severity rating will generally be that of the most severe stressor. However, in the case of multiple severe or extreme stressors, a higher rating should be considered. Each of the stressors should be noted and listed in the order of their importance.

Separate examples are given below for adults and for children and adolescents. These may be used as general guides for making the severity rating, the context in which the stressor(s) occurs being taken into account.

The code "0" should be used either when there is inadequate information about the presence or absence of psychosocial stressors to make a more definitive rating, or when the use of this axis is not appropriate because there has been no change in the person's condition (e.g., the person is being reevaluated after several months in the hospital because of a change of therapists).

Types of psychosocial stressors to be considered. To ascertain etiologically significant psychosocial stressors, the following areas may be considered:

Conjugal (marital and nonmarital): e.g., engagement, marriage, discord, separation, death of spouse.

Parenting: e.g., becoming a parent, friction with child, illness of child.

Other interpersonal: problems with one's friends, neighbors, associates, or nonconjugal family members, e.g., illness of best friend, discordant relationship with boss.

Occupational: includes work, school, homemaking, e.g., unemployment, retirement, school problems.

Living circumstances: e.g., change in residence, threat to personal safety, immigration.

Financial: e.g., inadequate finances, change in financial status.

Legal: e.g., arrest, imprisonment, lawsuit, or trial.

Developmental: phases of the life cycle, e.g., puberty, transition to adult status, menopause, "becoming 50."

Physical illness or injury: e.g., illness, accident, surgery, abortion. (Note: A physical disorder is listed on Axis III whenever it is related to the development or management of an Axis I or II disorder. A physical disorder can also be a psychosocial stressor if its impact is due to its meaning to the individual, in which case it would be listed on both Axis III and Axis IV.)

Other psychosocial stressors: e.g., natural or manmade disaster, persecution, unwanted pregnancy, out-of-wedlock birth, rape.

Family factors (children and adolescents): In addition to the above, for children and adolescents the following stressors may be considered: cold, hostile, intrusive, abusive, conflictual, or confusingly inconsistent relationship between parents or toward child; physical or mental illness in a family member; lack of parental guidance or excessively harsh or inconsistent parental control; insufficient, excessive, or confusing social or cognitive stimulation; anomalous family situation, e.g., complex or inconsistent parental custody and visitation arrangements; foster family; institutional rearing; loss of nuclear family members.

Axis V. Global Assessment of Functioning

Axis V permits the clinician to indicate his or her overall judgment of a person's psychological, social, and occupational functioning on a scale, the Global Assessment of Functioning Scale (GAF Scale)[1], that assesses mental health-illness. This scale appears on p. 12.

Ratings on the GAF Scale should be made for two time periods:

(1) Current—the level of functioning at the time of the evaluation.
(2) Past year—the highest level of functioning for at least a few months during the past year. For children and adolescents, this should include at least a month during the school year.

Ratings of current functioning will generally reflect the current need for treatment or care. Ratings of highest level of functioning during the past year frequently will have prognostic significance, because usually a person returns to his or her previous level of functioning after an episode of illness.

---

[1]The GAF Scale is a revision of the GAS (Endicott J, Spitzer RL, Fleiss J, et al: The Global Assessment Scale: A procedure for measuring overall severity of psychiatric disturbance. *Archives of General Psychiatry* 33:766-771, 1976) and the CGAS (Shaffer D, Gould MS, Brasic J, et al: Children's Global Assessment Scale [CGAS]. *Archives of General Psychiatry* 40:1228-1231, 1983), which are revisions of the Health-Sickness Rating Scale (Luborsky L: Clinicians' judgments of mental health. *Archives of General Psychiatry* 7:407-417, 1962).

Examples of How To Record the Results of a DSM-III-R Multiaxial Evaluation

Example 1

Axis I: 296.23   Major Depression, Single Episode, Severe without
                          Psychotic Features
            303.90   Alcohol Dependence
Axis II: 301.60   Dependent Personality Disorder (Provisional, rule out
                          Borderline Personality Disorder)
Axis III: Alcoholic cirrhosis of liver
Axis IV: Psychosocial stressors: anticipated retirement and change in residence, with loss of contact with friends
              Severity: 3—Moderate (predominantly enduring circumstances)
Axis V: Current GAF: 44
              Highest GAF past year: 55

Example 2

Axis I: 309.24   Adjustment Disorder with Anxious Mood
Axis II: V71.09   No diagnosis on Axis II
Axis III: None
Axis IV: Psychosocial stressors: Change of school
              Severity: 2—Mild (acute event)
Axis V: Current GAF: 70
              Highest GAF past year: 85

Example 3

Axis I: 295.94   Schizophrenia, Undifferentiated Type, Chronic with Acute
                        Exacerbation
Axis II: V40.00   Borderline Intellectual Functioning (Provisional)
Axis III: Late effects of viral encephalitis
Axis IV: Psychosocial stressors: death of mother
              Severity: 5—Extreme (acute event)
Axis V: Current GAF: 28
              Highest GAF past year: 40

TYPES OF INFORMATION IN THE TEXT

In order to ensure consistency and comprehensiveness in the descriptions of the disorders, information has been included under each of the headings below. In some instances, when many of the specific disorders, such as Psychoactive Substance Use Disorders, share common features, this information is included in the introduction to the entire section.

The first paragraph specifies the **essential features** of the disorder; these are the features that are generally required to make the diagnosis.

Associated features. Features that are often, but not invariably, present. These include both symptoms and coexisting disorders.

Age at onset. Age at which the disorder generally becomes apparent.

Course. The natural history of the disorder.

Impairment. Conceptualized primarily as impairment in social and occupational functioning.

Complications. Disorders or events (e.g., suicide) that may develop as a result of the disorder. In some cases the distinction among complications, impairment, and associated features is arbitrary.

Predisposing factors. Characteristics of a person that can be identified before the development of the disorder and place that person at higher risk for developing the disorder. Not included in this section are general societal or environmental conditions (such as poverty) that may predispose everyone exposed to those conditions to development of the disorder.

Prevalence. Often expressed as the proportion of adults who at some time in their lives will have a disturbance that meets the criteria for the disorder. This method of presentation has the advantage of being readily understandable, but it is highly dependent on the age at onset and the relative proportion of people in the population who have reached that age. The data are often presented as a range, based on more than a single study.
When data from epidemiologic studies are not available, the prevalence is stated in general terms preceded by "apparently" to indicate that the judgment is based on clinical experience. The expression *apparently rare* is applied to disorders that may not be seen by a clinician in many years of practice.

Sex ratio. The relative frequency with which the disorder is diagnosed in males and females.

Familial pattern. Frequency of the disorder among first-degree biologic relatives of those with the disorder compared with that among the general population. More frequent occurrence among those relatives does not, however, necessarily indicate a genetic mechanism.

Differential diagnosis. Disorders that should be distinguished from the disorder being discussed are indicated, generally in the order in which they appear in the classification.

EXPLANATION OF COMMONLY USED TERMS AND PHRASES

It cannot be established that an organic factor initiated and maintained the disturbance. This phrase is used for certain diagnoses to indicate that the diagnosis is made only when, after an appropriate evaluation, the clinician cannot identify an organic factor that is believed to have initiated *and* maintained the disturbance. In some cases, the presence of an etiologic organic factor can be established from the history alone. In other cases, physical examination or laboratory tests are necessary. For example, when a person presents with symptoms characteristic of Schizophrenia, the diagnosis can be made only when the clinician concludes, after an appropriate evaluation, that no organic factor (such as a psychoactive substance or a brain tumor) can be established to have initiated and maintained the disturbance.
It should be noted that the organic factor must not only have initiated the disturbance but be responsible for *maintaining* the disturbance as well. For example, the

diagnosis of Panic Disorder would still be appropriate in a situation in which the onset of the panic attacks was triggered by the use of cannabis, provided the panic attacks persisted for a significant period of time, such as one month, after use of the cannabis had stopped.

If a particular diagnosis is excluded because an organic factor that initiated and maintained the disturbance can be established, then the corresponding Organic Mental Disorder should be diagnosed. For example, if the diagnosis of Schizophrenia was excluded because of use of amphetamines, the diagnosis of an Organic Delusional Disorder should be made; if the diagnosis of a Major Depression was excluded because of a brain tumor, the diagnosis of an Organic Mood Disorder should be made.

The phrase *organic factor* is difficult to define precisely. However, in this context it refers to two major categories: (1) identifiable **exogenous** physical factors that affect the central nervous system, such as pharmacologic agents, infections, and trauma, and (2) identifiable **endogenous** factors, such as structural brain disease or metabolic disturbance. Genetically transmitted vulnerability and nonspecific abnormalities of central nervous system structure and function (including endocrinologic abnormalities) are generally **not** included as an organic factor in this context; these are present in only some people with the disorder, are present in some people without the disorder, and may be only associated features of the disorder, unrelated to the basic pathophysiologic process of the disturbance.

The fact that certain diagnoses are made only when an organic factor cannot be identified does not imply the absence of a fundamental biologic disturbance in these disorders. It should be understood that when we know more about the biologic mechanisms involved in such disorders as Schizophrenia, Bipolar Disorder, and Major Depression, we may be able to identify specific organic factors that are responsible for initiating and maintaining these disorders.

Occurrence is not exclusively during the course of [disorder]. This phrase is used in certain exclusion criteria to indicate that the diagnosis of the disorder being defined is not made if its defining symptoms or features have been present only when the other disorder was also present. For example, an exclusion criterion for Hypoactive Sexual Desire Disorder is "Occurrence is not exclusively during the course of a Major Depressive Episode," which means that if the lack of sexual desire was present only during a Major Depressive Episode, the additional diagnosis of Hypoactive Sexual Desire Disorder would not be made.

Not Otherwise Specified (NOS). This term is used to indicate a category within a class of disorders that is residual to the specific categories in that class, although it is recognized that in some settings the category may actually be more common than any of the specific disorders in that particular class.

Physical disorders. The term *physical disorders* is used to refer to any disorder listed in ICD-9-CM outside the chapter on mental disorders.

SPECIFYING CURRENT SEVERITY OF DISORDER

The current severity of a disorder may be specified, following the diagnosis, by the following terms (in parentheses): mild, moderate, severe, in partial remission (or residual state), in full remission.

Examples: Social Phobia (severe)
               Alcohol Dependence (in full remission)
               Attention-deficit Hyperactivity Disorder (residual state)

"Mild," "moderate," and "severe" should be used to indicate the severity of the current disorder (or provisional disorder) at the time of the evaluation when all of the diagnostic criteria are met. The distinction among mild, moderate, and severe should take into account the number and intensity of the signs and symptoms of the disorder and any resulting impairment in occupational or social functioning. For the following disorders, specific criteria for levels of severity are provided.

Attention-deficit Hyperactivity Disorder (p. 53)
Conduct Disorder (p. 55)
Oppositional Defiant Disorder (p. 58)
Dementia (p. 107)
Psychoactive Substance Dependence (p. 168)
Manic Episode (p. 218)
Major Depressive Episode (p. 223)
Panic Disorder with Agoraphobia (p. 239)
Paraphilias (p. 281)

For all the other disorders, the following guidelines may be used:

Mild: Few, if any, symptoms in excess of those required to make the diagnosis **and** symptoms result in only minor impairment in occupational functioning or in usual social activities or relationships with others.

Moderate: Symptoms or functional impairment between "mild" and "severe."

Severe: Several symptoms in excess of those required to make the diagnosis **and** symptoms markedly interfere with occupational functioning or with usual social activities or relationships with others.

In Partial Remission or **Residual State:** The full criteria for the disorder were previously met, but currently only some of the symptoms or signs of the illness are present. *In partial remission* should be used when there is the expectation that the person will completely recover (or have a complete remission) within the next few years, as, for example, in the case of a Major Depressive Episode. *Residual state* should be used when there is little expectation of a complete remission or recovery within the next few years, as, for example, in the case of Autistic Disorder or Attention-deficit Hyperactivity Disorder. (*Residual state* should not be used with Schizophrenia, since by tradition there is a specific residual type of Schizophrenia.) In some cases the distinction between *in partial remission* and *residual state* will be difficult to make.

In Full Remission: There are no longer any symptoms or signs of the disorder. The differentiation of *in full remission* from recovered (no current mental disorder) requires consideration of the length of time since the last period of disturbance, the total duration of the disturbance, and the need for continued evaluation or prophylactic treatment.

CHAPTER 3

THE DIAGNOSTIC CATEGORIES

Disorders Usually First Evident in Infancy, Childhood, or Adolescence

The disorders described in this chapter are those that usually appear and are first evident in infancy, childhood, or adolescence. There is no arbitrary age limit here that defines childhood and adolescence, and this section includes some disorders characteristic of older adolescents, such as Bulimia Nervosa, which may first appear in early adulthood.

In diagnosing an infant, child, or adolescent, the clinician should first consider the diagnoses included in this section. If an appropriate diagnosis cannot be found, disorders described elsewhere in this manual should be considered.

Because the *essential* features of Mood Disorders and Schizophrenia are the same in children and adults, there are no special categories corresponding to these disorders in this section of the classification. Therefore, if, for example, a child or adolescent has an illness that meets the criteria for Major Depression, Dysthymia, or Schizophrenia, these diagnoses should be given, regardless of the person's age. (In some instances, age-specific *associated* features that apply to infants, children, or adolescents are included in the text.)

Other diagnostic categories that are often appropriate for children and adolescents are the following (for a discussion of the diagnosis of Personality Disorders in children and adolescents, see p. 335):

Organic Mental Disorders	Somatoform Disorders
Psychoactive Substance Use Disorders	Sexual Disorders
	Adjustment Disorder
Schizophrenia	Psychological Factors Affecting Physical Condition
Mood Disorders	
Schizophreniform Disorder	Personality Disorders

Adults should be given diagnoses from this section if, as infants, children, or adolescents, they had symptoms of any of these disorders and the condition has persisted. Examples include the residual phase of Attention-deficit Hyperactivity Disorder and some cases of Conduct Disorder. Finally, some people may develop in adulthood a disorder, such as Anorexia Nervosa, that is included in this section because the disorder *usually* first develops in children or adolescents.

Many children who come to clinical attention have problems that do not warrant a diagnosis of a mental disorder. Such conditions can be noted with a V Code, such as Parent–Child Problem, Childhood or Adolescent Antisocial Behavior, or Other Specified Family Circumstances.

Children who are psychologically, physically, or sexually abused may react in a variety of ways. If the reaction constitutes a mental disorder, the following categories should be considered: Reactive Attachment Disorder of Infancy or Early Childhood, Post-traumatic Stress Disorder (generally for the older child), and Adjustment Disorder. (If the reaction is not sufficient to be considered a mental disorder, the situation can be coded as V61.20, Parent–Child Problem [child abuse].)

DEVELOPMENTAL DISORDERS (AXIS II)

The essential feature of this group of disorders is that the predominant disturbance is in the acquisition of cognitive, language, motor, or social skills. The disturbance may involve a general delay, as in Mental Retardation, or a delay or failure to progress in a specific area of skill acquisition, as in Specific Developmental Disorders, or multiple areas in which there are qualitative distortions of normal development, as in the Pervasive Developmental Disorders.

The course of the Developmental Disorders tends to be chronic, with some signs of the disorder persisting in a stable form (without periods of remission or exacerbation) into adult life. However, in many mild cases, adaptation or full recovery may occur.

MENTAL RETARDATION (AXIS II)

The essential features of this disorder are: (1) significantly subaverage general intellectual functioning, accompanied by (2) significant deficits or impairments in adaptive functioning, with (3) onset before the age of 18. The diagnosis is made regardless of whether or not there is a coexisting physical or other mental disorder.

General intellectual functioning. General intellectual functioning is defined as an intelligence quotient (IQ or IQ equivalent) obtained by assessment with one or more of the individually administered general intelligence tests (e.g., Wechsler Intelligence Scale for Children—Revised, Stanford Binet, Kaufman Assessment Battery for Children). Significantly subaverage intellectual functioning is defined as an IQ of 70 or below on an individually administered IQ test. Since any measurement is fallible, an IQ score is generally thought to involve an error of measurement of approximately five points; hence, an IQ of 70 is considered to represent a band or zone of 65 to 75.

Treating the IQ with some flexibility permits inclusion in the Mental Retardation category of people with IQs somewhat higher than 70 who exhibit significant deficits in adaptive behavior. It also permits exclusion from the diagnosis of those with IQs somewhat lower than 70 if the clinical judgment is that there are no significant deficits or impairments in adaptive functioning. An IQ level of 70 was chosen because most people with IQs below 70 require special services and care, particularly during the school-age years.

The arbitrary IQ ceiling values are based on data indicating a positive association between intelligence (as measured by IQ score) and adaptive behavior at lower IQ levels. This association declines at the mild and moderate levels of Mental Retardation.

Adaptive functioning. Adaptive functioning refers to the person's effectiveness in areas such as social skills, communication, and daily living skills, and how well the person meets the standards of personal independence and social responsibility expected of his or her age by his or her cultural group. Adaptive functioning in people with Mental Retardation (and in people without Mental Retardation) is influenced by personality characteristics, motivation, education, and social and vocational opportunities. Adaptive behavior is more likely to improve with remedial efforts than is IQ, which tends to remain more stable.

Useful scales have been designed to quantify adaptive functioning or behavior (e.g., the Vineland Adaptive Behavior Scales, American Association of Mental Deficiency Adaptive Behavior Scale). Ideally, these scales should be used in conjunction with a clinical judgment of general adaptation. If these scales are not available, clinical judgment of general adaptation alone, the person's age and cultural background being taken into consideration, may suffice.

Associated features. When a specific physical disorder is associated with Mental Retardation, the features of the physical disorder will, of course, also be present. For example, in cases of Mental Retardation associated with Down syndrome, the physical features of Down syndrome will be present. The more severe the Mental Retardation (especially if it is severe or profound), the greater the likelihood of associated abnormalities in one or more systems, such as the neurologic (e.g., seizures), neuromuscular, visual, auditory, and cardiovascular systems. These abnormalities may further impair the person's adaptive functioning. It should be noted, however, that in Mental Retardation associated with Down syndrome, social skills are likely to be higher than would be expected by the level of Mental Retardation.

Behavioral symptoms commonly seen in Mental Retardation include passivity, dependency, low self-esteem, low frustration tolerance, aggressiveness, poor impulse control, and stereotyped self-stimulating and self-injurious behavior. In some cases, these behaviors may be learned and conditioned by environmental factors; in other cases, they may be linked to an underlying physical disorder, such as self-injurious behavior associated with Lesch-Nyhan syndrome. At the present time there is no satisfactory subclassification of behavioral symptoms associated with Mental Retardation.

The prevalence of other mental disorders is at least three or four times greater among people with Mental Retardation than in the general population. Particularly common as associated diagnoses are Pervasive Developmental Disorders, Attention-deficit Hyperactivity Disorder, and Stereotypy/Habit Disorder.

Age at onset. By definition, Mental Retardation requires that onset be before age 18. When a similar clinical picture develops for the first time after the age of 18, the syndrome is a Dementia, not Mental Retardation, and is coded within the Organic Mental Disorders section of the classification (p. 103). An example would be a 19-year-old with previously normal intelligence who developed the clinical picture of Mental Retardation after sustaining brain damage in an automobile accident. However, a Dementia can be superimposed on previously existing Mental Retardation. An example would be a child with mild Mental Retardation whose functioning deteriorates after sustaining brain damage in an automobile accident. When the clinical picture develops before the age of 18 in a person who previously had normal intelligence, Mental Retardation and Dementia should both be diagnosed.

Course. The course of Mental Retardation is a function of both biologic factors, such as an underlying etiologic physical disorder, and environmental factors, such as educational and other opportunities, environmental stimulation, and appropriateness of management. If the underlying physical abnormality is static (as in fragile X syndrome), the course of the Mental Retardation is variable: with good environmental influences, functioning may improve; with poor environmental influences, it may deteriorate. If the underlying physical abnormality is progressive (as in a lipid storage disorder), functioning will tend to deteriorate, although with good environmental influences, the deterioration may proceed more slowly.

As a rule, children with Mental Retardation are no longer admitted to custodial-type institutions, and adults with Mental Retardation are only rarely thus institutionalized. As a result, the prognosis for Mental Retardation has improved dramatically in recent years. The majority of people with Mental Retardation now adapt well to life in the community, within the limits of their handicap.

Some people with mild Mental Retardation develop good adaptive skills and maintain jobs in competitive employment. For such people the diagnosis of Mental Retardation may no longer be justified, even if it was appropriate when they were of school age and their intellectual deficits limited their academic functioning.

Impairment. By definition, there is always impairment in adaptive functioning. The degree of impairment is correlated with the level of general intellectual functioning, the presence of associated features and complications, and educational and other environmental opportunities.

Complications. Other mental disorders, such as Depressive Disorders, psychotic disorders, and Personality Disorders, may be complications. The diagnosis of other mental disorders may be difficult because of cognitive and language deficits that may mask the clinical manifestations of the other disorders. For example, a person with Mental Retardation may have difficulty verbalizing depressive thoughts and feelings. For nonverbal people with Mental Retardation, the nonspecific diagnostic categories (e.g., Depressive Disorder Not Otherwise Specified), rather than the specific ones, may have to be employed.

People with Mental Retardation are particularly vulnerable to exploitation by others, such as being physically and sexually abused or being denied rights and opportunities.

Etiologic factors and familial pattern. Etiologic factors may be primarily biologic, psychosocial, or a combination of both. In approximately 30%–40% of the cases seen in clinical settings, no clear etiology can be determined despite extensive evaluation efforts. The following are the major causative factors in the remaining cases:

(1) hereditary factors (in approximately 5% of cases), such as inborn errors of metabolism (e.g., Tay-Sachs disease), other single-gene abnormalities (e.g., tuberous sclerosis), and chromosomal aberrations (e.g., translocation Down syndrome);

(2) early alterations of embryonic development (in approximately 30%), such as chromosomal changes (e.g., trisomy 21 syndrome), prenatal damage due to toxins (e.g., maternal alcohol consumption, infections) or unknown causes;

(3) pregnancy and perinatal problems (in approximately 10%), such as fetal malnutrition, prematurity, hypoxia, trauma;

(4) physical disorders acquired in childhood (in approximately 5%), such as infections, traumas, and lead poisoning;

(5) environmental influences and mental disorders (in approximately 15%-20%), such as deprivation of nurturance and of social, linguistic, and other stimulation, and complications of severe mental disorders (e.g., a drop in adaptive functioning in a person with a borderline-level IQ following early-onset Schizophrenia).

The prevalence of Mental Retardation due to known biologic factors is similar among children of upper and lower socioeconomic classes, except that certain etiologic factors are linked to lower socioeconomic status, such as lead poisoning and premature births. In cases in which no specific biologic causation can be identified, lower socioeconomic classes are overrepresented, and the Mental Retardation is usually milder (but all degrees of severity are represented).

The age at which a diagnosis of Mental Retardation is first made in a person depends on the degree of its severity and whether a physical disorder with characteristic phenotypic features is present. Thus, children with Severe Mental Retardation and children with Down syndrome are diagnosed earlier than children with mild retardation of unknown cause.

Prevalence. Recent studies suggest that at any one point in time, the prevalence rate of Mental Retardation is approximately 1%.

Sex ratio. Mental Retardation is more common among males, with a male:female ratio of approximately 1.5:1.

Differential diagnosis. The diagnosis of Mental Retardation should be made when the criteria are met, regardless of the presence of another diagnosis. In **Specific Developmental Disorders** (unassociated with Mental Retardation) there is a delay or failure of development in a specific area, such as reading or language, but in other areas of development the child is developing normally. In contrast, a child with Mental Retardation always has general delays in development in many areas.

In **Pervasive Developmental Disorders** there is qualitative impairment in the development of reciprocal social interaction, in the development of verbal and nonverbal communication skills, and in the development of imaginative activity. These abnormalities are not normal for any stage of development, whereas in Mental Retardation (unassociated with another disorder) there are generalized delays in development, but the person behaves as if he or she were passing through an earlier normal developmental stage.

Mental Retardation may, however, coexist with Specific Developmental Disorders (e.g., a severe language deficit out of proportion to other areas of development in an person with Mild Mental Retardation). People with a Pervasive Developmental Disorder also frequently have Mental Retardation (see discussion of Associated Features of Pervasive Developmental Disorders, p. 35).

The V code **Borderline Intellectual Functioning** is given when there is borderline intellectual functioning, which generally is in the IQ range of 71 to 84, and the diagnosis of Mental Retardation is not warranted. Differentiating Mild Mental Retardation from Borderline Intellectual Functioning requires careful consideration of all available information, including psychological test scores.

Diagnostic criteria for Mental Retardation

A. Significantly subaverage general intellectual functioning: an IQ of 70 or below on an individually administered IQ test (for infants, a clinical judgment of significantly subaverage intellectual functioning, since available intelligence tests do not yield numerical IQ values).

(continued)

Diagnostic criteria for Mental Retardation continued

B. Concurrent deficits or impairments in adaptive functioning, i.e., the person's effectiveness in meeting the standards expected for his or her age by his or her cultural group in areas such as social skills and responsibility, communication, daily living skills, personal independence, and self-sufficiency.

C. Onset before the age of 18.

Degrees of severity. There are four degrees of severity, reflecting the degree of intellectual impairment: Mild, Moderate, Severe, and Profound. IQ levels to be used as guides in distinguishing the four degrees of severity are:

Degree of severity	IQ
Mild	50-55 to approx. 70
Moderate	35-40 to 50-55
Severe	20-25 to 35-40
Profound	Below 20 or 25

317.00   Mild Mental Retardation

Mild Mental Retardation is roughly equivalent to what used to be referred to as the educational category of "educable." This group constitutes the largest segment of those with the disorder—about 85%. People with this level of Mental Retardation typically develop social and communication skills during the preschool years (ages 0–5), have minimal impairment in sensorimotor areas, and often are not distinguishable from normal children until a later age. By their late teens they can acquire academic skills up to approximately sixth-grade level; during their adult years, they usually achieve social and vocational skills adequate for minimum self-support, but may need guidance and assistance when under unusual social or economic stress. At the present time, virtually all people with Mild Mental Retardation can live successfully in the community, independently or in supervised apartments or group homes (unless there is an associated disorder that makes this impossible).

318.00   Moderate Mental Retardation

Moderate Mental Retardation is roughly equivalent to what used to be referred to as the educational category of "trainable." This former term should not be used since it wrongly implies that people with Moderate Mental Retardation cannot benefit from educational programs. This group constitutes 10% of the entire population of people with Mental Retardation.

Those with this level of Mental Retardation can talk or learn to communicate during the preschool years. They may profit from vocational training and, with moderate supervision, can take care of themselves. They can profit from training in social and occupational skills, but are unlikely to progress beyond the second grade level in academic subjects. They may learn to travel independently in familiar places. During adolescence, their difficulties in recognizing social conventions may interfere with peer relationships. In their adult years, they may be able to contribute to their own support by performing unskilled or semiskilled work under close supervision in sheltered workshops or in the competitive job market. They need supervision and guidance when under stress. They adapt well to life in the community, but usually in supervised group homes.

318.10   Severe Mental Retardation

This group constitutes 3%–4% of people with Mental Retardation. During the pre-school period, they display poor motor development, and they acquire little or no communicative speech. During the school-age period, they may learn to talk, and can be trained in elementary hygiene skills. They profit to only a limited extent from instruction in pre-academic subjects, such as familiarity with the alphabet and simple counting, but can master skills such as learning sight-reading of some "survival" words, such as "men" and "women" and "stop." In their adult years, they may be able to perform simple tasks under close supervision. Most adapt well to life in the community, in group homes or with their families, unless they have an associated handicap that requires specialized nursing or other care.

318.20   Profound Mental Retardation

This group constitutes approximately 1%–2% of people with Mental Retardation. During the early years, these children display minimal capacity for sensorimotor functioning. A highly structured environment, with constant aid and supervision, and an individualized relationship with a caregiver are required for optimal development. Motor development and self-care and communication skills may improve if appropriate training is provided. Currently, many of these people live in the community, in group homes, intermediate care facilities, or with their families. Most attend day programs, and some can perform simple tasks under close supervision in a sheltered workshop.

319.00   Unspecified Mental Retardation

This category should be used when there is a strong presumption of Mental Retardation but the person is untestable by standard intelligence tests. This may be the case when children, adolescents, or adults are too impaired or uncooperative to be tested. It may also be the case with infants when there is a clinical judgment of significantly subaverage intellectual functioning, but the available tests, such as the Bayley, Cattel, and others, do not yield IQ values. In general, the younger the age, the more difficult it is to make a diagnosis of Mental Retardation, except for those with profound impairment.

This category should not be used when the intellectual level is presumed to be above 70 (see V code for Borderline Intellectual Functioning, p. 359).

PERVASIVE DEVELOPMENTAL DISORDERS (AXIS II)

The disorders in this subclass are characterized by qualitative impairment in the development of reciprocal social interaction, in the development of verbal and nonverbal communication skills, and in imaginative activity. Often there is a markedly restricted repertoire of activities and interests, which frequently are stereotyped and repetitive. The severity and expression of these impairments vary greatly from child to child.

These disorders frequently are associated with a variety of other conditions. Distortions or delays in development are common in the following areas: intellectual skills, as measured by standardized intelligence tests (in most cases there is an associated diagnosis of Mental Retardation); comprehension of meaning in language and the production of speech (in addition to problems in the social use of speech for reciprocal communication); posture and movements; patterns of eating, drinking, or sleeping; and responses to sensory input.

Various diagnostic terms, including Atypical Development, Symbiotic Psychosis, Childhood Psychosis, Childhood Schizophrenia, and others, have been used to describe these disorders in the past. However, clinical descriptions have typically overlapped; and apart from Autistic Disorder, no generally recognized subtypes have yet emerged. Though some early investigators suggested that these disorders were continuous with adult psychoses (e.g., Schizophrenia), substantial research suggests that they are unrelated to the adult psychoses. For that reason, and the difficulties of assessing psychosis in childhood, the term *psychosis* has not been used here to label this group of disorders: Pervasive Developmental Disorders is used because it describes most accurately the core clinical disturbance in which many basic areas of psychological development are affected at the same time and to a severe degree.

This classification recognizes only one subgroup of the general category Pervasive Developmental Disorders: Autistic Disorder, also known as Infantile Autism and Kanner's syndrome. The evidence suggests, however, that this disorder is merely the most severe and prototypical form of the general category Pervasive Developmental Disorders. Cases that meet the general description of a Pervasive Developmental Disorder but not the specific criteria for Autistic Disorder are diagnosed as Pervasive Developmental Disorder Not Otherwise Specified (PDDNOS). Whereas in clinical settings Autistic Disorder is more commonly seen than PDDNOS, studies in England and the United States, using criteria similar to those in this manual, suggest that PDDNOS is more common than Autistic Disorder in the general population.

Qualitative impairment in reciprocal social interaction. This impairment is characterized by failure to develop interpersonal relationships and by lack of responsiveness to, or interest in, people. In infancy these deficiencies may be manifested by a failure to cuddle, by lack of eye contact and facial responsiveness, and by indifference or aversion to affection and physical contact. As a result, parents often suspect that the child is deaf (not realizing that deafness, by itself, is rarely associated with extreme social indifference). Adults may be treated as interchangeable, or the child may cling mechanically to a specific person. The attachment of some toddlers to their parent(s) may be bizarre, e.g., a child may seem to recognize his mother primarily on the basis of smell.

In some cases the disorder apparently follows a period of normal, or relatively normal, social development in the first years of life; but even in early childhood, there is invariably failure to develop cooperative play, imaginative play, and friendships. As the child grows older, however, greater awareness of, and social interest in, others may develop. Some of the least handicapped may eventually reach a stage in which they can become passively involved in other children's games or physical play, or include other children as "mechanical aids" in their own stereotyped activities.

Impairment in communication and imaginative activity. Impairment in communication includes both verbal and nonverbal skills. Language may be totally absent. When it develops, it is often characterized by: immature but essentially normal grammatical structure; delayed or immediate echolalia; pronoun reversals (e.g., use of "you" when "I" is intended); inability to name objects; inability to use abstract terms; idiosyncratic utterances whose meaning is clear only to those who are familiar with the child's past experiences (termed *metaphorical language* by Kanner); and abnormal speech melody, such as questionlike rises at ends of statements or monotonous tone of voice. Nonverbal communication, e.g., facial expression and gesture, is absent or minimal or, if present, is socially inappropriate in form.

Even when there are no gross abnormalities in language skills, communication is often impaired by circumstantiality and irrelevancies. A disturbance in the comprehension of language may be evidenced by an inability to understand jokes, puns, and sarcasm.

Impairment in imaginative activity may include absence of symbolic or fantasy play with toys or absence of playacting of adult roles, or imaginative activity may be restricted in content and repetitive and stereotyped in form. This is in marked contrast to the varied content of normal "pretend" play. For example, a child with the disorder may insist on lining up an exact number of playthings in the same manner over and over again, or repetitively mimic the actions of a television character.

Markedly restricted repertoire of activities and interests. This restriction may take various forms. In the younger child there may be resistance or even catastrophic reactions to minor changes in the environment, e.g., the child may scream when his or her place at the dinner table is changed. There is often attachment to objects, such as a string or rubber band. Motor stereotypies include hand-clapping, peculiar hand movements, rocking, and dipping and swaying movements of the whole body. In the older child there may be an insistence on following routines in a precise way, e.g., taking the same route to a favorite restaurant. There may be fascination with movement, such as passively staring at an electric fan or other rapidly revolving object. The child himself may be skillful at making all kinds of objects spin, so that he can watch them, or may spin himself around. The child may be exclusively interested in buttons, parts of the body, or playing with water.

Verbal stereotypies include repetition of words or phrases regardless of meaning. In older children, tasks involving long-term memory, for example, recall of the exact words of songs heard years before, train timetables, historical dates, or chemical formulae, may be excellent, but the information tends to be repeated over and over again, regardless of the social context and the appropriateness of the information.

Associated features. In general, the younger the child and the more severe the handicaps, the more associated features are likely to be present. They may include the following:

1. Abnormalities in the development of cognitive skills. The profile of specific skills is usually uneven, regardless of general level of intelligence. In most cases there is an associated diagnosis of Mental Retardation, most commonly in the moderate range (IQ 35-49).

2. Abnormalities of posture and motor behavior, such as stereotypies (arm-flapping, jumping, grimacing) in response to excitement, walking on tiptoe, odd hand and body postures, and poor motor coordination.

3. Odd responses to sensory input, such as ignoring some sensations (e.g., pain, heat, cold), displaying oversensitivity to certain sensations (e.g., covering ears to shut out some sounds; dislike of being touched), and being fascinated by some sensations (e.g., exaggerated reaction to lights or odors).

4. Abnormalities in eating, drinking, or sleeping (e.g., limiting diet to few foods, excessive drinking of fluids, recurrent awakening at night with rocking).

5. Abnormalities of mood (e.g., labile mood, giggling or weeping for no apparent reason, apparent absence of emotional reactions, lack of fear of real dangers, excessive fearfulness in response to harmless objects or events, generalized anxiety and tension).

6. Self-injurious behavior, such as head-banging, or finger-, hand-, or wrist-biting.

Other mental disorders, such as Major Depression, may occur during adolescence and adult life. They are most easily recognized in people who have sufficient speech to describe symptoms accurately.

Age at onset. Onset is reported by parents to be before age three in the great majority of cases. Very few cases are reported with an onset after five or six. However, it may be difficult to establish age at onset retrospectively unless those who cared for the child during the early years are able to give accurate information about language development, sociability, and play. Manifestations in infancy are more subtle and hard to define than those seen after two years of age. Parents of only children may be unaware of the problems until the child is observed with other children (for example, on entering school), and may then date the age at onset from that point, although a careful history often reveals that the abnormalities were present earlier. Parents may also date onset from a particular event, such as the birth of a sibling, or from the time when the child experienced a severe illness or accident or emotional trauma. In such cases, it is difficult to know whether subtle signs of the disorder may not have been present before the event.

In extremely rare cases, there is a period of apparently normal development followed by rapid distintegration of social and cognitive skills and development of the characteristic features of a Pervasive Developmental Disorder. Such cases have been termed Heller's syndrome or disintegrative psychosis, but according to this manual, should be classified as either Autistic Disorder or Pervasive Developmental Disorder Not Otherwise Specified.

Course. Manifestations of the disorder are, in almost all cases, lifelong, although they vary with chronological age and severity of the handicaps. Some children experience an improvement in social, language, and other skills at about age five to six years; in a few cases, this may be very marked.

Puberty can bring changes in either direction. Cognitive functions and social skills may decline or improve independently of each other. There is often an exacerbation of aggressive, oppositional, or other troublesome behavior, which may last for many years. A small minority of the children eventually are able to lead independent lives, with only minimal signs of the essential features of the disorder; but the social awkwardness and ineptness may persist. Most remain handicapped, with marked signs of the disorder. Factors related to long-term prognosis include IQ and the development of social and language skills.

Degree of impairment. The degree of impairment varies. In the majority of cases, a structured environment is necessary throughout life. In very rare cases, the person may complete college or even graduate education.

Complications. The major complication is the development of epileptic seizures. Most of those who develop seizures have an IQ below 50. In about 25% or more of cases of Autistic Disorder, there has been one or more episodes of seizure by the time the person reaches adulthood; in a sizable minority, onset of seizures is in adolescence.

In adolescence or early adult life, depression in response to partial realization of handicaps is common in those of higher levels of ability. Catatonic phenomena, particularly excitement or posturing, or an undifferentiated psychotic state with apparent delusions and hallucinations can occur in response to stress, but often clear rapidly if the stress is removed.

Prevalence. Studies in England and the United States, using criteria similiar to those in this manual, suggest that the prevalence of Autistic Disorder is approximately 4 to 5 children in every 10,000. Autistic Disorder was previously thought to be more common in upper socioeconomic classes, but studies suggest that this finding was a function of referral bias. The prevalence of Pervasive Developmental Disorder (Autistic Disorder and Pervasive Developmental Disorder Not Otherwise Specified) has been estimated at 10 to 15 children in every 10,000.

Sex ratio. Pervasive Developmental Disorder is more common among males than females, studies showing ratios ranging from 2:1 to 5:1. Most studies of Autistic Disorder show a ratio of 3:1 or 4:1.

Predisposing factors. A very wide range of pre-, peri- and postnatal conditions causing brain dysfunction are thought to predispose to the development of Pervasive Developmental Disorders. Autistic Disorder has been reported in association with maternal rubella, untreated phenylketonuria, tuberous sclerosis, anoxia during birth, encephalitis, infantile spasms, and fragile X syndrome. In the past, certain abnormalities of parental personality and child-rearing practices were thought to predispose to the development of Autistic Disorder, but controlled studies have not confirmed this view.

Familial pattern. Autistic Disorder is apparently more common in the siblings of children with the disorder than in the general population.

Differential diagnosis. Mental Retardation and Pervasive Developmental Disorder often coexist, but it should be understood that most people with even severe Mental Retardation do not have the essential features of Pervasive Developmental Disorder in that they are sociable and can communicate—even nonverbally if they have no speech. Differential diagnosis in people with severe or profound Mental Retardation may be difficult. When interest and pleasure in social approaches are evident, through eye contact, facial expression, bodily movements, and vocalizations, the diagnosis of Pervasive Developmental Disorder should not be made.

The diagnosis of **Schizophrenia** is extremely rare in childhood, whereas Pervasive Developmental Disorder is almost always first diagnosed in infancy or childhood. As adults, people with Pervasive Developmental Disorder may have many of the "negative symptoms" of the residual phase of Schizophrenia, such as social isolation and withdrawal, markedly peculiar behavior, blunted or inappropriate affect and oddities of language. The stereotyped, repetitive acting of a particular role—of an object, animal, or individual—by a person with Pervasive Developmental Disorder may be mistaken for a delusion. If the criteria for Autistic Disorder are met, the additional diagnosis of Schizophrenia should be made only in the rare instances in which prominent delusions or hallucinations meeting the criteria for Schizophrenia can be documented. Schizophrenia, however, preempts a diagnosis of Pervasive Developmental Disorder Not Otherwise Specified.

Hearing impairments and **Specific Developmental Language and Speech Disorders** affect the development of understanding and/or use of speech. Some **visual impairments** result in poor eye contact, and can be associated with staring at repetitive hand movements. Disorders involving only sensory and perceptual impairment can be differentiated from Pervasive Developmental Disorder by the presence of social interaction and a desire for communication appropriate for the person's mental age.

In **Schizoid and Schizotypal Personality Disorders** there are deficits in interpersonal relatedness. The diagnosis of Autistic Disorder preempts the diagnosis of these personality disorders. However, these personality disorders preempt the diagnosis of Pervasive Developmental Disorder Not Otherwise Specified.

In **Tic Disorders** and **Stereotypy/Habit Disorder** there are stereotyped body movements, but there is no qualitative impairment in reciprocal social interaction.

299.00   Autistic Disorder

The essential features constitute a severe form of Pervasive Developmental Disorder, with onset in infancy or childhood. The other features of the disorder are described above.

Diagnostic criteria for 299.00 Autistic Disorder

At least eight of the following sixteen items are present, these to include at least two items from A, one from B, and one from C.

Note: Consider a criterion to be met *only* if the behavior is abnormal for the person's developmental level.

A. Qualitative impairment in reciprocal social interaction as manifested by the following:

(The examples within parentheses are arranged so that those first mentioned are more likely to apply to younger or more handicapped, and the later ones, to older or less handicapped, persons with this disorder.)

(1) marked lack of awareness of the existence or feelings of others (e.g., treats a person as if he or she were a piece of furniture; does not notice another person's distress; apparently has no concept of the need of others for privacy)

(2) no or abnormal seeking of comfort at times of distress (e.g., does not come for comfort even when ill, hurt, or tired; seeks comfort in a stereo-typed way, e.g., says "cheese, cheese, cheese" whenever hurt)

(3) no or impaired imitation (e.g., does not wave bye-bye; does not copy mother's domestic activities; mechanical imitation of others' actions out of context)

(4) no or abnormal social play (e.g., does not actively participate in simple games; prefers solitary play activities; involves other children in play only as "mechanical aids")

(5) gross impairment in ability to make peer friendships (e.g., no interest in making peer friendships; despite interest in making friends, demonstrates lack of understanding of conventions of social interaction, for example, reads phone book to uninterested peer)

B. Qualitative impairment in verbal and nonverbal communication, and in imaginative activity, as manifested by the following:

(The numbered items are arranged so that those first listed are more likely to apply to younger or more handicapped, and the later ones, to older or less handicapped, persons with this disorder.)

(1) no mode of communication, such as communicative babbling, facial expression, gesture, mime, or spoken language

(2) markedly abnormal nonverbal communication, as in the use of eye-to-eye gaze, facial expression, body posture, or gestures to initiate or modulate social interaction (e.g., does not anticipate being held, stiffens when held, does not look at the person or smile when making a social approach, does not greet parents or visitors, has a fixed stare in social situations)

Diagnostic criteria for 299.00 Autistic Disorder continued

   (3) absence of imaginative activity, such as playacting of adult roles, fantasy characters, or animals; lack of interest in stories about imaginary events
   (4) marked abnormalities in the production of speech, including volume, pitch, stress, rate, rhythm, and intonation (e.g., monotonous tone, questionlike melody, or high pitch)
   (5) marked abnormalities in the form or content of speech, including stereo-typed and repetitive use of speech (e.g., immediate echolalia or mechanical repetition of television commercial); use of "you" when "I" is meant (e.g., using "You want cookie?" to mean "I want a cookie"); idiosyncratic use of words or phrases (e.g., "Go on green riding" to mean "I want to go on the swing"); or frequent irrelevant remarks (e.g., starts talking about train schedules during a conversation about sports)
   (6) marked impairment in the ability to initiate or sustain a conversation with others, despite adequate speech (e.g., indulging in lengthy monologues on one subject regardless of interjections from others)

C. Markedly restricted repertoire of activities and interests, as manifested by the following:

   (1) stereotyped body movements, e.g., hand-flicking or -twisting, spinning, head-banging, complex whole-body movements
   (2) persistent preoccupation with parts of objects (e.g., sniffing or smelling objects, repetitive feeling of texture of materials, spinning wheels of toy cars) or attachment to unusual objects (e.g., insists on carrying around a piece of string)
   (3) marked distress over changes in trivial aspects of environment, e.g., when a vase is moved from usual position
   (4) unreasonable insistence on following routines in precise detail, e.g., insisting that exactly the same route always be followed when shopping
   (5) markedly restricted range of interests and a preoccupation with one narrow interest, e.g., interested only in lining up objects, in amassing facts about meteorology, or in pretending to be a fantasy character

D. Onset during infancy or childhood.

Specify if childhood onset (after 36 months of age).

299.80   Pervasive Developmental Disorder Not Otherwise Specified

This category should be used when there is a qualitative impairment in the development of reciprocal social interaction and of verbal and nonverbal communication skills, but the criteria are not met for Autistic Disorder, Schizophrenia, or Schizotypal or Schizoid Personality Disorder. Some people with this diagnosis will exhibit a markedly restricted repertoire of activities and interests, but others will not.

SPECIFIC DEVELOPMENTAL DISORDERS (AXIS II)

This subclass is for disorders that are characterized by inadequate development of specific academic, language, speech, and motor skills and that are not due to demonstrable physical or neurologic disorders, a Pervasive Developmental Disorder,

Mental Retardation, or deficient educational opportunities. For example, a marked delay in language development in an otherwise normal child would be classified as a Specific Developmental Disorder, but a delay in language development in a child with a Pervasive Developmental Disorder would be attributed to the Pervasive Developmental Disorder and therefore would not be classified as a Specific Developmental Disorder. Similarly, a marked delay in learning to read experienced by an otherwise normal child with adequate educational opportunities would be classified as a Specific Developmental Disorder, whereas a delay in learning to read commensurate with general delays in development would be classified as Mental Retardation, not as a Specific Developmental Disorder.

The diagnosis of an Academic Skills Disorder (Developmental Arithmetic, Expressive Writing, and Reading Disorders) is made with the aid of standardized, individually administered tests that measure both the level of development of the impaired skill and the person's intellectual capacity. In diagnosing Developmental Expressive and Receptive Language Disorders, it is necessary to compare scores obtained from standardized measures of expressive or receptive language with scores obtained from standardized measures of nonverbal intellectual capacity.

It should be noted that a diagnosis of Mental Retardation in a child does not preclude the additional diagnosis of a Specific Developmental Disorder. For example, a child with an IQ of 60 should, with adequate schooling, be able to read simple materials. If the child's ability to read is markedly below what would be expected given an IQ of 60, both Mental Retardation and Developmental Reading Disorder should be diagnosed.

When a child has more than one Specific Developmental Disorder, all should be diagnosed. A Specific Developmental Disorder that appears to be caused by another Specific Developmental Disorder should be separately diagnosed. For example, a child with Developmental Receptive Language Disorder may show deficits in the development of arithmetic skills that are apparently related to the language disorder (i.e., a lack of understanding of numerical terms). In this example, the child would be diagnosed as having both Developmental Receptive Language Disorder and Developmental Arithmetic Disorder.

The inclusion of these categories in a classification of "mental disorders" is controversial, since many of the children with these disorders have no other signs of psychopathology. Further, the detection and treatment of many of these disorders usually take place within schools rather than the mental health system. However, these conditions are strongly associated with Axis I disorders and conform to the DSM-III-R concept of mental disorder (see p. 401).

Although many of the clinical features seen in Specific Developmental Disorders represent functional levels that are normal for very young children (e.g., inability to do arithmetic), there is no implication that children with these disorders will "catch up" over time. In fact, children with more severe forms of these disorders frequently continue to show signs of the disturbance in adolescence and adulthood; and the relevant diagnosis should be noted when an adult still has clinically significant signs of the disorder.

Impairment. All of the Specific Developmental Disorders are associated with impairment in academic functioning in children who are in school; impairment is most marked when language is affected. If the child is not in school, there is, by definition, impairment in activities of daily living.

Predisposing factors. There is some evidence that perinatal injury of various kinds predisposes to the development of Specific Developmental Disorders.

Complications. A common complication of Developmental Expressive or Receptive Language Disorder is an Academic Skills Disorder. A common complication of Academic Skills Disorders is Conduct Disorder.

Sex ratio. No information is available for Developmental Arithmetic and Developmental Coordination Disorders. The other Specific Developmental Disorders are from two to four times more common in males than in females.

Academic Skills Disorders

315.10 Developmental Arithmetic Disorder

The essential feature of this disorder is marked impairment in the development of arithmetic skills that is not explainable by Mental Retardation, inadequate schooling, or hearing or visual defects. The diagnosis is made only if this impairment significantly interferes with academic achievement or with activities of daily living that require arithmetic skills.

There are a number of different types of skills that may be impaired in Developmental Arithmetic Disorder. These include: "linguistic" skills (such as understanding or naming mathematical terms, understanding or naming mathematical operations or concepts, and coding written problems into mathematical symbols); "perceptual" skills (such as recognizing or reading numerical symbols or arithmetic signs, and clustering objects into groups); "attention" skills (such as copying figures correctly, remembering to add in "carried" numbers, and observing operational signs); and "mathematical" skills (such as following sequences of mathematical steps, counting objects, and learning multiplication tables).

Associated features. Various associated features have been reported, including: Developmental Receptive Language Disorder, Developmental Reading Disorder, Developmental Expressive Writing Disorder, Developmental Coordination Disorder, and memory and attention deficits.

Age at onset. This disorder is usually apparent by the time the child is eight years old (third grade). In some children the disorder is apparent as early as six years (first grade); in others it may not occur until age ten (fifth grade) or later.

Course. No information.

Prevalence. The prevalence is unknown, but the disorder is less common than Developmental Reading Disorder.

Familial pattern. No information.

Differential diagnosis. In **Mental Retardation,** deficits in arithmetic achievement are commensurate with the general impairment in intellectual functioning. However, in unusual cases of Mild Mental Retardation, arithmetic skills may be significantly below the expected level, given the person's schooling and level of Mental Retardation. In such cases the additional diagnosis of Developmental Arithmetic Disorder should be made, since treatment of the arithmetic difficulties can be particularly helpful to the child's chances for employment in adulthood.

Inadequate schooling can result in poor performance on standardized arithmetic tests. In such cases, however, there is likely to be a history of many school changes or absences, or most other children in the school are likely to have similar difficulty.

Diagnostic criteria for 315.10 Developmental Arithmetic Disorder

A. Arithmetic skills, as measured by a standardized, individually administered test, are markedly below the expected level, given the person's schooling and intellectual capacity (as determined by an individually administered IQ test).

B. The disturbance in A significantly interferes with academic achievement or activities of daily living requiring arithmetic skills.

C. Not due to a defect in visual or hearing acuity or a neurologic disorder.

315.80   Developmental Expressive Writing Disorder

The essential feature of this disorder is marked impairment in the development of expressive writing skills that is not explainable by Mental Retardation or inadequate schooling and that is not due to a visual or hearing defect or a neurologic disorder. The diagnosis is made only if this impairment significantly interferes with academic achievement or with activities of daily living that require expressive writing skills. The impairment in the ability to compose written texts may be marked by spelling errors, grammatical or punctuation errors within sentences, or poor paragraph organization.

Associated features. Common associated disorders are Developmental Reading Disorder, Developmental Expressive and Receptive Language Disorder, Developmental Arithmetic Disorder, Developmental Coordination Disorder, and Disruptive Behavior Disorders.

Age at onset. In severe cases, the disorder is apparent by age seven (second grade); in less severe cases, the disorder may not be apparent until age ten (fifth grade) or later.

Course and prevalence. Little attention has been given to Developmental Expressive Writing Disorder until recently. Consequently, there is no systematically collected information about course and prevalence. However, it is estimated that the disorder is probably as common as Developmental Reading Disorder and has a similar course.

Familial pattern. A history of Developmental Language Disorders and Academic Skills Disorders in first-degree biologic relatives is common.

Differential diagnosis. In **Mental Retardation**, difficulty composing written texts is commensurate with the general impairment in intellectual functioning. However, in some cases of Mild Mental Retardation, expressive writing skills may be significantly below the expected level, given the person's schooling and level of Mental Retardation. In such cases the additional diagnosis of Developmental Expressive Writing Disorder should be made, since treatment of the writing difficulties can be particularly helpful to the child's chances for employment in adulthood.

Impaired vision or hearing may affect expressive writing ability, and should be ruled out through audiometric or visual screening tests. **Impairment in motor coordination**, observed in Developmental Coordination Disorder and certain physical disorders, may produce illegible handwriting, but spelling and expression of thoughts in writing may not be affected.

Inadequate schooling can result in poor written expression abilities. In such cases, however, there is likely to be a history of many school changes or absences, or most other children in the school are likely to have similar difficulty.

Diagnostic criteria for 315.80 Developmental Expressive Writing Disorder

A. Writing skills, as measured by a standardized, individually administered test, are markedly below the expected level, given the person's schooling and intellectual capacity (as determined by an individually administered IQ test).

B. The disturbance in A significantly interferes with academic achievement or activities of daily living requiring the composition of written texts (spelling words and expressing thoughts in grammatically correct sentences and organized paragraphs).

C. Not due to a defect in visual or hearing acuity or a neurologic disorder.

315.00 Developmental Reading Disorder

The essential feature of this disorder is marked impairment in the development of word recognition skills and reading comprehension that is not explainable by Mental Retardation or inadequate schooling and that is not due to a visual or hearing defect or a neurologic disorder. The diagnosis is made only if this impairment significantly interferes with academic achievement or with activities of daily living that require reading skills.

Oral reading is characterized by omissions, distortions, and substitutions of words and by slow, halting reading. Reading comprehension is also affected. This disorder has been referred to as "dyslexia."

Associated features. Deficits in expressive language and speech discrimination are usually present, and may be severe enough to warrant the additional diagnosis of Developmental Expressive or Receptive Language Disorder. Developmental Expressive Writing Disorder is often present. In some cases there is a discrepancy between verbal and performance intelligence scores. Visual perceptual deficits are seen in only about 10% of cases. Disruptive Behavior Disorders may also be present, particularly in older children and adolescents.

Age at onset. The disorder is usually apparent by age seven (second grade). In severe cases, evidence of reading difficulty may be apparent as early as age six (first grade). Sometimes Developmental Reading Disorder may be compensated for in the early elementary grades, particularly when it is associated with high scores on intelligence tests. In this case, the disorder may not be apparent until age nine (fourth grade) or later.

Course. With reading therapy, if the disorder is mild, there often are no signs of the disorder in adulthood. If the disorder is severe, even with treatment many signs of the disorder remain for life.

Prevalence. Estimates of the prevalence of the disorder in school-age children have ranged from 2% to 8%.

Familial pattern. The disorder is more common among first-degree biologic relatives than in the general population.

Differential diagnosis. In **Mental Retardation,** reading difficulty is commensurate with the general impairment in intellectual functioning. However, in some cases of Mild Mental Retardation, the reading level is significantly below the expected level given the person's schooling and level of Mental Retardation. In such cases the additional diagnosis of Developmental Reading Disorder should be made, since treatment of the reading difficulties can be particularly helpful to the child's chances for employment in adulthood.

Inadequate schooling can result in poor performance on standardized reading tests. In such cases, however, there is likely to be a history of many school changes or absences, or most other children in the school are likely to have similar difficulty.

Impaired vision or hearing may affect reading ability, and can be ruled out through audiometric or visual screening tests.

Diagnostic criteria for 315.00 Developmental Reading Disorder

A. Reading achievement, as measured by a standardized, individually administered test, is markedly below the expected level, given the person's schooling and intellectual capacity (as determined by an individually administered IQ test).

B. The disturbance in A significantly interferes with academic achievement or activities of daily living requiring reading skills.

C. Not due to a defect in visual or hearing acuity or a neurologic disorder.

Language and Speech Disorders

315.39   Developmental Articulation Disorder

The essential feature of this disorder is a consistent failure to make correct articulations of speech sounds, at the developmentally appropriate age, that is not due to a Pervasive Developmental Disorder, Mental Retardation, impairment of the oral speech mechanism, or neurologic, intellectual, or hearing impairments. The disorder is manifested by frequent misarticulations, substitutions, or omissions of speech sounds, giving the impression of "baby talk."

The speech sounds that are most frequently misarticulated are those acquired later in the developmental sequence (r, sh, th, f, z, l, and ch); but in more severe cases or in younger children, sounds such as b, m, t, d, n, and h may be mispronounced. One or many speech sounds may be affected, but vowel sounds are not among them.

There is a considerable range in the severity of the disturbance. The child's speech may be completely intelligible, partially intelligible, or unintelligible.

Associated features. Other Specific Developmental Disorders are commonly present, including: Developmental Expressive Language Disorder, Developmental Receptive Language Disorder, Developmental Reading Disorder, and Developmental Coordination Disorder. Functional Enuresis may also be present.

A delay in reaching speech milestones (such as "first word" and "first sentence") has been reported in some children with Developmental Articulation Disorder, but most children with this disorder begin speaking at the appropriate age.

Age at onset. In severe cases, the disorder is recognized at about age three. In less severe cases, the disorder may not be apparent until age six.

Course. With speech therapy, complete recovery occurs in virtually all cases. In milder cases, spontaneous recovery may occur before the age of eight years.

Prevalence. A conservative estimate is that approximately 10% of children below age eight, and approximately 5% of children aged eight years or older, have the disorder.

Familial pattern. The disorder is more common among first-degree biologic relatives than in the general population.

Differential diagnosis. Misarticulations caused by **physical abnormalities** can be ruled out by physical examination: if there is a **hearing impairment,** audiometric testing will reveal an abnormality; with **dysarthria** or **apraxia,** there will be muscular weaknesses, oral mechanism defects, or a neurologic disorder, and there may be problems with chewing or sucking, drooling, and rate of speech.

In **Mental Retardation** there is a general impairment in intellectual functioning that is not present in Developmental Articulation Disorder. In **Pervasive Developmental Disorders** there are pervasive behavioral abnormalities not present in Developmental Articulation Disorder.

Diagnostic criteria for 315.39 Developmental Articulation Disorder

A. Consistent failure to use developmentally expected speech sounds. For example, in a three-year-old, failure to articulate p, b, and t, and in a six-year-old, failure to articulate r, sh, th, f, z, and l.

B. Not due to a Pervasive Developmental Disorder, Mental Retardation, defect in hearing acuity, disorders of the oral speech mechanism, or a neurologic disorder.

315.31 Developmental Expressive Language Disorder

The essential feature of this disorder is marked impairment in the development of expressive language that is not explainable by Mental Retardation or inadequate schooling and that is not due to a Pervasive Developmental Disorder, hearing impairment, or a neurologic disorder. The diagnosis is made only if this impairment significantly interferes with academic achievement or with activities of daily living that require the expression of verbal (or sign) language.

The linguistic features of Developmental Expressive Language Disorder are varied and depend on the severity of the disorder and the age of the child. Nonlinguistic functioning, however, is usually within normal limits. Among the expressive language limitations that may be present are: limited size of vocabulary, difficulty acquiring new words, vocabulary errors (such as substitutions, circumlocutions, overgeneralizations or jargon), shortened sentences, simplified grammatical structures, limited varieties of grammatical structures (such as verb forms), limited varieties of sentence types (such as imperatives, questions, etc.), omissions of critical parts of sentences, unusual word order, tangential responses, and slow rate of language development (speech beginning late, and advancement through stages of language development progressing slowly).

Associated features. Developmental Articulation Disorder is often present. In older children, school and learning problems (particularly in tasks involving perceptual or sequencing skills) may be present. A history of delay in reaching some motor milestones, Developmental Coordination Disorder, and Functional Enuresis are not uncommon. Emotional problems, social withdrawal, and behavioral difficulties may be present.

Age at onset. Severe forms usually occur before age three and are easily recognized. Less severe forms may not occur until early adolescence, when language ordinarily becomes more complex.

Course. For a young child with mild Developmental Expressive Language Disorder, the prognosis is very good. As many as 50% of the children with this disorder may spontaneously catch up in their expressive language abilities before they reach school age and thus not require any specialized help. In more severe cases, recovery is slower; but most children with Developmental Expressive Language Disorder not complicated by Developmental Receptive Language Disorder do acquire normal language abilities by late adolescence.

Prevalence. Estimates range from 3% to 10% of school-age children.

Familial pattern. It appears that the disorder is more likely to occur in people who have a family history of Developmental Articulation Disorder or other Specific Developmental Disorders.

Differential diagnosis. In **Mental Retardation** there may be impaired language functioning, but it is associated with the general impairment in intellectual functioning. **Impaired hearing** may also produce abnormal expressive language functioning, and should be ruled out by audiometric testing. In **Pervasive Developmental Disorders,** in which expressive language impairment may be present, there is little or no attempt to communicate nonverbally (e.g., through gestures). **Elective Mutism** involves limited expressive output that may mimic Developmental Expressive Language Disorder, but upon formal testing, comprehension is found to be within normal limits. **Acquired aphasia** is distinguished from Developmental Expressive Language Disorder by a history of onset associated with head trauma, seizures, or EEG abnormalities, or by "hard" neurologic signs such as hemiplegia.

Diagnostic criteria for 315.31 Developmental Expressive Language Disorder

A. The score obtained from a standardized measure of expressive language is substantially below that obtained from a standardized measure of nonverbal intellectual capacity (as determined by an individually administered IQ test).

B. The disturbance in A significantly interferes with academic achievement or activities of daily living requiring the expression of verbal (or sign) language. This may be evidenced in severe cases by use of a markedly limited vocabulary, by speaking only in simple sentences, or by speaking only in the present tense. In less severe cases, there may be hesitations or errors in recalling certain words, or errors in the production of long or complex sentences.

C. Not due to a Pervasive Developmental Disorder, defect in hearing acuity, or a neurologic disorder (aphasia).

315.31   Developmental Receptive Language Disorder

The essential feature of this disorder is marked impairment in the development of language comprehension that is not explainable by Mental Retardation or inadequate schooling and that is not due to a Pervasive Developmental Disorder, hearing impairment, or neurologic disorder. The diagnosis is made only if this impairment significantly interferes with academic achievement or with activities of daily living that require comprehension of verbal (or sign) language.

The comprehension deficit varies depending on the severity of the disorder and the age of the child. In mild cases there may be only difficulties in understanding particular types of words (such as spatial terms) or statements (for example, complex "if–then" sentences). In more severe cases, there may be multiple disabilities, including an inability to understand basic vocabulary or simple sentences, and deficits in various areas of auditory processing (e.g., discrimination of sounds, association of sounds and symbols, storage, recall, and sequencing).

Associated features. Developmental Articulation Disorder, Developmental Expressive Language Disorder, and Academic Skills Disorders are often present. Less commonly present are Functional Enuresis, Developmental Coordination Disorder, Attention-deficit Hyperactivity Disorder, EEG abnormalities, and other social and behavioral problems.

Age at onset. The disorder typically appears before the age of four years. Severe forms of the disorder are apparent by age two; mild forms of the disorder, however, may not be evident until the child is seven (second grade) or older, when language ordinarily becomes more complex.

Course. Although many children with Developmental Receptive Language Disorder do eventually acquire normal language abilities, some of the more severely affected do not.

Prevalence. Estimates range from 3% to 10% of school-age children.

Familial pattern. No information.

Differential diagnosis. Mental Retardation involves impaired language comprehension that is commensurate with the general impairment in intellectual functioning. **Hearing impairment,** identified by audiometric testing, may also produce abnormal functioning in language comprehension. In **Pervasive Developmental Disorders,** when there is impairment in language comprehension, there are usually few or no attempts to communicate nonverbally (e.g., through gestures) and little or no imaginary play. **Elective Mutism** involves limited expressive output that may suggest Developmental Receptive Language Disorder, but upon formal testing, comprehension is found to be within normal limits. **Acquired aphasia** is distinguished from Developmental Receptive Language Disorder by a history of onset associated with head trauma, seizures, or EEG abnormalities, or by "hard" neurologic signs such as hemiplegia.

Diagnostic criteria for 315.31 Developmental Receptive Language Disorder

A. The score obtained from a standardized measure of receptive language is substantially below that obtained from a standardized measure of nonverbal intellectual capacity (as determined by an individually administered IQ test).

B. The disturbance in A significantly interferes with academic achievement or activities of daily living requiring the comprehension of verbal (or sign) language. This may be manifested in more severe cases by an inability to understand simple words or sentences. In less severe cases, there may be difficulty in understanding only certain types of words, such as spatial terms, or an inability to comprehend longer or more complex statements.

C. Not due to a Pervasive Developmental Disorder, defect in hearing acuity, or a neurologic disorder (aphasia).

Motor Skills Disorder

315.40 Developmental Coordination Disorder

The essential feature of this disorder is a marked impairment in the development of motor coordination that is not explainable by Mental Retardation and that is not due to a known physical disorder. The diagnosis is made only if this impairment significantly interferes with academic achievement or with activities of daily living.

The manifestations of this disorder vary with age and development: young children exhibit clumsiness and delays in developmental motor milestones (including tying shoelaces, buttoning shirts, and zipping pants); older children display difficulties with the motor aspects of puzzle assembly, model-building, playing ball, and printing or handwriting.

Associated features. Commonly associated problems include delays in other nonmotor milestones, Developmental Articulation Disorder, and Developmental Receptive and Expressive Language Disorders.

Age at onset. Recognition of the disorder usually occurs when the child first attempts such tasks as running, holding a knife and fork, or buttoning clothes.

Course. The course is variable. In some cases, lack of coordination continues through adolescence and adulthood.

Prevalence. Prevalence has been estimated to be as high as 6% for children in the age range of 5-11 years.

Familial pattern. No information.

Differential diagnosis. In **specific neurologic disorders** that may be associated with problems in coordination (e.g., cerebral palsy, progressive lesions of the cerebellum), there is definite neural damage and abnormal findings on conventional neurologic examination. In **Attention-deficit Hyperactivity Disorder,** there may be falling, bumping into things, or knocking things over because of distractibility and impulsiveness. In **Mental Retardation,** there may be delays in motor milestones, but these are associated with the general impairment in intellectual functioning. Similarly, in **Pervasive Developmental Disorders,** an abnormal gait and delays in motor milestones are part of a marked and pervasive history of abnormal development.

Diagnostic criteria for 315.40 Developmental Coordination Disorder

A. The person's performance in daily activities requiring motor coordination is markedly below the expected level, given the person's chronological age and intellectual capacity. This may be manifested by marked delays in achieving motor milestones (walking, crawling, sitting), dropping things, "clumsiness," poor performance in sports, or poor handwriting.

B. The disturbance in A significantly interferes with academic achievement or activities of daily living.

C. Not due to a known physical disorder, such as cerebral palsy, hemiplegia, or muscular dystrophy.

315.90   Specific Developmental Disorder Not Otherwise Specified

Disorders in the development of language, speech, academic, and motor skills that do not meet the criteria for a Specific Developmental Disorder. Examples include aphasia with epilepsy acquired in childhood ("Landau syndrome") and specific developmental difficulties in spelling.

OTHER DEVELOPMENTAL DISORDERS (AXIS II)

315.90   Developmental Disorder Not Otherwise Specified

Disorders in development that do not meet the criteria for either Mental Retardation or a Pervasive or a Specific Developmental Disorder.

DISRUPTIVE BEHAVIOR DISORDERS

This subclass of disorders is characterized by behavior that is socially disruptive and is often more distressing to others than to the people with the disorders. The subclass includes Attention-deficit Hyperactivity Disorder, Oppositional Defiant Disorder, and Conduct Disorder. Studies have indicated that in both clinic and community samples, the symptoms of these disorders covary to a high degree. In the literature the behaviors that these disorders encompass have been referred to as "externalizing" symptoms.

314.01   Attention-deficit Hyperactivity Disorder (ADHD)

The essential features of this disorder are developmentally inappropriate degrees of inattention, impulsiveness, and hyperactivity. People with the disorder generally display some disturbance in each of these areas, but to varying degrees.

Manifestations of the disorder usually appear in most situations, including at home, in school, at work, and in social situations, but to varying degrees. Some people, however, show signs of the disorder in only one setting, such as at home or at school. Symptoms typically worsen in situations requiring sustained attention, such as listening to a teacher in a classroom, attending meetings, or doing class assignments or chores at home. Signs of the disorder may be minimal or absent when the person is receiving frequent reinforcement or very strict control, or is in a novel setting or a one-to-one situation (e.g., being examined in the clinician's office, or interacting with a videogame).

In the *classroom or workplace*, inattention and impulsiveness are evidenced by not sticking with tasks sufficiently to finish them and by having difficulty organizing and completing work correctly. The person often gives the impression that he or she is not listening or has not heard what has been said. Work is often messy, and performed carelessly and impulsively.

Impulsiveness is often demonstrated by blurting out answers to questions before they are completed, making comments out of turn, failing to await one's turn in group tasks, failing to heed directions fully before beginning to respond to assignments, interrupting the teacher during a lesson, and interrupting or talking to other children during quiet work periods.

Hyperactivity may be evidenced by difficulty remaining seated, excessive jumping about, running in classroom, fidgeting, manipulating objects, and twisting and wiggling in one's seat.

At *home*, inattention may be displayed in failure to follow through on others' requests and instructions and in frequent shifts from one uncompleted activity to another. Problems with impulsiveness are often expressed by interrupting or intruding on other family members and by accident-prone behavior, such as grabbing a hot pan from the stove or carelessly knocking over a pitcher. Hyperactivity may be evidenced by an inability to remain seated when expected to do so (situations in which this is the case vary greatly from home to home) and by excessively noisy activities.

With *peers*, inattention is evident in failure to follow the rules of structured games or to listen to other children. Impulsiveness is frequently demonstrated by failing to await one's turn in games, interrupting, grabbing objects (not with malevolent intent), and engaging in potentially dangerous activities without considering the possible consequences, e.g., riding a skateboard over extremely rough terrain. Hyperactivity may be shown by excessive talking and by an inability to play quietly and to regulate one's activity to conform to the demands of the game (e.g., in playing "Simon Says," the child keeps moving about and talking to peers when he or she is expected to be quiet).

Age-specific features. In preschool children, the most prominent features are generally signs of gross motor overactivity, such as excessive running or climbing. The child is often described as being on the go and "always having his motor running." Inattention and impulsiveness are likely to be shown by frequent shifting from one activity to another. In older children and adolescents, the most prominent features tend to be excessive fidgeting and restlessness rather than gross motor overactivity. Inattention and impulsiveness may contribute to failure to complete assigned tasks or instructions, or careless performance of assigned work. In adolescents, impulsiveness is often displayed in social activities, such as initiating a diverting activity on the spur of the moment instead of attending to a previous commitment (e.g., joy riding instead of doing homework).

Associated features. Associated features vary as a function of age, and include low self-esteem, mood lability, low frustration tolerance, and temper outbursts. Academic underachievement is characteristic of most children with this disorder.

In clinic samples, some or all of the symptoms of Oppositional Defiant Disorder, Conduct Disorder, and Specific Developmental Disorders are often present. Functional Encopresis and Functional Enuresis are sometimes seen. Although Tourette's Disorder is relatively rare in children with ADHD, in clinic samples many children with Tourette's Disorder are found to have ADHD as well.

Nonlocalized, "soft," neurologic signs and motor-perceptual dysfunctions (e.g., poor eye-hand coordination) may be present.

Age at onset. In approximately half of the cases, onset of the disorder is before age four. Frequently the disorder is not recognized until the child enters school.

Course. In the majority of cases manifestations of the disorder persist throughout childhood. Oppositional Defiant Disorder or Conduct Disorder often develops later in childhood in those with ADHD. Among those who develop Conduct Disorder, a significant number are found to have Antisocial Personality Disorder in adulthood. Follow-up studies of clinic samples indicate that approximately one-third of children with ADHD continue to show some signs of the disorder in adulthood. Studies have indicated that the following features predict a poor course: coexisting Conduct Disorder, low IQ, and severe mental disorder in the parents.

Impairment. Some impairment in social and school functioning is common.

Complications. School failure is the major complication.

Predisposing factors. Central nervous system abnormalities, such as the presence of neurotoxins, cerebral palsy, epilepsy, and other neurologic disorders, are thought to be predisposing factors. Disorganized or chaotic environments and child abuse or neglect may be predisposing factors in some cases.

Prevalence. The disorder is common; it may occur in as many as 3% of children.

Sex ratio. In clinic samples, the disorder is from six to nine times more common in males than in females. In community samples, multiple signs of the disorder occur only three times more often in males than in females.

Familial pattern. The disorder is believed to be more common in first-degree biologic relatives of people with the disorder than in the general population. Among family members, the following disorders are thought to be overrepresented: Specific Developmental Disorders, Alcohol Dependence or Abuse, Conduct Disorder, and Antisocial Personality Disorder.

Differential diagnosis. Age-appropriate overactivity, as is seen in some particularly active children, does not have the haphazard and poorly organized quality characteristic of the behavior of children with Attention-deficit Hyperactivity Disorder. Children in **inadequate, disorganized,** or **chaotic environments** may appear to have difficulty in sustaining attention and in goal-directed behavior. In such cases it may be impossible to determine whether the disorganized behavior is primarily a function of the chaotic environment or whether it is due largely to the child's psychopathology (in which case the diagnosis of Attention-deficit Hyperactivity Disorder may be warranted).

In **Mental Retardation** there may be many of the features of ADHD because of the generalized delay in intellectual development. The additional diagnosis of ADHD is made only if the relevant symptoms are excessive for the child's mental age.

Symptoms characteristic of ADHD are often observed in **Pervasive Developmental Disorders;** in these cases a diagnosis of ADHD is preempted.

In **Mood Disorders** there may be psychomotor agitation and difficulty in concentration that are difficult to distinguish from the hyperactivity and attentional difficulties seen in Attention-deficit Hyperactivity Disorder. Therefore, it is important to consider the diagnosis of a Mood Disorder before making the diagnosis of Attention-deficit Hyperactivity Disorder.

Signs of impulsiveness and hyperactivity are not present in **Undifferentiated Attention-deficit Disorder**.

Diagnostic criteria for 314.01 Attention-deficit Hyperactivity Disorder

Note: Consider a criterion met only if the behavior is considerably more frequent than that of most people of the same mental age.

A. A disturbance of at least six months during which at least eight of the following are present:

   (1) often fidgets with hands or feet or squirms in seat (in adolescents, may be limited to subjective feelings of restlessness)
   (2) has difficulty remaining seated when required to do so
   (3) is easily distracted by extraneous stimuli
   (4) has difficulty awaiting turn in games or group situations
   (5) often blurts out answers to questions before they have been completed
   (6) has difficulty following through on instructions from others (not due to oppositional behavior or failure of comprehension), e.g., fails to finish chores
   (7) has difficulty sustaining attention in tasks or play activities
   (8) often shifts from one uncompleted activity to another
   (9) has difficulty playing quietly
   (10) often talks excessively
   (11) often interrupts or intrudes on others, e.g., butts into other children's games
   (12) often does not seem to listen to what is being said to him or her
   (13) often loses things necessary for tasks or activities at school or at home (e.g., toys, pencils, books, assignments)

Diagnostic criteria for 314.01 Attention-deficit Hyperactivity Disorder continued

(14) often engages in physically dangerous activities without considering possible consequences (not for the purpose of thrill-seeking), e.g., runs into street without looking

Note: The above items are listed in descending order of discriminating power based on data from a national field trial of the DSM-III-R criteria for Disruptive Behavior Disorders.

B.   Onset before the age of seven.

C.   Does not meet the criteria for a Pervasive Developmental Disorder.

Criteria for severity of Attention-deficit Hyperactivity Disorder:

Mild: Few, if any, symptoms in excess of those required to make the diagnosis **and** only minimal or no impairment in school and social functioning.

Moderate: Symptoms or functional impairment intermediate between "mild" and "severe."

Severe: Many symptoms in excess of those required to make the diagnosis **and** significant and pervasive impairment in functioning at home and school and with peers.

Conduct Disorder

312.20   group type
312.00   solitary aggressive type
312.90   undifferentiated type

The essential feature of this disorder is a persistent pattern of conduct in which the basic rights of others and major age-appropriate societal norms or rules are violated. The behavior pattern typically is present in the home, at school, with peers, and in the community. The conduct problems are more serious than those seen in Oppositional Defiant Disorder.

Physical aggression is common. Children or adolescents with this disorder usually initiate aggression, may be physically cruel to other people or to animals, and frequently deliberately destroy other people's property (this may include fire-setting). They may engage in stealing with confrontation of the victim, as in mugging, purse-snatching, extortion, or armed robbery. At later ages, the physical violence may take the form of rape, assault, or, in rare cases, homicide.

Covert stealing is common. This may range from "borrowing" others' possessions to shoplifting, forgery, and breaking into someone else's house, building, or car. Lying and cheating in games or in schoolwork are common. Often a youngster with this disorder is truant from school, and may run away from home.

Associated features. Regular use of tobacco, liquor, or nonprescribed drugs and sexual behavior that begins unusually early for the child's peer group in his or her milieu are common. The child may have no concern for the feelings, wishes, and well-being of others, as shown by callous behavior, and may lack appropriate feelings of guilt or remorse. Such a child may readily inform on his or her companions and try to place blame for misdeeds on them.

Self-esteem is usually low, though the person may project an image of "toughness." Poor frustration tolerance, irritability, temper outbursts, and provocative recklessness are frequent characteristics. Symptoms of anxiety and depression are common, and may justify additional diagnoses.

Academic achievement, particularly in reading and other verbal skills, is often below the level expected on the basis of intelligence and age, and may justify the additional diagnosis of a Specific Developmental Disorder. Attentional difficulties, impulsiveness, and hyperactivity are very common, especially in childhood, and may justify the additional diagnosis of Attention-deficit Hyperactivity Disorder.

Age at onset. Onset is usually prepubertal, particularly of the Solitary Aggressive Type. Postpubertal onset is more common among females than males.

Course. The course is variable, mild forms frequently showing improvement over time and severe forms tending to be chronic. Early onset is associated with greater risk of continuation into adult life as Antisocial Personality Disorder. In some cases there may be adequate social functioning in adulthood, but persistence of illegal activity, which may be considered to be Adult Antisocial Behavior (V Code). Finally, many people with Conduct Disorder in childhood, particularly the Group Type, achieve reasonable social and occupational adjustment as adults.

Impairment. The degree of impairment varies from mild to severe. It may preclude attendance in an ordinary school classroom or living at home or in a foster home. When antisocial behavior is extreme, institutionalization, with its temporary loss of autonomy, may be necessary.

Complications. Complications include school suspension, legal difficulties, Psychoactive Substance Use Disorders, venereal diseases, unwanted pregnancy, high rates of physical injury from accidents, fights (and retaliation by victims), and suicidal behavior.

Predisposing factors. The following conditions have been noted as likely predisposing factors: antecedent Attention-deficit Hyperactivity Disorder or Oppositional Defiant Disorder, parental rejection, inconsistent management with harsh discipline, early institutional living, frequent shifting of parent figures (foster parents, relatives, or stepparents), absence of a father or presence of a father with Alcohol Dependence, large family size, and association with a delinquent subgroup.

Prevalence and sex ratio. It is estimated that approximately 9% of males and 2% of females under the age of 18 have the disorder.

Familial pattern. The disorder is more common in children of adults with Antisocial Personality Disorder and Alcohol Dependence than in the general population.

Differential diagnosis. Isolated acts of antisocial behavior do not justify a diagnosis of Conduct Disorder, and may be coded as Childhood or Adolescent Antisocial Behavior (V Codes). The behavior qualifies for a diagnosis of Conduct Disorder only if the antisocial behavior continues over a period of at least six months, and thus represents a repetitive and persistent pattern. When such a pattern exists, there will usually be obvious impairment in social and school functioning of a type not generally observed when the antisocial behavior represents an isolated act.

Though **Oppositional Defiant Disorder** includes some of the features observed in Conduct Disorder, such as disobedience and opposition to authority figures, the basic rights of others and major age-appropriate societal norms or rules are not violated as they are in Conduct Disorder.

The irritability and antisocial behavior often seen in Bipolar Disorder in children or adolescents can erroneously be considered symptoms of Conduct Disorder. However, manic episodes are usually brief, whereas Conduct Disorder tends to persist.

Attention-deficit Hyperactivity Disorder and **Specific Developmental Disorders** are common associated diagnoses, and should also be noted when present.

Diagnostic criteria for Conduct Disorder

A. A disturbance of conduct lasting at least six months, during which at least three of the following have been present:

   (1) has stolen without confrontation of a victim on more than one occasion (including forgery)
   (2) has run away from home overnight at least twice while living in parental or parental surrogate home (or once without returning)
   (3) often lies (other than to avoid physical or sexual abuse)
   (4) has deliberately engaged in fire-setting
   (5) is often truant from school (for older person, absent from work)
   (6) has broken into someone else's house, building, or car
   (7) has deliberately destroyed others' property (other than by fire-setting)
   (8) has been physically cruel to animals
   (9) has forced someone into sexual activity with him or her
   (10) has used a weapon in more than one fight
   (11) often initiates physical fights
   (12) has stolen with confrontation of a victim (e.g., mugging, purse-snatching, extortion, armed robbery)
   (13) has been physically cruel to people

   Note: The above items are listed in descending order of discriminating power based on data from a national field trial of the DSM-III-R criteria for Disruptive Behavior Disorders.

B. If 18 or older, does not meet criteria for Antisocial Personality Disorder.

Criteria for severity of Conduct Disorder:

Mild: Few if any conduct problems in excess of those required to make the diagnosis, **and** conduct problems cause only minor harm to others.

Moderate: Number of conduct problems and effect on others intermediate between "mild" and "severe."

Severe: Many conduct problems in excess of those required to make the diagnosis, **or** conduct problems cause considerable harm to others, e.g., serious physical injury to victims, extensive vandalism or theft, prolonged absence from home.

Types
The predominant clinical features of the three types presented here largely correspond to categories derived from empirical studies. These types refer to the conduct problems alone, not to any coexisting mental disorders, which should also be diagnosed when present. Each of the types can occur in mild, moderate, or severe form.

The Solitary Aggressive Type corresponds, roughly, to the DSM-III concept of Undersocialized Aggressive Type. Children with this type of Conduct Disorder often make little attempt to conceal their antisocial behavior; they are often socially isolated. The Group Type is more common and corresponds, roughly, to the DSM-III concept of Socialized Nonaggressive Type, although in the DSM-III-R type, physical aggression may be present. Usually these children claim loyalty to the members of their group. Note that although the Undifferentiated Type is defined here as a residual group, it may be far more common than either of the other two types.

312.20   group type
The essential feature is the predominance of conduct problems occurring mainly as a group activity with peers. Aggressive physical behavior may or may not be present.

312.00   solitary aggressive type
The essential feature is the predominance of aggressive physical behavior, usually toward both adults and peers, initiated by the person (not as a group activity).

312.90   undifferentiated type
This a subtype for children or adolescents with Conduct Disorder with a mixture of clinical features that cannot be classified as either Solitary Aggressive Type or Group Type.

313.81   Oppositional Defiant Disorder
The essential feature of this disorder is a pattern of negativistic, hostile, and defiant behavior without the more serious violations of the basic rights of others that are seen in Conduct Disorder. The diagnosis is made only if the oppositional and defiant behavior is much more common than that seen in other people of the same mental age.

Children with this disorder commonly are argumentative with adults, frequently lose their temper, swear, and are often angry, resentful, and easily annoyed by others. They frequently actively defy adult requests or rules and deliberately annoy other people. They tend to blame others for their own mistakes or difficulties.

Manifestations of the disorder are almost invariably present in the home, but may not be present at school or with other adults or peers. In some cases, features of the disorder, from the beginning of the disturbance, are displayed in areas outside the home; in other cases, they start in the home, but later develop in areas outside the home. Typically, symptoms of the disorder are more evident in interactions with adults or peers whom the child knows well. Thus, children with the disorder are likely to show little or no signs of the disorder when examined clinically.

Usually the person does not regard himself or herself as oppositional or defiant, but justifies his or her behavior as a response to unreasonable circumstances.

Associated features. Associated features vary as a function of age, and include low self-esteem, mood lability, low frustration tolerance, and temper outbursts. There may be heavy use of illegal psychoactive substances, such as cannabis and alcohol (before the legal age). Use of tobacco is common. Often Attention-deficit Hyperactivity Disorder is also present.

Age at onset. Although precursors may appear in early childhood, the disorder, as defined, typically begins by eight years, and usually not later than early adolescence.

Course. The course is unknown. In many cases the disturbance evolves into Conduct Disorder or a Mood Disorder.

Impairment. Impairment is usually greatest within the home.

Complications. Conduct Disorder is a common complication.

Predisposing factors and prevalence. No information.

Sex ratio. Before puberty, the disorder is more common in males than in females; in postpubertal children the sex ratio is probably equal.

Familial pattern. No information.

Differential diagnosis. In **Conduct Disorder** all of the features of Oppositional Defiant Disorder are likely to be present; for that reason, Conduct Disorder preempts the diagnosis of Oppositional Defiant Disorder. In a **psychotic disorder**, such as Schizophrenia, the features of Oppositional Defiant Disorder may be seen, particularly during the prodromal phase; and a psychotic disorder therefore preempts the diagnosis of Oppositional Defiant Disorder. Features of Oppositional Defiant Disorder may be seen during the course of **Dysthymia,** or a **Manic, Hypomanic,** or **Major Depressive Episode**, but in such cases the additional diagnosis of Oppositional Defiant Disorder is not made.

Diagnostic criteria for 313.81 Oppositional Defiant Disorder

Note: Consider a criterion met only if the behavior is considerably more frequent than that of most people of the same mental age.

A. A disturbance of at least six months during which at least five of the following are present:

   (1) often loses temper
   (2) often argues with adults
   (3) often actively defies or refuses adult requests or rules, e.g., refuses to do chores at home
   (4) often deliberately does things that annoy other people, e.g., grabs other children's hats
   (5) often blames others for his or her own mistakes
   (6) is often touchy or easily annoyed by others
   (7) is often angry and resentful
   (8) is often spiteful or vindictive
   (9) often swears or uses obscene language

(continued)

> **Diagnostic criteria for 313.81 Oppositional Defiant Disorder continued**
>
> **Note:** The above items are listed in descending order of discriminating power based on data from a national field trial of the DSM-III-R criteria for Disruptive Behavior Disorders.
>
> B. Does not meet the criteria for Conduct Disorder, and does not occur exclusively during the course of a psychotic disorder, Dysthymia, or a Major Depressive, Hypomanic, or Manic Episode.
>
> **Criteria for severity of Oppositional Defiant Disorder:**
>
> **Mild:** Few, if any, symptoms in excess of those required to make the diagnosis **and** only minimal or no impairment in school and social functioning.
>
> **Moderate:** Symptoms or functional impairment intermediate between "mild" and "severe."
>
> **Severe:** Many symptoms in excess of those required to make the diagnosis **and** significant and pervasive impairment in functioning at home and school and with other adults and peers.

ANXIETY DISORDERS OF CHILDHOOD OR ADOLESCENCE

This subclass includes disorders in which anxiety is the predominant clinical feature. In the first two categories, Separation Anxiety Disorder and Avoidant Disorder of Childhood or Adolescence, the anxiety is focused on specific situations. In the third category, Overanxious Disorder, the anxiety is generalized to a variety of situations.

309.21 Separation Anxiety Disorder

The essential feature of this disorder is excessive anxiety, for at least two weeks, concerning separation from those to whom the child is attached. When separation occurs, the child may experience anxiety to the point of panic. The reaction is beyond that expected for the child's developmental level. Onset of the disorder is before age 18. The diagnosis is not made if the anxiety occurs exclusively during the course of a Pervasive Developmental Disorder, Schizophrenia, or any other psychotic disorder.

Children with Separation Anxiety Disorder are uncomfortable when they travel independently away from the house or from other familiar areas. They may refuse to visit or sleep at friends' homes, to go on errands, or to attend camp or school. (It should be noted that some cases of school refusal are not due to separation anxiety; in such cases, usually in adolescence, the child actually fears the school situation because of anxiety about social or academic performance, whether or not he or she is accompanied by a parent.) Children with Separation Anxiety Disorder may be unable to stay in a room by themselves, and may display "clinging" behavior, staying close to the parent, "shadowing" the parent around the house. Physical complaints, such as stomachaches, headaches, nausea, and vomiting, are common when separation is anticipated or occurs. Cardiovascular symptoms such as palpitations, dizziness, and faintness are rare in younger children, but may occur in adolescents.

When separated from significant others to whom they are attached, these children are often preoccupied with morbid fears that accidents or illness will befall those to whom they are attached or themselves. They often express fear of being lost and never being reunited with their parents. The exact nature of the fantasized mishaps varies. In general, young children have less specific, more amorphous concerns. As the child becomes older, the fears may become systematized around identifiable potential dangers. Many children, even some older ones, do not report fears of definite threats, but only pervasive anxiety about ill-defined dangers or death. Children also typically exhibit anticipatory anxiety when separation is threatened or impending; young children experience distress only when separation actually occurs.

Children with this disorder often have fears of animals, monsters, and situations that are perceived as presenting danger to the integrity of the family or themselves. Consequently, they may have exaggerated fears of muggers, burglars, kidnappers, car accidents, or plane travel. Concerns about dying and death are common.

These children often have difficulty going to sleep, and may insist that someone stay with them until they fall asleep. They may make their way to their parents' bed (or that of another significant person, such as a sibling); if entry to the parental bedroom is barred, they may sleep outside the parents' door. Nightmares, whose content expresses the child's morbid fears, may occur.

Some children do not experience morbid apprehension about possible harm befalling them or those close to them, but instead are extremely homesick and uncomfortable, to the point of misery, or even panic, when away from home. These children yearn to return home, and are preoccupied with reunion fantasies. When not with a major attachment figure, children with this disorder may exhibit recurrent instances of social withdrawal, apathy, sadness, or difficulty concentrating on work or play. Occasionally, a child may become violent toward a person who is forcing separation. Children with Separation Anxiety Disorder may refuse to see relatives or former friends in order to avoid having to account for their difficulties in, or absence from, school or from other activities that they avoided.

Adolescents with this disorder, especially boys, may deny overconcern about their mother or their wish to be with her; yet their behavior reflects anxiety about separation: they are reluctant or unable to leave the home or the parent, and feel comfortable only in situations in which no separation is demanded.

Although the disorder represents a form of phobia, it is not included among the Phobic Disorders because it has unique features and is characteristically associated with childhood.

Associated features. Fear of the dark is common, and some children have fixed fears that may appear bizarre. For example, they may report that they see and feel eyes staring at them in the dark, that mythical animals are glaring at them, or that bloody creatures are reaching for them.

Depressed mood frequently is present, and may become more persistent over time, justifying an additional diagnosis of Dysthymia or Major Depression.

Children with this disorder are often described as demanding, intrusive, and in need of constant attention. They may complain that no one loves them or cares about them and that they wish they were dead, especially if separation is enforced. Others are described as unusually conscientious, compliant, and eager to please.

When no demands for separation are made, children with Separation Anxiety Disorder typically have no interpersonal difficulties.

Age at onset. The age at onset may be as early as preschool age; by definition, it is before the age of 18. Onset in adolescence is rare.

Course. Typically there are periods of exacerbation and remission over a period of several years. In some cases both the anxiety about possible separation and the avoidance of situations involving separation (e.g., going away to college) persist for many years.

Impairment. In its severe form, the disorder may be very incapacitating, in that the child is unable to attend school and function independently in a variety of areas.

Complications. The child often undergoes elaborate physical examinations and medical procedures because of numerous somatic complaints. When school refusal occurs, common complications are academic difficulties and social avoidance.

Predisposing factors. No specific premorbid personality disturbance is associated with Separation Anxiety Disorder. In most cases the disorder develops after some life stress, typically a loss, the death of a relative or pet, an illness of the child or a relative, or a change in the child's environment, such as a school change or a move to a new neighborhood.

Children with this disorder tend to come from families that are close-knit and caring. The etiologic significance of this familial pattern is not clear. Neglected children are underrepresented among those with Separation Anxiety Disorder.

Prevalence. The disorder is apparently not uncommon.

Sex ratio. The disorder is apparently equally common in males and females.

Familial pattern. The disorder is apparently more common in first-degree biologic relatives than in the general population, and may be more frequent in children of mothers with Panic Disorder.

Differential diagnosis. In **early childhood some degree of separation anxiety** is a normal phenomenon, and clinical judgment must be used in distinguishing this from the clearly excessive reaction to separation seen in Separation Anxiety Disorder. In **Overanxious Disorder,** anxiety is not focused on separation. In **Pervasive Developmental Disorders** or **Schizophrenia,** anxiety about separation may occur, but is viewed as due to these conditions rather than as a separate disorder. In **Major Depression** occurring in children, the diagnosis of Separation Anxiety Disorder should also be made when the criteria for both disorders are met. **Panic Disorder with Agoraphobia** is uncommon before age 18, and the fear is of being incapacitated by a panic attack rather than of separation from parental figures. In some cases of Panic Disorder with Agoraphobia in adolescents or young adults, however, many of the symptoms of Separation Anxiety Disorder may be present. In **Conduct Disorder,** truancy is common, but the child stays away from the home, and anxiety about separation is usually not present.

Diagnostic criteria for 309.21 Separation Anxiety Disorder

A. Excessive anxiety concerning separation from those to whom the child is attached, as evidenced by at least three of the following:

> **Diagnostic criteria for 309.21 Separation Anxiety Disorder continued**
>
> (1) unrealistic and persistent worry about possible harm befalling major attachment figures or fear that they will leave and not return
>
> (2) unrealistic and persistent worry that an untoward calamitous event will separate the child from a major attachment figure, e.g., the child will be lost, kidnapped, killed, or be the victim of an accident
>
> (3) persistent reluctance or refusal to go to school in order to stay with major attachment figures or at home
>
> (4) persistent reluctance or refusal to go to sleep without being near a major attachment figure or to go to sleep away from home
>
> (5) persistent avoidance of being alone, including "clinging" to and "shadowing" major attachment figures
>
> (6) repeated nightmares involving the theme of separation
>
> (7) complaints of physical symptoms, e.g., headaches, stomachaches, nausea, or vomiting, on many school days or on other occasions when anticipating separation from major attachment figures
>
> (8) recurrent signs or complaints of excessive distress in anticipation of separation from home or major attachment figures, e.g., temper tantrums or crying, pleading with parents not to leave
>
> (9) recurrent signs of complaints of excessive distress when separated from home or major attachment figures, e.g., wants to return home, needs to call parents when they are absent or when child is away from home
>
> B. Duration of disturbance of at least two weeks.
>
> C. Onset before the age of 18.
>
> D. Occurrence not exclusively during the course of a Pervasive Developmental Disorder, Schizophrenia, or any other psychotic disorder.

313.21   Avoidant Disorder of Childhood or Adolescence

The essential feature of this disorder is an excessive shrinking from contact with unfamiliar people that is of sufficient severity to interfere with social functioning in peer relationships and that is of at least six months' duration. This is coupled with a clear desire for social involvement with familiar people, such as peers the person knows well and family members. Relationships with family members and other familiar figures are warm and satisfying. The diagnosis is not made if the disturbance is sufficiently pervasive and persistent to warrant the diagnosis of Avoidant Personality Disorder.

A child with this disorder is likely to appear socially withdrawn, embarrassed, and timid when in the company of unfamiliar people and will become anxious when even a trivial demand is made to interact with strangers. When social anxiety is severe, the child may be inarticulate or mute, even if his or her communication skills are unimpaired.

Associated features. Children with this disorder are generally unassertive and lack self-confidence. In adolescence, inhibition of normal psychosexual activity is common. The disorder rarely occurs alone: children with this disorder usually have another Anxiety Disorder, such as Overanxious Disorder.

Age at onset. The disorder typically appears during the early school years, within the context of increased opportunities for social contact. It may, however, develop as early as two and a half years, after "stranger anxiety," as a normal developmental phenomenon, should have disappeared.

Course. The course seems variable: some children improve spontaneously, whereas others experience an episodic or chronic course. How often this disorder becomes chronic and continues into adulthood, as a Social Phobia, Generalized Type, or Avoidant Personality Disorder, is unknown.

Impairment. Age-appropriate socialization skills may not develop. The impairment in social functioning is often severe.

Predisposing factors. There is some evidence that Specific Developmental Disorders involving language and speech may predispose to the development of this disorder.

Complications. The most serious complication is failure to form social bonds beyond the family, with resulting feelings of isolation and depression.

Prevalence. The disorder is not common.

Sex ratio. The disorder is apparently more common in females than in males.

Familial pattern. There is some evidence that Anxiety Disorders may be more common in the mothers of children with the disorder.

Differential diagnosis. Socially reticent children are slow to warm up to unfamiliar people, but after a short time can respond, and suffer no impairment in peer interaction. In **Separation Anxiety Disorder,** the anxiety is focused on separation from the home or major attachment figures rather than on contact with unfamiliar people per se, but both disorders may be present. In **Overanxious Disorder,** anxiety is not focused on contact with unfamiliar people, but, again, both disorders may be present. In **Major Depression** and **Dysthymia**, social withdrawal is commonly present, but is generalized. In **Adjustment Disorder with Withdrawal,** the withdrawal is related to a recent psychosocial stressor and lasts less than six months.

The diagnosis is not made if the disturbance is sufficiently pervasive and persistent to warrant the diagnosis of **Avoidant Personality Disorder**.

Diagnostic criteria for 313.21 Avoidant Disorder of Childhood or Adolescence

A. Excessive shrinking from contact with unfamiliar people, for a period of six months or longer, sufficiently severe to interfere with social functioning in peer relationships.

B. Desire for social involvement with familiar people (family members and peers the person knows well), and generally warm and satisfying relations with family members and other familiar figures.

Diagnostic criteria for 313.21 Avoidant Disorder of Childhood or Adolescence continued

C. Age at least 2½ years.

D. The disturbance is not sufficiently pervasive and persistent to warrant the diagnosis of Avoidant Personality Disorder.

313.00   Overanxious Disorder

The essential feature of this disorder is excessive or unrealistic anxiety or worry for a period of six months or longer. A child with this disorder tends to be extremely self-conscious; to worry about future events, such as examinations, the possibility of injury, or inclusion in peer group activities, or about meeting expectations, such as deadlines, keeping appointments, or performing chores; and to be concerned even about past behavior. Because of his or her anxieties, the child may spend an inordinate amount of time inquiring about the discomforts or dangers of a variety of situations and need much reassurance. For example, routine visits to the doctor may be anticipated with excessive worry about minor procedures. The child may also be overly anxious about competence in a number of areas and, especially, about what others will think of his or her performance.

In some cases physical concomitants of anxiety are apparent: the child may complain of a lump in the throat, or experience gastrointestinal distress, headache, shortness of breath, nausea, dizziness, or other somatic discomforts. Difficulty falling asleep is common. The child may constantly appear nervous or tense.

Preoccupation with a neighbor or adult school figure who seems "mean" or critical has been observed. As the child becomes older, such preoccupations usually focus on more general forms of judgment, such as peer, social, or athletic acceptance, and school grades.

If another Axis I disorder is present (e.g., Separation Anxiety Disorder, Phobic Disorder, Obsessive Compulsive Disorder), the anxiety and worry extend beyond the focus of that disorder. For example, if Separation Anxiety Disorder is present, the anxiety and worry are not exclusively related to separation.

A diagnosis of Overanxious Disorder is not made if the disturbance occurs only during the course of a psychotic disorder or a Mood Disorder.

Associated features. Social and Simple Phobia may also be present. Children with this disorder may refuse to attend school because of their anxiety in that setting. They often seem hypermature because of their "precocious" concerns. Perfectionist tendencies, with obsessional self-doubt, may be evident; the child may be excessively conformist and overzealous in seeking approval. Sometimes excessive motor restlessness or nervous habits, such as nail-biting or hair-pulling, are observed. The child may be reluctant to engage in age-appropriate activities in which there are demands for performance, such as sports.

Course. The onset may be sudden or gradual, with exacerbations associated with stress. The disorder may persist into adult life as an Anxiety Disorder, such as Generalized Anxiety Disorder or a Social Phobia.

Age at onset. No information.

Impairment. In unusually severe cases, this disorder can be incapacitating and result in inability to meet realistic demands at home and in school.

Complications. Complications may include unnecessary medical evaluations for somatic symptoms.

Predisposing factors. This disorder seems to be more common in eldest children, in small families, in upper socioeconomic groups, and in families in which there is a concern about achievement even when the child functions at an adequate or superior level.

Prevalence. The disorder is not uncommon. Most of the children without the additional diagnosis of Separation Anxiety Disorder seen in clinical settings are 13 years or older; those with both disorders are usually under 13.

Sex. The disorder is apparently equally common in males and in females.

Familial pattern. There is some evidence that Anxiety Disorders are more common among mothers of children with Overanxious Disorder than mothers of children with other mental disorders.

Differential diagnosis. In cases of **Separation Anxiety Disorder** unassociated with **Overanxious Disorder,** the anxiety is focused solely on situations involving separation. Children with only **Attention-deficit Hyperactivity Disorder** may appear nervous and jittery, but are not unduly concerned about the future. The two disorders may coexist however. In **Adjustment Disorder with Anxious Mood,** the anxiety is related to a recent psychosocial stressor and lasts less than six months.

Overanxious Disorder should not be diagnosed when the anxiety is a symptom of a **psychotic disorder** or a **Mood Disorder.**

Diagnostic criteria for 313.00 Overanxious Disorder

A. Excessive or unrealistic anxiety or worry, for a period of six months or longer, as indicated by the frequent occurrence of at least four of the following:

   (1) excessive or unrealistic worry about future events
   (2) excessive or unrealistic concern about the appropriateness of past behavior
   (3) excessive or unrealistic concern about competence in one or more areas, e.g., athletic, academic, social
   (4) somatic complaints, such as headaches or stomachaches, for which no physical basis can be established
   (5) marked self-consciousness
   (6) excessive need for reassurance about a variety of concerns
   (7) marked feelings of tension or inability to relax

Diagnostic criteria for 313.00 Overanxious Disorder continued

B. If another Axis I disorder is present (e.g., Separation Anxiety Disorder, Phobic Disorder, Obsessive Compulsive Disorder), the focus of the symptoms in A are not limited to it. For example, if Separation Anxiety Disorder is present, the symptoms in A are not exclusively related to anxiety about separation. In addition, the disturbance does not occur only during the course of a psychotic disorder or a Mood Disorder.

C. If 18 or older, does not meet the criteria for Generalized Anxiety Disorder.

D. Occurrence not exclusively during the course of a Pervasive Developmental Disorder, Schizophrenia, or any other psychotic disorder.

EATING DISORDERS

This subclass of disorders is characterized by gross disturbances in eating behavior; it includes Anorexia Nervosa, Bulimia Nervosa, Pica, and Rumination Disorder of Infancy. Anorexia Nervosa and Bulimia Nervosa are apparently related disorders, typically beginning in adolescence or early adult life. Pica and Rumination Disorder of Infancy are primarily disorders of young children and are probably unrelated to Anorexia Nervosa and Bulimia Nervosa.

Simple obesity is included in ICD-9-CM as a physical disorder, and is not in this section since it is not generally associated with any distinctly psychological or behavioral syndrome. However, when there is evidence that psychological factors are of importance in the etiology or course of a particular case of obesity, this can be indicated by noting Psychological Factors Affecting Physical Condition (p. 333).

307.10 Anorexia Nervosa

The essential features of this disorder are: refusal to maintain body weight over a minimal normal weight for age and height; intense fear of gaining weight or becoming fat, even though underweight; a distorted body image; and amenorrhea (in females). (The term *anorexia* is a misnomer since loss of appetite is rare.)

The disturbance in body image is manifested by the way in which the person's body weight, size, or shape is experienced. People with this disorder say they "feel fat," or that parts of their body are "fat," when they are obviously underweight or even emaciated. They are preoccupied with their body size and usually dissatisfied with some feature of their physical appearance.

The weight loss is usually accomplished by a reduction in total food intake, often with extensive exercising. Frequently there is also self-induced vomiting or use of laxatives or diuretics. (In such cases Bulimia Nervosa may also be present.)

The person usually comes to professional attention when weight loss (or failure to gain expected weight) is marked. An example is weighing less than 85% of expected weight (85% is provided as an arbitrary but useful guide). By the time the person is profoundly underweight, there are other signs, such as hypothermia, bradycardia, hypotension, edema, lanugo (neonatal-like hair), and a variety of metabolic changes. In most cases amenorrhea follows weight loss, but it is not unusual for amenorrhea to appear before noticeable weight loss has occurred.

Associated features. Some people with this disorder cannot exert continuous control over their intended voluntary restriction of food intake and have bulimic episodes (eating binges), often followed by vomiting. Many of these people also have Bulimia Nervosa.

Other peculiar behaviors concerning food are common. For example, people with Anorexia Nervosa often prepare elaborate meals for others, but tend to limit themselves to a narrow selection of low-calorie foods. In addition, they may hoard, conceal, crumble, or throw away food.

Most people with this disorder steadfastly deny or minimize the severity of their illness and are uninterested in, or resistant to, therapy. Many of the adolescents have delayed psychosexual development, and adults have a markedly decreased interest in sex. Compulsive behavior, such as hand-washing, may be present during the illness and may justify the additional diagnosis of Obsessive Compulsive Disorder.

Age at onset. Age at onset is usually early to late adolescence, although it can range from prepuberty to the early 30s (rare).

Sex ratio. This disorder occurs predominantly in females (95%).

Prevalence. Studies of samples from different populations have reported a range of from 1 in 800 to as many as 1 in 100 females between the ages of 12 and 18.

Course. The course may be unremitting until death, episodic, or, most commonly, consist of a single episode, with return to normal weight.

Impairment. The severe weight loss often necessitates hospitalization to prevent death by starvation.

Complications. Follow-up studies indicate mortality rates of between 5% and 18%.

Familial pattern. The disorder is more common among sisters and mothers of those with the disorder than among the general population. Several studies have reported a higher than expected frequency of Major Depression and Bipolar Disorder among first-degree biologic relatives of people with Anorexia Nervosa.

Predisposing factors. In some people the onset of illness is associated with a stressful life situation. Many of these people are described as having been overly perfectionist, "model children." About one-third of them are mildly overweight before onset of the illness.

Differential diagnosis. In **Depressive Disorders** and **certain physical disorders,** weight loss can occur, but there is no disturbance of body image or intense fear of obesity.

In **Schizophrenia** there may be bizarre eating patterns; however, the full syndrome of Anorexia Nervosa is rarely present; when it is, both diagnoses should be given.

In **Bulimia Nervosa** (without associated Anorexia Nervosa) there may be a fear of fatness, and weight loss may be substantial, but the weight does not fall below a minimal normal weight. In some instances Anorexia Nervosa occurs in a person with Bulimia Nervosa, in which case both diagnoses are given.

Diagnostic criteria for 307.10 Anorexia Nervosa

A. Refusal to maintain body weight over a minimal normal weight for age and height, e.g., weight loss leading to maintenance of body weight 15% below that expected; or failure to make expected weight gain during period of growth, leading to body weight 15% below that expected.

B. Intense fear of gaining weight or becoming fat, even though underweight.

C. Disturbance in the way in which one's body weight, size, or shape is experienced, e.g., the person claims to "feel fat" even when emaciated, believes that one area of the body is "too fat" even when obviously underweight.

D. In females, absence of at least three consecutive menstrual cycles when otherwise expected to occur (primary or secondary amenorrhea). (A woman is considered to have amenorrhea if her periods occur only following hormone, e.g., estrogen, administration.)

307.51   Bulimia Nervosa

The essential features of this disorder are: recurrent episodes of binge eating (rapid consumption of a large amount of food in a discrete period of time); a feeling of lack of control over eating behavior during the eating binges; self-induced vomiting, use of laxatives or diuretics, strict dieting or fasting, or vigorous exercise in order to prevent weight gain; and persistent overconcern with body shape and weight. In order to qualify for the diagnosis, the person must have had, on average, a minimum of two binge eating episodes a week for at least three months.

Eating binges may be planned. The food consumed during a binge often has a high caloric content, a sweet taste, and a texture that facilitates rapid eating. The food is usually eaten as inconspicuously as possible, or secretly. The food is usually gobbled down quite rapidly, with little chewing. Once eating has begun, additional food may be sought to continue the binge. A binge is usually terminated by abdominal discomfort, sleep, social interruption, or induced vomiting. Vomiting decreases the physical pain of abdominal distention, allowing either continued eating or termination of the binge, and often reduces post-binge anguish. In some cases vomiting may itself be desired, so that the person will binge in order to vomit, or will vomit after eating a small amount of food. Although eating binges may be pleasurable, disparaging self-criticism and a depressed mood often follow.

People with Bulimia Nervosa invariably exhibit great concern about their weight and make repeated attempts to control it by dieting, vomiting, or the use of cathartics or diuretics. Frequent weight fluctuations due to alternating binges and fasts are common. Often these people feel that their life is dominated by conflicts about eating.

Associated features. Although most people with Bulimia Nervosa are within a normal weight range, some may be slightly underweight, and others may be overweight. A depressed mood that may be part of a Depressive Disorder is commonly observed. Some people with this disorder are subject to Psychoactive Substance Abuse or Dependence, most frequently involving sedatives, amphetamines, cocaine, or alcohol.

Age at onset. The disorder usually begins in adolescence or early adult life.

Course. The usual course, in clinic samples, is chronic and intermittent over a period of many years. Usually the binges alternate with periods of normal eating, or with periods of normal eating and fasts. In extreme cases, however, there may be alternate binges and fasts, with no periods of normal eating.

Familial pattern. Frequently the parents of people with this disorder are obese. Several studies have reported a higher than expected frequency of Major Depression in first-degree biologic relatives of people with Bulimia Nervosa.

Impairment and complications. Bulimia Nervosa is seldom incapacitating, except in a few people who spend their entire day in binge eating and vomiting. Dental erosion is a common complication of the vomiting. Electrolyte imbalance and dehydration can occur, and may cause serious physical complications, such as cardiac arrhythmias and, occasionally, sudden death. Rare complications include esophageal tears and gastric ruptures.

Prevalence and sex ratio. A recent study of college freshman indicated that 4.5% of the females and 0.4% of the males had a history of Bulimia.

Predisposing factors. There is some evidence that obesity in adolescence predisposes to the development of the disorder in adulthood.

Differential diagnosis. In **Anorexia Nervosa** there is severe weight loss, but in Bulimia Nervosa (without associated Anorexia Nervosa) the weight fluctuations are rarely so extreme as to be life-threatening. In some instances Anorexia Nervosa occurs in a person with Bulimia Nervosa, in which case both diagnoses are given. In **Schizophrenia** there may be unusual eating behavior, but the full syndrome of Bulimia Nervosa is rarely present; when it is, both diagnoses should be given. In **certain neurologic diseases,** such as **epileptic equivalent seizures, central nervous system tumors, Klüver-Bucy-like syndromes,** and **Kleine-Levin syndrome,** there are abnormal eating patterns, but the diagnosis of Bulimia Nervosa is rarely warranted; when it is, both diagnoses should be given. Binge eating is often a feature of **Borderline Personality Disorder** in females. If the full criteria for Bulimia Nervosa are met, both diagnoses should be given.

Diagnostic criteria for 307.51 Bulimia Nervosa

A. Recurrent episodes of binge eating (rapid consumption of a large amount of food in a discrete period of time).

B. A feeling of lack of control over eating behavior during the eating binges.

Diagnostic criteria for 307.51 Bulimia Nervosa continued

C. The person regularly engages in either self-induced vomiting, use of laxatives or diuretics, strict dieting or fasting, or vigorous exercise in order to prevent weight gain.

D. A minimum average of two binge eating episodes a week for at least three months.

E. Persistent overconcern with body shape and weight.

307.52   Pica

The essential feature is the persistent eating of a nonnutritive substance. Infants with the disorder typically eat paint, plaster, string, hair, or cloth. Older children may eat animal droppings, sand, insects, leaves, or pebbles. There is no aversion to food.

Associated features. There are no regularly associated features.

Age at onset. Age at onset is usually from 12 to 24 months, but may be earlier.

Course. Pica usually remits in early childhood, but may persist into adolescence or, rarely, continue through adulthood.

Impairment. None.

Complications. Lead poisoning may result from the ingestion of paint or paint-soaked plaster; hairball tumors may cause intestinal obstruction. Toxoplasma or toxocara infections may follow ingestion of feces or dirt.

Predisposing factors. Mental Retardation, neglect, and poor supervision may be predisposing factors.

Prevalence and sex ratio. Pica is rare in normal adults, but is occasionally seen in young children, in persons with Mental Retardation, and in pregnant females.

Familial pattern. No information.

Differential diagnosis. In **Autistic Disorder, Schizophrenia,** and **certain physical disorders,** such as **Kleine-Levin syndrome,** nonnutritive substances may be eaten. In such instances Pica should not be noted as an additional diagnosis.

Diagnostic criteria for 307.52 Pica

A. Repeated eating of a nonnutritive substance for at least one month.

B. Does not meet the criteria for either Autistic Disorder, Schizophrenia, or Kleine-Levin syndrome.

307.53 Rumination Disorder of Infancy

The essential feature of this disorder is repeated regurgitation of food, with weight loss or failure to gain expected weight, developing after a period of normal functioning. Partially digested food is brought up into the mouth without nausea, retching, disgust, or associated gastrointestinal disorder. The food is then ejected from the mouth or chewed and reswallowed. A characteristic position of straining and arching the back, with the head held back, is observed. The infant makes sucking movements with his or her tongue and gives the impression of gaining considerable satisfaction from the activity.

Associated features. The infant is generally irritable and hungry between episodes of regurgitation.

Age at onset. The disorder usually appears between 3 and 12 months of age. In children with Mental Retardation, it occasionally begins later.

Course. The disorder is potentially fatal. A mortality rate from malnutrition as high as 25% has been reported. In severe cases, although the infant is apparently hungry and ingests large amounts of food, progressive malnutrition occurs because regurgitation immediately follows the feedings. Spontaneous remissions are thought to be common.

Impairment. If failure to gain expected weight or severe malnutrition develops, developmental delays in all spheres often occur, and impairment can be severe.

Complications. A frequent complication of this disorder is that the caretaker becomes discouraged by failure to feed the infant successfully, and then becomes alienated from the child. The noxious odor of the regurgitated material may cause the caretaker to avoid the infant, which results in understimulation.

Predisposing factors and familial pattern. No information.

Prevalence. The disorder is apparently very rare.

Sex ratio. The disorder is equally common in males and in females.

Differential diagnosis. Congenital anomalies, such as **pyloric stenosis,** or **infections of the gastrointestinal system,** can cause regurgitation of food, and need to be ruled out by appropriate physical examinations and laboratory tests.

Diagnostic criteria for 307.53 Rumination Disorder of Infancy

A. Repeated regurgitation, without nausea or associated gastrointestinal illness, for at least one month following a period of normal functioning.

B. Weight loss or failure to make expected weight gain.

307.50   Eating Disorder Not Otherwise Specified

Disorders of eating that do not meet the criteria for a specific Eating Disorder.

Examples:

(1) a person of average weight who does not have binge eating episodes, but frequently engages in self-induced vomiting for fear of gaining weight
(2) all of the features of Anorexia Nervosa in a female except absence of menses
(3) all of the features of Bulimia Nervosa except the frequency of binge eating episodes

GENDER IDENTITY DISORDERS

The essential feature of the disorders included in this subclass is an incongruence between assigned sex (i.e., the sex that is recorded on the birth certificate) and gender identity. Gender identity is the sense of knowing to which sex one belongs, that is, the awareness that "I am a male," or "I am a female." Gender identity is the private experience of gender role, and gender role is the public expression of gender identity. Gender role can be defined as everything that one says and does to indicate to others or to oneself the degree to which one is male or female.

Some forms of gender identity disturbance are on a continuum, whereas others may be discrete. When gender identity disturbance is mild, the person is aware that he is a male or that she is a female, but discomfort and a sense of inappropriateness about the assigned sex are experienced. When severe, as in Transsexualism, the person not only is uncomfortable with the assigned sex but has the sense of belonging to the opposite sex.

Disturbance in gender identity is rare, and should not be confused with the far more common phenomena of feelings of inadequacy in fulfilling the expectations associated with one's gender role. An example of the latter would be a person who perceives himself or herself as being sexually unattractive yet experiences himself or herself unambiguously as a man or a woman in accordance with his or her assigned sex.

Although people who first present clinically with gender identity problems may be of any age, in the vast majority of cases the onset of the disorder can be traced back to childhood. In rare cases, however, an adult will present clinically for the first time with a gender identity problem and report that the first signs of the disturbance were in adult life.

302.60   Gender Identity Disorder of Childhood

The essential features of this disorder are persistent and intense distress in a child about his or her assigned sex and the desire to be, or insistence that he or she is, of the other sex. (This disorder is not merely a child's nonconformity to stereotypic sex-role behavior as, for example, in "tomboyishness" in girls or "sissyish" behavior in boys, but rather a profound disturbance of the normal sense of maleness or femaleness.) In addition, in a girl there is either persistent marked aversion to normative feminine clothing and insistence on wearing stereotypic masculine clothing, or persistent repudiation of her female anatomic characteristics. In a boy, there is either preoccupation with female stereotypic activities, or persistent repudiation of his male anatomic characteristics. This diagnosis is not given after the onset of puberty.

Girls with this disorder regularly have male companions and an avid interest in sports and rough-and-tumble play; they show no interest in dolls or playing "house" (unless they play the father or another male role). More rarely, a girl with this disorder refuses to urinate in a sitting position, claims that she has, or will grow, a penis, does not want to grow breasts or menstruate, or asserts that she will grow up to become a man (not merely in role).

Boys with this disorder usually are preoccupied with female stereotypic activities. They may have a preference for dressing in girls' or women's clothes, or may improvise such items from available material when genuine articles are unavailable. (The cross-dressing typically does not cause sexual excitement, as in Transvestic Fetishism.) They often have a compelling desire to participate in the games and pastimes of girls. Female dolls are often their favorite toy, and girls are regularly their preferred playmates. When playing "house," the role of a female is typically adopted. Rough-and-tumble play or sports are generally avoided. Gestures and actions are often judged against a cultural stereotype of femininity, and the boy is usually subjected to male peer group teasing and rejection, whereas the same rarely occurs among girls until adolescence. Boys with this disorder may assert that they will grow up to become women (not merely in role). In rare cases a boy with this disorder claims that his penis or testes are disgusting or will disappear, or that it would be better not to have a penis or testes.

Some children refuse to attend school because of teasing or pressure to dress in attire stereotypical of their assigned sex. Most children with this disorder deny being disturbed by it, except that it brings them into conflict with the expectations of their family or peers.

Associated features. Some of these children, particularly girls, show no other signs of psychopathology. Others may display serious signs of disturbance, such as social withdrawal, separation anxiety, or depression.

Age at onset and course. The majority of the boys with this disorder begin to develop it before their fourth birthday. Social ostracism increases during the early grades of school, and social conflict is significant at about age seven or eight. During the later grade-school years, grossly feminine behavior may lessen. Studies indicate that from one-third to two-thirds or more of boys with the disorder develop a homosexual orientation during adolescence.

For females the age at onset is also early, but most give up an exaggerated insistence on male activities and attire during late childhood or adolescence. A minority retain a masculine identification, and some of these develop a homosexual orientation.

Whereas most adult people with Transsexualism report having had a gender identity problem during childhood, prospective studies of children with Gender Identity Disorder of Childhood indicate that very few develop Transsexualism in adolescence or adulthood.

Complications. In a small number of cases, the disorder becomes continuous with Transsexualism or Gender Identity Disorder of Adolescence or Adulthood, Nontranssexual Type.

Impairment. Positive peer relations with members of the same sex are absent or difficult to establish. The amount of impairment varies from none to extreme, and is related to the degree of associated psychopathology and the reaction of peers and family to the person's behavior.

Prevalence. The disorder is apparently uncommon.

Sex ratio. In clinic samples there are many more boys with this disorder than girls. The sex ratio in the general population is unknown.

Familial pattern. No information.

Predisposing factors. Studies indicate that characteristics of the child, the parents, or of other social agents, such as parental substitutes and siblings, may be predisposing factors for the development of the disorder. In boys, the characteristics may include "feminine" physical features, an aversion to rough-and-tumble play, separation anxiety, and a history of early hospitalization. The relevant characteristics of parents and other influential people in the child's environment may include weak reinforcement of normative gender-role behavior, absence or unavailability of a father, and encouragement of extreme physical and psychological closeness with her son by a mother. In girls, a strong interest in rough-and-tumble play on the part of the child and weak reinforcement of normative gender-role behavior by the parents may contribute to the development of the disorder.

Differential diagnosis. Children whose behavior merely does not fit the cultural stereotype of masculinity or femininity should not be given this diagnosis unless the full syndrome is present. **Physical abnormalities of the sex organs** are rarely associated with Gender Identity Disorder of Childhood; when they are present, the physical disorder should be noted on Axis III.

Diagnostic criteria for 302.60 Gender Identity Disorder of Childhood

For Females:
A. Persistent and intense distress about being a girl, and a stated desire to be a boy (not merely a desire for any perceived cultural advantages from being a boy), or insistence that she is a boy.

B. Either (1) or (2):

   (1) persistent marked aversion to normative feminine clothing and insistence on wearing stereotypical masculine clothing, e.g., boys' underwear and other accessories

   (2) persistent repudiation of female anatomic structures, as evidenced by at least one of the following:

   (a) an assertion that she has, or will grow, a penis
   (b) rejection of urinating in a sitting position
   (c) assertion that she does not want to grow breasts or menstruate

C. The girl has not yet reached puberty.

For Males:
A. Persistent and intense distress about being a boy and an intense desire to be a girl or, more rarely, insistence that he is a girl.

B. Either (1) or (2):

   (1) preoccupation with female stereotypical activities, as shown by a preference for either cross-dressing or simulating female attire, or by an intense desire to participate in the games and pastimes of girls and rejection of male stereotypical toys, games, and activities

(continued)

Diagnostic criteria for 302.60 Gender Identity Disorder of Childhood continued

    (2) persistent repudiation of male anatomic structures, as indicated by at least one of the following repeated assertions:

        (a) that he will grow up to become a woman (not merely in role)
        (b) that his penis or testes are disgusting or will disappear
        (c) that it would be better not to have a penis or testes

C. The boy has not yet reached puberty.

302.50   Transsexualism

The essential features of this disorder are a persistent discomfort and sense of inappropriateness about one's assigned sex in a person who has reached puberty. In addition, there is persistent preoccupation, for at least two years, with getting rid of one's primary and secondary sex characteristics and acquiring the sex characteristics of the other sex. Therefore, the diagnosis is not made if the disturbance is limited to brief periods of stress. Invariably there is the wish to live as a member of the other sex. In the rare cases in which physical intersexuality or a genetic abnormality is present, such a condition should be noted on Axis III.

People with this disorder usually complain that they are uncomfortable wearing the clothes of their assigned sex and therefore dress in clothes of the other sex. Often they engage in activities that in our culture tend to be associated with the other sex. These people often find their genitals repugnant, which may lead to persistent requests for sex reassignment by hormonal and surgical means.

To varying degrees, the behavior, dress, and mannerisms become those of the other sex. With cross-dressing and hormonal treatment (and for males, electrolysis), some males and some females with the disorder will appear relatively indistinguishable from members of the other sex. However, even after sex reassignment, many people still have some physical features of their originally assigned sex that the alert observer can recognize.

Cross-culturally, the Hijra of India and the corresponding group in Burma may have conditions that, according to this manual, would be diagnosed as male-to-female Transsexualism. The Hijra, however, traditionally undergo castration, not hormonal and surgical feminization (creation of a vagina).

Associated features. Generally there is a moderate to severe coexisting personality disturbance. Frequently the person experiences considerable anxiety and depression, which he or she may attribute to the inability to live in the role of the desired sex.

Course. Without treatment, the course of the disorder is chronic, but cases with apparently spontaneous remission do occur. The long-term outcome of combined psychiatric, hormonal, and surgical sex-reassignment treatment is not well known. Many people function better for years after such treatment, but a number of cases in which re-reassignment has been desired have also been reported.

People who have female-to-male Transsexualism appear to represent a more homogeneous group than those who have male-to-female Transsexualism in that they are more likely to have a history of homosexuality and a more stable course, with or without treatment.

Age at onset. People who develop Transsexualism almost invariably report having had a gender identity problem in childhood. Some assert that they were secretly aware of their gender problem, but that it was not evident to their family and friends. Although onset of the full syndrome is most often in late adolescence or early adult life, in some cases the disorder has a later onset.

Impairment and complications. Frequently, social and occupational functioning are markedly impaired, partly because of associated psychopathology and partly because of problems encountered in attempting to live in the desired gender role. Depression is common, and can lead to suicide attempts. In rare instances, males may mutilate their genitals.

Predisposing factors. Extensive, pervasive childhood femininity in a boy or childhood masculinity in a girl increases the likelihood of Transsexualism. It seems usually to develop within the context of a disturbed relationship with one or both parents. Some cases of Gender Identity Disorder of Adolescence or Adulthood, Nontranssexual Type, evolve into Transsexualism.

Prevalence. The estimated prevalence is one per 30,000 for males and one per 100,000 for females.

Sex ratio. Males seek help at clinics specializing in the treatment of this disorder more commonly than do females. The ratio varies from as high as 8:1 to as low as 1:1.

Familial pattern. No information.

Differential diagnosis. Some people with disturbed gender identity may, in isolated periods of stress, wish to belong to the other sex and to be rid of their own genitals. In such cases a diagnosis of **Gender Identity Disorder Not Otherwise Specified** should be considered, since the diagnosis of Transsexualism is made only when the disturbance has been continuous for at least two years. In **Schizophrenia** there may be delusions of belonging to the other sex, but this is rare. The insistence by a person with Transsexualism that he or she is of the other sex is, strictly speaking, not a delusion, since what is invariably meant is that the person *feels like* a member of the other sex rather than truly believes that he or she *is* a member of the other sex. In very rare cases, however, Schizophrenia and Transsexualism may coexist.

In both **Transvestic Fetishism** and **Gender Identity Disorder of Adolescence or Adulthood, Nontranssexual Type**, there may be cross-dressing. But unless these disorders evolve into Transsexualism, there is no wish to be rid of one's own genitals.

Types. The disorder is subdivided according to the history of sexual orientation, as asexual, homosexual (toward same sex), heterosexual (toward opposite sex), or unspecified. In the first, "asexual," the person reports never having had strong sexual feelings. Often there is an additional history of little or no sexual activity or pleasure derived from the genitals. In the second group, "homosexual," a predominantly homosexual arousal pattern preceding the onset of the Transsexualism is acknowledged, although often such people deny that the orientation is homosexual because of their conviction that they are "really" of the other sex. In the third group, "heterosexual," the person claims to have had a heterosexual orientation.

Diagnostic criteria for 302.50 Transsexualism

A. Persistent discomfort and sense of inappropriateness about one's assigned sex.

B. Persistent preoccupation for at least two years with getting rid of one's primary and secondary sex characteristics and acquiring the sex characteristics of the other sex.

C. The person has reached puberty.

Specify history of sexual orientation: **asexual, homosexual, heterosexual,** or **unspecified.**

302.85 Gender Identity Disorder of Adolescence or Adulthood, Nontranssexual Type (GIDAANT)

The essential features of this disorder are a persistent or recurrent discomfort and sense of inappropriateness about one's assigned sex, and persistent or recurrent cross-dressing in the role of the other sex, either in fantasy or in actuality, in a person who has reached puberty. This disorder differs from Transvestic Fetishism in that the cross-dressing is not for the purpose of sexual excitement; it differs from Transsexualism in that there is no persistent preoccupation (for at least two years) with getting rid of one's primary and secondary sex characteristics and acquiring the sex characteristics of the other sex.

Some people with this disorder once had Transvestic Fetishism, but no longer experience sexual arousal with cross-dressing. Other people with this disorder are homosexuals who cross-dress. This disorder is common among female impersonators.

Cross-dressing phenomena range from occasional solitary wearing of female clothes to extensive feminine identification in males and masculine identification in females, and involvement in a transvestic subculture. More than one article of clothing of the other sex is involved, and the person may dress entirely as a member of the opposite sex. The degree to which the cross-dressed person appears as a member of the other sex varies, depending on mannerisms, body habitus, and cross-dressing skill. When not cross-dressed, the person usually appears as an unremarkable member of his or her assigned sex.

Associated features. Anxiety and depression are common, but are often attenuated when the person is cross-dressing.

Age at onset and course. Age at onset and course are variable. In most cases, before puberty there was a history of some or all of the features of Gender Identity Disorder of Childhood. However, by definition, GIDAANT is diagnosed only once puberty has been reached. The initial experience may involve partial or total cross-dressing; when it is partial, it often progresses to total. Cross-dressing, although intermittent in the beginning, often becomes more frequent, and may become habitual. A small number of people with GIDAANT, as the years pass, want to dress and live permanently as the other sex, and the disorder may evolve into Transsexualism.

Impairment. Unless there is another diagnosis in addition to GIDAANT, the impairment is generally restricted to conflicts with family members and other people regarding the cross-dressing.

Complications. The major complication is Transsexualism.

Predisposing factors. As noted above, both Gender Identity Disorder of Childhood and Transvestic Fetishism sometimes evolve into GIDAANT.

Prevalence. Although its prevalence is unknown, the disorder is probably more common than Transsexualism.

Sex ratio. The disorder is more common in males.

Familial pattern. No information.

Differential diagnosis. In **Transvestic Fetishism**, the cross-dressing is for the purpose of sexual excitement. In **Transsexualism**, there is a persistent (for more than two years) wish to get rid of one's primary and secondary sex characteristics and acquire the sex characteristics of the other sex. In those rare instances in which a person with GIDAANT develops Transsexualism, the diagnosis of GIDAANT is changed accordingly.

Subtypes. The disorder is subdivided according to the history of sexual orientation, as asexual, homosexual (toward same sex), heterosexual (toward opposite sex), or unspecified. In the first, "asexual," the person reports never having had strong sexual feelings. Often there is an additional history of little or no sexual activity or pleasure derived from the genitals. In the second group, "homosexual," a predominantly homosexual arousal pattern preceding the onset of the GIDAANT is acknowledged. In the third group, "heterosexual," the person claims to have had a heterosexual orientation.

Diagnostic criteria for 302.85 Gender Identity Disorder of Adolescence or Adulthood, Nontranssexual Type (GIDAANT)

A. Persistent or recurrent discomfort and sense of inappropriateness about one's assigned sex.

B. Persistent or recurrent cross-dressing in the role of the other sex, either in fantasy or actuality, but not for the purpose of sexual excitement (as in Transvestic Fetishism).

C. No persistent preoccupation (for at least two years) with getting rid of one's primary and secondary sex characteristics and acquiring the sex characteristics of the other sex (as in Transsexualism).

D. The person has reached puberty.

Specify history of sexual orientation: **asexual, homosexual, heterosexual,** or **unspecified.**

302.85   Gender Identity Disorder Not Otherwise Specified

Disorders in gender identity that are not classifiable as a specific Gender Identity Disorder.

Examples:

    (1) children with persistent cross-dressing without the other criteria for Gender Identity Disorder of Childhood

    (2) adults with transient, stress-related cross-dressing behavior

    (3) adults with the clinical features of Transsexualism of less than two years' duration

    (4) people who have a persistent preoccupation with castration or peotomy without a desire to acquire the sex characteristics of the other sex

TIC DISORDERS

Tics are the essential feature of the three disorders in this subclass: Tourette's Disorder, Chronic Motor or Vocal Tic Disorder, and Transient Tic Disorder. There is evidence from genetic and other studies that Tourette's Disorder and Chronic Motor or Vocal Tic Disorder represent different symptomatic expressions of the same underlying disorder. However, they are included in this manual as separate disorders because they generally involve different degrees of impairment (the former being more disabling) and they have different treatment implications.

A tic is an involuntary, sudden, rapid, recurrent, nonrhythmic, stereotyped, motor movement or vocalization. It is experienced as irresistible, but can be suppressed for varying lengths of time. All forms of tics are often exacerbated by stress and usually are markedly diminished during sleep. They may become attenuated during some absorbing activities, such as reading or sewing.

Both *motor* and *vocal tics* may be classified as either *simple* or *complex*, although the boundaries are not well defined. Common *simple motor tics* are eye-blinking, neck-jerking, shoulder-shrugging, and facial grimacing. Common *simple vocal tics* are coughing, throat-clearing, grunting, sniffing, snorting, and barking. Common *complex motor tics* are facial gestures, grooming behaviors, hitting or biting self, jumping, touching, stamping, and smelling an object. Common *complex vocal tics* are repeating words or phrases out of context, coprolalia (use of socially unacceptable words, frequently obscene), palilalia (repeating one's own sounds or words), and echolalia (repeating the last-heard sound, word, or phrase of another person, or a last-heard sound). Other complex tics include echokinesis (imitation of the movements of someone who is being observed).

Associated features. Discomfort in social situations, shame, self-consciousness, and depressed mood are common, especially with Tourette's Disorder.

Predisposing factors. A controversy exists as to whether or not the onset of some cases of Tic Disorders is precipitated by exposure to phenothiazines, head trauma, or the administration of central nervous system stimulants. It is estimated that in one-third of cases of Tourette's Disorder, the severity of the tics is exacerbated by administration of central nervous system stimulants, which may be a dose-related phenomenon.

Impairment. Social, academic, and occupational functioning may be impaired because of rejection by others or anxiety about having tics in social situations. In addition, in severe cases of Tourette's Disorder, the tics themselves may interfere with daily activities, such as reading or writing. Although most people with Tourette's Disorder do not have marked impairment, in general the impairment is more severe than in Chronic Motor or Vocal Tic Disorder. Impairment in Transient Tic Disorder rarely is marked.

Differential diagnosis of tics. Tics should be distinguished from **other movement disturbances.** *Choreiform movements* are dancing, random, irregular, nonrepetitive movements. *Dystonic movements* are slower, twisting movements interspersed with prolonged states of muscular tension. *Athetoid movements* are slow, irregular, writhing movements, most frequently in the fingers and toes, but often involving the face and neck. *Myoclonic movements* are brief, shocklike muscle contractions that may affect parts of muscles or muscle groups, but not synergistically. *Hemiballismic movements* are intermittent, coarse, large amplitude, unilateral movements of the limbs. *Spasms* are stereotypic, slower, and more prolonged than tics, and involve groups of muscles. *Hemifacial spasm* consists of irregular, repetitive, unilateral jerks of facial muscles. *Synkinesis* consists of movements of the corner of the mouth when the person intends to close the eye, and its converse. *Dyskinesias*, such as tardive dyskinesia, are oral-buccal-lingual masticatory movements of the face and choreoathetoid movements of the limbs.

Stereotyped movements (see Stereotypy/Habit Disorder, p. 93), such as head-banging, rocking, or repetitive hand movements, are apparently intentional behaviors and are often rhythmic. **Compulsions**, as in Obsessive Compulsive Disorder, are differentiated from tics in that they are intentional behaviors, whereas tics are involuntary.

307.23   Tourette's Disorder

The essential features of this disorder are multiple motor and one or more vocal tics. These may appear simultaneously, or at different periods during the illness. The tics occur many times a day, nearly every day or intermittently throughout a period of more than one year. The anatomic location, number, frequency, complexity, and severity of the tics change over time.

The tics typically involve the head and, frequently, other parts of the body, such as the torso and upper and lower limbs. The vocal tics include various sounds such as clicks, grunts, yelps, barks, sniffs, and coughs, or words. Coprolalia, a complex vocal tic involving the uttering of obscenities, is present in up to a third of cases. Complex motor tics involving touching, squatting, deep knee bends, retracing steps, and twirling when walking are often present.

In approximately half the cases, the first symptoms to appear are bouts of a single tic, most frequently eye-blinking, less frequently tics involving another part of the face or the body. Initial symptoms can also include tongue protrusion, squatting, sniffing, hopping, skipping, throat-clearing, stuttering, uttering sounds or words, and coprolalia. Other cases begin with multiple symptoms, which may include any combination of the previously described tics, and various noises such as barks, grunts, screams, yelps, or snorts.

Associated features. There may be other symptoms, such as mental coprolalia (sudden, intrusive, senseless thoughts of socially unacceptable or obscene words, phrases, or sentences that differ from true obsessions in that no attempt is made to ignore, suppress, or neutralize the thoughts), obsessions, and compulsions.

In clinical samples, other mental disorders are frequently associated with Tourette's Disorder, particularly Attention-deficit Hyperactivity Disorder and Obsessive Compulsive Disorder. It is not clear if this co-morbidity also exists in representative community samples.

Age at onset. The median age at onset is 7 years, and the great majority have an onset before age 14. The disorder may appear as early as one year of age.

Course. The disorder is usually lifelong, though periods of remission lasting from weeks to years may occur. In some cases, the severity and frequency of the symptoms diminish during adolescence and adulthood, and the symptoms do not vary in severity over time as much as before. In other cases, the symptoms of the disorder disappear entirely, usually by early adulthood.

Complications. Complications include physical injury, such as blindness due to retinal detachment (from head-banging or striking oneself), orthopedic problems (from knee-bending, neck-jerking, or head-turning), skin problems (from picking), and, in rare cases, self-mutilation (from head-banging).

Prevalence. The estimated lifetime prevalence rate is at least 0.5 per thousand.

Sex ratio. The disorder is at least three times more common in males than in females.

Familial pattern. Tic Disorders are more common among first-degree biologic relatives of people with Tourette's Disorder than among the general population. Evidence suggests that Tourette's Disorder and Chronic Motor or Vocal Tic Disorder may be inherited as a single autosomal dominant disorder.

In addition, there is some evidence that Obsessive Compulsive Disorder is more common in first-degree biologic relatives of people with Tourette's Disorder than in the general population and is another expression of the same underlying disorder.

Differential diagnosis. See differential diagnosis of tics, page 79. **Amphetamine Intoxication, many neurologic disorders (such as cerebrovascular accidents, Lesch-Nyhan syndrome, Wilson's disease, Sydenham's chorea, Huntington's chorea, and multiple sclerosis), Organic Mental Disorders**, and **Schizophrenia** may present with abnormal motor movements. These disorders can readily be differentiated from Tourette's Disorder because they have distinguishing symptoms, signs, clinical course, and physiologic abnormalities as revealed by laboratory tests; and none of them involve vocalizations similar to the clicks, grunts, yelps, barks, sniffs, coughs, and words of Tourette's Disorder.

Diagnostic criteria for 307.23 Tourette's Disorder

A. Both multiple motor and one or more vocal tics have been present at some time during the illness, although not necessarily concurrently.

B. The tics occur many times a day (usually in bouts), nearly every day or intermittently throughout a period of more than one year.

C. The anatomic location, number, frequency, complexity, and severity of the tics change over time.

D. Onset before age 21.

E. Occurrence not exclusively during Psychoactive Substance Intoxication or known central nervous system disease, such as Huntington's chorea and postviral encephalitis.

307.22   Chronic Motor or Vocal Tic Disorder

The essential features of this disorder are either motor or vocal tics, but not both (as in Tourette's Disorder). The other characteristics of the disorder are generally the same as Tourette's Disorder, except that the severity of the symptoms and the functional impairment are usually much less.

Familial pattern. Both Chronic Motor or Vocal Tic Disorder and Tourette's Disorder frequently occur in the same families and appear to be genetically related.

Differential diagnosis. In **Transient Tic Disorder,** the duration of the disturbance is always less than one year. In **Tourette's Disorder** there are both motor and vocal tics. A rare disorder of adolescence and adulthood, sometimes referred to as "psychogenic cough," or "chronic cough of adolescence," is distinguished from Chronic Motor or Vocal Tic Disorder by the monosymptomatic and intentional nature of the symptom.

Diagnostic criteria for 307.22 Chronic Motor or Vocal Tic Disorder

A. Either motor or vocal tics, but not both, have been present at some time during the illness.

B. The tics occur many times a day, nearly every day, or intermittently throughout a period of more than one year.

C. Onset before age 21.

D. Occurrence not exclusively during Psychoactive Substance Intoxication or known central nervous system disease, such as Huntington's chorea and postviral encephalitis.

307.21   Transient Tic Disorder

The essential feature of this disorder is single or multiple motor and/or vocal tics that occur many times a day, nearly every day for at least two weeks, but for no longer than twelve consecutive months. (Thus, the diagnosis is not made if there is a history of Tourette's or Chronic Motor or Vocal Tic Disorder, both of which require a duration of at least one year.)

The most common tic is eye-blinking or another facial tic. However, the whole head, torso, or limbs may be involved. In addition, there may be vocal tics. A person may have only one or a number of tics; if the latter, the tics may be performed simultaneously, sequentially, or randomly.

Age at onset. Age at onset is always during childhood or early adolescence, and may be as early as two years of age.

Course. The tics may disappear permanently, or recur, especially during periods of stress. In rare cases, after a period of partial remission, the person may develop either Tourette's Disorder or Chronic Motor or Vocal Tic Disorder.

Complications. No information.

Prevalence. Surveys of schoolchildren have reported that from 5% to 24% have had a history of some kind of tic. However, since these surveys do not specify a minimum or a maximum duration, it is not known how applicable these findings are to the prevalence of Tic Disorders as defined in this manual.

Sex ratio. Most studies find the disorder three times more common in males than in females.

Familial pattern. Tic Disorders are apparently more common in first-degree biological relatives of people with Transient Tic Disorder than in the general population.

Differential diagnosis. In **Tourette's Disorder** and **Chronic Motor or Vocal Tic Disorder,** the duration of the disturbance is at least one year. See differential diagnosis of tics (p. 79) and Tourette's Disorder (p. 80).

Diagnostic criteria for 307.21 Transient Tic Disorder

A. Single or multiple motor and/or vocal tics.

B. The tics occur many times a day, nearly every day for at least two weeks, but for no longer than twelve consecutive months.

C. No history of Tourette's or Chronic Motor or Vocal Tic Disorder.

D. Onset before age 21.

E. Occurrence not exclusively during Psychoactive Substance Intoxication or known central nervous system disease, such as Huntington's chorea and postviral encephalitis.

Specify: single episode or **recurrent**.

307.20   Tic Disorder Not Otherwise Specified

Tics that do not meet the criteria for a specific Tic Disorder. An example is a Tic Disorder with onset in adulthood.

ELIMINATION DISORDERS

307.70   Functional Encopresis

The essential feature of this disorder is repeated involuntary (or, much more rarely, intentional) passage of feces into places not appropriate for that purpose (e.g., clothing or floor). In order to make the diagnosis, the event must occur at least once a month for at least six months, the chronologic and mental age of the child must be at least four years, and physical disorders that can cause fecal incontinence, such as aganglionic megacolon, must be ruled out.

The stool may be of normal or near-normal consistency, or liquid, as in the case of overflow incontinence secondary to functional fecal retention. When the passage of feces is involuntary rather than intentional, it is often related to constipation, impaction, or retention with subsequent overflow. The constipation may develop because the child, for psychological reasons, avoids defecating, because of either anxiety about defecating in a particular place or a more general pattern of oppositional behavior. In other children, the constipation develops for physiologic reasons, such as dehydration associated with a febrile illness or medication. Once constipation has developed, it may be complicated by an anal fissure, painful defecation, and further fecal retention.

Functional Encopresis is generally referred to as *primary* if it has not been preceded by a period of fecal continence lasting at least one year, and *secondary* if it has been preceded by a period of fecal continence lasting at least one year.

Associated features. Very often the child feels ashamed or embarrassed, and may wish to avoid situations that might lead to embarrassment, such as camp or even school. When the incontinence is clearly deliberate, antisocial and other psychopathological features are common. Smearing feces may be deliberate, and should be differentiated from smearing that takes place accidentally in the child's attempt to clear or hide feces passed involuntarily. Twenty-five percent of children with Functional Encopresis also have Functional Enuresis.

Course. Functional Encopresis rarely becomes chronic, but, unless treated, can persist for years.

Age at onset. By definition, primary Functional Encopresis begins by age four. Secondary Functional Encopresis usually begins between the ages of four and eight.

Impairment. The amount of impairment directly attributable to the disorder is primarily a function of the effect on the child's self-esteem; the degree of social ostracism by peers; and anger, punishment, and rejection on the part of caretakers.

Complications. None.

Predisposing factors. Inadequate, inconsistent toilet training and psychosocial stress, such as entering school and the birth of a sibling, may be predisposing factors.

Prevalence. It is estimated that approximately 1% of five-year-olds have the disorder. Primary Functional Encopresis apparently is more common in lower socioeconomic classes.

Sex ratio. The disorder is more common in males than in females.

Familial pattern. No information.

Differential diagnosis. Functional Encopresis must be differentiated from **structural organic causes of encopresis,** such as **aganglionic megacolon**, which need to be ruled out by physical examination and laboratory procedures.

Diagnostic criteria for 307.70 Functional Encopresis

  A. Repeated passage of feces into places not appropriate for that purpose (e.g., clothing, floor), whether involuntary or intentional. (The disorder may be overflow incontinence secondary to functional fecal retention.)

(continued)

Diagnostic criteria for 307.70 Functional Encopresis continued

B. At least one such event a month for at least six months.

C. Chronologic and mental age, at least four years.

D. Not due to a physical disorder, such as aganglionic megacolon.

Specify primary or secondary type.

Primary type: the disturbance was not preceded by a period of fecal continence lasting at least one year.

Secondary type: the disturbance was preceded by a period of fecal continence lasting at least one year.

307.60   Functional Enuresis

The essential feature of this disorder is repeated involuntary or intentional voiding of urine during the day or at night into bed or clothes, after an age at which continence is expected. In order to make the diagnosis, etiologic physical disorders must be ruled out. The disorder is somewhat arbitrarily defined by at least two such events per month for children between the ages of five and six, and at least once a month for older children.

Functional Enuresis is often referred to as *primary* if it has not been preceded by a period of urinary continence lasting at least one year, and *secondary* if it has been preceded by a period of urinary continence lasting at least one year. Either of the above types may be *nocturnal* (most common), defined as the passage of urine during sleep time only, *diurnal*, defined as the passage of urine during waking hours, or *both* diurnal and nocturnal.

In most cases of nocturnal Functional Enuresis, the child awakens with no memory of a dream and no memory of having urinated. Typically the disturbance occurs during the first third of the night. In a few cases the voiding takes place during the rapid eye movement (REM) stage of sleep, and in such cases the child may recall a dream that involved the act of urinating.

Associated features. Although the great majority of children with Functional Enuresis do not have a coexisting mental disorder, the prevalence of coexisting mental disorders is greater in those with Functional Enuresis than in the general population. Functional Encopresis, Sleepwalking Disorder, and Sleep Terror Disorder may also be present.

Course. Most children with the disorder become continent by adolescence, but in approximately 1% of cases, the disorder continues into adulthood.

Age at onset. Primary Functional Enuresis by definition begins by age five. In most cases of secondary Functional Enuresis, onset is between the ages of five and eight.

Impairment. The amount of impairment directly attributable to the disorder is primarily a function of the effect on the child's self-esteem; the degree of social ostracism by peers; and anger, punishment, and rejection on the part of caretakers.

Complications. None.

Predisposing factors. Among predisposing factors are delay in the development of the supporting musculature of the bladder, and impaired ability of the bladder to adapt to urinary filling without changes in intravesical pressure, resulting in a lower bladder volume threshold for involuntary voiding; delayed or lax toilet training; and psychosocial stress, in particular, hospitalization between the ages of two and four, entering school, and the birth of a sibling.

Prevalence and sex ratio. The prevalence of Functional Enuresis as defined here is: at age 5, 7% for males, and 3% for females; at age 10, 3% for males, and 2% for females; and at age 18, 1% for males, and almost nonexistent for females.

Familial pattern. Approximately 75% of all children with Functional Enuresis have a first-degree biologic relative who has, or has had, the disorder. The concordance for the disorder is greater in monozygotic than in dizygotic twins.

Differential diagnosis. Organic causes of enuresis such as diabetes, seizure disorder, and urinary tract infection should be ruled out by appropriate physical examinations.

Diagnostic criteria for 307.60 Functional Enuresis

A. Repeated voiding of urine during the day or night into bed or clothes, whether involuntary or intentional.

B. At least two such events per month for children between the ages of five and six, and at least one event per month for older children.

C. Chronologic age at least five, and mental age at least four.

D. Not due to a physical disorder, such as diabetes, urinary tract infection, or a seizure disorder.

Specify primary or secondary type.

  Primary type: the disturbance was not preceded by a period of urinary continence lasting at least one year.

  Secondary type: the disturbance was preceded by a period of urinary continence lasting at least one year.

Specify nocturnal only, diurnal only, or **nocturnal and diurnal.**

SPEECH DISORDERS NOT ELSEWHERE CLASSIFIED

307.00   Cluttering

The essential feature of Cluttering is a disturbance of fluency involving an abnormally rapid rate and erratic rhythm of speech that impedes intelligibility. Faulty phrasing patterns are usually present so that there are bursts of speech consisting of groups of words that are not related to the grammatical structure of the sentence. The affected person is usually unaware of any communication impairment.

Associated features. Common associated features include: (a) articulation errors (with sounds or syllables being omitted, substituted, or transposed); (b) expressive language errors involving lapses in syntax (*Example*: entire words may be omitted, or replaced with "uh"); (c) Academic Skills Disorders; (d) Attention-deficit Hyperactivity Disorder; and (e) auditory-perceptual or visual-motor impairments.

Age at onset. Usual onset of the disorder is after the age of seven.

Course, impairment, complications, predisposing factors, prevalence, and sex ratio. No information.

Familial pattern. There may be a family history of Cluttering or of impairment in spoken or written language.

Differential diagnosis. Normal childhood dysfluency is an intermittent and transient condition occurring around the age of two years. **Stuttering and spastic dysphonia** are characterized by an awareness or distress about the speech dysfluency that is not present in Cluttering.

Diagnostic criteria for 307.00 Cluttering

A disorder of speech fluency involving both the rate and the rhythm of speech and resulting in impaired speech intelligibility. Speech is erratic and dysrhythmic, consisting of rapid and jerky spurts that usually involve faulty phrasing patterns (e.g., alternating pauses and bursts of speech that produce groups of words unrelated to the grammatical structure of the sentence).

307.00   Stuttering

The essential feature of this disorder is a marked impairment in speech fluency characterized by frequent repetitions or prolongations of sounds or syllables. Various other types of speech dysfluencies may also be involved, including blocking of sounds or interjections of words or sounds. The extent of the disturbance varies from situation to situation and is more severe when there is special pressure to communicate, as during a job interview. There are anecdotal reports that in even the most severe cases, Stuttering is often absent during oral reading, singing, or talking to inanimate objects or to pets. In the United States, stammering is not distinguished from Stuttering.

Associated features. With the initial onset of the disorder, the speaker is usually unaware of the problem. Later, awareness and even fearful anticipation of the problem occur. The speaker may attempt to avoid stuttering by: (1) linguistic mechanisms (e.g., altering the rate of speech, avoiding certain speech situations such as telephoning or public speaking, or avoiding certain words or sounds); and (2) motor movements accompanying the speech dysfluencies (eye blinks, tics, tremors of the lips or face, jerking of the head, breathing movements, or fist clenching).

Other disorders commonly associated with Stuttering in childhood include Developmental Articulation Disorder, Developmental Expressive Language Disorder, Attention-deficit Hyperactivity Disorder, and Anxiety Disorders.

Age at onset. Stuttering begins during the course of speech and language development. Retrospective studies of people with Stuttering report onset typically between ages two and seven (with peak onset at around age five). Onset occurs before age ten in 98% of cases.

Course. The onset of Stuttering is usually insidious, covering many months during which time episodic, unnoticed speech dysfluencies become a chronic problem. Typically, the disturbance starts gradually, with repetition of initial consonants, whole words that are usually the first words of a phrase, or long words. The child is generally not aware of the Stuttering. As the disorder progresses, the repetitions become more frequent, and the Stuttering occurs on the most important words or phrases. As the child becomes aware of the speech difficulty, mechanisms for avoiding the dysfluencies, motor responses, and emotional responses may appear.

Approximately 80% of people with Stuttering recover (60% spontaneously), recovery typically occurring before age 16. Aside from gender, recovery being more common in females, no factors (including treatment, age at onset, or severity) have been shown to be clearly associated with recovery.

Impairment and complications. Impairment of social functioning may result from associated anxiety, frustration, or low self-esteem. In adults, limitation in occupational choice or advancement is the principal complication.

Predisposing factors. Recent research involving family and twin studies provides strong evidence of a genetic factor in the etiology of Stuttering. The presence of Developmental Articulation or Developmental Expressive Language Disorder, or a family history of these, increases the likelihood of Stuttering. Stress or anxiety have been shown to exacerbate Stuttering, but are not thought to play a role in the etiology.

Prevalence. Approximately 5% of children have Stuttering. Stuttering is more common in younger children than in older ones, an estimated 10% of elementary-school-age children being affected. The prevalence for adults is estimated at 1%.

Sex ratio. The male-to-female ratio is approximately three to one.

Familial pattern. There is a strong familial incidence, some studies reporting as many as 50% of first-degree biologic relatives being affected. There is high concordance in monozygotic twins.

Differential diagnosis. Stuttering must be distinguished from **normal childhood dysfluency**, an intermittent speech dysfluency with no associated features occurring around age two. The clinical features are virtually indistinguishable from Stuttering. Therefore, most speech pathologists consider stuttering behavior, when it occurs before age three, to be "normal childhood dysfluency" rather than Stuttering. **Cluttering** is distinguished from Stuttering by a rapid rate of speech, severe impairment of speech intelligibility, and lack of awareness of the disturbance. **Spastic dysphonia**, a speech disorder similar to Stuttering, is distinguished from the latter by the presence of an abnormal pattern of breathing.

Diagnostic criteria for 307.00 Stuttering

Frequent repetitions or prolongations of sounds or syllables that markedly impair the fluency of speech.

OTHER DISORDERS OF INFANCY, CHILDHOOD, OR ADOLESCENCE

313.23   Elective Mutism

The essential feature of this disorder is persistent refusal to talk in one or more major social situations, including school, despite ability to comprehend spoken language and to speak. The refusal to talk is not a symptom of Social Phobia, Major Depression, or a psychotic disorder, such as Schizophrenia.

The child with Elective Mutism may communicate via gestures, by nodding or shaking the head, or, in some cases, by monosyllabic or short, monotone utterances. Most commonly the child will not speak at school, but will talk normally within the home. Less commonly the child refuses to speak in nearly all social situations.

Children with this disorder generally have normal language skills, though some have delayed language development and abnormalities of articulation.

Associated features. Speech disorders may be present, such as Developmental Articulation Disorder, Developmental Expressive or Receptive Language Disorder, or a physical disorder that causes abnormalities of articulation. Excessive shyness, social isolation and withdrawal, clinging, school refusal, compulsive traits, negativism, temper tantrums, or other controlling or oppositional behavior, particularly at home, may be observed.

Age at onset. Although onset is usually before age five, the disturbance may come to clinical attention only with entry into school.

Course. In most cases the disturbance lasts only a few weeks or months; in a few, it continues for several years.

Impairment. There may be severe impairment in social and school functioning.

Complications. School failure and teasing or scapegoating by peers are common complications.

Predisposing factors. Maternal overprotection, Language and Speech Disorders, Mental Retardation, immigration, and hospitalization or trauma before age three may predispose to Elective Mutism.

Prevalence. The disorder is apparently rare: it is found in fewer than 1% of child-guidance, clinical, and school-social-casework referrals.

Sex ratio. The disorder is slightly more common in females than in males.

Familial pattern. No information.

Differential diagnosis. In **Severe** or **Profound Mental Retardation, Pervasive Developmental Disorder,** and **Developmental Expressive Language Disorder,** there may be inability to speak, but not a refusal to do so.

Children in families who have emigrated to a country of a different language may refuse to speak the new language. When comprehension of the new language is adequate but the refusal to speak persists, Elective Mutism should be diagnosed.

Diagnostic criteria for 313.23 Elective Mutism

A. Persistent refusal to talk in one or more major social situations (including at school).

B. Ability to comprehend spoken language and to speak.

313.82 Identity Disorder

The essential feature of this disorder is severe subjective distress regarding inability to integrate aspects of the self into a relatively coherent and acceptable sense of self. There is uncertainty about a variety of issues relating to identity, including long-term goals, career choice, friendship patterns, sexual orientation and behavior, religious identification, moral value systems, and group loyalties. These symptoms last at least three months and result in impairment in social or occupational (including academic) functioning. The disturbance does not occur exclusively during the course of another mental disorder, such as a Mood Disorder, Schizophrenia, or Schizophreniform Disorder; the disturbance is not sufficiently pervasive and persistent to warrant the diagnosis of Borderline Personality Disorder.

The uncertainty regarding long-term goals may be expressed as inability to choose or adopt a life pattern, for example, one dedicated to material success, or service to the community, or even some combination of the two. Conflict regarding career choice may be expressed as inability to decide on a career or as inability to pursue an apparently chosen occupation. Conflict regarding friendship patterns may be expressed in an inability to decide the kinds of people with whom to be friendly and the degree of intimacy to permit. Conflict regarding values and loyalties may include concerns about religious identification, patterns of sexual behavior, and moral issues. The person experiences these conflicts as irreconcilable aspects of his or her personality and, as a result, fails to perceive himself or herself as having a coherent identity. Frequently the disturbance is epitomized by the person's asking, "Who am I?"

Associated features. Mild anxiety and depression are common and are usually related to inner preoccupations rather than external events. Self-doubt and doubt about the future are usually present, and take the form of either difficulty in making choices or impulsive experimentation. Negative or oppositional patterns are often chosen in an attempt to establish an independent identity distinct from family or other close people. Such attempts may include transient experimental phases of widely divergent behavior as the person "tries on" various roles.

Age at onset. The most common age at onset is late adolescence, when people generally become detached from their family value systems and attempt to establish independent identities. (This diagnosis appears in this section of the manual because the usual onset is in adolescence.) As value systems change, this disorder may also appear in young adulthood, or even in middle age, if a person begins to question earlier life decisions.

Course. Frequently there is a phase with acute onset, which either resolves over a period of time or becomes chronic. In other instances the onset is more gradual. If the disorder begins in adolescence, it is usually resolved by the mid-20s. If it becomes chronic, however, the person may be unable to make a career commitment, or may fail to form lasting emotional attachments, with resulting frequent shifts in jobs, relationships, and career directions.

Impairment. The degree of impairment varies. Usually there is some interference in both occupational (including academic) and social functioning, with deterioration in friendships and family relationships.

Complications. Educational achievement and work performance below that appropriate to the person's intellectual ability may result from this disorder.

Prevalence. No information. The disorder is apparently more common now than several decades ago, perhaps because today there are more options regarding values, behavior, and life-styles and more conflict between adolescent peer values and parental or societal values.

Predisposing factors, sex ratio, and familial pattern. No information.

Differential diagnosis. Normal conflicts associated with maturing, such as "adolescent turmoil" or "middle-age crisis," are usually not associated with severe distress and impairment in occupational or social functioning. Nevertheless, if the criteria are met, the diagnosis of Identity Disorder should be given regardless of the person's developmental stage.

In **Schizophrenia, Schizophreniform Disorder,** and **Mood Disorder,** there frequently are marked disturbances in identity, but these diagnoses preempt the diagnosis of Identity Disorder.

In **Borderline Personality Disorder,** identity disturbances are only one of several important areas of disturbance, and there is often considerable mood disturbance. If the disturbance is sufficiently pervasive and persistent to warrant the diagnosis of Borderline Personality Disorder, then that diagnosis preempts the diagnosis of Identity Disorder. What appears initially to be Identity Disorder may later turn out to have been an early manifestation of one of the disorders noted above.

Diagnostic criteria for 313.82 Identity Disorder

A. Severe subjective distress regarding uncertainty about a variety of issues relating to identity, including three or more of the following:

(1) long-term goals
(2) career choice
(3) friendship patterns

Diagnostic criteria for 313.82 Identity Disorder continued

  (4) sexual orientation and behavior
  (5) religious identification
  (6) moral value systems
  (7) group loyalties

B. Impairment in social or occupational (including academic) functioning as a result of the symptoms in A.

C. Duration of the disturbance of at least three months.

D. Occurrence not exclusively during the course of a Mood Disorder or of a psychotic disorder, such as Schizophrenia.

E. The disturbance is not sufficiently pervasive and persistent to warrant the diagnosis of Borderline Personality Disorder.

313.89   Reactive Attachment Disorder of Infancy or Early Childhood

The essential feature of this disorder is markedly disturbed social relatedness in most contexts that begins before the age of five and is not due to Mental Retardation or a Pervasive Developmental Disorder, such as Autistic Disorder. The disturbance in social relatedness is presumed to be due to grossly pathogenic care that preceded the onset of the disturbance.

The disturbance may take the form of either persistent failure to initiate or respond in an age-expected manner to most social interactions or (in an older child) indiscriminate sociability, e.g., excessive familiarity with relative strangers, as shown by making requests and displaying affection. Some severe forms of this disorder, in which there is lack of weight gain and motor development, have been called "failure to thrive" or "hospitalism."

Infants with this disorder present with poorly developed social responsiveness. Visual tracking of eyes and faces and responding to the caregiver's voice may not be established by two months of age; attention, interest, and gaze reciprocity may be absent. At four to five months, the infant may fail to express pleasure by smiling, participate in playful, simple games with the caregiver or observer, or attempt vocal and visual reciprocity (e.g., turn his or her head toward the side from which the voice of the caregiver or observer comes). At six to ten months, the infant may fail to reach out when he or she is to be picked up, reach spontaneously for the caregiver, crawl toward the caregiver, establish visual or vocal communication with the caregiver, begin to imitate the caregiver, or display any of the usual more subtle facial expressions of joy, coyness, curiosity, surprise, fear, anger, or attentiveness.

The child often is apathetic; staring, weak cry, poor muscle tone, weak rooting and grasping reactions to attempts to feed, and low spontaneous motility are commonly observed. Excessive sleep and a rather generalized lack of interest in the environment are frequent manifestations of the disorder.

Often such infants are noticed by a pediatrician because of failure to thrive physically. Since these infants frequently do not receive well-baby care, the reason for the visit to the pediatrician may be a complicating physical illness, usually infectious, or an associated feeding problem (e.g., rumination) or injury. The head circumference is generally normal, and failure to gain weight, if present, is disproportionately greater than the failure (if any) to gain in length.

The diagnosis of Reactive Attachment Disorder of Infancy or Early Childhood can be made only in the presence of clear evidence of grossly pathogenic care. This frequently requires either a home visit, observation of the spontaneous emotional and social interaction between the caregiver and the infant during both feeding and non-feeding periods, or reports from other observers. Parental reports may not be reliable, particularly when there is suspected child abuse. The pathogenic care may include persistent disregard of the child's basic emotional needs for comfort, stimulation, and affection. For example, the caregiver may be overly harsh, or consistently ignore the child. Some caregivers may persistently disregard the child's physical needs, failing to feed the child adequately, or to protect the child from physical danger or assault (including sexual abuse). Repeated and frequent changes of the primary caregiver so that stable attachments are not possible may also be an etiologic factor.

It is pathognomonic of this disorder that, except in cases of extreme neglect with consequent severe physical complications (e.g., starvation, dehydration, or other inter-current physical complications that can cause death before therapeutic measures can take hold), the clinical picture can be substantially improved by adequate care. (Such care need not be provided by a single person to be effective; it can include hospitalization, for example.) Such a therapeutic response is ultimate confirmation of the diagnosis.

Associated features. Feeding disturbances may be present, in particular, rumination, regurgitation, and vomiting. Such disturbances may be related to psychosocial deprivation and may, in turn, be a central factor in malnutrition. There may be sleep disturbances, and hypersensitivity to touch and sound.

Age at onset. By definition, the age at onset is before age five. Beyond this age, children do not develop this clinical picture in response to grossly pathogenic care. The diagnosis can be made as early as in the first month of life.

Course, impairment, and complications. If care remains grossly inadequate, severe malnutrition, intercurrent infection, and death can occur. As noted above, however, the disorder is reversible with appropriate treatment and does not recur if affectionate and developmentally appropriate care is provided, preferably by a primary caregiver.

Predisposing factors. All factors that interfere with early emotional attachment of the child to a primary caregiver can predispose to this disorder. In terms of the caregiver, these include: severe depression, isolation and lack of support systems, obsessions of infanticide that make the caregiver stay away from the infant, impulse-control difficulties, and extreme deprivation or abuse during the caregiver's own childhood.

Babies that are "difficult" or very lethargic may frustrate the caregiver excessively and discourage appropriate caregiver behavior. Other factors that predispose to the disorder are lack of affectionate body-to-body contact during the first weeks of life, such as a prolonged period in an incubator or other early separations from a caring adult.

Prevalence, sex ratio, and familial pattern. No information.

Differential diagnosis. The diagnosis of Reactive Attachment Disorder of Infancy or Early Childhood is not made if the disturbance in social relatedness is attributed to either **Mental Retardation** or a **Pervasive Developmental Disorder,** such as **Autistic Disorder**.

Children with a variety of **severe neurologic abnormalities,** such as **deafness, blindness, profound multisensory defects, major central nervous system disease,** or **severe chronic physical illness,** may have very specific needs and few means of satisfying them, and thus may suffer minor secondary attachment disturbances. However, markedly disturbed social relatedness is generally not present.

In **psychosocial dwarfism** there may also be apathy, parental neglect, and disappearance of symptoms with hospitalization. However, in psychosocial dwarfism there rarely is a history of grossly pathogenic care.

Diagnostic criteria for 313.89 Reactive Attachment Disorder of Infancy or Early Childhood

A. Markedly disturbed social relatedness in most contexts, beginning before the age of five, as evidenced by either (1) or (2):

   (1) persistent failure to initiate or respond to most social interactions (e.g., in infants, absence of visual tracking and reciprocal play, lack of vocal imitation or playfulness, apathy, little or no spontaneity; at later ages, lack of or little curiosity and social interest)
   (2) indiscriminate sociability, e.g., excessive familiarity with relative strangers by making requests and displaying affection

B. The disturbance in A is not a symptom of either Mental Retardation or a Pervasive Developmental Disorder, such as Autistic Disorder.

C. Grossly pathogenic care, as evidenced by at least one of the following:

   (1) persistent disregard of the child's basic emotional needs for comfort, stimulation, and affection. *Examples*: overly harsh punishment by caregiver; consistent neglect by caregiver.
   (2) persistent disregard of the child's basic physical needs, including nutrition, adequate housing, and protection from physical danger and assault (including sexual abuse)
   (3) repeated change of primary caregiver so that stable attachments are not possible, e.g., frequent changes in foster parents

D. There is a presumption that the care described in C is responsible for the disturbed behavior in A; this presumption is warranted if the disturbance in A began following the pathogenic care in C.

Note: If failure to thrive is present, code it on Axis III.

307.30 Stereotypy/Habit Disorder

The essential features of this disorder are intentional and repetitive behaviors that are nonfunctional, i.e., serve no constructive, socially acceptable purpose. The behaviors may include: body-rocking, head-banging, hitting or biting parts of one's own body (e.g., face-slapping, hand-biting), skin-picking or -scratching, teeth-grinding (bruxism), bodily manipulations (e.g., incessant nose-picking, hair-pulling, eye- and anus-poking), noncommunicative, repetitive vocalizations, breath-holding, hyperventilation, and swallowing air (aerophagia). Frequently the behaviors are performed in a rhythmic fashion.

The diagnosis is given only when the disturbance either causes physical injury to the child or markedly interferes with normal activities. The diagnosis is not given when a Pervasive Developmental Disorder or a Tic Disorder is present.

Associated features. Stereotypy/Habit Disorder, especially in its more severe forms, is frequently associated with Mental Retardation. Stereotypic "blindism" behaviors are seen in some congenitally blind people, such as head-rocking and other maneuvers to create sensory stimuli (pressing the eyeballs, directing eyes at strong light source, smelling objects and persons). Characteristic self-restraint behaviors, such as keeping hands inside the shirt, are seen in people who injure themselves with these behaviors.

Age at onset. Behaviors such as thumb-sucking, rocking (especially before falling asleep), and bruxism may be observed in normal infants and young children. The pathologic Stereotypy/Habit Disorder is usually first seen in childhood, and may intensify in adolescence.

Course. The course may be brief if it is apparently linked to an episodic disorder, such as a brief psychotic episode. It may be chronic if linked to a chronic disorder, such as severe or profound Mental Retardation. The course is likely to be chronic if there are treatment or environmental factors that maintain the symptoms, such as a caregiver's paying attention to the self-injurious behavior. In some children with Mental Retardation, the symptoms disappear in later childhood, especially with treatment. Stereotypy/Habit Disorder associated with disorders of the central nervous system, such as Lesch-Nyhan syndrome, are more likely to be refractory to treatment.

Impairment. Severe forms may interfere with self-care and other skills. Depending on the type of behavior, the disorder may result in social rejection. Complications (see below) may lead to physical impairment.

Complications. In extreme cases, severe mutilation and life-threatening injuries may result. Self-inflicted wounds may become infected and lead to septicemia. Severe eye-poking or -hitting may produce retinal detachment and blindness. Scarring from chronic, self-inflicted injuries may limit limb movement or be disfiguring in other ways. Some people with Lesch-Nyhan syndrome may virtually amputate distal parts of the upper limbs through biting.

Predisposing factors. People with severe or profound Mental Retardation, especially those who have multiple handicaps, are more predisposed to develop Stereotypy/Habit Disorder than those with milder Mental Retardation. The disorder is more common in nonstimulating institutional environments, where it may serve the adaptive function of attracting staff attention. It may be associated with sensory handicaps (blindness and deafness, especially when congenital), degenerative and central nervous system disorders (Lesch-Nyhan syndrome, temporal lobe epilepsy, postencephalitic syndrome), and other mental disorders in their most severe forms (e.g., Schizophrenia and Obsessive Compulsive Disorder). It may be induced by certain psychoactive substances such as amphetamine, in which case both the diagnosis Stereotypy/Habit Disorder and Psychoactive Substance-induced Organic Mental Disorder should be made.

Prevalence. No information. Self-injurious behaviors have been estimated to occur in 10% to 23% of institutionalized people with Mental Retardation.

Differential diagnosis. Self-stimulating behaviors, such as rocking (especially before falling asleep) and thumb-sucking, are common in normal infants and young children. Stereotypy/Habit Disorder should not be diagnosed if the behavior occurs in the context of a **Pervasive Developmental Disorder**. The stereotyped behavior present in **Tic Disorders** is involuntary, even though it can be suppressed for varying periods of time.

Diagnostic criteria for 307.30 Stereotypy/Habit Disorder

A. Intentional, repetitive, nonfunctional behaviors, such as hand-shaking or -waving, body-rocking, head-banging, mouthing of objects, nail-biting, picking at nose or skin.

B. The disturbance either causes physical injury to the child or markedly interferes with normal activities, e.g., injury to head from head-banging; inability to fall asleep because of constant rocking.

C. Does not meet the criteria for either a Pervasive Developmental Disorder or a Tic Disorder.

314.00   Undifferentiated Attention-deficit Disorder

This is a residual category for disturbances in which the predominant feature is the persistence of developmentally inappropriate and marked inattention that is not a symptom of another disorder, such as Mental Retardation or Attention-deficit Hyperactivity Disorder, or of a disorganized and chaotic environment. Some of the disturbances that in DSM-III would have been categorized as Attention Deficit Disorder without Hyperactivity would be included in this category. Research is necessary to determine if this is a valid diagnostic category and, if so, how it should be defined.

Organic
Mental Syndromes
and Disorders

This chapter includes the following:

(1) A discussion of the concepts of organic mental syndrome and organic mental disorder, p. 97

(2) A description of the organic mental syndromes:
Delirium, p. 100
Dementia, p. 103
Amnestic Syndrome, p. 108
Organic Delusional Syndrome, p. 109
Organic Hallucinosis, p. 110
Organic Mood Syndrome, p. 111
Organic Anxiety Syndrome, p. 113
Organic Personality Syndrome, p. 114
Intoxication, p. 116
Withdrawal, p. 118
Organic Mental Syndrome Not Otherwise Specified, p. 119

(3) A description of the DSM-III-R Organic Mental Disorders:
Dementias Arising in the Senium and Presenium, p. 119
Psychoactive Substance-induced Organic Mental Disorders, p. 123
Organic Mental Disorders Associated with Axis III
    Physical Disorders or Conditions, or Whose Etiology is Unknown, p. 162

The Concepts of Organic Mental Syndrome and Organic Mental Disorder

In DSM-III-R a distinction is made between organic *mental syndromes* and organic *mental disorders*. "Organic mental syndrome" is used to refer to a constellation of psychological or behavioral signs and symptoms without reference to etiology (e.g., Organic Anxiety Syndrome, Dementia); "organic mental disorder" designates a particular organic mental syndrome in which the etiology is known or presumed (e.g., Alcohol Withdrawal Delirium, Multi-infarct Dementia). In the DSM-III-R classification the term *disorder* is used when an organic mental syndrome is associated with an Axis III physical disorder or condition, as in Organic Delusional Disorder due to a brain tumor. *Disorder* is also used when the etiology is unknown, although, strictly speaking, in such a case it would be more correct to use *syndrome*.

The essential feature of all these disorders is a psychological or behavioral abnormality associated with transient or permanent dysfunction of the brain. Organic Mental Disorders are diagnosed (a) by recognizing the presence of one of the Organic Mental Syndromes, as described below, and (b) by demonstrating, by means of the history, physical examination, or laboratory tests, the presence of a specific organic factor (or factors) judged to be etiologically related to the abnormal mental state. In certain cases with the characteristic symptoms of a dementia or a delirium, however, a reasonable inference of an organic factor can be made from the clinical features alone if the disturbance cannot be accounted for by any nonorganic mental disorder. For example, in some cases it is reasonable to assume the presence of an organic factor to account for characteristic symptoms of Dementia if all nonorganic mental disorders that could account for the symptoms, such as Major Depression, have been ruled out. Similarly, in some cases it is reasonable to assume the presence of an organic factor to account for the characteristic features of a Delirium if all nonorganic disorders that could account for the symptoms, such as a Manic Episode, have been ruled out.

Organic Mental Disorders are a heterogeneous group; therefore, no single description can characterize them all. The differences in clinical presentation reflect differences in the localization, mode of onset, progression, duration, and nature of the underlying pathophysiologic process.

Differentiation of Organic Mental Disorders as a separate class does not imply that nonorganic ("functional") mental disorders are somehow independent of brain processes. On the contrary, it is assumed that all psychological processes, normal and abnormal, depend on brain function. Limitations in our knowledge, however, sometimes make it impossible to determine whether a particular mental disorder in a particular person should be considered an Organic Mental Disorder (because it is due to brain dysfunction of *known* organic etiology) or whether it should be diagnosed as other than an Organic Mental Disorder (because it is more adequately accounted for as a response to psychological or social factors [as in Adjustment Disorder] or because the presence of a specific organic factor has not been established [as in Schizophrenia]).

The organic factor responsible for an Organic Mental Disorder may be a primary disease of the brain or a systemic illness that secondarily affects the brain. It may also be a psychoactive substance or toxic agent that is either currently disturbing brain function or has left some long-lasting effect. Withdrawal of a psychoactive substance that was previously regularly used by the person is another cause of Organic Mental Disorder.

The most common Organic Mental Syndromes are Delirium, Dementia, Intoxication, and Withdrawal. These syndromes display great variability among people and in the same person over time. More than one Organic Mental Syndrome may be present in a person simultaneously (e.g., Delirium superimposed upon Dementia), and one Organic Mental Syndrome may succeed another (e.g., thiamine-deficiency Delirium [Wernicke's encephalopathy] followed by Alcohol Amnestic Disorder [Korsakoff's syndrome]).

Associated features. A wide variety of different emotional, motivational, and behavioral abnormalities are associated with Organic Mental Disorders. It is often impossible to decide whether the symptoms are the direct result of damage to the brain or are a reaction to the cognitive deficits and other psychological changes that constitute the essential features of these disorders.

Severe emotional disturbances may accompany cognitive impairment in a person who views it as a loss, a serious threat to self-esteem, or both. Anxiety, depression, irritability, and shame of varying degrees of intensity may be present.

Obsessive compulsive people tend to be particularly intolerant of, and disturbed by, their reduced cognitive capacity or by perceptual abnormalities, such as hallucinations. They tend to react with a fear of loss of control. There may also be severe depression leading to suicide attempts. Other people cope with memory and other cognitive deficits by marked orderliness, which helps them maintain some degree of control. Such people insist on keeping things in exactly the same places, keeping detailed notes and diaries to counteract forgetfulness, and avoiding situations in which their deficits could be exposed. Some people resort to circumstantiality and confabulation in an effort to conceal gaps in memory.

Paranoid attitudes and actual delusions may be exhibited by habitually suspicious people who feel threatened by their cognitive impairment. They may accuse others of maliciously misplacing or stealing their possessions. Irritability and outbursts of temper, sometimes with physical aggression, may occur. Some people are euphoric; others, apathetic.

Decreased control over sexual, aggressive, and acquisitive impulses may accompany cognitive impairment. Social judgment may be impaired, and result in inappropriate behavior that provokes retaliation. Inappropriate sexual advances, exhibitionistic acts, stealing, ravenous eating, and other manifestations of faulty impulse control may be exhibited.

These associated features reflect the person's personality, education level, and interpersonal relations as well as the type and severity of the cognitive impairment or abnormality. They are not necessarily correlated with the degree of cognitive impairment: A person with a relatively mild cognitive impairment may display conspicuous emotional and behavioral disturbance. Severe and widespread brain dysfunction, such as follows extensive neuronal destruction or metabolic dysfunction, may produce apathy, lethargy, incontinence of urine or feces, diminished psychomotor activity, somnolence, or blunting of affect.

Emotional and behavioral disturbances may result in social isolation, by withdrawal or ostracism; and this, in turn, tends to aggravate the cognitive disability.

Age at onset. Organic Mental Disorders may occur at any age. Delirium is most apt to occur at the extremes of the life cycle; Dementia is most common in the elderly.

Course. Since Organic Mental Disorders encompass such a wide range of psychopathological syndromes and organic etiologies, no single course characterizes them all. Onset may be sudden, as in the case of Delirium associated with an acute infection or Dementia resulting from major head trauma, or it may be insidious, as in Primary Degenerative Dementia of the Alzheimer Type or the personality disturbance sometimes associated with temporal lobe epilepsy.

The course is also extremely variable. It may be steadily or irregularly progressive, episodic, static, or rapidly or gradually resolving. A major factor in determining the course is the nature of the underlying pathology. Metabolic disorders, psychoactive substance intoxications and withdrawals, and systemic illnesses tend to cause temporary brain dysfunction, and may be followed by full recovery. Pathological processes causing structural damage to the brain are more likely to cause permanent residual impairment.

ORGANIC MENTAL SYNDROMES

The Organic Mental Syndromes can be grouped into six categories:

(1) **Delirium and Dementia,** in which cognitive impairment is relatively global;

(2) **Amnestic Syndrome and Organic Hallucinosis,** in which relatively selective areas of cognition are impaired;

(3) **Organic Delusional Syndrome, Organic Mood Syndrome, and Organic Anxiety Syndrome,** which have features resembling Schizophrenic, Mood, and Anxiety Disorders;

(4) **Organic Personality Syndrome,** in which the personality is affected;

(5) **Intoxication and Withdrawal,** in which the disorder is associated with ingestion of or reduction in use of a psychoactive substance and does not meet the criteria for any of the previous syndromes (Strictly speaking, these two Organic Mental Syndromes are etiologically rather than descriptively defined.);

(6) **Organic Mental Syndrome Not Otherwise Specified,** which constitutes a residual category for any other Organic Mental Syndrome not classifiable as one of the previous syndromes.

Delirium
The essential features of Delirium are reduced ability to maintain attention to external stimuli and to appropriately shift attention to new external stimuli, and disorganized thinking, as manifested by rambling, irrelevant, or incoherent speech. The syndrome also involves a reduced level of consciousness, sensory misperceptions, disturbances of the sleep-wake cycle and level of psychomotor activity, disorientation to time, place, or person, and memory impairment. The onset is relatively rapid, and the course typically fluctuates. The total duration is usually brief.

Some reserve the term *delirium* for a particular, agitated variety of confusional state with vivid visual hallucinations. In this manual, however, Delirium is intended to include the broad spectrum of clinical states having in common the essential features described above.

In Delirium there is difficulty sustaining and shifting attention. The person is easily distracted by irrelevant stimuli, and is unable to shift attention to a new stimulus when it is appropriate to do so. Questions must be repeated several times because of the person's inability to focus attention. It may be difficult, or impossible, to engage him or her in conversation because attention wanders or because the person is perseverating in response to earlier questions.

The person with Delirium cannot maintain a coherent stream of thought. Thinking loses its usual clarity and direction toward a goal; it appears fragmented and disjointed. In mild Delirium, this may be manifested by slight or moderate acceleration or slowing of thought; in severe Delirium, thinking is totally disorganized. This disturbance is reflected in speech that, in some cases, is rambling or irrelevant, and in others, pressured and incoherent, with unpredictable switching from subject to subject. It is also reflected in defective reasoning and impaired goal-directed behavior. Although other cognitive disturbances, particularly disorientation and memory impairment, are also commonly present in Delirium, the person may be so inattentive and incoherent that these mental functions cannot be meaningfully assessed.

Perceptual disturbances are common and result in various misinterpretations, illusions, and hallucinations. For example, the banging of a door may be mistaken for a pistol shot (misinterpretation); the folds of the bedclothes may appear to be animate objects (illusion); or the person may "see" a group of people hovering over the bed when no one is actually there (hallucination). Although sensory misperceptions and hallucinations are most commonly visual, they may occur in other sensory modalities as well. Misperceptions range from simple and uniform to highly complex. There are often both a delusional conviction of the reality of hallucinations and an emotional and behavioral response in keeping with their content.

The sleep-wake cycle is almost invariably disturbed. This frequently involves some depression in the level of consciousness, ranging from simple drowsiness, through increasing stages of torpor, to stupor or semicoma. On the other hand, some people with Delirium are hypervigilant and have difficulty falling asleep. Fluctuations from hypersomnolence to insomnia and reversals of the customary sleep-wake cycle may also be present. Vivid dreams and nightmares are common, and may merge with hallucinations.

Psychomotor activity may also be disturbed. Many people are restless and hyperactive. Groping or picking at the bedclothes, attempting to get out of bed, striking out at nonexistent objects, and sudden changes of position are manifestations of increased psychomotor activity. On the other hand, there may be decreased psychomotor activity, with sluggishness and even certain features resembling catatonic stupor. Psychomotor activity often shifts abruptly from one of these extremes to another.

Disorientation to time and place is common; disorientation to person is uncommon. In mild delirium, disorientation to time may be the first symptom to appear.

Memory disturbance, particularly recent memory, is invariably present. For a discussion of this clinical feature and its assessment, see Dementia, p. 104.

Associated features. Emotional disturbances are very common and quite variable. They include anxiety, fear, depression, irritability, anger, euphoria, and apathy. Some people maintain the same emotional tone throughout the course of the Delirium whereas others experience rapid and unpredictable changes from one emotional state to another. Fear is very commonly experienced, sometimes as the result of threatening hallucinations or poorly systematized delusions. If fear is marked, the person may attempt to flee his or her surroundings without regard to possible injury, or may attack those who are falsely viewed as threatening. Severely depressed feelings may also lead to self-destructive acts. Crying, calls for help, cursing, muttering, moaning, and other vocal productions, particularly prominent at night, are further manifestations of the disturbed emotional state of people with Delirium.

Neurologic signs are comparatively uncommon in Delirium. An important exception, however, is the presence of abnormal movements. Various forms of tremor are frequently present. Asterixis, a peculiar flapping movement of the hyperextended hands, was originally described in hepatic encephalopathy, but may be found in other delirious states as well. Autonomic signs (tachycardia, sweating, flushed face, dilated pupils, and elevated blood pressure) commonly occur.

Other disorders of higher cortical function in Delirium include dysnomia (inability to name objects) and dysgraphia (impaired ability to write).

Age at onset. Delirium can occur at any age, but is especially common in children and after the age of 60.

Course. Delirium usually develops over a short period of time. Sometimes it begins quite abruptly, e.g., after a head injury or following a seizure. At other times it is preceded, for hours or days, by certain prodromal symptoms. These include restlessness, difficulty thinking clearly, hypersensitivity to auditory and visual stimuli, nocturnal insomnia, daytime hypersomnolence, vivid dreams, and nightmares. The slower evolution is more likely if systemic illness or metabolic imbalance underlies the Delirium.

Fluctuation in symptoms is one of the hallmarks of Delirium. Typically, the person is worse during sleepless nights or in the dark. So-called "lucid intervals," periods during which he or she is more attentive and coherent, may occur at any time, but are most common in the morning. These fluctuations help distinguish Delirium from other Organic Mental Syndromes.

The duration of an episode of Delirium is usually brief, about one week; it is rare for Delirium to persist for more than a month. If the underlying disorder is promptly corrected or is self-limited, recovery from Delirium may be complete. On the other hand, if the underlying disorder persists, the clinical syndrome of Delirium gradually shifts to some other, more stable, Organic Mental Syndrome, or may cause death.

Complications. Injuries may be sustained from falling out of bed or attempting to flee frightening hallucinations. Agitation may interfere with proper medical management. If inadequately or belatedly treated, Delirium may lead to a Dementia or, more rarely, an Amnestic Syndrome or Organic Personality Syndrome.

Etiologic factors. The causes of Delirium usually lie outside the nervous system and include: systemic infections; metabolic disorders such as hypoxia, hypercarbia, hypoglycemia, ionic imbalances, hepatic or renal disease, or thiamine deficiency; postoperative states; and psychoactive substance intoxication and withdrawal. Delirium also occurs in hypertensive encephalopathy, following seizures, and on regaining consciousness following head trauma. Certain focal lesions of the right parietal lobe and inferomedial surface of the occipital lobe may present as Delirium.

Predisposing factors. The immature or aging brain is more susceptible to the development of Delirium. Preexisting brain damage or a previous history of Delirium appears to increase the chances of a person's developing this syndrome.

Differential diagnosis. Schizophrenia, Schizophreniform Disorder, and other psychotic disorders may also be marked by hallucinations, delusions, and disordered thinking. In Delirium, however, these symptoms are extremely random and haphazard, without evidence of systematization. The course fluctuates, and there are reduced ability to maintain and shift attention appropriately and, often, impairment in memory and orientation. Finally, in Delirium there is frequently a generalized slowing of background activity on the electroencephalogram, and the syndrome's cause is obviously organic.

Whereas memory impairment is common in both **Dementia** and Delirium, in Dementia the person is alert. Often, however, the two syndromes coexist, and it may be difficult to decide how much of the clinical picture to ascribe to one syndrome and how much to the other. One cannot diagnose Dementia in the presence of significant Delirium because the symptoms of Delirium interfere with proper assessment of Dementia. Both diagnoses are given only when there is a definite history of preexisting Dementia. When there is uncertainty as to whether the symptoms in a given person are basically those of Delirium or Dementia, it is best to make a provisional diagnosis of Delirium. This should lead to a more active therapeutic approach, and with time the proper diagnosis will become apparent.

Factitious Disorder with Psychological Symptoms simulating an Organic Mental Syndrome might, under rare circumstances, present a problem in the differential diagnosis of Delirium. The person with Factitious Disorder shows inconsistencies in tests of mental status. A normal electroencephalogram also helps to exclude Delirium.

Diagnostic criteria for Delirium

A. Reduced ability to maintain attention to external stimuli (e.g., questions must be repeated because attention wanders) and to appropriately shift attention to new external stimuli (e.g., perseverates answer to a previous question).

B. Disorganized thinking, as indicated by rambling, irrelevant, or incoherent speech.

C. At least two of the following:

> (1) reduced level of consciousness, e.g., difficulty keeping awake during examination
>
> (2) perceptual disturbances: misinterpretations, illusions, or hallucinations
>
> (3) disturbance of sleep-wake cycle with insomnia or daytime sleepiness
>
> (4) increased or decreased psychomotor activity
>
> (5) disorientation to time, place, or person
>
> (6) memory impairment, e.g., inability to learn new material, such as the names of several unrelated objects after five minutes, or to remember past events, such as history of current episode of illness

D. Clinical features develop over a short period of time (usually hours to days) and tend to fluctuate over the course of a day.

E. Either (1) or (2):

> (1) evidence from the history, physical examination, or laboratory tests of a specific organic factor (or factors) judged to be etiologically related to the disturbance
>
> (2) in the absence of such evidence, an etiologic organic factor can be presumed if the disturbance cannot be accounted for by any nonorganic mental disorder, e.g., Manic Episode accounting for agitation and sleep disturbance

---

Dementia

The essential feature of Dementia is impairment in short- and long-term memory, associated with impairment in abstract thinking, impaired judgment, other disturbances of higher cortical function, or personality change. The disturbance is severe enough to interfere significantly with work or usual social activities or relationships with others. The diagnosis of Dementia is not made if these symptoms occur only in the presence of reduced ability to maintain or shift attention to external stimuli, as in Delirium; however, Delirium and Dementia may coexist.

As in all Organic Mental Syndromes, an underlying causative organic factor is always assumed. In certain clinical states, e.g., Primary Degenerative Dementia of the Alzheimer Type, however, it may be impossible to establish a *specific* organic factor as the definitive cause of the disturbance. These conditions may nevertheless be diagnosed as Dementia if (a) the impairment in memory is associated with either impaired abstract thinking or judgment, other disturbances of higher cortical functioning, or personality change, (*b*) a diligent search for a specific organic etiologic factor has been made, and (*c*) all nonorganic diagnoses that could account for the disturbance have been ruled out (e.g., Major Depression accounting for the cognitive impairment).

In the past, the term *Dementia* often implied a progressive or irreversible course. The definition of Dementia in this manual, however, is based on clinical symptoms alone, and carries no connotation concerning prognosis. Dementia may be progressive, static, or remitting. The reversibility of a Dementia is a function of the underlying pathology and of the availability and timely application of effective treatment.

Memory impairment is usually the most prominent symptom initially. In mild Dementia there is moderate memory loss, more marked for recent events, such as forgetting names, telephone numbers, directions, conversations, and events of the day. In more severe cases, only highly learned material is retained, and new information is rapidly forgotten. The person may leave a task unfinished because of forgetting to return to it after an interruption. This may cause a person to leave the water running in the sink or to neglect turning off the stove. In advanced stages of Dementia, memory impairment is often so severe that the person forgets the names of close relatives, his or her own occupation, schooling, birthday, or, occasionally, even his or her own name. Memory disturbance may be formally documented by demonstrating difficulty in learning new information (short-term memory deficit) and in remembering past personal information or facts of common knowledge (long-term memory deficit). The former is tested by asking the person to memorize the names of several unrelated objects, or a brief sentence, and then to repeat them after a few minutes of distraction; the latter is tested by asking about events that happened in the past, such as one's birthplace, or past Presidents.

Impairment in abstract thinking takes many forms. The person has trouble coping with novel tasks, especially if pressed for time. He or she may try to avoid situations and tasks that require the processing of new and complex information. The deficit is sometimes formally assessed by asking the person with Dementia to find similarities or differences between related words.

Impaired judgment and impulse control are also commonly observed. Coarse language, inappropriate jokes, neglect of personal appearance and hygiene, and a general disregard for the conventional rules of social conduct are evidence of bad judgment and poor impulse control. A previously cautious businesswoman may embark on a reckless business venture. An elderly man who never married may make sexual advances to strangers. A retiree may shoplift without considering the consequences. Marked impairment of judgment and impulse control is particularly characteristic of certain Dementias that affect primarily the frontal lobes.

Dementia also involves a variety of disturbances of higher cortical function. Although language is unaffected by some neurologic disorders that cause Dementia, in others it is abnormal. It may appear vague, stereotyped, and imprecise, with long circumlocutory phrases; or there may be signs of aphasia, such as difficulty naming objects. In severe forms of Dementia, the person may be virtually mute. So-called "constructional ability" is often disturbed, and can be demonstrated by having the person copy three-dimensional figures, assemble blocks, or arrange sticks in specific designs. Agnosias (failure to recognize or identify objects despite intact sensory function) and apraxias (inability to carry out motor activities despite intact comprehension and motor function) may also be present.

Personality change is often observed in Dementia, and may involve either an alteration or an accentuation of premorbid traits. A common pattern is for a normally active person to become increasingly apathetic and withdrawn; his or her range of social involvement narrows, the personality loses its sparkle, and the person is described by others as "not himself (or herself)." Another pattern of change is for a previously neat and meticulous person to become slovenly and unconcerned about his or her appearance. On the other hand, some people display an accentuation of preexisting obsessive compulsive, histrionic, impulsive, or paranoid traits. Irritability and cantankerousness are also common features of Dementia.

Associated features. When Dementia is mild and the person has some grasp of his or her deteriorating faculties, he or she may react with marked anxiety or depression. Attempts to conceal or compensate for subjectively perceived intellectual deficits are very common. This may result in excessive orderliness, social withdrawal, or a tendency to relate events in minute detail so as to avoid exposure of gaps in memory. Paranoid ideation may occasionally be quite marked and result in false accusations and verbal or physical attacks. The habitually jealous person who develops a Dementia may develop a delusion of marital infidelity and actually assault his or her spouse.

People with Dementia are especially vulnerable to physical and psychosocial stressors. For example, minor surgery, bereavement, or retirement may considerably aggravate intellectual deficits.

Age at onset. Dementia is found predominantly in the elderly, although certain specific etiologic factors (see below) may cause Dementia at any age. The diagnosis of Dementia may be made at any time after the IQ is fairly stable (usually by age three or four). Thus, if a child at age four developed a chronic neurologic disorder that interfered with previously acquired functions so as to significantly lower intellectual and adaptive functioning, he or she would be considered to have both Dementia and Mental Retardation. In such a case both diagnoses should be made, Mental Retardation being listed first because of its greater relevance to management.

Course. The mode of onset and subsequent course of Dementia depend on the underlying etiology. When Dementia is a result of some clearly defined episode of neurologic disease, such as cerebral hypoxia or encephalitis, or of head trauma, it may begin quite suddenly, but then remain relatively stationary for a long time. Primary Degenerative Dementia of the Alzheimer Type, on the other hand, is usually insidious in onset and slowly progresses to death, with a generally deteriorating course over a period of several years. Dementia resulting from brain tumors, subdural hematomas, and metabolic factors may also have a gradual onset. When the underlying disorder can be treated, as in hypothyroidism, subdural hematoma, normal-pressure hydrocephalus, and tertiary neurosyphilis, Dementia can be arrested or even reversed. However, the more widespread the structural damage to the brain, the less likely is clinical improvement.

Impairment. By definition, Dementia is diagnosed only when the loss of intellectual function is sufficiently severe to interfere with social or occupational functioning, although the degree of impairment may vary. In advanced Dementia the person becomes totally oblivious to his or her surroundings and requires constant care.

Complications. People with Dementia may wander and become lost. They may, occasionally, do harm to themselves or others. Delirium is frequently a complication of Dementia. People with severe Dementia are susceptible to accidents and infectious diseases, which often prove fatal.

Etiologic factors. Primary Degenerative Dementia of the Alzheimer Type appears to be the most common Dementia. Other causes include: vascular disease (Multi-infarct Dementia); central nervous system infections (including tertiary neurosyphilis, tuberculous and fungal meningitis, viral encephalitis, human immunodeficiency virus (HIV)-related disorders [e.g., Acquired Immune Deficiency Syndrome (AIDS), AIDS-related Complex (ARC)], and Jakob-Creutzfeldt disease); brain trauma (especially chronic subdural hematoma); toxic-metabolic disturbances (such as pernicious anemia, folic-acid deficiency, hypothyroidism, bromide intoxication); normal-pressure hydrocephalus; neurologic diseases such as Huntington's chorea, multiple sclerosis, Pick's disease, cerebellar degeneration, progressive supranuclear palsy, and Parkinson's disease; and postanoxic or posthypoglycemic states.

Differential diagnosis. The **normal process of aging** has been associated in a number of studies with a variety of different changes in intellectual function. The nature of these changes and whether they should be considered true decrements of function, however, remain controversial. The diagnosis of Dementia is warranted only if there is demonstrable evidence of memory impairment that, along with the other features of Dementia, is of sufficient severity to interfere with social or occupational functioning. Dementia is not synonymous with aging.

In **Delirium** there is also memory impairment; the difference is that in Dementia the person is alert. The clinical course of these two syndromes also differs. In Delirium, symptoms typically fluctuate, whereas in Dementia, they are relatively stable. An Organic Mental Disorder persisting in unchanged form for more than a few months suggests Dementia rather than Delirium. (See also the differential diagnosis of Delirium, p. 102.)

Schizophrenia, especially when chronic, may be associated with some degree of intellectual deterioration. The absence of identifiable brain pathology helps rule out the additional diagnosis of Dementia.

People with a **Major Depressive Episode** may complain of memory impairment, difficulty thinking and concentrating, and an overall reduction in intellectual abilities. They may also perform poorly on mental-status examination and neuropsychological testing. These features may suggest a possible diagnosis of Dementia, and this phenomenon has been called "pseudodementia" or "the dementia syndrome of depression."

Abnormalities of mood in Dementia are less frequent and, when present, less pervasive than in depression. The clinical history may help to differentiate the two conditions. In depressive pseudodementia, the onset can frequently be dated with some precision, and symptoms usually progress more rapidly than in true Dementia. In addition, there may be a history of previous mental illness.

It has been suggested that in "the dementia syndrome of depression," the mood disturbance unmasks an underlying structural abnormality in the central nervous system, resulting in the clinical features of Dementia. In the absence of evidence of a specific organic etiologic factor, if the symptoms suggesting a Major Depressive Episode are at least as prominent as those suggesting Dementia, it is best to diagnose Major Depressive Episode and to assume that the symptoms suggesting Dementia are secondary to the depression. A therapeutic trial with an antidepressant drug or electroconvulsive therapy (ECT) (if not contraindicated) may clarify the diagnosis in that if the disorder is actually a Major Depressive Episode, cognitive impairment usually resolves as the mood improves.

Factitious Disorder with Psychological Symptoms may mimic Dementia, but rarely.

Diagnostic criteria for Dementia

A. Demonstrable evidence of impairment in short- and long-term memory. Impairment in short-term memory (inability to learn new information) may be indicated by inability to remember three objects after five minutes. Long-term memory impairment (inability to remember information that was known in the past) may be indicated by inability to remember past personal information (e.g., what happened yesterday, birthplace, occupation) or facts of common knowledge (e.g., past Presidents, well-known dates).

B. At least one of the following:

(1) impairment in abstract thinking, as indicated by inability to find similarities and differences between related words, difficulty in defining words and concepts, and other similar tasks

(2) impaired judgment, as indicated by inability to make reasonable plans to deal with interpersonal, family, and job-related problems and issues

(3) other disturbances of higher cortical function, such as aphasia (disorder of language), apraxia (inability to carry out motor activities despite intact comprehension and motor function), agnosia (failure to recognize or identify objects despite intact sensory function), and "constructional difficulty" (e.g., inability to copy three-dimensional figures, assemble blocks, or arrange sticks in specific designs)

(4) personality change, i.e., alteration or accentuation of premorbid traits

C. The disturbance in A and B significantly interferes with work or usual social activities or relationships with others.

D. Not occurring exclusively during the course of Delirium.

E. Either (1) or (2):

(1) there is evidence from the history, physical examination, or laboratory tests of a specific organic factor (or factors) judged to be etiologically related to the disturbance

(2) in the absence of such evidence, an etiologic organic factor can be presumed if the disturbance cannot be accounted for by any nonorganic mental disorder, e.g., Major Depression accounting for cognitive impairment

Criteria for severity of Dementia:

Mild: Although work or social activities are significantly impaired, the capacity for independent living remains, with adequate personal hygiene and relatively intact judgment.

Moderate: Independent living is hazardous, and some degree of supervision is necessary.

Severe: Activities of daily living are so impaired that continual supervision is required, e.g., unable to maintain minimal personal hygiene; largely incoherent or mute.

Amnestic Syndrome

The essential feature of this syndrome is impairment in short- and long-term memory that is attributed to a specific organic factor. The diagnosis is not made if the memory impairment exists in the context of reduced ability to maintain and shift attention (Delirium) or is associated with impairment in abstract thinking, impaired judgment, other disturbances of higher cortical function, or personality change (Dementia).

As in Dementia, the person with an Amnestic Syndrome has both an ongoing inability to learn new material (short-term memory deficit) and an inability to recall material that was known in the past (long-term memory deficit). For a discussion of these clinical features and their assessment, see Dementia, p. 104.

In Amnestic Syndrome, events of the very remote past are better recalled than more recent events. For example, a person may remember in vivid detail a hospital stay that took place a decade before the examination, but may have no idea that he or she is currently in the hospital. So-called "immediate memory" (e.g., digit span), however, is *not* impaired in Amnestic Syndrome.

Associated features. A significant degree of amnesia nearly always results in disorientation. Confabulation, the recitation of imaginary events to fill in gaps in memory, is often observed, and when present, tends to disappear with time. Most people with this syndrome lack insight into their memory deficit, and may explicitly deny it, despite evidence to the contrary. Others acknowledge a problem, but appear unconcerned. Apathy, lack of initiative, and emotional blandness are common. Although the person is superficially friendly and agreeable, his or her affect is shallow.

When Amnestic Syndrome is the result of Alcohol Dependence and vitamin deficiency (see Alcohol Amnestic Disorder, p. 133), other neurologic complications of alcohol ingestion and malnutrition, such as peripheral neuropathy and cerebellar ataxia, may also be observed.

Course. The mode of onset depends on the etiology. In most cases it is fairly sudden. The subsequent course, also a function of the etiology, is usually one of chronicity.

Impairment. Impairment in social and occupational functioning is usually moderate to severe.

Complications. Any complications are the direct result of the person's memory impairment. For example, the person's forgetting to extinguish a lighted cigarette may cause a fire.

Etiologic factors. Amnestic Syndrome may result from any pathologic process that causes bilateral damage to certain diencephalic and medial temporal structures (e.g., mammillary bodies, fornix, hippocampal complex). Examples include head trauma, surgical intervention, hypoxia, infarction in the territory of the posterior cerebral arteries, and herpes simplex encephalitis. The most common form of Amnestic Syndrome is that associated with thiamine deficiency and chronic use of alcohol.

Prevalence. The syndrome is apparently uncommon.

Differential diagnosis. Delirium and **Dementia** also involve memory impairment. In Delirium, however, the memory impairment is associated with impaired attention; and in Dementia, there are other major cognitive deficits as well.

In **Factitious Disorder with Psychological Symptoms,** memory testing often yields inconsistent results. Furthermore, there is no organic etiologic factor.

Diagnostic criteria for Amnestic Syndrome

A. Demonstrable evidence of impairment in both short- and long-term memory; with regard to long-term memory, very remote events are remembered better than more recent events. Impairment in short-term memory (inability to learn new information) may be indicated by inability to remember three objects after five minutes. Long-term memory impairment (inability to remember information that was known in the past) may be indicated by inability to remember past personal information (e.g., what happened yesterday, birthplace, occupation) or facts of common knowledge (e.g., past Presidents, well-known dates).

B. Not occurring exclusively during the course of Delirium, and does not meet the criteria for Dementia (i.e., no impairment in abstract thinking or judgment, no other disturbances of higher cortical function, and no personality change).

C. There is evidence from the history, physical examination, or laboratory tests of a specific organic factor (or factors) judged to be etiologically related to the disturbance.

Organic Delusional Syndrome

The essential feature of this syndrome is prominent delusions that are due to a specific organic factor. The diagnosis is not made if the delusions occur in the context of reduced ability to maintain and shift attention to external stimuli, as in Delirium.

The nature of the delusions is variable and depends, to some extent, on the etiology. Persecutory delusions are the most common type. Amphetamine use may cause a highly organized paranoid delusional state indistinguishable from the active phase of Schizophrenia. Some people with cerebral lesions develop the delusion that a limb of their body is missing.

In Organic Delusional Syndrome, hallucinations may be present, but are usually not prominent. When prominent hallucinations coexist with prominent delusions, both Organic Delusional Syndrome and Organic Hallucinosis may be diagnosed.

Associated features. Mild cognitive impairment is often observed. As in Schizophrenia, almost any symptom may occur as an associated feature. The person may appear perplexed, disheveled, or eccentrically dressed. Speech may be rambling or incoherent. Abnormalities of psychomotor activity may occur, with either hyperactivity (pacing, rocking), or apathetic immobility. Ritualistic, stereotyped behavior, sometimes associated with magical thinking, may also be observed. A dysphoric mood is common.

Impairment. Impairment in social and occupational functioning is usually severe.

Complications. The person may harm himself or herself or others while reacting to delusions.

Etiologic factors. These are diverse. A number of substances—e.g., amphetamines, cannabis, and hallucinogens—may cause this syndrome. Some people with temporal lobe epilepsy have an interictal Organic Delusional Syndrome that is almost indistinguishable from Schizophrenia. A paranoid Organic Delusional Syndrome has been described in some cases of Huntington's chorea. Certain cerebral lesions, particularly of the right hemisphere, may result in this syndrome.

Differential diagnosis. Nonorganic psychotic disorders such as **Schizophrenia** or **Delusional Disorders** must be distinguished from Organic Delusional Syndrome. Differentiation rests primarily on evidence, gathered from the history, physical examination, or laboratory tests, of a specific organic factor judged to be etiologically related to the delusions. The appearance of delusions *de novo* in a person over the age of 35 years without a known history of Schizophrenia or Delusional Disorder should always alert the diagnostician to the possibility of an Organic Delusional Syndrome. On the other hand, the fact that a person has a previous history of nonorganic psychosis does not mean that one should neglect consideration of an Organic Delusional Syndrome, especially if there is concern about a possible organic factor (for example, the ingestion of a hallucinogen).

In **Organic Hallucinosis,** hallucinations are prominent. Delusions, if present, are related in content to the hallucinations. In **Organic Mood Syndrome,** symptoms resembling those of Mood Disorders predominate. Delusions and hallucinations, if present, are related in content to the mood disturbance.

Diagnostic criteria for Organic Delusional Syndrome

A. Prominent delusions.

B. There is evidence from the history, physical examination, or laboratory tests of a specific organic factor (or factors) judged to be etiologically related to the disturbance.

C. Not occurring exclusively during the course of Delirium.

Organic Hallucinosis

The essential feature of Organic Hallucinosis is the presence of prominent persistent or recurrent hallucinations that are due to a specific organic factor. The diagnosis is not made if hallucinations occur in the context of reduced ability to maintain and shift attention to external stimuli, as in Delirium.

Hallucinations may occur in any modality, but certain organic factors tend to produce hallucinations of a particular type. For example, hallucinogens most commonly cause visual hallucinations, whereas alcohol tends to induce auditory hallucinations. People who are blind as a result of cataracts may develop visual hallucinations; those who are deaf as a result of otosclerosis may have auditory hallucinations. Hallucinations vary from very simple and unformed to highly complex and organized.

The person may be aware that the hallucinations are not real, or may have a firm delusional conviction of their reality. Delusions, however, are not the major feature of this syndrome, and are restricted to the content of the hallucinations or to the belief that the hallucinations are real. Further elaboration of delusional material (for example, the development of systematized persecutory delusions to account for the hallucinations, or delusions not related to the hallucinations) suggests an Organic Delusional Syndrome, which may be an additional diagnosis.

Associated features. These features vary according to the etiology, the environment, and individual differences in response. Organic Hallucinosis in congenial surroundings may be a pleasant experience; in other circumstances, the hallucinations may be fraught with anxiety, depression, or other dysphoric affects.

Course. The course depends on the underlying etiology. When associated with ingestion of a hallucinogen, the hallucinosis may be for as brief a period as a few hours. Untreated cataracts or otosclerosis may cause a chronic Hallucinosis. If the syndrome is the result of temporary sensory deprivation, the duration may be quite brief.

Impairment. The degree of impairment is a function of the underlying etiology and the extent to which the person acts on the basis of the hallucinations.

Complications. Accidents may occur when the person attempts to flee from frightening hallucinations.

Etiologic factors. Use of hallucinogens and prolonged use of alcohol are the most common causes of this syndrome. Sensory deprivation, as in blindness or deafness, is another cause. Seizure foci, especially in the temporal and occipital lobes, may also cause the syndrome.

Differential diagnosis. In **Delirium,** hallucinations, if present, occur in association with reduced ability to maintain and shift attention to external stimuli. In **Dementia,** hallucinations, if present, are associated with memory impairment. In **Organic Delusional Syndrome,** hallucinations, if present, are usually not prominent; when prominent hallucinations coexist with prominent delusions, both Organic Delusional Syndrome and Organic Hallucinosis may be diagnosed.

Schizophrenia and **Mood Disorders** may involve hallucinations, but no specific organic factor can be demonstrated.

Hypnagogic and **hypnopompic hallucinations** may occur in people without a mental disorder, but they occur only upon falling asleep or upon awakening.

Diagnostic criteria for Organic Hallucinosis

A. Prominent persistent or recurrent hallucinations.

B. There is evidence from the history, physical examination, or laboratory tests of a specific organic factor (or factors) judged to be etiologically related to the disturbance.

C. Not occurring exclusively during the course of Delirium.

Organic Mood Syndrome

The essential feature of this syndrome is a prominent and persistent depressed, elevated, or expansive mood, resembling either a Manic Episode or a Major Depressive Episode, that is due to a specific organic factor. The diagnosis is not made if the disturbance in mood occurs in the context of reduced ability to maintain and shift attention, as in Delirium.

The clinical phenomenology of this syndrome is similar to that of a Manic or Major Depressive Episode (p. 214 and p. 218). The severity of the disturbance may range from mild to severe. If delusions or hallucinations are present, they are similar to those described under Mood Disorders.

Associated features. Mild cognitive impairment is often observed. Any of the features associated with the Mood Disorders may also be present. If the mood is depressed, these features may include fearfulness, anxiety, irritability, brooding, excessive somatic concerns, panic attacks, suspiciousness, and a tearful, sad appearance. Delusions of persecution or worthlessness can occur. If the mood is manic, irritability and lability of mood may be present. Hallucinations and delusions are more common in the manic form than in the depressed form.

Impairment. Minimal to severe impairment can result.

Complications. See Manic and Major Depressive Episodes (p. 216 and p. 221).

Etiologic factors. This syndrome is usually caused by toxic or metabolic factors. Certain substances, notably reserpine, methyldopa, and some of the hallucinogens, are apt to cause a depressive syndrome. Endocrine disorders are another important etiologic factor, and may produce either depressive or manic syndromes. Examples are hyper- and hypothyroidism and hyper- and hypoadrenocorticalism. Carcinoma of the pancreas is sometimes associated with a depressive syndrome, possibly due to neuropeptides in the gastrointestinal tract that are identical with those found in the brain. Viral illness may also cause a depressive syndrome. Structural disease of the brain, such as may result from hemispheric strokes, is a common cause of Organic Mood Syndrome.

Differential diagnosis. In **Mood Disorders,** no specific organic factor can be demonstrated. When an episode of mood disturbance follows the taking of a psychoactive substance, such as reserpine, the causal relationship between the ingestion of the substance and the mood disturbance may not be clear. A history of previous Mood Disorder in the person or in family members suggests that the substance merely triggered a Mood Disorder in a person who was particularly vulnerable to the organic factor. On the other hand, the absence of a history of previous Mood Disorder in the person or family members suggests an Organic Mood Syndrome.

Diagnostic criteria for Organic Mood Syndrome

A. Prominent and persistent depressed, elevated, or expansive mood.

B. There is evidence from the history, physical examination, or laboratory tests of a specific organic factor (or factors) judged to be etiologically related to the disturbance.

C. Not occurring exclusively during the course of Delirium.

Specify: manic, depressed, or **mixed.**

Organic Anxiety Syndrome

The essential feature of this syndrome is prominent, recurrent, panic attacks or generalized anxiety caused by a specific organic factor. The diagnosis is not made if the anxiety occurs only during the course of Delirium, in which there is reduced ability to maintain attention to external stimuli and to appropriately shift attention to new external stimuli.

The clinical phenomenology of this syndrome is similar to that of Panic Disorder or Generalized Anxiety Disorder (p. 235 and p. 251). The severity of the disturbance may range from mild to severe, depending on the rapidity of onset, the severity of the pathophysiologic process, and the psychosocial setting.

Associated features. Mild cognitive impairment, especially in the ability to sustain attention, is often observed.

Course. The course of the illness depends on the underlying etiology. Although it is expected that recovery will result when the etiologic factor is removed, in some cases there may be residual symptoms of anxiety resulting from actual structural damage, a long recovery period, or other factors as yet not understood.

Impairment. Minimal to severe impairment can result, depending on the etiologic factor and the person's particular vulnerability.

Complications. If the underlying organic etiology is not reversed, other organic mental syndromes may develop. For example, recurrent bouts of hypoglycemia may affect cerebral function and result in Organic Anxiety Syndrome, but may also eventually lead to Dementia.

Etiologic factors. This syndrome is usually caused by endocrine disorders or the use of psychoactive substances. Examples of such endocrine disorders are: hyper- and hypothyroidism, pheochromocytoma, fasting hypoglycemia, and hypercortisolism. Organic Anxiety Syndrome is also commonly caused by intoxication from stimulants such as caffeine, cocaine, and amphetamines, or withdrawal from substances that depress the central nervous system, such as alcohol and sedatives. Brain tumors in the vicinity of the third ventricle and epilepsy involving the diencephalon are unusual but established etiologies. Other etiologic factors may include pulmonary embolus, chronic obstructive pulmonary disease, aspirin intolerance, collagen-vascular disease, and brucellosis. Vitamin B_{12} deficiency, demyelinating disease, and heavy metal intoxication are less likely to present with anxiety as the only symptom, but this can occur.

Differential diagnosis. In **Anxiety Disorders,** no specific organic factor can be demonstrated. In **Organic Mood Syndrome,** there is a prominent and persistent disturbance in mood; in some instances this may coexist with Organic Anxiety Syndrome, in which case both diagnoses are given. Global impairment of cognitive functioning is evident in **Delirium** and **Dementia.** Anxiety may be present in **Organic Personality Syndrome,** but it is not as prominent as the change in personality.

Anxiety is an associated symptom of many mental disorders. In order to diagnose Organic Anxiety Syndrome, there must be evidence of both prominent anxiety symptoms and an organic factor that is judged to be etiologically related to the disturbance. Such a judgment will be influenced by the extent to which the etiologic factor and the anxiety covary, the age at onset of the disturbance (the onset of most of the Anxiety Disorders is before age 35), and a family history of organic factors, such as hyperthyroidism, that are known to cause Organic Anxiety Syndrome.

Diagnostic criteria for Organic Anxiety Syndrome

A. Prominent, recurrent, panic attacks (criteria A, C, and D of Panic Disorder, p. 237) or generalized anxiety (criterion D of Generalized Anxiety Disorder, p. 253).

B. There is evidence from the history, physical examination, or laboratory tests of a specific organic factor (or factors) judged to be etiologically related to the disturbance.

C. Not occurring exclusively during the course of Delirium.

Organic Personality Syndrome

The essential feature of this syndrome is a persistent personality disturbance, either lifelong or representing a change or accentuation of a previously characteristic trait, that is due to a specific organic factor. Affective instability, recurrent outbursts of aggression or rage, markedly impaired social judgment, marked apathy and indifference, or suspiciousness or paranoid ideation are common. Organic Personality Syndrome in a young child may occur before the development of an enduring style of relating to the environment (personality); in such cases the syndrome is recognized by significant changes in the child's usual behavior patterns.

The clinical syndrome in a particular person depends principally on the nature and localization of the pathologic process. A common pattern is characterized by affective instability and impairment in social judgment. The person may be belligerent or have temper outbursts that are grossly out of proportion to any precipitating psychosocial stressors. Socially inappropriate actions, such as sexual indiscretions, may be engaged in with little concern for the consequences.

Another pattern is characterized by marked apathy and indifference. The person may have no interest in his or her usual hobbies and may appear unconcerned with events occurring in the immediate environment. (Both of these patterns may be associated with damage to the frontal lobes, and for this reason are sometimes referred to as "frontal lobe syndromes.")

Another recognized pattern, seen in some people with temporal lobe epilepsy, is a marked tendency toward humorless verbosity in both writing and speech, religiosity, and, occasionally, exaggerated aggressiveness. The major personality change may be the development of suspiciousness or paranoid ideation.

If outbursts of aggression or rage are the predominant feature, this should be noted as *Explosive Type*.

Associated features. Mild cognitive impairment and irritability may be present.

Course. The course depends on the etiology. It may be of short duration if it results from a medication or psychoactive substance use or is due to a tumor that was removed soon after the disorder developed. If it is secondary to structural damage to the brain, it is likely to be long-standing. Occasionally an Organic Personality Syndrome is the first symptom of a disease process that eventually causes a Dementia. For example, in multiple sclerosis, an Organic Personality Syndrome may precede the eventual development of a Dementia.

Impairment. The degree of impairment is variable. Though the person's cognitive function may be relatively intact, his or her poor judgment may cause such difficulties that he or she may require constant supervision, or even custodial care.

Complications. Socially unacceptable behavior may lead to social ostracism or legal difficulties. Impulsive or explosive behavior may be dangerous to the person and to others.

Etiologic factors. Organic Personality Syndrome is usually due to structural damage to the brain. Common causes are neoplasms (for example, meningiomas pressing on the frontal lobes), head trauma, and cerebrovascular disease. A characteristic Organic Personality Syndrome has been described as an interictal phenomenon in some people with temporal lobe epilepsy. Multiple sclerosis and Huntington's chorea are sometimes associated with this syndrome. Rather uncommon causes are endocrine disorders (thyroid and adrenocortical disease) and ingestion of certain psychoactive substances.

Differential diagnosis. In **Dementia,** personality change is but one facet of an overall syndrome that also includes significant impairment in memory, and usually in judgment and abstract thinking as well. Occasionally, personality change may be the first sign of an Organic Mental Syndrome that eventually evolves into Dementia. In these instances the initial diagnosis of Organic Personality Syndrome will have to be changed to Dementia as memory and other cognitive deficits increase and become the predominant feature.

In **Schizophrenia, Delusional Disorders, Mood Disorders,** and **Impulse Control Disorders Not Elsewhere Classified,** marked personality changes may occur. In these disorders, however, no specific organic factor is judged etiologically related to the personality change.

Diagnostic criteria for Organic Personality Syndrome

A. A persistent personality disturbance, either lifelong or representing a change or accentuation of a previously characteristic trait, involving at least one of the following:

    (1) affective instability, e.g., marked shifts from normal mood to depression, irritability, or anxiety
    (2) recurrent outbursts of aggression or rage that are grossly out of proportion to any precipitating psychosocial stressors
    (3) markedly impaired social judgment, e.g., sexual indiscretions
    (4) marked apathy and indifference
    (5) suspiciousness or paranoid ideation

B. There is evidence from the history, physical examination, or laboratory tests of a specific organic factor (or factors) judged to be etiologically related to the disturbance.

C. This diagnosis is not given to a child or adolescent if the clinical picture is limited to the features that characterize Attention-deficit Hyperactivity Disorder (see p. 50).

(continued)

Diagnostic criteria for Organic Personality Syndrome continued

D. Not occurring exclusively during the course of Delirium, and does not meet the criteria for Dementia.

Specify explosive type if outbursts of aggression or rage are the predominant feature.

Intoxication

The essential features of Intoxication are maladaptive behavior and a substance-specific syndrome that are due to the recent ingestion of a psychoactive substance. Evidence for the recent ingestion of the psychoactive substance can be obtained by history, physical examination (e.g., smell of alcohol), or toxicologic analysis of body fluids (e.g., urine or blood). The clinical picture does not correspond to any of the other specific Organic Mental Syndromes, such as Delirium, Organic Delusional Syndrome, Organic Hallucinosis, Organic Mood Syndrome, or Organic Anxiety Syndrome. (Intoxication may, however, be superimposed on any Organic Mental Syndrome except Delirium.)

As used here, the concept of Intoxication is a residual category for a clinical picture, caused by an exogenous psychoactive substance, that does not correspond to any of the specific Organic Mental Syndromes. Thus, use of amphetamine that caused rapidly developing persecutory delusions would be diagnosed as Amphetamine Delusional Disorder; only the relatively milder clinical picture, without the full symptomatic picture of a Delusional Syndrome, would be diagnosed as Amphetamine Intoxication. Similar states caused by endogenous substances (such as ketone bodies in diabetic acidosis) should be coded in the category Organic Mental Syndrome NOS (see p. 163) since they are associated with an Axis III physical disorder or condition.

Although the specific clinical picture is determined by the nature of the psychoactive substance used, the most common changes involve disturbances of perception, wakefulness, attention, thinking, judgment, emotional control, and psychomotor behavior. It should be noted that more than one psychoactive substance may produce a similar or identical syndrome. For example, Amphetamine and Cocaine Intoxication can both present with maladaptive behavioral changes and tachycardia, pupillary dilation, elevated blood pressure, perspiration or chills, and nausea or vomiting.

As used here, Intoxication refers to a mental disorder and requires the presence of maladaptive behavior. It should be noted that when used in the physiologic sense, the term *intoxication* is broader in scope than this definition implies. Therefore, recreational use of psychoactive substances that causes physiologic and psychological changes but does not result in maladaptive behavior is not considered Intoxication. For example, social drinking frequently causes loquacity, euphoria, and slurred speech; but this should not be considered Intoxication unless maladaptive behavior, such as fighting, impaired judgment, or impaired social or occupational functioning, results.

Associated features. The particular psychoactive substance used, the person's expectations, preintoxication personality and biologic state, and the environmental circumstances of the psychoactive substance use determine the associated features. For example, Cannabis Intoxication may be intensified in a person expecting religious revelations from the substance. Intoxication in public places may result in belligerent behavior or accidents. Withdrawn people may use intoxication as a means of achieving further social withdrawal (as in a "solitary drinker"). People with depression may become suicidal or experience increased dysphoria when intoxicated.

Course. The rapidity of onset and the duration of an Intoxication depend on: the amount of the psychoactive substance consumed, how rapidly it was consumed, the person's tolerance (innate or acquired), body size (in general, the larger the person, the larger the quantity required to induce intoxication), and the half-life of the particular psychoactive substance. In the case of alcohol, other considerations are the specific beverage consumed (distilled spirits produce higher blood levels than the same amount of alcohol consumed in the same period in the form of beer or wine) and whether the alcohol is combined with food.

Intoxication usually lasts for a few hours, but may last several days. In rare instances a person may continue taking the psychoactive substance, so that he or she remains intoxicated for even longer periods.

Impairment. During the intoxicated state, the person has, by definition, some maladaptive behavioral changes. This impairment in ability to function may be inconsequential if it occurs at a time when the person has no social or occupational responsibilities. On the other hand, impairment may be marked if the intoxication occurs when the person has major social or occupational responsibilities.

Complications. Excessive ingestion of psychoactive substances that have a depressant effect on the nervous system may result in coma or death. Psychoactive substances that act as stimulants may cause seizures. During the intoxicated state the person may fall or become involved in an automobile accident.

For some of the psychoactive substances, an initial Intoxication may develop into a specific Organic Mental Syndrome. For example, Amphetamine Intoxication may develop into Amphetamine Delirium, or methyl alcohol Intoxication may lead to a Dementia.

Differential diagnosis. When the criteria for **Delirium, Organic Hallucinosis, Organic Delusional Syndrome**, or **Organic Mood Syndrome** are met following the ingestion of a psychoactive substance, these conditions are diagnosed, because Intoxication is a residual category.

Many **neurologic diseases** can produce symptoms, such as slurred speech and incoordination, that resemble an Intoxication.

Diagnostic criteria for Intoxication

A. Development of a substance-specific syndrome due to recent ingestion of a psychoactive substance. (**Note:** More than one substance may produce similar or identical syndromes.)

B. Maladaptive behavior during the waking state due to the effect of the substance on the central nervous system, e.g., belligerence, impaired judgment, impaired social or occupational functioning.

C. The clinical picture does not correspond to any of the other specific Organic Mental Syndromes, such as Delirium, Organic Delusional Syndrome, Organic Hallucinosis, Organic Mood Syndrome, or Organic Anxiety Syndrome.

Withdrawal

The essential feature of Withdrawal is the development of a substance-specific syndrome that follows the cessation of, or reduction in, intake of a psychoactive substance that the person previously used regularly. (Strictly speaking, in the case of fetal alcohol syndrome, it is the mother, not the infant, who has ingested the psychoactive substance.) Evidence for the cessation of, or reduction in, use of a psychoactive substance may be obtained by history or by toxicologic analysis of body fluids (e.g., urine or blood). The clinical picture does not correspond to any of the other specific Organic Mental Syndromes, such as Delirium, Organic Hallucinosis, Organic Delusional Syndrome, Organic Mood Syndrome, or Organic Anxiety Syndrome. (Withdrawal may, however, be superimposed on any Organic Mental Syndrome except Delirium.) Thus, a clinical syndrome of disorientation, perceptual disturbance, and psychomotor agitation following cessation of alcohol use is termed *Alcohol Withdrawal Delirium*, and only the milder clinical picture associated with cessation of alcohol use is termed *Uncomplicated Alcohol Withdrawal*.

The syndrome that develops varies according to the psychoactive substance the person was using. Common symptoms include anxiety, restlessness, irritability, insomnia, and impaired attention.

Associated features. The nature of the psychoactive substance determines the associated features, which may range from disturbing physiologic symptoms, such as nausea and vomiting following cessation of heavy alcohol intake, to diffuse malaise, such as that following chronic use of certain sedatives, or a compelling desire to resume taking the substance. There may be changes in sleep patterns and mood, as can be seen after withdrawal from amphetamines or corticosteroids, or convulsions after Sedative Withdrawal.

Course. Withdrawal is usually self-limited to no more than a few days or, at most, several weeks, except when complicated by the development of another Organic Mental Syndrome.

Impairment. Impairment varies from mild, as in Nicotine Withdrawal, to severe, as may be the case in Uncomplicated Alcohol Withdrawal or Opioid Withdrawal.

Complications. In order to avoid painful withdrawal symptoms, the person may continue to use the psychoactive substance. Illegal behavior, such as stealing to pay for heroin, may result from efforts to obtain the substance.

Differential diagnosis. Many physical disorders have symptoms that resemble those of Withdrawal. For example, the symptoms of influenza are very similar to those of Opioid Withdrawal.

Diagnostic criteria for Withdrawal

A. Development of a substance-specific syndrome that follows the cessation of, or reduction in, intake of a psychoactive substance that the person previously used regularly.

B. The clinical picture does not correspond to any of the other specific Organic Mental Syndromes, such as Delirium, Organic Delusional Syndrome, Organic Hallucinosis, Organic Mood Syndrome, or Organic Anxiety Syndrome.

Organic Mental Syndrome Not Otherwise Specified

Syndromes which do not meet the criteria for any of the other Organic Mental Syndromes and in which there are maladaptive changes during the waking state, with evidence, from either physical examination, laboratory tests, or history, of a specific organic factor that is judged to be etiologically related to the disturbance, should be diagnosed Organic Mental Syndrome NOS. Examples include the "neurasthenic" picture associated with early Addison's disease and unusual disturbances of consciousness or behavior occurring during seizures.

ORGANIC MENTAL DISORDERS

The Organic Mental Disorders can be grouped into three categories. Since, by tradition, disorders that are related either to aging of the brain or to the ingestion of a substance are classified as mental disorders, the first two categories, beginning on this page, describe Dementias Arising in the Senium and Presenium (Primary Degenerative Dementia of the Alzheimer Type and Multi-infarct Dementia) and the various Psychoactive Substance-induced Organic Mental Disorders. The final category, beginning on page 162, lists Organic Mental Disorders whose etiology or pathophysiologic process is an Axis III physical disorder or condition, or is unknown.

DEMENTIAS ARISING IN THE SENIUM AND PRESENIUM

Certain degenerative Dementias have traditionally been referred to as Senile and Presenile Dementias, the distinction being arbitrarily based on an age at onset over 65. Nearly all of these cases are associated with the histopathologic changes of Alzheimer's disease. Although the definitive diagnosis of Alzheimer's disease is dependent on histopathologic data, there is growing consensus that there is a high correlation between this pathology and a particular clinical picture. For this reason, this manual contains a single category that encompasses the syndrome of Primary Degenerative Dementia of the Alzheimer Type. It should be noted that Alzheimer's disease itself is a physical disorder, and therefore is not included in this manual of mental disorders; it should, however, be recorded on Axis III. Primary Degenerative Dementia of the Alzheimer Type is subtyped according to the age at onset, for the purpose of historical continuity and to maintain compatibility with ICD-9-CM.

If in a particular case the clinician believes that there is a distinct clinical picture that differs from that associated with Alzheimer's disease, or that some other specific pathology is involved, such as a brain tumor, Huntington's chorea, or vitamin B_{12} deficiency, the category of Senile or Presenile Dementia NOS should be used, and the specific disease should be noted on Axis III.

In DSM-II, the Dementia associated with vascular disease was called Psychosis with Cerebral Arteriosclerosis. However, the presence of the Dementia appears to be related to repeated infarcts of the brain rather than to the extent of the cerebral arteriosclerosis. At autopsy the brain shows multiple infarcts of various ages. For this reason, the category is here termed *Multi-infarct Dementia*.

290.xx   Primary Degenerative Dementia of the Alzheimer Type

The essential feature of this condition is the presence of Dementia of insidious onset and a generally progressive, deteriorating course for which all other specific causes have been excluded by the history, physical examination, and laboratory tests. The Dementia involves a multifaceted loss of intellectual abilities, such as memory, judgment, abstract thought, and other higher cortical functions, and changes in personality and behavior. (See p. 103 for a description of the essential and associated features of Dementia.)

Phenomenologic subtypes. The clinical picture is sometimes complicated by the presence of significant depressive features or of delusions. More rarely there may be superimposed Delirium. These additional features, when present, should be noted with the appropriate codes (p. 121).

Age at onset. Senile onset (after age 65) is much more common than presenile onset. Few cases develop before the age of 49.

Course. The onset is insidious, and the course is generally progressive and deteriorating. In the early stages, memory impairment may be the only apparent cognitive deficit. There may also be subtle personality changes, such as the development of apathy, lack of spontaneity, and a quiet withdrawal from social interactions. People usually remain neat and well-groomed, and, aside from an occasional irritable outburst, are cooperative and behave in a socially appropriate way. With progression to the middle stage of the disease, various cognitive disturbances become quite apparent, and behavior and personality are more obviously affected. By the late stage, the person may be completely mute and inattentive. At this point he or she is totally incapable of caring for himself or herself. This stage leads inevitably to death. With senile onset, the average duration of symptoms, from onset to death, is about five years.

Impairment and complications. See Dementia, p. 105.

Pathology. In the majority of cases, the brain is atrophied, with widened cortical sulci and enlarged cerebral ventricles. This may be demonstrated in life by computer-assisted tomography or pneumoencephalography. Microscopic examination usually reveals three histopathologic changes: senile plaques, neurofibrillary tangles, and granulovacuolar degeneration of neurons. These are the changes classically described in Alzheimer's disease. Rare cases have the histologic features of mixed vascular and degenerative disease.

Predisposing factors. Down syndrome predisposes to Alzheimer's disease.

Prevalence. Between 2% and 4% of the population over the age of 65 is estimated to have Primary Degenerative Dementia of the Alzheimer Type. The prevalence increases with increasing age, particularly after 75.

Sex ratio. The disorder is slightly more common in females than in males.

Familial pattern. First-degree biologic relatives of people with presenile onset of the disorder are more likely to develop Dementia than members of the general population. In rare cases, Primary Degenerative Dementia of the Alzheimer Type is inherited as a dominant trait.

Differential diagnosis. The **normal process of aging** has been associated in a number of studies with certain decrements in intellectual functioning. The nature and significance of these changes are controversial. The diagnosis of Primary Degenerative

Dementia of the Alzheimer Type should be limited to cases in which there is clear evidence of progressive and significant deterioration of intellectual and social or occupational functioning. (See Dementia, differential diagnosis, p. 106, for discussion.)

Subdural hematoma, normal-pressure hydrocephalus, cerebral neoplasm, Parkinson's disease, vitamin B$_{12}$ deficiency, hypothyroidism, Psychoactive Substance Intoxication, and other specific and possibly treatable physical disorders that may cause Dementia need to be ruled out by the history, physical examination, and appropriate laboratory tests.

In **Multi-infarct Dementia** the clinical course is more variable and typically progresses in stepwise fashion, with focal neurologic signs and systemic evidence of vascular disease. In occasional cases the two disorders may coexist, and both diagnoses should be recorded.

Elderly people with a Major Depressive Episode may have features strongly suggesting Dementia. For a discussion of this important problem in differential diagnosis, see Major Depressive Episode (p. 221) and Dementia (p. 106).

Diagnostic criteria for Primary Degenerative Dementia of the Alzheimer Type

A. Dementia (see p. 107).

B. Insidious onset with a generally progressive deteriorating course.

C. Exclusion of all other specific causes of Dementia by history, physical examination, and laboratory tests.

Note: Code 331.00 Alzheimer's disease on Axis III.

Types

Primary Degenerative Dementia of the Alzheimer Type, Senile Onset (after age 65)

290.30 with delirium
290.20 with delusions
290.21 with depression
290.00 uncomplicated

Primary Degenerative Dementia of the Alzheimer Type, Presenile Onset (age 65 and below)

290.11 with delirium
290.12 with delusions
290.13 with depression
290.10 uncomplicated

290.4x Multi-infarct Dementia

The essential feature of this disorder is a Dementia due to significant cerebrovascular disease. There is a stepwise deterioration in intellectual functioning that, early in the course, leaves some intellectual functions relatively intact ("patchy" deterioration). Focal neurologic signs and symptoms are also present.

The onset is typically abrupt. The course is stepwise and fluctuating, with rapid changes, rather than uniformly progressive. The pattern of deficits is "patchy," depending on which regions of the brain have been destroyed. Certain cognitive functions may be affected early, whereas others remain relatively unimpaired. The Dementia typically involves disturbances in memory, abstract thinking, judgment, impulse control, and personality. See Dementia, p. 103.

The focal neurologic signs commonly seen include weaknesses in the limbs, reflex asymmetries, extensor plantar responses, dysarthria, and small-stepped gait.

Vascular disease is always presumed to be present and responsible for both the Dementia and the focal neurologic signs. Evidence of cerebral and systemic vascular disease may be apparent on physical examination. Hypertension, carotid bruit, funduscopic abnormalities, or an enlarged heart may be present. These conditions should be noted on Axis III.

Associated features. Pseudobulbar palsy with fleeting episodes of laughing and crying (sham emotion), dysarthria, and dysphagia (trouble swallowing) are very common. There may be periods of increased confusion, possibly related to further vascular insults.

Age at onset. The onset of Multi-infarct Dementia is apparently earlier than that of Primary Degenerative Dementia of the Alzheimer Type.

Course. As noted above, the course is erratic. Early treatment of hypertension and vascular disease may prevent further progression.

Pathology. The brain shows multiple and extensive localized areas of softening. There may also be a variety of pathological changes in the cerebral vessels.

Predisposing factors. The most significant factor is arterial hypertension. Extracranial vascular disease of the great vessels in the neck and valvular disease of the heart may be sources of cerebral emboli.

Prevalence. Multi-infarct Dementia is apparently much less common than Primary Degenerative Dementia of the Alzheimer Type.

Sex ratio. The disorder is apparently more common in males.

Familial pattern. No information.

Differential diagnosis. A single stroke may cause a relatively circumscribed change in mental state, e.g., an aphasia following damage to the left hemisphere, or an Amnestic Syndrome from infarction in the distribution of the posterior cerebral arteries. As a general rule, a single stroke does not cause Dementia. Multi-infarct Dementia results from the occurrence of multiple strokes, at different times.

In **Primary Degenerative Dementia of the Alzheimer Type** the course is uniformly progressive rather than stepwise, as in Multi-infarct Dementia, and there is usually no evidence of cerebrovascular disease. In some instances both Multi-infarct Dementia and Primary Degenerative Dementia of the Alzheimer Type may coexist, with clinical features of both; in such cases both diagnoses should be recorded.

Types

Multi-infarct Dementia

290.41 with delirium
290.42 with delusions
290.43 with depression
290.40 uncomplicated

Diagnostic criteria for Multi-infarct Dementia

A. Dementia (see p. 107).

B. Stepwise deteriorating course with "patchy" distribution of deficits (i.e., affecting some functions, but not others) early in the course.

C. Focal neurologic signs and symptoms (e.g., exaggeration of deep tendon reflexes, extensor plantar response, pseudobulbar palsy, gait abnormalities, weakness of an extremity, etc.).

D. Evidence from history, physical examination, or laboratory tests of significant cerebrovascular disease (recorded on Axis III) that is judged to be etiologically related to the disturbance.

290.00 Senile Dementia Not Otherwise Specified
     Note: Specify etiology on Axis III if known.
Dementias associated with an organic factor and arising after age 65 that cannot be classified as a specific Dementia, e.g., as Primary Degenerative Dementia of the Alzheimer Type, Senile Onset, or Dementia Associated with Alcoholism.

290.10 Presenile Dementia Not Otherwise Specified
     Note: Specify etiology on Axis III if known (e.g., Pick's disease, Jakob-Creutzfeldt disease).
Dementias associated with an organic factor and arising before age 65 that cannot be classified as a specific Dementia, e.g., Primary Degenerative Dementia of the Alzheimer Type, Presenile Onset.

PSYCHOACTIVE SUBSTANCE-INDUCED ORGANIC MENTAL DISORDERS

This section of the classification deals with the various Organic Mental Syndromes caused by the direct effects of various psychoactive substances on the nervous system. These disorders are distinguished from the Psychoactive Substance Use Disorders, which refer to the behavior associated with taking psychoactive substances that affect the central nervous system. In most cases the diagnosis of these Organic Mental Disorders will be made in people who also have a Psychoactive Substance Use Disorder.

This section includes those Psychoactive Substance-induced Organic Mental Disorders caused by the eleven classes of substances that most commonly are taken nonmedicinally to alter mood or behavior: alcohol; amphetamines or similarly acting sympathomimetics; caffeine; cannabis; cocaine; hallucinogens; inhalants; nicotine;

opioids; phencyclidine (PCP) or similarly acting arylcyclohexylamines; and sedatives, hypnotics, or anxiolytics. Although some of these substances also have a legitimate medicinal purpose, they may, under unsupervised circumstances, cause Organic Mental Disorders. In addition, there is a residual class for Organic Mental Disorders caused by other or unspecified psychoactive substances. These eleven classes of psychoactive substances appear in alphabetical order. However, the following classes share many similar features:

alcohol and sedatives, anxiolytics, or hypnotics;

cocaine and amphetamine or similarly acting sympathomimetics;

hallucinogens and phencyclidine (PCP) or similarly acting arylcyclohexylamines.

For each class of psychoactive substance, the specific disorders described represent the types of Organic Mental Syndrome known to be caused by that class of psychoactive substance. For example, whereas alcohol causes many different syndromes, the current evidence suggests that caffeine causes only one.

Organic Mental Syndromes Associated with Psychoactive Substances

	Intoxication	Withdrawal	Delirium	Withdrawal delirium	Delusional disorder	Mood disorder	Other syndromes
Alcohol	x	x		x			[1]
Amphetamine and related substances	x	x	x		x		
Caffeine	x						
Cannabis	x				x		
Cocaine	x	x	x		x		
Hallucinogen	x (hallucinosis)				x	x	[2]
Inhalant	x						
Nicotine		x					
Opioid	x	x					
Phencyclidine (PCP) and related substances	x		x		x	x	[3]
Sedative, hypnotic, or anxiolytic	x	x		x			[4]

[1]Alcohol Idiosyncratic Intoxication, Alcohol Hallucinosis, Alcohol Amnestic Disorder, Dementia Associated with Alcoholism.
[2]Posthallucinogen Perception Disorder.
[3]Phencyclidine (PCP) or Similarly Acting Arylcyclohexylamine Organic Mental Disorder NOS.
[4]Sedative, Hypnotic or Anxiolytic Amnestic Disorder.

The descriptions of these disorders often do not include many categories of information, such as age at onset, predisposing factors, prevalence, and sex ratio. This information is frequently available in the corresponding portion of the section on Psychoactive Substance Use Disorders. The description of impairment for each of the individual Organic Mental Syndromes can be found in the preceding section. For many of the Psychoactive Substance-induced Organic Mental Disorders, a predisposing factor is prolonged heavy use with the development of dependence. Since this is obvious, only other predisposing factors are noted, when known.

Recording specific diagnoses. Whenever possible, the clinician should record the name of the specific psychoactive substance rather than the name of the entire class of substances, using the code number for the appropriate class. *Examples*: the clinician should record 305.70 Amphetamine Intoxication (rather than Amphetamine or Similarly Acting Sympathomimetic Intoxication); 292.00 Uncomplicated Pentobarbital Withdrawal (rather than Sedative, Hypnotic, or Anxiolytic Withdrawal); 292.81 Atropine Delirium (rather than Other or Unspecified Psychoactive Substance Delirium).

In order for the DSM-III-R classification to be compatible with ICD-9-CM, some diagnoses in this subclass share the same code number. For example, Phencyclidine Intoxication, Inhalant Intoxication, and Caffeine Intoxication all share the code 305.90. Codes used for more than one DSM-III-R diagnosis are followed by an asterisk in the classification.

The use of laboratory tests in the diagnosis of Psychoactive Substance-induced Organic Mental Disorders and Psychoactive Substance Use Disorders. For many years, tests for urine and blood toxicology have been used as aids in the diagnosis and treatment of Psychoactive Substance Use Disorders. Toxicologic procedures differ in their degree of accuracy, but in recent years their accuracy has been significantly improved.

At the present time, if toxicologic tests are to be used, two different procedures should be utilized in determining the presence or absence of a psychoactive substance in the urine. The first procedure should be a screening test that has great sensitivity (few false negatives); examples of such a procedure are thin-layer chromatography (TLC) and immune assay tests. However, screening procedures that are highly sensitive are often not very specific (many false positives). Therefore, positive results obtained with the screening procedure should then be confirmed by a second procedure that may be less sensitive, but is far more specific for the substances detected by the screening procedure. The tests that are more specific are often more expensive than the screening tests. The procedures with greater specificity include gas chromatography and high-performance liquid chromatography; for forensic work, gas chromatography/mass spectrometry is the procedure of choice.

Toxicologic procedures may be helpful in several circumstances. In the case of acute intoxication, blood and urine tests can help in determining the etiologic psychoactive substance. Often the clinical signs and symptoms of intoxication from various psychoactive substances are similar, and specific confirmation can therefore be made only by toxicology. In addition, people often take a number of different psychoactive substances, and it may be very difficult to determine clinically which substances are present without toxicologic analyses. People with a Psychoactive Substance Use Disorder often buy drugs illicitly, and therefore may not know the specific contents of those drugs, since in street drugs substitution and contamination are frequent. Toxicologic procedures may be helpful in determining the psychoactive substances that are present so that the most appropriate treatment can be initiated.

Denial and withholding of information are common problems when taking histories from people with Psychoactive Substance Use Disorders. If the use has not taken place within a day or two before the clinical evaluation, the person may not appear intoxicated, which makes it very difficult to determine clinically whether or not psychoactive substances have been used. Since most psychoactive substances can be detected in the urine for up to 48 hours or longer after use, the toxicologic examination of urine for psychoactive substances can be helpful in determining whether or not the person has been truthful and can thus aid in treatment.

Urine toxicologic tests can be useful in the differential diagnosis of psychosis and depression. The acute effects of most psychoactive substances can mimic many mental disorders. Testing urine for the presence of psychoactive substances can help eliminate the need to consider acute intoxication as a causative factor in the diagnosis of the current episode of illness. When a psychoactive substance is detected that has the ability to produce the clinical syndrome that is present, then intoxication from use of a psychoactive substance must be included in the differential diagnosis, and further investigation must be undertaken to determine whether or not it is the etiologic agent of the presenting symptoms.

Although most psychoactive substances and their metabolites clear the urine within 48 hours of the time they are ingested, in chronic users certain metabolites may be present for a longer period. If the person presents with a confusing withdrawal syndrome, urine tests may be helpful in determining the class of drugs from which the person is withdrawing and make it possible to initiate appropriate treatment. They also may be helpful in differentiating a withdrawal syndrome from other mental disorders, since withdrawal symptoms can mimic the symptoms of mental disorders unrelated to use of a psychoactive substance.

The blood level of a psychoactive substance can be helpful in determining if the person has a high tolerance to a given class of psychoactive substances. For example, if the person presents with a blood alcohol level of over 150 mg/dl and is not showing signs of Alcohol Intoxication, this indicates a significant tolerance to alcohol and, therefore, that the person is probably a chronic user of alcohol or other sedatives, hypnotics, or anxiolytics.

Another approach that can be used to determine tolerance is to challenge the person with a known intoxicant. Pentobarbital has been utilized for this purpose. The person who does not show any signs of intoxication from a dose of pentobarbital of 200 mg or higher has a significant tolerance to sedatives, hypnotics, or anxiolytics and needs to be treated appropriately to prevent a withdrawal syndrome. In cases in which opioid tolerance or dependence cannot be clearly confirmed by history, the use of an antagonist drug such as naloxone may be helpful. The administration of a test dose of naloxone of 0.4 mg parenterally will precipitate an acute withdrawal reaction in a person who is tolerant to and dependent on opioids. Failure to produce the withdrawal syndrome indicates that the person is not tolerant to or dependent on opioids.

Knowing whether or not the person has taken a psychoactive substance may also prove to be very important in doing other types of testing. Intoxication and withdrawal interfere with psychological test batteries, and it is usually appropriate to wait ten days to two weeks after detoxification before initiating these tests. The dexamethasone suppression test and thyroid studies may also be interfered with if there has been recent drug use. Therefore, these tests should not be performed in a person who is actively using a psychoactive substance or undergoing withdrawal.

ALCOHOL-INDUCED ORGANIC MENTAL DISORDERS

See p. 173 for a description of Alcohol Dependence and Abuse.

This section includes Organic Mental Disorders attributed to the ingestion of alcohol. Although ICD-9-CM has a category for Alcoholic Jealousy, the literature does not provide sufficient evidence to support the existence of this syndrome as an independent entity. The concept "alcoholic jealousy" can be expressed in DSM-III-R terms by a diagnosis of Alcohol Dependence and an additional diagnosis of Delusional Disorder, Persecutory Type.

303.00   Alcohol Intoxication

The essential feature of this disorder is maladaptive behavioral changes due to recent ingestion of alcohol. These changes may include aggressiveness, impaired judgment, impaired attention, irritability, euphoria, depression, emotional lability, and other manifestations of impaired social or occupational functioning. Characteristic physiologic signs include slurred speech, incoordination, unsteady gait, nystagmus, and flushed face.

The diagnosis is not made when there is evidence that the amount of alcohol ingested was insufficient to cause intoxication in most people, as in Alcohol Idiosyncratic Intoxication (p. 128).

Associated features. The person's usual behavior may be accentuated or altered. For example, a person who tends to be somewhat suspicious may, under the influence of alcohol, become markedly paranoid. On the other hand, people who are ordinarily withdrawn and uncomfortable in social situations may become exceptionally convivial.

Alcohol Intoxication is sometimes associated with an amnesia for the events that occurred during the course of the intoxication ("blackouts").

Course. Although alcohol is basically a central nervous system depressant, its initial behavioral effects are often viewed as "disinhibitory" phenomena. Thus, early in the course of Alcohol Intoxication, a person may appear exceptionally bright, expansive, and hyperactive, with a subjective sensation of well-being and increased mental alertness. With further intoxication, however, the person may slow down and become depressed, withdrawn, and dull, and even lose consciousness.

The duration of an episode of Alcohol Intoxication depends on a variety of factors, including the amount and type of alcoholic beverage consumed, how rapidly it was ingested, and whether or not it was taken with food. Since only a small percentage of alcohol is excreted, the rate at which alcohol is metabolized—approximately 5-10 ml of absolute alcohol per hour—plays a very important role in determining the length of a period of intoxication. The development of short-term tolerance may also influence the course of Alcohol Intoxication, so that a person may appear less intoxicated after many hours of drinking than after a few hours. There is considerable individual variation in susceptibility to intoxication with alcohol. Some people show intoxication with blood alcohol levels as low as 30 mg/dl, whereas others appear unintoxicated with levels as high as 150 mg/dl.

The signs of intoxication are more marked when the blood alcohol level is rising than when it is falling. Most people become intoxicated at blood alcohol levels between 100 and 200 mg/dl. Death has been reported at levels ranging from 400 to 700 mg/dl. Alcohol usually exerts its fatal effect either by a direct depression of respiration or by aspiration of vomitus.

Complications. Highway accidents are a major complication of Alcohol Intoxication. Approximately half of all highway fatalities involve either a driver or a pedestrian who has been drinking. Intoxication also causes falls and numerous household and industrial accidents. Moreover, it is frequently associated with the commission of criminal acts. More than one-half of all murderers and their victims are believed to have been intoxicated at the time of the act. One study indicates that about one-fourth of all suicides occur while the person is drinking alcohol.

Alcohol Intoxication frequently results in physical disorders. Falls and accidents result in fractures, subdural hematomas, and other forms of brain trauma. Exposure to extreme weather leads to frostbite and sunburn. Alcohol Intoxication may also possibly suppress immune mechanisms and thus predispose to infections.

Differential diagnosis. Alcohol use without intoxication may produce some changes (e.g., increased sociability and loquacity), but does not involve such maladaptive behavior as impaired judgment and irritability.

Intoxication due to sedatives, hypnotics, and anxiolytics has the same clinical picture as Alcohol Intoxication. Since a person may be ingesting both alcohol and other psychoactive substances, the presence of alcohol on the breath does not exclude the possibility that another psychoactive substance is responsible for the intoxication.

Certain neurologic diseases, such as **cerebellar ataxias** or **multiple sclerosis,** may have some of the physiologic signs and symptoms of Alcohol Intoxication.

In **Alcohol Idiosyncratic Intoxication,** a marked change in behavior follows ingestion of an amount of alcohol that is insufficient to cause Alcohol Intoxication in most people.

Diagnostic criteria for 303.00 Alcohol Intoxication

A. Recent ingestion of alcohol (with no evidence suggesting that the amount was insufficient to cause intoxication in most people).

B. Maladaptive behavioral changes, e.g., disinhibition of sexual or aggressive impulses, mood lability, impaired judgment, impaired social or occupational functioning.

C. At least one of the following signs:

   (1) slurred speech
   (2) incoordination
   (3) unsteady gait
   (4) nystagmus
   (5) flushed face

D. Not due to any physical or other mental disorder.

291.40   Alcohol Idiosyncratic Intoxication

The essential feature of this disorder is a marked behavioral change—usually to aggressiveness—that is due to the recent ingestion of an amount of alcohol insufficient to induce intoxication in most people. There is usually subsequent amnesia for the period of intoxication. The behavior is atypical of the person when not drinking—for example, a shy, retiring, mild-mannered person may, after one weak alcoholic drink, become belligerent and assaultive.

This disorder has also been called "pathological intoxication."

Age at onset. No information.

Course. The change in behavior begins either while the person is drinking or shortly thereafter (within minutes). The duration is quite brief, and the condition ceases within a few hours. The person returns to his or her normal state as the blood alcohol level falls, but may have amnesia for the period of intoxication.

Prevalence. Apparently uncommon.

Predisposing factors. A few people with this disorder have been reported to have temporal lobe spikes on an electroencephalogram after receiving small amounts of alcohol. Although the reports are only anecdotal, it is thought that people with brain damage lose "tolerance" for alcohol and behave abnormally after drinking small amounts. The types of brain injury most often associated with this syndrome are from trauma and encephalitis. The loss of tolerance may be temporary or permanent. It is also reported that people who are unusually fatigued or have a debilitating physical illness may have a low tolerance to alcohol and respond inappropriately to small amounts. In addition, advancing age may be associated with reduced tolerance to alcohol.

Differential diagnosis. Other exogenous agents, especially **sedatives, hypnotics, and anxiolytics,** may occasionally cause abrupt changes in behavior. **Temporal lobe epilepsy,** during the interictal period, may be associated with fits of destructive rage. In **Malingering,** the person may wish to avoid responsibility for aggressive behavior, claiming that it occurred while he or she was intoxicated from a small amount of alcohol.

Diagnostic criteria for 291.40 Alcohol Idiosyncratic Intoxication

A. Maladaptive behavioral changes, e.g., aggressive or assaultive behavior, occurring within minutes of ingesting an amount of alcohol insufficient to induce intoxication in most people.

B. The behavior is atypical of the person when not drinking.

C. Not due to any physical or other mental disorder.

291.80 Uncomplicated Alcohol Withdrawal

The essential features of this disorder are certain characteristic symptoms such as a coarse tremor of hands, tongue, or eyelids; nausea or vomiting; malaise or weakness; autonomic hyperactivity (such as tachycardia, sweating, and elevated blood pressure); anxiety, depressed mood, or irritability; transient hallucinations (generally poorly formed) or illusions; headache; and insomnia. These symptoms follow within several hours after cessation of or reduction in alcohol ingestion by a person who has been drinking alcohol for several days or longer. The diagnosis is not made if the disturbance meets the criteria for Alcohol Withdrawal Delirium.

Associated features. Dry mouth is a common symptom. The complexion is often puffy and blotchy, and there may be mild peripheral edema. When nausea or vomiting is present, there may also be gastritis. Sleep is often fitful and disturbed by "bad dreams."

Age at onset. Most people with Alcohol Dependence begin drinking in their teens or early adulthood and develop their first withdrawal symptoms in their 20s or 30s.

Course. Withdrawal symptoms begin shortly after cessation of or reduction in drinking and almost always disappear within five to seven days unless Alcohol Withdrawal Delirium develops.

Complications. Major motor seizures ("rum fits") may occur. People with a pre-existing history of epilepsy are more apt to develop withdrawal seizures.

Predisposing factors. Malnutrition, fatigue, preexisting depression, and concomitant physical illness may aggravate the syndrome.

Differential diagnosis. In **Alcohol Withdrawal Delirium** there are the disturbances in attention and other symptoms characteristic of Delirium.
In **Alcohol Hallucinosis** the hallucinations are vivid and persistent, whereas if they occur in Uncomplicated Alcohol Withdrawal, they are brief and poorly formed.
Sedative, Hypnotic, or Anxiolytic Withdrawal produces a syndrome essentially identical with that of Uncomplicated Alcohol Withdrawal. **Hypoglycemia** and **diabetic ketoacidosis** result in symptoms similar to those of Alcohol Withdrawal. **Essential tremor** may suggest the tremulousness of Uncomplicated Alcohol Withdrawal.

Diagnostic criteria for 291.80 Uncomplicated Alcohol Withdrawal

A. Cessation of prolonged (several days or longer) heavy ingestion of alcohol or reduction in the amount of alcohol ingested, followed within several hours by coarse tremor of hands, tongue, or eyelids, and at least one of the following:

    (1) nausea or vomiting
    (2) malaise or weakness
    (3) autonomic hyperactivity, e.g., tachycardia, sweating, elevated blood pressure
    (4) anxiety
    (5) depressed mood or irritability
    (6) transient hallucinations or illusions
    (7) headache
    (8) insomnia

B. Not due to any physical or other mental disorder, such as Alcohol Withdrawal Delirium.

291.00   Alcohol Withdrawal Delirium

The essential feature of this disorder is a Delirium (p. 100) that develops after recent cessation of or reduction in alcohol consumption, usually within one week. Marked autonomic hyperactivity, often indicated by tachycardia and sweating, is present.

This disorder has also been called "delirium tremens."

Associated features. Vivid hallucinations, which may be visual, auditory, or tactile, are common. Delusions and agitated behavior are also frequently present. There may be a coarse, irregular tremor. Fever may also occur.

Age at onset. The first episode of this disorder usually occurs after 5 to 15 years of heavy drinking.

Course. Onset is usually on the second or third day following cessation of or reduction in drinking. Occasionally it occurs earlier; it rarely appears more than a week after abstinence. Unless complicated by some other illness, the syndrome most often runs its course in two to three days. If seizures also occur as the result of the withdrawal from alcohol ("rum fits"), they always precede the development of Delirium.

Complications. See Delirium (p. 102).

Predisposing factors. The presence of a concomitant physical illness predisposes to this syndrome. A physically healthy person seldom develops Delirium during withdrawal from alcohol.

Prevalence. This syndrome is much less common than Uncomplicated Alcohol Withdrawal.

Differential diagnosis. See Delirium (p. 102).

Diagnostic criteria for 291.00 Alcohol Withdrawal Delirium

A.   Delirium (p. 103) developing after cessation of heavy alcohol ingestion or a reduction in the amount of alcohol ingested (usually within one week).

B.   Marked autonomic hyperactivity, e.g., tachycardia, sweating.

C.   Not due to any physical or other mental disorder.

291.30   Alcohol Hallucinosis

The essential feature of this disorder is an Organic Hallucinosis (see p. 110) in which vivid and persistent hallucinations develop shortly (usually within 48 hours) after cessation of or reduction in alcohol ingestion by a person who apparently has Alcohol Dependence. The hallucinations may be auditory or visual. The auditory hallucinations are usually voices and, less commonly, unformed sounds such as hissing or buzzing.

In the majority of cases, the content of the hallucinations is unpleasant and disturbing. However, the hallucinatory content may be benign and leave the person undisturbed. The voices may address the person directly, but more often they discuss him or her in the third person.

Age at onset. Although first episodes have been reported in people in their early to mid-20s, more typically onset is at about age 40 and follows 10 years or more of heavy drinking.

Course. Onset may accompany a gradual decrease in blood alcohol levels toward the end of an extended period of Alcohol Intoxication. However, the disturbance most often develops soon after cessation of drinking, usually within the first 48 hours, although occasionally somewhat later. The disorder may last several weeks or months. With the evolution of the chronic form, which may be recognized as early as a week after onset of the illness, the person becomes quiet and resigned despite the fact that the hallucinations persist. Ideas of reference and other poorly systematized persecutory delusions become prominent. At this stage the illness may be clinically indistinguishable from Schizophrenia, with vague and illogical thinking, tangential associations, and inappropriate affect. There is some evidence that the chronic form is more likely to develop from repeated episodes of the disorder.

Impairment. Impairment may be severe, as the person responds to the hallucinations as though they were real.

Complications. In an effort to avoid the consequences of threatening voices, the person may harm himself or herself or others.

Predisposing factors. This disorder occurs only following prolonged, heavy ingestion of alcohol in people who apparently have Alcohol Dependence. Contrary to previously held beliefs, there is no evidence that Schizophrenia predisposes to the development of this disorder.

Prevalence. Apparently rare.

Sex ratio. The disorder is apparently four times more common in males than in females.

Familial pattern. No information.

Differential diagnosis. See Organic Hallucinosis (p. 111). In **Schizophrenia** there is no temporal relation of psychotic symptoms to the cessation of alcohol use, and the course is chronic. Moreover, the age at onset of Alcohol Hallucinosis is later than in Schizophrenia, and both the family background and the premorbid personality are not typical of those in Schizophrenia. In **Uncomplicated Alcohol Withdrawal**, hallucinations and illusions may be present, but they are brief and poorly formed.

Diagnostic criteria for 291.30 Alcohol Hallucinosis

A. Organic Hallucinosis (p. 111) with vivid and persistent hallucinations (auditory or visual) developing shortly (usually within 48 hours) after cessation of or reduction in heavy ingestion of alcohol in a person who apparently has Alcohol Dependence.

B. No Delirium as in Alcohol Withdrawal Delirium.

C. Not due to any physical or other mental disorder.

291.10 Alcohol Amnestic Disorder

The essential feature of this disorder is an Amnestic Syndrome (see p. 108) apparently due to the vitamin deficiency associated with prolonged, heavy ingestion of alcohol. Alcohol Amnestic Disorder due to thiamine deficiency is also known as Korsakoff's syndrome.

Associated features. Neurologic disturbances such as peripheral neuropathy, cerebellar ataxia, and myopathy are among the associated features.

Course. Alcohol Amnestic Disorder often follows an acute episode of Wernicke's encephalopathy, a neurologic disease manifested by confusion, ataxia, eye-movement abnormalities (gaze palsies, nystagmus), and other neurologic signs. Gradually these manifestations subside, but a major impairment of memory, Alcohol Amnestic Disorder, remains. If Wernicke's disease is treated early with large doses of thiamine, Alcohol Amnestic Disorder may not develop.

Once Alcohol Amnestic Disorder becomes established, it usually persists indefinitely, though there may be slight improvement over a long period of time.

Impairment. Impairment is usually quite severe, and life-long custodial care may be necessary.

Complications. See Amnestic Syndrome (p. 108).

Predisposing factors. Alcohol Dependence (by definition).

Prevalence. The disorder is apparently rare, perhaps because of the routine administration of thiamine during detoxification.

Differential diagnosis. See Amnestic Syndrome (p. 108). In **Dementia Associated with Alcoholism,** the disturbance is not limited to memory impairment.

Diagnostic criteria for 291.10 Alcohol Amnestic Disorder

A. Amnestic Syndrome (p. 109) following prolonged, heavy ingestion of alcohol.

B. Not due to any physical or other mental disorder.

291.20 Dementia Associated with Alcoholism

The essential feature of this disorder is the development of a Dementia (see p. 103) following prolonged and heavy ingestion of alcohol, for which all other causes of Dementia have been excluded. In order to exclude transient effects of intoxication and withdrawal, this diagnosis should not be made until at least three weeks have elapsed since cessation of alcohol ingestion.

The etiologic role of alcohol in the Dementia associated with prolonged, heavy ingestion of alcohol is controversial.

Associated features. See Alcohol Dependence (p. 173) and Dementia (p. 103).

Age at onset. This syndrome rarely begins before the age of 35 since many years of heavy drinking are apparently necessary to produce Dementia.

Course. No information.

Impairment. Mild cognitive deficits demonstrable only by neuropsychological testing have been reported in some people with Alcohol Dependence. As this diagnosis involves a Dementia, by definition there is always some impairment in social or occupational functioning. When impairment is severe, the person becomes totally oblivious of his or her surroundings and requires constant care.

Complications. See Dementia.

Predisposing factors. Alcohol Dependence (by definition).

Prevalence. Mild, sometimes reversible, intellectual impairment is commonly found when a specific search is made in people with chronic Alcohol Dependence. The severe form of this disorder is apparently rare.

Differential diagnosis. See Dementia (p. 106). Dementia Associated with Alcoholism is distinguished from **Alcohol Amnestic Disorder** by the presence of cognitive deficits other than in the sphere of memory alone. It is distinguished from **other causes of Dementia** by failure to demonstrate a specific etiology other than alcohol use.

Diagnostic criteria for 291.20 Dementia Associated with Alcoholism

A. Dementia (p. 107) following prolonged, heavy ingestion of alcohol and persisting at least three weeks after cessation of alcohol ingestion.

B. Exclusion, by history, physical examination, and laboratory tests, of all causes of Dementia other than prolonged heavy use of alcohol.

AMPHETAMINE- OR SIMILARLY ACTING SYMPATHOMIMETIC-INDUCED ORGANIC MENTAL DISORDERS

See p. 175 for a description of substances in this class and Amphetamine- or Similarly Acting Sympathomimetic Dependence and Abuse.

305.70 Amphetamine or Similarly Acting Sympathomimetic Intoxication

The essential features of this disorder are maladaptive behavioral changes and specific physical symptoms due to recent use of amphetamine or similarly acting sympathomimetic substances. The maladaptive behavioral changes may include fighting, grandiosity, hypervigilance, psychomotor agitation, impaired judgment, and impaired social or occupational functioning. The physical symptoms may include tachycardia, pupillary dilation, elevated blood pressure, perspiration or chills, and nausea and vomiting. The maladaptive behavioral changes and physical symptoms begin no longer than one hour after administration, and may occur within a few seconds.

Associated features. If taken intravenously, amphetamine or similarly acting sympathomimetics produce a characteristic "rush" of well-being and confidence. If the intoxication is severe, there is likely to be confusion, rambling or even incoherent speech, anxiety, and apprehension. There may be headache and palpitations. Intoxication with high doses of substances in this class may be associated with transient ideas of reference, paranoid ideation, a subjective sense of "profound thoughts," increased sexual interest, ringing in the ears, hearing one's name called, and a sensation of insects crawling up the skin (formication) or seeing insects. Increased curiosity and bizarre behavior, such as sorting objects into various piles, are sometimes observed. Stereotyped movements of mouth and tongue may be noted.

When the immediate psychoactive effects of high doses of substances in this class have subsided, they are replaced by unpleasant rebound effects (the "crash"), including a dysphoric mood and a craving for the substance. Other possible symptoms of the "crash" include anxiety, tremulousness, irritability, and feelings of fatigue and depression. (When the "crash" extends beyond 24 hours after the last use of the substance, the condition is classified as Amphetamine or Similarly Acting Sympathomimetic Withdrawal.)

Course. The course of Amphetamine or Similarly Acting Sympathomimetic Intoxication is usually self-limited, with full recovery within 48 hours.

Complications. Syncope or chest pain may occur. There may be seizures following large doses. Death may result from cardiac arrhythmias or respiratory paralysis.

Amphetamine or Similarly Acting Sympathomimetic Delusional Disorder has developed if delusions or hallucinations persist beyond the time of direct substance effect. On occasion, intoxication from this class of psychoactive substances may develop into a Delirium.

Differential diagnosis. Manic episodes may present with symptoms similar to those seen in Amphetamine or Similarly Acting Sympathomimetic Intoxication. **Cocaine Intoxication** and **Phencyclidine (PCP) Intoxication** may cause a similar clinical picture, and can be distinguished from Amphetamine Intoxication only by the presence of amphetamine metabolites in a urine specimen or amphetamine in plasma.

Diagnostic criteria for 305.70 Amphetamine or Similarly Acting Sympathomimetic Intoxication

A. Recent use of amphetamine or a similarly acting sympathomimetic.

B. Maladaptive behavioral changes, e.g., fighting, grandiosity, hypervigilance, psychomotor agitation, impaired judgment, impaired social or occupational functioning.

C. At least two of the following signs within one hour of use:

    (1) tachycardia
    (2) pupillary dilation
    (3) elevated blood pressure
    (4) perspiration or chills
    (5) nausea or vomiting

(continued)

Diagnostic criteria for 305.70 Amphetamine or Similarly Acting Sympathomimetic Intoxication continued

D. Not due to any physical or other mental disorder.

Note: When the differential diagnosis must be made without a clear-cut history or toxicologic analysis of body fluids, it may be qualified as "Provisional."

292.00   Amphetamine or Similarly Acting Sympathomimetic Withdrawal

The essential features of this disorder are dysphoric mood (e.g., depression, irritability, anxiety) and fatigue, insomnia or hypersomnia, or psychomotor agitation due to abrupt cessation of prolonged (several days or longer) heavy use of amphetamine or a similarly acting sympathomimetic or reduction in the amount of the substance used. The symptoms persist more than 24 hours after cessation of substance use.

Associated features. Paranoid and suicidal ideation may be present.

Course. The symptoms usually reach a peak in two to four days, although depression and irritability may persist for months.

Complications. Suicide is the major complication.

Differential Diagnosis. A coexisting **Depressive Disorder** should be considered if a depressive syndrome persists for several weeks.

Diagnostic criteria for 292.00 Amphetamine or Similarly Acting Sympathomimetic Withdrawal

A. Cessation of prolonged (several days or longer) heavy use of amphetamine or a similarly acting sympathomimetic, or reduction in the amount of substance used, followed by dysphoric mood (e.g., depression, irritability, anxiety) and at least one of the following, persisting more than 24 hours after cessation of substance use:

(1) fatigue
(2) insomnia or hypersomnia
(3) psychomotor agitation

B. Not due to any physical or other mental disorder, such as Amphetamine or Similarly Acting Sympathomimetic Delusional Disorder.

Note: When the differential diagnosis must be made without a clear-cut history or toxicologic analysis of body fluids, it may be qualified as "Provisional."

292.81   Amphetamine or Similarly Acting Sympathomimetic Delirium

The essential feature is a Delirium (see p. 100) developing within 24 hours of intake of amphetamine or a similarly acting sympathomimetic.

Associated features. Tactile and olfactory hallucinations may be present. Affect is often labile. Violent or aggressive behavior is common, and restraint may be required.

Course. Delirium usually occurs within one hour of substance use and is over in about six hours. When the substance is taken intravenously, the onset is almost immediate. More rarely, the Delirium follows a period of Intoxication. When the other pharmacologic effects of the substance have worn off, the Delirium disappears completely.

Complications. See Amphetamine or Similarly Acting Sympathomimetic Intoxication (p. 135).

Prevalence. This disorder is not as common as Amphetamine or Similarly Acting Sympathomimetic Delusional Disorder.

Differential diagnosis. See differential diagnosis of Delirium (p. 102).

Diagnostic criteria for 292.81 Amphetamine or Similarly Acting Sympathomimetic Delirium

A. Delirium (p. 103) developing within 24 hours of use of amphetamine or a similarly acting sympathomimetic.

B. Not due to any physical or other mental disorder.

Note: When the differential diagnosis must be made without a clear-cut history or toxicologic analysis of body fluids, it may be qualified as "Provisional."

292.11   Amphetamine or Similarly Acting Sympathomimetic Delusional Disorder

The essential feature of this disorder is an Organic Delusional Syndrome (see p. 109), with rapidly developing persecutory delusions as the predominant clinical feature, developing shortly after use of amphetamine or a similarly acting sympathomimetic.

Associated features. Distortion of body image and misperception of people's faces may occur. Initially, suspiciousness and curiosity may be experienced with pleasure, but may later induce aggressive or violent action against "enemies." The hallucination of bugs or vermin crawling in or under the skin (formication) can lead to scratching and extensive skin excoriations.

Course. Delusions can linger for a week or more, but occasionally last for over a year.

Impairment, complications, and differential diagnosis. See Organic Delusional Syndrome, p. 109-110.

> **Diagnostic criteria for 292.11 Amphetamine or Similarly Acting Sympathomimetic Delusional Disorder**
>
> A. Organic Delusional Syndrome (p. 110) developing shortly after use of amphetamine or a similarly acting sympathomimetic.
>
> B. Rapidly developing persecutory delusions are the predominant clinical feature.
>
> C. Not due to any physical or other mental disorder.
>
> **Note:** When the differential diagnosis must be made without a clear-cut history or toxicologic analysis of body fluids, it may be qualified as "Provisional."

CAFFEINE-INDUCED ORGANIC MENTAL DISORDER

The consumption of caffeine, especially in the form of coffee, tea, cola, chocolate, and cocoa, is ubiquitous in the United States. Other common sources of caffeine are over-the-counter analgesics, "cold" preparations, and stimulants. Although the existence of a caffeine withdrawal headache is well established, the syndrome is usually not severe enough to warrant clinical attention.

305.90   Caffeine Intoxication
The essential features of this disorder are such characteristic effects of recent use of caffeine-containing substances as restlessness, nervousness, excitement, insomnia, flushed face, diuresis, and gastrointestinal complaints. These symptoms appear in some people following ingestion of as little as 250 mg of caffeine per day, whereas others require much larger doses. At levels of more than 1 g/day, there may be muscle twitching, rambling flow of thought and speech, cardiac arrhythmia, periods of inexhaustibility, and psychomotor agitation. Mild sensory disturbances such as ringing in the ears and flashes of light have been reported at higher doses. With doses exceeding 10 g of caffeine, grand mal seizures and respiratory failure may result in death.

This disorder has been called Caffeinism.

A rough guide to calculating caffeine intake follows: coffee contains 100-150 mg of caffeine per cup; tea is about half as strong; a glass of cola is about a third as strong. Most caffeine-containing prescriptions and over-the-counter medications are one-third to one-half the strength of a cup of coffee. Two notable exceptions are migraine medications and over-the-counter stimulants that contain 100 mg per tablet.

Complications. Complications include developing or aggravating gastrointestinal and heart disease. Caffeine can produce epigastric distress and, occasionally, peptic ulcer and hematemesis. In addition to arrhythmia with extremely high doses, the substance can cause marked hypotension and circulatory failure.

Differential diagnosis. Manic episodes, Panic Disorder, and **Generalized Anxiety Disorder** can cause a clinical picture similar to that of Caffeine Intoxication. The temporal relationship of the symptoms to caffeine use establishes the diagnosis.

Diagnostic criteria for 305.90 Caffeine Intoxication

A. Recent consumption of caffeine, usually in excess of 250 mg.

B. At least five of the following signs:

    (1) restlessness
    (2) nervousness
    (3) excitement
    (4) insomnia
    (5) flushed face
    (6) diuresis
    (7) gastrointestinal disturbance
    (8) muscle twitching
    (9) rambling flow of thought and speech
    (10) tachycardia or cardiac arrhythmia
    (11) periods of inexhaustibility
    (12) psychomotor agitation

C. Not due to any physical or other mental disorder, such as an Anxiety Disorder.

CANNABIS-INDUCED ORGANIC MENTAL DISORDERS

See p. 176 for a description of the different forms of cannabis and Cannabis Dependence and Abuse.

305.20 Cannabis Intoxication

The essential features of this disorder are maladaptive behavioral changes and specific physical symptoms due to the recent use of cannabis. Maladaptive behavioral effects may include euphoria, anxiety, suspiciousness or paranoid ideation, sensation of slowed time (five minutes may seem like an hour), impaired judgment, and social withdrawal. Inappropriate laughter, panic attacks, and dysphoric affects may occur, primarily in people who have not developed tolerance to the substance. The person may believe that he or she is dying or going crazy. Adverse reactions are more likely to occur in people with rigid personalities, in people who have had a psychotic disorder, or in circumstances considered to be threatening, such as the possibility of a police raid.

Conjunctival injection and tachycardia are almost always present, although tachycardia is not as prominent when the person is a chronic user of cannabis. Other physical symptoms include increased appetite, often for "junk food," and a dry mouth.

Associated features. Depersonalization or derealization may occur. Hallucinations are rare except when very high blood levels are reached. (In such circumstances the substance acts as a hallucinogen. Because this rarely occurs, a separate diagnosis of Cannabis Hallucinosis is not included in this classification.)

Course. Intoxication occurs almost immediately after smoking marijuana, peaks within a half hour, and usually lasts about three hours. Orally ingested cannabis is more slowly absorbed and reaches a lower peak blood level, and has longer-lasting effects.

Complications. Automobile accidents may occur because of impaired motor coordination.

Differential diagnosis. Other Psychoactive Substance-induced Intoxications should be considered. The person with Cannabis Intoxication will sometimes have the characteristic sweet smell of burned cannabis on his or her clothing. **Alcohol Intoxication** frequently decreases appetite, increases aggressive behavior, produces nystagmus or ataxia, and is associated with the smell of alcohol, whereas these symptoms are rare in Cannabis Intoxication. **Hallucinogens** in low doses cause a clinical picture that resembles Cannabis Intoxication. If administration was by smoking, this would indicate Cannabis Intoxication, since hallucinogens are not smoked; if administration was by ingestion, Cannabis Intoxication must still be considered.

Diagnostic criteria for 305.20 Cannabis Intoxication

A. Recent use of cannabis.

B. Maladaptive behavioral changes, e.g., euphoria, anxiety, suspiciousness or paranoid ideation, sensation of slowed time, impaired judgment, social withdrawal.

C. At least two of the following signs developing within two hours of cannabis use:

 (1) conjunctival injection
 (2) increased appetite
 (3) dry mouth
 (4) tachycardia

D. Not due to any physical or other mental disorder.

Note: When the differential diagnosis must be made without a clear-cut history or toxicologic analysis of body fluids, it may be qualified as "Provisional."

292.11 Cannabis Delusional Disorder

The essential feature of this disorder is an Organic Delusional Syndrome (see p. 109), usually with persecutory delusions, developing shortly after cannabis use.

Associated features. Marked anxiety, emotional lability, depersonalization, and subsequent amnesia for the episode can occur. Associated physical symptoms are the same as those seen in Cannabis Intoxication.

Course. The disorder usually remits within a day, but in some cases may persist for a few days.

Prevalence. The disorder is apparently rare.

Differential diagnosis. See Organic Delusional Syndrome, p. 110.

> **Diagnostic criteria for 292.11 Cannabis Delusional Disorder**
>
> A. Organic Delusional Syndrome (p. 110) developing shortly after cannabis use.
>
> B. Not due to any physical or other mental disorder.
>
> **Note:** When the differential diagnosis must be made without a clear-cut history or toxicologic analysis of body fluids, it may be qualified as "Provisional."

COCAINE-INDUCED ORGANIC MENTAL DISORDERS

See p. 177 for a description of the different forms of cocaine and Cocaine Dependence and Abuse.

305.60   Cocaine Intoxication

The essential features of this disorder are maladaptive behavioral changes and other specific signs due to the recent use of cocaine. The maladaptive behavioral changes may include euphoria, fighting, grandiosity, hypervigilance, psychomotor agitation, impaired judgment, and impaired social or occupational functioning. The other specific signs may include tachycardia, pupillary dilation, elevated blood pressure, perspiration or chills, nausea and vomiting, and visual or tactile hallucinations. The maladaptive behavioral changes and other specific signs begin no later than one hour after administration, and may occur within a few seconds.

Associated features. If taken intravenously, cocaine produces a characteristic "rush" of well-being, confidence, and, in some cases, euphoria. If the intoxication is severe, confusion, rambling or even incoherent speech, anxiety, and apprehension are likely to be present. There may be headache and palpitations. Intoxication with high doses of cocaine may be associated with transient ideas of reference, paranoid ideation, a subjective sense of "profound thoughts," increased sexual interest, ringing in the ears, hearing one's name called, and a sensation of insects crawling up the skin (formication) or seeing insects. Increased curiosity and bizarre behavior, such as sorting objects into various piles, may be observed. Stereotyped movements of mouth and tongue are sometimes noted.

When the immediate psychoactive effects of high doses of cocaine have subsided, they are replaced by unpleasant rebound effects (the "crash"), including a dysphoric mood and a craving for cocaine. Other symptoms of the "crash" may include anxiety, tremulousness, irritability, and feelings of fatigue and depression. (When the "crash" extends beyond 24 hours after the last use of cocaine, it becomes Cocaine Withdrawal.)

Course. The course of Cocaine Intoxication is usually self-limited, with full recovery within 48 hours.

Complications. Syncope or chest pain may occur. There may be seizures following large doses. Death may result from cardiac arrhythmias or respiratory paralysis. Cocaine Delusional Disorder has developed if delusions or hallucinations persist beyond the time of direct substance effect. On occasion, Cocaine Intoxication may develop into Cocaine Delirium.

Differential diagnosis. Manic episodes may present with symptoms similar to those seen in Cocaine Intoxication. **Amphetamine Intoxication** and **Phencyclidine (PCP) Intoxication** may cause a similar clinical picture, and can be distinguished from Cocaine Intoxication only by the presence of cocaine metabolites in a urine specimen or cocaine in plasma.

Diagnostic criteria for 305.60 Cocaine Intoxication

A. Recent use of cocaine.

B. Maladaptive behavioral changes, e.g., euphoria, fighting, grandiosity, hyper-vigilance, psychomotor agitation, impaired judgment, impaired social or occupational functioning.

C. At least two of the following signs within one hour of using cocaine:

   (1) tachycardia
   (2) pupillary dilation
   (3) elevated blood pressure
   (4) perspiration or chills
   (5) nausea or vomiting
   (6) visual or tactile hallucinations

D. Not due to any physical or other mental disorder.

Note: When the differential diagnosis must be made without a clear-cut history or toxicologic analysis of body fluids, it may be qualified as "Provisional."

292.00 Cocaine Withdrawal
The essential features of this disorder are dysphoric mood (e.g., depression, irritability, anxiety) and fatigue, insomnia or hypersomnia, or psychomotor agitation due to abrupt cessation of prolonged (several days or longer) heavy use of cocaine or reduction in the amount of cocaine used. The symptoms persist more than 24 hours after cessation of substance use.

Associated features. Paranoid and suicidal ideation may be present.

Course. The symptoms usually reach a peak in two to four days, although depression and irritability may persist for months.

Complications. Suicide is the major complication.

Differential diagnosis. A coexisting **Depressive Disorder** should be considered if a depressive syndrome persists for several weeks.

Diagnostic criteria for 292.00 Cocaine Withdrawal

A. Cessation of prolonged (several days or longer) heavy use of cocaine, or reduction in the amount of cocaine used, followed by dysphoric mood (e.g.,

Diagnostic criteria for 292.00 Cocaine Withdrawal continued

> depression, irritability, anxiety) and at least one of the following, persisting more than 24 hours after cessation of substance use:
>
> (1) fatigue
> (2) insomnia or hypersomnia
> (3) psychomotor agitation
>
> B. Not due to any physical or other mental disorder, such as Cocaine Delusional Disorder.
>
> **Note:** When the differential diagnosis must be made without a clear-cut history or toxicologic analysis of body fluids, it may be qualified as "Provisional."

292.81 Cocaine Delirium

The essential feature of this disorder is a Delirium (see p. 100) developing within 24 hours of intake of cocaine.

Associated features. Tactile and olfactory hallucinations may be present. Affect is often labile. Violent or aggressive behavior is common, and restraint may be required.

Course. Delirium usually occurs within one hour of substance use and is over in about six hours. When the substance is taken intravenously, the onset is almost immediate. More rarely, the Delirium follows a period of intoxication. When the other pharmacologic effects of the substance have worn off, the Delirium disappears completely.

Complications. See Cocaine Intoxication (p. 141).

Prevalence. This disorder is not as common as Cocaine Delusional Disorder.

Differential diagnosis. See differential diagnosis of Delirium (p. 102).

Diagnostic criteria for 292.81 Cocaine Delirium

> A. Delirium (p. 103) developing within 24 hours of use of cocaine.
>
> B. Not due to any physical or other mental disorder.
>
> **Note:** When the differential diagnosis must be made without a clear-cut history or toxicologic analysis of body fluids, it may be qualified as "Provisional."

292.11 Cocaine Delusional Disorder

The essential feature of this disorder is an Organic Delusional Syndrome (see p. 109), with rapidly developing persecutory delusions as the predominant clinical feature, appearing shortly after use of cocaine.

Associated features. Distortion of body image and misperception of people's faces may occur. Initially, suspiciousness and curiosity may be experienced with pleasure, but may later induce aggressive or violent action against "enemies." The hallucination of bugs or vermin crawling in or under the skin (formication) can lead to scratching and extensive skin excoriations.

Course. Delusions can linger for a week or more, but occasionally last for over a year.

Impairment, complications, and differential diagnosis. See Organic Delusional Syndrome, p. 109-110.

Diagnostic criteria for 292.11 Cocaine Delusional Disorder

A. Organic Delusional Syndrome (p. 110) developing shortly after use of cocaine.

B. Rapidly developing persecutory delusions are the predominant clinical feature.

C. Not due to any physical or other mental disorder.

Note: When the differential diagnosis must be made without a clear-cut history or toxicologic analysis of body fluids, it may be qualified as "Provisional."

HALLUCINOGEN-INDUCED ORGANIC MENTAL DISORDERS

See p. 179 for a description of the different forms of hallucinogens and Hallucinogen Dependence and Abuse.

305.30   Hallucinogen Hallucinosis

The essential features of this disorder are maladaptive behavioral changes, characteristic perceptual changes, and physical signs due to recent hallucinogen use. The maladaptive behavioral effects may take the form of marked anxiety or depression, ideas of reference, fear of losing one's mind, paranoid ideation, impaired judgment, or impaired social or occupational functioning.

The perceptual changes include subjective intensification of perceptions, depersonalization, derealization, illusions, hallucinations, and synesthesias (e.g., seeing colors when a loud sound occurs). These occur in a state of full wakefulness and alertness. There may be hyperacusis and overattention to detail. The illusions may involve distortions of the person's body image. The hallucinations are usually visual, often of geometric forms and figures, sometimes of persons and objects. More rarely, auditory and tactile hallucinations are experienced.

Physical symptoms include pupillary dilation, tachycardia, sweating, palpitations, blurring of vision, tremors, and incoordination.

This category is called a Hallucinosis even though it is recognized that frequently, with low doses, the perceptual changes do not include hallucinations.

Associated features. The associated features are heavily influenced by the setting in which the syndrome occurs, the dose, and the expectations and personality of the individual. Euphoria is common. Usually the person realizes that the perceptual changes are due to the effect of the hallucinogen. More rarely, the person is convinced that he or she has lost his or her sanity, and will not regain it.

Imagery and thoughts are often dominated by mystical or religious experiences. For example, the person may believe that he or she has achieved certain insights not possible otherwise.

Course. The onset is usually within an hour of use. In the case of LSD, the most commonly used hallucinogen, the disorder lasts from 8 to 12 hours. For other hallucinogens the duration may range from under an hour to a day or two—at most, three days.

Complications. In rare cases the person acts irrationally, and may harm himself or herself or others. "Flashback" hallucinations (recurrent hallucinations after the hallucinogen is no longer present in the body) can occur, and in such cases a diagnosis of Post-hallucinogen Perception Disorder should be considered. Hallucinogen Delusional Disorder and Hallucinogen Mood Disorder are also possible complications.

Differential diagnosis. See Organic Hallucinosis, p. 111. Various **Psychoactive Substance-induced Intoxications,** such as that due to **cannabis,** cause clinical pictures similar to the Hallucinogen Hallucinosis that results from low doses. In such cases, if an adequate history is not available, urine or blood toxicologic analyses should be used to make the diagnosis.

Diagnostic criteria for 305.30 Hallucinogen Hallucinosis

A. Recent use of a hallucinogen.

B. Maladaptive behavioral changes, e.g., marked anxiety or depression, ideas of reference, fear of losing one's mind, paranoid ideation, impaired judgment, impaired social or occupational functioning.

C. Perceptual changes occurring in a state of full wakefulness and alertness, e.g., subjective intensification of perceptions, depersonalization, derealization, illusions, hallucinations, synesthesias.

D. At least two of the following signs:

   (1) pupillary dilation
   (2) tachycardia
   (3) sweating
   (4) palpitations
   (5) blurring of vision
   (6) tremors
   (7) incoordination

E. Not due to any physical or other mental disorder.

Note: When the differential diagnosis must be made without a clear-cut history or toxicologic analysis of body fluids, it may be qualified as "Provisional."

292.11   Hallucinogen Delusional Disorder

The essential feature of this disorder is an Organic Delusional Syndrome (see p. 109) that develops shortly after hallucinogen use. The Organic Delusional Syndrome emerges during or following Hallucinogen Hallucinosis (p. 144). All of the perceptual changes described in Hallucinogen Hallucinosis may occur; but, in addition, the person has a delusional conviction that the disturbed perceptions and thoughts correspond to reality.

Course. The course is variable, and may range from a brief, transitory experience to a long-lasting psychotic episode that is difficult to distinguish from a nonorganic psychotic disorder, such as Schizophreniform Disorder.

Complications. See Hallucinogen Hallucinosis, p. 144.

Differential diagnosis. See Organic Delusional Syndrome, p. 110. A preexisting **nonorganic psychotic disorder** should be considered if Hallucinogen Delusional Disorder persists.

Diagnostic criteria for 292.11 Hallucinogen Delusional Disorder

A.   Organic Delusional Syndrome (p. 110) developing shortly after hallucinogen use.

B.   Not due to any physical or other mental disorder, such as Schizophrenia.

Note: When the differential diagnosis must be made without a clear-cut history or toxicologic analysis of body fluids, it may be qualified as "Provisional."

292.84   Hallucinogen Mood Disorder

The essential feature of this disorder is an Organic Mood Syndrome (see p. 111) that develops shortly after hallucinogen use (usually within one or two weeks) and persists more than 24 hours after cessation of such use.

Typically, the mood emerges shortly after the hallucinogen use. Most common is the appearance of depression or anxiety; elation is rare. The depressive features often include feelings of self-reproach or excessive or inappropriate guilt, accompanied by fearfulness, tension, and physical restlessness. The person may be unable to stop talking and have difficulty sleeping. People with this disorder are frequently preoccupied with thoughts that they have destroyed their brains, that they have driven themselves crazy, and will be unable to return to their normal state. These thoughts are without delusional conviction. When there is elation, it is often accompanied by grandiosity, decreased need for sleep, distractibility, increased activity, and loquacity.

Course. The course is variable, and may range from a brief, transitory experience to a long-lasting episode that is difficult to distinguish from a Mood Disorder.

Complications. Suicide may be a complication.

Differential diagnosis. A person with a preexisting **Mood Disorder** may take a hallucinogen to elevate his or her mood and then become more depressed. In such cases it may be difficult or impossible to determine if the increased disturbance in mood is due to the substance or is merely an exacerbation of the Mood Disorder. See Organic Mood Syndrome, p. 112.

Diagnostic criteria for 292.84 Hallucinogen Mood Disorder

A. Organic Mood Syndrome (p. 112) developing shortly after hallucinogen use (usually within one or two weeks), and persisting more than 24 hours after cessation of such use.

B. Not due to any physical or other mental disorder.

Note: When the differential diagnosis must be made without a clear-cut history or toxicologic analysis of body fluids, it may be qualified as "Provisional."

292.89   Posthallucinogen Perception Disorder

The essential feature of this disorder is the reexperiencing, following cessation of use of a hallucinogen, of one or more of the same perceptual symptoms that were experienced while intoxicated with the hallucinogen. Usually the symptoms last for just a few seconds. More rarely, they may progress and be experienced throughout the day for years. The diagnosis is made only when these symptoms cause marked distress.

The most common symptoms are geometric hallucinations, hallucinations of formed objects (e.g., a face), auditory hallucinations of sounds or voices, false perceptions of movement in the peripheral visual fields, flashes of colors, intensified colors, trails of images from moving objects, positive afterimages, halos around objects, and macropsia and micropsia (objects appearing larger and smaller than thay actually are). Less common are paresthesias, often described as tingling in the head, and auditory "trailing" (echoing of ordinary sounds). The symptoms are often triggered by emergence into a dark environment, use of cannabis, or use of a phenothiazine. The symptoms can sometimes be brought on by intention.

The person with this disorder generally recognizes that the current symptoms are the same as the perceptual symptoms that were previously experienced while taking a hallucinogen. Even in the presence of distinct hallucinations, the person has insight into the pathologic nature of the symptoms.

Associated features. Lack of sexual interest is common.

Course. Approximately half of the people who have this disorder experience a remission within months. Many of the others continue to experience symptoms of the disorder for several years.

Complications. Complications include suicidal behavior, Major Depression, and Panic Disorder.

Prevalence. Mild and transient perceptual disturbances following the use of a hallucinogen may be common. The prevalence of severe forms that would qualify for Posthallucinogen Perception Disorder is unknown.

Differential diagosis. The diagnosis can be made only if the following conditions have been considered: **anatomic lesions and infections of the brain, Delirium, Dementia, sensory (visual) epilepsies, Schizophrenia, entoptic imagery,** and **hypnopompic hallucinations.**

Diagnostic criteria for 292.89 Posthallucinogen Perception Disorder

A. The reexperiencing, following cessation of use of a hallucinogen, of one or more of the perceptual symptoms that were experienced while intoxicated with the hallucinogen, e.g., geometric hallucinations, false perceptions of movement in the peripheral visual fields, flashes of color, intensified colors, trails of images from moving objects, positive afterimages, halos around objects, macropsia, and micropsia.

B. The disturbance in A causes marked distress.

C. Other causes of the symptoms, such as anatomic lesions and infections of the brain, Delirium, Dementia, sensory (visual) epilepsies, Schizophrenia, entoptic imagery, and hypnopompic hallucinations, have been ruled out.

INHALANT-INDUCED ORGANIC MENTAL DISORDER

See p. 180 for a description of substances in this class and Inhalant Dependence and Abuse.

Excluded from this classification are anesthetic gases (e.g., nitrous oxide, ether) and short-acting vasodilators such as the amyl- and butylnitrites. Although these substances are often used for their psychoactive effects, they present a different intoxication picture, and they are usually used by a population with etiologic and clinical factors that differ from those who abuse inhalants. Use of these other substances should be classified under 292.90, Other or Unspecified Psychoactive Substance Organic Mental Disorder.

305.90 Inhalant Intoxication

The essential features of this disorder are maladaptive behavioral changes and characteristic physical signs following recent use of an inhalant. The maladaptive behavioral changes may include belligerence, assaultiveness, apathy, impaired judgment, and impaired social or occupational functioning. Physical signs include dizziness, nystagmus, slurred speech, unsteady gait, lethargy, depressed reflexes, tremor, blurred vision or diplopia, stupor or coma, and euphoria. High acute doses or chronic heavy use of inhalants may induce characteristic neurologic signs, such as incoordination, generalized muscle weakness, and psychomotor retardation.

The symptoms of mild to moderate Inhalant Intoxication are very similar to those of Alcohol and Sedative, Hypnotic, or Anxiolytic Intoxications. Inhalant Intoxication, however, is somewhat more likely than Alcohol or Sedative, Hypnotic, or Anxiolytic Intoxication to be associated with behavioral and psychological symptoms such as aggressiveness, impulsiveness, or impaired judgment.

Associated features. Inhalants often leave visible external signs of use, including a rash around the nose and mouth, breath odors, and residue on the face, hands, and clothing. Eye irritation is common (redness, swelling, tearing), and there may be irritation of the throat, lungs, and nose (coughing, gagging, or sinus discharge). Nausea and headache may occur early in intoxication and subsequent to it.

Course. Because of rapid distribution via the lungs, intoxication onset is quick, often within five minutes, and the duration is short, with cessation of symptoms from one to one and a half hours after the last administration. As with alcohol and barbiturates, the initial effects may be disinhibitory, and the later effects, inhibitory. The pattern of intoxication episodes is highly variable, but chronic users report staying high for several hours at a time or throughout the day. Because the substances are inhaled, the user can titrate the dose to maintain a constant level of intoxication. Heavier "binges" may be embedded in the chronic pattern.

Complications. All of the complications resulting from impaired motor ability noted for alcohol apply to Inhalant Intoxication (e.g., accidents, head trauma). Less-well-documented, anecdotal reports suggest an association with criminal acts and self-destructive behavior. Death may occur from central nervous system depression or, unlike in the case of alcohol and sedatives, from cardiac arrhythmia. Certain hydrocarbons may sensitize the heart muscle to epinephrine, and a sudden shock may then lead to ventricular fibrillation and sudden death. Rare cases of suffocation, resulting from loss of consciousness while the head is covered with a plastic bag (in order to inhale the psychoactive substance) or from aspiration of gastric contents, have been reported.

Sex ratio. Males are only slightly more likely to experiment with inhalants than females, but males are overrepresented in clinic samples of inhalant users.

Differential diagnosis. Alcohol and Sedative, Hypnotic, or Anxiolytic Intoxications present similar symptoms, and should be considered. Breath odor and/or residues on body or clothing may be important differentiating clues, but should not be relied upon exclusively. People who chronically use inhalants are likely to be frequent and heavy users of other drugs, which further complicates the diagnostic picture. Concomitant use of alcohol may also make the differentiation difficult. Tremor and muscle weakness can indicate more severe Inhalant Intoxication, particularly in the chronic user, and may be differentiating signs. Industrial workers may occasionally be accidentally exposed to volatile chemicals and suffer physiologic intoxication. In this case, Inhalant Intoxication should not be diagnosed in the absence of the maladaptive behavior criterion.

Diagnostic criteria for 305.90 Inhalant Intoxication

A. Recent use of an inhalant.

B. Maladaptive behavioral changes, e.g., belligerence, assaultiveness, apathy, impaired judgment, impaired social or occupational functioning.

C. At least two of the following signs:

   (1) dizziness
   (2) nystagmus
   (3) incoordination

(continued)

Diagnostic criteria for 305.90 Inhalant Intoxication continued

    (4) slurred speech
    (5) unsteady gait
    (6) lethargy
    (7) depressed reflexes
    (8) psychomotor retardation
    (9) tremor
  (10) generalized muscle weakness
  (11) blurred vision or diplopia
  (12) stupor or coma
  (13) euphoria

D. Not due to any physical or other mental disorder.

Note: When the differential diagnosis must be made without a clear-cut history or toxicologic analysis of body fluids, it may be qualified as "Provisional."

NICOTINE-INDUCED ORGANIC MENTAL DISORDER

292.00   Nicotine Withdrawal

See p. 181 for a description of the different forms of nicotine and Nicotine Dependence.

The essential feature of this disorder is a characteristic withdrawal syndrome due to the abrupt cessation of or reduction in the use of nicotine-containing substances (e.g., cigarettes, cigars, and pipes, chewing tobacco, or nicotine gum) that has been at least moderate in duration and amount. The syndrome includes craving for nicotine; irritability, frustration, or anger; anxiety; difficulty concentrating; restlessness; decreased heart rate; and increased appetite or weight gain.

In many heavy cigarette-smokers, changes in mood and performance that are related to withdrawal can be detected within two hours after the last tobacco use. The sense of craving appears to reach a peak within the first 24 hours after cessation of tobacco use, and gradually declines thereafter over a few days to several weeks. In any given case it is difficult to distinguish a withdrawal effect from the emergence of psychological traits that were suppressed, controlled, or altered by the effects of nicotine or from a behavioral reaction (e.g., frustration) to the loss of a reinforcer.

Mild symptoms of withdrawal may occur after switching to low tar/nicotine cigarettes and after stopping the use of smokeless (chewing) tobacco or nicotine gum.

Associated features. Increased slow rhythms on an EEG, decreased catecholamines, decreased metabolic rate, tremor, increased coughing, REM change, gastrointestinal disturbance, headaches, insomnia, and impairment of performance on tasks requiring vigilance are commonly associated features of Nicotine Withdrawal.

Course. The symptoms begin within 24 hours of cessation of or reduction in nicotine use and usually decrease in intensity over a period of a few days to several weeks. Some former nicotine users report that craving for the substance continues for longer periods.

Complications. Whether severe Nicotine Withdrawal decreases the ability to stop smoking or remain abstinent from smoking is unknown.

Differential diagnosis. The diagnosis of Nicotine Withdrawal is usually self-evident from the person's history, and disappearance of the symptoms if smoking is resumed is confirmatory. However, **withdrawal from other psychoactive substances** may take place simultaneously, and produce similar symptoms.

Diagnostic criteria for 292.00 Nicotine Withdrawal

A. Daily use of nicotine for at least several weeks.

B. Abrupt cessation of nicotine use, or reduction in the amount of nicotine used, followed within 24 hours by at least four of the following signs:

   (1) craving for nicotine
   (2) irritability, frustration, or anger
   (3) anxiety
   (4) difficulty concentrating
   (5) restlessness
   (6) decreased heart rate
   (7) increased appetite or weight gain

OPIOID-INDUCED ORGANIC MENTAL DISORDERS

See p. 182 for a description of substances in this class and Opioid Dependence and Abuse.

305.50   Opioid Intoxication

The essential features of this disorder are maladaptive behavioral changes and specific neurologic signs due to the recent use of an opioid.

The initial maladaptive behavioral changes from intravenous opioids occur within 2 to 5 minutes after use and often include euphoria that may last 10 to 30 minutes. This is followed by a longer period (two to six hours, depending upon the type of opioid, the dose, and the previous history of drug-taking) of lethargy, somnolence, and apathy or dysphoria. Other maladaptive behavioral effects during the period of intoxication include impaired judgment and impaired social and occupational functioning. Unlike in Alcohol Intoxication, aggression and violence are rare.

Pupillary constriction is always present (or dilation due to anoxia from a severe overdose). Other neurologic signs commonly observed are drowsiness, slurred speech, and impairment in attention and memory.

Associated features. Pupillary constriction may lead to reduced visual acuity. The inhibitory effect of the psychoactive substance on gastrointestinal motility may cause constipation. There may be analgesia.

For many people, the effect of taking an opioid for the first time is dysphoric rather than euphoric, and nausea and vomiting may result.

Course. The factors involved in the rapidity of onset and the duration of intoxication are discussed in the text on Intoxication as an Organic Mental Syndrome (p. 117).

Complications. The most serious complication is opioid poisoning, manifested by coma, shock, pinpoint pupils, and depressed respiration, with the possibility of death from respiratory arrest. This syndrome can be rapidly reversed by intravenous administration of a narcotic antagonist such as naloxone, nalorphine, or levallorphan if this treatment is given before irreversible brain anoxia has occurred.

Other complications are similar to those of Alcohol Intoxication (see p. 128), but are less commonly seen.

Differential diagnosis. Other Psychoactive-induced Substance Intoxications may cause a similar clinical picture. Sedatives and alcohol are most likely to be confused in this regard. **Alcohol** and **Sedative, Hypnotic, or Anxiolytic Intoxication** can be distinguished by the absence of pupillary constriction in the former and by toxicologic analysis of body fluids. Mild **Hallucinogen Hallucinosis** may occasionally cause a similar picture. **Cocaine, amphetamines,** and **hallucinogens** cause pupillary dilation; but unless the person is in a state of severe intoxication, the possibility that this dilation is a sign of Opioid Intoxication is unlikely.

Diagnostic criteria for 305.50 Opioid Intoxication

A. Recent use of an opioid.

B. Maladaptive behavioral changes, e.g., initial euphoria followed by apathy, dysphoria, psychomotor retardation, impaired judgment, impaired social or occupational functioning.

C. Pupillary constriction (or pupillary dilation due to anoxia from severe overdose) and at least one of the following signs:

   (1) drowsiness
   (2) slurred speech
   (3) impairment in attention or memory

D. Not due to any physical or other mental disorder.

Note: When the differential diagnosis must be made without a clear-cut history, testing with an opioid antagonist, or toxicologic analysis of body fluids, it may be qualified as "Provisional."

292.00 Opioid Withdrawal

The essential feature of this disorder is a characteristic withdrawal syndrome due to recent cessation of or reduction in use of an opioid. The syndrome includes lacrimation, rhinorrhea, pupillary dilation, piloerection, sweating, diarrhea, yawning, mild hypertension, tachycardia, fever, and insomnia.

The symptoms and signs of Opioid Withdrawal may be precipitated by the abrupt cessation of opioid administration after a one- or two-week period of continuous use or by administration of a narcotic antagonist (e.g., naloxone or nalorphine) after therapeutic doses of an opioid given four times a day for as short a period of time as three or four days.

Associated features. Common associated features include restlessness, irritability, depression, tremor, weakness, nausea, vomiting, and muscle and joint pains. These symptoms, together with the symptoms noted above, resemble the clinical picture of influenza.

Depending on the observer and the environment, there may be complaints, pleas, demands, and manipulations all directed toward the goal of obtaining more opioids. A need for analgesia may be simulated, or the withdrawal symptoms may be exaggerated.

Course. Mild Opioid Withdrawal may occur following abrupt withdrawal of analgesic doses of morphine after seven to ten days of administration. However, it is relatively uncommon for opioid craving to occur in the context of analgesic administration for pain from physical disorders or associated with surgery. The withdrawal symptoms with full-blown craving for opioids usually occur secondary to abrupt withdrawal in people with Opioid Dependence. In the case of morphine or heroin, the first withdrawal signs are usually noted within six to eight hours of the previous dose, reach a peak on the second or third day, and disappear in seven to ten days.

The withdrawal syndrome from meperidine begins more quickly after the last dose, reaches a peak within 8 to 12 hours, and is over within 4 or 5 days. Methadone withdrawal may not begin for one to three days after the last dose, and its severity depends on the degree of dependence. The symptoms are usually over by the 10th to 14th day.

Withdrawal symptoms from semisynthetic and synthetic opioids are qualitatively similar to those from morphine, the general rule being that substances with a short duration of action tend to produce short, intense withdrawal syndromes, whereas substances that are more slowly eliminated produce withdrawal syndromes that are prolonged, but milder. However, narcotic antagonist-precipitated withdrawal following administration of long-acting substances can be quite severe.

Complications. Death rarely occurs unless the person has a severe physical disorder, such as cardiac disease.

Differential diagnosis. Influenza is remarkably similar in its clinical picture to Opioid Withdrawal.

Withdrawals from other psychoactive substances and **mixed withdrawals,** especially **Sedative, Hypnotic, or Anxiolytic Withdrawal,** can be differentiated from Opioid Withdrawal by testing blood and urine and by taking a careful history, bearing in mind that people giving such a history are often unreliable. Third-party confirmation is extremely valuable.

Diagnostic criteria for 292.00 Opioid Withdrawal

A. Cessation of prolonged (several weeks or more) moderate or heavy use of an opioid, or reduction in the amount of opioid used (or administration of an

(continued)

Diagnostic criteria for 292.00 Opioid Withdrawal continued

opioid antagonist after a brief period of use), followed by at least three of the following:

(1) craving for an opioid
(2) nausea or vomiting
(3) muscle aches
(4) lacrimation or rhinorrhea
(5) pupillary dilation, piloerection, or sweating
(6) diarrhea
(7) yawning
(8) fever
(9) insomnia

B. Not due to any physical or other mental disorder.

Note: When the differential diagnosis must be made without a clear-cut history or toxicologic analysis of body fluids, it may be qualified as "Provisional."

PHENCYCLIDINE (PCP)- OR SIMILARLY ACTING ARYLCYCLOHEXYLAMINE-INDUCED ORGANIC MENTAL DISORDERS

See p. 183 for a description of substances in this class and Phencyclidine (PCP) or Similarly Acting Arylcyclohexylamine Dependence and Abuse.

305.90 Phencyclidine (PCP) or Similarly Acting Arylcyclohexylamine Intoxication

The essential features of this disorder are maladaptive behavioral changes and specific physical signs due to the recent use of phencyclidine (PCP) or a similarly acting arylcyclohexylamine. The symptoms begin within one hour of oral use of the substance; if smoked, insufflated, or taken intravenously, onset may be within five minutes. The maladaptive behavioral changes include belligerence, assaultiveness, impulsiveness, unpredictability, psychomotor agitation, impaired judgment, and impaired social or occupational functioning. The physical symptoms include vertical and horizontal nystagmus, increased blood pressure or heart rate, numbness or diminished responsiveness to pain, ataxia, dysarthria, muscle rigidity, seizures, and hyperacusis.

The effects of this class of psychoactive substances are generally dose related, although there is great variability among individuals. The effects usually range from a mild, "floaty" euphoria and numbness after ingesting less than 5 mg of phencyclidine to muscle rigidity, hypertension, and a noncommunicative state following a dose of 5-10 mg, and coma, convulsions, and possible death after a dose of 20 mg or more.

Associated features. Intoxication may be accompanied by repetitive motor movements, including facial grimacing, muscle rigidity on stimulation, and repeated episodes of vomiting. There may also be hallucinations, paranoid ideation, and bizarre or violent behavior.

Course. In most cases, people who are acutely confused following use of phencyclidine or a similarly acting arylcyclohexylamine are alert and oriented within three to four hours of admission to an emergency room. Chronic users of phencyclidine report feeling intoxicated for four to six hours after ingesting the usual "street" dose. Effects can last for several days.

Complications. Death from respiratory depression can occur following a high dose. Suicide is not uncommon during acute intoxication. While a person is recovering from an intoxicated state, depression, irritability, and nervousness often occur.

Differential diagnosis. Other Psychoactive Substance-induced Intoxications that cause a similar clinical picture, such as those due to amphetamines and hallucinogens, may be ruled out by the presence of phencyclidine or a similarly acting arylcyclohexylamine in the urine or plasma.

Diagnostic criteria for 305.90 Phencyclidine (PCP) or Similarly Acting Arylcyclohexylamine Intoxication

A. Recent use of phencyclidine or a similarly acting arylcyclohexylamine.

B. Maladaptive behavioral changes, e.g., belligerence, assaultiveness, impulsiveness, unpredictability, psychomotor agitation, impaired judgment, impaired social or occupational functioning.

C. Within an hour (less when smoked, insufflated ["snorted"], or used intravenously), at least two of the following signs:

(1) vertical or horizontal nystagmus
(2) increased blood pressure or heart rate
(3) numbness or diminished responsiveness to pain
(4) ataxia
(5) dysarthria
(6) muscle rigidity
(7) seizures
(8) hyperacusis

D. Not due to any physical or other mental disorder, e.g., Phencyclidine (PCP) or Similarly Acting Arylcyclohexylamine Delirium.

Note: When the differential diagnosis must be made without a clear-cut history or toxicologic analysis of body fluids, it may be qualified as "Provisional."

292.81 Phencyclidine (PCP) or Similarly Acting Arylcyclohexylamine Delirium

The essential feature of this disorder is a Delirium (see p. 100) developing shortly after use of phencyclidine (PCP) or a similarly acting arylcyclohexylamine. The Delirium may occur within 24 hours after use or may emerge following recovery from an overdose up to a week after the substance has been taken.

Associated features. See Phencyclidine or Similarly Acting Arylcyclohexylamine Intoxication (p. 154).

Course. The Delirium may last up to a week, with waxing and waning that are probably a reflection of excretion into and reabsorption from the stomach.

Complications. See Phencyclidine or Similarly Acting Arylcyclohexylamine Intoxication (p. 155).

Prevalence. This disorder is not as common as Intoxication from this class of psychoactive substances.

Differential diagnosis. See differential diagnosis of Delirium (p. 102).

Diagnostic criteria for 292.81 Phencyclidine (PCP) or Similarly Acting Arylcyclohexylamine Delirium

A. Delirium (p. 103) developing shortly after use of phencyclidine or a similarly acting arylcyclohexylamine.

B. Not due to any physical or other mental disorder.

Note: When the differential diagnosis must be made without a clear-cut history or toxicologic analysis of body fluids, it may be qualified as "Provisional."

292.11   Phencyclidine (PCP) or Similarly Acting Arylcyclohexylamine Delusional Disorder

The features are essentially the same as those in Cocaine Delusional Disorder (see p. 143).

Diagnostic criteria for 292.11 Phencyclidine (PCP) or Similarly Acting Arylcyclohexylamine Delusional Disorder

A. Organic Delusional Syndrome (p. 110) developing shortly after use of phencyclidine or a similarly acting arylcyclohexylamine, or emerging up to a week after an overdose.

B. Not due to any physical or other mental disorder, such as Schizophrenia.

Note: When the differential diagnosis must be made without a clear-cut history or toxicologic analysis of body fluids, it may be qualified as "Provisional."

292.84   Phencyclidine (PCP) or Similarly Acting Arylcyclohexylamine Mood Disorder

The essential feature of this disorder is an Organic Mood Syndrome (see p. 111) that develops shortly after use of phencyclidine (PCP) or a similarly acting arylcyclohexylamine (usually within one or two weeks) and persists more than 24 hours after cessation of substance use.

Typically, the mood emerges shortly after use of the psychoactive substance. Most common is the appearance of depression or anxiety; elation is rare. The depressive features often include feelings of self-reproach or excessive or inappropriate guilt, accompanied by fearfulness, tension, and physical restlessness. The person may be unable to stop talking and have difficulty sleeping. Such people are frequently preoccupied with thoughts that they have destroyed their brains, that they have driven themselves crazy, and will be unable to return to their normal state. These thoughts are without delusional conviction. Elation is often accompanied by grandiosity, decreased need for sleep, distractibility, increased activity, and loquacity.

Course. The course is variable, and may range from a brief, transitory experience to a long-lasting episode that is difficult to distinguish from a Mood Disorder.

Complications. Suicide may be a complication.

Differential diagnosis. A person with a preexisting **Mood Disorder** may take PCP or a similarly acting arylcyclohexylamine to elevate his or her mood and then become more depressed. In such cases it may be difficult or impossible to determine if the increased disturbance in mood is due to the psychoactive substance or is merely an exacerbation of the Mood Disorder. See Organic Mood Syndrome, p. 112.

Diagnostic criteria for 292.84 Phencyclidine (PCP) or Similarly Acting Arylcyclohexylamine Mood Disorder

A. Organic Mood Syndrome (p. 112) developing shortly after use of phencyclidine or a similarly acting arylcyclohexylamine (usually within one or two weeks) and persisting more than 24 hours after cessation of substance use.

B. Not due to any physical or other mental disorder.

Note: When the differential diagnosis must be made without a clear-cut history or toxicologic analysis of body fluids, it may be qualified as "Provisional."

292.90   Phencyclidine (PCP) or Similarly Acting Arylcyclohexylamine Organic Mental Disorder Not Otherwise Specified

The essential feature of this disorder is recent use of phencyclidine (PCP) or a similarly acting arylcyclohexylamine that has resulted in an illness that involves features of several Organic Mental Syndromes or a progression from one Organic Mental Syndrome to another. For example, a person may simultaneously have prominent delusions, hallucinations, and signs of disorientation, or may initially have a Delirium, followed by an Organic Delusional Syndrome.

Diagnostic criteria for 292.90 Phencyclidine (PCP) or Similarly Acting Arylcyclohexylamine Organic Mental Disorder Not Otherwise Specified

A. Recent use of phencyclidine or a similarly acting arylcyclohexylamine.

B. The resulting illness involves features of several Organic Mental Syndromes or a progression from one Organic Mental Syndrome to another, e.g., initially there is Delirium, followed by an Organic Delusional Syndrome.

C. Not due to any physical or other mental disorder.

Note: When the differential diagnosis must be made without a clear-cut history or toxicologic analysis of body fluids, it may be qualified as "Provisional."

SEDATIVE-, HYPNOTIC-, OR ANXIOLYTIC-INDUCED ORGANIC MENTAL DISORDERS

See p. 184 for a description of substances in this class and Sedative, Hypnotic, or Anxiolytic Dependence and Abuse.

305.40   Sedative, Hypnotic, or Anxiolytic Intoxication

The essential features of this disorder are maladaptive behavioral changes and characteristic physical signs due to the recent use of a sedative, hypnotic, or anxiolytic. The maladaptive behavioral changes may include disinhibition of sexual or aggressive impulses, mood lability, impaired judgment, and impaired social or occupational functioning. Characteristic physical signs include: slurred speech, incoordination, unsteady gait, and impairment in attention or memory.

The essential and associated features are similar to those of Alcohol Intoxication, though there is no syndrome of Idiosyncratic Intoxication. On the whole, intoxication with this class of substances is less likely to result in displays of aggression or violence than is the case with Alcohol Intoxication. This is partly due to the less rapid absorption rate of these substances compared with that of alcohol, but may also be due to the fact that a higher proportion of people with Alcohol Intoxication are males, and that the settings in which alcohol is ingested (e.g., bars) are more likely to be associated with displays of aggression.

Course. As in Alcohol Intoxication, the initial behavioral effects are usually disinhibitory. If the person continues to use the psychoactive substance, inhibitory effects will supervene.

The factors involved in rapidity of onset and duration of the intoxication are discussed in the text on Intoxication as an Organic Mental Syndrome (see p. 117).

Complications. The complications described under Alcohol Intoxication can also occur with these substances, although they are less commonly seen. In contrast to their wide margin of safety when used alone, benzodiazepines in combination with alcohol appear to be particularly dangerous, and accidental overdoses have been reported.

Accidental overdoses have also been reported in people who deliberately abuse barbiturates and other nonbenzodiazepine sedatives, such as methaqualone. With repeated use in search of euphoria, tolerance develops to the sedative effects, and a progressively higher dose is used. However, tolerance to brain-stem-depressant effects develops much more slowly, and as the person takes more drug to achieve euphoria, there may be a sudden onset of respiratory depression and hypotension, which may result in death.

Diagnostic criteria for 305.40 Sedative, Hypnotic, or Anxiolytic Intoxication

A. Recent use of a sedative, hypnotic, or anxiolytic.

B. Maladaptive behavioral changes, e.g., disinhibition of sexual or aggressive impulses, mood lability, impaired judgment, impaired social or occupational functioning.

C. At least one of the following signs:

   (1) slurred speech
   (2) incoordination
   (3) unsteady gait
   (4) impairment in attention or memory

D. Not due to any physical or other mental disorder.

Note: When the differential diagnosis must be made without a clear-cut history or toxicologic analysis of body fluids, it may be qualified as "Provisional."

292.00 Uncomplicated Sedative, Hypnotic, or Anxiolytic Withdrawal

The essential features of this disorder are certain characteristic symptoms such as nausea or vomiting, malaise or weakness, autonomic hyperactivity (e.g, tachycardia, sweating), anxiety or irritability, orthostatic hypotension, coarse tremor of the hands, tongue, and eyelids, marked insomnia, and grand mal seizures. These symptoms develop following cessation of prolonged (several weeks or more) moderate or heavy use of a sedative, hypnotic, or anxiolytic or a reduction in the amount of the substance that was regularly used.

These features are similar to those of Uncomplicated Alcohol Withdrawal, and may vary from a relatively mild syndrome to a severe syndrome with seizures, depending on the dose and duration of use. Withdrawal has been reported in people receiving as little as 15 mg of diazepam (or its equivalent in other benzodiazepines) daily for eight months or more, but is more likely to be found with cessation of doses in the range of 40 mg daily of diazepam or its equivalent. At doses in the range of 100 mg of diazepam or more, withdrawal seizures have been observed. Alternatively, myoclonic jerks may be present. Since myoclonic jerks can be mistaken for attempts to simulate seizures, they may be mistaken for Malingering.

The onset of benzodiazepine withdrawal is usually within two to three days after cessation of use; but with long-acting drugs such as diazepam, there may be a latency of five to six days before the withdrawal syndrome appears.

Diagnostic criteria for 292.00 Uncomplicated Sedative, Hypnotic, or Anxiolytic Withdrawal

A. Cessation of prolonged (several weeks or more) moderate or heavy use of a sedative, hypnotic, or anxiolytic, or reduction in the amount of substance used, followed by at least three of the following:

   (1) nausea or vomiting
   (2) malaise or weakness
   (3) autonomic hyperactivity, e.g., tachycardia, sweating
   (4) anxiety or irritability
   (5) orthostatic hypotension
   (6) coarse tremor of hands, tongue, and eyelids
   (7) marked insomnia
   (8) grand mal seizures

B. Not due to any physical or other mental disorder, such as Sedative, Hypnotic, or Anxiolytic Withdrawal Delirium.

Note: When the differential diagnosis must be made without a clear-cut history or toxicologic analysis of body fluids, it may be qualified as "Provisional."

292.00   Sedative, Hypnotic, or Anxiolytic Withdrawal Delirium

The essential feature of this disorder is a Delirium (see p. 100) that develops after cessation of or reduction in heavy use of a sedative, hypnotic, or anxiolytic, usually within one week. Marked autonomic hyperactivity, such as tachycardia and sweating, is observed.

Associated features. Vivid hallucinations, which may be visual, auditory, or tactile, are common. Delusions and agitated behavior are also frequently present. There may be a coarse, irregular tremor. Fever may also occur.

Age at onset. The first episode of this disorder usually occurs after 5 to 15 years of heavy sedative, hypnotic, or anxiolytic use.

Course. The onset is usually on the second or third day after cessation of or reduction in substance use. Occasionally it occurs earlier; it rarely appears more than a week after abstinence. Unless complicated by some other illness, the syndrome most often runs its course in two to three days. If seizures also occur as the result of withdrawal from the substance, they always precede the development of Delirium.

Complications. See Delirium (p. 102).

Predisposing factors. The presence of a concomitant physical illness predisposes to this syndrome. A physically healthy person seldom develops Delirium during withdrawal from sedatives, hypnotics, or anxiolytics.

Prevalence. This syndrome is much less common than Uncomplicated Sedative, Hypnotic, or Anxiolytic Withdrawal, and is also much less common than Alcohol Withdrawal Delirium.

Differential diagnosis. See Delirium (p. 102).

Diagnostic criteria for 292.00 Sedative, Hypnotic, or Anxiolytic Withdrawal Delirium

A. Delirium (p. 103) developing after the cessation of heavy use of a sedative, hypnotic, or anxiolytic, or a reduction in the amount of substance used (usually within one week).

B. Autonomic hyperactivity, e.g., tachycardia, sweating.

C. Not due to any physical or other mental disorder.

Note: When the differential diagnosis must be made without a clear-cut history or toxicologic analysis of body fluids, it may be qualified as "Provisional."

292.83   Sedative, Hypnotic, or Anxiolytic Amnestic Disorder

The essential feature of this disorder is an Amnestic Syndrome (see p. 108) following prolonged heavy use of a sedative, hypnotic, or anxiolytic.

Age at onset. There is some evidence that the age at onset is in the 20s. The earlier onset compared with that of Alcohol Amnestic Disorder may be due to the more common earlier age at onset of heavy use of this class of psychoactive substances compared with alcohol.

Course. The course is variable. Unlike in Alcohol Amnestic Disorder, full recovery may occur.

Impairment, complications, and differential diagnosis. See Amnestic Syndrome (p. 108).

Diagnostic criteria for 292.83 Sedative, Hypnotic, or Anxiolytic Amnestic Disorder

A. Amnestic Syndrome (p. 109) following prolonged heavy use of a sedative, hypnotic, or anxiolytic.

B. Not due to any physical or other mental disorder.

Note: When the differential diagnosis must be made without a clear-cut history or toxicologic analysis of body fluids, it may be qualified as "Provisional."

Other or Unspecified Psychoactive Substance-induced Organic Mental Disorders

These codes are to be used when a person develops an Organic Mental Syndrome apparently due to use of a psychoactive substance if:

(1) the substance cannot be classified in any of the eleven previously listed categories (*Examples:* Levo-dopa Delusional Disorder, Anticholinergic Delirium);
(2) the syndrome is caused by an unknown substance (*Example:* an intoxication after taking a bottle of unlabeled pills).

Following the listing of each of the diagnoses in this section, the reader is directed to the page listing the diagnostic criteria for the appropriate Organic Mental Syndrome.

305.90   **Other or Unspecified Psychoactive Substance Intoxication (p. 117)**
292.00   **Other or Unspecified Psychoactive Substance Withdrawal (p. 118)**
292.81   **Other or Unspecified Psychoactive Substance Delirium (p. 103)**
292.82   **Other or Unspecified Psychoactive Substance Dementia (p. 107)**
292.83   **Other or Unspecified Psychoactive Substance Amnestic Disorder (p. 109)**
292.11   **Other or Unspecified Psychoactive Substance Delusional Disorder (p. 110)**
292.12   **Other or Unspecified Psychoactive Substance Hallucinosis (p. 111)**
292.84   **Other or Unspecified Psychoactive Substance Mood Disorder (p. 112)**
292.89   **Other or Unspecified Psychoactive Substance Anxiety Disorder (p. 114)**
292.89   **Other or Unspecified Psychoactive Substance Personality Disorder (p. 115)**
292.90   **Other or Unspecified Psychoactive Substance Organic Mental Disorder Not Otherwise Specified (p. 119)**

ORGANIC MENTAL DISORDERS ASSOCIATED WITH AXIS III PHYSICAL DISORDERS OR CONDITIONS, OR WHOSE ETIOLOGY IS UNKNOWN

These codes permit identification of specific Organic Mental Disorders on Axis I associated with physical disorders recorded on Axis III. Examples include Delirium (Axis I) associated with pneumonia (Axis III), and Dementia (Axis I) associated with brain tumor (Axis III). Following the name of each of the Organic Mental Disorders is the page listing the diagnostic criteria for the corresponding syndrome.

293.00   **Delirium (p. 103)**
294.10   **Dementia (p. 107)**
294.00   **Amnestic Disorder (p. 109)**
293.81   **Organic Delusional Disorder (p. 110)**
293.82   **Organic Hallucinosis (p. 111)**
293.83   **Organic Mood Disorder (p. 112)**
            Specify: **manic, depressed, or mixed.**

294.80 **Organic Anxiety Disorder (p. 114)**
310.10 **Organic Personality Disorder (p. 115)**
       Specify **if explosive type.**
294.80 **Organic Mental Disorder Not Otherwise Specified (p. 119)**

Psychoactive Substance Use Disorders

In our society, use of certain substances to modify mood or behavior under certain circumstances is generally regarded as normal and appropriate. Such use includes recreational drinking of alcohol, in which a majority of adult Americans participate, and the use of caffeine, in the form of coffee or tea, as a stimulant. On the other hand, there are wide cultural variations. In some groups even the recreational use of alcohol is frowned upon, whereas in other groups the use of various illegal substances for mood-altering effects has become widely accepted. In addition, certain psychoactive substances are used medically for the alleviation of pain, relief of tension, or to suppress appetite.

This diagnostic class deals with symptoms and maladaptive behavioral changes associated with more or less regular use of psychoactive substances that affect the central nervous system. These behavioral changes would be viewed as extremely undesirable in almost all cultures. Examples include continued use of the psychoactive substance despite the presence of a persistent or recurrent social, occupational, psychological, or physical problem that the person knows may be exacerbated by that use and the development of serious withdrawal symptoms following cessation of or reduction in use of a psychoactive substance. These conditions are here conceptualized as mental disorders, and are therefore to be distinguished from nonpathological psychoactive substance use, such as the moderate imbibing of alcohol or the use of certain substances for appropriate medical purposes.

The disorders classified in this section are to be distinguished from Psychoactive Substance-induced Organic Mental Disorders because Psychoactive Substance Use Disorders refer to the maladaptive behavior associated with more or less regular use of the substances whereas Psychoactive Substance-induced Organic Mental Disorders describe the direct acute or chronic effects of such substances on the central nervous system. Almost invariably, people who have a Psychoactive Substance Use Disorder will also have a Psychoactive Substance-induced Organic Mental Disorder, such as Intoxication or Withdrawal.

For all classes of psychoactive substances, pathological use is categorized as either Psychoactive Substance Dependence or the residual diagnosis of Psychoactive Substance Abuse. For a discussion of the role of toxicologic analysis of body fluids in the diagnosis of Psychoactive Substance Use Disorders, see p. 125.

PSYCHOACTIVE SUBSTANCE DEPENDENCE

The essential feature of this disorder is a cluster of cognitive, behavioral, and physiologic symptoms that indicate that the person has impaired control of psychoactive substance use and continues use of the substance despite adverse consequences. The symptoms of the dependence syndrome include, but are not limited to, the physiologic symptoms of tolerance and withdrawal (as in DSM-III). Some people with physiologic tolerance and withdrawal may not have the dependence syndrome as defined here. For example, many surgical patients develop a tolerance to prescribed opioids and experience withdrawal symptoms without showing any signs of impaired control of their use of opioids. Conversely, other people may show signs of severely impaired control of psychoactive substance use (e.g., of cannabis) without clear signs of physiologic tolerance or withdrawal. Some heavy coffee-drinkers are physiologically dependent on caffeine and exhibit both tolerance and withdrawal. However, such use is generally not associated with dependence as defined here, and few, if any, of these people have difficulty switching to decaffeinated coffee or coffee substitutes. Therefore, Caffeine Dependence is not included in this classification of mental disorders. In contrast, Caffeine Intoxication is often clinically significant, and therefore is included (as a Psychoactive Substance-induced Organic Mental Disorder).

The symptoms of the dependence syndrome are the same across all categories of psychoactive substances, but for some classes some of the symptoms are less salient, and in a few instances do not apply (e.g., withdrawal symptoms do not occur in Hallucinogen Dependence). At least three of the nine characteristic symptoms of dependence are necessary to make the diagnosis. In addition, the diagnosis of the dependence syndrome requires that some symptoms of the disturbance have persisted for at least one month, or have occurred repeatedly over a longer period of time, as in binge drinking.

Dependence as defined here is conceptualized as having different degrees of severity, and guidelines for mild, moderate, and severe dependence and dependence in partial or full remission are provided.

Symptoms of Dependence

The following are the characteristic symptoms of dependence. It should be noted that not all nine symptoms must be present for the diagnosis of Dependence, and for some classes of psychoactive substances, certain of these symptoms do not apply.

1. The person finds that when he or she actually takes the psychoactive substance, it is often in larger amounts or over a longer period than originally intended. For example, the person may decide to take only one drink of alcohol, but after taking this first drink, continues to drink until severely intoxicated.

2. The person recognizes that the substance use is excessive, and has attempted to reduce or control it, but has been unable to do so (as long as the substance is available). In other instances the person may want to reduce or control his or her substance use, but has never actually made an effort to do so.

3. A great deal of time is spent in activities necessary to procure the substance (including theft), taking it, or recovering from its effects. In mild cases the person may spend several hours a day taking the substance, but continue to be involved in other activities. In severe cases, virtually all of the user's daily activities revolve around obtaining, using, and recuperating from the effects of the substance.

4. The person may suffer intoxication or withdrawal symptoms when he or she is expected to fulfill major role obligations (work, school, homemaking). For example, the person may be intoxicated when working outside the home or when expected to take

care of his or her children. In addition, the person may be intoxicated or have withdrawal symptoms in situations in which substance use is physically hazardous, such as driving a car or operating machinery.

5. Important social, occupational, or recreational activities are given up or reduced because of substance use. The person may withdraw from family activities and hobbies in order to spend more time with substance-using friends, or to use the substance in private.

6. With heavy and prolonged substance use, a variety of social, psychological, and physical problems occur, and are exacerbated by continued use of the substance. Despite having one or more of these problems (and recognizing that use of the substance causes or exacerbates them), the person continues to use the substance.

7. Significant tolerance, a markedly diminished effect with continued use of the same amount of the substance, occurs. The person will then take greatly increased amounts of the substance in order to achieve intoxication or the desired effect. This is distinguished from the marked personal differences in initial sensitivity to the effects of a particular substance.

The degree to which tolerance develops varies greatly across classes of substances. Many cigarette-smokers consume more than 20 cigarettes a day, an amount that would have produced definite symptoms of toxicity when they first started smoking. Many heavy users of cannabis are not aware of tolerance to it, although tolerance has been demonstrated in some people. Whether there is tolerance to phencyclidine (PCP) and related substances is unclear. Heavy users of alcohol at the peak of their tolerance can consume only about 50% more than they originally needed in order to experience the effects of intoxication. In contrast, heavy users of opioids often increase the amount of opioids consumed to tenfold the amount they originally used—an amount that would be lethal to a nonuser. When the psychoactive substance used is illegal and perhaps mixed with various diluents or with other substances, tolerance may be difficult to determine.

8. With continued use, characteristic withdrawal symptoms develop when the person stops or reduces intake of the substance. The withdrawal symptoms vary greatly across classes of substances. Marked and generally easily measured physiologic signs of withdrawal are common with alcohol, opioids, sedatives, hypnotics, and anxiolytics. Such signs are less obvious with amphetamines, cocaine, nicotine, and cannabis, but intense subjective symptoms can occur upon withdrawal from heavy use of these substances. No significant withdrawal is seen even after repeated use of hallucinogens; withdrawal from PCP and related substances has not yet been described in humans, although it has been demonstrated in animals. (See the specific withdrawal syndromes in Psychoactive Substance-induced Organic Mental Disorders.)

9. After developing unpleasant withdrawal symptoms, the person begins taking the substance in order to relieve or avoid those symptoms. This typically involves using the substance throughout the day, beginning soon after awakening. This symptom is generally not present with cannabis, hallucinogens, and PCP.

Diagnostic criteria for Psychoactive Substance Dependence

A. At least three of the following:

(1) substance often taken in larger amounts or over a longer period than the person intended

(continued)

Diagnostic criteria for Psychoactive Substance Dependence continued

    (2) persistent desire or one or more unsuccessful efforts to cut down or control substance use

    (3) a great deal of time spent in activities necessary to get the substance (e.g., theft), taking the substance (e.g., chain smoking), or recovering from its effects

    (4) frequent intoxication or withdrawal symptoms when expected to fulfill major role obligations at work, school, or home (e.g., does not go to work because hung over, goes to school or work "high," intoxicated while taking care of his or her children), or when substance use is physically hazardous (e.g., drives when intoxicated)

    (5) important social, occupational, or recreational activities given up or reduced because of substance use

    (6) continued substance use despite knowledge of having a persistent or recurrent social, psychological, or physical problem that is caused or exacerbated by the use of the substance (e.g., keeps using heroin despite family arguments about it, cocaine-induced depression, or having an ulcer made worse by drinking)

    (7) marked tolerance: need for markedly increased amounts of the substance (i.e., at least a 50% increase) in order to achieve intoxication or desired effect, or markedly diminished effect with continued use of the same amount

    Note: The following items may not apply to cannabis, hallucinogens, or phencyclidine (PCP):

    (8) characteristic withdrawal symptoms (see specific withdrawal syndromes under Psychoactive Substance-induced Organic Mental Disorders)

    (9) substance often taken to relieve or avoid withdrawal symptoms

B. Some symptoms of the disturbance have persisted for at least one month, or have occurred repeatedly over a longer period of time.

Criteria for Severity of Psychoactive Substance Dependence:

Mild: Few, if any, symptoms in excess of those required to make the diagnosis, and the symptoms result in no more than mild impairment in occupational functioning or in usual social activities or relationships with others.

Moderate: Symptoms or functional impairment between "mild" and "severe."

Severe: Many symptoms in excess of those required to make the diagnosis, and the symptoms markedly interfere with occupational functioning or with usual social activities or relationships with others.[1]

In Partial Remission: During the past six months, some use of the substance and some symptoms of dependence.

In Full Remission: During the past six months, either no use of the substance, or use of the substance and no symptoms of dependence.

---

[1]Because of the availability of cigarettes and other nicotine-containing substances and the absence of a clinically significant nicotine intoxication syndrome, impairment in occupational or social functioning is not necessary for a rating of severe Nicotine Dependence.

PSYCHOACTIVE SUBSTANCE ABUSE

Psychoactive Substance Abuse is a residual category for noting maladaptive patterns of psychoactive substance use that have never met the criteria for dependence for that particular class of substance. The maladaptive pattern of use is indicated by either (1) continued use of the psychoactive substance despite knowledge of having a persistent or recurrent social, occupational, psychological, or physical problem that is caused or exacerbated by use of the substance or (2) recurrent use of the substance in situations when use is physically hazardous (e.g., driving while intoxicated). The diagnosis is made only if some symptoms of the disturbance have persisted for at least one month or have occurred repeatedly over a longer period of time.

This diagnosis is most likely to be applicable to people who have only recently started taking psychoactive substances and to involve substances, such as cannabis, cocaine, and hallucinogens, that are less likely to be associated with marked physiologic signs of withdrawal and the need to take the substance to relieve or avoid withdrawal symptoms.

Examples of situations in which this category would be appropriate are as follows:

1. A college student binges on cocaine every few weekends. These periods are followed by a day or two of missing school because of "crashing." There are no other symptoms.

2. A middle-aged man repeatedly drives his car when intoxicated with alcohol. There are no other symptoms.

3. A woman keeps drinking alcohol even though her physician has told her that it is responsible for exacerbating the symptoms of a duodenal ulcer. There are no other symptoms.

Diagnostic criteria for Psychoactive Substance Abuse

A. A maladaptive pattern of psychoactive substance use indicated by at least one of the following:

    (1) continued use despite knowledge of having a persistent or recurrent social, occupational, psychological, or physical problem that is caused or exacerbated by use of the psychoactive substance

    (2) recurrent use in situations in which use is physically hazardous (e.g., driving while intoxicated)

B. Some symptoms of the disturbance have persisted for at least one month, or have occurred repeatedly over a longer period of time.

C. Never met the criteria for Psychoactive Substance Dependence for this substance.

CLASSES OF PSYCHOACTIVE SUBSTANCES

Nine classes of psychoactive substances are associated with both abuse and dependence: alcohol; amphetamine or similarly acting sympathomimetics; cannabis; cocaine; hallucinogens; inhalants; opioids; phencyclidine (PCP) or similarly acting arylcyclohexylamines; and sedatives, hypnotics, or anxiolytics. Dependence (but not abuse) is seen with nicotine. (Although Nicotine Abuse is logically possible, according to the definition of abuse noted above, in practice virtually no one who has not previously been dependent on nicotine uses nicotine-containing substances in a maladaptive way, e.g., episodic use of cigarettes that exacerbates a physical disorder.)

In this chapter, these ten classes of psychoactive substances appear in alphabetical order, although the following classes share similar features:

alcohol and sedatives, anxiolytics or hypnotics;

cocaine and amphetamine or similarly acting sympathomimetics;

hallucinogens and phencylidine (PCP) or similarly acting arylcyclohexylamines.

USE OF MULTIPLE SUBSTANCES

Psychoactive Substance Abuse and Dependence often involve several substances, either simultaneously or sequentially. For example, people with Cocaine Dependence frequently use alcohol, anxiolytics, or opioids to counteract lingering dysphoric anxiety symptoms. People with Opioid or Cannabis Abuse or Dependence usually have several other Psychoactive Substance Use Disorders, particularly of sedatives, hypnotics, or anxiolytics, amphetamines or similarly acting sympathomimetics, and cocaine.

When a person's condition meets the criteria for more than one Psychoactive Substance Use Disorder, multiple diagnoses should be made. The Polysubstance Dependence diagnosis is reserved for noting a period of at least six months during which the person was repeatedly using at least three categories of psychoactive substances (not including nicotine and caffeine), but no single psychoactive substance predominated. Further, during this period the dependence criteria were met for psychoactive substances (as a group), but not for any specific substance.

RECORDING SPECIFIC DIAGNOSES

The clinician should record the name of the specific psychoactive substance rather than the name of the class of substances, using the code number for the appropriate class. For example, the clinician should write 305.70 Amphetamine Abuse (rather than Amphetamine or Similarly Acting Sympathomimetic Abuse), 304.10 Diazepam Dependence (rather than Sedative, Hypnotic, or Anxiolytic Dependence), and 305.90 Cogentin Abuse (rather than Psychoactive Substance Abuse NOS).

OTHER FEATURES OF PSYCHOACTIVE SUBSTANCE USE DISORDERS

Route of administration. The route of administration of a psychoactive substance is an important variable in determining the likelihood that its use will lead to dependence or abuse. It may also affect the particular pattern of psychoactive substance use, i.e., determine whether periodic binges or daily use is more likely. In general, routes of administration that produce more rapid and efficient absorption of the substance into the bloodstream tend to increase the likelihood of an escalating pattern of substance use that leads to dependence. In addition, for some substances there is an increased likelihood of a binge pattern of use, i.e., a form of episodic use consisting of compressed time periods of continuous high dose use followed by one or more days of nonuse. For example, a person is much more likely to develop dependence on cocaine and develop a binge pattern of use when the substance is smoked or taken intravenously than when it is "sniffed" or taken orally.

Routes of administration that quickly deliver a large amount of the substance to the brain are also associated with higher levels of substance consumption, with a resulting increased likelihood of toxic effects. For example, the user of intravenous amphetamines is much more likely to consume large amounts of the substance and to develop a Psychoactive Substance-induced Organic Mental Disorder than the person who takes the substance only orally or intranasally.

Duration of psychoactive effects. The duration of psychoactive effects associated with a particular psychoactive substance is also an important variable in determining the likelihood that use of the substance will lead to dependence or abuse and a pattern of binge use. In general, relatively short-acting psychoactive substances, such as amphetamine, cocaine, and certain anxiolytics, tend to be more commonly used than substances with similar psychoactive effects, but longer action. Consequently, the shorter-acting psychoactive substances have a particularly high potential for the development of dependence or abuse.

Associated features. Repeated episodes of Psychoactive Substance-induced Intoxication are almost invariably present in Psychoactive Substance Abuse or Dependence, although for some substances it is possible to develop dependence without ever exhibiting frank intoxication (e.g., alcohol).

Personality disturbance and disturbance of mood are often present, and may be intensified by the Psychoactive Substance Use Disorder. For example, antisocial personality traits may be accentuated by the need to obtain money to purchase illegal substances. Anxiety or depression associated with Borderline Personality Disorder may be intensified as the person uses a psychoactive substance in an unsuccessful attempt to treat his or her mood disturbance.

In chronic abuse or dependence, mood lability and suspiciousness, both of which can contribute to violent behavior, are common.

Age at onset. Alcohol Abuse and Dependence usually appear in the 20s, 30s, and 40s. Dependence on amphetamine or similarly acting sympathomimetics, cannabis, cocaine, hallucinogens, nicotine, opioids, and phencyclidine (PCP) or similarly acting arylcyclohexylamines more commonly begin in the late teens and 20s. When a Psychoactive Substance Use Disorder begins in early adolescence, it is often associated with Conduct Disorder and failure to complete school.

Complications. The abuse or dependence associated with each class of psychoactive substances may cause an Organic Mental Syndrome. For example, prolonged Alcohol Dependence may cause Alcohol Withdrawal Delirium, Alcohol Amnestic Disorder, or Alcohol Hallucinosis. Similarly, Hallucinogen Delusional Disorder may be a complication of chronic hallucinogen use. Complications of the specific intoxication states, such as traffic accidents and physical injury due to Alcohol Intoxication, have been noted in the Organic Mental Disorders section.

Frequently there is a deterioration in the general level of physical health. Malnutrition and a variety of other physical disorders may result from failure to maintain physical health by proper diet and adequate personal hygiene.

Use of contaminated needles for intravenous administration of amphetamines, cocaine, and opioids can cause hepatitis, tetanus, vasculitis, septicemia, subacute bacterial endocarditis, embolic phenomena, malaria, and Human Immunodeficiency Virus (HIV)-related disorders (e.g., Acquired Immune Deficiency Syndrome [AIDS], AIDS-related Complex [ARC]). Materials used to "cut" the substances can cause toxic or allergic reactions. Using cocaine intranasally ("snorting") sometimes causes erosion of the nasal septum. Cocaine use can result in sudden death from cardiac arrhythmias, myocardial infarction, a cerebrovascular accident, or respiratory arrest.

Physical complications of chronic Alcohol Dependence include hepatitis, cirrhosis, peripheral neuropathy, gastritis, and a variety of reproductive disorders. In addition, chronic Alcohol Dependence increases the risk and severity of heart disease, pneumonia, tuberculosis, and neurologic disorders. The long-term potential for respiratory disorder with chronic cannabis use is controversial. The long-term physical complications from chronic and heavy nicotine use are discussed on page 182.

Depressive symptoms are a frequent complication of Psychoactive Substance Use Disorders and partly account for the high rate of suicide by people with these disorders. Suicide associated with alcohol and other psychoactive substances can occur in both intoxicated and sober states.

Long-term dependence on certain psychoactive substances, particularly cannabis, hallucinogens, and PCP, is often associated with a generalized reduction in goal-directed behaviors, e.g., going to school, work, and the pursuit of hobbies, even when the person does not take the substance for long periods of time. This is often accompanied by depression, anxiety, irritability, and mild deficits in cognitive functioning, e.g., difficulty concentrating. This has been called the "amotivational syndrome." It is unclear whether this syndrome is the direct consequence of the chronic effect of the psychoactive substances on the central nervous system or whether it is an expression of preexisting psychopathology.

Impairment. Impairment in social and occupational functioning is frequently marked, particularly with dependence.

Course. Brief, self-limited episodes of dependence or abuse may occur, particularly during periods of psychosocial stress. More commonly, the course is chronic, lasting several years, with periods of exacerbation and partial or full remission.

Predisposing factors. Conduct Disorder in children, and Personality Disorders, particularly Antisocial Personality Disorder, predispose to the development of Psychoactive Substance Use Disorders. Children of people who themselves have Psychoactive Substance Use Disorders are at higher risk for developing these disorders.

Sex ratio. Psychoactive Substance Use Disorders are diagnosed more commonly in males than in females.

Differential Diagnosis. For a discussion of the role of toxicologic analysis of body fluids in the differential diagnosis of Psychoactive Substance Use Disorders, see p. 125.

Nonpathologic psychoactive substance use for recreational or medical purposes is not associated with the dependence syndrome, or a maladaptive pattern of use (abuse).

Repeated episodes of Psychoactive Substance-induced Intoxication are almost invariably present in Psychoactive Substance Abuse and Dependence, although for some substances (e.g., alcohol) it is possible to develop dependence without ever exhibiting frank intoxication (e.g., alcohol). However, one or more episodes of Psychoactive Substance-induced Intoxication alone are not sufficient for a diagnosis of either Psychoactive Substance Dependence or Abuse.

DESCRIPTIONS OF PSYCHOACTIVE SUBSTANCE USE DISORDERS

Diagnostic criteria for dependence categories will be found on p. 167. Diagnostic criteria for abuse categories are on p. 169.

303.90   Alcohol Dependence
305.00   Alcohol Abuse

See Alcohol-induced Organic Mental Disorders (p. 127) for a description of Alcohol Intoxication, Alcohol Idiosyncratic Intoxication, Uncomplicated Alcohol Withdrawal, Alcohol Withdrawal Delirium, Alcohol Hallucinosis, Alcohol Amnestic Disorder, and Dementia Associated with Alcoholism.

Most adults in the United States are light drinkers. About 35% abstain, 55% drink fewer than three alcoholic drinks a week, and only 11% consume an average of one ounce or more of alcohol a day.

Drinking patterns vary by age and sex. For both males and females, the prevalence of drinking is highest and abstention is lowest in the 21-34-year age range. At all ages, two to five times more males than females are "heavy" drinkers, although, because of differences in weight and body water, different standards should be used to define "heavy" drinking in females. For ages 65 years and older, abstainers exceed drinkers in both sexes, and only 7% of males and 2% of females are considered heavy drinkers.

Most alcohol is consumed by a small percentage of people: 10% of drinkers consume 50% of the total amount of alcohol consumed.

Patterns of use. There are three main patterns of chronic Alcohol Abuse or Dependence. The first consists of regular daily intake of large amounts; the second, of regular heavy drinking limited to weekends; the third, of long periods of sobriety interspersed with binges of daily heavy drinking lasting for weeks or months. It is a mistake to associate one of these particular patterns exclusively with "alcoholism."

Some investigators divide alcoholism into "species" depending on the pattern of drinking. One species, so-called gamma alcoholism, is common in the United States and conforms to the stereotype of the alcoholism seen in people who are active in Alcoholics Anonymous. Gamma alcoholism involves problems with "control": once the person with gamma alcoholism begins to drink, he or she is unable to stop until poor health or depleted financial resources prevent further drinking. Once the "bender" is terminated, however, the person is able to abstain from alcohol for varying lengths of time.

Gamma alcoholism is often compared with a "species" of alcoholism common in France. In this, the person with alcoholism is not aware of lack of control: he or she *must* drink a given quantity of alcohol every day, but there is no compulsion to exceed that amount. The person may not recognize that he or she has an alcohol problem until, for some reason, he or she has to stop drinking and develops withdrawal symptoms.

Although these two pure types of alcoholism do exist, they do not conform to the pattern of drinking seen in most people with Alcohol Abuse or Dependence in the United States.

Associated features. Alcohol Dependence and Abuse are often associated with use and abuse of other psychoactive drugs, including cannabis, cocaine, heroin, amphetamines, and various sedatives and hypnotics. Frequent and often simultaneous use of alcohol plus several of the above substances is most commonly seen in adolescents and people under 30. Use and abuse of benzodiazepines combined with alcohol are more common in middle life. Although benzodiazepines are contraindicated in the treatment of alcoholism, these agents are often prescribed by a physician in a misguided attempt to stop or reduce a patient's drinking.

Whether most people with Alcohol Dependence are at particular risk to develop dependence or abuse of other drugs is not definitely known, but certainly some are. Nicotine Dependence is especially common.

Alcohol Dependence is often associated with depression, but usually the depression appears to be a consequence, not a cause, of the drinking. In Bipolar Disorder, alcohol intake increases more often during Manic Episodes than during depressions. Anxiety Disorders—particularly agoraphobia in females and Social Phobia in males—occur in a sizable minority of people with Alcohol Abuse or Dependence, their onset often preceding the heavy drinking.

Course. The natural history of alcoholism seems to be somewhat different in males and females. In males the onset is usually in the late teens or the 20s, the course is insidious, and the person may not be fully aware of his dependence on alcohol until the 30s. The first hospitalization usually occurs in the late 30s or 40s. In males, symptoms of Alcohol Dependence or Abuse rarely occur for the first time after age 45. If they do occur, a Mood Disorder or Organic Mental Disorder should be considered as a source of symptoms.

Alcohol Dependence has a higher "spontaneous" remission rate than is often recognized. The frequency of admissions to psychiatric hospitals for alcoholism drops markedly in the sixth and seventh decades of life, as do first arrests for alcohol-related offenses. Although the mortality rate among people with Alcohol Dependence is perhaps two to three times that of the general population, this is probably insufficient to account for the apparent decrease in problem drinking in middle and late middle life.

Females with Alcohol Dependence have been studied less extensively than males, but the evidence suggests that the course of the disorder is more variable in females. The onset often occurs later, and spontaneous remission apparently is less frequent. Females with alcoholism are also more likely to have a history of a Mood Disorder.

Drinking problems may occur in various sequences. Frequently, after years of heavy problem-free drinking, a person may experience many problems in a brief period.

As people drink more over days, months, and years, they gradually *need* to drink more to obtain the same effect. This is called tolerance. A person with severe chronic Alcohol Dependence may be able to drink, at most, twice as much as a teetotaler of similar age and health. Compared with tolerance for morphine, which can be considerable, tolerance for alcohol is modest.

More striking than "acquired" tolerance may be inborn tolerance. People vary widely in the amount of alcohol they can tolerate, independently of their drinking experience. Some people, however hard they try, cannot drink more than a small amount of alcohol without developing a headache, upset stomach, or dizziness. Others seem able to drink large amounts with hardly any bad effects; they appear to have been born with this capacity, not to have developed it entirely from practice.

Differences in tolerance for alcohol apply not only to people but to racial groups. For example, many Orientals develop flushing of the skin, sometimes with nausea, after drinking only a small amount of alcohol.

Prevalence. A community study in the United States, conducted from 1981 to 1983 and using DSM-III criteria, indicated that approximately 13% of the adult population had had Alcohol Abuse or Dependence at some time in their lives.

Familial Pattern. Alcohol Dependence tends to cluster in families. Recent evidence, based on adoption studies, indicates that the transmission of Alcohol Dependence from generation to generation does not require environmental exposure to family members with alcohol problems: it occurs at increased rates even when the children are reared by adoptive parents without alcohol problems, which suggests a genetic influence in the disorder.

304.40 Amphetamine or Similarly Acting Sympathomimetic Dependence
305.70 Amphetamine or Similarly Acting Sympathomimetic Abuse

See Amphetamine- or Similarly Acting Sympathomimetic-induced Organic Mental Disorders (p. 134) for a description of Amphetamine or Similarly Acting Sympathomimetic Intoxication, Withdrawal, Delirium, and Delusional Disorder.

This group includes all of the substances of the substituted phenylethylamine structure, such as amphetamine, dextroamphetamine, and methamphetamine ("Speed"), and those with structures different from the substituted phenylethylamine that have amphetaminelike action, such as methylphenidate and some substances used as appetite suppressants ("diet pills"). These substances are typically taken orally or intravenously, though methamphetamine is frequently taken by nasal inhalation (like cocaine).

The patterns of use, associated features, and course of Amphetamine Dependence and Abuse are very similar to those of Cocaine Dependence and Abuse since both substances are potent central nervous system stimulants with similar psychoactive and sympathomimetic effects. Controlled studies have shown that experienced users are unable to distinguish amphetamine from cocaine. One of the few differences between the two classes of substances is that the psychoactive effects of amphetamine last longer and its peripheral sympathomimetic effects may be more potent.

Patterns of use. Many people who develop Amphetamine Dependence or Abuse first start using amphetamine or related substances for their appetite-suppressant effect in an attempt at weight control.

Amphetamine Dependence and Abuse are usually characterized by either episodic or chronic daily, or almost daily, use. In episodic use, the amphetamine use tends to be separated by several days of nonuse, e.g., the substance may be used on weekends and once or twice during the week. "Bingeing" is a common form of episodic use consisting of compressed time periods of continuous high-dose use followed by one or more days of nonuse, e.g., consumption of several grams or more of amphetamine during a single 48-hour period, followed by a one- or two-day recuperation period, and then another binge. Binges tend to terminate only when the user collapses from physical exhaustion or when amphetamine supplies are depleted. Binges are generally followed by an extremely intense and unpleasant "crash" (see p. 135) requiring at least two or more days of recuperation. In some cases the "crash" may extend into Amphetamine Withdrawal (see p. 136) lasting several days.

Chronic daily, or almost daily, use may be at high or low doses. Use may be throughout the course of a day or be restricted to certain hours, e.g., only during working hours or only during the evening. In this pattern there are usually no wide fluctuations in the amount of amphetamine used on successive occasions, but there is often a general increase in doses over time.

Associated features. Often the user of amphetamine also abuses or is dependent on alcohol or a sedative, hypnotic, or anxiolytic, which is taken in an attempt to alleviate the unpleasant aftereffects of Amphetamine Intoxication.

Psychological and behavioral changes associated with Amphetamine Abuse and Dependence include depression, irritability, anhedonia, anergia, and social isolation.

Sexual dysfunction, paranoid ideation, attentional disturbances, and memory problems may also occur.

Course. Intravenous administration of amphetamine tends to engender a rapid progression from infrequent amphetamine use to Amphetamine Abuse or Dependence, often within only a few weeks or months. Intranasal administration of amphetamine flakes tends to engender a more gradual progression to Amphetamine Abuse or Dependence, which may not be clearly evident for months or years after initial use.

Amphetamine Abuse and Dependence are usually associated with a progressive tolerance to the desired effects of the substance, which leads to use of increasing doses. Continuing use produces a progressive diminution in pleasurable effects and a corresponding increase in dysphoric effects. Eventually, a point is reached at which the person still craves the amphetamine, despite the absence of substance-induced euphoria because of tolerance, and an accumulation of unpleasant adverse effects from the continued drug-taking. Continuing use of amphetamine appears to be driven by persistent craving for the substance rather than attempts to avoid or alleviate withdrawal symptoms (as is typically seen in Opioid Dependence).

Prevalence. A community study in the United States, conducted from 1981 to 1983 and using DSM-III criteria, indicated that approximately 2% of the adult population had had Amphetamine or Similarly Acting Sympathomimetic Abuse at some time in their lives.

304.30   Cannabis Dependence
305.20   Cannabis Abuse
See Cannabis-induced Organic Mental Disorders (p. 139) for a description of Cannabis Intoxication and Delusional Disorder.

This group includes all substances with psychoactive properties derived from the cannabis plant plus chemically similar synthetic substances. In the United States the most commonly used substances are marijuana, hashish, and, occasionally, purified delta-9-tetrahydrocannabinol (THC), the major psychoactive ingredient in these substances. These psychoactive substances are almost always smoked, but may also be taken orally, sometimes mixed with food.

The THC content of the marijuana that is generally available varies greatly. The THC content of illicit marijuana has increased significantly since the late 1960s, from an average of approximately 1%–5% to as much as 10%–15% by the mid 1980s. The greater potency of current marijuana supplies may be contributing to an increasing prevalence of Cannabis Dependence and associated disorders.

Patterns of use. Cannabis is regarded by many people as a substance of low abuse potential that is extremely unlikely to cause any problems with continued use. For that reason, many people start using the substance without any appreciation of its capacity to induce dependence.

Cannabis Dependence is usually characterized by daily, or almost daily, use of the substance. In Cannabis Abuse, the person uses the substance episodically, but shows evidence of maladaptive behavior, such as driving while impaired by Cannabis Intoxication.

Since impairment in social and occupational functioning and the development of related physical disorders in Cannabis Dependence are less than those typically seen with other psychoactive substances, such as alcohol, cocaine, and heroin, people with Cannabis Dependence and Abuse rarely seek treatment for these disorders.

Associated features. Cannabis is used in combination with other substances, particularly alcohol and cocaine. Psychological symptoms associated with Cannabis Dependence include lethargy, anhedonia, and attentional and memory problems.

Course. Cannabis Dependence or Abuse usually develops with repeated use over a substantial period of time; rapid development following initial use is rare. Tolerance may develop to some of the substance's psychoactive effects and thus promote increased levels of consumption. However, this is usually not marked, and rarely is there an abrupt escalation of the amount of the substance consumed with each use. Typically, it is the frequency rather than the absolute amount of cannabis used that increases over time. With chronic heavy use there is often a diminution or loss of the pleasurable effects of the substance. There may be a corresponding increase in dysphoric effects, but this is not seen as frequently as in chronic heavy use of amphetamine or cocaine.

Prevalence. Cannabis is the most widely used illicit psychoactive substance in the United States. A community study in the United States, conducted from 1981 to 1983 and using DSM-III criteria, indicated that approximately 4% of the adult population had had Cannabis Abuse at some time in their lives.

304.20   Cocaine Dependence
305.60   Cocaine Abuse

See Cocaine-induced Organic Mental Disorders (p. 141) for a description of Cocaine Intoxication, Withdrawal, Delirium, and Delusional Disorder.

Several different types of coca preparations are used for their psychoactive properties: coca leaves (chewed), coca paste (smoked), cocaine hydrochloride powder (inhaled or injected), and cocaine alkaloid—"freebase" or "crack" (smoked).

The chewing of coca leaves is a practice generally limited to native populations in Central and South American cocaine-producing countries. In order to achieve the mild stimulant effects from chewing the leaves, the cocaine alkaloid from the leaf is released by simultaneously chewing a piece of another plant that contains an alkaline substance. This practice has rarely been known to cause an Organic Mental Syndrome or Abuse or Dependence.

Coca paste is a crude extract of the coca leaf prepared by adding organic solvents, such as kerosene or gasoline combined with sulfuric acid. Coca paste is usually smoked in a pipe, or is sometimes mixed in a cigarette with tobacco or cannabis. The availability of coca paste has been limited almost exclusively to cocaine-producing countries in Central and South America, in some of which this highly toxic and addictive form of cocaine, contaminated by the solvents used in the extraction process, has been causing increasing mental and physical disorders among the native populations.

As with all smokable forms of cocaine, the intensity of psychoactive effects and the addiction potential of the substance are maximized by its extremely rapid and efficient absorption by the lungs and subsequent circulation to the brain within only a few seconds after inhalation of the smoke.

The most commonly used form of cocaine in the United States is cocaine hydrochloride powder, which is usually inhaled through the nostrils, and then absorbed into the bloodstream through the mucous membranes. Cocaine hydrochloride is soluble in water, and thus can also be administered by intravenous injection; it is sometimes mixed with heroin in the same syringe, yielding a drug combination known as a "speedball." This mixture is particularly dangerous since the cocaine and heroin act synergistically in depressing respiratory function. Cocaine powder is not smoked because the substance decomposes at the temperatures required for smoking.

The prevalence of smoking cocaine in its alkaloid form began to increase rapidly in the United States in about 1984. The cocaine alkaloid is extracted or "freed" from the powdered hydrochloride salt through use of one of several different reagents, such as ether, ammonia, or sodium bicarbonate (baking soda). When the user performs the extraction from cocaine powder, the resulting cocaine alkaloid is commonly called "freebase." Cocaine in this form has a much lower volatility point, and therefore is not destroyed by the heat necessary to change it into a gas, as is the case with cocaine hydrochloride. When cocaine is purchased in its alkaloid form, it is commonly called "crack" or "rock," although pharmacologically it is the same as "freebase" cocaine. The appeal of smokable cocaine is due to a combination of factors, including its familiar and seemingly benign method of administration and its extremely rapid and potent psychoactive effects.

Patterns of use. Cocaine Abuse and Dependence are associated with two different patterns of use: episodic, and chronic daily, or almost daily, use. In episodic use, the cocaine use tends to be separated by two or more days of nonuse, e.g., it may be used on weekends and once or twice during the week. "Bingeing" is a common form of episodic use consisting of compressed time periods of continuous high-dose use, e.g., consumption of several grams or more of cocaine during a single 48-hour period. Bingeing is most commonly associated with cocaine smoking and intravenous use. Binges tend to terminate only when the user collapses from physical exhaustion or when cocaine supplies are depleted. Binges are generally followed by an extremely intense and unpleasant "crash" (see p. 135) requiring at least two or more days of recuperation. In some cases the "crash" may extend into Cocaine Withdrawal (see p. 142) lasting several days.

Chronic daily, or almost daily, use may be at high or low doses. Use may be throughout the course of a day or be restricted to certain hours, e.g., only during working hours or only during the evening. In this pattern there are usually no wide fluctuations in the amount of cocaine used on successive days, but there is often a general increase in doses used over time.

Associated features. Often the user of cocaine also abuses or is dependent on alcohol or a sedative, hypnotic, or anxiolytic, which is taken in an attempt to alleviate the unpleasant aftereffects of Cocaine Intoxication.

Psychological and behavioral changes associated with Cocaine Abuse and Dependence include depression, irritability, anhedonia, anergia, and social isolation. Sexual dysfunction, paranoid ideation, attentional disturbances, and memory problems may also occur.

Course. Cocaine smoking and intravenous administration of cocaine tend to engender rapid progression from infrequent cocaine use to Cocaine Abuse or Dependence, often within only a few weeks or months. Intranasal administration of cocaine tends to result in more gradual progression to Cocaine Abuse or Dependence, which may not be clearly evident for months or years following initial use.

Cocaine Abuse and Dependence are usually associated with a progressive tolerance of the desirable effects of the substance, which leads to use of increasing doses. With continuing use there is a progressive diminution in pleasurable effects and a corresponding increase in dysphoric effects. Eventually, a point is reached at which the person still craves the cocaine despite the absence of substance-induced euphoria because of tolerance, and an accumulation of unpleasant adverse effects caused by the continued drug-taking. Continuing use of cocaine appears to be driven by persistent craving and urges for the substance rather than attempts to avoid or alleviate withdrawal symptoms (as is typically seen in Opioid Dependence).

Prevalence. A community study in the United States, conducted from 1981 to 1983 and using DSM-III criteria (which did not contain a category for Cocaine Dependence), indicated that approximately 0.2% of the adult population had had Cocaine Abuse at some time in their lives. Because of the broadened criteria for Dependence included in this manual, and because of the definite increase in use in recent years, the prevalence of Cocaine Dependence is believed to be far higher than this now.

304.50 Hallucinogen Dependence
305.30 Hallucinogen Abuse
See Hallucinogen-induced Organic Mental Disorders (p. 144) for a description of Hallucinogen Hallucinosis, Hallucinogen Delusional Disorder, Hallucinogen Mood Disorder, and Post-hallucinogen Perception Disorder.

This group includes two types of psychoactive substances, both of which have hallucinogenic properties: substances structurally related to 5-hydroxytryptamine (e.g., lysergic acid diethylamine [LSD] and dimethyltryptamine [DMT]), and substances related to catecholamine (e.g., mescaline). Phencyclidine (PCP), although it is sometimes referred to as an hallucinogen, is classified separately since it rarely causes a pure hallucinosis.

Hallucinogens are taken orally.

Pattern of use. Most people are introduced to a hallucinogen by "experimenting" with the substance. Some find the hallucinosis extremely dysphoric and stop using the substance, whereas others enjoy the experience and continue its use. Use is almost always episodic, because the psychoactive effects of these substances impair normal cognitive and perceptual functions so markedly that the user generally must set aside time from normal daily activities to take the substance. In addition, frequent use may lead to rapid development of marked tolerance, which makes it virtually impossible to take enough of the substance on a daily basis to obtain the desired effects. For these reasons, abuse is much more common than dependence.

Associated features. Hallucinogens are frequently contaminated with other drugs, such as PCP and amphetamine. In addition, users frequently smoke cannabis and abuse alcohol.

Course. The course is unpredictable, and is probably related to the nature of the underlying pathology that played a role in onset of its use. Most people rapidly resume their former life-style after only a brief period of abuse or dependence.

Prevalence. Among people seeking help for dependence on psychoactive substances, the use of hallucinogens as the predominant substance is extremely rare. A community study in the United States, conducted from 1981 to 1983 and using DSM-III criteria, indicated that approximately 0.3% of the adult population had had Hallucinogen Abuse at some time in their lives.

304.60   Inhalant Dependence
305.90   Inhalant Abuse

See Inhalant-induced Organic Mental Disorders (p. 148) for a description of Inhalant Intoxication.

Included in this classification are disorders induced by inhaling, through the mouth or nose, the aliphatic and aromatic hydrocarbons found in substances such as gasoline, glue, paint, paint thinners, and spray paints. Less commonly used are the halogenated hydrocarbons found in cleaners, typewriter correction fluid, and spray-can propellants and other volatile compounds containing esters, ketones, and glycols. These volatile substances are available in a wide variety of commercial products, and may be used interchangeably, depending on availability and personal preference. There may be subtle differences in the psychoactive and physical effects of the different compounds, but not enough is known about their differential effects to distinguish among them. All are capable of producing Intoxication.

Most compounds that are inhaled are a mixture of several substances that can produce psychoactive effects. Therefore, under most circumstances, it is difficult to ascertain the exact substance responsible for the disorder. Unless there is clear evidence that a single, unmixed substance has been used, the general term "inhalant" should be used in recording the diagnosis.

Specifically excluded from these diagnoses are dependence patterns resulting from the use of anesthetic gases (e.g., nitrous oxide, ether) and short-acting vasodilators such as amyl or butyl nitrite. These should be listed under 304.90 Psychoactive Substance Dependence NOS.

Patterns of use. Several methods are used to inhale intoxicating vapors. Most commonly, a rag soaked with the substance is applied to the mouth and nose and the vapors are breathed in. The substance may also be placed in a paper or plastic bag, and the gases in the bag inhaled. Substances may also be inhaled directly from containers, or from aerosols sprayed in the mouth or nose. There are rare reports of using heating compounds to accelerate vaporization. The inhalants reach the lungs, bloodstream, and target sites very rapidly. Use of different methods combined with varying concentrations of inhalants in the products used cause highly variable concentrations in the body, making it extremely difficult to match dose to effect.

The background of inhalant users is generally marked by considerable family dysfunction (separation, poor supervision, Alcohol or other Psychoactive Substance Dependence), and school or work adjustment problems (delinquency, truancy, poor grades, dropping out of school, unemployment). There is a higher incidence of inhalant use among minority youth living in economically depressed areas, although dependence has been documented among all racial, gender, and socioeconomic groups.

The pattern of development of Inhalant Dependence is related to age. Inhalants are sometimes used by quite young children, 9–13 years old, generally with a group of peers who are likely to use alcohol and cannabis as well. Inhalant use may increase gradually over time until inhalants become the preferred substance, and the peer group meets frequently to use inhalants together. Older adolescents and young adults who have Inhalant Dependence are likely to have used many different substances as adolescents and to have gradually increased inhalant use until inhalants have become the preferred substance.

Cases have also been reported of the development of dependence in industrial workers who have long-term exposure and access to volatile compounds. In these instances a worker may begin to use the compound intentionally for its psychoactive effects and subsequently develop a pattern diagnosable as dependence.

Associated features. Users of inhalants nearly always use other psychoactive substances as well. When Inhalant Dependence exists, however, it is usually clear that inhalants are the preferred substance, and inhalants are used regularly whereas other substances are used only sporadically. Even occasional users of inhalants are likely to have significant physical and mental problems.

Course. Younger children diagnosed as having Inhalant Dependence may use inhalants several times a week, often on weekends and after school. Severe dependence in young adults may involve varying periods of intoxication throughout each day and occasional periods of heavier use that may last several days. This pattern may persist for many years, with recurrent need for treatment. Users of inhalants may have a preferred level or degree of intoxication, and the method of administration allows a user to maintain that specific level for several hours. Chronic heavy users of inhalants may develop renal and hepatic complications.

Tolerance to inhalants has been reported, but may be merely increased use over time, with more periods of intoxication and increased preference for higher levels of intoxication. Withdrawal has also been reported, but there is inadequate evidence to substantiate its existence.

Prevalence. No information.

305.10   Nicotine Dependence
See Nicotine-Induced Organic Mental Disorders (p. 150) for a description of Nicotine Withdrawal.

Patterns of use. At present, the most common form of Nicotine Dependence is associated with the inhalation of cigarette smoke. Pipe- and cigar-smoking, the use of snuff, and the chewing of tobacco are less likely to lead to Nicotine Dependence. The more rapid onset of nicotine effects with cigarette-smoking leads to a more intensive habit pattern that is more difficult to give up because of the frequency of reinforcement and the greater physical dependence on nicotine.

Associated features. People with this disorder are often distressed because of their inability to stop nicotine use, particularly when they have serious physical symptoms that are aggravated by nicotine. Some people who have Nicotine Dependence may have difficulty remaining in social or occupational situations in which smoking is prohibited.

Course. The course of Nicotine Dependence is variable. Most people repeatedly attempt to give up nicotine use without success. In some the dependence is brief, in that when they experience concern about nicotine use, they promptly make an effort to stop smoking and are successful, though in many cases they may experience a period of Nicotine Withdrawal lasting from days to weeks. Studies of treatment outcome suggest that the relapse rate is greater than 50% in the first 6 months, and at least 70% within the first 12 months. After a year's abstinence, subsequent relapse is unlikely.

The difficulty in giving up nicotine use definitively, particularly cigarettes, may be due to the unpleasant nature of the withdrawal syndrome, the deeply engrained nature of the habit, the repeated effects of nicotine, which rapidly follow the inhalation of cigarette smoke (75,000 puffs per year for a pack-a-day smoker), and the likelihood that a desire to use nicotine is elicited by environmental cues, such as the ubiquitous presence of other smokers and the widespread availability of cigarettes. When efforts to give up smoking are made, Nicotine Withdrawal may develop.

Impairment. Since nicotine, unlike alcohol, rarely causes any clinically significant state of intoxication, there is no impairment in social or occupational functioning as an immediate and direct consequence of its use.

Complications. The most common complications are bronchitis, emphysema, coronary artery disease, peripheral vascular disease, and a variety of cancers.

Prevalence and sex ratio. A large proportion of the adult population of the United States has Nicotine Dependence, the prevalence among males being greater than that among females. Among teen-age smokers, males are affected approximately as often as females.

Familial pattern. Cigarette smoking among first-degree biologic relatives of people with Nicotine Dependence is more common than among the general population. Evidence for a genetic factor has been documented, but the effect is modest.

304.00   Opioid Dependence
305.50   Opioid Abuse

See Opioid-induced Organic Mental Disorders (p. 151) for a description of Opioid Intoxication and Withdrawal.

This group includes natural opioids, such as heroin and morphine, and synthetics with morphinelike action, which act on opiate receptors. These compounds are prescribed as analgesics, anesthetics, or cough-suppressants. They include codeine, hydromorphone, meperidine, methadone, oxycodone, and others. Several other compounds that have both direct opiatelike agonist effects and antagonist effects are included in this class of substances because they often produce the same physiologic and behavioral effects as pure opioids, e.g., pentazocine and buprenorphine. Prescription opiates are typically taken orally in pill form, but can also be taken intravenously; heroin is typically taken intravenously, but can also be taken by nasal inhalation or smoking. Regular use of these substances leads to remarkably high levels of tolerance.

Although methadone is included in this class, people properly supervised in a methadone maintenance program should not develop any of the Opioid-induced Organic Mental Disorders. When the criteria for one of these diagnoses are met, this indicates that there has been nonmedical use of methadone, in which case the appropriate diagnosis should be made.

Patterns of use. There are two patterns of development of dependence and abuse. In one, which is relatively infrequent, the person originally obtained an opioid by prescription, from a physician, for the treatment of pain or cough-suppression, but has gradually increased the dose and frequency of use on his or her own. The person continues to justify the substance use on the basis of treatment of symptoms, but substance-seeking behavior becomes prominent, and the person may go to several physicians in order to obtain sufficient supplies of the substance.

A second pattern that leads to dependence or abuse involves young people in their teens or early 20s who, with a group of peers, use opioids obtained from illegal sources. Some use an opioid alone to obtain a "high," or euphoria. Others use these substances in combination with amphetamines, cannabis, hallucinogens, or sedatives to enhance the euphoria or to counteract the depressant effect of the opioid. In this pattern, the first use of opioids may have been preceded by a period of "polysubstance use," which may have involved alcohol, amphetamines, cannabis, hallucinogens, nicotine, sedatives, hypnotics, anxiolytics, or prescription and nonprescription cough syrups. The use of these other psychoactive substances generally continues after the use of opioids is established.

Course. Once a pattern of Opioid Abuse or Dependence is established, substance procurement and use generally dominate the person's life.

In Opioid Dependence, the course is a function of the context of the addiction. For example, the vast majority of people who became dependent on heroin in Vietnam did not return to their addiction when back in the United States. In contrast, it is believed that most people who become dependent on opioids in the United States become involved in a chronic behavioral pattern, marked by remissions while in treatment or prison or when the substance is scarce and relapses on returning to a familiar environment in which these substances are available and friends or colleagues also use them.

In the United States, in this century, people with Opioid Dependence have had a high annual death rate (approximately 10 per 1,000) because of the physical complications of the disorder and a life-style often associated with violence. Among those who survive, increasing abstinence is observed with the passage of years, dependence coming to an end, on average, within about nine years after its onset. However, for many people with Opioid Dependence, the dependence continues throughout life.

Prevalence. A community study in the United States, conducted from 1981 to 1983 and using DSM-III criteria, indicated that approximately 0.7% of the adult population had had Opioid Abuse or Dependence at some time in their lives.

304.50   Phencyclidine (PCP) or Similarly Acting Arylcyclohexylamine Dependence
305.90   Phencyclidine (PCP) or Similarly Acting Arylcyclohexylamine Abuse

See Phencyclidine (PCP)- or Similarly Acting Arylcyclohexylamine-induced Organic Mental Disorders (p. 154) for a description of Phencyclidine (PCP) or Similarly Acting Arylcyclohexylamine Intoxication, Delirium, Delusional Disorder, Mood Disorder, and Organic Mental Disorder NOS.

This group of psychoactive substances includes phencyclidine (PCP) and similarly acting compounds such as ketamine (Ketalar) and the thiophene analogue of phencyclidine (TCP). These substances can be taken orally or intravenously, or can be smoked or inhaled. Within this class of substances, phencyclidine is the most commonly used. It is sold on the street under a variety of names, the most common of which are PCP, PeaCe Pill, and angel dust.

Patterns of use. Most people are introduced to PCP when it is present as a contaminant of other illegal psychoactive substances, such as amphetamine and related substances, cannabis, cocaine, or hallucinogens. The person suspects that PCP is the active ingredient and then seeks PCP specifically. PCP is usually taken episodically in binges and "runs" that can last several days. However, there are some people who chronically use the substance on a daily basis.

Whether or not tolerance and withdrawal symptoms develop with use of these substances is currently unclear.

Associated features. Many heavy users of PCP are also heavy users of alcohol and cannabis.

Course. Usually abuse or dependence develops after only a short period of occasional use of the psychoactive substance. The "experimental" user either finds the substance too unpredictable in its effects and abandons further use, or quickly becomes a heavy user and develops abuse or dependence. The motivation for continued use of the substance is apparently its euphoric effect, not avoidance or relief of withdrawal symptoms.

Prevalence. The use of PCP as the predominant substance among people seeking help for dependence on psychoactive substances is relatively rare.

304.10   Sedative, Hypnotic, or Anxiolytic Dependence
305.40   Sedative, Hypnotic, or Anxiolytic Abuse

See Sedative-, Hypnotic-, or Anxiolytic-induced Organic Mental Disorders (p. 158) for a description of Sedative, Hypnotic, or Anxiolytic Intoxication, Withdrawal, Withdrawal Delirium, and Amnestic Disorder.

Hypnotics, or "sleeping pills," include benzodiazepines such as flurazepam, triazolam, and temazepam, and other substances unrelated to benzodiazepines, such as ethchlorvynol, glutethimide, chloral hydrate, methaqualone, and the barbiturates. Benzodiazepines are also used for the treatment of anxiety and are the most commonly prescribed psychoactive medications.

Although these psychoactive substances differ widely in their mechanisms of action, rates of absorption, metabolism, and distribution in the body, at some dose and at some duration of use, they are all capable of producing similar syndromes of intoxication and withdrawal. Substances in this category are usually taken orally.

Patterns of use. There are two patterns of development of dependence and abuse. In one, the person originally obtained the psychoactive substance by prescription from a physician for treatment of anxiety or insomnia, but has gradually increased the dose and frequency of use on his or her own. The person continues to justify the use on the basis of treating symptoms, but substance-seeking behavior becomes prominent, and the person may go to several doctors in order to obtain sufficient supplies of the substance. Tolerance can be remarkable, with doses of more than 100 mg of diazepam daily producing little sedation.

It should be noted that there are people who continue to take benzodiazepine medication according to a physician's direction for a legitimate medical indication such as symptoms of chronic severe anxiety. These people would not ordinarily develop symptoms that meet the criteria for dependence because they are not preoccupied with obtaining the substance, and its use does not interfere with their performing their normal social or occupational roles. On the contrary, the benzodiazepine may make normal functioning possible. Nevertheless, these people are likely to develop "physical dependence" on benzodiazepines in the pharmacologic sense because a withdrawal syndrome would ensue if the use of the substance were terminated abruptly.

A second pattern, more frequent than the first, that leads to dependence involves young people in their teens or early 20s who, with a group of peers, use substances obtained from illegal sources. The initial objective is to obtain a "high," or euphoria, when the substance is used alone. Others use these substances in combination with opioids to enhance the euphoria or to counteract the stimulant effects of cocaine or amphetamine. An initial pattern of intermittent use at parties can lead to daily use and remarkable levels of tolerance. Ingestion of doses of 500 to 1,500 mg of diazepam or its equivalent have been observed, and there is evidence of strong substance-seeking behavior and resort to illegal sources of supply.

Course. The most common course is heavy daily use that results in dependence. A significant number of people with dependence eventually stop using the substance and recover completely, even from the physical complications of the disorder.

Prevalence. A community study in the United States, conducted from 1981 to 1983 and using DSM-III criteria, indicated that approximately 1.1% of the adult population had had Sedative, Hypnotic, or Anxiolytic Abuse or Dependence at some time in their lives.

304.90   Polysubstance Dependence
This category should be used when, for a period of at least six months, the person has repeatedly used at least three categories of psychoactive substances (not including nicotine and caffeine), but no single psychoactive substance has predominated. During this period the criteria have been met for dependence on psychoactive substances as a group, but not for any specific substance.

304.90   Psychoactive Substance Dependence Not Otherwise Specified
This is a residual category for disorders in which there is dependence on a psychoactive substance that cannot be classified according to any of the previous categories (e.g., anticholinergics), or for use as an initial diagnosis in cases of dependence in which the specific substance is not yet known.

305.90   Psychoactive Substance Abuse Not Otherwise Specified
This is a residual category for disorders in which there is abuse of a psychoactive substance that cannot be classified according to any of the previous categories (e.g., anticholinergics), or for use as an initial diagnosis in cases of abuse in which the specific substance is not yet known.

Schizophrenia

The essential features of this disorder are the presence of characteristic psychotic symptoms during the active phase of the illness and functioning below the highest level previously achieved (in children or adolescents, failure to achieve the expected level of social development), and a duration of at least six months that may include characteristic prodromal or residual symptoms. At some phase of the illness Schizophrenia always involves delusions, hallucinations, or certain characteristic disturbances in affect and the form of thought. The diagnosis is made only when it cannot be established that an organic factor initiated and maintained the disturbance. The diagnosis is not made if the symptoms are due to a Mood Disorder or Schizoaffective Disorder.

Some approaches to defining Schizophrenia have emphasized the tendency toward a deteriorating course (Kraepelin), underlying disturbances in certain psychological processes (Bleuler), or pathognomonic symptoms (Schneider). In this manual the concept is not limited to illnesses with a deteriorating course, although a minimal duration of illness is required since some evidence suggests that illnesses of briefer duration (here called Schizophreniform Disorder) are likely to have different external correlates, such as family history and likelihood of recurrence. The approach taken here excludes illnesses without overt psychotic features, which have sometimes been referred to as Latent, Borderline, or Simple Schizophrenia. Such conditions are likely to be diagnosed in this manual as Personality Disorders, e.g., a Schizotypal Personality Disorder. People who develop a major depressive or manic syndrome for an extended period relative to the duration of the disturbance are not classified as having Schizophrenia, but rather as having either a Mood or Schizoaffective Disorder.

Thus, this manual utilizes clinical criteria that include both a minimal duration and a characteristic symptom picture to identify a group of conditions that has validity in terms of differential response to somatic therapy, presence of a familial pattern, and a tendency toward onset in early adult life, recurrence, and deterioration in social and occupational functioning.

Functioning below highest level previously achieved. During the course of the disturbance, functioning in such areas as work, social relations, and self-care is markedly below the highest level achieved before onset of the disorder. If the onset is in childhood or adolescence, there is failure to achieve the expected level of social development. This diagnostic requirement is included so that people with an isolated symptom, such as an encapsulated delusion, but without a reduction in social or work functioning, are not given the diagnosis of Schizophrenia, which typically involves impairment in more than one area of functioning.

Characteristic symptoms involving multiple psychological processes. Invariably there are characteristic disturbances in several of the following areas: content and form of thought, perception, affect, sense of self, volition, relationship to the external world, and psychomotor behavior. It should be noted that no single feature is invariably present or seen only in Schizophrenia.

Content of thought. The major disturbance in the content of thought involves delusions that are often multiple, fragmented, or bizarre (i.e., involving a phenomenon that in the person's culture would be regarded as totally implausible, e.g., thought broadcasting, or being controlled by a dead person). Simple persecutory delusions involving the belief that others are spying on, spreading false rumors about, or planning to harm the person are common. Delusions of reference, in which events, objects, or other people are given particular and unusual significance, usually of a negative or pejorative nature, are also common. For example, the person may be convinced that a television commentator is mocking him.

Certain delusions are observed far more frequently in Schizophrenia than in other psychotic disorders. These include, for instance, the belief or experience that one's thoughts, as they occur, are broadcast from one's head to the external world so that others can hear them (thought broadcasting); that thoughts that are not one's own are inserted into one's mind (thought insertion); that thoughts have been removed from one's head (thought withdrawal); or that one's feelings, impulses, thoughts, or actions are not one's own, but are imposed by some external force (delusions of being controlled). Less commonly, somatic, grandiose, religious, and nihilistic delusions are observed.

Form of thought. A disturbance in the form of thought is often present. This has been referred to as "formal thought disorder," and is different from a disorder in the content of thought. The most common example of this is loosening of associations, in which ideas shift from one subject to another, completely unrelated or only obliquely related subject, without the speaker's displaying any awareness that the topics are unconnected. Statements that lack a meaningful relationship may be juxtaposed, or the person may shift idiosyncratically from one frame of reference to another. When loosening of associations is severe, the person may become incoherent, that is, his or her speech may become incomprehensible.

There may be poverty of content of speech, in which speech is adequate in amount, but conveys little information because it is vague, overly abstract, or overly concrete, repetitive, or stereotyped. The listener can recognize this disturbance by noting that little if any information has been conveyed although the person has spoken at some length. Less common disturbances include neologisms, perseveration, clanging, and blocking.

Perception. The major disturbances in perception are various forms of hallucinations. Although these occur in all modalities, the most common are auditory hallucinations, which frequently involve many voices the person perceives as coming from outside his or her head. The voices may be familiar, and often make insulting remarks; they may be single or multiple. Voices speaking directly to the person or commenting on his or her ongoing behavior are particularly characteristic. Command hallucinations may be obeyed, which sometimes creates danger for the person or others. Occasionally, the auditory hallucinations are of sounds rather than voices.

Tactile hallucinations may be present, and typically involve electrical, tingling, or burning sensations. Somatic hallucinations, such as the sensation of snakes crawling inside the abdomen, are occasionally experienced. Visual, gustatory, and olfactory hallucinations also occur, but with less frequency, and, in the absence of auditory hallucinations, always raise the possibility of an Organic Mental Disorder. Other perceptual abnormalities include sensations of bodily change; hypersensitivity to sound, sight, and smell; illusions; and synesthesias.

Affect. The disturbance often involves flat or inappropriate affect. In flat affect, there are virtually no signs of affective expression; the voice is usually monotonous and the face, immobile. The person may complain that he or she no longer responds with normal emotional intensity or, in extreme cases, no longer has feelings. In inappropriate affect, the affect is clearly discordant with the content of the person's speech or ideation. For example, while discussing being tortured by electrical shocks, a person with Schizophrenia, Disorganized Type, may laugh or smile. Sudden and unpredictable changes in affect involving inexplicable outbursts of anger may occur.

Although these affective disturbances are almost invariably part of the clinical picture, their presence is often difficult to detect except when they are in an extreme form. Furthermore, antipsychotic drugs have effects that may appear similar to the affective flattening seen in Schizophrenia.

Sense of self. The sense of self that gives the normal person a feeling of individuality, uniqueness, and self-direction is frequently disturbed in Schizophrenia. This is sometimes referred to as a loss of ego boundaries, and frequently is evidenced by extreme perplexity about one's own identity and the meaning of existence, or by some of the specific delusions described above, particularly those involving control by an outside force.

Volition. The characteristic disturbances in volition are most readily observed in the residual phase. There is nearly always some disturbance in self-initiated, goal-directed activity, which may grossly impair work or other role functioning. This may take the form of inadequate interest, drive, or ability to follow a course of action to its logical conclusion. Marked ambivalence regarding alternative courses of action can lead to near-cessation of goal-directed activity.

Impaired interpersonal functioning and relationship to the external world. Difficulty in interpersonal relationships is almost invariably present. Often this takes the form of social withdrawal and emotional detachment. When the person is severely preoccupied with egocentric and illogical ideas and fantasies and distorts or excludes the external world, the condition has been referred to as "autism." Some with the disorder, during a phase of the illness, cling to other people, intrude upon strangers, and fail to recognize that excessive closeness makes other people uncomfortable and likely to pull away.

Psychomotor behavior. Various disturbances in psychomotor behavior are observed, particularly in the chronically severe and acutely florid forms of the disorder. There may be a marked decrease in reactivity to the environment, with a reduction in spontaneous movements and activity. In extreme cases the person appears unaware of the nature of the environment (as in catatonic stupor); may maintain a rigid posture and resist efforts to be moved (as in catatonic rigidity); may make apparently purposeless and stereotyped, excited motor movements not influenced by external stimuli (as in catatonic excitement); may voluntarily assume inappropriate or bizarre postures (as in catatonic posturing); or may resist and actively counteract instructions or attempts to be moved (as in catatonic negativism). In addition, odd mannerisms, grimacing, or waxy flexibility may be present.

Associated features. Almost any symptom can occur as an associated feature. The person may appear perplexed, disheveled, or eccentrically groomed or dressed. Abnormalities of psychomotor activity—e.g., pacing, rocking, or apathetic immobility—are common. Frequently there is poverty of speech, that is, a restriction in the amount of spontaneous speech, so that replies to questions tend to be brief, concrete, and unelaborated. Ritualistic or stereotyped behavior associated with magical thinking often occurs. Dysphoric mood is common, and may take the form of depression, anxiety, anger, or a mixture of these. Depersonalization, derealization, ideas of reference, and illusions are often present, as are hypochrondiacal concerns, which may or may not be delusional. Typically, no disturbance in the sensorium is evident, although during a period of exacerbation of the disorder, the person may be confused or even disoriented, or have memory impairment.

Age at onset. Onset is usually during adolescence or early adulthood, but the disorder may begin in middle or late adult life. Many studies indicate a somewhat earlier onset in males than in females.

Course. As noted previously, the diagnosis of Schizophrenia requires that continuous signs of the illness have been present for at least six months, which always includes an active phase with psychotic symptoms. When active or positive symptoms are prominent, negative symptoms, such as social withdrawal and lack of initiative, may be present, but difficult to identify. If the active phase lasts more than six months, it is not necessary to identify a distinct prodromal or residual phase, even though prodromal/residual symptoms have usually been present.

The development of the active phase of the illness is generally preceded by a *prodromal phase* in which there is a clear deterioration from a previous level of functioning. This phase is characterized by social withdrawal, impairment in role functioning, peculiar behavior, neglect of personal hygiene and grooming, blunted or inappropriate affect, disturbances in communication, bizarre ideation, unusual perceptual experiences, and lack of initiative, interests, or energy. Friends and relatives often describe the onset of prodromal symptoms as a change in personality or as no longer "being the same person." The length of this prodromal phase is extremely variable, and its onset may be difficult to date accurately. The prognosis is especially poor when the prodromal phase has taken an insidious, downhill course over many years.

During the *active phase*, psychotic symptoms—e.g., delusions, hallucinations, loosening of associations, incoherence, and catatonic behavior—are prominent. The specific psychotic symptoms are noted in criterion A of the diagnostic criteria (p. 194). In order to make the diagnosis, the psychotic symptoms must persist for at least one week, unless they are successfully treated. Onset of the active phase, either initially or as an exacerbation of a preexisting active phase, may be associated with a psychosocial stressor.

Usually a *residual phase* follows the active phase of the illness. The clinical picture of this phase is similar to that of the prodromal phase, except that affective blunting or flattening and impairment in role functioning tend to be more common in the residual phase. During this phase some of the psychotic symptoms, such as delusions or hallucinations, may persist, but may no longer be accompanied by strong affect.

A return to full premorbid functioning in this disorder is not common. Full remissions do occur, but their frequency is currently a subject of controversy. The most common course is probably one of acute exacerbations with residual impairment between episodes. Residual impairment often increases between episodes during the initial years of the disorder. There is some evidence, however, that in many people with the disorder, the residual symptoms become attenuated in the later phases of the illness.

Numerous studies have indicated a group of factors associated with good prognosis, including absence of premorbid personality disturbance, adequate premorbid social functioning, precipitating events, abrupt onset, onset in mid-life, a clinical picture that involves confusion, and a family history of Mood Disorder.

Because knowledge of the course is very important for planning treatment, and because differences in course may reflect fundamental differences among people with Schizophrenia, a separate digit is provided for coding the course as Subchronic, Chronic, Subchronic with Acute Exacerbation, Chronic with Acute Exacerbation, or In Remission (for criteria, see p. 195).

Since a six-month duration of illness is required for the diagnosis, there is no acute type. (The DSM-III-R diagnosis of Schizophreniform Disorder is the nearest equivalent of the ICD-9-CM concept Acute Schizophrenic Episode. Frequently, an episode of Schizophreniform Disorder will persist for more than six months, in which case the diagnosis should be changed to Schizophrenia.)

Impairment. Invariably, at some point in the disorder as described above, there is impairment in several areas of routine daily functioning, such as work, social relations, and self-care. Supervision may be required to ensure that nutritional and hygienic needs are met and to protect the person from the consequences of poor judgment, cognitive impairment, or actions based on delusions or in response to hallucinations. Between episodes of illness the extent of disability may range from none to disability so severe that institutional care is required.

Complications. Although violent acts performed by people with this disorder often attract public attention, whether their frequency is actually greater than in the general population is not known. What is known is that the life expectancy of people with Schizophrenia is shorter than that of the general population because of an increased suicide rate and death from a variety of other causes.

Premorbid personality. The premorbid personalities of people who develop Schizophrenia are often described as suspicious, introverted, withdrawn, eccentric, or impulsive; Paranoid, Schizoid, Schizotypal, or Borderline Personality Disorder may be present. In such cases, since it can have prognostic significance, the Personality Disorder should be noted on Axis II, followed by "(Premorbid)."

Predisposing factors. The diagnosis is made more commonly among the lower socioeconomic groups. The reasons for this are unclear, but may involve downward social drift, lack of upward socioeconomic mobility, and high stress.

Certain patterns of family interaction have been hypothesized to predispose to the development, onset, relapse, or chronicity of Schizophrenia; but interpretations of the evidence supporting these hypotheses are controversial.

Prevalence. Studies in Europe and Asia, using a relatively narrow concept of Schizophrenia, have reported a lifetime prevalence rate of from 0.2% to almost 1%. Studies in the United States that have used broader criteria and surveyed urban populations have reported higher rates.

Sex ratio. The disorder is apparently equally common in both sexes.

Familial pattern. All investigators have found a higher prevalence of the disorder in first-degree biologic relatives of people with Schizophrenia than would be expected in the general population. Included are studies in which the adopted offspring of people with Schizophrenia have been reared by parents who do not have the disorder. Twin studies consistently show a higher concordance rate of Schizophrenia in monozygotic than in dizygotic twins. However, the experience of being a monozygotic twin does not in itself appear to predispose to the development of Schizophrenia. Although genetic factors have been proven to be involved in the development of the illness, the existence of a substantial discordance rate, even in monozygotic twins, indicates the importance of nongenetic factors.

Differential diagnosis. The diagnosis is made only when it cannot be established that an organic factor initiated and maintained the disturbance. **Organic Mental Disorders** often present with symptoms that suggest Schizophrenia, such as delusions, hallucinations, incoherence, and flat or inappropriate affect. In particular, **Organic Delusional Syndromes, such as those due to amphetamines or phencyclidine**, may cross-sectionally be identical in symptomatology with Schizophrenia. Even though an active phase of Schizophrenia may begin with confusion, the presence of persistent disorientation or memory impairment strongly suggests an Organic Mental Disorder. (Of course, it is possible for a person with Schizophrenia to have a superimposed Organic Mental Disorder.) (See also discussion of etiologic factors of Organic Delusional Syndrome, p. 110.)

Differential diagnosis of Schizophrenia from the psychotic forms of **Mood Disorder** (particularly Bipolar Disorder), and **Schizoaffective Disorder** is of special importance because of the different long-term treatment implications. The differential diagnosis can be difficult, because mood disturbance, particularly with depressive symptoms, is common during all three phases of Schizophrenia. If episodes of marked mood disturbance are present and are confined to the *residual* phase, an additional diagnosis of either **Depressive Disorder NOS** or **Bipolar Disorder NOS** should be considered. An example would be a person with Schizophrenia, Residual Type, Chronic, who develops a superimposed Major Depressive Syndrome of several months' duration without any psychotic symptoms.

If either a full depressive or manic syndrome is present at some time during the *active* phase, Schizoaffective Disorder and a Mood Disorder with Psychotic Features must be ruled out. If the total duration of all episodes of a mood syndrome are *brief* relative to the duration of Schizophrenia (active and residual phases), then the mood disturbance is considered an associated feature of Schizophrenia, and no additional diagnosis need be made. If the total duration of the mood disturbance is *not brief*, then a diagnosis of Schizophrenia is not made, and Schizoaffective Disorder and Mood Disorder with Psychotic Features must be considered.

If delusions or hallucinations (or catatonic symptoms in the case of a Manic Episode) occur exclusively during periods of mood disturbance, the diagnosis is **Mood Disorder with Psychotic Features.** However, if delusions or hallucinations are present for at least two weeks in the absence of mood symptoms, a diagnosis of **Schizoaffective**

Disorder is made. If loose associations, incoherence, catatonic symptoms, and flat affect (in the absence of delusions and hallucinations) overlap with the mood syndrome, then diagnoses of both **Psychotic Disorder NOS** and **Depressive or Bipolar Disorder NOS** are made. **Psychotic Disorder NOS** is also diagnosed in those unusual instances in which one of the psychotic symptoms of Schizophrenia, such as an encapsulated bizarre delusion, is present, but there is apparently no diminution in functioning from the highest previous level.

In **Schizophreniform Disorder**, by definition the duration of the illness is less than six months. The cross-sectional symptom picture may be indistinguishable from Schizophrenia, but emotional turmoil and confusion are more likely to occur in Schizophreniform Disorder. It should be noted that the six-month duration of illness required for Schizophrenia refers to a *continuous* period of illness. Thus, a person with several episodes of Schizophreniform Disorder from each of which there has been full recovery would not be diagnosed as having Schizophrenia merely because the total period of illness exceeded six months.

Delusional Disorder is distinguished from Schizophrenia by the absence of prominent hallucinations, incoherence, loosening of associations, or bizarre delusions (such as delusions of being controlled or thought broadcasting).

In **Autistic Disorder** there often are disturbances in communication and in affect that suggest Schizophrenia. However, the additional diagnosis of Schizophrenia is made only if prominent delusions or hallucinations are also present. Schizophrenia occurring in a child preempts the residual diagnosis of **Pervasive Developmental Disorder NOS.**

In **Obsessive Compulsive Disorder** and **Hypochondriasis,** the person may have overvalued ideas that are difficult to distinguish from delusions; but people with these disorders generally recognize, at least to some degree, that their symptoms and thinking are irrational, even if they are dominated by them.

In **Factitious Disorder with Psychological Symptoms**, "psychotic" symptoms are intentionally produced, and are likely to be present only when the person thinks he or she is being observed.

In **Personality Disorders, especially Schizotypal, Borderline, Schizoid,** and **Paranoid** types, transient psychotic symptoms may be present. However, a return within hours or days to the usual level of functioning distinguishes these disorders from Schizophrenia. It is more difficult to distinguish severe forms of Paranoid and Schizotypal Personality Disorders from Schizophrenia because of the difficulty in determining whether the paranoid ideation is of delusional intensity and whether the oddities of communication and perception are severe enough to meet the criteria for Schizophrenia. Furthermore, it is often difficult to differentiate the prodromal phase of Schizophrenia from manifestations of some of the Personality Disorders since both Personality Disorders and Schizophrenia usually develop during adolescence or early adult life.

Beliefs or experiences of members of religious or other cultural groups may be difficult to distinguish from delusions or hallucinations. When such experiences are shared and accepted by a cultural group, they should not be considered evidence of psychosis.

In **Mental Retardation**, low level of social functioning, oddities of behavior, and impoverished affect and cognition all may suggest Schizophrenia. Both diagnoses should be made in the same person only when there is certainty that the symptoms suggesting Schizophrenia, such as delusions or hallucinations, are definitely present and are not the result of difficulties in communication.

Diagnostic criteria for Schizophrenia

A. Presence of characteristic psychotic symptoms in the active phase: either (1), (2), or (3) for at least one week (unless the symptoms are successfully treated):

(1) two of the following:

(a) delusions
(b) prominent hallucinations (throughout the day for several days or several times a week for several weeks, each hallucinatory experience not being limited to a few brief moments)
(c) incoherence or marked loosening of associations
(d) catatonic behavior
(e) flat or grossly inappropriate affect

(2) bizarre delusions (i.e., involving a phenomenon that the person's culture would regard as totally implausible, e.g., thought broadcasting, being controlled by a dead person)
(3) prominent hallucinations [as defined in (1)(b) above] of a voice with content having no apparent relation to depression or elation, or a voice keeping up a running commentary on the person's behavior or thoughts, or two or more voices conversing with each other

B. During the course of the disturbance, functioning in such areas as work, social relations, and self-care is markedly below the highest level achieved before onset of the disturbance (or, when the onset is in childhood or adolescence, failure to achieve expected level of social development).

C. Schizoaffective Disorder and Mood Disorder with Psychotic Features have been ruled out, i.e., if a Major Depressive or Manic Syndrome has ever been present during an active phase of the disturbance, the total duration of all episodes of a mood syndrome has been brief relative to the total duration of the active and residual phases of the disturbance.

D. Continuous signs of the disturbance for at least six months. The six-month period must include an active phase (of at least one week, or less if symptoms have been successfully treated) during which there were psychotic symptoms characteristic of Schizophrenia (symptoms in A), with or without a prodromal or residual phase, as defined below.

Prodromal phase: A clear deterioration in functioning before the active phase of the disturbance that is not due to a disturbance in mood or to a Psychoactive Substance Use Disorder and that involves at least two of the symptoms listed below.

Residual phase: Following the active phase of the disturbance, persistence of at least two of the symptoms noted below, these not being due to a disturbance in mood or to a Psychoactive Substance Use Disorder.

Prodromal or Residual Symptoms:

(1) marked social isolation or withdrawal
(2) marked impairment in role functioning as wage-earner, student, or homemaker

Diagnostic criteria for Schizophrenia continued

    (3) markedly peculiar behavior (e.g., collecting garbage, talking to self in public, hoarding food)

    (4) marked impairment in personal hygiene and grooming

    (5) blunted or inappropriate affect

    (6) digressive, vague, overelaborate, or circumstantial speech, or poverty of speech, or poverty of content of speech

    (7) odd beliefs or magical thinking, influencing behavior and inconsistent with cultural norms, e.g., superstitiousness, belief in clairvoyance, telepathy, "sixth sense," "others can feel my feelings," overvalued ideas, ideas of reference

    (8) unusual perceptual experiences, e.g., recurrent illusions, sensing the presence of a force or person not actually present

    (9) marked lack of initiative, interests, or energy

Examples: Six months of prodromal symptoms with one week of symptoms from A; no prodromal symptoms with six months of symptoms from A; no prodromal symptoms with one week of symptoms from A and six months of residual symptoms.

E. It cannot be established that an organic factor initiated and maintained the disturbance.

F. If there is a history of Autistic Disorder, the additional diagnosis of Schizophrenia is made only if prominent delusions or hallucinations are also present.

Classification of course. The course of the disturbance is coded in the fifth digit:

1-Subchronic. The time from the beginning of the disturbance, when the person first began to show signs of the disturbance (including prodromal, active, and residual phases) more or less continuously, is less than two years, but at least six months.

2-Chronic. Same as above, but more than two years.

3-Subchronic with Acute Exacerbation. Reemergence of prominent psychotic symptoms in a person with a subchronic course who has been in the residual phase of the disturbance.

4-Chronic with Acute Exacerbation. Reemergence of prominent psychotic symptoms in a person with a chronic course who has been in the residual phase of the disturbance.

5-In Remission. When a person with a history of Schizophrenia is free of all signs of the disturbance (whether or not on medication), "in Remission" should be coded. Differentiating Schizophrenia in Remission from No Mental Disorder requires consideration of overall level of functioning, length of time since the last episode of disturbance, total duration of the disturbance, and whether prophylactic treatment is being given.

0-Unspecified.

When the course is noted as "in Remission," the phenomenologic type should describe the last exacerbation of Schizophrenia, e.g., "295.25 Schizophrenia, Catatonic Type, in Remission." When the phenomenology of the last exacerbation is unknown, it should be noted as "Undifferentiated."

Specify late onset if the disturbance (including the prodromal phase) develops after age 45.

Types

The types are defined by the cross-sectional clinical picture. Some are less stable over time than others, and their prognostic and treatment implications are variable. The diagnosis of a particular type should be based on the predominant clinical picture that occasioned the most recent evaluation or admission to clinical care.

295.2x Catatonic Type

The essential feature of this type is marked psychomotor disturbance, which may involve stupor, negativism, rigidity, excitement, or posturing. Sometimes there is rapid alternation between the extremes of excitement and stupor. Associated features include stereotypies, mannerisms, and waxy flexibility. Mutism is particularly common.

During catatonic stupor or excitement, the person needs careful supervision to avoid hurting himself or herself or others. Medical care may be needed because of malnutrition, exhaustion, hyperpyrexia, or self-inflicted injury.

Although this type was very common several decades ago, it is now rare in Europe and North America.

Diagnostic criteria for 295.2x Catatonic Type

A type of Schizophrenia in which the clinical picture is dominated by any of the following:

(1) catatonic stupor (marked decrease in reactivity to the environment and/or reduction in spontaneous movements and activity) or mutism

(2) catatonic negativism (an apparently motiveless resistance to all instructions or attempts to be moved)

(3) catatonic rigidity (maintenance of a rigid posture against efforts to be moved)

(4) catatonic excitement (excited motor activity, apparently purposeless and not influenced by external stimuli)

(5) catatonic posturing (voluntary assumption of inappropriate or bizarre postures)

295.1x Disorganized Type

The essential features of this type are incoherence, marked loosening of associations, or grossly disorganized behavior, and, in addition, flat or grossly inappropriate affect. There are no systematized delusions (as in Paranoid Type), although fragmentary delusions or hallucinations, in which the content is not organized into a coherent theme, are common.

Associated features include grimaces, mannerisms, hypochondriacal complaints, extreme social withdrawal, and other oddities of behavior.

This clinical picture is usually associated with extreme social impairment, poor premorbid personality, an early and insidious onset, and a chronic course without significant remissions.

In other classifications this type is termed Hebephrenic.

Diagnostic criteria for 295.1x Disorganized Type

A type of Schizophrenia in which the following criteria are met:

A. Incoherence, marked loosening of associations, or grossly disorganized behavior.

B. Flat or grossly inappropriate affect.

C. Does not meet the criteria for Catatonic Type.

295.3x   Paranoid Type

The essential feature of this type of Schizophrenia is preoccupation with one or more systematized delusions or with frequent auditory hallucinations related to a single theme. In addition, symptoms characteristic of the Disorganized and Catatonic Types, such as incoherence, flat or grossly inappropriate affect, catatonic behavior, or grossly disorganized behavior, are absent. When all exacerbations of the disorder meet the criteria for Paranoid Type, the clinician should specify *Stable Type*.

Associated features include unfocused anxiety, anger, argumentativeness, and violence. Often a stilted, formal quality or extreme intensity in interpersonal interactions is noted.

The impairment in functioning may be minimal if the delusional material is not acted upon. Onset tends to be later in life than the other types, and the distinguishing characteristics may be more stable over time. Some evidence suggests that the prognosis for the Paranoid Type, particularly with regard to occupational functioning and capacity for independent living, may be considerably better than for the other types of Schizophrenia.

Diagnostic criteria for 295.3x Paranoid Type

A type of schizophrenia in which there are:

A. Preoccupation with one or more systematized delusions or with frequent auditory hallucinations related to a single theme.

B. *None* of the following: incoherence, marked loosening of associations, flat or grossly inappropriate affect, catatonic behavior, grossly disorganized behavior.

Specify stable type if criteria A and B have been met during all past and present active phases of the illness.

295.9x   Undifferentiated Type

The essential features of the Undifferentiated Type of Schizophrenia are prominent psychotic symptoms (i.e., delusions, hallucinations, incoherence, or grossly disorganized behavior) that cannot be classified in any category previously listed or that meet the criteria for more than one category.

Diagnostic criteria for 295.9x Undifferentiated Type

A type of Schizophrenia in which there are:

A. Prominent delusions, hallucinations, incoherence, or grossly disorganized behavior.

B. Does not meet the criteria for Paranoid, Catatonic, or Disorganized Type.

295.6x   Residual Type

This category should be used when there has been at least one episode of Schizophrenia, but the clinical picture that occasioned the evaluation or admission to clinical care is without prominent psychotic symptoms, though signs of the illness persist. Emotional blunting, social withdrawal, eccentric behavior, illogical thinking, and mild loosening of associations are common. If delusions or hallucinations are present, they are not prominent, and are not accompanied by strong affect.

The course of this type is either chronic or subchronic, since "acute exacerbation," by definition, involves prominent psychotic symptoms, and "in remission" implies no signs of the illness.

Diagnostic criteria for 295.6x Residual Type

A type of Schizophrenia in which there are:

A. Absence of prominent delusions, hallucinations, incoherence, or grossly disorganized behavior.

B. Continuing evidence of the disturbance, as indicated by two or more of the residual symptoms listed in criterion D of Schizophrenia.

Delusional (Paranoid) Disorder

297.10   Delusional (Paranoid) Disorder

The essential feature of this disorder is the presence of a persistent, nonbizarre delusion that is not due to any other mental disorder, such as Schizophrenia, Schizophreniform Disorder, or a Mood Disorder. The diagnosis is made only when it cannot be established that an organic factor initiated and maintained the disturbance.

Apart from the delusion or its ramifications, behavior is not obviously odd or bizarre. Auditory or visual hallucinations, if present, are not prominent. This category was called Paranoid Disorder in DSM-III. However, since delusions are the primary symptom of this disorder and the term *paranoid* has multiple other meanings, which can cause confusion, the term *Delusional Disorder* is used in this manual.

Current evidence from demographic, family, and follow-up studies suggests that Delusional Disorder is probably distinct from both Schizophrenia and Mood Disorders. The differentiation of Delusional Disorder from severe Paranoid Personality Disorder is less clear.

Types and associated features. The following delusional themes are commonly seen in Delusional Disorder: erotomanic, grandiose, jealous, persecutory, and somatic. The type of Delusional Disorder is based on the predominant delusional theme. Cases presenting with more than one delusional theme are frequent.

Erotomanic Type. The central theme of an erotic delusion is that one is loved by another. The delusion usually concerns idealized romantic love and spiritual union rather than sexual attraction. The person about whom this conviction is held is usually of higher status, such as a famous person or a superior at work, and may even be a complete stranger. Efforts to contact the object of the delusion, through telephone calls, letters, gifts, visits, and even surveillance and stalking are common, though occasionally the person keeps the delusion secret.

Whereas in clinical samples most of the cases are female, in forensic samples most are male. Some people with this disorder, particularly males, come into conflict with the law in their efforts to pursue the object of their delusion, or in a misguided effort to ''rescue'' him or her from some imagined danger. The prevalence of erotic delusions is such as to be a significant source of harassment to public figures.

Grandiose Type. Grandiose delusions usually take the form of the person's being convinced that he or she possesses some great, but unrecognized, talent or insight, or has made some important discovery, which he or she may take to various governmental agencies (e.g., the Federal Bureau of Investigation or the U.S. Patent Office). Less common is the delusion that one has a special relationship with a prominent person, such as being the daughter of a movie star or an advisor to the President, or that one is the prominent person, in which case the actual person, if alive, is regarded as an imposter. Grandiose delusions may have a religious content, and people with these delusions can become leaders of religious cults.

Jealous Type. When delusions of jealousy are present, a person is convinced, without due cause, that his or her spouse or lover is unfaithful. Small bits of "evidence," such as disarrayed clothing or spots on the sheets, may be collected and used to justify the delusion. Almost invariably the person with the delusion confronts his or her spouse or lover and may take extraordinary steps to intervene in the imagined infidelity. These attempts may include restricting the autonomy of the spouse or lover by insisting that he or she never leave the house unaccompanied, secretly following the spouse or lover, or investigating the other "lover." The person with the delusion may physically attack the spouse or lover and, more rarely, the other "lover."

Persecutory Type. This is the most common type. The persecutory delusion may be simple or elaborate, and usually involves a single theme or series of connected themes, such as being conspired against, cheated, spied upon, followed, poisoned or drugged, maliciously maligned, harassed, or obstructed in the pursuit of long-term goals. Small slights may be exaggerated and become the focus of a delusional system. In certain cases the focus of the delusion is some injustice that must be remedied by legal action ("querulous paranoia"), and the affected person often engages in repeated attempts to obtain satisfaction by appeal to the courts and other government agencies. People with persecutory delusions are often resentful and angry, and may resort to violence against those they believe are hurting them.

Somatic Type. Somatic delusions occur in several forms. Most common are convictions that the person emits a foul odor from his or her skin, mouth, rectum, or vagina; that he or she has an infestation of insects on or in the skin; that he or she has an internal parasite; that certain parts of his or her body are, contrary to all evidence, misshapen and ugly; or that certain parts of his or her body (e.g., the large intestine) are not functioning. People with somatic delusions usually consult nonpsychiatric physicians for treatment of their perceived somatic conditions.

Age at onset. The age at onset of Delusional Disorder is generally middle or late adult life, but can be at a younger age. In most studies average age at onset has been found to be between 40 and 55.

Course. The course is quite variable. In certain cases, especially of the Persecutory Type, the disorder is chronic. However, even in such cases, waxing and waning of concern with the delusion are common. In other cases, full periods of remission may be followed by subsequent relapses. In yet other cases, the disorder remits within a few months, often without subsequent relapse.

Impairment. Impairment in daily functioning is rare. Intellectual and occupational functioning are usually satisfactory, even when the disorder is chronic. Social and marital functioning, on the other hand, are often impaired. A common characteristic of people with Delusional Disorder is the apparent normality of their behavior and appearance when their delusional ideas are not being discussed or acted upon.

Complications. No information.

Predisposing factors. Immigration, emigration, deafness, and other severe stresses may predispose to the development of Delusional Disorder. There is some evidence that low socioeconomic status also increases the risk of developing this disorder. People with Paranoid, Schizoid, or Avoidant Personality Disorder may also be more likely to develop Delusional Disorder.

Prevalence. Delusional Disorder is relatively uncommon. The best estimate for the population prevalence of the disorder is around 0.03%, which, because of its late age at onset, suggests a lifetime morbidity risk of between 0.05% and 0.1%.

Sex ratio. Delusional Disorder is apparently slightly more common in females than males.

Familial pattern. No information is available regarding the familial pattern of Delusional Disorder itself. However, there is limited evidence that cases of Avoidant and Paranoid Personality Disorders may be especially common among first-degree biologic relatives of people with Delusional Disorder.

Differential diagnosis. The diagnosis is made only when it cannot be established that an organic factor initiated and maintained the disturbance. **Organic Mental Disorders** often present with symptoms that suggest Delusional Disorder. In particular, in the early phase of a **Dementia,** there may be simple persecutory delusions. **Organic Delusional Syndromes,** such as those due to amphetamines or a brain tumor, may cross-sectionally be identical in symptomatology to Delusional Disorder. (See also discussion of etiologic factors of Organic Delusional Syndrome, p. 110.)

In **Schizophrenia, Paranoid Type,** or **Schizophreniform Disorder,** there are certain symptoms, such as prominent hallucinations and bizarre delusions (e.g., delusions of control, or of thought broadcasting, thought withdrawal, or thought insertion), that are not present in Delusional Disorder. Although delusions that others are attempting to control the person's behavior are common in both Delusional Disorder and Schizophrenia, the *experience* of being controlled by alien forces suggests Schizophrenia or Schizophreniform Disorder. Compared with Schizophrenia, Delusional Disorder usually produces less impairment in occupational and social functioning.

The differential diagnosis with **Mood Disorders with Psychotic Features** can be difficult, as the psychotic features associated with Mood Disorders most commonly involve nonbizarre delusions, and prominent hallucinations are unusual. Therefore, the differential diagnosis depends on the temporal relationship of the mood disturbance and the delusions. In a Mood Disorder with Psychotic Features, the onset of the mood disturbance usually precedes the appearance of psychotic symptoms and is present after their remission. Furthermore, in Mood Disorders, the mood symptoms are usually severe. Although depressive symptoms are common in Delusional Disorder, they occur after the onset of the delusions, are usually mild in nature, and often remit while the delusional symptoms persist.

Specifically, if the total duration of all mood disturbances has been *brief* relative to the total duration of the delusional disturbance, then the mood disturbance is considered to be an associated feature of a Delusional Disorder, and no additional diagnosis of a Mood Disorder is given. However, if the total duration of all mood syndromes has *not* been brief relative to the duration of the delusional disturbance, then a diagnosis of a Mood Disorder with Psychotic Features or Psychotic Disorder NOS must be considered. If the delusions are present only during episodes of mood disturbance, then a diagnosis of either Bipolar Disorder with Psychotic Features or Major Depression with Psychotic Features should be made. If the nonbizarre delusions persist in the absence of any mood disturbance, then diagnoses of both Psychotic Disorder NOS and Mood Disorder NOS are made. An example of this would be a person with a five-year history of a fixed persecutory delusion who for most of that time also had recurrent depressive episodes.

Body Dysmorphic Disorder involves a preoccupation with some imagined defect in appearance, but, unlike in Delusional Disorder, Somatic Type, the belief is not of delusional intensity, i.e., the person can acknowledge the possibility that he or she may be exaggerating the extent of the defect or that there may be no defect at all.

In **Paranoid Personality Disorder** there may be paranoid ideation or pathologic jealousy, but there are no delusions. Whenever a person with a Delusional Disorder has a preexisting Personality Disorder, including Paranoid Personality Disorder, the Personality Disorder should be listed on Axis II, followed by "Premorbid" in parentheses.

A diagnosis of **Psychotic Disorder NOS** is made if the duration of nonbizarre delusions is less than a month and there is no apparent psychosocial stressor (as in Brief Reactive Psychosis).

Diagnostic criteria for 297.10 Delusional Disorder

A. Nonbizarre delusion(s) (i.e., involving situations that occur in real life, such as being followed, poisoned, infected, loved at a distance, having a disease, being deceived by one's spouse or lover) of at least one month's duration.

B. Auditory or visual hallucinations, if present, are not prominent [as defined in Schizophrenia, A(1)(b)].

C. Apart from the delusion(s) or its ramifications, behavior is not obviously odd or bizarre.

D. If a Major Depressive or Manic Syndrome has been present during the delusional disturbance, the total duration of all episodes of the mood syndrome has been brief relative to the total duration of the delusional disturbance.

E. Has never met criterion A for Schizophrenia, and it cannot be established that an organic factor initiated and maintained the disturbance.

Specify type: The following types are based on the predominant delusional theme. If no single delusional theme predominates, specify as **Unspecified Type**.

Erotomanic Type
Delusional Disorder in which the predominant theme of the delusion(s) is that a person, usually of higher status, is in love with the subject.

Diagnostic criteria for 297.10 Delusional Disorder continued

Grandiose Type
Delusional Disorder in which the predominant theme of the delusion(s) is one of inflated worth, power, knowledge, identity, or special relationship to a deity or famous person.

Jealous Type
Delusional Disorder in which the predominant theme of the delusion(s) is that one's sexual partner is unfaithful.

Persecutory Type
Delusional Disorder in which the predominant theme of the delusion(s) is that one (or someone to whom one is close) is being malevolently treated in some way. People with this type of Delusional Disorder may repeatedly take their complaints of being mistreated to legal authorities.

Somatic Type
Delusional Disorder in which the predominant theme of the delusion(s) is that the person has some physical defect, disorder, or disease.

Unspecified Type
Delusional Disorder that does not fit any of the previous categories, e.g., persecutory and grandiose themes without a predominance of either; delusions of reference without malevolent content.

Psychotic Disorders Not Elsewhere Classified

This diagnostic class is for psychotic disorders that cannot be classified as either an Organic Mental Disorder, Schizophrenia, Delusional Disorder, or a Mood Disorder with Psychotic Features. There are four specific categories: Brief Reactive Psychosis, Schizophreniform Disorder, Schizoaffective Disorder, and Induced Psychotic Disorder. Finally, there is a residual category, Psychotic Disorder Not Otherwise Specified, for psychotic disorders that do not meet the criteria for any specific psychotic disorder or about which there is inadequate information to make a specific diagnosis. (For a definition of "psychotic," see p. 404.)

298.80 Brief Reactive Psychosis

The essential feature of this disorder is sudden onset of psychotic symptoms of at least a few hours', but no more than one month's, duration, with eventual full return to premorbid level of functioning. The psychotic symptoms appear shortly after one or more events that, singly or together, would be markedly stressful to almost anyone in similar circumstances in that person's culture. The precipitating event(s) may be any major stress, such as the loss of a loved one or the psychological trauma of combat. Invariably there is emotional turmoil, manifested by rapid shifts from one intense affect to another, or overwhelming perplexity or confusion, which the person may acknowledge or which can be judged from the way he or she responds to questions and requests.

To avoid misdiagnosis when a more pervasive disorder is actually involved, Brief Reactive Psychosis should not be diagnosed if any of the prodromal symptoms of Schizophrenia were present before onset of the disturbance or if the person had Schizotypal Personality Disorder. In addition, the diagnosis is not made if the disturbance is due to a psychotic Mood Disorder or if an organic factor initiated and maintained the disturbance.

Associated features. Behavior may be bizarre and may include peculiar postures, outlandish dress, screaming, or muteness. Suicidal or aggressive behavior may also be present. Speech may include inarticulate gibberish or repetition of nonsensical phrases. Affect is often inappropriate. Transient hallucinations or delusions are common. Silly or obviously confabulated answers may be given to factual questions. Disorientation and impairment in recent memory often occur.

Age at onset. The disorder usually appears in adolescence or early adulthood.

Course. The psychotic symptoms generally subside in a day or two. By definition, this diagnosis is not applicable if the psychotic symptoms persist for more than one month. Transient secondary effects, such as loss of self-esteem and mild depression, may persist beyond the one month, but there is eventually full return to the premorbid level of functioning.

Impairment. Supervision may be required to ensure that nutritional and hygienic needs are met and that the person is protected from the consequences of poor judgment, cognitive impairment, or acting on the basis of delusions.

Predisposing factors. Preexisting psychopathology may predispose to the development of this disorder. People with Paranoid, Histrionic, Narcissistic, Schizotypal, or Borderline Personality Disorder are thought to be particularly vulnerable to its development. By definition, situations involving major stress predispose to development of this disorder.

Complications, prevalence, sex ratio, and familial pattern. No information.

Differential diagnosis. The diagnosis is made only when it cannot be established that an organic factor initiated and maintained the disturbance. Organic Mental Disorders, particularly **Delirium, Organic Delusional Syndrome,** or **Intoxication,** can be distinguished from this disorder only on the basis of historical or laboratory information that indicates a known organic factor. (See also discussion of etiologic factors of Organic Delusional Syndrome, p. 110.)

Although by definition this diagnosis is not made if the psychotic symptoms persist for more than one month, the diagnosis can be made soon after onset of the disturbance, without waiting for the expected recovery. In such instances the diagnosis should be qualified as "provisional." If the disturbance continues beyond one month, the diagnosis should be changed to either **Schizophreniform Disorder, Delusional Disorder, Mood Disorder,** or **Psychotic Disorder NOS.**

Manic and Major Depressive Episodes may follow a major psychosocial stressor. The diagnosis of a Manic or Major Depressive Episode preempts the diagnosis of Brief Reactive Psychosis, and should be made when the relevant criteria are met, whether or not the condition is associated with a psychosocial stressor.

People with a **Personality Disorder** may, under stress, develop Brief Reactive Psychosis, in which case both diagnoses should be made.

An episode of **Factitious Disorder with Psychological Symptoms** may have apparently psychotic symptoms and may also be precipitated by a psychosocial stressor, but in such cases there is evidence that the symptoms are intentionally produced.

When **Malingering** presents with apparently psychotic symptoms, there is usually evidence that the illness was feigned for an understandable goal.

Diagnostic criteria for 298.80 Brief Reactive Psychosis

A. Presence of at least one of the following symptoms indicating impaired reality testing (not culturally sanctioned):

Diagnostic criteria for 298.80 Brief Reactive Psychosis continued

      (1) incoherence or marked loosening of associations
      (2) delusions
      (3) hallucinations
      (4) catatonic or disorganized behavior

B. Emotional turmoil, i.e., rapid shifts from one intense affect to another, or overwhelming perplexity or confusion.

C. Appearance of the symptoms in A and B shortly after, and apparently in response to, one or more events that, singly or together, would be markedly stressful to almost anyone in similar circumstances in the person's culture.

D. Absence of the prodromal symptoms of Schizophrenia, and failure to meet the criteria for Schizotypal Personality Disorder before onset of the disturbance.

E. Duration of an episode of the disturbance of from a few hours to one month, with eventual full return to premorbid level of functioning. (When the diagnosis must be made without waiting for the expected recovery, it should be qualified as "provisional.")

F. Not due to a psychotic Mood Disorder (i.e., no full mood syndrome is present), and it cannot be established that an organic factor initiated and maintained the disturbance.

295.40 Schizophreniform Disorder

The essential features of this disorder are identical with those of Schizophrenia, with the exception that the duration, including prodromal, active, and residual phases, is less than six months. Originally, the term *Schizophreniform Disorder* was applied to schizophrenia-like psychoses with a good outcome. In an attempt to convey that concept, the clinician can supplement the diagnosis of Schizophreniform Disorder with additional specification of the presence of good prognostic features. These features have been identified from a large descriptive literature as those that most consistently identify people with schizophrenia-like symptoms who tend to have a good outcome. The presence of at least two of these symptoms suggests, but by no means guarantees, a relatively good prognosis.

Schizophreniform Disorder is currently classified outside the category of Schizophrenia because the evidence linking Schizophreniform Disorder to typical Schizophrenia remains unclear. There is consistent evidence that people with symptoms similar to those of Schizophrenia of less than six months' duration have a better outcome than those with a more prolonged disturbance. Information from family and genetic studies is contradictory: some studies suggest that Schizophreniform Disorder is distinct from classic Schizophrenia, and others suggest that the two are closely related.

The diagnosis of Schizophreniform Disorder is made under two conditions. In the first, the diagnosis is applied to an episode of illness (of less than six months' duration) from which the person has already recovered. In this case, the diagnosis can be made without qualification. In the second instance, the diagnosis is applied to a person who, although still symptomatic, has been so for less than six months. In this case, the diagnosis should be qualified as "provisional," because there is no certainty that the person will actually recover from the disturbance within the required six-month period. (The diagnosis should be changed to Schizophrenia if the clinical picture persists beyond six months.)

Differential diagnosis. Since the diagnostic criteria for **Schizophrenia** and Schizophreniform Disorder differ primarily in terms of duration of the illness, most of the discussion of the differential diagnosis of Schizophrenia (p. 192) applies also to Schizophreniform Disorder, except that the clinical picture in Schizophreniform Disorder is more often characterized by emotional turmoil, fear, confusion, and particularly vivid hallucinations.

Brief Reactive Psychosis usually does not present with the characteristic psychotic symptoms of the active phase of Schizophrenia. However, in those rare instances in which the criteria for both Brief Reactive Psychosis and Schizophreniform Disorder are met (e.g., three weeks of bizarre delusions apparently triggered by a markedly stressful event, without any of the prodromal symptoms of Schizophrenia), the diagnosis of Brief Reactive Psychosis preempts the diagnosis of Schizophreniform Disorder.

Diagnostic criteria for 295.40 Schizophreniform Disorder

A. Meets criteria A and C of Schizophrenia (p. 194).

B. An episode of the disturbance (including prodromal, active, and residual phases) lasts less than six months. (When the diagnosis must be made without waiting for recovery, it should be qualified as "provisional.")

C. Does not meet the criteria for Brief Reactive Psychosis, and it cannot be established that an organic factor initiated and maintained the disturbance.

Specify: without good prognostic features or **with good prognostic features,** i.e., with at least two of the following:
   (1) onset of prominent psychotic symptoms within four weeks of first noticeable change in usual behavior or functioning
   (2) confusion, disorientation, or perplexity at the height of the psychotic episode
   (3) good premorbid social and occupational functioning
   (4) absence of blunted or flat affect

295.70 Schizoaffective Disorder

The term *Schizoaffective Disorder* has been used in many different ways since it was first introduced as a subtype of Schizophrenia, and represents one of the most confusing and controversial concepts in psychiatric nosology. The approach taken in this manual emphasizes the temporal relationship of schizophrenic and mood symptoms. This diagnostic category should be considered for conditions that do not meet the criteria for either Schizophrenia or a Mood Disorder, but that at one time have presented with both a schizophrenic and a mood disturbance and, at another time, with psychotic symptoms but without mood symptoms. The diagnosis is made only when it cannot be established that an organic factor initiated and maintained the disturbance.

Although far from definitive, this description of Schizoaffective Disorder appears to have tentative validity from prognostic, treatment, and family studies as delimiting an entity that appears to be distinct from Mood Disorder. The relationship of Schizoaffective Disorder, as described here, to Schizophrenia remains unclear. Family studies suggest that this disorder may bear a close relationship to Schizophrenia. The distinction between Bipolar and Depressive Types of Schizoaffective Disorder may be important. Several lines of evidence suggest that Schizoaffective Disorder, Bipolar Type, may be more closely related to a Mood Disorder than is Schizoaffective Disorder, Depressive Type.

Since the DSM-III-R term *Mood Disorders* has replaced the DSM-III term *Affective Disorders*, the name of this category should more properly be "Schizomood Disorder." However, the term *Schizoaffective Disorder* is retained for the sake of historical continuity.

Age at onset. Detailed information is lacking, but the typical age at onset is probably in early adulthood.

Course. Studies have suggested that there is some tendency toward a chronic course. The prognosis appears to be somewhat better than that for Schizophrenia, but not nearly so good as that for Mood Disorder.

Prevalence. Detailed information is lacking here as well, but this disorder appears to be less common than Schizophrenia.

Sex ratio. No information.

Familial pattern. Several studies have suggested that there is an increased risk of Schizophrenia in first-degree biologic relatives of people with this disorder. There may also be an increased risk of Mood Disorder in relatives of some people with this disorder, although this has not been firmly established.

Differential diagnosis. The diagnosis is made only when it cannot be established that an organic factor initiated and maintained the disturbance. **Organic Mental Disorders** can present with both bizarre psychotic symptoms and a prominent mood disturbance. (See also discussions of etiologic factors of Organic Delusional Syndrome, p. 110, and Organic Mood Syndrome, p. 112.)

When a disturbance involves both the characteristic symptoms of the active phase of **Schizophrenia** and prominent mood symptoms, the differential diagnosis depends on the temporal relationship of the mood and the psychotic symptoms. In Schizophrenia, either the total duration of all episodes of mood disturbance is brief relative to the total duration of the disturbance, or the mood disturbance occurs only during the residual phase of the disorder.

In **Mood Disorder with Psychotic Features**, there is never a period of at least two weeks in which delusions or hallucinations are present without prominent mood symptoms.

In **Delusional Disorder** the psychotic features are limited to nonbizarre delusions.

Diagnostic criteria for 295.70 Schizoaffective Disorder

A. A disturbance during which, at some time, there is either a Major Depressive or a Manic Syndrome concurrent with symptoms that meet the A criterion of Schizophrenia.

B. During an episode of the disturbance, there have been delusions or hallucinations for at least two weeks, but no prominent mood symptoms.

C. Schizophrenia has been ruled out, i.e., the duration of all episodes of a mood syndrome has not been brief relative to the total duration of the psychotic disturbance.

D. It cannot be established that an organic factor initiated and maintained the disturbance.

Specify: bipolar type (current or previous Manic Syndrome) or
         depressive type (no current or previous Manic Syndrome)

297.30   Induced Psychotic Disorder

The essential feature of this disorder is a delusional system that develops in a second person as a result of a close relationship with another person (the primary case) who already has a psychotic disorder with prominent delusions. The same delusions are at least partly shared by both persons. This diagnosis is not made in people who present evidence of a psychotic disorder (or the prodromal symptoms of Schizophrenia) immediately before onset of the delusion.

The content of the delusion is usually within the realm of possibility, and often is based on common past experiences of the two people. Occasionally, bizarre delusions may be induced. Usually the primary person with the psychotic disorder is the dominant one in the relationship and gradually imposes his or her delusional system on the more passive and initially healthy second person. These people usually have lived together a long time, and are isolated from contact with other people.

Associated features. If the relationship with the primary person who has the psychotic disorder is interrupted, usually the delusional beliefs in the second person will diminish or disappear. Although most commonly seen in relationships of only two people (known as *Folie à deux*), cases have been reported involving up to twelve people in a family. People with this disorder rarely seek treatment, and secondary cases are usually brought to light when the primary person receives treatment.

Age at onset. Variable.

Course. The course is usually chronic in that this disorder occurs almost invariably in relationships that are longstanding and resistant to being altered by external forces.

Impairment. Impairment is generally less severe than for Delusional Disorder or Schizophrenia, as often only a portion of the primary person's delusional system is adopted.

Prevalence. Rare.

Sex ratio. More common among females.

Complications and familial pattern. No information.

Differential Diagnosis. In **Delusional Disorder, Schizophrenia,** and **Schizoaffective Disorder,** there is either no close relationship with a dominant person who has a psychotic disorder or, if there is such a person, the psychotic symptoms (or prodromal symptoms, in the case of Schizophrenia) precede the onset of any shared delusions.

Diagnostic criteria for 297.30 Induced Psychotic Disorder

A. A delusion develops (in a second person) in the context of a close relationship with another person, or persons, with an already established delusion (the primary case).

B. The delusion in the second person is similar in content to that in the primary case.

C. Immediately before onset of the induced delusion, the second person did not have a psychotic disorder or the prodromal symptoms of Schizophrenia.

298.90 Psychotic Disorder Not Otherwise Specified (Atypical Psychosis)

Disorders in which there are psychotic symptoms (delusions, hallucinations, incoherence, marked loosening of associations, catatonic excitement or stupor, or grossly disorganized behavior) that do not meet the criteria for any other nonorganic psychotic disorder. This category should also be used for psychoses about which there is inadequate information to make a specific diagnosis. (This is preferable to "Diagnosis Deferred," and can be changed if more information becomes available.) This diagnosis is made only when it cannot be established that an organic factor initiated and maintained the disturbance.

Examples:

(1) psychoses with unusual features, e.g., persistent auditory hallucinations as the only disturbance

(2) postpartum psychoses that do not meet the criteria for an Organic Mental Disorder, psychotic Mood Disorder, or any other psychotic disorder

(3) psychoses with confusing clinical features that make a more specific diagnosis impossible

Mood Disorders

The essential feature of this group of disorders is a disturbance of mood, accompanied by a full or partial Manic or Depressive Syndrome, that is not due to any other physical or mental disorder. Mood refers to a prolonged emotion that colors the whole psychic life; it generally involves either depression or elation. In DSM-III this diagnostic class was called Affective Disorders.

The organization of the text for the Mood Disorders departs from the usual method of presentation in order to avoid redundancy, and includes the following:

Terminology used in the classification of Mood Disorders, p. 213
Subclassification of Mood Disorders, p. 214
Manic Episode, p. 214
Hypomanic Episode, p. 218
Major Depressive Episode, p. 218
   Chronic Type, p. 224
   Melancholia, p. 224
   Seasonal pattern, p. 224
BIPOLAR DISORDERS, p. 225
   Bipolar Disorder, p. 225
   Cyclothymia, p. 226
   Bipolar Disorder NOS, p. 228
DEPRESSIVE DISORDERS, p. 228
   Major Depression, p. 228
   Dysthymia, p. 230
   Depressive Disorder NOS, p. 233

Terminology used in classification of Mood Disorders. A *mood syndrome* (depressive or manic) is a group of mood and associated symptoms that occur together for a minimal duration of time. For example, the Major Depressive Syndrome is defined as depressed mood or loss of interest, of at least two weeks' duration, accompanied by several associated symptoms, such as weight loss and difficulty concentrating. Mood syndromes can occur as part of a Mood Disorder, as part of a nonmood psychotic disorder (e.g., Schizoaffective Disorder), or as part of an Organic Mental Disorder (e.g., Organic Mood Disorder).

A *mood episode* (major depressive, manic, or hypomanic) is a mood syndrome that is not due to a known organic factor and is not part of a nonmood psychotic disorder (e.g., Schizophrenia, Schizoaffective Disorder, or Delusional Disorder). For example, a Major Depressive Episode is a Major Depressive Syndrome (as defined above) in which it cannot be established that an organic factor initiated and maintained the disturbance and the presence of a nonmood psychotic disorder has been ruled out.

A *mood disorder* is determined by the pattern of mood episodes. For example, the diagnosis of Major Depression is made when there have been one or more Major Depressive Episodes without a history of a Manic or unequivocal Hypomanic Episode.

Subclassification of Mood Disorders. Mood Disorders are divided into Bipolar Disorders and Depressive Disorders. The essential feature of Bipolar Disorders is the presence of one or more Manic or Hypomanic Episodes (usually with a history of Major Depressive Episodes). The essential feature of Depressive Disorders is one or more periods of depression without a history of either Manic or Hypomanic Episodes.

There are two Bipolar Disorders: Bipolar Disorder, in which there is one or more Manic Episodes (usually with one or more Major Depressive Episodes); and Cyclothymia, in which there are numerous Hypomanic Episodes and numerous periods with depressive symptoms. Disorders with Hypomanic and full Major Depressive Episodes, sometimes referred to as "Bipolar II," are included in the residual category of Bipolar Disorder NOS.

There are two Depressive Disorders: Major Depression, in which there is one or more Major Depressive Episodes; and Dysthymia, in which there is a history of a depressed mood more days than not for at least two years and in which, during the first two years of the disturbance, the condition did not meet the criteria for a Major Depressive Episode. In many cases of Dysthymia, there are superimposed Major Depressions.

The current state of Major Depression or Bipolar Disorder is described with a fifth-digit code. If the criteria for a Major Depressive or Manic Episode are currently met, the episode is subclassified as either: mild, moderate, severe without psychotic features, or with psychotic features. If the criteria are currently not met, the fifth-digit code indicates whether the disorder is in partial or in full remission.

In addition, a current Major Depressive Episode can be specified as:

melancholic type—a typically severe form of a Major Depressive Episode that is believed to be particularly responsive to somatic therapy (see p. 224 for criteria); or

chronic—the current episode has lasted two consecutive years without a period of two months or longer in which there have been no depressive symptoms.

For Bipolar Disorder, Bipolar Disorder NOS, Recurrent Major Depression, and Depressive Disorder NOS, a further specification is:

seasonal pattern—a regular cyclic relationship between onset of the mood episodes and a particular 60-day period of the year (see p. 224 for criteria).

Manic Episode

The essential feature of a Manic Episode is a distinct period during which the predominant mood is either elevated, expansive, or irritable, and there are associated symptoms of the Manic Syndrome. The disturbance is sufficiently severe to cause marked impairment in occupational functioning or in usual social activities or relationships with others, or to require hospitalization to prevent harm to self or others. The associated symptoms include inflated self-esteem or grandiosity (which may be delusional), decreased need for sleep, pressure of speech, flight of ideas, distractibility, increased involvement in goal-directed activity, psychomotor agitation, and excessive involvement in pleasurable activities which have a high potential for painful consequences that the person often does not recognize. The diagnosis is made only if it cannot be established that an organic factor initiated and maintained the disturbance. In addition, the diagnosis is not made if the disturbance is superimposed on Schizophrenia, Schizophreniform Disorder, Delusional Disorder, or Psychotic Disorder NOS, or if the criteria for Schizoaffective Disorder are met.

The elevated mood may be described as euphoric, unusually good, cheerful, or high, often having an infectious quality for the uninvolved observer, but recognized as excessive by those who know the person well. The expansive quality of the mood disturbance is characterized by unceasing and unselective enthusiasm for interacting with people and seeking involvement with other aspects of the environment. Although elevated mood is considered the prototypic symptom, the predominant mood disturbance may be irritability, which may be most apparent when the person is thwarted.

Characteristically, there is inflated self-esteem, ranging from uncritical self-confidence to marked grandiosity, which may be delusional. For instance, the person may give advice on matters about which he or she has no special knowledge, such as how to run a mental hospital or the United Nations. Despite lack of any particular talent, the person may start a novel, compose music, or seek publicity for some impractical invention. Grandiose delusions involving a special relationship to God or some well-known figure from the political, religious, or entertainment world are common.

Almost invariably there is a decreased need for sleep; the person awakens several hours before the usual time, full of energy. When the sleep disturbance is severe, the person may go for days without any sleep at all, yet not feel tired.

Manic speech is typically loud, rapid, and difficult to interrupt. Often it is full of jokes, puns, plays on words, and amusing irrelevancies. It may become theatrical, with dramatic mannerisms and singing. Sounds rather than meaningful conceptual relationships may govern word choice (clanging). If the person's mood is more irritable than expansive, his or her speech may be marked by complaints, hostile comments, and angry tirades.

Frequently there is flight of ideas, i.e., a nearly continuous flow of accelerated speech, with abrupt changes from topic to topic, usually based on understandable associations, distracting stimuli, or plays on words. When flight of ideas is severe, speech may be disorganized and incoherent. However, loosening of associations and incoherence may occur even when there is no flight of ideas, particularly if the person is on medication.

Distractibility is usually present, and is evidenced by rapid changes in speech or activity as a result of responding to various irrelevant external stimuli, such as background noise, or signs or pictures on the wall.

The increase in goal-directed activity often involves excessive planning of, and participation in, multiple activities (e.g., sexual, occupational, political, religious). Almost invariably there is increased sociability, which includes efforts to renew old acquaintanceships and calling friends at all hours of the night. The person does not recognize the intrusive, domineering, and demanding nature of these interactions. Frequently, expansiveness, unwarranted optimism, grandiosity, and lack of judgment lead to such activities as buying sprees, reckless driving, foolish business investments, and sexual behavior unusual for the person. Often the activities have a disorganized, flamboyant, or bizarre quality, for example, dressing in colorful or strange garments, wearing excessive, poorly applied makeup, or distributing candy, money, or advice to passing strangers.

Associated features. Frequently the person does not recognize that he or she is ill and resists all efforts to be treated. Another common associated feature is lability of mood, with rapid shifts to anger or depression. The depression, expressed by tearfulness, suicidal threats, or other depressive symptoms, may last moments, hours, or, more rarely, days. Occasionally the depressive and manic symptoms occur simultaneously, or may alternate rapidly within a few days. Less often, in Bipolar Disorder, Mixed, the depressive symptoms are prominent and last at least a full day, and there is the full symptom picture of both Manic and Major Depressive Episodes.

When delusions or hallucinations are present, their content is usually clearly consistent with the predominant mood (mood-congruent). God's voice may be heard explaining that the person has a special mission. Persecutory delusions may be based on the idea that the person is being persecuted because of some special relationship or attribute. Less commonly, the content of the hallucinations or delusions has no apparent relationship to the predominant mood (mood-incongruent).

Catatonic symptoms, such as stupor, mutism, negativism, and posturing, may be present.

Age at onset. Retrospective studies indicate that the mean age at onset is in the early 20s. However, some studies indicate that a sizable number of new cases appear after age 50.

Course. Manic Episodes typically begin suddenly, with a rapid escalation of symptoms over a few days. The episodes usually last from a few days to months, and are briefer and end more abruptly than Major Depressive Episodes.

Impairment. By definition, there is considerable impairment in social and occupational functioning. Often there is a need for protection from the consequences of poor judgment and hyperactivity, which often results in involuntary hospitalization.

Complications. The most common complications of a Manic Episode are Psychoactive Substance Abuse and the consequences of actions resulting from impaired judgment, such as financial losses and illegal activities.

Predisposing factors. Frequently Manic Episodes follow psychosocial stressors. Antidepressant somatic treatment (drugs or ECT) may precipitate a Manic Episode. Childbirth sometimes precipitates a Manic Episode.

Differential diagnosis of Manic Episode. The diagnosis is made only when it cannot be established that an organic factor initiated and maintained the disturbance. **Organic Mood Syndromes** with mania may be due to such psychoactive substances as amphetamines or steroids, or to some other known organic factor, such as multiple sclerosis (see discussion of etiologic factors of Organic Mood Syndrome, p. 112). A Manic Episode should be diagnosed in cases that are apparently precipitated by somatic antidepressant treatment (e.g., drugs, ECT). Some investigators consider a postpartum Manic Episode to have an "organic" etiology. However, because of the difficulty of distinguishing the psychological and physiologic stresses associated with pregnancy and delivery, in this classification such episodes are not considered Organic Mood Syndromes, and should be diagnosed as Manic Episodes.

In **Attention-deficit Hyperactivity Disorder** there is persistent excessive activity and restlessness that may suggest a Manic Episode. However, the mood is not abnormally expansive or elevated and the disturbance does not have the relatively clear onset that is characteristic of a Manic Episode.

In **Schizophrenia, Paranoid Type,** there may be irritability, anger, and psychotic symptoms that are difficult to distinguish from similar features of a Manic Episode. In such instances it may be necessary to rely on features that, on a statistical basis, are associated differentially with the two conditions. For example, the diagnosis of a Manic Episode is more likely if there is a family history of Mood Disorder, good premorbid adjustment, and a previous episode of a Mood Disorder from which there was complete recovery.

In **Hypomanic Episodes** the mood disturbance is not sufficiently severe to cause marked impairment in social or occupational functioning or to require hospitalization.

Diagnostic criteria for Manic Episode

Note: A "Manic Syndrome" is defined as including criteria A, B, and C below. A "Hypomanic Syndrome" is defined as including criteria A and B, but not C, i.e., no marked impairment.

A. A distinct period of abnormally and persistently elevated, expansive, or irritable mood.

B. During the period of mood disturbance, at least three of the following symptoms have persisted (four if the mood is only irritable) and have been present to a significant degree:

(1) inflated self-esteem or grandiosity
(2) decreased need for sleep, e.g., feels rested after only three hours of sleep
(3) more talkative than usual or pressure to keep talking
(4) flight of ideas or subjective experience that thoughts are racing
(5) distractibility, i.e., attention too easily drawn to unimportant or irrelevant external stimuli
(6) increase in goal-directed activity (either socially, at work or school, or sexually) or psychomotor agitation
(7) excessive involvement in pleasurable activities which have a high potential for painful consequences, e.g., the person engages in unrestrained buying sprees, sexual indiscretions, or foolish business investments

C. Mood disturbance sufficiently severe to cause marked impairment in occupational functioning or in usual social activities or relationships with others, or to necessitate hospitalization to prevent harm to self or others.

D. At no time during the disturbance have there been delusions or hallucinations for as long as two weeks in the absence of prominent mood symptoms (i.e., before the mood symptoms developed or after they have remitted).

E. Not superimposed on Schizophrenia, Schizophreniform Disorder, Delusional Disorder, or Psychotic Disorder NOS.

F. It cannot be established that an organic factor initiated and maintained the disturbance. **Note:** Somatic antidepressant treatment (e.g., drugs, ECT) that apparently precipitates a mood disturbance should not be considered an etiologic organic factor.

(continued)

Diagnostic criteria for Manic Episode continued

Manic Episode codes: fifth-digit code numbers and criteria for severity of current state of Bipolar Disorder, Manic or Mixed:

1-Mild: Meets minimum symptom criteria for a Manic Episode (or almost meets symptom criteria if there has been a previous Manic Episode).

2-Moderate: Extreme increase in activity or impairment in judgment.

3-Severe, without Psychotic Features: Almost continual supervision required in order to prevent physical harm to self or others.

4-With Psychotic Features: Delusions, hallucinations, or catatonic symptoms. If possible, **specify** whether the psychotic features are *mood-congruent* or *mood-incongruent*.

Mood-congruent psychotic features: Delusions or hallucinations whose content is entirely consistent with the typical manic themes of inflated worth, power, knowledge, identity, or special relationship to a deity or famous person.

Mood-incongruent psychotic features: Either (a) or (b):

(a) Delusions or hallucinations whose content does *not* involve the typical manic themes of inflated worth, power, knowledge, identity, or special relationship to a deity or famous person. Included are such symptoms as persecutory delusions (not directly related to grandiose ideas or themes), thought insertion, and delusions of being controlled.

(b) Catatonic symptoms, e.g., stupor, mutism, negativism, posturing.

5-In Partial Remission: Full criteria were previously, but are not currently, met; some signs or symptoms of the disturbance have persisted.

6-In Full Remission: Full criteria were previously met, but there have been no significant signs or symptoms of the disturbance for at least six months.

0-Unspecified.

Hypomanic Episode

The essential feature of a Hypomanic Episode is a distinct period in which the predominant mood is either elevated, expansive, or irritable and there are associated symptoms of the Manic Syndrome. By definition, the disturbance is not severe enough to cause marked impairment in social or occupational functioning or to require hospitalization (as required in the diagnosis of a Manic Episode). The associated features of Hypomanic Episodes are similar to those of a Manic Episode except that delusions are never present and all other symptoms tend to be less severe than in Manic Episodes.

Major Depressive Episode

The essential feature of a Major Depressive Episode is either depressed mood (or possibly, in children or adolescents, an irritable mood) or loss of interest or pleasure in all, or almost all, activities, and associated symptoms, for a period of at least two weeks. The symptoms represent a change from previous functioning and are relatively persistent, that is, they occur for most of the day, nearly every day, during at least a two-week period. The associated symptoms include appetite disturbance, change in weight, sleep disturbance, psychomotor agitation or retardation, decreased energy, feelings of worthlessness or excessive or inappropriate guilt, difficulty thinking or concentrating, and recurrent thoughts of death, or suicidal ideation or attempts. The diagnosis is made only if it cannot be established that an organic factor initiated and maintained the disturbance and the disturbance is not the normal reaction to the loss of a loved one (Uncomplicated Bereavement). In addition, the diagnosis is not made if the disturbance is superimposed on Schizophrenia, Schizophreniform Disorder, Delusional Disorder, or Psychotic Disorder NOS, or if the criteria for Schizoaffective Disorder are met.

A person with depressed mood will usually describe feeling depressed, sad, hopeless, discouraged, "down in the dumps," or some other colloquial equivalent. In some cases, although the person may deny feeling depressed, the presence of depressed mood can be inferred from others' observing that the person looks sad or depressed.

Loss of interest or pleasure is probably always present in a Major Depressive Episode to some degree, and is often described by the person as not being as interested in usual activities as previously, "not caring anymore," or, more rarely, a painful inability to experience pleasure. The person may not complain of loss of interest or pleasure, but family members generally will notice withdrawal from friends and family and neglect of avocations that were previously a source of pleasure.

Appetite is frequently disturbed, loss of appetite being the more common, but increased appetite sometimes being evident. When loss of appetite is severe, there may be significant weight loss or, in the case of children, failure to make expected weight gains. When appetite is markedly increased, there may be significant weight gain.

Sleep is commonly disturbed, the more frequent complaint being insomnia, but sometimes hypersomnia. The insomnia may involve difficulty falling asleep (initial insomnia), waking up during sleep and then returning to sleep only with difficulty (middle insomnia), or early morning awakening (terminal insomnia). Hypersomnia may involve sleeping for a longer period of time than is usual, daytime sleepiness, or taking excessive naps. Sometimes the sleep disturbance, rather than the depressed mood or loss of interest or pleasure, is the main symptom that brings the person into treatment (see Sleep Disorders, p. 297).

Psychomotor agitation takes the form of inability to sit still, pacing, hand-wringing, pulling or rubbing of hair, skin, clothing, or other objects. Psychomotor retardation may take the form of slowed speech, increased pauses before answering, soft or monotonous speech, slowed body movements, a markedly decreased amount of speech (poverty of speech), or muteness. A decrease in energy level is almost invariably present, and is experienced as sustained fatigue even in the absence of physical exertion. The smallest task may seem difficult or impossible to accomplish.

The sense of worthlessness varies from feelings of inadequacy to completely unrealistic negative evaluations of one's worth. The person may reproach himself or herself for minor failings that are exaggerated and search the environment for cues confirming the negative self-evaluation. Guilt may be expressed as an excessive reaction to either current or past failings or as exaggerated responsibility for some untoward or tragic event. The sense of worthlessness or guilt may be of delusional proportions.

Difficulty in concentrating, slowed thinking, and indecisiveness are frequent. The person may complain of memory difficulty and appear easily distracted.

Thoughts of death (not just fear of dying) are common. Often there is the belief that the person or others would be better off dead. There may be suicidal thoughts, with or without a specific plan, or suicide attempts.

Associated features. Commonly associated features include tearfulness, anxiety, irritability, brooding or obsessive rumination, excessive concern with physical health, panic attacks, and phobias.

When delusions or hallucinations are present, their content is usually clearly consistent with the predominant mood (mood-congruent). A common delusion is that one is being persecuted because of a moral transgression or some personal inadequacy. There may be nihilistic delusions of world or personal destruction, somatic delusions of cancer or other serious illness, or delusions of poverty. Hallucinations, when present, are usually transient and not elaborate, and may involve voices that berate the person for his or her shortcomings or sins.

Less commonly the content of the hallucinations or delusions has no apparent relationship to the mood disturbance (mood-incongruent). This is particularly the case with persecutory delusions, in which the person may be at a loss to explain why he or she should be the object of persecution. Less common mood-incongruent psychotic symptoms include thought insertion, thought broadcasting, and delusions of control.

Age-specific features. Although the essential features of a Major Depressive Episode are similar in children, adolescents, and adults, there are some differences.

In prepubertal children with a Major Depressive Episode, somatic complaints, psychomotor agitation, and mood-congruent hallucinations (usually only a single voice talking to the child) are particularly frequent.

In children with a Major Depressive Episode, Anxiety Disorders of Childhood (Separation Anxiety Disorder, Overanxious Disorder, and Avoidant Disorder of Childhood or Adolescence) and phobias are common.

In adolescents, negativistic or frankly antisocial behavior and use of alcohol or illicit drugs may be present and justify the additional diagnoses of Oppositional Defiant Disorder, Conduct Disorder, or Psychoactive Substance Abuse or Dependence. Feelings of wanting to leave home or of not being understood and approved of, restlessness, grouchiness, and aggression are common. Sulkiness, a reluctance to cooperate in family ventures, and withdrawal from social activities, with retreat to one's room, are frequent. School difficulties are likely. There may be inattention to personal appearance and increased emotionality, with particular sensitivity to rejection in love relationships.

In elderly adults some of the symptoms of depression, e.g., disorientation, memory loss, and distractibility, may suggest Dementia. Loss of interest or pleasure in the person's usual activities may appear as apathy; difficulty in concentration, as inattentiveness. These symptoms make the differential diagnosis of "pseudodementia" (due to depression) from true Dementia (an Organic Mental Disorder) particularly difficult (p. 106).

Age at onset. The average age at onset is in the late 20s, but a Major Depressive Episode may begin at any age, including infancy.

Course. The onset of a Major Depressive Episode is variable, the symptoms usually developing over days to weeks; in some cases, however, it may be sudden (e.g., when associated with severe psychosocial stress). In some instances prodromal symptoms—e.g., generalized anxiety, panic attacks, phobias, or mild depressive symptoms—may occur over a period of several months.

The duration of a Major Depressive Episode is also variable. Untreated, the episode typically lasts six months or longer. Usually there is a complete remission of symptoms, and general functioning returns to the premorbid level; but in a large proportion of cases, some symptoms of the episode persist for as long as two years without a period of two months or longer without significant depressive symptoms. These episodes are specified as *Chronic Type.*

Impairment. In Major Depressive Episodes the degree of impairment varies, but there is always some interference in social and occupational functioning. If impairment is severe, the person may be totally unable to function socially or occupationally, or even to feed or clothe himself or herself or maintain minimal personal hygiene.

Complications. The most serious complication of a Major Depressive Episode is suicide.

Predisposing factors. Chronic physical illness and Psychoactive Substance Dependence, particularly Alcohol and Cocaine Dependence, apparently predispose to the development of a Major Depressive Episode. Frequently a Major Depressive Episode follows a psychosocial stressor, particularly death of a loved one, marital separation, or divorce. Childbirth sometimes precipitates a Major Depressive Episode.

Differential diagnosis of Major Depressive Episode. The diagnosis is made only when it cannot be established that an organic factor initiated and maintained the disturbance. An **Organic Mood Syndrome with depression** may be due to substances such as reserpine, to infectious diseases such as influenza, or to hypothyroidism (see discussion of etiologic factors of Organic Mood Syndrome, p. 112). Some investigators consider a postpartum depressive episode to have an "organic" etiology. However, because of the difficulty of separating the psychological and physiologic stresses associated with pregnancy and delivery, in this classification such episodes are not considered Organic Mood Syndromes, and are diagnosed as Major Depressive Episodes.
Primary Degenerative Dementia of the Alzheimer Type and **Multi-infarct Dementia,** because of the presence of disorientation, apathy, and complaints of difficulty concentrating or of memory loss, may be difficult to distinguish from a Major Depressive Episode occurring in the elderly. If the presenting symptoms suggesting Dementia are significantly more prominent than the depressive ones, then the diagnosis should be **Dementia with depression.** If the symptoms suggesting a Major Depressive Episode are at least as prominent as those suggesting Dementia, it is best to diagnose a Major Depressive Episode and assume that the symptoms suggesting Dementia represent a **pseudodementia** that is a manifestation of the Major Depressive Episode. In such cases the successful treatment of the Major Depressive Episode often results in disappearance of the symptoms suggesting Dementia, which indicates that the appropriate diagnosis was Major Depression. If the symptoms of the Dementia persist, this suggests that the appropriate diagnosis was **Dementia with depression.**
If a **psychological reaction to the functional impairment associated with a physical illness** that does not involve the central nervous system causes a depression that meets the full criteria for a Major Depressive Episode, the Major Depression should be recorded on Axis I, the physical disorder on Axis III, and the severity of the psychosocial stressor on Axis IV. Examples would include the psychological reaction to amputation of a leg or to the development of a life-threatening or incapacitating illness.
In **Schizophrenia** there are usually some depressive symptoms. If an episode of depression is superimposed on the residual phase of Schizophrenia, or if it occurs briefly during the active phase, the additional diagnosis of either Depressive Disorder NOS or Adjustment Disorder with Depressed Mood may be made, but not Major Depression. A person with **Schizophrenia, Catatonic Type,** may appear to be with-

drawn and depressed, and it may be difficult to distinguish this condition from Major Depression with psychomotor retardation. An amobarbital interview can often be helpful in making this distinction. However, when the differential is still unclear, it may be necessary to rely on symptoms that, on a statistical basis, are associated differentially with the two disorders. For example, the diagnosis of a Major Depressive Episode is more likely if there is a family history of Mood Disorder, good premorbid adjustment, and a previous episode of mood disturbance from which there was complete recovery.

In **Schizoaffective Disorder** there are periods of at least two weeks during which there have been delusions or hallucinations in the absence of prominent mood disturbance.

Uncomplicated Bereavement is distinguished from a Major Depressive Episode and is not considered a mental disorder even when associated with the full depressive syndrome. However, morbid preoccupation with worthlessness, suicidal ideation, marked functional impairment or psychomotor retardation, or prolonged duration suggests that bereavement is complicated by a Major Depressive Episode.

Diagnostic criteria for Major Depressive Episode

Note: A "Major Depressive Syndrome" is defined as criterion A below.

A. At least five of the following symptoms have been present during the same two-week period and represent a change from previous functioning; at least one of the symptoms is either (1) depressed mood, or (2) loss of interest or pleasure. (Do not include symptoms that are clearly due to a physical condition, mood-incongruent delusions or hallucinations, incoherence, or marked loosening of associations.)

   (1) depressed mood (or can be irritable mood in children and adolescents) most of the day, nearly every day, as indicated either by subjective account or observation by others

   (2) markedly diminished interest or pleasure in all, or almost all, activities most of the day, nearly every day (as indicated either by subjective account or observation by others of apathy most of the time)

   (3) significant weight loss or weight gain when not dieting (e.g., more than 5% of body weight in a month), or decrease or increase in appetite nearly every day (in children, consider failure to make expected weight gains)

   (4) insomnia or hypersomnia nearly every day

   (5) psychomotor agitation or retardation nearly every day (observable by others, not merely subjective feelings of restlessness or being slowed down)

   (6) fatigue or loss of energy nearly every day

   (7) feelings of worthlessness or excessive or inappropriate guilt (which may be delusional) nearly every day (not merely self-reproach or guilt about being sick)

   (8) diminished ability to think or concentrate, or indecisiveness, nearly every day (either by subjective account or as observed by others)

   (9) recurrent thoughts of death (not just fear of dying), recurrent suicidal ideation without a specific plan, or a suicide attempt or a specific plan for committing suicide

Diagnostic criteria for Major Depressive Episode continued

B. (1) It cannot be established that an organic factor initiated and maintained the disturbance

(2) The disturbance is not a normal reaction to the death of a loved one (Uncomplicated Bereavement)

Note: Morbid preoccupation with worthlessness, suicidal ideation, marked functional impairment or psychomotor retardation, or prolonged duration suggest bereavement complicated by Major Depression.

C. At no time during the disturbance have there been delusions or hallucinations for as long as two weeks in the absence of prominent mood symptoms (i.e., before the mood symptoms developed or after they have remitted).

D. Not superimposed on Schizophrenia, Schizophreniform Disorder, Delusional Disorder, or Psychotic Disorder NOS.

Major Depressive Episode codes: fifth-digit code numbers and criteria for severity of current state of Bipolar Disorder, Depressed, or Major Depression:

1-Mild: Few, if any, symptoms in excess of those required to make the diagnosis, **and** symptoms result in only minor impairment in occupational functioning or in usual social activities or relationships with others.

2-Moderate: Symptoms or functional impairment between "mild" and "severe."

3-Severe, without Psychotic Features: Several symptoms in excess of those required to make the diagnosis, **and** symptoms markedly interfere with occupational functioning or with usual social activities or relationships with others.

4-With Psychotic Features: Delusions or hallucinations. If possible, **specify** whether the psychotic features are *mood-congruent* or *mood-incongruent.*

Mood-congruent psychotic features: Delusions or hallucinations whose content is entirely consistent with the typical depressive themes of personal inadequacy, guilt, disease, death, nihilism, or deserved punishment.

Mood-incongruent psychotic features: Delusions or hallucinations whose content does *not* involve typical depressive themes of personal inadequacy, guilt, disease, death, nihilism, or deserved punishment. Included here are such symptoms as persecutory delusions (not directly related to depressive themes), thought insertion, thought broadcasting, and delusions of control.

5-In Partial Remission: Intermediate between "In Full Remission" and "Mild," **and** no previous Dysthymia. (If Major Depressive Episode was superimposed on Dysthymia, the diagnosis of Dysthymia alone is given once the full criteria for a Major Depressive Episode are no longer met.)

6-In Full Remission: During the past six months no significant signs or symptoms of the disturbance.

0-Unspecified.

(continued)

Diagnostic criteria for Major Depressive Episode continued

Specify chronic if current episode has lasted two consecutive years without a period of two months or longer during which there were no significant depressive symptoms.

Specify if current episode is **Melancholic Type**.

Diagnostic criteria for Melancholic Type

The presence of at least five of the following:

(1) loss of interest or pleasure in all, or almost all, activities
(2) lack of reactivity to usually pleasurable stimuli (does not feel much better, even temporarily, when something good happens)
(3) depression regularly worse in the morning
(4) early morning awakening (at least two hours before usual time of awakening)
(5) psychomotor retardation or agitation (not merely subjective complaints)
(6) significant anorexia or weight loss (e.g., more than 5% of body weight in a month)
(7) no significant personality disturbance before first Major Depressive Episode
(8) one or more previous Major Depressive Episodes followed by complete, or nearly complete, recovery
(9) previous good response to specific and adequate somatic antidepressant therapy, e.g., tricyclics, ECT, MAOI, lithium

Diagnostic criteria for seasonal pattern

A. There has been a regular temporal relationship between the onset of an episode of Bipolar Disorder (including Bipolar Disorder NOS) or Recurrent Major Depression (including Depressive Disorder NOS) and a particular 60-day period of the year (e.g., regular appearance of depression between the beginning of October and the end of November).

Note: Do not include cases in which there is an obvious effect of seasonally related psychosocial stressors, e.g., regularly being unemployed every winter.

B. Full remissions (or a change from depression to mania or hypomania) also occurred within a particular 60-day period of the year (e.g., depression disappears from mid-February to mid-April).

C. There have been at least three episodes of mood disturbance in three separate years that demonstrated the temporal seasonal relationship defined in A and B; at least two of the years were consecutive.

D. Seasonal episodes of mood disturbance, as described above, outnumbered any nonseasonal episodes of such disturbance that may have occurred by more than three to one.

BIPOLAR DISORDERS

296.6x Bipolar Disorder, Mixed
296.4x Bipolar Disorder, Manic
296.5x Bipolar Disorder, Depressed
The essential feature of Bipolar Disorder is one or more Manic Episodes (see p. 214), usually accompanied by one or more Major Depressive Episodes (see p. 218).

Bipolar Disorder is subclassified in the fourth digit as either mixed, manic, or depressed, depending on the clinical features of the current episode (or most recent episode if the disorder is currently in partial or full remission). In addition, Bipolar Disorder is subclassified in the fifth digit according to the current state of the disturbance. If the criteria are currently met for a Manic Episode or Major Depressive Episode, the severity of the episode is indicated as either mild, moderate, severe without psychotic features, or with psychotic features. If the criteria are not currently met, the fifth digit indicates whether the disturbance is in partial or full remission.

Course. In Bipolar Disorder the initial episode that occasioned hospitalization is usually manic. Both the Manic and Major Depressive Episodes are more frequent than the Major Depressive Episodes in Major Depression, Recurrent. Frequently a Manic or Major Depressive Episode is immediately followed by a short episode of the other kind. In many cases there are two or more complete cycles (a Manic and a Major Depressive Episode that succeed each other without a period of remission) within a year. Such cases have been called "rapid cycling." In rare cases over long periods of time, there is an alternation of the two kinds of episodes without any intervening period of normal mood.

There is evidence that cases of Bipolar Disorder with a mixed or rapid cycling episode have a much more chronic course than those without this type of episode.

Prevalence. It is estimated that from 0.4% to 1.2% of the adult population have had Bipolar Disorder.

Sex ratio. Recent epidemiologic studies in the United States indicate that the disorder is equally common in males and in females (unlike Major Depression, which is more common in females).

Familial pattern. Bipolar Disorder has clearly been shown to occur at much higher rates in first-degree biologic relatives of people with Bipolar Disorder than in the general population.

Differential diagnosis. In **Cyclothymia** there are numerous periods of Hypomanic Episodes and numerous periods of depressed mood or loss of interest or pleasure that do not meet the criteria for a Major Depressive Episode. If a Manic Episode occurs after the first two years of Cyclothymia, the additional diagnosis of Bipolar Disorder is given.

Diagnostic criteria for Bipolar Disorders

296.6x Bipolar Disorder, Mixed

For fifth digit, use the Manic Episode codes (p. 218) to describe current state.

(continued)

Diagnostic criteria for Bipolar Disorders continued

A. Current (or most recent) episode involves the full symptomatic picture of both Manic and Major Depressive Episodes (except for the duration requirement of two weeks for depressive symptoms) (p. 217 and p. 222), intermixed or rapidly alternating every few days.

B. Prominent depressive symptoms lasting at least a full day.

Specify if **seasonal pattern** (see p. 224).

296.4x Bipolar Disorder, Manic

For fifth digit, use the Manic Episode codes (p. 218) to describe current state.

Currently (or most recently) in a Manic Episode (p. 217). (If there has been a previous Manic Episode, the current episode need not meet the full criteria for a Manic Episode.)

Specify if **seasonal pattern** (see p. 224).

296.5x Bipolar Disorder, Depressed

For fifth digit, use the Major Depressive Episode codes (p. 223) to describe current state.

A. Has had one or more Manic Episodes (p. 217).

B. Currently (or most recently) in a Major Depressive Episode (p. 222). (If there has been a previous Major Depressive Episode, the current episode need not meet the full criteria for a Major Depressive Episode.)

Specify if **seasonal pattern** (see p. 224).

301.13 Cyclothymia

The essential feature of this disorder is a chronic mood disturbance, of at least two years' duration (one year for children and adolescents), involving numerous Hypomanic Episodes and numerous periods of depressed mood or loss of interest or pleasure of insufficient severity or duration to meet the criteria for a Major Depressive or a Manic Episode. In order to make the diagnosis, there must be a two-year period (one year for children and adolescents) in which the person is never without hypomanic or depressive symptoms for more than two months. The diagnosis is not made if there is clear evidence of either a Manic Episode or a Major Depressive Episode during the first two years of the disturbance. (A Manic Episode would indicate Bipolar Disorder; a Major Depressive Episode, without a Manic Episode, would indicate Bipolar Disorder NOS.) In addition, the diagnosis is not made if the disturbance is superimposed on a chronic psychotic disorder, such as Schizophrenia or Delusional Disorder, or if it is initiated and maintained by a specific organic factor or substance.

The boundaries between Cyclothymia and Bipolar Disorder and Bipolar Disorder NOS are not well defined, and some investigators believe that Cyclothymia is a mild form of Bipolar Disorder.

Associated features. Associated features are similar to those of Manic Episode (p. 216) and Major Depressive Episode (p. 220) except that, by definition, there is no marked impairment in social or occupational functioning during the Hypomanic Episodes. In fact, in some cases the person is particularly productive in occupational situations and socially effective during Hypomanic Episodes. However, many people experience social difficulties in their interpersonal relationships and academic and occupational pursuits because of the recurrent cycles of mood swings.

Psychoactive Substance Abuse is common as a result of self-treatment with sedatives and alcohol during the depressed periods and the self-indulgent use of stimulants and psychedelic substances during the hypomanic periods.

Age at onset. The disorder usually begins in adolescence or early adult life.

Course. The disorder usually is without clear onset and has a chronic course. Often the person develops Bipolar Disorder.

Impairment. During periods of depression, social and occupational functioning are invariably impaired, although not as severely as in a Major Depressive Episode.

Complications. See Manic Episode (p. 216) and Major Depressive Episode (p. 221). Frequently Manic and Major Depressive Episodes are complications of this disorder.

Predisposing factors. No information.

Prevalence. Studies have reported a lifetime prevalence of from 0.4% to 3.5%.

Sex ratio. In clinical samples the disorder is apparently equally common in males and in females.

Familial pattern. Major Depression and Bipolar Disorder may be more common among first-degree biologic relatives of people with Cyclothymia than among the general population.

Differential diagnosis. See differential diagnosis of a Manic Episode (p. 216). If a Manic Episode or a Major Depressive Episode occurs during the first two years of what appears to be Cyclothymia, the diagnosis of either **Bipolar Disorder** (for a Manic Episode) or **Bipolar Disorder NOS** (for a Major Depressive Episode) is given. In **Borderline Personality Disorder** there are often marked shifts in mood, from depression to irritability or anxiety, that may suggest Hypomanic Episodes. However, the characteristic associated symptoms of a Hypomanic Episode, such as less need for sleep and racing thoughts, are rarely present.

Diagnostic criteria for 301.13 Cyclothymia

A. For at least two years (one year for children and adolescents), presence of numerous Hypomanic Episodes (all of the criteria for a Manic Episode, p. 217, except criterion C that indicates marked impairment) and numerous periods with depressed mood or loss of interest or pleasure that did not meet criterion A of Major Depressive Episode.

(continued)

Diagnostic criteria for 301.13 Cyclothymia continued

B. During a two-year period (one year in children and adolescents) of the disturbance, never without hypomanic or depressive symptoms for more than two months at a time.

C. No clear evidence of a Major Depressive Episode or Manic Episode during the first two years of the disturbance (or one year in children and adolescents).

Note: After this minimum period of Cyclothymia, there may be superimposed Manic or Major Depressive Episodes, in which case the additional diagnosis of Bipolar Disorder or Bipolar Disorder NOS should be given.

D. Not superimposed on a chronic psychotic disorder, such as Schizophrenia or Delusional Disorder.

E. It cannot be established that an organic factor initiated and maintained the disturbance, e.g., repeated intoxication from drugs or alcohol.

296.70 Bipolar Disorder Not Otherwise Specified

Disorders with manic or hypomanic features that do not meet the criteria for any specific Bipolar Disorder.

Examples:

(1) at least one Hypomanic Episode and at least one Major Depressive Episode, but never either a Manic Episode or Cyclothymia. Such cases have been referred to as "Bipolar II."

(2) one or more Hypomanic Episodes, but without Cyclothymia or a history of either a Manic or a Major Depressive Episode

(3) a Manic Episode superimposed on Delusional Disorder, residual Schizophrenia, or Psychotic Disorder NOS

Specify if **seasonal pattern** (see p. 224).

DEPRESSIVE DISORDERS

296.2x Major Depression, Single Episode
296.3x Major Depression, Recurrent

The essential feature of Major Depression is one or more Major Depressive Episodes (see p. 218) without a history of either a Manic Episode (see p. 214) or an unequivocal Hypomanic Episode. Major Depression is subclassified in the fourth digit as either Single Episode or Recurrent. In addition, it is subclassified in the fifth digit to indicate the current state of the disturbance. If the criteria are currently met for a Major Depressive Episode, the severity of the episode is indicated as either mild, moderate, severe without psychotic features, or with psychotic features. If these criteria are not currently met, the fifth digit indicates whether the disturbance is in partial or full remission.

Course. Some people have only a single episode, with full return to premorbid functioning. However, it is estimated that over 50% of people who initially have Major Depression, Single Episode, will eventually have another Major Depressive Episode, the illness then meeting the criteria for Major Depression, Recurrent. People with

Major Depression, Recurrent, are at greater risk of developing Bipolar Disorder than are those with a single episode of Major Depression. People with Major Depression superimposed on Dysthymia (often referred to as "double depression") are at greater risk for having a recurrence of a Major Depressive Episode than those who have only Major Depression.

The course of Major Depression, Recurrent, is variable. Some people have episodes separated by many years of normal functioning; others have clusters of episodes; and still others have increasingly frequent episodes as they grow older. Functioning usually returns to the premorbid level between episodes. In 20% to 35% of cases, however, there is a chronic course, with considerable residual symptomatic and social impairment. Some of these cases continue to meet the criteria for a Major Depressive Episode throughout the course of the disturbance (specified as *Chronic Type*); the others are coded as being in partial remission.

Prevalence. Studies of Major Depression in the United States and Europe, using criteria similar to those in this manual, report a wide range of values for the proportion of the adult population that has had the disorder. The range for females is from 9% to 26%; that for males, 5% to 12%. Studies examining the proportion of the adult population that currently has the disorder report rates ranging from 4.5% to 9.3% for females and 2.3% to 3.2% for males.

There is evidence that prevalence of the disorder has increased in the age cohorts that came to maturity after the Second World War.

Sex ratio. In almost all studies of Major Depression in adults in industrialized countries, the disorder is estimated to be twice as common in females as in males (unlike Bipolar Disorder which is equally common in males and in females).

Familial pattern. Most family studies have shown that Major Depression is 1.5 to 3 times more common among first-degree biologic relatives of people with this disorder than among the general population.

Differential diagnosis. See differential diagnosis of a Major Depressive Episode (p. 221). A history of a **Manic Episode** or an **unequivocal Hypomanic Episode** precludes the diagnosis of Major Depression. In the first two years of **Dysthymia** (or one year for children and adolescents), there is no clear evidence of a Major Depressive Episode. However, later in the course of Dysthymia, or before its onset, there may be Major Depression.

Diagnostic criteria for Major Depression

296.2x Major Depression, Single Episode

For fifth digit, use the Major Depressive Episode codes (p. 223) to describe current state.

A. A single Major Depressive Episode (p. 222).

B. Has never had a Manic Episode (p. 217) or an unequivocal Hypomanic Episode (see p. 217).

(continued)

Diagnostic criteria for Major Depression continued

Specify if **seasonal pattern** (see p. 224).

296.3x Major Depression, Recurrent

For fifth digit, use the Major Depressive Episode codes (p. 223) to describe current state.

A. Two or more Major Depressive Episodes (p. 222), each separated by at least two months of return to more or less usual functioning. (If there has been a previous Major Depressive Episode, the current episode of depression need not meet the full criteria for a Major Depressive Episode.)

B. Has never had a Manic Episode (p. 217) or an unequivocal Hypomanic Episode (see p. 217).

Specify if **seasonal pattern** (see p. 224).

300.40   Dysthymia (or Depressive Neurosis)

The essential feature of this disorder is a chronic disturbance of mood involving depressed mood (or possibly an irritable mood in children or adolescents), for most of the day more days than not, for at least two years (one year for children and adolescents). In addition, during these periods of depressed mood there are some of the following associated symptoms: poor appetite or overeating, insomnia or hypersomnia, low energy or fatigue, low self-esteem, poor concentration or difficulty making decisions, and feelings of hopelessness.

In order to make the diagnosis, there must be a two-year (one-year for children or adolescents) period in which the person is never without depressive symptoms for more than two months. The diagnosis is not made if there is clear evidence of a Major Depressive Episode during this minimum period of the disturbance. In addition, the diagnosis is not made if the disturbance is superimposed on a chronic psychotic disorder, such as Schizophrenia or Delusional Disorder, or if the disturbance is sustained by a specific organic factor or substance, for example, prolonged administration of an antihypertensive medication.

Dysthymia frequently seems to be a consequence of a preexisting, chronic, nonmood Axis I or Axis III disorder, e.g., Anorexia Nervosa, Somatization Disorder, Psychoactive Substance Dependence, an Anxiety Disorder, or rheumatoid arthritis. Such cases of Dysthymia are specified as *Secondary Type*; cases of Dysthymia that are apparently not related to a preexisting chronic disorder are specified as *Primary Type*. Cases of Dysthymia that develop before the age of 21 are specified as *early onset*; cases that develop at or after age 21 are specified as *late onset*. Some investigators believe that the early onset primary type represents a distinct nosologic entity.

The boundaries of Dysthymia with Major Depression are unclear, particularly in children and adolescents.

Associated features. Associated features (and age-specific associated features) are similar to those of Major Depressive Episode (p. 220), except that by definition there are no delusions or hallucinations.

Often an associated personality disturbance warrants an additional diagnosis of a Personality Disorder on Axis II.

Age at onset. This disorder usually begins in childhood, adolescence, or early adult life, and for this reason has often been referred to as Depressive Personality.

Course. The disorder usually begins without clear onset and has a chronic course. In clinical settings, people with this disorder usually have superimposed Major Depression, which often is the reason for the person's currently seeking treatment.

Impairment and complications. The impairment in social and occupational functioning is usually mild or moderate because of the chronicity rather than the severity of the depressive syndrome. Therefore, hospitalization is rarely required unless there is a suicide attempt or a superimposed Major Depression. The complications are similar to those of Major Depression, although, because of the chronicity of this disorder, there may be a greater likelihood of developing Psychoactive Substance Dependence or Abuse.

In children and adolescents, social interaction with peers and adults is frequently affected. Children with depression often react negatively or shyly to praise and frequently respond to positive relationships with negative behaviors (sometimes as testing, sometimes as manifestations of unexpressed resentment and anger). School performance and progress may be deleteriously affected.

Predisposing factors. By definition, predisposing factors for the *secondary type* include chronic nonmood Axis I and Axis III disorders. In addition, chronic psychosocial stressors may predispose to both *primary* and *secondary* types.

In children and adolescents, predisposing factors are the presence of Attention-deficit Hyperactivity Disorder, Conduct Disorder, Mental Retardation, a severe Specific Developmental Disorder, or an inadequate, disorganized, rejecting, and chaotic environment.

Prevalence. This disorder is apparently common.

Sex ratio. Among adults the disorder is apparently more common in females. In children it seems to occur equally frequently in both sexes.

Familial pattern. There is evidence that the disorder is more common among first-degree biologic relatives of people with Major Depression than among the general population.

Differential diagnosis. The differential diagnosis of Dysthymia and Major Depression is particularly difficult, since the two disorders share similar symptoms and differ only in duration and severity.

Usually Major Depression consists of one or more discrete Major Depressive Episodes that can be distinguished from the person's usual functioning, whereas Dysthymia is characterized by a chronic mild depressive syndrome that has been present for many years. When Dysthymia is of many years' duration, the mood disturbance cannot be distinguished from the person's "usual" functioning. If the initial onset of what appears to be Dysthymia directly follows a Major Depressive Episode, the correct diagnosis is **Major Depression in Partial Remission**. The diagnosis of Dysthymia can be made following Major Depression only if there has been a full remission of the Major Depressive Episode lasting at least six months before the development of Dysthymia.

People with Dysthymia frequently have a superimposed Major Depression (often referred to as "double depression"). When a Major Depression is superimposed on preexisting Dysthymia (which has been present for at least two years), both diagnoses should be recorded since it is likely that the person will continue to have Dysthymia after he or she has recovered from the Major Depression.

Often there is evidence of a coexisting personality disturbance. When a person meets the criteria for both Dysthymia and a **Personality Disorder,** both diagnoses should be made. This disorder is particularly common in people with Borderline, Histrionic, Narcissistic, Avoidant, and Dependent Personality Disorders.

Normal fluctuations of mood are not as frequent or severe as the depressed mood in Dysthymia, and there is no interference with social functioning.

Diagnostic criteria for 300.40 Dysthymia

A. Depressed mood (or can be irritable mood in children and adolescents) for most of the day, more days than not, as indicated either by subjective account or observation by others, for at least two years (one year for children and adolescents)

B. Presence, while depressed, of at least two of the following:

   (1) poor appetite or overeating
   (2) insomnia or hypersomnia
   (3) low energy or fatigue
   (4) low self-esteem
   (5) poor concentration or difficulty making decisions
   (6) feelings of hopelessness

C. During a two-year period (one-year for children and adolescents) of the disturbance, never without the symptoms in A for more than two months at a time.

D. No evidence of an unequivocal Major Depressive Episode during the first two years (one year for children and adolescents) of the disturbance.

   Note: There may have been a previous Major Depressive Episode, provided there was a full remission (no significant signs or symptoms for six months) before development of the Dysthymia. In addition, after these two years (one year in children or adolescents) of Dysthymia, there may be superimposed episodes of Major Depression, in which case both diagnoses are given.

E. Has never had a Manic Episode (p. 217) or an unequivocal Hypomanic Episode (see p. 217).

F. Not superimposed on a chronic psychotic disorder, such as Schizophrenia or Delusional Disorder.

G. It cannot be established that an organic factor initiated and maintained the disturbance, e.g., prolonged administration of an antihypertensive medication.

Diagnostic criteria for 300.40 Dysthymia continued

Specify primary or **secondary type:**

Primary type: the mood disturbance is not related to a preexisting, chronic, nonmood, Axis I or Axis III disorder, e.g., Anorexia Nervosa, Somatization Disorder, a Psychoactive Substance Dependence Disorder, an Anxiety Disorder, or rheumatoid arthritis.

Secondary type: the mood disturbance is apparently related to a preexisting, chronic, nonmood Axis I or Axis III disorder.

Specify early onset or **late onset:**

Early onset: onset of the disturbance before age 21.

Late onset: onset of the disturbance at age 21 or later.

311.00   Depressive Disorder Not Otherwise Specified

Disorders with depressive features that do not meet the criteria for any specific Mood Disorder or Adjustment Disorder with Depressed Mood.

Examples:

(1) a Major Depressive Episode superimposed on residual Schizophrenia
(2) a recurrent, mild, depressive disturbance that does not meet the criteria for Dysthymia
(3) non-stress-related depressive episodes that do not meet the criteria for a Major Depressive Episode

Specify if **seasonal pattern** (see p. 224).

Anxiety Disorders (or Anxiety and Phobic Neuroses)

The characteristic features of this group of disorders are symptoms of anxiety and avoidance behavior. In Panic Disorder and Generalized Anxiety Disorder, anxiety is usually the predominant symptom, and avoidance behavior is almost always present in Panic Disorder with Agoraphobia. In Phobic Disorders anxiety is experienced if the person confronts the dreaded object or situation. In Obsessive Compulsive Disorder anxiety is experienced if the person attempts to resist the obsessions or compulsions. Avoidance behavior is almost always present in Phobic Disorders, and frequently present in Obsessive Compulsive Disorder. The classification of Post-traumatic Stress Disorder is controversial since the predominant symptom is the reexperiencing of a trauma, not anxiety or avoidance behavior. However, anxiety symptoms and avoidance behavior are extremely common, and symptoms of increased arousal are invariably present.

Although anxiety related to separation from parental figures is a form of phobic reaction, it is classified as Separation Anxiety Disorder and is in the section Disorders Usually First Evident in Infancy, Childhood, or Adolescence (p. 27). Similarly, phobic avoidance limited to sexual activities is classified as Sexual Aversion Disorder and is in the section Sexual Disorders (p. 293).

Recent studies indicate that Anxiety Disorders are those most frequently found in the general population, Simple Phobia being the most common Anxiety Disorder in the general population, but Panic Disorder the most common among people seeking treatment. Panic Disorder, Phobic Disorders, and Obsessive Compulsive Disorder are all apparently more common among first-degree biologic relatives of people with each of these disorders than among the general population.

300.21 Panic Disorder with Agoraphobia
300.01 Panic Disorder without Agoraphobia

The essential features of these disorders are recurrent panic attacks, i.e., discrete periods of intense fear or discomfort, with at least four characteristic associated symptoms. The diagnoses are made only when it cannot be established that an organic factor initiated and maintained the disturbance.

The panic attacks usually last minutes or, more rarely, hours. The attacks, at least initially, are unexpected, i.e., they do not occur immediately before or on exposure to a situation that almost always causes anxiety (as in Simple Phobia). In addition, the attacks are not triggered by situations in which the person is the focus of others' attention (as in Social Phobia). The "unexpected" aspect of the panic attacks is an essential feature of the disorder, although later in the course of the disturbance certain situations, e.g., driving a car or being in a crowded place, may become associated with having a panic attack. These situations increase the likelihood of an attack's occurring at some time while the person is in that situation, although not immediately upon entering the situation, as in Simple Phobia. In such a situation, the person fears having a panic attack, but is uncertain about when it may occur, or if it will occur at all.

Panic attacks typically begin with the sudden onset of intense apprehension, fear, or terror. Often there is a feeling of impending doom. Much more rarely, the person does not experience the attack as anxiety, but only as intense discomfort. During most panic attacks there are more than six associated symptoms. (Attacks involving four or more symptoms are arbitrarily defined as panic attacks; attacks involving fewer than four symptoms are limited symptom attacks. See Agoraphobia without History of Panic Disorder, p. 240.)

The symptoms experienced during an attack are: shortness of breath (dyspnea) or smothering sensations; dizziness, unsteady feelings, or faintness; choking; palpitations or accelerated heart rate; trembling or shaking; sweating; nausea or abdominal distress; depersonalization or derealization; numbness or tingling sensations (paresthesias); flushes (hot flashes) or chills; chest pain or discomfort; fear of dying; and fear of going crazy or of doing something uncontrolled during the attack.

In the great majority of cases of Panic Disorder seen in clinical settings, the person has developed some symptoms of Agoraphobia. Agoraphobia is the fear of being in places or situations from which escape might be difficult (or embarrassing) or in which help might not be available in the event of a panic attack. As a result of this fear, there are either travel restrictions or need for a companion when away from home, or there is endurance of agoraphobic situations despite intense anxiety. Common agoraphobic situations include being outside the home alone, being in a crowd or standing in a line, being on a bridge, and traveling in a bus, train, or car. (Agoraphobia also includes those unusual cases in which persistent avoidance behavior originated during an active phase of Panic Disorder, but the person does not attribute subsequent avoidance behavior to fear of having a panic attack.)

Associated features. The person often develops varying degrees of nervousness and apprehension between attacks, usually focused on the fear of having another attack. A coexisting Depressive Disorder is often present.

Age at onset. The average age at onset is in the late 20s.

Course. Typically there are recurrent panic attacks several times a week or even daily. In very rare instances there is only a single attack, followed by a persistent fear of having another attack. The disorder may be limited to a single brief period lasting several weeks or months, may recur several times, or, more typically (particularly in Panic Disorder with Agoraphobia), may last for years, with varying periods of partial or full remission and exacerbation. During periods of partial remission, there may be recurrent limited symptom attacks (as defined above).

Impairment. Panic Disorder without Agoraphobia may be associated with no or only limited impairment in social and occupational functioning. Panic Disorder with Agoraphobia, by definition, is associated with varying degrees of constriction in life-style. When the Agoraphobia is severe, the person is nearly or completely housebound or unable to leave the house unaccompanied.

Complications. Complications include Psychoactive Substance Use Disorders, particularly alcohol and anxiolytics.

Predisposing factors. Separation Anxiety Disorder in childhood and sudden loss of social supports or disruption of important interpersonal relationships apparently predispose to the development of this disorder.

Prevalence. The disorder is common. In clinical settings Panic Disorder with Agoraphobia is much more common than Panic Disorder without Agoraphobia.

Sex ratio. In clinical samples, Panic Disorder without Agoraphobia is about equally common in males and in females; Panic Disorder with Agoraphobia is about twice as common in females as in males.

Differential diagnosis. The diagnosis is made only when it cannot be established that an organic factor initiated and maintained the disturbance. **Physical disorders** such as hypoglycemia, pheochromocytoma, and hyperthyroidism, all of which can cause similar symptoms, must be considered (see discussion of etiologic factors of Organic Anxiety Syndrome, p. 113).

In **withdrawal** from some substances, such as barbiturates, and in some **Psychoactive Substance-induced Intoxications,** such as those due to **caffeine** or **amphetamines,** there may be panic attacks. Panic Disorder should not be diagnosed when the panic attacks are due to ingestion of a psychoactive substance.

During a **Major Depressive Episode** there may be recurrent unexpected panic attacks, in which case diagnoses of both a Mood Disorder and Panic Disorder should be made. Similarly, if recurrent panic attacks occur during the course of **Somatization Disorder,** the additional diagnosis of Panic Disorder should be made.

Typically, people with Panic Disorder develop varying degrees of nervousness and apprehension between attacks. When this is focused on the fear of having another attack (as is usually the case), the additional diagnosis of **Generalized Anxiety Disorder** is not made. More rarely, however, the focus of concern may not be fear of having another panic attack, in which case the diagnosis of Generalized Anxiety Disorder should be considered.

In **Simple Phobia,** the person may develop panic attacks if exposed to the phobic stimulus. However, in such situations the panic attack occurs immediately before or upon exposure to the phobic situation and its intensity varies as the phobic stimulus approaches or withdraws. In Panic Disorder, by contrast, even when the attacks are associated with certain situations, such as being outside the home alone or standing in line, the person is never certain just when an attack will occur in that situation, or if it will occur at all. In **Social Phobia,** the person may develop panic attacks that are triggered only by being the focus of others' attention, whereas in Panic Disorder, the panic attacks are not, by definition, thus triggered. People with Panic Disorder may, however, have an unrelated Simple Phobia or Social Phobia.

Diagnostic criteria for Panic Disorder

A. At some time during the disturbance, one or more panic attacks (discrete periods of intense fear or discomfort) have occurred that were (1) unex-

(continued)

Diagnostic criteria for Panic Disorder continued

pected, i.e., did not occur immediately before or on exposure to a situation that almost always caused anxiety, and (2) not triggered by situations in which the person was the focus of others' attention.

B. Either four attacks, as defined in criterion A, have occurred within a four-week period, or one or more attacks have been followed by a period of at least a month of persistent fear of having another attack.

C. At least four of the following symptoms developed during at least one of the attacks:

(1) shortness of breath (dyspnea) or smothering sensations
(2) dizziness, unsteady feelings, or faintness
(3) palpitations or accelerated heart rate (tachycardia)
(4) trembling or shaking
(5) sweating
(6) choking
(7) nausea or abdominal distress
(8) depersonalization or derealization
(9) numbness or tingling sensations (paresthesias)
(10) flushes (hot flashes) or chills
(11) chest pain or discomfort
(12) fear of dying
(13) fear of going crazy or of doing something uncontrolled

Note: Attacks involving four or more symptoms are panic attacks; attacks involving fewer than four symptoms are limited symptom attacks (see Agoraphobia without History of Panic Disorder, p. 241).

D. During at least some of the attacks, at least four of the C symptoms developed suddenly and increased in intensity within ten minutes of the beginning of the first C symptom noticed in the attack.

E. It cannot be established that an organic factor initiated and maintained the disturbance, e.g., Amphetamine or Caffeine Intoxication, hyperthyroidism.

Note: Mitral valve prolapse may be an associated condition, but does not preclude a diagnosis of Panic Disorder.

Types of Panic Disorder

Diagnostic criteria for 300.21 Panic Disorder with Agoraphobia

A. Meets the criteria for Panic Disorder.

B. Agoraphobia: Fear of being in places or situations from which escape might be difficult (or embarrassing) or in which help might not be available in the event of a panic attack. (Include cases in which persistent avoidance behavior originated during an active phase of Panic Disorder, even if the person does not attribute the avoidance behavior to fear of having a panic attack.) As a

Diagnostic criteria for 300.21 Panic Disorder with Agoraphobia continued

result of this fear, the person either restricts travel or needs a companion when away from home, or else endures agoraphobic situations despite intense anxiety. Common agoraphobic situations include being outside the home alone, being in a crowd or standing in a line, being on a bridge, and traveling in a bus, train, or car.

Specify current severity of agoraphobic avoidance:

Mild: Some avoidance (or endurance with distress), but relatively normal lifestyle, e.g., travels unaccompanied when necessary, such as to work or to shop; otherwise avoids traveling alone.

Moderate: Avoidance results in constricted life-style, e.g., the person is able to leave the house alone, but not to go more than a few miles unaccompanied.

Severe: Avoidance results in being nearly or completely housebound or unable to leave the house unaccompanied.

In Partial Remission: No current agoraphobic avoidance, but some Agoraphobic avoidance during the past six months.

In Full Remission: No current agoraphobic avoidance and none during the past six months.

Specify current severity of panic attacks:

Mild: During the past month, either all attacks have been limited symptom attacks (i.e., fewer than four symptoms), or there has been no more than one panic attack.

Moderate: During the past month attacks have been intermediate between ''mild'' and ''severe.''

Severe: During the past month, there have been at least eight panic attacks.

In Partial Remission: The condition has been intermediate between ''In Full Remission'' and ''Mild.''

In Full Remission: During the past six months, there have been no panic or limited symptom attacks.

Diagnostic criteria for 300.01 Panic Disorder without Agoraphobia

A. Meets the criteria for Panic Disorder.

B. Absence of Agoraphobia, as defined above.

Specify current severity of panic attacks, as defined above.

300.22 Agoraphobia without History of Panic Disorder

The essential feature of this disorder is Agoraphobia without a history of Panic Disorder. Agoraphobia is the fear of being in places or situations from which escape might be difficult (or embarrassing), or in which help might not be available in the event of suddenly developing a symptom(s) that could be incapacitating or extremely embarrassing. As a result of this fear, the person either restricts travel or needs a companion when away from home, or else endures agoraphobic situations despite intense anxiety. Common agoraphobic situations include being outside the home alone, being in a crowd or standing in a line, being on a bridge, and traveling in a bus, train, or car.

Usually the person is afraid of having a *limited symptom attack*, that is, developing a single or small number of symptoms, such as becoming dizzy or falling, depersonalization or derealization, loss of bladder or bowel control, vomiting, or having cardiac distress. In some of these cases, such symptoms have occurred in the past, and the person may be preoccupied with fears of their recurrence. In other cases, the person has never experienced the symptom(s), but nevertheless fears that the symptom "could" develop and incapacitate him or her or be extremely embarrassing. In a small number of cases the person fears feeling incapacitated in some way, but is unable to specify what symptom he or she fears.

It is unclear whether Agoraphobia without History of Panic Disorder with limited symptom attacks represents a variant of Panic Disorder with Agoraphobia, and whether the same disorder without limited symptom attacks represents a disorder that is unrelated to Panic Disorder.

Associated features. Personality disturbance, particularly features of Avoidant Personality Disorder, may be present.

Age at onset. Age at onset is variable, but the disorder most commonly begins in the 20s or 30s.

Course. Typically, the disorder persists for years.

Impairment. In clinical samples the impairment is usually severe.

Complications. Some people subsequently develop Panic Disorder.

Predisposing factors. No information.

Prevalence. In clinical samples the disorder is rare. It may, however, be more common in the general population.

Sex ratio. The disorder is diagnosed far more commonly in females than in males.

Differential diagnosis. In a **psychotic disorder with persecutory features,** the person may avoid situations that he or she believes make him or her vulnerable to being attacked. In **severe Major Depressive Episode,** the person may avoid situations that he or she experiences as overwhelming. In neither of these cases, however, does the person fear suddenly developing a symptom that would be extremely embarrassing or incapacitating.

In **Panic Disorder with Agoraphobia,** the panic attacks may be in full remission while the agoraphobia persists, but a history of Panic Disorder would preclude a current diagnosis of Agoraphobia without History of Panic Disorder. (Note: Panic

Disorder does not preclude a preexisting diagnosis of Agoraphobia without History of Panic Disorder.) In extremely severe cases of **Social Phobia,** the person may avoid the same kinds of situations that are avoided in Agoraphobia without History of Panic Disorder. The motivation, however, is to avoid doing something or acting in a way that would be embarrassing or humiliating rather than to avoid the sudden development of a symptom.

Diagnostic criteria for 300.22 Agoraphobia without History of Panic Disorder

A. Agoraphobia: Fear of being in places or situations from which escape might be difficult (or embarrassing) or in which help might not be available in the event of suddenly developing a symptom(s) that could be incapacitating or extremely embarrassing. Examples include: dizziness or falling, depersonalization or derealization, loss of bladder or bowel control, vomiting, or cardiac distress. As a result of this fear, the person either restricts travel or needs a companion when away from home, or else endures agoraphobic situations despite intense anxiety. Common agoraphobic situations include being outside the home alone, being in a crowd or standing in a line, being on a bridge, and traveling in a bus, train, or car.

B. Has never met the criteria for Panic Disorder.

Specify with or **without limited symptom attacks** (see p. 240).

300.23 Social Phobia

The essential feature of this disorder is a persistent fear of one or more situations (the social phobic situations) in which the person is exposed to possible scrutiny by others and fears that he or she may do something or act in a way that will be humiliating or embarrassing. The social phobic fear may be circumscribed, such as fears of being unable to continue talking while speaking in public, choking on food when eating in front of others, being unable to urinate in a public lavatory, or having a hand tremble when writing in the presence of others. In other cases the social phobic fears may involve most social situations, such as general fears of saying foolish things or not being able to answer questions in social situations.

If an Axis III or another Axis I disorder is present, the social phobic fear is unrelated to it, e.g., the fear is not of having a panic attack (as in Panic Disorder), stuttering (as in Stuttering), trembling (as in Parkinson's disease), or exhibiting abnormal eating behavior (as in Anorexia Nervosa or Bulimia Nervosa).

During some phase of the disturbance, exposure to the specific phobic stimulus (or stimuli) almost invariably provokes an immediate anxiety response. Thus, for example, the person with a Social Phobia of public speaking, when forced to give a talk, will almost invariably have an immediate anxiety response, such as feeling panicky, sweating, and having tachycardia and difficulty breathing.

Marked anticipatory anxiety occurs if the person is confronted with the necessity of entering into the social phobic situation, and such situations are therefore usually avoided. Less commonly, the person forces himself or herself to endure the social phobic situation, but it is experienced with intense anxiety. Usually the person fears that others will detect signs of anxiety in the social phobic situation. A vicious cycle may be created in which the irrational fear generates anxiety that impairs performance, thus increasing the motivation to avoid the phobic situation. Invariably the person recognizes that his or her fear is excessive or unreasonable.

The diagnosis of a Social Phobia is made only if the avoidant behavior interferes with occupational functioning or with usual social activities or relationships with others, or if there is marked distress about having the fear.

Associated features. Panic Disorder and Simple Phobia frequently coexist with Social Phobia.

Age at onset. The disorder often begins in late childhood or early adolescence.

Course. The disorder is usually chronic, and may be exacerbated if the anxiety impairs performance in the feared situation.

Impairment. Unless the disorder is severe, it is rarely, in itself, incapacitating, although there is usually some interference with occupational functioning or with usual social activities or relationships with others. Considerable inconvenience may result from the need to avoid the phobic situation, e.g., avoiding a trip if it necessitates the use of a public lavatory. Fear of public speaking may interfere with professional advancement.

Complications. People with this disorder are prone to episodic abuse of alcohol, barbiturates, and anxiolytics. When social or occupational functioning is severely impaired, a depressive disorder may be a complication.

Predisposing factors. No information.

Prevalence. Social Phobia with the circumscribed symptoms of fear of eating in public, writing in public, or using public lavatories is relatively rare. However, Social Phobia involving fear of public speaking and Social Phobia involving a generalized fear of most social situations are common.

Sex ratio. In clinical samples the disorder is apparently more common in males than in females.

Familial pattern. No information.

Differential diagnosis. Avoidance of certain social situations that are normally a source of some distress, which is common in many people with "normal" fear of public speaking, does not justify a diagnosis of Social Phobia. In **Avoidant Personality Disorder,** there may be marked anxiety and avoidance of most social situations. In such cases both Social Phobia and Avoidant Personality Disorder should be considered.

In **Simple Phobia** there is also a circumscribed phobic stimulus, but it is not a social situation involving the possibility of humiliation or embarrassment. In **Panic Disorder with Agoraphobia,** the person may avoid certain social situations, such as restaurants, because of a fear of the embarrassment of having a panic attack in that situation. In such a case the additional diagnosis of a Social Phobia is not made. However, people with Panic Disorder can also have an unrelated Social Phobia, which may have been present before the development of the Panic Disorder.

Diagnostic criteria for 300.23 Social Phobia

A. A persistent fear of one or more situations (the social phobic situations) in which the person is exposed to possible scrutiny by others and fears that he or she may do something or act in a way that will be humiliating or embarrassing. Examples include: being unable to continue talking while speaking in public, choking on food when eating in front of others, being unable to urinate in a public lavatory, hand-trembling when writing in the presence of others, and saying foolish things or not being able to answer questions in social situations.

B. If an Axis III or another Axis I disorder is present, the fear in A is unrelated to it, e.g., the fear is not of having a panic attack (Panic Disorder), stuttering (Stuttering), trembling (Parkinson's disease), or exhibiting abnormal eating behavior (Anorexia Nervosa or Bulimia Nervosa).

C. During some phase of the disturbance, exposure to the specific phobic stimulus (or stimuli) almost invariably provokes an immediate anxiety response.

D. The phobic situation(s) is avoided, or is endured with intense anxiety.

E. The avoidant behavior interferes with occupational functioning or with usual social activities or relationships with others, or there is marked distress about having the fear.

F. The person recognizes that his or her fear is excessive or unreasonable.

G. If the person is under 18, the disturbance does not meet the criteria for Avoidant Disorder of Childhood or Adolescence.

Specify generalized type if the phobic situation includes most social situations, and also consider the additional diagnosis of Avoidant Personality Disorder.

300.29 Simple Phobia

The essential feature of this disorder is a persistent fear of a circumscribed stimulus (object or situation) other than fear of having a panic attack (as in Panic Disorder) or of humiliation or embarrassment in certain social situations (as in Social Phobia). Simple Phobias are sometimes referred to as "specific" phobias. The most common Simple Phobias in the general population, though not necessarily among those seeking treatment, involve animals, particularly dogs, snakes, insects, and mice. Other Simple Phobias involve witnessing blood or tissue injury (blood-injury phobia), closed spaces (claustrophobia), heights (acrophobia), and air travel.

During some phase of the disturbance, exposure to the simple phobic stimulus (or stimuli) almost invariably provokes an immediate anxiety response. Thus, for example, a person with a Simple Phobia of cats, when forced to confront a cat, will almost invariably have an immediate anxiety response, such as feeling panicky, sweating, and having tachycardia and difficulty breathing. Anxiety increases or decreases in a fairly predictable manner with changes in the location or nature of the phobic stimulus (e.g., height of the building, nearness of the cat, size or behavior of the dog).

Marked anticipatory anxiety occurs if the person is confronted with the necessity of entering into the simple phobic situation, and such situations are therefore usually avoided. Less commonly, the person forces himself or herself to endure the simple phobic situation, but it is experienced with intense anxiety. Invariably the person recognizes that his or her fear is excessive or unreasonable.

The diagnosis of a Simple Phobia is made only if the avoidant behavior interferes with the person's normal routine or with usual social activities or relationships with others, or if there is marked distress about having the fear.

Associated features. Unrelated Social Phobia and Panic Disorder with or without Agoraphobia are often present. Blood-injury phobias are frequently associated with vasovagal fainting on exposure to the phobic stimulus.

Age at onset. Age at onset varies, but animal phobias nearly always begin in childhood; blood-injury phobias most frequently begin in adolescence or early adulthood; circumscribed phobias of heights, driving, closed spaces, and air travel appear to begin most frequently in the fourth decade of life.

Course. Most simple phobias that start in childhood disappear without treatment. However, those that persist into adulthood rarely remit without treatment.

Impairment. Impairment may be minimal if the phobic object is rare and easily avoided, such as fear of snakes in someone living in the city. Impairment may be considerable if the phobic object is common and cannot be avoided, such as a fear of elevators in someone living in a large city who must use elevators at work.

Complications and predisposing factors. No information.

Prevalence. Simple Phobias are common in the general population; but since they rarely result in marked impairment, people with this disorder seldom seek treatment.

Sex ratio. The disorder is more often diagnosed in females.

Differential diagnosis. In **Schizophrenia** certain activities may be avoided in response to delusions, but in such a situation the person does not recognize that the fear is excessive or unreasonable.

In **Post-traumatic Stress Disorder,** phobic avoidance of stimuli associated with the trauma is frequently present. In **Obsessive Compulsive Disorder,** phobic avoidance of certain situations that are associated with anxiety about dirt or contamination is frequent. The diagnosis of Simple Phobia should not be made in either of these cases.

Diagnostic criteria for 300.29 Simple Phobia

A. A persistent fear of a circumscribed stimulus (object or situation) other than fear of having a panic attack (as in Panic Disorder) or of humiliation or embarrassment in certain social situations (as in Social Phobia).

   Note: Do not include fears that are part of Panic Disorder with Agoraphobia or Agoraphobia without History of Panic Disorder.

B. During some phase of the disturbance, exposure to the specific phobic stimulus (or stimuli) almost invariably provokes an immediate anxiety response.

Diagnostic criteria for 300.29 Simple Phobia continued

C. The object or situation is avoided, or endured with intense anxiety.

D. The fear or the avoidant behavior significantly interferes with the person's normal routine or with usual social activities or relationships with others, or there is marked distress about having the fear.

E. The person recognizes that his or her fear is excessive or unreasonable.

F. The phobic stimulus is unrelated to the content of the obsessions of Obsessive Compulsive Disorder or the trauma of Post-traumatic Stress Disorder.

300.30   Obsessive Compulsive Disorder (or Obsessive Compulsive Neurosis)

The essential feature of this disorder is recurrent obsessions or compulsions sufficiently severe to cause marked distress, be time-consuming, or significantly interfere with the person's normal routine, occupational functioning, or usual social activities or relationships with others.

Obsessions are persistent ideas, thoughts, impulses, or images that are experienced, at least initially, as intrusive and senseless—for example, a parent having repeated impulses to kill a loved child, or a religious person having recurrent blasphemous thoughts. The person attempts to ignore or suppress such thoughts or impulses or to neutralize them with some other thought or action. The person recognizes that the obsessions are the product of his or her own mind, and are not imposed from without (as in the delusion of thought insertion).

The most common obsessions are repetitive thoughts of violence (e.g., killing one's child), contamination (e.g., becoming infected by shaking hands), and doubt (e.g., repeatedly wondering whether one has performed some act, such as having hurt someone in a traffic accident).

Compulsions are repetitive, purposeful, and intentional behaviors that are performed in response to an obsession, according to certain rules, or in a stereotyped fashion. The behavior is designed to neutralize or to prevent discomfort or some dreaded event or situation. However, either the activity is not connected in a realistic way with what it is designed to neutralize or prevent, or it is clearly excessive. The act is performed with a sense of subjective compulsion that is coupled with a desire to resist the compulsion (at least initially). The person recognizes that his or her behavior is excessive or unreasonable (this may not be true for young children and may no longer be true for people whose obsessions have evolved into overvalued ideas) and does not derive pleasure from carrying out the activity, although it provides a release of tension. The most common compulsions involve hand-washing, counting, checking, and touching.

When the person attempts to resist a compulsion, there is a sense of mounting tension that can be immediately relieved by yielding to the compulsion. In the course of the illness, after repeated failure at resisting the compulsions, the person may give in to them and no longer experience a desire to resist them.

Associated features. Depression and anxiety are common. Frequently there is phobic avoidance of situations that involve the content of the obsessions, such as dirt or contamination. For example, a person with obsessions about dirt may avoid public restrooms; a person with obsessions about contamination may avoid shaking hands with strangers.

Age at onset. Although the disorder usually begins in adolescence or early adulthood, it may begin in childhood.

Course. The course is usually chronic, with waxing and waning of symptoms.

Impairment. Impairment is often moderate or severe. In some cases acting according to the compulsions may become the major life activity.

Complications. Complications include Major Depression and the abuse of alcohol and anxiolytics.

Predisposing factors. No information.

Prevalence. Although the disorder was previously thought to be relatively rare in the general population, recent community studies indicate that mild forms of the disorder may be relatively common.

Sex ratio. This disorder is equally common in males and in females.

Differential diagnosis. Some activities, such as **eating (e.g., Eating Disorders), sexual behavior (e.g., Paraphilias), gambling (e.g., Pathological Gambling), or drinking (e.g., Alcohol Dependence or Abuse), when engaged in excessively** may be referred to as "compulsive." However, the activities are not true compulsions because the person derives pleasure from the particular activity, and may wish to resist it only because of its secondary deleterious consequences.

In a Major Depressive Episode, **obsessive brooding** about potentially unpleasant circumstances, or about possible alternative actions, is common. However, these symptoms lack the quality of being experienced as senseless because the person generally regards the ideation as meaningful, although possibly excessive. Therefore, these are not true obsessions.

In some cases of Obsessive Compulsive Disorder, the obsession becomes an overvalued idea, such as the almost unshakable belief that one is contaminating other people. Such overvalued ideas may be bizarre and suggest **Schizophrenia.** However, the person with Obsessive Compulsive Disorder who has an overvalued idea can usually, after considerable discussion, acknowledge the possibility that his or her belief may be unfounded. In contrast, the person with a true delusion usually has a fixed conviction that cannot be shaken.

In **Schizophrenia,** stereotyped behavior is common, but it is usually due to delusions rather than to true compulsions. However, in some cases of Obsessive Compulsive Disorder, there may be bizarre delusions and other symptoms unrelated to the disorder that justify the additional diagnosis of Schizophrenia.

In some people with **Tourette's Disorder,** an associated diagnosis is Obsessive Compulsive Disorder.

Diagnostic criteria for 300.30 Obsessive Compulsive Disorder

A. Either obsessions or compulsions:

Obsessions: (1), (2), (3), and (4):

(1) recurrent and persistent ideas, thoughts, impulses, or images that are experienced, at least initially, as intrusive and senseless, e.g., a parent's having repeated impulses to kill a loved child, a religious person's having recurrent blasphemous thoughts

(2) the person attempts to ignore or suppress such thoughts or impulses or to neutralize them with some other thought or action

(3) the person recognizes that the obsessions are the product of his or her own mind, not imposed from without (as in thought insertion)

(4) if another Axis I disorder is present, the content of the obsession is unrelated to it, e.g., the ideas, thoughts, impulses, or images are not about food in the presence of an Eating Disorder, about drugs in the presence of a Psychoactive Substance Use Disorder, or guilty thoughts in the presence of a Major Depression

Compulsions: (1), (2), and (3):

(1) repetitive, purposeful, and intentional behaviors that are performed in response to an obsession, or according to certain rules or in a stereotyped fashion

(2) the behavior is designed to neutralize or to prevent discomfort or some dreaded event or situation; however, either the activity is not connected in a realistic way with what it is designed to neutralize or prevent, or it is clearly excessive

(3) the person recognizes that his or her behavior is excessive or unreasonable (this may not be true for young children; it may no longer be true for people whose obsessions have evolved into overvalued ideas)

B. The obsessions or compulsions cause marked distress, are time-consuming (take more than an hour a day), or significantly interfere with the person's normal routine, occupational functioning, or usual social activities or relationships with others.

309.89   Post-traumatic Stress Disorder

The essential feature of this disorder is the development of characteristic symptoms following a psychologically distressing event that is outside the range of usual human experience (i.e., outside the range of such common experiences as simple bereavement, chronic illness, business losses, and marital conflict). The stressor producing this syndrome would be markedly distressing to almost anyone, and is usually experienced with intense fear, terror, and helplessness. The characteristic symptoms involve re-experiencing the traumatic event, avoidance of stimuli associated with the event or numbing of general responsiveness, and increased arousal. The diagnosis is not made if the disturbance lasts less than one month.

The most common traumata involve either a serious threat to one's life or physical integrity; a serious threat or harm to one's children, spouse, or other close relatives and friends; sudden destruction of one's home or community; or seeing another person who has recently been, or is being, seriously injured or killed as the result of an accident or physical violence. In some cases the trauma may be learning about a serious threat or harm to a close friend or relative, e.g., that one's child has been kidnapped, tortured, or killed.

The trauma may be experienced alone (e.g., rape or assault) or in the company of groups of people (e.g., military combat). Stressors producing this disorder include natural disasters (e.g., floods, earthquakes), accidental disasters (e.g., car accidents with serious physical injury, airplane crashes, large fires, collapse of physical structures), or deliberately caused disasters (e.g., bombing, torture, death camps). Some stressors frequently produce the disorder (e.g., torture), and others produce it only occasionally (e.g., natural disasters or car accidents). Sometimes there is a concomitant physical component of the trauma, which may even involve direct damage to the central nervous system (e.g., malnutrition, head injury). The disorder is apparently more severe and longer lasting when the stressor is of human design. The specific stressor and its severity should be recorded on Axis IV (p. 18).

The traumatic event can be reexperienced in a variety of ways. Commonly the person has recurrent and intrusive recollections of the event or recurrent distressing dreams during which the event is reexperienced. In rare instances there are dissociative states, lasting from a few seconds to several hours, or even days, during which components of the event are relived, and the person behaves as though experiencing the event at that moment. There is often intense psychological distress when the person is exposed to events that resemble an aspect of the traumatic event or that symbolize the traumatic event, such as anniversaries of the event.

In addition to the reexperiencing of the trauma, there is persistent avoidance of stimuli associated with it, or a numbing of general responsiveness that was not present before the trauma. The person commonly makes deliberate efforts to avoid thoughts or feelings about the traumatic event and about activities or situations that arouse recollections of it. This avoidance of reminders of the trauma may include psychogenic amnesia for an important aspect of the traumatic event.

Diminished responsiveness to the external world, referred to as "psychic numbing" or "emotional anesthesia," usually begins soon after the traumatic event. A person may complain of feeling detached or estranged from other people, that he or she has lost the ability to become interested in previously enjoyed activities, or that the ability to feel emotions of any type, especially those associated with intimacy, tenderness, and sexuality, is markedly decreased.

Persistent symptoms of increased arousal that were not present before the trauma include difficulty falling or staying asleep (recurrent nightmares during which the traumatic event is relived are sometimes accompanied by middle or terminal sleep disturbance), hypervigilance, and exaggerated startle response. Some complain of difficulty in concentrating or in completing tasks. Many report changes in aggression. In mild cases this may take the form of irritability with fears of losing control. In more severe forms, particularly in cases in which the survivor has actually committed acts of violence (as in war veterans), the fear is conscious and pervasive, and the reduced capacity for modulation may express itself in unpredictable explosions of aggressive behavior or an inability to express angry feelings.

Symptoms characteristic of Post-traumatic Stress Disorder, or physiologic reactivity, are often intensified or precipitated when the person is exposed to situations or activities that resemble or symbolize the original trauma (e.g., cold snowy weather or uniformed guards for survivors of death camps in cold climates; hot, humid weather for veterans of the South Pacific).

Age-specific features. Occasionally, a child may be mute or refuse to discuss the trauma, but this should not be confused with inability to remember what occurred. In younger children, distressing dreams of the event may, within several weeks, change into generalized nightmares of monsters, of rescuing others, or of threats to self or others. Young children do not have the sense that they are reliving the past; reliving the trauma occurs in action, through repetitive play.

Diminished interest in significant activities and constriction of affect both may be difficult for children to report on themselves, and should be carefully evaluated by reports from parents, teachers, and other observers. A symptom of Post-traumatic Stress Disorder in children may be a marked change in orientation toward the future. This includes the sense of a foreshortened future, for example, a child may not expect to have a career or marriage. There may also be "omen formation," that is, belief in an ability to prophesy future untoward events.

Children may exhibit various physical symptoms, such as stomachaches and headaches, in addition to the specific symptoms of increased arousal noted above.

Associated features. Symptoms of depression and anxiety are common, and in some instances may be sufficiently severe to be diagnosed as an Anxiety or Depressive Disorder. Impulsive behavior can occur, such as suddenly changing place of residence, unexplained absences, or other changes in life-style. There may be symptoms of an Organic Mental Disorder, such as failing memory, difficulty in concentrating, emotional lability, headache, and vertigo. In the case of a life-threatening trauma shared with others, survivors often describe painful guilt feelings about surviving when others did not, or about the things they had to do in order to survive.

Age at onset. The disorder can occur at any age, including during childhood.

Course and subtypes. Symptoms usually begin immediately or soon after the trauma. Reexperiencing symptoms may develop after a latency period of months or years following the trauma, though avoidance symptoms have usually been present during this period.

Impairment and complications. Impairment may be either mild or severe and affect nearly every aspect of life. Phobic avoidance of situations or activities resembling or symbolizing the original trauma may interfere with interpersonal relationships such as marriage or family life. Emotional lability, depression, and guilt may result in self-defeating behavior or suicidal actions. Psychoactive Substance Use Disorders are common complications.

Predisposing factors. Several studies indicate that preexisting psychopathological conditions predispose to the development of this disorder. However, the disorder can develop in people without any such preexisting conditions, particularly if the stressor is extreme.

Prevalence, sex ratio, and familial pattern. No information.

Differential diagnosis. If an **Anxiety, Depressive,** or **Organic Mental Disorder** develops following the trauma, these diagnoses should also be made.

In **Adjustment Disorder** the stressor is usually less severe and within the range of common experience; and the characteristic symptoms of Post-traumatic Stress Disorder, such as reexperiencing the trauma, are absent.

Diagnostic criteria for 309.89 Post-traumatic Stress Disorder

A. The person has experienced an event that is outside the range of usual human experience and that would be markedly distressing to almost anyone, e.g., serious threat to one's life or physical integrity; serious threat or harm to one's children, spouse, or other close relatives and friends; sudden destruction of one's home or community; or seeing another person who has recently been, or is being, seriously injured or killed as the result of an accident or physical violence.

B. The traumatic event is persistently reexperienced in at least one of the following ways:

   (1) recurrent and intrusive distressing recollections of the event (in young children, repetitive play in which themes or aspects of the trauma are expressed)
   (2) recurrent distressing dreams of the event
   (3) sudden acting or feeling as if the traumatic event were recurring (includes a sense of reliving the experience, illusions, hallucinations, and dissociative [flashback] episodes, even those that occur upon awakening or when intoxicated)
   (4) intense psychological distress at exposure to events that symbolize or resemble an aspect of the traumatic event, including anniversaries of the trauma

C. Persistent avoidance of stimuli associated with the trauma or numbing of general responsiveness (not present before the trauma), as indicated by at least three of the following:

   (1) efforts to avoid thoughts or feelings associated with the trauma
   (2) efforts to avoid activities or situations that arouse recollections of the trauma
   (3) inability to recall an important aspect of the trauma (psychogenic amnesia)
   (4) markedly diminished interest in significant activities (in young children, loss of recently acquired developmental skills such as toilet training or language skills)
   (5) feeling of detachment or estrangement from others
   (6) restricted range of affect, e.g., unable to have loving feelings
   (7) sense of a foreshortened future, e.g., does not expect to have a career, marriage, or children, or a long life

D. Persistent symptoms of increased arousal (not present before the trauma), as indicated by at least two of the following:

   (1) difficulty falling or staying asleep
   (2) irritability or outbursts of anger
   (3) difficulty concentrating
   (4) hypervigilance
   (5) exaggerated startle response
   (6) physiologic reactivity upon exposure to events that symbolize or resemble an aspect of the traumatic event (e.g., a woman who was raped in an elevator breaks out in a sweat when entering any elevator)

> **Diagnostic criteria for 309.89 Post-traumatic Stress Disorder continued**
>
> E.   Duration of the disturbance (symptoms in B, C, and D) of at least one month.
>
> **Specify delayed onset** if the onset of symptoms was at least six months after the trauma.

300.02   Generalized Anxiety Disorder

The essential feature of this disorder is unrealistic or excessive anxiety and worry (apprehensive expectation) about two or more life circumstances, e.g., worry about possible misfortune to one's child (who is in no danger) and worry about finances (for no good reason), for six months or longer, during which the person has been bothered by these concerns more days than not. In children and adolescents this may take the form of anxiety and worry about academic, athletic, and social performance. When the person is anxious, there are many signs of motor tension, autonomic hyperactivity, and vigilance and scanning. (Symptoms that are present only during panic attacks are not considered in making the diagnosis.)

In diagnosing the disorder, other disorders that are frequently associated with generalized anxiety need to be ruled out. Thus, the diagnosis is not made if the worry and anxiety occur exclusively during the course of a Mood Disorder or a psychotic disorder; nor is it made if the anxiety symptoms are sustained by a specific organic factor (e.g., hyperthyroidism, Caffeine Intoxication).

The diagnosis can be made if another Axis I disorder is also present provided the focus of the anxiety and worry is unrelated to that disorder, e.g., the worry is not about having a panic attack (as in Panic Disorder), being embarrassed or humiliated in public (as in Social Phobia), being contaminated (as in Obsessive Compulsive Disorder), or gaining weight (as in Anorexia Nervosa).

The symptoms of *motor tension* seen in Generalized Anxiety Disorder include: trembling, twitching, or feeling shaky; muscle tension and aches or soreness; restlessness; and easy fatigability.

Symptoms of *autonomic hyperactivity* include: shortness of breath or smothering sensations; palpitations or accelerated heart rate (tachycardia); sweating, or cold clammy hands; dry mouth; dizziness or lightheadedness; nausea, diarrhea, or other abdominal distress; flushes (hot flashes) or chills; frequent urination; and trouble swallowing or a "lump in the throat."

Symptoms of *vigilance and scanning* include: feeling keyed up or on edge; exaggerated startle response; difficulty concentrating or mind going blank because of anxiety; trouble falling or staying asleep; and irritability.

Associated features. Mild depressive symptoms are common. An associated and unrelated Panic Disorder or a Depressive Disorder is often present.

Impairment. Impairment in social or occupational functioning is rarely more than mild.

Complications. No information.

Age at onset. Age at onset is variable, but most commonly is in the 20s and 30s.

Course. In clinical samples the disorder is usually found to have been present for many years.

Predisposing factors. In clinical samples the disorder sometimes seems to follow a Major Depressive Episode.

Prevalence. When other disorders that could account for the anxiety symptoms are ruled out, the disorder is not commonly diagnosed in clinical samples.

Sex ratio. In clinical samples the disorder is apparently equally common in females and in males.

Familial pattern. No information.

Differential diagnosis. This diagnosis is made only when it cannot be established that an organic factor initiated and maintained the disturbance. **Physical disorders, such as hyperthyroidism,** and **Organic Mental Disorders,** such as **Caffeine Intoxication,** must be considered, as they can cause an identical clinical picture (see discussion of etiologic factors of Organic Anxiety Syndrome, p. 113).

In **Adjustment Disorder with Anxious Mood,** the full symptom picture required to meet the criteria for Generalized Anxiety Disorder is generally not present, the duration of the disturbance is less than six months, and a psychosocial stressor must be recognized.

In **psychotic disorders, Eating Disorders, Anxiety Disorders, Depressive Disorders,** and many other mental disorders, anxiety and worry are often prominent symptoms, but usually are clearly related to the underlying disorder. The additional diagnosis of Generalized Anxiety Disorder should be considered only when the focus of persistent anxiety and worry is unrelated to any other Axis I disorder.

Diagnostic criteria for 300.02 Generalized Anxiety Disorder

A. Unrealistic or excessive anxiety and worry (apprehensive expectation) about two or more life circumstances, e.g., worry about possible misfortune to one's child (who is in no danger) and worry about finances (for no good reason), for a period of six months or longer, during which the person has been bothered more days than not by these concerns. In children and adolescents, this may take the form of anxiety and worry about academic, athletic, and social performance.

B. If another Axis I disorder is present, the focus of the anxiety and worry in A is unrelated to it, e.g., the anxiety or worry is not about having a panic attack (as in Panic Disorder), being embarrassed in public (as in Social Phobia), being contaminated (as in Obsessive Compulsive Disorder), or gaining weight (as in Anorexia Nervosa).

C. The disturbance does not occur only during the course of a Mood Disorder or a psychotic disorder.

Diagnostic criteria for 300.02 Generalized Anxiety Disorder continued

D. At least 6 of the following 18 symptoms are often present when anxious (do not include symptoms present only during panic attacks):

Motor tension

  (1) trembling, twitching, or feeling shaky
  (2) muscle tension, aches, or soreness
  (3) restlessness
  (4) easy fatigability

Autonomic hyperactivity

  (5) shortness of breath or smothering sensations
  (6) palpitations or accelerated heart rate (tachycardia)
  (7) sweating, or cold clammy hands
  (8) dry mouth
  (9) dizziness or lightheadedness
  (10) nausea, diarrhea, or other abdominal distress
  (11) flushes (hot flashes) or chills
  (12) frequent urination
  (13) trouble swallowing or "lump in throat"

Vigilance and scanning

  (14) feeling keyed up or on edge
  (15) exaggerated startle response
  (16) difficulty concentrating or "mind going blank" because of anxiety
  (17) trouble falling or staying asleep
  (18) irritability

E. It cannot be established that an organic factor initiated and maintained the disturbance, e.g., hyperthyroidism, Caffeine Intoxication.

300.00 Anxiety Disorder Not Otherwise Specified

Disorders with prominent anxiety or phobic avoidance that are not classifiable as a specific Anxiety Disorder or as an Adjustment Disorder with Anxious Mood.

Somatoform Disorders

The essential features of this group of disorders are physical symptoms suggesting physical disorder (hence, Somatoform) for which there are no demonstrable organic findings or known physiologic mechanisms, and for which there is positive evidence, or a strong presumption, that the symptoms are linked to psychological factors or conflicts. Unlike in Factitious Disorder or Malingering, the symptom production in Somatoform Disorders is not intentional, i.e., the person does not experience the sense of controlling the production of the symptoms. Although the symptoms of Somatoform Disorders are "physical," the specific pathophysiologic processes involved are not demonstrable or understandable by existing laboratory procedures and are conceptualized most clearly by means of psychological constructs. For that reason, these are classified as mental disorders.

The first disorder in this category is Body Dysmorphic Disorder (previously called Dysmorphophobia), a disorder characterized by preoccupation with some imagined defect in physical appearance. The next disorder, Conversion Disorder, refers to a condition in which psychological factors are judged to be etiologically related to a loss or alteration of physical functioning that suggests a physical disorder. Hypochondriasis involves preoccupation with the fear of having, or the belief that one has, a serious disease. Somatization Disorder is a chronic, polysymptomatic disorder that begins early in life and that was previously referred to as either Hysteria or Briquet's Syndrome. Somatoform Pain Disorder is characterized by preoccupation with pain that is not attributable to any other mental or physical disorder. Undifferentiated Somatoform Disorder is for clinical conditions that resemble Somatization Disorder, but do not meet the full criteria for that disorder.

300.70 Body Dysmorphic Disorder (Dysmorphophobia)

The essential feature of this disorder is preoccupation with some imagined defect in appearance in a normal-appearing person. The most common complaints involve facial flaws, such as wrinkles, spots on the skin, excessive facial hair, shape of nose, mouth, jaw, or eyebrows, and swelling of the face. More rarely the complaint involves the appearance of the feet, hands, breasts, back, or some other part of the body. In some cases a slight physical anomaly is present, but the person's concern is grossly excessive.

In the past this disorder was called Dysmorphophobia; but since the disturbance does not involve phobic avoidance, that term was a misnomer. The term *Dysmorphophobia* has also been used to include cases in which the belief in a defect in appearance is of delusional intensity. It is unclear, however, whether the two different disorders can be distinguished by whether or not the belief is a delusion (as in DSM-III-R), or whether there are merely two variants of the same disorder. In this manual, a belief in a defect in appearance that is of delusional intensity is classified as Delusional Disorder, Somatic Subtype.

Associated features. A history of repeated visits to plastic surgeons or dermatologists in an effort to correct the imagined defect is common. A depressive syndrome and obsessive compulsive personality traits are frequent. Often there is avoidance of social or occupational situations because of anxiety about the imagined defect.

Age at onset. The most common age at onset is from adolescence through the third decade.

Course. The disorder usually persists for several years.

Impairment. Social and occupational functioning may be impaired, but marked disruption is uncommon.

Complications. Unnecessary surgical procedures may be a complication.

Prevalence. The disorder may actually be more common than it was previously thought to be.

Predisposing factors, sex ratio, and familial pattern. No information.

Differential diagnosis. In normal adolescence, **concern about minor defects in appearance**, such as acne, is common, but not grossly excessive. In **Major Depression, Avoidant Personality Disorder,** and **Social Phobia,** the person may exaggerate defects in appearance, but this symptom is not the predominant disturbance. In **Delusional Disorder, Somatic Subtype,** the person's belief in the defect is of delusional intensity.

In **Anorexia Nervosa** and in **Transsexualism,** the respective unfounded beliefs about body weight and gender-related physical characteristics do not warrant the diagnosis of Body Dysmorphic Disorder.

Diagnostic criteria for 300.70 Body Dysmorphic Disorder

A. Preoccupation with some imagined defect in appearance in a normal-appearing person. If a slight physical anomaly is present, the person's concern is grossly excessive.

B. The belief in the defect is not of delusional intensity, as in Delusional Disorder, Somatic Type (i.e., the person can acknowledge the possibility that he or she may be exaggerating the extent of the defect or that there may be no defect at all).

C. Occurrence not exclusively during the course of Anorexia Nervosa or Transsexualism.

300.11   Conversion Disorder (or Hysterical Neurosis, Conversion Type)

The essential feature of this disorder is an alteration or loss of physical functioning that suggests physical disorder, but that instead is apparently an expression of a psychological conflict or need. The symptoms of the disturbance are not intentionally produced (as in Factitious Disorder or Malingering) and, after appropriate investigation, cannot be explained by any physical disorder or known pathophysiologic mechanism. Conversion Disorder is not diagnosed when conversion symptoms are limited to pain (see Somatoform Pain Disorder, p. 264) or to a disturbance in sexual functioning (see Sexual Pain Disorders, p. 294), or are merely one of the symptoms of Somatization Disorder (p. 261).

The most obvious and "classic" conversion symptoms are those that suggest neurologic disease, such as paralysis, aphonia, seizures, coordination disturbance, akinesia, dyskinesia, blindness, tunnel vision, anosmia, anesthesia, and paresthesia. More rarely, conversion symptoms may involve the autonomic or endocrine system. Vomiting as a conversion symptom can represent revulsion and disgust. Pseudocyesis (false pregnancy) can represent both a wish for, and a fear of, pregnancy.

The definition of this disorder is unique in this classification in that it implies specific mechanisms to account for the disturbance. Two mechanisms have been suggested to explain what the person derives from having a conversion symptom.

In one mechanism, the person achieves "primary gain" by keeping an internal conflict or need out of awareness. In such cases there is a temporal relationship between an environmental stimulus that is apparently related to a psychological conflict or need and initiation or exacerbation of the symptom. For example, after an argument, inner conflict about the expression of rage may be expressed as "aphonia" or as a "paralysis" of the arm; or if the person views a traumatic event, a conflict about acknowledging that event may be expressed as "blindness." In such cases the symptom has a symbolic value that is a representation and partial solution of the underlying psychological conflict.

In the other mechanism, the person achieves "secondary gain" by avoiding a particular activity that is noxious to him or her and getting support from the environment that otherwise might not be forthcoming. For example, with a "paralyzed" hand, a soldier can avoid firing a gun; or a person with marked dependency needs may develop "blindness," or inability to walk or stand (astasia-abasia), even though all leg movements can be performed normally, to prevent desertion by a spouse.

A conversion symptom is likely to involve a single symptom during a given episode, but may vary in site and nature if there are subsequent episodes.

Associated features. Usually the symptom develops in a setting of extreme psychological stress and appears suddenly. Histrionic personality traits (p. 348) are common, but not invariably present. *La belle indifférence*, an attitude toward the symptom that suggests a relative lack of concern, out of keeping with the severe nature of the impairment, is sometimes present. This feature has little diagnostic value, however, since it is also found in some seriously ill medical patients who are stoic about their situation.

Age at onset. The usual age at onset is in adolescence or early adulthood, but the symptom may appear for the first time during middle age, or even in the later decades of life.

Course. The course of Conversion Disorder (as distinct from conversion symptoms that are part of other disorders, such as Somatization Disorder) is unknown, but probably is usually of short duration, with abrupt onset and resolution. Recurrence of an episode of Conversion Disorder usually predicts a chronic course.

Some people given an initial diagnosis of conversion symptoms are later found to have a neurologic disorder. Apparently, in some of these instances the earliest symptoms of the neurologic disorder predisposed to the development of a concomitant conversion symptom. In other instances the original diagnosis of a conversion symptom was incorrect and represented a missed diagnosis of true organic pathology.

Impairment and complications. The effect of this disorder on the person's life is usually marked and frequently impedes normal life activities. Prolonged loss of function may produce real and serious complications, such as contractures or disuse atrophy from conversion paralysis. When associated with Dependent Personality Disorder, the conversion symptom may enhance the development of a chronic sick role. Unnecessary diagnostic or therapeutic medical procedures may themselves produce disfigurement or incapacity.

Predisposing factors. Antecedent physical disorders (which may provide a prototype for the symptoms, e.g., pseudoseizures in people with epilepsy), exposure to other people with real physical symptoms or conversion symptoms, and extreme psychosocial stress (e.g., warfare or the recent death of a significant figure) are predisposing factors. Histrionic and Dependent Personality Disorders also increase vulnerability to the disorder.

Prevalence. Although Conversion Disorder was apparently common several decades ago, it is now rarely encountered. Most cases are seen on neurology or orthopedic wards and in military settings, especially in wartime.

Sex ratio. No definite information is available; but one particular conversion symptom, globus hystericus, the feeling of a lump in the throat that interferes with swallowing, is apparently more common in females.

Familial pattern. No information.

Differential diagnosis. Some **physical disorders that present with vague, multiple, somatic symptoms, such as multiple sclerosis or systemic lupus erythematosus,** may, early in their course, be misdiagnosed as conversion symptoms. A diagnosis of Conversion Disorder is suggested if the symptoms are inconsistent with the actual known physical disorder—for example, motor signs of good function in a supposedly paralyzed part of the body, or complaints obviously inconsistent with the anatomical distribution of the nervous system. Another example would be "anesthesia" of the hand conforming to the concept of the hand rather than to the functional area served by a specific part of the nervous system. In another example, a person with conversion blindness may be found to have normal pupillary responses and evoked potentials as measured by an EEG. Resolution of symptoms through suggestion, hypnosis, or amobarbital interview suggests a conversion symptom. Temporary improvement due to suggestion has little diagnostic value since this may also occur with true physical illness.

In **undiagnosed physical disorder**, physical symptoms are present that are not explainable by a known physical disorder, but there is no evidence that they serve a psychological purpose. **Physical disorders in which psychological factors often play an** important role, such as irritable colon or bronchial asthma, should not be diagnosed as Conversion Disorders since there is demonstrable organic pathology or a pathophysiologic mechanism to account for the disorder.

Somatization Disorder and, more rarely, Schizophrenia may have conversion *symptoms.* However, the diagnosis of Conversion Disorder should not be made when such symptoms are due to either of these more pervasive disorders.

In many of the Sexual Dysfunctions, it is difficult to determine whether the symptom, such as impotence in the male or lack of sexual excitement in the female, represents a physiologic reaction to anxiety or a direct expression of a psychological conflict or need (conversion symptom). For this reason, and in order to group all of the sexual disturbances together, conversion symptoms involving sexual dysfunction are not coded as Conversion Disorder, but rather as Sexual Dysfunction.

Some somatoform pain can be conceptualized as a conversion symptom; but because of the different course and treatment implications, all such cases should be coded as Somatoform Pain Disorder.

In Hypochondriasis, typically there are physical symptoms, but there is no actual loss or distortion of bodily functions.

In Factitious Disorder with Physical Symptoms, the symptoms are intentionally produced, and the simulated illness rarely takes the form of neurologic symptoms that are likely to be confused with conversion symptoms. However, distinguishing conversion seizures from seizures as a manifestation of Factitious Disorder is often extremely difficult.

In Malingering the symptoms are intentionally produced in pursuit of a goal that is obviously recognizable given the person's environmental circumstance; this goal frequently involves the prospect of material reward or the avoidance of unpleasant work or duty.

Diagnostic criteria for 300.11 Conversion Disorder

A. A loss of, or alteration in, physical functioning suggesting a physical disorder.

B. Psychological factors are judged to be etiologically related to the symptom because of a temporal relationship between a psychosocial stressor that is apparently related to a psychological conflict or need and initiation or exacerbation of the symptom.

C. The person is not conscious of intentionally producing the symptom.

D. The symptom is not a culturally sanctioned response pattern and cannot, after appropriate investigation, be explained by a known physical disorder.

E. The symptom is not limited to pain or to a disturbance in sexual functioning.

Specify: single episode or recurrent.

300.70   Hypochondriasis (or Hypochondriacal Neurosis)

The essential feature of this disorder is preoccupation with the fear of having, or the belief that one has, a serious disease, based on the person's interpretation of physical signs or sensations as evidence of physical illness. A thorough physical evaluation does not support the diagnosis of any physical disorder that can account for the physical signs or sensations or for the person's unwarranted interpretation of them, although a coexisting physical disorder may be present. The unwarranted fear or belief of having a disease persists despite medical reassurance, but is not of delusional intensity, in that the person can acknowledge the possibility that he or she may be exaggerating the extent of the feared disease or that there may be no disease at all.

The preoccupation may be with bodily functions, such as heartbeat, sweating, or peristalsis, or with minor physical abnormalities, such as a small sore or an occasional cough. The person interprets these sensations or signs as evidence of a serious disease. The feared disease, or diseases, may involve several body systems, at different times or simultaneously. Alternatively, there may be preoccupation with a specific organ or a single disease, as in "cardiac neurosis," in which the person fears or believes that he or she has heart disease.

Associated features. The medical history is often presented in great detail and at length. "Doctor-shopping" and deterioration in "doctor–patient" relationships, with frustration and anger on both sides, are common. People with this disorder often believe they are not getting proper care.

Anxiety and depressed mood and obsessive compulsive personality traits are frequently observed.

Age at onset. The disorder can begin at any age. The most common age at onset is between 20 and 30 years.

Course. The course is usually chronic, with waxing and waning of symptoms. However, recovery occurs in many cases.

Impairment. There is usually some impairment in social or occupational functioning. Social relations are often strained because the person is preoccupied with the disease. There may be no effect on functioning at work if the person limits the preoccupation with physical complaints to nonwork time; otherwise, the preoccupation may cause the person to miss work or interfere with his or her work efficiency. Impairment is severe when the person adopts an invalid life-style and becomes bedridden.

Complications. Complications are secondary to efforts to obtain medical care. Because of the multiple physical symptoms without organic basis, true organic pathology may be missed. In addition, when the person goes from doctor to doctor, there is the danger of repeated diagnostic procedures that carry risks of their own, such as exploratory surgery.

Predisposing factors. Past experience with true organic disease, in oneself or a family member, and psychosocial stressors apparently predispose to development of this disorder.

Prevalence. This disorder is commonly seen in general medical practice. Because people with the disorder are often offended at the suggestion that their fears or beliefs may be unwarranted, they frequently refuse referral for mental health care, and are not often seen in mental health facilities.

Sex ratio. The disorder is equally common in males and in females.

Familial pattern. No information.

Differential diagnosis. The most important differential diagnostic consideration is **true organic disease,** such as early stages of neurologic disorders (e.g., multiple sclerosis), endocrine disorders (e.g., thyroid or parathyroid disease), and illnesses that frequently affect multiple body systems (e.g., systemic lupus erythematosus). However, the presence of true organic disease does not rule out the possibility of coexisting Hypochondriasis.

In **some psychotic disorders, such as Schizophrenia and Major Depression with Psychotic Features,** there may be somatic delusions of having a physical disease. In Hypochondriasis the belief of having a disease generally does not have the fixed quality of a true somatic delusion in that usually the person with Hypochondriasis can entertain the possibility that the feared disease is not present. This distinction may be difficult to make on initial evaluation.

In **psychotic disorders, Dysthymia, Panic Disorder, Generalized Anxiety Disorder, Obsessive Compulsive Disorder,** and **Somatization Disorder** there may be hypochondriacal concerns, but rarely will there be longstanding preoccupation with hypochondriacal symptoms. In Somatization Disorder there tends to be preoccupation with symptoms rather than fear of having a specific disease or diseases. When the criteria for any of these disorders are met and the criteria for Hypochondriasis are also met, both diagnoses should be given.

Diagnostic criteria for 300.70 Hypochondriasis

A. Preoccupation with the fear of having, or the belief that one has, a serious disease, based on the person's interpretation of physical signs or sensations as evidence of physical illness.

B. Appropriate physical evaluation does not support the diagnosis of any physical disorder that can account for the physical signs or sensations or the person's unwarranted interpretation of them, **and** the symptoms in A are not just symptoms of panic attacks.

C. The fear of having, or belief that one has, a disease persists despite medical reassurance.

D. Duration of the disturbance is at least six months.

E. The belief in A is not of delusional intensity, as in Delusional Disorder, Somatic Type (i.e., the person can acknowledge the possibility that his or her fear of having, or belief that he or she has, a serious disease is unfounded).

300.81 Somatization Disorder

The essential features of this disorder are recurrent and multiple somatic complaints, of several years' duration, for which medical attention has been sought, but that apparently are not due to any physical disorder. The disorder begins before the age of 30 and has a chronic but fluctuating course.

Complaints are often presented in a dramatic, vague, or exaggerated way, or are part of a complicated medical history in which many physical diagnoses have been considered. Those affected frequently receive medical care from a number of physicians, sometimes simultaneously. (Although most people without mental disorders have aches and pains and other physical complaints at various times, they rarely bring them to medical attention.) Complaints invariably involve the following organ systems or types of symptoms: conversion or pseudoneurologic symptoms (e.g., paralysis, blindness), gastrointestinal discomfort (e.g., abdominal pain), female reproductive difficulties (e.g., painful menstruation), psychosexual problems (e.g., sexual indifference), pain (e.g., back pain), and cardiopulmonary symptoms (e.g., dizziness).

Associated features. Anxiety and depressed mood are extremely frequent. In fact, many people with this disorder who seek mental health care do so because of depressive symptoms, which may include suicide threats and attempts. Antisocial behavior and occupational, interpersonal, and marital difficulties are common. Hallucinations are also reported, usually of hearing one's name called. Reality testing, however, is intact. Histrionic Personality Disorder and, more rarely, Antisocial Personality Disorder often are also present.

Age at onset. Symptoms usually begin in the teen years or, rarely, in the 20s. Menstrual difficulties may be one of the earliest symptoms in females, although preadolescents and adolescents may present with seizures, depressive symptoms, headache, abdominal pain, or a plethora of other physical symptoms.

Course. This is a chronic but fluctuating disorder that rarely remits spontaneously. A year seldom passes without some medical attention.

Impairment and complications. Because of constant consultation of doctors, numerous medical evaluations are undergone, both in and out of the hospital; there is frequently unwitting submission to unnecessary surgery. These people run the risk of Psychoactive Substance Use Disorders involving various prescribed medicines. Because of depressive symptoms, they may experience long periods of incapacity and frequently threaten or attempt suicide. Completed suicide, when it occurs, is usually associated with Psychoactive Substance Abuse. People with this disorder often lead lives as chaotic and complicated as their medical histories.

Predisposing factors. No information.

Prevalence. Studies have reported widely different lifetime prevalence rates, ranging from 0.2% to 2% among females, depending on whether the interviewer is a physician and on demographic variables in the samples studied.

Sex ratio. The disorder is rarely diagnosed in males.

Familial pattern. Somatization Disorder is observed in 10% to 20% of female first-degree biologic relatives of females with Somatization Disorder. The male relatives of females with this disorder show an increased risk of Antisocial Personality Disorder and Psychoactive Substance Use Disorders. Adoption studies indicate that both genetic and environmental factors contribute to the risk of this group of disorders, because both biologic and adoptive parents with any of the disorders increase the risk of Antisocial Personality Disorder, Psychoactive Substance Use Disorders, and Somatization Disorder.

Differential diagnosis. It is necessary to rule out **physical disorders that present with vague, multiple, and confusing somatic symptoms, e.g., hyperparathyroidism, porphyria, multiple sclerosis, and systemic lupus erythematosus.** The onset of multiple physical symptoms late in life is almost always due to physical disease.

Schizophrenia with multiple somatic delusions needs to be differentiated from the nondelusional somatic complaints of people with Somatization Disorder. In rare instances, people with Somatization Disorder also have Schizophrenia, in which case both diagnoses should be noted.

In **Panic Disorder** there are also cardiopulmonary symptoms, but these occur only within the context of panic attacks. However, Panic Disorder may coexist with Somatization Disorder, so when the physical symptoms do not occur only during panic attacks, both diagnoses may be made.

In **Conversion Disorder** one or more conversion symptoms occur in the absence of the full clinical picture of Somatization Disorder.

In **Factitious Disorder with Physical Symptoms** the person has a sense of controlling production of the symptoms.

Diagnostic criteria for 300.81 Somatization Disorder

A. A history of many physical complaints or a belief that one is sickly, beginning before the age of 30 and persisting for several years.

B. At least 13 symptoms from the list below. To count a symptom as significant, the following criteria must be met:

   (1) no organic pathology or pathophysiologic mechanism (e.g., a physical disorder or the effects of injury, medication, drugs, or alcohol) to account for the symptom or, when there is related organic pathology, the complaint or resulting social or occupational impairment is grossly in excess of what would be expected from the physical findings
   (2) has not occurred only during a panic attack
   (3) has caused the person to take medicine (other than over-the-counter pain medication), see a doctor, or alter life-style

Symptom list:

Gastrointestinal symptoms:

   (1) **vomiting (other than during pregnancy)**
   (2) abdominal pain (other than when menstruating)
   (3) nausea (other than motion sickness)
   (4) bloating (gassy)
   (5) diarrhea
   (6) intolerance of (gets sick from) several different foods

Pain symptoms:

   (7) **pain in extremities**
   (8) back pain
   (9) joint pain
   (10) pain during urination
   (11) other pain (excluding headaches)

(continued)

Diagnostic criteria for 300.81 Somatization Disorder continued

Cardiopulmonary symptoms:

(12) **shortness of breath when not exerting oneself**
(13) palpitations
(14) chest pain
(15) dizziness

Conversion or pseudoneurologic symptoms:

(16) **amnesia**
(17) **difficulty swallowing**
(18) loss of voice
(19) deafness
(20) double vision
(21) blurred vision
(22) blindness
(23) fainting or loss of consciousness
(24) seizure or convulsion
(25) trouble walking
(26) paralysis or muscle weakness
(27) urinary retention or difficulty urinating

Sexual symptoms for the major part of the person's life after opportunities for sexual activity:

(28) **burning sensation in sexual organs or rectum (other than during intercourse)**
(29) sexual indifference
(30) pain during intercourse
(31) impotence

Female reproductive symptoms judged by the person to occur more frequently or severely than in most women:

(32) **painful menstruation**
(33) irregular menstrual periods
(34) excessive menstrual bleeding
(35) vomiting throughout pregnancy

Note: The seven items in boldface may be used to screen for the disorder. The presence of two or more of these items suggests a high likelihood of the disorder.

307.80   Somatoform Pain Disorder

The essential feature of this disorder is preoccupation with pain in the absence of adequate physical findings to account for the pain or its intensity.

The pain symptom either is inconsistent with the anatomical distribution of the nervous system or, if it mimics a known disease entity (as in angina or sciatica), cannot, after extensive diagnostic evaluation, be adequately accounted for by organic pathology. Similarly, no pathophysiologic mechanism accounts for the pain, as in tension headaches caused by muscle spasm.

In some cases there may be evidence that psychological factors are etiologically involved in the pain, as when there is a clear temporal relationship between an environmental stimulus that is apparently related to a psychological conflict or need and initiation or exacerbation of the pain. In other cases the evidence may be the pain's permitting the person to avoid some activity that is noxious to him or her or to get support from the environment that otherwise might not be forthcoming. In still other cases, there may be no direct evidence of an etiologic role of psychological factors.

Associated features. Somatoform Pain Disorder may be accompanied by other localized sensory or motor-function changes, such as paresthesias and muscle spasm. Characteristic are frequent visits to physicians to obtain relief despite medical reassurance (doctor-shopping), excessive use of analgesics without relief of the pain, requests for surgery, and assumption of the role of invalid. The person usually refuses to consider the contribution of psychological factors to the pain. In some cases the pain has symbolic significance, such as pain mimicking angina in a person whose father died of heart disease. A past history of conversion symptoms is common. Histrionic personality traits (see p. 348) are seldom present, nor is *la belle indifférence*, though concern about the pain symptom is usually less intense than its stated severity. Symptoms of depression are frequent (particularly anhedonia and insomnia), and in many cases an associated diagnosis of Major Depression is warranted.

Age at onset. This disorder can occur at any stage of life, from childhood to old age, but most frequently has its onset in the 30s and 40s.

Course. The pain usually appears suddenly and increases in severity over a few weeks or months. In most cases the symptom has persisted for many years by the time the person comes to the attention of the mental health profession.

Impairment. Typically, the person becomes very incapacitated and has to quit working. An invalid role is often assumed.

Complications. The most serious complications are iatrogenic; they include dependence on minor tranquilizers and narcotic analgesics and repeated, unsuccessful, surgical interventions.

Predisposing factors. In about half of the cases, the pain develops immediately following a physical trauma. There is some evidence that among people with Somatoform Pain Disorder, a greater than would be expected proportion began working at an unusually early age, held jobs that were physically strenuous or overly routinized, were "workaholics," and rarely took time off from work for vacations.

Prevalence. No information, although the disorder is probably common in general medical practice.

Sex ratio. The disorder is diagnosed almost twice as frequently in females as in males.

Familial pattern. There is some evidence that first-degree biologic relatives of people with this disorder have had more painful injuries and illnesses, depression, and Alcohol Dependence than occur in the general population.

Differential diagnosis. The **dramatic presentation of organic pain,** which may seem excessive to an observer because of minimal physical findings, is not sufficient for diagnosing this disorder, and may be only a function of histrionic personality traits or a culturally-determined style of communication.

People with **Somatization Disorder, Depressive Disorders,** or **Schizophrenia** may complain of various aches and pains, but pain rarely dominates the clinical picture.

In **Malingering,** the symptoms are intentionally produced in pursuit of a goal that is obviously recognizable, given the person's environmental circumstances. For example, a person with Opioid Dependence complains of pain in order to obtain opioids.

The **pain associated with muscle contraction headaches ("tension headaches")** is not to be diagnosed as Somatoform Pain Disorder because there is a pathophysiologic mechanism that accounts for the pain.

Diagnostic criteria for 307.80 Somatoform Pain Disorder

A. Preoccupation with pain for at least six months.

B. Either (1) or (2):

    (1) appropriate evaluation uncovers no organic pathology or pathophysiologic mechanism (e.g., a physical disorder or the effects of injury) to account for the pain

    (2) when there is related organic pathology, the complaint of pain or resulting social or occupational impairment is grossly in excess of what would be expected from the physical findings

---

300.70 Undifferentiated Somatoform Disorder

This is a category for clinical pictures that do not meet the full symptom picture of Somatization Disorder. There is either a single circumscribed symptom, such as difficulty in swallowing, or, more commonly, multiple physical complaints, such as fatigue, loss of appetite, and gastrointestinal problems. Like Somatization Disorder, the symptoms are not explainable on the basis of demonstrable organic findings or a known pathophysiologic mechanism, and are apparently linked to psychological factors. The diagnosis is not made if the disturbance is of less than six months' duration or if it occurs only during the course of another Somatoform Disorder, such as Somatoform Pain Disorder, a Sexual Pain Disorder, a Mood Disorder, an Anxiety Disorder, a Sleep Disorder, or a psychotic disorder, such as Schizophrenia.

Although Undifferentiated Somatoform Disorder is defined here as residual to Somatization Disorder, it is far more common than Somatization Disorder itself.

Associated features. Anxiety and depressed mood are common.

Age at onset. No information.

Course. Unlike in Somatization Disorder, the course is variable and often is recurrent or limited to a single episode (of at least six months' duration).

Impairment and complications. Impairment is generally less than that in Somatization Disorder.

Predisposing factors. No information.

Sex ratio. Unlike in Somatization Disorder, there is no evidence that this disorder is much more common in females.

Differential diagnosis. In **Somatization Disorder**, there is the requirement of a minimum number of characteristic symptoms, of several years' duration, and onset before age 30. In **Adjustment Disorder with Physical Complaints**, the duration is less than six months. In **Psychological Factors Affecting Physical Condition**, the physical complaints are of an Axis III condition or disorder.

Diagnostic criteria for 300.70 Undifferentiated Somatoform Disorder

A. One or more physical complaints, e.g., fatigue, loss of appetite, gastrointestinal or urinary complaints.

B. Either (1) or (2):

(1) appropriate evaluation uncovers no organic pathology or pathophysiologic mechanism (e.g., a physical disorder or the effects of injury, medication, drugs, or alcohol) to account for the physical complaints

(2) when there is related organic pathology, the physical complaints or resulting social or occupational impairment is grossly in excess of what would be expected from the physical findings

C. Duration of the disturbance is at least six months.

D. Occurrence not exclusively during the course of another Somatoform Disorder, a Sexual Dysfunction, a Mood Disorder, an Anxiety Disorder, a Sleep Disorder, or a psychotic disorder.

300.70 Somatoform Disorder Not Otherwise Specified

Disorders with somatoform symptoms that do not meet the criteria for any specific Somatoform Disorder or Adjustment Disorder with Physical Complaints.

Examples:

(1) an illness involving nonpsychotic hypochondriacal symptoms of less than six months' duration
(2) an illness involving non-stress-related physical complaints of less than six months' duration

Dissociative Disorders (or Hysterical Neuroses, Dissociative Type)

The essential feature of these disorders is a disturbance or alteration in the normally integrative functions of identity, memory, or consciousness. The disturbance or alteration may be sudden or gradual, and transient or chronic. If it occurs primarily in identity, the person's customary identity is temporarily forgotten, and a new identity may be assumed or imposed (as in Multiple Personality Disorder), or the customary feeling of one's own reality is lost and is replaced by a feeling of unreality (as in Depersonalization Disorder). If the disturbance occurs primarily in memory, important personal events cannot be recalled (as in Psychogenic Amnesia and Psychogenic Fugue).

Depersonalization Disorder has been included in the Dissociative Disorders because the feeling of one's own reality, an important component of identity, is lost. Some, however, question this inclusion because disturbance in memory is absent.

Although Sleepwalking Disorder has the essential feature of a Dissociative Disorder, it is classified as a Sleep Disorder.

300.14 Multiple Personality Disorder

The essential feature of this disorder is the existence within the person of two or more distinct personalities or personality states. Personality is here defined as a relatively enduring pattern of perceiving, relating to, and thinking about the environment and one's self that is exhibited in a wide range of important social and personal contexts. Personality states differ only in that the pattern is not exhibited in as wide a range of contexts. In classic cases, there are at least two fully developed personalities; in other cases, there may be only one distinct personality and one or more personality states. In classic cases, the personalities and personality states each have unique memories, behavior patterns, and social relationships; in other cases, there may be varying degrees of sharing of memories and commonalities in behavior or social relationships. In children and adolescents, classic cases with two or more fully developed personalities are not as common as they are in adults. In adults, the number of personalities or personality states in any one case varies from two to over one hundred, with occasional cases of extreme complexity. Approximately half of recently reported cases have ten personalities or fewer, and half have over ten. (In the text below, both personality and personality states will be subsumed under the term *personality*.)

At least two of the personalities, at some time and recurrently, take full control of the person's behavior. The transition from one personality to another is usually sudden (within seconds to minutes), but, rarely, may be gradual (over hours or days). The transition is often triggered by psychosocial stress or idiosyncratically meaningful social or environmental cues. Transitions may also occur when there are conflicts among the personalities or in connection with a plan they have agreed upon. A transition may also be elicited by hypnosis or an amobarbital interview.

Often personalities are aware of some or all of the others to varying degrees, and some may experience the others as friends, companions, or adversaries. Some personalities may be aware of the existence of other personalities, but not have any direct interaction with them. Some may be unaware of the existence of the others. At any given moment, only one personality interacts with the external environment, and none or any number of the other personalities may actively perceive (i.e., "listen in on") or influence all or part of what is going on. The personality that presents itself for treatment often has little or no knowledge of the existence of the other personalities.

Most of the personalities are aware of lost periods of time or distortions in their experience of time. For example, the person may be aware of periods of amnesia or periods of confusion about his or her experience of time. Some admit to these experiences if asked, but few volunteer such information because they fear being called liars or being considered "crazy." Others are unaware of their amnestic experiences, confabulate memories that cover the amnestic periods, or have access to the memories of the other personalities, which they report as if they were their own.

The individual personalities may be quite discrepant in attitude, behavior, and self-image, and may even represent opposites. But they may also differ only in alternating approaches to a major problem area. For example, a quiet, retiring spinster may alternate with a flamboyant, promiscuous, bar habituée; or a person may have one personality that responds to aggression with childlike fright and flight, another that responds with masochistic submission, and yet another that responds with counterattack. At different periods in the person's life, any of the different personalities may vary in the proportion of time that they control the person's behavior.

Associated features. One or more of the personalities may function with a reasonable degree of adaptation (e.g., be gainfully employed) while alternating with another personality that is clearly dysfunctional or appears to have a specific mental disorder. Studies have demonstrated that various personalities in the same person may have different physiologic characteristics and different responses to psychological tests. Different personalities may, for example, have different eyeglass prescriptions, different responses to the same medication, and different IQs. One or more of the personalities may report being of the opposite sex, of a different race or age, or from a different family than the other personalities. Each personality displays behaviors characteristic of its sense of its stated age.

One or more of the personalities may be aware of hearing or having heard the voice(s) of one or more of the other personalities, or may report having talked with or engaged in activities with one or more of the other personalities. These internal conversations and the belief that one has engaged in activities with another personality when the latter is actually a dissociated aspect of the person must be differentiated from other forms of hallucinatory and delusional experiences.

The personalities often exist in groups of two or more, all of whom represent the same period of life (e.g., adolescence). When this occurs, one or more may have the role of protector of another member or members of the group.

Most often the personalities have proper names, usually different from the first name, and sometimes different from both the first and last names, of the individual. Often the names have symbolic meaning, for example, "Melody" as the name of a personality that expresses itself through music. Occasionally, one (or more) of the personalities is unnamed, or is given the name of its function, for example, "The Protector."

Frequently, one or more of the personalities exhibits symptoms suggesting a coexisting mental disorder, for example, changes of mood suggesting a Mood Disorder, complaints of anxiety suggesting an Anxiety Disorder, or marked disturbance in personality functioning suggesting Borderline Personality Disorder. It is often unclear whether these represent coexisting disorders or merely associated features of Multiple Personality Disorder.

Age at onset. Onset of Multiple Personality Disorder is almost invariably in childhood, but most cases do not come to clinical attention until much later.

Course. The disorder tends to be chronic, although over time the frequency of switching between the personalities often decreases.

Impairment. The degree of impairment varies from mild to severe, depending primarily on the nature of, and relationships among, the personalities and only secondarily on their number.

Complications. Suicide attempts, self-mutilation, externally directed violence (including child abuse, assault, or rape), and Psychoactive Substance Dependence Disorders are possible complications of this disorder.

Predisposing factors. Several studies indicate that in nearly all cases, the disorder has been preceded by abuse (often sexual) or another form of severe emotional trauma in childhood.

Prevalence. Recent reports suggest that this disorder is not nearly so rare as it has commonly been thought to be.

Sex ratio. In several studies of psychiatric patients, the disorder has been diagnosed from three to nine times more frequently in females than in males.

Familial pattern. Several studies have demonstrated that the disorder is more common in first-degree biologic relatives of people with the disorder than in the general population.

Differential diagnosis. Psychogenic Fugue and **Psychogenic Amnesia** may be confused with Multiple Personality Disorder, but do not have its characteristic repeated shifts in identity, and usually are limited to a single, brief episode.

Psychotic disorders may be confused with Multiple Personality Disorder because the person reports being controlled or influenced by others, or hearing or talking with voices (of other personalities). These symptoms may be interpreted by the clinician as the delusions or hallucinations of **Schizophrenia** or of a **Mood Disorder with Psychotic Features.**

The **belief that one is possessed** by another person, spirit, or entity may occur as a symptom of Multiple Personality Disorder. In such cases the complaint of being "possessed" is actually the experience of the alternate personality's influence on the person's behavior and mood. However, the feeling that one is "possessed" may also be a delusion in a psychotic disorder, such as Schizophrenia, not a symptom of a Dissociative Disorder.

Borderline Personality Disorder may coexist with Multiple Personality Disorder. However, often the person with Multiple Personality Disorder is incorrectly diagnosed as having only Borderline Personality Disorder because the alternation of the personalities is mistakenly thought to be the instability of mood, self-image, and interpersonal behavior that characterizes Borderline Personality Disorder. Similarly, **other mental disorders** may coexist with or obscure the presence of Multiple Personality Disorder.

Malingering can present a difficult diagnostic dilemma, which often can be resolved only by obtaining additional data from ancillary sources, such as hospital and police records and family members, employers, and friends.

Diagnostic criteria for 300.14 Multiple Personality Disorder

A. The existence within the person of two or more distinct personalities or personality states (each with its own relatively enduring pattern of perceiving, relating to, and thinking about the environment and self).

B. At least two of these personalities or personality states recurrently take full control of the person's behavior.

300.13   Psychogenic Fugue

The essential feature of this disorder is sudden, unexpected travel away from home or customary work locale with assumption of a new identity and an inability to recall one's previous identity. Perplexity and disorientation may occur. Following recovery, there is no recollection of events that took place during the fugue. The diagnosis is not made in the presence of an Organic Mental Disorder.

In some cases the disorder may be manifested by the assumption of a completely new identity during the fugue, usually marked by more gregarious and uninhibited traits than characterized the former personality, which typically is quiet and altogether ordinary. In such instances the person may give himself or herself a new name, take up a new residence, and engage in complex social activities that are well integrated and do not suggest the presence of a mental disorder. In most cases, however, the fugue is less elaborate, and consists of little more than brief, apparently purposeful travel. Social contacts in these cases are minimal or even avoided; the new identity, although present, is incomplete. Occasionally there are outbursts of violence against property or another person. In all cases of fugue, however, the person's travel and behavior must appear more purposeful than the confused wandering that may be seen in Psychogenic Amnesia.

Associated features. No information.

Age at onset. Variable.

Predisposing factors and course. Heavy alcohol use may predispose to the development of the disorder. Psychogenic Fugue typically follows severe psychosocial stress, such as marital quarrels, personal rejections, military conflict, or a natural disaster. Usually the fugue is of brief duration—hours to days—and involves a limited amount of travel; more rarely, it continues for many months and involves complex but unobtrusive travel over thousands of miles and across numerous national borders. Usually, recovery is rapid; recurrences are rare.

Impairment. The degree of impairment varies with the duration of the fugue and the extent to which it causes subsequent social distress to the person and his or her associates. When violent behavior has occurred, the social, legal, and other personal sequelae depend on the nature of the violent act. In most cases impairment is minimal and transient.

Complications. None.

Prevalence. Although apparently rare, the disorder is most common in wartime, or in the wake of a natural disaster.

Sex ratio and familial pattern. No information.

Differential diagnosis. In **Multiple Personality Disorder** there are characteristic repeated shifts of identity, and the disorder is not limited to a single episode, as is usually the case with Psychogenic Fugue. In addition, a history of identity disturbance since childhood is often present in Multiple Personality Disorder, whereas in Psychogenic Fugue the onset of the identity disturbance generally coincides with that of the fugue.

In **Psychogenic Amnesia,** sudden failure to recall important personal events, including one's personal identity, occurs; but purposeful travel and the assumption of a new identity, partial or complete, are not present.

In **temporal lobe epilepsy,** there is no assumption of a new identity. Mood is dysphoric, and typically, temporal lobe epilepsy is not precipitated by psychosocial stress.

Malingering, in which there is feigned inability to recall one's previous activity and identity, is exceedingly difficult to distinguish from Psychogenic Fugue. Careful questioning under hypnosis or during an amobarbital interview may provide useful information, although some people continue to malinger even under hypnosis or amobarbital.

Diagnostic criteria for 300.13 Psychogenic Fugue

A. The predominant disturbance is sudden, unexpected travel away from home or one's customary place of work, with inability to recall one's past.

B. Assumption of a new identity (partial or complete).

C. The disturbance is not due to Multiple Personality Disorder or to an Organic Mental Disorder (e.g., partial complex seizures in temporal lobe epilepsy).

300.12 Psychogenic Amnesia

The essential feature of this disorder is sudden inability to recall important personal information, an inability not due to an Organic Mental Disorder. The extent of the disturbance is too great to be explained by ordinary forgetfulness. The diagnosis is not made if the person travels to another locale and assumes a new identity, in which case the diagnosis is Psychogenic Fugue, or if the amnesia is a symptom of Multiple Personality Disorder.

There are four types of disturbance in recall. In *localized* (or circumscribed) amnesia, the most common type, there is failure to recall all events occurring during a circumscribed period of time, usually the first few hours following a profoundly disturbing event. For example, the uninjured survivor of a car accident that killed his immediate family may not be able to recall anything that happened from the time of the accident until two days later. Somewhat less common is *selective* amnesia, failure to recall some, but not all, of the events occurring during a circumscribed period of time. In the illustration above, the uninjured survivor might recall making the funeral arrangements, but not concurrent discussions with family members. The least common types of disturbance in recall are *generalized* amnesia, in which failure of recall encompasses the person's entire life, and *continuous* amnesia, in which the person cannot recall events subsequent to a specific time up to and including the present.

During an ongoing amnestic episode, perplexity, disorientation, and purposeless wandering may occur. When the period of time for which there is amnesia is in the past, the person is usually aware of the disturbance in recall.

Associated features. During the amnestic period there may be indifference toward the memory disturbance. Post-traumatic Stress Disorder may also be present.

Age at onset and sex ratio. The disorder is most often observed in adolescent and young adult females, but rarely in the elderly. Military sources provide many clinical reports describing the disorder in young males during war.

Course and predisposing factors. Amnesia begins suddenly, usually following severe psychosocial stress. The stress often involves a threat of physical injury or death. In other instances the stress is due to the unacceptability of certain impulses or acts, such as an extramarital affair. In still other instances, the person may be in a subjectively intolerable life situation, such as having been abandoned by a spouse.

Termination of the amnesia is typically abrupt. Recovery is complete, and recurrences are rare.

Impairment. The degree of impairment varies from mild to severe in proportion to the duration of the amnestic episode and the importance of forgotten events to the person's social functioning. The impairment is usually minimal and temporary, since rapid recovery is the rule.

Complications. None.

Prevalence. The disorder is rarely diagnosed under normal circumstances; it is more common in wartime and during natural disasters.

Familial pattern. No information.

Differential diagnosis. The onset of a memory disturbance in an **Organic Mental Disorder** usually has no relationship to stress, and the disturbance is more marked for recent than for remote events. Memory impairment caused by organic factors usually disappears very slowly, if at all; full return of memory is rare. Furthermore, attention deficits and disturbances of affect are frequently present.

In **Psychoactive Substance-induced Intoxication** there can be blackouts with failure to recall events that occurred during the intoxication. The organic factor (the substance taken) and the failure to achieve full return of memory clearly distinguish it from Psychogenic Amnesia.

In **Alcohol Amnestic Disorder**, short-term (not immediate) memory is impaired, i.e., events can be recalled immediately after they occur, but not after the passage of a few minutes. This type of memory disturbance is not seen in Psychogenic Amnesia. In addition, blunted affect, confabulation, and lack of awareness of the memory impairment are common in Alcohol Amnestic Disorder.

In **postconcussion amnesia**, the disturbance of recall, though circumscribed, is often retrograde, encompassing a period of time before the head trauma, whereas in Psychogenic Amnesia the disturbance of recall is almost always anterograde. Retrograde amnesia following head trauma can usually be distinguished from rare cases of Psychogenic Amnesia with retrograde amnesia by diagnostic use of hypnosis or an amobarbital interview; prompt recovery of the lost memories suggests a psychogenic basis for the disturbance.

In **epilepsy**, the memory impairment is sudden in onset, motor abnormalities are usually present during the episode, and repeated EEGs typically reveal anomalies.

In **catatonic stupor**, mutism may suggest Psychogenic Amnesia, but failure of recall is nearly always absent, and there usually are other characteristic catatonic symptoms, such as rigidity, posturing, and negativism.

Malingering involving simulated amnesia presents a particularly difficult diagnostic dilemma. Attention to the possibility that the amnesia is feigned is crucial. Careful questioning under hypnosis or during an amobarbital interview may provide useful information, although one may encounter confabulation, and some people continue to malinger even under hypnosis or during an amobarbital interview.

Diagnostic criteria for 300.12 Psychogenic Amnesia

A. The predominant disturbance is an episode of sudden inability to recall important personal information that is too extensive to be explained by ordinary forgetfulness.

B. The disturbance is not due to Multiple Personality Disorder or to an Organic Mental Disorder (e.g., blackouts during Alcohol Intoxication).

300.60 Depersonalization Disorder (or Depersonalization Neurosis)

The essential feature of this disorder is the occurrence of persistent or recurrent episodes of depersonalization sufficiently severe to cause marked distress. The diagnosis is not made when the symptom of depersonalization is secondary to any other disorder, such as Panic Disorder or Agoraphobia without History of Panic Disorder.

The symptom of depersonalization involves an alteration in the perception or experience of the self in which the usual sense of one's own reality is temporarily lost or changed. This is manifested by a feeling of detachment from and being an outside observer of one's mental processes or body, or of feeling like an automaton or as if in a dream. Various types of sensory anesthesia and a sensation of not being in complete control of one's actions, including speech, are often present. All of these feelings are ego dystonic, and the person maintains intact reality testing.

The onset of depersonalization is usually rapid; its disappearance is usually gradual.

Associated features. Derealization is frequently present. This is evidenced by a strange alteration in the perception of one's surroundings so that a sense of the reality of the external world is lost. Alterations in the size or shape of objects in the external world are commonly perceived. People may seem dead or mechanical.

Other common associated features include dizziness, depression, obsessive rumination, somatic concerns, anxiety, fear of going insane, and a disturbance in the subjective sense of time. There is often the feeling that recall is difficult or slow.

Age at onset. The disorder usually begins in adolescence or early adult life. Onset after the age of 40 is uncommon.

Course. The course is generally chronic and marked by remissions and exacerbations. Most often the exacerbations occur when there is mild anxiety or depression.

Impairment. The degree of impairment may vary from minimal to severe. It may be exacerbated by the presence of associated features such as anxiety or fear of insanity.

Complications. Hypochondriasis or a Psychoactive Substance Use Disorder may be a complication of this disorder.

Predisposing factors. Severe stress, such as military combat or an auto accident, may predispose to Depersonalization Disorder.

Prevalence. Single brief episodes of depersonalization may occur at some time in as many as 70% of young adults. However, the prevalence of Depersonalization Disorder, that is, of persistent or recurrent episodes sufficiently severe to cause marked distress, is unknown.

Sex ratio and familial pattern. No information.

Differential diagnosis. The **symptom of depersonalization**, even if recurrent, that does not cause any social or occupational impairment, must be distinguished from Depersonalization Disorder.

In **Schizophrenia, Mood Disorders, Organic Mental Disorders** (especially **Intoxication** and **Withdrawal**), **Anxiety Disorders, Personality Disorders,** and **epilepsy,** depersonalization may be a symptom. In such cases, the additional diagnosis of Depersonalization Disorder is not made.

Diagnostic criteria for 300.60 Depersonalization Disorder

A. Persistent or recurrent experiences of depersonalization as indicated by either (1) or (2):

   (1) an experience of feeling detached from, and as if one is an outside observer of, one's mental processes or body

   (2) an experience of feeling like an automaton or as if in a dream

(continued)

> **Diagnostic criteria for 300.60 Depersonalization Disorder** continued
>
> B. During the depersonalization experience, reality testing remains intact.
>
> C. The depersonalization is sufficiently severe and persistent to cause marked distress.
>
> D. The depersonalization experience is the predominant disturbance and is not a symptom of another disorder, such as Schizophrenia, Panic Disorder, or Agoraphobia without History of Panic Disorder but with limited symptom attacks of depersonalization, or temporal lobe epilepsy.

300.15   Dissociative Disorder Not Otherwise Specified

Disorders in which the predominant feature is a dissociative symptom (i.e., a disturbance or alteration in the normally integrative functions of identity, memory, or consciousness) that does not meet the criteria for a specific Dissociative Disorder.

Examples:

(1) Ganser's syndrome: the giving of "approximate answers" to questions, commonly associated with other symptoms such as amnesia, disorientation, perceptual disturbances, fugue, and conversion symptoms

(2) cases in which there is more than one personality state capable of assuming executive control of the individual, but not more than one personality state is sufficiently distinct to meet the full criteria for Multiple Personality Disorder, or cases in which a second personality never assumes complete executive control

(3) trance states, i.e., altered states of consciousness with markedly diminished or selectively focused responsiveness to environmental stimuli. In children this may occur following physical abuse or trauma

(4) derealization unaccompanied by depersonalization

(5) dissociated states that may occur in people who have been subjected to periods of prolonged and intense coercive persuasion (e.g., brainwashing, thought reform, or indoctrination while the captive of terrorists or cultists)

(6) cases in which sudden, unexpected travel and organized, purposeful behavior with inability to recall one's past are not accompanied by the assumption of a new identity, partial or complete

Sexual Disorders

The Sexual Disorders are divided into two groups. The Paraphilias are characterized by arousal in response to sexual objects or situations that are not part of normative arousal-activity patterns and that in varying degrees may interfere with the capacity for recipro-cal, affectionate sexual activity. The Sexual Dysfunctions are characterized by inhi-bitions in sexual desire or the psychophysiologic changes that characterize the sexual response cycle. Finally, there is a residual class, Other Sexual Disorders, for disorders in sexual functioning that are not classifiable in any of the specific categories.

PARAPHILIAS

The essential feature of disorders in this subclass is recurrent intense sexual urges and sexually arousing fantasies generally involving either (1) nonhuman objects, (2) the suffering or humiliation of oneself or one's partner (not merely simulated), or (3) children or other nonconsenting persons. The diagnosis is made only if the person has acted on these urges, or is markedly distressed by them. In other classifications these disorders are referred to as Sexual Deviations. The term *Paraphilia* is preferable because it correctly emphasizes that the deviation (para) lies in that to which the person is attracted (philia).

For some people with a Paraphilia, paraphilic fantasies or stimuli may always be necessary for erotic arousal and are always included in sexual activity, if not actually acted out alone or with a partner. In other cases the paraphilic preferences occur only episodically, for example, during periods of stress; at other times the person is able to function sexually without paraphilic fantasies or stimuli.

The imagery in a paraphilic fantasy is frequently the stimulus for sexual excitement in people without a Paraphilia. For example, female undergarments are sexually excit-ing for many men; such fantasies and urges are paraphilic only when the person acts on them or is markedly distressed by them.

The imagery in a Paraphilia, e.g., of being humiliated by one's partner, may be relatively harmless and acted out with a consenting partner. More likely it is not shared by the partner, who consequently feels erotically excluded from the sexual interaction. In more extreme form, paraphilic imagery is acted out with a nonconsenting partner, and may be injurious to the partner (as in Sexual Sadism) or to the self (as in Sexual Masochism).

The Paraphilias included here are, by and large, conditions that have been specifically identified by previous classifications. Some of them are relatively common in clinics that specialize in the treatment of Paraphilias and other sexual behavior problems (e.g., Pedophilia, Voyeurism, and Exhibitionism); others are much less commonly seen in such settings (e.g., Sexual Masochism and Sexual Sadism). Because some of these disorders are associated with nonconsenting partners, they are of legal and social significance. People with these disorders tend not to regard themselves as ill, and usually come to the attention of mental health professionals only when their behavior has brought them into conflict with sexual partners or society.

The specific Paraphilias described here are: (1) Exhibitionism, (2) Fetishism, (3) Frotteurism, (4) Pedophilia, (5) Sexual Masochism, (6) Sexual Sadism, (7) Transvestic Fetishism, and (8) Voyeurism. Finally, there is a residual category, Paraphilia Not Otherwise Specified, for noting the many other Paraphilias that are less commonly encountered, or have not been sufficiently described to date to warrant inclusion as specific categories.

People with a Paraphilia commonly suffer from several varieties: in clinical settings that specialize in the treatment of Paraphilias, people with these disorders have an average of from three to four different Paraphilias. People with Paraphilias may also have other mental disorders, such as Psychoactive Substance Use Disorders or various Personality Disorders. In such cases multiple diagnoses should be made.

Criteria for the severity of the manifestations of a specific Paraphilia are provided. These guidelines distinguish, first, people who do not act on their paraphilic urge(s) from those who do. It is recognized, however, that this distinction in some cases may be more a function of various personality traits (such as the presence or absence of antisocial personality traits), the severity of psychosocial stressors, and the presence of a Psychoactive Substance Use Disorder than of factors inherent in the Paraphilia itself. The second distinction made in these guidelines is between people who have occasionally acted on a paraphilic urge and those who repeatedly do so. Again, the factors noted above rather than ones inherent in the Paraphilia itself may be involved in this distinction.

Among other clinical considerations besides severity of the manifestations are the degree to which the person requires the paraphilic imagery or fantasy for sexual arousal, the extent to which the person has harmed others or himself or herself, the degree of subjective distress, and, finally, the social or occupational impairment that is the direct result of Paraphilia-related behavior.

Associated features. Specific paraphilic imagery is selectively focused on and sought out by people with one or more Paraphilias. The person may select an occupation or develop a hobby or volunteer work that brings him into contact with the desired stimuli (e.g., selling women's shoes or lingerie in Fetishism, working with children in Pedophilia, or driving an ambulance in Sexual Sadism). The person may selectively view, read, purchase, or collect photographs, films, and textual depictions focusing on his preferred type of paraphilic stimulus.

The preferred stimulus, even within a particular Paraphilia, may be highly specific, such as ten-year-old blond boys with a light complexion and thin habitus. People who do not have a consenting partner with whom their fantasies can be acted out may purchase the services of prostitutes or others who provide specialized Paraphilia-related services (e.g., "bondage and domination" or "cross-dressing lessons") or may act out their fantasies with unwilling victims.

Frequently people with these disorders assert that the behavior causes them no distress and that their only problem is the reaction of others to their behavior. Others report extreme guilt, shame, and depression at having to engage in an unusual sexual activity that is socially unacceptable or that they regard as immoral. There is often impairment in the capacity for reciprocal, affectionate sexual activity, and Sexual Dysfunctions may be present. Personality disturbances, particularly emotional immaturity, are also frequent, and may be severe enough to warrant an Axis II diagnosis of a Personality Disorder.

Impairment. Social and sexual relationships may suffer if others, such as a spouse (approximately one-half of the people with Paraphilias seen clinically are married), become aware of the unusual sexual behavior. In addition, if the person engages in sexual activity with a partner who refuses to cooperate in the unusual behavior, such as fetishistic or sadistic behavior, sexual excitement may be inhibited and the relationship may suffer. In some instances the unusual behavior, e.g., exhibitionistic acts or the collection of fetishes, may become the major sexual activity in the person's life.

Complications. In Sexual Masochism, the person may suffer serious physical damage. Paraphilias involving another person, particularly Voyeurism, Exhibitionism, Frotteurism, Pedophilia, and Sexual Sadism, often lead to arrest and incarceration. Sexual offenses against children constitute a significant proportion of all reported criminal sex acts. People with Exhibitionism, Pedophilia, and Voyeurism make up the majority of apprehended sex offenders.

Predisposing factors. With the exception of Pedophilia (see p. 285) and Transvestic Fetishism (see p. 289), there is no information about predisposing factors.

Prevalence. The disorders are rarely diagnosed in general clinical facilities. However, judging from the large commercial market in paraphilic pornography and paraphernalia, the prevalence in the community is believed to be far higher than that indicated by statistics from clinical facilities. Because of the highly repetitive nature of paraphilic behavior, a large percentage of the population has been victimized by people with Paraphilias.

Sex ratio. Except for Sexual Masochism, in which the sex ratio is estimated to be 20 males for each female, the other Paraphilias are practically never diagnosed in females, but some cases have been reported.

Familial pattern. No information.

Criteria for severity of manifestations of a specific Paraphilia

Mild: The person is markedly distressed by the recurrent paraphilic urges but has never acted on them.

Moderate: The person has occasionally acted on the paraphilic urge.

Severe: The person has repeatedly acted on the paraphilic urge.

302.40   Exhibitionism

The essential feature of this disorder is recurrent, intense, sexual urges and sexually arousing fantasies, of at least six months' duration, involving the exposure of one's genitals to a stranger. The person has acted on these urges, or is markedly distressed by them. Sometimes the person masturbates while exposing himself (or fantasizing exposing himself).

If the person acts on these urges, there is no attempt at further sexual activity with the stranger, and therefore people with this disorder are usually not physically dangerous to the victim. In some cases, the desire to surprise or shock the observer is consciously perceived or close to conscious awareness. In other cases, the person has the sexually arousing fantasy that the person observing him will become sexually aroused. The condition apparently occurs only in males, and the victims are almost entirely female (children or adults).

Age at onset and course. The disorder usually occurs before age 18, although it can begin at a much later age. Few arrests are made in the older age groups, which suggests that the condition becomes less severe after age 40.

Differential diagnosis. In **Pedophilia,** exposure may occur as a prelude to sexual activity with the child. **Public urination,** sometimes offered as an explanation by a person with Exhibitionism, needs to be ruled out.

Diagnostic criteria for 302.40 Exhibitionism

A. Over a period of at least six months, recurrent intense sexual urges and sexually arousing fantasies involving the exposure of one's genitals to an unsuspecting stranger.

B. The person has acted on these urges, or is markedly distressed by them.

302.81   Fetishism

The essential feature of this disorder is recurrent, intense, sexual urges and sexually arousing fantasies, of at least six months' duration, involving the use of nonliving objects (fetishes). The person has acted on these urges, or is markedly distressed by them. Among the more common fetish objects are bras, women's underpants, stockings, shoes, boots, or other wearing apparel. The person with Fetishism frequently masturbates while holding, rubbing, or smelling the fetish object, or may ask his sexual partner to wear the object during their sexual encounters. Usually the fetish is required or strongly preferred for sexual excitement, and in its absence there may be erectile failure in males.

The diagnosis is not made when the fetishes are limited to articles of female clothing used in cross-dressing, as in Transvestic Fetishism, or when the object is genitally stimulating because it has been designed for that purpose, e.g., a vibrator.

Age at onset. Usually the disorder begins by adolescence, although the fetish may have been endowed with special significance earlier, in childhood. Once established, the disorder tends to be chronic.

Differential diagnosis. Nonpathologic sexual experimentation can involve sexual arousal by nonhuman objects, but this stimulus for sexual excitement is neither persistently preferred nor required.

In **Transvestic Fetishism** the sexual arousal is limited to articles of female clothing used in cross-dressing.

Diagnostic criteria for 302.81 Fetishism

A. Over a period of at least six months, recurrent intense sexual urges and sexually arousing fantasies involving the use of nonliving objects by themselves (e.g., female undergarments).

   Note: The person may at other times use the nonliving object with a sexual partner.

B. The person has acted on these urges, or is markedly distressed by them.

C. The fetishes are not only articles of female clothing used in cross-dressing (Transvestic Fetishism) or devices designed for the purpose of tactile genital stimulation (e.g., vibrator).

302.89 Frotteurism

The essential feature of this disorder is recurrent, intense, sexual urges and sexually arousing fantasies, of at least six months' duration, involving touching and rubbing against a nonconsenting person. It is the touching, not the coercive nature of the act, that is sexually exciting. The person has acted on these urges, or is markedly distressed by them. Some authorities distinguish Frotteurism (rubbing) from Toucherism (fondling). In this manual, both are included within this category.

The person with Frotteurism usually commits frottage in crowded places, such as on busy sidewalks or in public transportation vehicles, from which he can more easily escape arrest. The person usually selects a victim with a body habitus very attractive to him who is wearing tight-fitting clothes. He rubs his genitals against the victim's thighs and buttocks or fondles her genitalia or breasts with his hands. While doing this he usually fantasizes an exclusive, caring relationship with his victim. However, he recognizes that in order to avoid possible prosecution, he must escape detection after touching his victim. The victim may not initially protest the frottage because she cannot imagine that such a provocative sexual act would be committed in such a public place.

Age at onset. Usually the disorder begins by adolescence. Some people with Frotteurism report that they first became interested in touching others while observing others committing acts of frottage.

Course. Most acts of frottage occur when the person is 15 to 25 years of age, after which there is a gradual decline in its frequency.

Differential diagnosis. Normal sexual activity includes sexual excitement from touching or fondling one's sexual partner. By contrast, the person with Frotteurism fondles an unsuspecting, nonconsenting partner. In **Mental Retardation** or **Schizophrenia**, there may be a deficiency in judgment, social skills, or impulse control that, in rare instances, leads to isolated touching of others. However, such behavior is generally not repetitive, and is not associated with attempts by the person to escape detection after touching the victim.

Diagnostic criteria for 302.89 Frotteurism

A. Over a period of at least six months, recurrent intense sexual urges and sexually arousing fantasies involving touching and rubbing against a nonconsenting person. It is the touching, not the coercive nature of the act, that is sexually exciting.

B. The person has acted on these urges, or is markedly distressed by them.

302.20 Pedophilia

The essential feature of this disorder is recurrent, intense, sexual urges and sexually arousing fantasies, of at least six months' duration, involving sexual activity with a prepubescent child. The person has acted on these urges, or is markedly distressed by them. The age of the child is generally 13 or younger. The age of the person is arbitrarily set at age 16 years or older and at least 5 years older than the child. For late adolescents with the disorder, no precise age difference is specified, and clinical judgment must be used; both the sexual maturity of the child and the age difference must be taken into account.

People with Pedophilia generally report an attraction to children of a particular age range, which may be as specific as within a range of only one or two years. Those attracted to girls usually prefer eight-to-ten-year-olds, whereas those attracted to boys usually prefer slightly older children. Attraction to girls is apparently twice as common as attraction to boys. Many people with Pedophilia are sexually aroused by both young boys and young girls.

Some people with Pedophilia are sexually attracted only to children (exclusive type), whereas others are sometimes attracted to adults (nonexclusive type).

People with this disorder who act on their urges with children may limit their activity to undressing the child and looking, exposing themselves, masturbating in the presence of the child, or gentle touching and fondling of the child. Others, however, perform fellatio or cunnilingus on the child or penetrate the child's vagina, mouth, or anus with their fingers, foreign objects, or penis, and use varying degrees of force to achieve these ends. These activities are commonly explained with excuses or rationalizations that they have "educational value" for the child, that the child derives "sexual pleasure" from them, or that the child was "sexually provocative"—themes that are also common in pedophilic pornography.

The person may limit his activities to his own children, stepchildren, or relatives, or may victimize children outside his family. Some people with the disorder threaten the child to prevent disclosure. Others, particularly those who frequently victimize children, develop complicated techniques for obtaining children, which may include winning the trust of a child's mother, marrying a woman with an attractive child, trading children with others with the disorder, or, in rare instances, bringing foster children from nonindustrialized countries or abducting children from strangers.

Except in cases in which the disorder is associated with Sexual Sadism, the person may be generous and very attentive to the child's needs in all respects other than the sexual victimization in order to gain the child's affection, interest, and loyalty and to prevent the child from reporting the sexual activity.

Age at onset. The disorder usually begins in adolescence, although some people with Pedophilia report that they did not become aroused by children until middle age.

Course. The course is usually chronic, especially in those attracted to boys. The frequency of pedophilic behavior often fluctuates with psychosocial stress. The recidivism rate for people with Pedophilia involving a preference for the same sex is roughly twice that of those who prefer the opposite sex.

Predisposing factors. Many people with this disorder were themselves victims of sexual abuse in childhood.

Differential diagnosis. Isolated sexual acts with children do not necessarily warrant the diagnosis of Pedophilia. Such acts may be precipitated by marital discord, recent loss, or intense loneliness. In such instances the desire for sex with a child may be understood as a substitute for a preferred but unavailable adult. When pedophilic behavior involves a family member (incest), a diagnosis of Pedophilia should be made if the diagnostic criteria are met. In such cases there often is pedophilic behavior with children outside the family. In **Mental Retardation, Organic Personality Syndrome, Alcohol Intoxication,** or **Schizophrenia** there may be a decrease in judgment, social skills, or impulse control, particularly in the elderly, that, in rare instances, leads to isolated sexual acts with children; but in such cases sexual activity with children is generally not the consistently preferred method for achieving sexual satisfaction.

In **Exhibitionism,** exposure may be to a child, but the act is not a prelude to further sexual activity with the child. **Sexual Sadism** may, in rare instances, be associated with Pedophilia, in which case both diagnoses are warranted.

Diagnostic criteria for 302.20 Pedophilia

A. Over a period of at least six months, recurrent intense sexual urges and sexually arousing fantasies involving sexual activity with a prepubescent child or children (generally age 13 or younger).

B. The person has acted on these urges, or is markedly distressed by them.

C. The person is at least 16 years old and at least 5 years older than the child or children in A.

   Note: Do not include a late adolescent involved in an ongoing sexual relationship with a 12- or 13-year-old.

Specify: same sex, opposite sex, or **same and opposite sex.**

Specify if **limited to incest.**

Specify: exclusive type (attracted only to children), or **nonexclusive type.**

302.83 Sexual Masochism

The essential feature of this disorder is recurrent, intense, sexual urges and sexually arousing fantasies, of at least six months' duration, involving the act (real, not simulated) of being humiliated, beaten, bound, or otherwise made to suffer. The person has acted on these urges, or is markedly distressed by them.

Some people with this disorder are bothered by their masochistic fantasies, which may be invoked during sexual intercourse or masturbation, but not otherwise acted upon. In such cases the masochistic fantasies usually involve being raped while being held or bound by others so that there is no possibility of escape. Others act on the masochistic sexual urges by themselves (e.g., through binding themselves, sticking themselves with pins, shocking themselves electrically, or self-mutilation) or with a partner. Masochistic acts that may be sought with a partner include restraint (physical bondage), blindfolding (sensory bondage), paddling, spanking, whipping (flagellation), beating, electrical shocks, cutting, "pinning and piercing" (infibulation), and humiliation (such as being urinated or defecated upon, being forced to crawl and bark like a dog, or being subjected to verbal abuse). Forced cross-dressing may be sought for its humiliating associations. The term *infantilism* is sometimes used to describe a desire to be treated as a helpless infant and clothed in diapers.

One particularly dangerous form of Sexual Masochism, called "hypoxyphilia," involves sexual arousal by oxygen deprivation. In this form, the person produces oxygen deprivation by means of a noose, ligature, plastic bag, mask, chemical (often a volatile nitrite that produces a temporary decrease in brain oxygenation by peripheral vasodilation), or chest compression, but allows himself the opportunity to escape asphyxiation before consciousness is lost. People engaging in such behavior report that the activity is accompanied by sexual fantasies in which they asphyxiate or harm others, others asphyxiate or harm them, or they escape near brushes with death. Oxygen depriving activities may be engaged in alone or with a partner. Because of equipment malfunction, errors in the placement of the noose or ligature, or other mistakes, accidental deaths sometimes occur. Data from the United States, England, Australia, and Canada indicate that there are 1 to 2 such deaths per million population detected and reported each year.

Some men with Sexual Masochism also have Fetishism, Transvestic Fetishism, or Sexual Sadism.

Age at onset. Masochistic sexual fantasies are likely to have been present in childhood. The age at which masochistic activities with partners first begin is variable, but is commonly by early adulthood.

Course. The disorder is usually chronic, and the person tends to repeat the same masochistic act. Some people with the disorder may engage in masochistic acts for many years without increasing the potential injuriousness of their acts. Others, however, increase the severity of the masochistic acts over time or during periods of stress, which may eventually result in the person's death.

Differential diagnosis. Masochistic fantasies of being bound, beaten, raped, or otherwise humiliated facilitate sexual excitement in some people. The diagnosis of Sexual Masochism is made only if the person is markedly distressed by such fantasies, or has acted on them. Cross-dressing is present in **Transvestic Fetishism**, and may also be present in Sexual Masochism. In the latter, however, it is the humiliation of being forced to cross-dress, not the garments themselves, that is sexually exciting.

Accidental death during masochistic sexual acts must be differentiated from **suicide** and **homicide.**

Self-defeating personality traits, such as the need to be disappointed or humiliated, are distinguished from Sexual Masochism by the fact that they are not associated with sexual excitement.

Diagnostic criteria for 302.83 Sexual Masochism

A. Over a period of at least six months, recurrent intense sexual urges and sexually arousing fantasies involving the act (real, not simulated) of being humiliated, beaten, bound, or otherwise made to suffer.

B. The person has acted on these urges, or is markedly distressed by them.

302.84 Sexual Sadism

The essential feature of this disorder is recurrent, intense, sexual urges and sexually arousing fantasies, of at least six months' duration, involving acts (real, not simulated) in which the psychological or physical suffering (including humiliation) of the victim is sexually exciting. The person has acted on these urges, or is markedly distressed by them.

Some people with this disorder are bothered by their sadistic fantasies, which may be invoked during sexual activity, but not otherwise acted upon; in such cases the sadistic fantasies usually involve having complete control over the victim, who is terrified by anticipation of the impending sadistic act. Others act on the sadistic sexual urges with a consenting partner (who may have Sexual Masochism) who willingly suffers pain or humiliation. Still other people with Sexual Sadism act on their sadistic sexual urges with nonconsenting victims. In all of these cases, it is the suffering of the victim that is sexually arousing.

Sadistic fantasies or acts may involve activities that indicate the dominance of the person over his victim (e.g., forcing the victim to crawl, or keeping the victim in a cage), or restraint, blindfolding, paddling, spanking, whipping, pinching, beating, burning, electrical shocks, rape, cutting or stabbing, strangulation, torture, mutilation, or killing.

Age at onset. Sadistic sexual fantasies are likely to have been present in childhood. The age at onset of sadistic activities is variable, but is commonly by early adulthood.

Course. The condition is usually chronic in its extreme form. When Sexual Sadism is practiced with nonconsenting partners, the activity is likely to be repeated until the person with Sexual Sadism is apprehended.

Some people with the disorder may engage in sadistic acts for many years without a need to increase the potential for inflicting serious physical damage. Usually, however, the severity of the sadistic acts increases over time. When the disorder is severe, and when it is associated with Antisocial Personality Disorder and sadistic personality traits, these people may seriously injure or kill their victims.

Differential diagnosis. Rape or other sexual assault may be committed by people with this disorder. In such instances the suffering inflicted on the victim is far in excess of that necessary to gain compliance, and the visible pain of the victim is sexually arousing. In most cases of rape, however, the rapist is not motivated by the prospect of inflicting suffering, and he may even lose sexual desire while observing the victim's suffering. Studies of rapists indicate that fewer than 10% have Sexual Sadism. Some rapists are apparently sexually aroused by coercing or forcing a nonconsenting person to engage in intercourse and are able to maintain sexual arousal even while observing the victim's suffering. However, unlike the person with Sexual Sadism, such people do not find the victim's suffering sexually arousing.

Sadistic acts also occur in the absence of sexual arousal in a variety of crimes, in torture used to interrogate prisoners, in cult rituals, and in people with sadistic personality traits.

Diagnostic criteria for 302.84 Sexual Sadism

A. Over a period of at least six months, recurrent intense sexual urges and sexually arousing fantasies involving acts (real, not simulated) in which the psychological or physical suffering (including humiliation) of the victim is sexually exciting to the person.

B. The person has acted on these urges, or is markedly distressed by them.

302.30 Transvestic Fetishism

The essential feature of this disorder is recurrent, intense, sexual urges and sexually arousing fantasies, of at least six months' duration, involving cross-dressing. The person has acted on these urges, or is markedly distressed by them. Usually the person keeps a collection of women's clothes that he intermittently uses to cross-dress when alone. While cross-dressed, he usually masturbates and imagines other males' being attracted to him as a woman in his female attire.

This disorder has been described only in heterosexual males. The diagnosis is not made in cases in which the disturbance has evolved into Gender Identity Disorder of Adolescence or Adulthood, Nontranssexual Type, or Transsexualism.

Transvestic phenomena range from occasional solitary wearing of female clothes to extensive involvement in a transvestic subculture. Some men wear a single item of women's apparel (e.g., underwear or hosiery) under their masculine attire. When more than one article of women's clothing are involved, the man may wear makeup and dress entirely as a woman.

The degree to which the cross-dressed person appears to be a woman varies, depending on mannerisms, body habitus, and cross-dressing skill. When not cross-dressed, he is usually unremarkably masculine. Although the basic preference is heterosexual, rarely has the person had sexual experience with several women, and he may have engaged in occasional homosexual acts.

An associated feature may be the presence of Sexual Masochism.

Age at onset and course. The disorder typically begins with cross-dressing in childhood or early adolescence. In many cases the cross-dressing is not done in public until adulthood. The initial experience may involve partial or total cross-dressing; when it is partial, it often progresses to complete cross-dressing. A favored article of clothing may become erotic in itself and may be used habitually, first in masturbation, and later in intercourse.

In some people sexual arousal by clothing tends to disappear, although the cross-dressing continues as an antidote to anxiety. In such cases the diagnosis should be changed to Gender Identity Disorder of Adolescence or Adulthood, Nontranssexual Type. A small number of people with Transvestic Fetishism, as the years pass, want to dress and live permanently as women, and desire surgical or hormonal sex reassignment. In such cases the diagnosis should be changed to Transsexualism.

Predisposing factors. According to the folklore of people with this condition, "petticoat punishment," the punishment of humiliating a boy by dressing him in the clothes of a girl, is common in the history of those who later develop this disorder.

Differential diagnosis. Cross-dressing for the relief of tension or gender discomfort may be done without directly causing sexual excitement. This should not be diagnosed as Transvestic Fetishism; the diagnosis of **Gender Identity Disorder of Adolescence or Adulthood, Nontranssexual Type** should be considered. In **male homosexuality** there may be occasional cross-dressing to attract another male or to masquerade in theatrical fashion as a female. However, the act of cross-dressing does not cause sexual arousal. In **female impersonators,** unless Transvestic Fetishism is also involved, the act of cross-dressing does not cause sexual arousal, and interference with the cross-dressing does not result in intense frustration.

In **Transsexualism** there is persistent discomfort and a sense of inappropriateness about one's assigned sex and preoccupation with getting rid of one's primary and secondary sex characteristics and acquiring the sex characteristics of the other sex. No sexual excitement is associated with the cross-dressing. The person with Transvestic Fetishism considers himself to be basically male, whereas the originally anatomically male Transsexual has a female sexual identity. In the rare instances in which Transvestic Fetishism evolves into Transsexualism, the diagnosis of Transvestic Fetishism is changed to Transsexualism.

Fetishism is not diagnosed when sexual arousal by nonhuman objects is limited to articles of female clothing used in cross-dressing. In **Sexual Masochism** (not associated with Tranvestic Fetishism) the person may desire to be forced to cross-dress because of its humiliating associations, but the garments themselves do not cause sexual arousal.

Diagnostic criteria for 302.30 Transvestic Fetishism

A. Over a period of at least six months, in a heterosexual male, recurrent intense sexual urges and sexually arousing fantasies involving cross-dressing.

B. The person has acted on these urges, or is markedly distressed by them.

C. Does not meet the criteria for Gender Identity Disorder of Adolescence or Adulthood, Nontranssexual Type, or Transsexualism.

302.82　Voyeurism

The essential feature of this disorder is recurrent, intense, sexual urges and sexually arousing fantasies, of at least six months' duration, involving the act of observing unsuspecting people, usually strangers, who are either naked, in the process of disrobing, or engaging in sexual activity. The person has acted on these urges, or is markedly distressed by them.

The act of looking ("peeping") is for the purpose of achieving sexual excitement, and no sexual activity with the person is sought. Orgasm, usually produced by masturbation, may occur during the voyeuristic activity, or later in response to the memory of what the person has witnessed. Often these people enjoy the fantasy of having a sexual experience with the observed person, but in reality this does not occur. In its severe form, peeping constitutes the exclusive form of sexual activity.

Age at onset. Usually the onset of voyeuristic behavior is before age 15.

Course. The course tends to be chronic.

Differential diagnosis. Normal sexual activity often includes sexual excitement from observing nudity, disrobing, or sexual activity. However, it is not with an unsuspecting partner, and it is usually a prelude to further sexual activity with the person observed. Furthermore, the person with Voyeurism is aroused by the secretive, illegal nature of his peeping. **Watching pornography,** filmed or live, causes sexual excitement; but in pornography, the people who are being observed know that they are being seen, even though the observer may *pretend* that the people are unsuspecting.

Diagnostic criteria for 302.82 Voyeurism

A. Over a period of at least six months, recurrent intense sexual urges and sexually arousing fantasies involving the act of observing an unsuspecting person who is naked, in the process of disrobing, or engaging in sexual activity.

B. The person has acted on these urges, or is markedly distressed by them.

302.90 Paraphilia Not Otherwise Specified
Paraphilias that do not meet the criteria for any of the specific categories.

Examples:

  (1) Telephone scatologia (lewdness)
  (2) Necrophilia (corpses)
  (3) Partialism (exclusive focus on part of body)
  (4) Zoophilia (animals)
  (5) Coprophilia (feces)
  (6) Klismaphilia (enemas)
  (7) Urophilia (urine)

SEXUAL DYSFUNCTIONS

The essential feature of this subclass is inhibition in the appetitive or psychophysiologic changes that characterize the complete sexual response cycle. Ordinarily this diagnostic category will be applied only when the disturbance is a major part of the clinical picture, even though it may not be part of the chief complaint. The diagnosis is not made if the Sexual Dysfunction is attributed entirely to organic factors, such as a physical disorder or a medication, or if it is due to another Axis I mental disorder. In some cases multiple diagnoses may be appropriate, such as Hypoactive Sexual Desire Disorder and Sexual Aversion Disorder.

The complete sexual response cycle can be divided into the following phases:

1. *Appetitive.* This consists of fantasies about sexual activity and a desire to have sexual activity.

2. *Excitement.* This consists of a subjective sense of sexual pleasure and accompanying physiologic changes. The major changes in the male consist of penile tumescence, leading to erection, and the appearance of Cowper's gland secretion. The major changes in the female consist of vasocongestion in the pelvis, vaginal lubrication, and swelling of the external genitalia. Other changes include development of the orgasmic platform, i.e., narrowing of the outer third of the vagina by increased pubococcygeal muscle tension and vasocongestion; vasocongestion of the labia minora; breast tumescence; and lengthening and widening of the inner two-thirds of the vagina.

3. *Orgasm.* This consists of a peaking of sexual pleasure, with release of sexual tension and rhythmic contraction of the perineal muscles and pelvic reproductive organs. In the male there is the sensation of ejaculatory inevitability, which is followed by emission of semen, caused by contractions of the prostate, seminal vesicles, and urethra. In the female there are contractions, not always subjectively experienced as such, of the wall of the outer third of the vagina. In both the male and the female there is often generalized muscular tension or contractions, such as involuntary pelvic thrusting.

4. *Resolution.* This consists of a sense of general relaxation, well-being, and muscular relaxation. During this phase males are physiologically refractory to further erection and orgasm for a variable period of time. In contrast, females may be able to respond to additional stimulation almost immediately.

Inhibitions in the response cycle may occur at one or more of these phases, although inhibition in the resolution phase is rarely of primary clinical significance. Whenever more than one Sexual Dysfunction is present, they should all be recorded, in order of clinical significance.

The particular manifestations of each of the Sexual Dysfunctions are noted in the diagnostic criteria. In most instances there will be a disturbance in both the subjective sense of pleasure or desire and objective performance. More rarely there may be subjective disturbance alone, without any objective signs of dysfunction, or, conversely, inhibition in performance without any acknowledged subjective distress.

In the diagnostic criteria, no attempt is made to specify a minimum proportion or type of sexual encounter in which the dysfunction must occur in order for the diagnosis to be given. This judgment has to be made by the clinician, who must take into account various factors such as frequency and chronicity of the symptom, subjective distress, and effect on other areas of functioning. The phrase "persistent or recurrent" in the diagnostic criteria is a shorthand method of designating the need for such a clinical judgment.

All of the dysfunctions may be psychogenic only or psychogenic and biogenic, lifelong or acquired (developing after a period of normal functioning), and generalized or situational (limited to certain situations or with certain partners). Although in most instances the dysfunctions occur during sexual activity with a partner, in some cases it may be appropriate to identify dysfunctions that occur during masturbation.

Associated features. Frequently there are no other obvious signs of disturbance. This is particularly the case in Hypoactive Sexual Desire Disorder, since it does not necessarily involve impairment in performance. In other cases there may be a vague sense of not living up to some ill-defined concept of normality, or there may be a variety of complaints, such as depression, anxiety, guilt, shame, frustration, and somatic symptoms. Almost invariably a fear of failure and the development of a "spectator" attitude (self-monitoring), with extreme sensitivity to the reaction of the sexual partner, are present. This may further impair performance and satisfaction and lead to secondary avoidance of sexual activity and impaired communication with the sexual partner.

Age at onset. The most common age at onset is early adulthood, although Premature Ejaculation more commonly begins with the first sexual encounters. The most common age of clinical presentation is late 20s and early 30s, a few years after establishment of a sustained sexual relationship. However, the initial appearance of a disorder, particularly Male Erectile Disorder, may be later in adult life.

Course. The course is extremely variable. As previously noted, all of the dysfunctions may be lifelong or acquired (develop after a period of normal functioning). They may be limited to a single, short-lived episode, or present a recurrent pattern of episodic dysfunction. Hypoactive Sexual Desire Disorder may develop as a reaction to any of the other Sexual Dysfunctions.

Impairment. Sexual Dysfunctions, even when severe, are rarely associated with impairment in occupational functioning, but the relationship with a sexual partner may suffer.

Complications. The major complications consist of disrupted marital or other sexual relationships.

Predisposing factors. There is no empirical evidence of an association between certain personality traits and the presence of one or more Sexual Dysfunctions. Anxiety, excessively high subjective standards of sexual performance, and unusual sensitivity to real or imagined rejection by a sexual partner predispose to the development of acquired Sexual Dysfunctions. Any negative attitude toward sexuality, due to particular experiences, internal conflicts, or adherence to rigid cultural values, predisposes to the Sexual Dysfunctions. General psychopathology may predispose to the development of lifelong Sexual Dysfunctions.

Prevalence. Although their exact prevalence is not known, most of these disorders are believed to be common, particularly in their milder forms. Studies in Europe and the United States indicate that in the young adult population, approximately 8% of the males have Male Erectile Disorder. It has been estimated that approximately 20% of the total population have Hypoactive Sexual Desire Disorder, 30% of the male population have Premature Ejaculation and that approximately 30% of the female population have Inhibited Female Orgasm.

Sex ratio. The sex ratio varies for the particular dysfunction. Hypoactive Sexual Desire Disorder and Inhibited Orgasm are more common in females. Although Dyspareunia is defined so that it can occur in males, it rarely does.

Familial pattern. No information.

Differential diagnosis. When a **physical disorder** partially accounts for the symptoms of a Sexual Dysfunction but psychological factors also contribute to the disturbance, both diagnoses should be given (the physical disorder being recorded on Axis III), and the Sexual Dysfunction should be specified as psychogenic and biogenic. For example, diminished sexual desire that is partly secondary to diabetes can be diagnosed as Hypoactive Sexual Desire Disorder if it is judged to involve performance anxiety as well. The measurement of nocturnal penile tumescence associated with REM sleep is a useful diagnostic technique for evaluating the degree to which a physical disorder is etiologically related to the disturbance. Disturbed sexual performance that is chronic, invariable over time, and independent of situation also suggests the presence of an etiologically significant physical disorder. In many instances the underlying physical disorder may not have been previously diagnosed.

If **another Axis I mental disorder,** for example, Major Depression, is the primary cause of a disturbance in sexual functioning, such as loss of sexual desire, a Sexual Dysfunction should **not** be diagnosed. However, in some instances it will not be clear whether the disturbance in sexual functioning antedates the other mental disorder (in which case it should also be diagnosed) or whether it is secondary to the other mental disorder (in which case it should not be diagnosed). Frequently, a **Personality Disorder** may coexist with a Sexual Dysfunction, and may even be conceptualized as etiologic. In such cases the Sexual Dysfunction should be recorded on Axis I and the Personality Disorder, on Axis II. If a **V Code Condition** such as Marital Problem or Other Interpersonal Problem is the primary cause of a disturbance in functioning, the Sexual Dysfunction should be diagnosed and both conditions noted.

If **sexual stimulation** is **inadequate** in either focus, intensity, or duration, the diagnosis of Sexual Dysfunction involving excitement or orgasm is not made.

Specify: psychogenic only, or **psychogenic and biogenic.** (Note: If biogenic only, code on Axis III.)

Specify: lifelong or **acquired**

Specify: generalized or **situational**

Sexual Desire Disorders

Diagnostic criteria for 302.71 Hypoactive Sexual Desire Disorder

A. Persistently or recurrently deficient or absent sexual fantasies and desire for sexual activity. The judgment of deficiency or absence is made by the clinician, taking into account factors that affect sexual functioning, such as age, sex, and the context of the person's life.

B. Occurrence not exclusively during the course of another Axis I disorder (other than a Sexual Dysfunction), such as Major Depression.

Diagnostic criteria for 302.79 Sexual Aversion Disorder

A. Persistent or recurrent extreme aversion to, and avoidance of, all or almost all, genital sexual contact with a sexual partner.

B. Occurrence not exclusively during the course of another Axis I disorder (other than a Sexual Dysfunction), such as Obsessive Compulsive Disorder or Major Depression.

Sexual Arousal Disorders

Diagnostic criteria for 302.72 Female Sexual Arousal Disorder

A. Either (1) or (2):

    (1) persistent or recurrent partial or complete failure to attain or maintain the lubrication-swelling response of sexual excitement until completion of the sexual activity

    (2) persistent or recurrent lack of a subjective sense of sexual excitement and pleasure in a female during sexual activity

B. Occurrence not exclusively during the course of another Axis I disorder (other than a Sexual Dysfunction), such as Major Depression.

Diagnostic criteria for 302.72 Male Erectile Disorder

A. Either (1) or (2):

    (1) persistent or recurrent partial or complete failure in a male to attain or maintain erection until completion of the sexual activity

    (2) persistent or recurrent lack of a subjective sense of sexual excitement and pleasure in a male during sexual activity

B. Occurrence not exclusively during the course of another Axis I disorder (other than a Sexual Dysfunction), such as Major Depression.

Orgasm Disorders

Diagnostic criteria for 302.73 Inhibited Female Orgasm

A. Persistent or recurrent delay in, or absence of, orgasm in a female following a normal sexual excitement phase during sexual activity that the clinician judges to be adequate in focus, intensity, and duration. Some females are able to experience orgasm during noncoital clitoral stimulation, but are unable to experience it during coitus in the absence of manual clitoral stimulation. In most of these females, this represents a normal variation of the female sexual response and does not justify the diagnosis of Inhibited Female Orgasm. However, in some of these females, this does represent a psychological inhibition that justifies the diagnosis. This difficult judgment is assisted by a thorough sexual evaluation, which may even require a trial of treatment.

B. Occurrence not exclusively during the course of another Axis I disorder (other than a Sexual Dysfunction), such as Major Depression.

Diagnostic criteria for 302.74 Inhibited Male Orgasm

A. Persistent or recurrent delay in, or absence of, orgasm in a male following a normal sexual excitement phase during sexual activity that the clinician, taking into account the person's age, judges to be adequate in focus, intensity, and duration. This failure to achieve orgasm is usually restricted to an inability to reach orgasm in the vagina, with orgasm possible with other types of stimulation, such as masturbation.

B. Occurrence not exclusively during the course of another Axis I disorder (other than a Sexual Dysfunction), such as Major Depression.

Diagnostic criteria for 302.75 Premature Ejaculation

Persistent or recurrent ejaculation with minimal sexual stimulation or before, upon, or shortly after penetration and before the person wishes it. The clinician must take into account factors that affect duration of the excitement phase, such as age, novelty of the sexual partner or situation, and frequency of sexual activity.

Sexual Pain Disorders

Diagnostic criteria for 302.76 Dyspareunia

A. Recurrent or persistent genital pain in either a male or a female before, during, or after sexual intercourse.

B. The disturbance is not caused exclusively by lack of lubrication or by Vaginismus.

Diagnostic criteria for 306.51 Vaginismus

A. Recurrent or persistent involuntary spasm of the musculature of the outer third of the vagina that interferes with coitus.

B. The disturbance is not caused exclusively by a physical disorder, and is not due to another Axis I disorder.

302.70   Sexual Dysfunction Not Otherwise Specified
Sexual Dysfunctions that do not meet the criteria for any of the specific Sexual Dysfunctions.

Examples:

   (1) no erotic sensation, or even complete anesthesia, despite normal physiologic component of orgasm
   (2) the female analogue of Premature Ejaculation
   (3) genital pain occurring during masturbation

OTHER SEXUAL DISORDERS

302.90 Sexual Disorder Not Otherwise Specified

Sexual Disorders that are not classifiable in any of the previous categories. In rare instances, this category may be used concurrently with one of the specific diagnoses when both are necessary to explain or describe the clinical disturbance.

Examples:

   (1) marked feelings of inadequacy concerning body habitus, size and shape of sex organs, sexual performance, or other traits related to self-imposed standards of masculinity or femininity
   (2) distress about a pattern of repeated sexual conquests or other forms of nonparaphilic sexual addiction, involving a succession of people who exist only as things to be used
   (3) persistent and marked distress about one's sexual orientation

Sleep Disorders

Described in this chapter are disorders of sleep that are chronic (of more than one month's duration), not the transient disturbances of sleep that are a normal part of everyday life. Thus, insomnia for a few nights, apparently caused by a psychosocial stressor, would not be diagnosed here (though if it were accompanied by other clinically significant features, it might be considered an Adjustment Disorder).

Sleep disturbances are a common symptom of many mental and physical disorders, such as Depressive Disorders and physical conditions causing pain or other discomfort, and can be associated with the taking of certain medications. In addition, sleep disturbances may initiate or exacerbate other physical or mental disorders. When the sleep disturbance is related in any of these ways to another mental disorder or to a physical disorder, it is here diagnosed as a Sleep Disorder if the sleep disturbance is the predominant complaint. (The other mental or physical disorder should, of course, be listed as well.)

Sleep Disorders are divided into two major subgroups: the Dyssomnias and the Parasomnias. In the Dyssomnias, the predominant disturbance is in the amount, quality, or timing of sleep. In the Parasomnias, the predominant disturbance is an abnormal event occurring during sleep.

The classification of Sleep Disorders presented here does not include certain physical disorders that a more comprehensive classification of Sleep Disorders would include. For example, hypersomnia related to such well-recognized physical disorders as sleep apnea and narcolepsy is classified here under the single rubric of Hypersomnia Related to a Known Organic Factor; the sleep apnea or narcolepsy should be noted as an additional diagnosis on Axis III. In a more comprehensive classification of Sleep Disorders, sleep apnea and narcolepsy would be considered Sleep Disorders in their own right. Similarly, such a classification would include a separate category for Nocturnal Enuresis, which in DSM-III-R is included with the childhood disorders as Functional Enuresis.

The criteria for the Sleep Disorders presented here do not include data from laboratory procedures such as sleep recordings. However, such procedures may be necessary in some people to firmly establish the diagnosis of certain Sleep Disorders, such as a sleep disturbance related to sleep apnea or to another physical disorder.

The term *daytime* is used below to denote the major period of wakefulness, although it is recognized that for some people who work night shifts, the major period of wakefulness is at night. The term *primary* as used in Primary Insomnia and Primary

Hypersomnia means that the Sleep Disorder appears to be independent of any other known physical or mental condition; it does not imply that the disorder either precedes another disorder or is more important than an associated disorder.

DYSSOMNIAS

The essential feature of this group of Sleep Disorders is a disturbance in the amount, quality, or timing of sleep. The Dyssomnias include three groups of disorders: Insomnia Disorders, Hypersomnia Disorders, and Sleep-Wake Schedule Disorder. In the Insomnia Disorders, sleep is deficient in the quantity or quality necessary for normal daytime functioning. In the Hypersomnia Disorders, the person feels excessively sleepy when awake, despite sleep of normal length. In Sleep-Wake Schedule Disorder, there is a mismatch between the person's sleep-wake pattern and the pattern that is normal for his or her environment.

Insomnia Disorders

The essential feature of these disorders is a predominant complaint of difficulty in initiating or maintaining sleep, or of not feeling rested after sleep that is apparently adequate in amount (nonrestorative sleep). The disturbance occurs at least three times a week for at least one month and is sufficiently severe to result in either a complaint of significant daytime fatigue or the observation by others of some symptom that is attributable to the sleep disturbance, e.g., irritability or impaired daytime functioning. An Insomnia Disorder is not diagnosed if the insomnia occurs only during the course of Sleep-Wake Schedule Disorder or a Parasomnia.

There are three Insomnia Disorders: Insomnia Related to Another Mental Disorder (Nonorganic), Insomnia Related to a Known Organic Factor, and Primary Insomnia.

There is great variability in the normal length of time it takes a person to fall asleep or in the amount of sleep normally required for a person to feel alert and rested. For the vast majority of people, sleep begins within 30 minutes of creating an environment that encourages sleep ("going to bed") and lasts from four to ten hours. Typically, a young person with an Insomnia Disorder complains that it takes too long to fall asleep. An older person complains that he or she awakens too frequently, or is unable to stay asleep long enough to feel rested the next day. In some cases a person with insomnia complains only of nonrestorative sleep, despite apparently having no difficulty falling asleep or staying asleep.

Associated features. Various nonspecific complaints are common, among them disturbances in mood, memory, and concentration.

Age at onset. An Insomnia Disorder can begin at any age, but such disorders become increasingly common with advancing age. This is particularly true for Insomnia Related to a Known Organic Factor.

Course. The course of Insomnia Related to a Another Mental Disorder (Nonorganic) and Insomnia Related to a Known Organic Factor generally follows the course of the related condition. The course of Primary Insomnia varies; it may be relatively brief (although, by definition, it is of at least one month's duration), particularly if the disorder is precipitated by a psychosocial stressor, or, at the other extreme, it may be unrelenting and last for decades.

Impairment. In rare cases there may be no obvious impairment in social or occupational functioning; but typically, some impairment results from an Insomnia Disorder.

More rarely, because the person is unable to function efficiently during his or her waking hours, social or occupational functioning may be seriously disrupted.

Complications. Complications are primarily those that result from treatment with pharmacologic agents, such as sedatives or hypnotics (prescribed or taken on one's own), from alcohol consumed to induce sleep, or from stimulants taken to increase alertness.

Predisposing factors. Insomnia of different kinds is apparently more common in people with increased levels of stress and psychopathology. There is some evidence that people who seem to lack awareness of their own emotions are predisposed to the development of Insomnia Disorders. Many people who in later life develop an Insomnia Disorder were light sleepers as children.

Prevalence. The prevalence of Insomnia Disorders as defined here is unknown. However, about 15% of the general population consider insomnia a serious problem, for which professional help is occasionally sought. In clinical settings, Insomnia Related to Another Mental Disorder (Nonorganic) is more common than the other two Insomnia Disorders.

Sex ratio. Insomnia Disorders Related to Another Mental Disorder (Nonorganic) are more common in females than in males.

Familial pattern. No information.

Differential diagnosis. Insomnia is a common symptom of **many mental and physical disorders.** The additional diagnosis of an Insomnia Disorder is considered only when the sleep disturbance is the predominant complaint. For example, when the chief complaint of a person with Dysthymia is of severe and chronic insomnia, both diagnoses (Insomnia Related to Another Mental Disorder [Nonorganic] and Dysthymia) should be given. On the other hand, when insomnia is associated with Dysthymia, but is not the chief complaint, an Insomnia Disorder should not be diagnosed as an additional disorder.

In **Sleep-Wake Schedule Disorder,** insomnia disappears if the person is allowed to sleep according to his or her own circadian sleep-wake pattern.

In **Hypersomnia Disorders,** insomnia may be present, but the predominant complaint is hypersomnia. For example, in Hypersomnia related to either sleep apnea or narcolepsy, the person typically is bothered primarily by excessive daytime sleepiness, although he or she may also complain of frequent nocturnal awakenings.

Some **people who normally require little sleep** may complain of insomnia. The diagnosis of Insomnia Disorder is made only if the presumed lack of sleep results in significant daytime fatigue or impaired functioning.

Diagnostic criteria for Insomnia Disorders

A. The predominant complaint is of difficulty in initiating or maintaining sleep, or of nonrestorative sleep (sleep that is apparently adequate in amount, but leaves the person feeling unrested).

(continued)

Diagnostic criteria for Insomnia Disorders continued

B. The disturbance in A occurs at least three times a week for at least one month and is sufficiently severe to result in either a complaint of significant daytime fatigue or the observation by others of some symptom that is attributable to the sleep disturbance, e.g., irritability or impaired daytime functioning.

C. Occurrence not exclusively during the course of Sleep-Wake Schedule Disorder or a Parasomnia.

307.42   Insomnia Related to Another Mental Disorder (Nonorganic)

The essential feature is an Insomnia Disorder that is judged to be related to another Axis I or Axis II mental disorder (nonorganic). Common nonorganic Axis I disorders that may be present with an Insomnia Disorder are Depressive Disorders, Anxiety Disorders, and Adjustment Disorder with Anxious Mood. A common Axis II disorder that may present with an Insomnia Disorder is Obsessive Compulsive Personality Disorder.

This diagnosis should be made when an Insomnia Disorder is apparently due to the emotional reaction of the person to a life-threatening physical disorder, such as Major Depression or Adjustment Disorder with Anxious Mood in response to a myocardial infarction.

Diagnostic criteria for 307.42 Insomnia Related to Another Mental Disorder (Nonorganic)

Insomnia Disorder, as defined by criteria A, B, and C above, that is related to another Axis I or Axis II mental disorder, such as Major Depression, Generalized Anxiety Disorder, Adjustment Disorder with Anxious Mood, or Obsessive Compulsive Personality Disorder. This category is not used if the Insomnia Disorder is related to an Axis I disorder involving a known organic factor, such as a Psychoactive Substance Use Disorder (e.g., Amphetamine Dependence).

780.50   Insomnia Related to a Known Organic Factor

The essential feature is an Insomnia Disorder that is related to a known organic factor, such as a physical condition, the use of certain medications, or a Psychoactive Substance Use Disorder. This diagnosis is not made if the Insomnia Disorder is due to the person's emotional reaction to a physical condition, not to the condition itself.

Many physical disorders and conditions that are associated with an Insomnia Disorder, such as arthritis, Parkinson's disease, or angina, disturb sleep through pain and discomfort. These physical disorders are generally symptomatic both when one is awake and during sleep. Other physical disorders are symptomatic only during sleep, and can be diagnosed directly only during sleep. For example, in a person with sleep apnea, waking respiratory functions are typically within normal limits; but during sleep, there are frequent respiratory pauses, often associated with oxygen desaturation and cardiac arrhythmias. In myoclonus, periodic leg twitches may disturb sleep, although muscle and neuronal functioning when awake is generally normal.

An Insomnia Disorder can also be associated with prolonged use of certain medications, such as amphetamines or other stimulants, steroids, central adrenergic blocking agents, and bronchodilators. In addition, an Insomnia Disorder can be associated with a Psychoactive Substance Use Disorder, such as Alcohol Dependence or Amphetamine Dependence.

Diagnostic criteria for 780.50 Insomnia Related to a Known Organic Factor

Insomnia Disorder, as defined by criteria A, B, and C above, that is related to a known organic factor, such as a physical disorder (e.g., sleep apnea, arthritis), a Psychoactive Substance Use Disorder (e.g., Amphetamine Dependence), or a medication (e.g., prolonged use of decongestants).

The known organic factor should be listed on Axis III (if a physical disorder or use of a medication that does not meet the criteria for a Psychoactive Substance Use Disorder) or Axis I (if a Psychoactive Substance Use Disorder).

307.42   Primary Insomnia

The essential feature is an Insomnia Disorder whose persistence is apparently not related to another mental disorder or to a known organic factor, such as a physical condition, a Psychoactive Substance Use Disorder, or a medication.

Characteristically, the person worries excessively during the day about not being able to fall and stay asleep; this may become a major preoccupation. The person often makes intense efforts to fall asleep, but worries about these efforts' being unsuccessful, which increases tension or arousal; is able to fall asleep when he or she is not trying to sleep, for example, while watching television; and experiences a paradoxical improvement in sleep when away from his or her usual sleep environment.

Some people with Primary Insomnia report a lifelong pattern of poor sleep, often dating back to early childhood. Others develop the disorder later in life, often during a period of stressful life events.

Primary Insomnia may develop as a complication of either Insomnia Related to Another Mental Disorder or Insomnia Related to a Known Organic Factor. For example, a person with a painful, slowly healing, broken leg may develop Insomnia Related to a Known Organic Factor. If severe insomnia persists for at least a month after the painful physical condition has been resolved, the diagnosis should be changed to Primary Insomnia.

Diagnostic criteria for 307.42 Primary Insomnia

Insomnia Disorder, as defined by criteria A, B, and C above, that apparently is not maintained by any other mental disorder or any known organic factor, such as a physical disorder, a Psychoactive Substance Use Disorder, or a medication.

Hypersomnia Disorders

The essential feature of these disorders is either excessive daytime sleepiness or sleep attacks (not accounted for by an inadequate amount of sleep) or, more rarely, a prolonged transition to the fully awake state on awakening (sleep drunkenness). The disturbance occurs nearly every day for at least one month, or episodically for longer periods of time, and is sufficiently severe to result in impaired occupational functioning or impairment in usual social activities or relationships with others. A Hypersomnia Disorder is not diagnosed if the hypersomnia occurs only during the course of a Sleep-Wake Schedule Disorder.

There are three Hypersomnia Disorders: Hypersomnia Related to Another Mental Disorder (Nonorganic), Hypersomnia Related to a Known Organic Factor, and Primary Hypersomnia.

Daytime sleepiness is defined as a tendency to fall asleep very easily (typically in five minutes or less), at almost any time during the day, even following a normal or prolonged amount of sleep at night. Typically, in excessive daytime sleepiness the person falls asleep unintentionally at work, while driving, or at social gatherings. (Thus, excessive fatigue, listlessness, or excessive bedrest are *not* synonymous with sleepiness.) Sleep attacks are discrete periods of sudden, irresistible sleep. In sleep drunkenness, the person requires much more time to become fully alert upon awakening than would be normal, and during this prolonged transition may be ataxic and disoriented.

Usually the hypersomnia is present every day, as when related to sleep apnea or narcolepsy. More rarely, the hypersomnia is episodic, as in Kleine-Levin syndrome and some atypical forms of Major Depression.

Course. The course of Hypersomnia Related to Another Mental Disorder (Nonorganic) and Hypersomnia Related to a Known Organic Factor generally follows that of the related condition. Severity of the symptoms fluctuates considerably over time.

Impairment. Social and occupational impairment may vary from mild to severe.

Complications. Many people with Hypersomnia Disorders become demoralized or depressed. Accidental injury, e.g., from falling asleep while driving, is a common complication. Physiologic tolerance to stimulant medication given as a treatment may develop.

Prevalence. The lifetime prevalence rate of Hypersomnia Disorders has been estimated at 1%–2%.

Familial pattern. Most Hypersomnia Disorders, particularly when related to narcolepsy, are more common among first-degree biologic relatives of people with these disorders than among the general population.

Differential diagnosis. Hypersomnia may be associated with **many physical illnesses,** but is rarely the predominant complaint. Similarly, hypersomnia in **Depressive Disorders** is common, but is rarely the predominant complaint.

In **psychomotor epilepsy,** the seizures may mimic the sleep attacks of narcolepsy. During epileptic seizures, however, characteristic perseverative motor movements, such as repeated swallowing and rubbing the hands, may be observed.

Diagnostic criteria for Hypersomnia Disorders

A. The predominant complaint is either (1) or (2):

   (1) excessive daytime sleepiness or sleep attacks not accounted for by an inadequate amount of sleep

   (2) prolonged transition to the fully awake state on awakening (sleep drunkenness)

B. The disturbance in A occurs nearly every day for at least one month, or episodically for longer periods of time, and is sufficiently severe to result in impaired occupational functioning or impairment in usual social activities or relationships with others.

C. Occurrence not exclusively during the course of Sleep-Wake Schedule Disorder.

307.44   Hypersomnia Related to Another Mental Disorder (Nonorganic)

The essential feature of this disorder is hypersomnia that is apparently related to another mental disorder (nonorganic).

Hypersomnia (rather than insomnia) may be found in some Mood Disorders, especially in the depressive phase of Bipolar Disorder. Adolescents and young adults are more likely to have hypersomnia than are older adults, who typically complain of insomnia when depressed. In other mental disorders, such as Somatoform Disorders, Borderline Personality Disorder, and Schizophrenia, hypersomnia as a predominant complaint is rare, but can occur. Typically, the person attributes the excessive daytime sleepiness to nonrestorative sleep.

Age at onset. Hypersomnia related to atypical forms of Major Depression is usually apparent by the 20s.

Diagnostic criteria for 307.44 Hypersomnia Related to Another Mental Disorder (Nonorganic)

Hypersomnia, as defined by criteria A, B, and C above, that is related to another Axis I or II mental disorder, such as Major Depression or Dysthymia.

780.50   Hypersomnia Related to a Known Organic Factor

The essential feature of this disorder is hypersomnia related to a known organic factor, such as a physical condition, a Psychoactive Substance use Disorder, or a medication.

Some disorders related to a Hypersomnia Disorder are present when the person is awake or asleep (e.g., sleepiness associated with Psychoactive Substance Use Disorders, such as Cannabis Dependence, or prolonged use of certain medications, such as sedatives or antihypertensives). Other disorders associated with Hypersomnia are apparent only during sleep (e.g., sleep apnea and sleep-related myoclonus), and the person is generally not aware of what disturbs his or her sleep.

About 85% of cases of Hypersomnia seen in sleep disorders centers are diagnosed as Hypersomnia Related to a Known Organic Factor. About 50% of these cases are associated with sleep apnea; 25%, with narcolepsy; and 10%, with sleep-related myoclonus and "restless legs" syndrome.

Associated features. People with narcolepsy often have cataplexy (episodic loss of muscle tone, triggered by strong emotions, that can result in falls), hypnagogic or hypnopompic hallucinations, and sleep paralysis (inability to move while falling asleep or upon sudden awakening). People with obstructive sleep apnea are often obese and subject to systemic and pulmonary hypertension with cardiac arrhythmias. Less often, they suffer from impotence and headaches. In Kleine-Levin syndrome, the periods of hypersomnia are associated with increased eating and sexual drive.

Age at onset. Narcolepsy typically begins around the time of puberty (in most instances, before the age of 30); obstructive sleep apnea most commonly begins in middle adult life and becomes increasingly common with advancing age. Kleine-Levin syndrome has its onset in late adolescence. Hypersomnia related to a Psychoactive Substance Use Disorder is usually apparent by the 20s.

Impairment. The person with narcolepsy often strives continually to prevent attacks of cataplexy by exerting control over his or her emotions. This may lead to a generalized lack of expressiveness that interferes with social relations. Many people with severe obstructive sleep apnea display irritability and various degrees of cognitive impairment, such as distractibility, confusion, and deficits in perception and memory.

Predisposing factors. Obesity is a predisposing factor to the development of obstructive sleep apnea.

Sex ratio. Narcolepsy is equally common in males and females; Kleine-Levin syndrome is far more common in males; obstructive sleep apnea is rarer in premenopausal females than in males, but becomes equally common after menopause.

Diagnostic criteria for 780.50 Hypersomnia Related to a Known Organic Factor

Hypersomnia Disorder, as defined by criteria A, B, and C above, that is related to a known organic factor, such as a physical disorder (e.g., sleep apnea), a Psychoactive Substance Use Disorder (e.g., Cannabis Dependence), or a medication (e.g., prolonged use of sedatives or antihypertensives).

The known organic factor should be listed on Axis III (if a physical disorder or use of a medication that does not meet the criteria for a Psychoactive Substance Use Disorder) or Axis I (if a Psychoactive Substance Use Disorder).

780.54   Primary Hypersomnia

The essential feature of this disorder is hypersomnia whose persistence apparently is not related to another mental disorder or to a known organic factor, such as a physical condition, a Psychoactive Substance Use Disorder, or a medication.

In some cases the disorder may represent a response to nonrestorative sleep of unknown etiology. In other cases it may be a response to stress or part of a general pattern of adaptation characterized by lack of a sense of purpose in life.

Diagnostic criteria for 780.54 Primary Hypersomnia

Hypersomnia, as defined by criteria A, B, and C above, that is apparently not maintained by any other mental disorder or any known organic factor, such as a physical disorder, a Psychoactive Substance Use Disorder, or a medication.

Sleep-Wake Schedule Disorder

307.45   Sleep-Wake Schedule Disorder

Even when people live in environments in which cues about the time of day have been removed, most biologic functions still follow a rhythm with a period that lasts about 24 hours (circadian rhythm). The essential feature of Sleep-Wake Schedule Disorder is a mismatch between the normal sleep-wake schedule that is demanded by the person's environment and the person's circadian rhythm. This results in a complaint of either insomnia (the person attempts to sleep, but is unable to do so) or hypersomnia (the person is unable to remain alert when wakefulness is expected). However, if early in the development of Sleep-Wake Schedule Disorder the person is allowed to follow his or her own sleep-wake schedule, the insomnia or hypersomnia disappears.

Transient sleep-wake schedule mismatches commonly occur when people change time zones rapidly or occasionally stay up late for several days. For a diagnosis of Sleep-Wake Schedule Disorder to be made, the insomnia or hypersomnia must be sufficiently frequent and severe to meet the A and B criteria for Insomnia or Hypersomnia Disorder.

There are three types of Sleep-Wake Schedule Disorder: Frequently Changing Type, Advanced or Delayed Type, and Disorganized Type.

In the *Advanced or Delayed Type,* the essential feature is a Sleep-Wake Schedule Disorder in which onset and offset of sleep are considerably advanced or delayed in relation to what the person desires, usually the conventional schedule for the particular society. In some cases the person's sleep-wake schedule may occasionally appear to be normal only because medication or environmental demands interfere with sleep onset or offset. In such a case, for example, the person may have a sleep-wake schedule that is delayed about four hours, so that without medication or environmental demands, he or she would go to sleep at about 3 AM and awaken at about 11 AM. However, the person may actually have to awaken at 8 AM because of the need to be at work, or may go to sleep with a hypnotic at 11 PM. Though these hours are the conventional societal times for onset and offset of sleep, in this instance the person's onset and offset of sleep that would occur without medication or environmental demands would reveal an underlying Sleep-Wake Schedule Disorder.

In the advanced type, most evening activity is preempted by an obligatory early bedtime, and the person may awaken for the day at 3:00 AM or earlier. In the delayed type, the person has great difficulty arising in time to fulfill his or her morning obligations.

The delayed type is frequently observed in younger people with few rigidly scheduled work or social commitments (e.g., students or the unemployed). It is also frequent in "night people," i.e., those whose subjective arousal increases considerably at night, but who feel bad for a long time after the major sleep period has ended.

The advanced sleep pattern is often observed among older people. Because it also frequently results in early morning awakening, depression has to be differentiated from the advanced type of sleep by the presence of depressed mood or anhedonia and by other signs, such as loss of appetite and psychomotor disturbance.

In the *Disorganized Type*, the essential feature is a generally random or capricious pattern of sleep and wake times, in which there is no daily major sleep period. This type is seen in people who schedule their sleep hours haphazardly and snatch moments of sleep through the 24 hours. Some of these people may be elderly or bedridden and nap off and on throughout the day. The diagnosis should not be made in those rare people with a constitutionally low need for sleep whose sleep-wake schedules are irregular but cause no significant distress or interference with daytime functioning.

In the *Frequently Changing Type*, the essential feature is a Sleep-Wake Schedule Disorder apparently due to frequent changes in sleep and waking times. This is often associated with frequent airplane flights involving time-zone changes or with changing work schedules (shift work); sleep is then often divided into two or more periods (e.g., napping both before and after work). On weekends or on days off, the person may temporarily attempt to revert to a normal sleep-wake schedule and thus undermine a long-term circadian adaptation to the new work schedule.

For reasons as yet unknown, people vary greatly in their ability to tolerate frequently changing sleep-wake schedules. Some people work for years on rotating work shifts without experiencing any distress. In general, older people have more difficulty adjusting to frequent schedule changes.

"Night owls" seem to do better on shift work than those who typically rise early ("larks"). Some people attempt to force wakefulness during new work hours by drinking excessive amounts of coffee. Less frequently, sleep is forced, through hypnotics, to fit the newly adopted sleep hours. Another possible complication of the Frequently Changing Type of sleep schedule is that the person's social and family life may suffer considerable disruption.

Associated features. Nonspecific dysphoric symptoms, such as malaise and lack of energy, are common.

Age at onset. The period of the circadian rhythm normally lengthens during adolescence, which increases vulnerability to the Delayed Type of Sleep-Wake Schedule Disorder. In the elderly, the period of the circadian rhythm normally shortens, which increases the likelihood of the Advanced Type of Sleep-Wake Schedule Disorder. The Disorganized Type may occur at any age.

Course. The course of the Frequently Changing and Disorganized Types is generally determined by the person's life-style, i.e., whether or not he or she continues to do shift work, travel through different time zones, or have an irregular sleep-wake pattern.

Impairment. Impairment in social or occupational functioning varies from mild to severe.

Complications. Accidents, lapses of attention, and certain physical disorders such as gastric ulcers may increase when one is frequently forced to stay alert during the nadir of one's circadian rhythm.

Predisposing factors. By definition, a life-style that includes frequently changing or irregular sleep-wake patterns predisposes to this disorder. This includes frequent airplane flights across different time zones, shift work, erratic social schedules, or chaotic living conditions that result in frequent nighttime awakenings and daytime naps. At any given time, one in four working males and one in six working females have work schedules that are outside the typical 9-to-5 pattern. These figures, however, refer to merely a part of the population at risk for the Frequently Changing Type of Sleep-Wake Schedule Disorder.

Prevalence, sex ratio, and familial pattern. No information.

Differential diagnosis. Sleep-Wake Schedule Disorder is differentiated from **Insomnia Disorder** and **Hypersomnia Disorder** by the person's history and by the fact that Sleep-Wake Schedule Disorder typically improves if the person is allowed to follow his or her own sleep-wake schedule for a while.
    A disorganized sleep-wake schedule is observed in some people with a **psychotic or Personality Disorder.** The diagnosis of Sleep-Wake Schedule Disorder is made only if disturbed sleep is the predominant complaint.

Diagnostic criteria for 307.45 Sleep-Wake Schedule Disorder

Mismatch between the normal sleep-wake schedule for a person's environment and his or her circadian sleep-wake pattern, resulting in a complaint of either insomnia (criteria A and B of Insomnia Disorder) or hypersomnia (criteria A and B of Hypersomnia Disorder).

Specify Type:

Advanced or Delayed Type: Sleep-Wake Schedule Disorder with onset and offset of sleep considerably advanced or delayed (if sleep-wake schedule is not interfered with by medication or environmental demands) in relation to what the person desires (usually the conventional societal sleep-wake schedule).

Disorganized Type: Sleep-Wake Schedule Disorder apparently due to disorganized and variable sleep and waking times, resulting in absence of a daily major sleep period.

Frequently Changing Type: Sleep-Wake Schedule Disorder apparently due to frequently changing sleep and waking times, such as recurrent changes in work shifts or time zones.

Other Dyssomnias

307.40 Dyssomnia Not Otherwise Specified

Insomnias, hypersomnias, or sleep-wake schedule disturbances that cannot be classified in any of the specific categories noted above.

PARASOMNIAS

The essential feature of this group of disorders is an abnormal event that occurs either during sleep or at the threshold between wakefulness and sleep; the predominant complaint focuses on this disturbance, not on its effect on sleeping or wakefulness. For example, sleep apnea and dream anxiety attacks both occur during sleep; but the disturbance associated with sleep apnea is classified as a Dyssomnia because the person typically complains about excessive daytime sleepiness, whereas Dream Anxiety Disorder is classified as a Parasomnia because the person characteristically complains mainly about the dreams and the ensuing anxiety and less about the fact that these dreams interfere with sleeping.

From the perspective of a classification of Sleep Disorders, Functional Enuresis occurring during sleep is a Parasomnia. However, in DSM-III-R, Functional Enuresis (both daytime and nocturnal) is classified as a Disorder of Elimination in the major diagnostic class of Disorders Usually First Evident in Infancy, Childhood, or Adolescence (see p. 84).

Although rare, nocturnal seizure disorders (classified as a physical disorder) may mimic the symptoms of a Parasomnia, especially if the seizures do not occur at any particular time within the night. A waking clinical EEG does not rule out this possibility because, quite frequently, the waking EEG may be entirely normal whereas an EEG administered during certain sleep stages may show abnormalities, especially after a few hours of sleep have elapsed.

307.47 Dream Anxiety Disorder (Nightmare Disorder)

The essential feature is repeated awakenings from sleep with detailed recall of frightening dreams. These dreams are typically vivid and quite extended and usually include threats to survival, security, or self-esteem. Often there is a recurrence of the same or similar themes. The dream experience or the sleep disturbance resulting from the awakenings causes significant distress. Dream anxiety episodes often increase with mental stress, less often with physical fatigue, and, in a few cases, with changes in the sleep environment. This condition has also been called Nightmare Disorder. The diagnosis is not made if the disturbance is initiated and maintained by a specific organic factor, such as a medication.

Dream anxiety episodes occur during periods of REM sleep. Thus, although they may occur at almost any time during the night, they become more frequent toward the end of the night, when REM sleep is more abundant. During a typical dream anxiety episode, there is remarkably little autonomic agitation. Large body movements are rarely observed during the episode because the REM-related loss of muscle tone inhibits body movement, but they are often present during the awakening.

Upon awakening from the frightening dream, the person rapidly becomes oriented and alert. Usually, a detailed account of the dream experience can be given, both immediately upon awakening and in the morning. Many people who suffer nightmares have difficulty returning to sleep after awakening from a nightmare.

Associated features. No consistently associated psychopathology has been observed in children with Dream Anxiety Disorder. In contrast, adults with the disorder often display high levels of associated psychopathology. Some studies have suggested that the disorder is often associated with artistic ability. Others have indicated personality patterns of distrustfulness, alienation, estrangement, and oversensitivity. In many cases marked schizoid or borderline personality traits have been noted.

Age at onset. Over half the cases start before the age of 10, and in about two-thirds of cases, onset is before age 20. A major stressful life event seems to precede the onset of the disorder in about 60% of cases.

Course. The frequency of episodes is variable both within and among individuals. In many cases three or more nightmares per week are reported. Children frequently outgrow the disorder. If it begins in adulthood, however, the disorder often persists for decades.

Impairment. Generally, there is no major effect on daytime functioning.

Complications. No information.

Predisposing factors. The disorder is reported to be particularly common in people with frequent physical and mental health problems.

Prevalence. About 5% of the general population report a current complaint, and another 6% a past complaint, of nightmares. It is not clear what proportion of these would qualify for the diagnosis of Dream Anxiety Disorder.

Sex ratio. The disorder is more common in females.

Familial pattern. No information.

Differential diagnosis. The diagnosis is not made if the disturbance was initiated and maintained by a known organic factor. Certain drugs, including reserpine, thioridazine, mesoridazine, tricyclic antidepressants, and benzodiazepines, have been reported to occasionally cause nightmares. Abrupt withdrawal from REM-suppressant drugs (e.g., tricyclics) generally induces REM rebound, which may be associated with increased intensity of dreaming and with the possible occurrence of nightmares. If the nightmares are apparently due to any of these organic factors, a diagnosis of Parasomnia NOS should be made.

In **Sleep Terror Disorder** the disturbance typically occurs during the first third of sleep, there is excessive body movement and extreme autonomic discharge, and there is little detailed dream recall, either immediately following the episode or upon awakening in the morning.

Diagnostic criteria for 307.47 Dream Anxiety Disorder

A. Repeated awakenings from the major sleep period or naps with detailed recall of extended and extremely frightening dreams, usually involving threats to survival, security, or self-esteem. The awakenings generally occur during the second half of the sleep period.

B. On awakening from the frightening dreams, the person rapidly becomes oriented and alert (in contrast to the confusion and disorientation seen in Sleep Terror Disorder and some forms of epilepsy).

C. The dream experience or the sleep disturbance resulting from the awakenings causes significant distress.

D. It cannot be established that an organic factor initiated and maintained the disturbance, e.g., certain medications.

307.46   Sleep Terror Disorder

The essential features of this disorder are repeated episodes of abrupt awakening from sleep, usually beginning with a panicky scream. The episode usually occurs during the first third of the major sleep period (the interval of nonrapid eye movement [NREM] sleep that typically contains EEG delta activity, sleep stages 3 and 4) and lasts one to ten minutes. This condition has also been called Pavor Nocturnus.

During a typical episode, the person abruptly sits up in bed and has a frightened expression and signs of intense anxiety, dilated pupils, profuse perspiration, piloerection, rapid breathing, and a quick pulse. A person in this state is unresponsive to efforts of others to comfort him or her until the agitation and confusion subside. The person may then recount having had a sense of terror and fragmentary dream images before arousal, but rarely a vivid and complete dream sequence. Morning amnesia for the entire episode is the rule. Episodes are more likely to occur if the person is fatigued, or has experienced stress.

Before a severe episode, the sleep EEG delta waves may be higher in amplitude than usual for the NREM phase of sleep, and breathing and the heartbeat, slower. Onset of the episode is accompanied by a twofold to fourfold increase in heart rate, and the EEG quickly assumes a more awakelike pattern.

Associated features. There is no consistently associated psychopathology in children with this disorder. In contrast, adults with the disorder frequently have symptoms of other mental disorders, such as Generalized Anxiety Disorder.

Age at onset. Sleep Terror Disorder usually begins between the ages 4 and 12. When the disorder begins in adulthood, it usually begins in the 20s or 30s; onset after 40 is rare.

Course. Episodes are extremely variable in frequency both within and among individuals. They usually occur at intervals of days or weeks, but may occur on consecutive nights. In children the disorder usually gradually disappears in early adolescence. When the disorder begins in adulthood, the course is often chronic.

Impairment. Impairment is limited to avoidance of situations in which others might become aware of the disturbance, such as going to camp or visiting friends overnight.

Complications. Accidental injury during an episode may be a complication.

Predisposing factors. Febrile illness in childhood or early adolescence may be a predisposing factor.

Prevalence. It is estimated that 1% to 4% of children at some time have the disorder. A much higher percentage of children experience isolated episodes.

Sex ratio. The disorder is more common in males than in females.

Familial pattern. The disorder is apparently more common among first-degree biologic relatives of people with the disorder than among the general population.

Differential diagnosis. Dream Anxiety Disorder is distinguished from Sleep Terror Disorder by its appearance in the middle and latter thirds of the night, milder physiologic arousal and agitation, absence of a panicky scream upon awakening, and distinct recall of a detailed dream sequence. Parents may misinterpret the fearfulness and fragmentary imagery reports of Sleep Terror Disorder in their child as indicative of Dream Anxiety Disorder. **Hypnagogic hallucinations** may be associated with anxiety, but occur at sleep onset and consist of vivid images at the transition from wakefulness to sleep. **Epileptic seizures** during sleep, with postictal confusion, may present a clinical picture similar to Sleep Terror Disorder, and need to be ruled out by the presence of an abnormal sleep EEG at the time of the episode.

Diagnostic criteria for 307.46 Sleep Terror Disorder

A. A predominant disturbance of recurrent episodes of abrupt awakening (lasting 1-10 minutes) from sleep, usually occurring during the first third of the major sleep period and beginning with a panicky scream.

B. Intense anxiety and signs of autonomic arousal during each episode, such as tachycardia, rapid breathing, and sweating, but no detailed dream is recalled.

C. Relative unresponsiveness to efforts of others to comfort the person during the episode and, almost invariably, at least several minutes of confusion, disorientation, and perseverative motor movements (e.g., picking at pillow).

D. It cannot be established that an organic factor initiated and maintained the disturbance, e.g., brain tumor.

307.46   Sleepwalking Disorder

The essential features of this disorder are repeated episodes of a sequence of complex behaviors that progress to leaving the bed and walking about, without the person's being conscious of the episode or later remembering it. The episode usually occurs during the first third of the major sleep period (the interval of nonrapid eye movement [NREM] sleep that typically contains EEG delta activity, sleep stages 3 and 4) and lasts from a few minutes to about a half-hour.

During a typical episode, the person sits up and initially performs perseverative motor movements, such as picking at a blanket or sheet, then proceeds to semipurposeful motor acts, which, in addition to walking, may include dressing, opening doors, eating, and going to the bathroom. On some occasions the episode may terminate before the walking stage is reached.

During the episode the person has a blank, staring face, is relatively unresponsive to the efforts of others to influence the sleepwalking or to communicate with him or her, and can be awakened only with great difficulty. During sleepwalking, coordination is poor; but the person may be able to see and walk around objects in his or her path. It is a myth that during sleepwalking the person is careful and safe; in fact, he or she can stumble or lose balance and be injured by taking hazardous routes such as through windows or down fire escapes.

The walking behavior may terminate spontaneously, in which case the person awakens and is disoriented for several minutes. On the other hand, the person may return to bed without ever reaching consciousness, or may lie down in another place to continue sleeping, and be mystified the next morning at finding himself or herself there.

Upon awakening (either from the sleepwalking episode or the next morning), the person does not remember the route traversed and what happened during the episode. Fragmentary dream images may be recalled, but not complete dream sequences.

Sleep EEG slow waves usually increase in amplitude in stage 4 sleep just preceding the episode; but EEG flattening, i.e., arousal, may occur before the episode. In the usual case, as the person walks, the high-amplitude, slow-wave pattern gives way to a mixture of NREM stages and lower-amplitude EEG activity.

Sleepwalking is more likely to occur if the person is fatigued, or has experienced stress.

Associated features. Frenzied behavior or aggression toward persons or objects during sleepwalking is infrequent. Sleeptalking may accompany sleepwalking, but articulation is poor, and dialogue is rare.

People with Sleepwalking Disorder have a higher than normal incidence of other episodic disorders associated with deep NREM sleep, such as Sleep Terror Disorder. No consistently associated psychopathology has been observed in children with this disorder. In contrast, adults with the disorder frequently have symptoms of other mental disorders, such as Personality Disorders.

Age at onset. Sleepwalking Disorder usually begins between ages 6 and 12.

Course. Sleepwalking usually lasts several years in children and adolescents, whether it occurs infrequently or nightly. The great majority of children or adolescents with the disorder are asymptomatic by their 20s; when the disturbance begins in adulthood, it tends to be more chronic.

Impairment. Impairment is limited to avoidance of situations in which others might become aware of the disturbance, such as going to camp or visiting friends overnight.

Complications. Accidental injury during the episodes is the major complication.

Predisposing factors. Febrile illness as a child is a predisposing factor.

Prevalence. It is estimated that 1%–6% of children have the disorder at some time. As many as 15% of all children experience isolated episodes. Sleepwalking Disorder is rarer in adults.

Sex ratio. The disorder is apparently more common in males than in females.

Familial pattern. The disorder is more common among first-degree biologic relatives of people with Sleepwalking Disorder than among the general population. These relatives tend to be deep sleepers.

Differential diagnosis. Psychomotor epileptic seizures may occur at night and produce episodes of perseverative behaviors similar to those in sleepwalking except that the people almost never return to their own beds. Also, during epileptic attacks the person is unresponsive to environmental stimuli, and perseverative motor movements such as swallowing and rubbing the hands are more common. People with seizure disorders generally display such behaviors in the waking state as well, and the activity is associated with a recordable seizure discharge. However, seizure disorders do not preclude coexisting Sleepwalking Disorder.

Psychogenic Fugue is distinguishable from Sleepwalking Disorder on several counts: Psychogenic Fugue is rare in children, typically begins when the person is awake, lasts hours or days, is not characterized by disturbances of consciousness, and is usually associated with other evidence of severe psychopathology.

Sleep drunkenness (prolonged transition to a clear consciousness after awakening) may resemble Sleepwalking Disorder except that the former occurs after awakening and is often associated with aggressive behavior.

Diagnostic criteria for 307.46 Sleepwalking Disorder

A. Repeated episodes of arising from bed during sleep and walking about, usually occurring during the first third of the major sleep period.

B. While sleepwalking, the person has a blank, staring face, is relatively unresponsive to the efforts of others to influence the sleepwalking or to communicate with him or her, and can be awakened only with great difficulty.

C. On awakening (either from the sleepwalking episode or the next morning), the person has amnesia for the episode.

D. Within several minutes after awakening from the sleepwalking episode, there is no impairment of mental activity or behavior (although there may initially be a short period of confusion or disorientation).

E. It cannot be established that an organic factor initiated and maintained the disturbance, e.g., epilepsy.

307.40 Parasomnia Not Otherwise Specified

Disturbances during sleep that cannot be classified in any of the specific categories noted above. *Example*: Nightmares apparently caused by having taken or withdrawn from certain drugs.

Factitious Disorders

"Factitious" means not real, genuine, or natural. Factitious Disorders are therefore characterized by physical or psychological symptoms that are intentionally produced or feigned. The sense of intentionally producing a symptom is subjective, and can only be inferred by an outside observer.

The judgment that the symptom is intentionally produced is based, in part, on the person's ability to simulate illness in such a way that he or she is not likely to be discovered. This involves decisions as to timing and concealment that require a degree of judgment and intellectual activity suggestive of "voluntary" control. However, these acts have a compulsive quality in the sense that the person is unable to refrain from a particular behavior even if its dangers are known. The behaviors should therefore be considered "voluntary" only in the sense that they are deliberate and purposeful (intentional), but not in the sense that the acts can be controlled. Thus, in Factitious Disorders, behavior that appears to be under "voluntary" control is used to pursue goals that are involuntarily adopted.

The judgment that a particular behavior is intentionally produced is made by the exclusion of all other possible causes of the behavior. For example, a person presenting with hematuria is found to have anticoagulants in his possession; he denies having taken them, but blood studies are consistent with the ingestion of the anticoagulants. A reasonable inference is that the person may have taken the medication intentionally. A single episode of such behavior could be accidental rather than intentional. Repeated episodes would justify an inference of intentional production of the symptoms—a Factitious Disorder. The presence of factitious physical or psychological symptoms does not preclude the coexistence of true physical or psychological symptoms.

Factitious Disorders are distinguished from acts of malingering. In Malingering, the "patient" also produces the symptoms intentionally, but it is for a goal that is obviously recognizable when the environmental circumstances are known. For example, a claim of physical illness in order to avoid jury duty, standing trial, or conscription into the military would be classified as Malingering. Similarly, a hospitalized mental patient simulating an exacerbation of his or her illness in order to avoid transfer to another, less desirable facility would be an act of malingering. In contrast, in a Factitious Disorder there is a psychological need to assume the sick role, as evidenced by an absence of external incentives for the behavior. If the patient mentioned above were being transferred to an obviously more desirable facility, his or her simulated exacerbation of symptoms would be a Factitious Disorder. Whereas an act of malingering may, under

315

certain circumstances, be considered adaptive, by definition a diagnosis of a Factitious Disorder always implies psychopathology, most often a severe personality disturbance.

Factitious Disorders usually present with either physical or psychological symptoms. The chronic form of Factitious Disorder with Physical Symptoms, often referred to as the Münchausen syndrome, is the best known and most frequently reported of the Factitious Disorders.

301.51   Factitious Disorder with Physical Symptoms

The essential feature of this disorder is the intentional production of physical symptoms. The presentation may be total fabrication, as in complaints of acute abdominal pain in the absence of any such pain; self-inflicted, as in the production of abscesses by injection of saliva into the skin; an exaggeration or exacerbation of a preexisting physical condition, as in the acceptance of a penicillin injection despite a known previous history of an anaphylactic reaction; or any combination or variation of the above.

The best-studied form of this disorder has been called Münchausen syndrome. In this chronic form of the disorder, the person's plausible presentation of factitious physical symptoms is associated with multiple hospitalizations. The person's entire life may consist of either trying to get admitted to or staying in hospitals. Common clinical pictures include severe right lower quadrant pain associated with nausea and vomiting, dizziness and blacking out, massive hemoptysis, generalized rashes and abscesses, fevers of undetermined origin, bleeding secondary to ingestion of anticoagulants, and "lupuslike" syndromes. All organ systems are potential targets, and the symptoms presented are limited only by the person's medical knowledge, sophistication, and imagination.

People with this disorder usually present their history with great dramatic flair, but are extremely vague and inconsistent when questioned in more detail. They may indulge in uncontrollable, pathologic lying, in a manner intriguing to the listener, about any aspect of their history or symptoms (*pseudologia fantastica*). They often have extensive knowledge of medical terminology and hospital routines. Once admitted to a hospital, they can create havoc on the ward by demanding attention from hospital staff and by noncompliance with hospital routines and regulations. Complaints of pain and requests for analgesics are very common. After an extensive work-up of their initial chief complaints has proved negative, they often complain of other physical problems and produce more factitious symptoms. People with this disorder even eagerly undergo multiple invasive procedures and operations. While in the hospital, they usually have few visitors.

When confronted with evidence of their factitious symptoms, people with this disorder either deny the allegations or rapidly discharge themselves against medical advice. They will frequently be admitted to another hospital the same day. Their courses of hospitalizations often take them to numerous cities, states, countries, and even different continents. Eventually a point may be reached at which the person is "caught" producing factitious symptoms; he or she is recognized by someone from a previous admission or another hospital, or other hospitals are contacted and confirm multiple prior hospitalizations for factitious symptomatology.

Associated features. Psychoactive Substance Abuse, particularly of analgesics and sedatives, often medically prescribed, may be present.

Age at onset and course. Onset is usually in early adulthood, often with a hospitalization for true physical illness. In the chronic form of this disorder, a pattern of successive hospitalizations becomes a lifelong pattern.

Impairment. This disorder is extremely incapacitating. The course of chronic hospitalizations is obviously incompatible with the person's maintaining steady employment, maintaining family ties, and forming lasting interpersonal relationships.

Complications. Multiple hospitalizations frequently lead to iatrogenically induced physical conditions, such as the formation of scar tissue from unnecessary surgery, abscesses from numerous injections, and adverse drug reactions. People with the chronic form of this disorder may acquire a "gridiron abdomen" from multiple surgical procedures. Occasionally, people with this disorder will spend time in jail because of vagrancy or having committed an assault in a psychiatric hospital because of being transferred from a general hospital when the factitious nature of their symptoms was discovered.

Predisposing factors. Among predisposing factors are true physical disorders during childhood or adolescence leading to extensive medical treatment and hospitalization; a grudge against the medical profession, sometimes due to previous medical mismanagement; employment as a nurse, laboratory technician, or other medical paraprofessional; underlying dependent, exploitative, or self-defeating personality traits; and an important relationship with a physician in the past, e.g., a family member who was a physician, or seduction by a physician during childhood or adolescence.

Prevalence. Some believe the disorder is common but rarely recognized. Others believe that it is rare and that the few people with the chronic form of the disorder are being overreported because they appear to different physicians at different hospitals, often under different names.

Sex ratio. The disorder is apparently more common in males.

Familial pattern. No information.

Differential diagnosis. The major differential diagnostic consideration is obviously with **true physical disorder.** Considerable suspicion should be aroused if any combination of the following is noted in a person hospitalized for physical symptoms: *pseudologia fantastica*, with emphasis on dramatic presentation; disruptive behavior on the ward, including noncompliance with hospital rules and regulations and arguing excessively with the nurses and physicians; extensive knowledge of medical terminology and hospital routines; continued use of analgesics for "pain"; evidence of multiple surgical interventions, e.g., a "gridiron abdomen" or burr holes in the skull; extensive history of traveling; few, if any, visitors while hospitalized; and a fluctuating clinical course, with rapid production of "complications" or new "pathology" once the initial work-up proves negative.

In **Somatoform Disorders** there are also physical complaints not due to true physical disorder, but the symptoms are not intentionally produced.

People with **Malingering** may seek hospitalization by producing symptoms in attempts to obtain compensation, evade the police, or simply "get a bed for the night." However, the goal is usually apparent, and they can "stop" the symptoms when they are no longer useful to them.

Antisocial Personality Disorder is often incorrectly diagnosed on the basis of the *pseudologia fantastica*, a lack of close relations with others, and the occasionally associated histories of Psychoactive Substance Abuse and criminal activity. Antisocial Personality Disorder differs from this disorder in its earlier onset and its rare association with chronic hospitalization as a way of life.

Schizophrenia is often incorrectly diagnosed because of the bizarre life-style. However, the characteristic psychotic symptoms of Schizophrenia are not present.

Diagnostic criteria for 301.51 Factitious Disorder with Physical Symptoms

A.   Intentional production or feigning of physical (but not psychological) symptoms.

B.   A psychological need to assume the sick role, as evidenced by the absence of external incentives for the behavior, such as economic gain, better care, or physical well-being.

C.   Occurrence not exclusively during the course of another Axis I disorder, such as Schizophrenia.

300.16   Factitious Disorder with Psychological Symptoms

The essential feature of this disorder is intentional production or feigning of psychological (often psychotic) symptoms suggestive of mental disorder. The person's goal is apparently to assume the "patient" role and is not otherwise understandable in light of the person's environmental circumstances (as is the case in Malingering).

This disorder is often recognized by the pan-symptomatic complex of psychological symptoms that are presented and by the fact that the symptoms are worse when the person is aware of being observed. Such a person may claim depression and suicidal ideation following the death of a spouse (this not being confirmed by other informants), memory loss (recent and remote), hallucinations (auditory and visual), and dissociative and conversion symptoms. He or she may be extremely suggestible and admit to many additional symptoms the examiner mentions. Conversely, the person may be extremely negativistic and uncooperative when questioned. The psychological symptoms presented usually represent the person's concept of mental disorder, and may not conform to any of the recognized diagnostic categories.

Associated features. *Vorbeireden*, the symptom of giving approximate answers or talking past the point, may be present. This is to be considered when the person gives answers involving intellectual functions (such as calculations) that consistently are near misses of the correct response. When asked to multiply eight times eight, for example, the response may be "sixty-five." This phenomenon, however, is not specific to this disorder, and may be found in people with Schizophrenia or in persons without mental disorders who are exhausted or are being humorous.

Factitious Disorder with Psychological Symptoms is almost always superimposed on a severe Personality Disorder. The person may secretly use psychoactive substances for the purpose of producing symptoms that suggest a nonorganic mental disorder. Stimulants (amphetamines, cocaine, or caffeine) may be used to produce restlessness or insomnia; hallucinogens (LSD, mescaline, THC), to induce altered levels of consciousness and perception; analgesics (heroin, morphine), to induce euphoria; and hypnotics (barbiturates, alcohol), to induce lethargy. Combinations of the above substances can produce very bizarre presentations.

Age at onset, prevalence, and familial pattern. No information.

Sex ratio. The disorder is apparently more common in males.

Predisposing factors. Severe Personality Disorder is a predisposing factor.

Course. The course may be limited to one or more brief episodes, or may be chronic.

Impairment. Impairment tends to be severe.

Complications. Frequent hospitalizations are a complication.

Differential diagnosis. Differential diagnosis of this disorder from other mental disorders is extremely difficult. The clinician may notice that the total clinical picture is not characteristic of any recognized mental disorder. Psychological tests (e.g., projective tests, or the Bender-Gestalt) may be helpful when the responses elicited suggest a mixture of perceptual, cognitive, and intellectual impairment that is not characteristic of any mental disorder, but rather suggests the person's concept of mental disorder. There is a danger, however, that simulated bizarre responses will be taken at face value.

A true **Dementia** frequently has a demonstrable organic etiology or pathophysiologic process. In pseudodementia there are often near-miss, approximate answers rather than gross inability to answer questions correctly, as is often the case in a Factitious Disorder.

In a **true psychosis,** such as **Brief Reactive Psychosis or Schizophreniform Disorder,** the person's behavior on the ward will generally not differ markedly from his or her behavior in the clinician's office. In contrast, in a Factitious Disorder with psychotic features the person may appear to respond to auditory hallucinations only when under the impression that he or she is being watched.

For a discussion of the differential diagnosis with **Malingering,** see p. 360.

Diagnostic criteria for 300.16 Factitious Disorder with Psychological Symptoms

A. Intentional production or feigning of psychological (but not physical) symptoms.

B. A psychological need to assume the sick role, as evidenced by the absence of external incentives for the behavior, such as economic gain, better care, or physical well-being.

C. Occurrence not exclusively during the course of another Axis I disorder, such as Schizophrenia.

300.19   Factitious Disorder Not Otherwise Specified

Factitious Disorders that cannot be classified in any of the previous specific categories, e.g., a disorder with both factitious physical and factitious psychological symptoms.

Impulse Control Disorders Not Elsewhere Classified

This is a residual diagnostic class for disorders of impulse control that are not classified in other categories, e.g., Psychoactive Substance Use Disorders or Paraphilias.

The essential features of disorders of impulse control are:

1. Failure to resist an impulse, drive, or temptation to perform some act that is harmful to the person or others. There may or may not be conscious resistance to the impulse. The act may or may not be premeditated or planned.
2. An increasing sense of tension or arousal before committing the act.
3. An experience of either pleasure, gratification, or release at the time of committing the act. The act is ego-syntonic in that it is consonant with the immediate conscious wish of the individual. Immediately following the act there may or may not be genuine regret, self-reproach, or guilt.

This class contains five specific categories: Intermittent Explosive Disorder, Kleptomania, Pathological Gambling, Pyromania, and Trichotillomania.

312.34 Intermittent Explosive Disorder

The essential features of this disorder are discrete episodes of loss of control of aggressive impulses resulting in serious assaultive acts or destruction of property. The degree of aggressiveness expressed during the episodes is grossly out of proportion to any precipitating psychosocial stressors. There are no signs of generalized impulsivity or aggressiveness between the episodes.

Other disorders that are sometimes associated with loss of control of aggressive impulses must be ruled out before the diagnosis can be made. These include psychotic disorders, Organic Personality Syndrome, Antisocial or Borderline Personality Disorder, Conduct Disorder, or intoxication with a psychoactive substance.

The person may describe the episodes as "spells" or "attacks." The symptoms are said to appear within minutes or hours and, regardless of duration, remit almost as quickly. Genuine regret or self-reproach about the consequences of the action and the inability to control the aggressive impulse may follow each episode.

This category has been retained in DSM-III-R despite the fact that many doubt the existence of a clinical syndrome characterized by episodic loss of control that is not symptomatic of one of the disorders that must be ruled out before the diagnosis of Intermittent Explosive Disorder can be made.

Age at onset. The disorder may begin at any stage of life, but more commonly begins in the second or third decade.

Course. No information.

Impairment. Normal social relations may be impaired because of social ostracism that results from the unpredictable aggressive behavior.

Complications. Incarceration or chronic hospitalization may result.

Predisposing factors. No information.

Prevalence. The disorder is apparently very rare.

Sex ratio. The disorder is believed to be more common in males than in females. The males are likely to be seen in a correctional institution, and the females in a mental health facility.

Familial pattern. The disorder is apparently more common in first-degree biologic relatives of people with the disorder than in the general population.

Differential diagnosis. The diagnosis of Intermittent Explosive Disorder can be made only after other disorders that are sometimes associated with loss of control of aggressive impulses have been ruled out, such as a **psychotic disorder, Organic Personality Syndrome, Antisocial or Borderline Personality Disorder, Conduct Disorder,** or **intoxication with a psychoactive substance.**

Diagnostic criteria for 312.34 Intermittent Explosive Disorder

A. Several discrete episodes of loss of control of aggressive impulses resulting in serious assaultive acts or destruction of property.

B. The degree of aggressiveness expressed during the episodes is grossly out of proportion to any precipitating psychosocial stressors.

C. There are no signs of generalized impulsiveness or aggressiveness between the episodes.

D. The episodes of loss of control do not occur during the course of a psychotic disorder, Organic Personality Syndrome, Antisocial or Borderline Personality Disorder, Conduct Disorder, or intoxication with a psychoactive substance.

312.32 Kleptomania

The essential feature of this disorder is a recurrent failure to resist impulses to steal objects not needed for personal use or their monetary value; the objects taken are either given away, discarded, returned surreptitiously, or kept and hidden. Almost invariably the person has enough money to pay for the stolen objects. The person experiences an increasing sense of tension immediately before committing the act and intense gratification or relief while committing it. Although the theft does not occur when immediate arrest is probable (e.g., in full view of a policeman), it is not preplanned, and the chances of apprehension are not fully taken into account. The stealing is done without long-term planning and without assistance from, or collaboration with, others. Further, there is no association between the stealing and anger or vengeance.

The diagnosis is not made if the stealing is due to Conduct Disorder or Antisocial Personality Disorder.

Associated features. The person frequently displays signs of depression, anxiety, and guilt about the possibility or actuality of being apprehended and the resulting loss of status in society. Often, but not invariably, there are signs of personality disturbance.

Age at onset and course. The age at onset may be as early as childhood. The condition waxes and wanes and tends to be chronic; how often it remits is unknown.

Impairment and complications. Impairment is usually due to the legal consequences of being apprehended, the major complication of the disorder.

Prevalence. The disorder is apparently quite rare. Fewer than 5% of arrested shoplifters give a history that is consistent with the disorder; and in some of these cases, the history may be fabricated to conform to the stereotype of the disorder.

Predisposing factors and familial pattern. No information.

Sex ratio. The sex ratio is not known; but because shoplifting is more common among females, Kleptomania-related shoplifting is probably more common in females than in males.

Differential diagnosis. In **ordinary stealing** the act may be planned or impulsive, but the objects are stolen for their immediate use or monetary gain. In **Malingering,** there may be an attempt to simulate the disorder in order to avoid criminal prosecution for common thievery. In **Conduct Disorder, Antisocial Personality Disorder,** and **manic episodes**, stealing may occur; but in such cases, the act is obviously related to the more pervasive disorder. In **Schizophrenia**, stealing may be in response to delusions or hallucinations. In **Organic Mental Disorders**, it may occur because of failure to remember to pay for the object that has been taken.

Diagnostic criteria for 312.32 Kleptomania

A. Recurrent failure to resist impulses to steal objects not needed for personal use or their monetary value.

B. Increasing sense of tension immediately before committing the theft.

C. Pleasure or relief at the time of committing the theft.

D. The stealing is not committed to express anger or vengeance.

E. The stealing is not due to Conduct Disorder or Antisocial Personality Disorder.

312.31 Pathological Gambling

The essential features of this disorder are a chronic and progressive failure to resist impulses to gamble, and gambling behavior that compromises, disrupts, or damages personal, family, or vocational pursuits. The gambling preoccupation, urge, and activity increase during periods of stress. Problems that arise as a result of the gambling lead to an intensification of the gambling behavior. Characteristic problems include extensive indebtedness and consequent default on debts and other financial responsibilities, disrupted family relationships, inattention to work, and financially motivated illegal activities to pay for gambling.

Associated features. Generally, people with Pathological Gambling have the attitude that money causes and is also the solution to all their problems. As the gambling increases, the person is usually forced to lie in order to obtain money and to continue gambling. There is no serious attempt to budget or save money. When borrowing resources are strained, antisocial behavior in order to obtain money is likely.

People with this disorder are often overconfident, very energetic, easily bored, and "big spenders"; but there are times when they show obvious signs of personal stress, anxiety, and depression.

Age at onset and course. The disorder usually begins in adolescence in males, and later in life in females. It waxes and wanes, but tends to be chronic.

Impairment. The disorder is extremely incapacitating and results in failure to maintain financial solvency or provide basic support for oneself or one's family. The person may become alienated from family and acquaintances.

Complications. Psychoactive Substance Abuse and Dependence, suicide attempts, association with fringe or illegal groups (more common in males), civil court actions, and arrest for typically nonviolent crimes involving only property are among the possible complications.

Predisposing factors. Among the predisposing factors are inappropriate parental discipline (absence, inconsistency, or harshness); exposure to gambling activities as an adolescent; and a high family value placed on material and financial symbols and a lack of family emphasis on saving, planning, and budgeting. Females with this disorder are more likely than others to have a husband with Alcohol Dependence or who is often absent from the home.

Prevalence. Recent estimates place prevalence at 2%–3% percent of the adult population.

Sex ratio. The disorder is more common among males than females.

Familial pattern. Pathological Gambling and Alcohol Dependence are more common among the parents of people with Pathological Gambling than in the general population.

Differential diagnosis. In **social gambling,** gambling is with friends, and acceptable losses are predetermined.

During a **manic** or **hypomanic episode,** loss of judgment and excessive gambling may follow the onset of the mood disturbance. When maniclike mood changes occur in Pathological Gambling, they are generally related to winning streaks, and they are usually followed by depressive episodes because of subsequent gambling losses. Periods of depression tend to increase as the disorder progresses.

Problems with gambling are often associated with **Antisocial Personality Disorder,** and in Pathological Gambling antisocial behavior is frequent. In cases in which both disorders are present, both should be diagnosed.

Diagnostic criteria for 312.31 Pathological Gambling

Maladaptive gambling behavior, as indicated by at least four of the following:

(1) frequent preoccupation with gambling or with obtaining money to gamble

(2) frequent gambling of larger amounts of money or over a longer period of time than intended

(3) a need to increase the size or frequency of bets to achieve the desired excitement

(4) restlessness or irritability if unable to gamble

(5) repeated loss of money by gambling and returning another day to win back losses ("chasing")

(6) repeated efforts to reduce or stop gambling

(7) frequent gambling when expected to meet social or occupational obligations

(8) sacrifice of some important social, occupational, or recreational activity in order to gamble

(9) continuation of gambling despite inability to pay mounting debts, or despite other significant social, occupational, or legal problems that the person knows to be exacerbated by gambling

---

312.33 Pyromania

The essential features of this disorder are deliberate and purposeful (rather than accidental) fire-setting on more than one occasion; tension or affective arousal prior to setting the fires; and intense pleasure, gratification, or relief when setting the fires or witnessing or participating in their aftermath. In addition, there are fascination with, interest in, curiosity about, or attraction to fire and its situational context or associated characteristics (e.g., uses, consequences, exposure to fires). The fire-setting is not done for monetary gain, as an expression of sociopolitical ideology, to conceal criminal activity, to express anger or vengeance, to improve one's living circumstances, or in response to a delusion or hallucination.

Although the fire-setting results from a failure to resist an impulse, there may be considerable advance preparation for starting the fire, and the person may leave obvious clues. People with the disorder are often recognized as regular "watchers" at fires in their neighborhoods, frequently set off false alarms, and show interest in fire-fighting paraphernalia. Their fascination with fire leads some to seek employment or volunteer work in fire-fighting. They may be indifferent to the consequences of the fire for life or property, or they may get satisfaction from the resulting destruction.

Associated features. No information.

Age at onset. Onset is usually in childhood. When it is in adolescence or adulthood, the fire-setting tends to be more deliberately destructive.

Course. No information.

Impairment and complications. Impairment is usually due to the legal consequences of being apprehended, the major complication of the disorder.

Sex ratio. The disorder is diagnosed far more commonly in males than in females.

Predisposing factors, prevalence, and familial pattern. No information.

Differential diagnosis. Young children's experimentation and fascination with matches, lighters, and fire may be a part of their normal investigation of their environment.
In any mental disorder, fire-setting may occur, and must be differentiated from Pyromania. **Intentional fire-setting** may occur for profit, for sabotage, or to retaliate. "**Communicative arson**" is particularly relevant in **Schizophrenia** and **Bipolar Disorder;** fire-setting may be in response to delusions or hallucinations. In some **Organic Mental Disorders,** fire-setting may occur because of failure to appreciate the consequences of the act. In institutions, fire-setting may occur secondary to careless smoking.

Diagnostic criteria for 312.33 Pyromania

A. Deliberate and purposeful fire-setting on more than one occasion.

B. Tension or affective arousal before the act.

C. Fascination with, interest in, curiosity about, or attraction to fire and its situational context or associated characteristics (e.g., paraphernalia, uses, consequences, exposure to fires).

D. Intense pleasure, gratification, or relief when setting fires, or when witnessing or participating in their aftermath.

E. The fire-setting is not done for monetary gain, as an expression of sociopolitical ideology, to conceal criminal activity, to express anger or vengeance, to improve one's living circumstances, or in response to a delusion or hallucination.

312.39 Trichotillomania
The essential feature of this disorder is recurrent failure to resist impulses to pull out one's own hair. The diagnosis is not made when hair-pulling is associated with a preexisting inflammation of the skin or is in response to a delusion or hallucination.
   The person with this disorder experiences an increasing sense of tension immediately before engaging in the behavior and achieves a sense of release or gratification from pulling out the hair. The avulsion of hairs results in patchy areas of incomplete alopecia in easily accessible regions, principally the scalp. Other areas commonly

involved are the eyebrows, eyelashes, and beard. Less commonly the trunk, armpits, and pubic area may be involved. Hair loss often is characterized by short, broken strands appearing together with long, normal hairs in the affected areas. The surface of the scalp is normal, showing neither atrophy nor scarring.

Specific patterns and rituals involving the plucking of the hair and its disposition are common: Trichophagy or mouthing of the hair may follow the plucking. Pain is not routinely reported to accompany the hair-pulling; pruritus and tingling in the involved areas may be present.

Unlike in alopecia areata, regrowth of the hair is without pigmentary change, and a scalp biopsy will uncover signs of the traumatic nature of the disorder: catagen hairs, absence of inflammation and scarring, the presence of keratin plugs, and dilated follicular infundibula. Characteristic histopathologic changes in the hair follicle, known as trichomalacia, are demonstrated by biopsy, and help to distinguish the condition from other causes of alopecia.

Associated features. Longstanding denial of the behavior is commonly encountered, and the person often strives to conceal or camouflage the resultant alopecia. Head-banging, nail-biting, scratching, gnawing, excoriation, and other acts of self-mutilation may be present.

Age at onset. The disorder usually begins in childhood, but cases have been reported with onset as late as 62. Some suggest that adult onset is strongly linked to the presence of a psychotic disorder.

Course. The course of the disorder is not well known. In some cases it has been known to persist for more than two decades. Of people presenting for treatment, approximately one-third report a duration of one year or less. Frequent exacerbations and remissions are common.

Impairment and complications. Alopecia of the scalp, particularly the crown and occiput, is the major complication, and may in some cases progress to alopecia totalis.

Predisposing factors. Though the disorder is regarded as "multidetermined," onset has been linked to stressful situations in more than one-quarter of cases. Disturbances in mother–child relationships, fear of being left alone, and recent object loss are often cited as critical factors in the genesis of the condition. Psychoactive Substance Abuse may contribute to the development of this disorder.

Prevalence. There is no information about the prevalence of this disorder, but it may be more common than is currently believed. It is more common in people with Mental Retardation, and possibly more common in people with Schizophrenia or Borderline Personality Disorder. It has been suggested that eldest or only children are more often afflicted.

Familial pattern. There is no information on the familial pattern. Cases of afflicted siblings have not been reported to date, but one study of the disorder in children reported that 5 of 19 subjects had a family history of some form of alopecia.

Sex ratio. The available data are contradictory, but the disorder is apparently more common in females.

Differential diagnosis. Stroking and "fiddling with" the hair are common and normal activities. In **Obsessive Compulsive Disorder,** repetitive behaviors are seemingly purposeful and designed to prevent or produce some future event or situation. In **Factitious Disorder with Physical Symptoms,** medical attention and the "patient" role are actively sought, and the person deliberately simulates illness toward these ends. In **Psychological Factors Affecting Physical Condition,** psychological factors affect or contribute to (rather than create) the physical condition. In **Stereotypy/Habit Disorder,** movements are stereotyped and often rhythmic and the person usually does not seem distressed by the behavior.

In addition to the Axis I diagnosis of Trichotillomania, **alopecia** should be recorded on Axis III.

Diagnostic criteria for 312.39 Trichotillomania

A. Recurrent failure to resist impulses to pull out one's own hair, resulting in noticeable hair loss.

B. Increasing sense of tension immediately before pulling out the hair.

C. Gratification or a sense of relief when pulling out the hair.

D. No association with a preexisting inflammation of the skin, and not a response to a delusion or hallucination.

312.39 Impulse Control Disorder Not Otherwise Specified

Disorders of impulse control that do not meet the criteria for a specific Impulse Control Disorder.

Adjustment Disorder

The essential feature of this disorder is a maladaptive reaction to an identifiable psycho-social stressor, or stressors, that occurs within three months after onset of the stressor, and has persisted for no longer than six months. The maladaptive nature of the reaction is indicated either by impairment in occupational (including school) functioning or in usual social activities or relationships with others or by symptoms that are in excess of a normal and expectable reaction to the stressor. The disturbance is not merely one instance of a pattern of overreaction to stress or an exacerbation of one of the mental disorders previously described in this manual. It is assumed that the disturbance will remit soon after the stressor ceases or, if the stressor persists, when a new level of adaptation is achieved. The severity of the stressor and the specific stressor should be noted on Axis IV (see p. 18).

The stressors may be single, such as divorce, or multiple, such as marked business difficulties and marital problems. They may be recurrent, e.g., associated with seasonal business crises, or continuous, e.g., caused by residence in a deteriorating neighborhood or the psychosocial stress associated with a chronic illness. They can occur in a family setting, e.g., in discordant intrafamilial relationships. They may affect only a particular person, e.g., in a psychological reaction to a physical illness, or they may affect a group or community, e.g., as in a natural disaster, or persecution based on racial, social, religious, or other group affiliation. Some stressors may accompany specific developmental events, such as going to school, leaving the parental home, getting married, becoming a parent, failing to attain occupational goals, and retirement.

The severity of the reaction is not completely predictable from the intensity of the stressor. People who are particularly vulnerable may have a more severe form of the disorder following only a mild or moderate stressor, whereas others may have only a mild form of the disorder in response to a marked and continuing stressor.

This category should not be used if the disturbance meets the criteria for a specific mental disorder, such as a specific Anxiety or Mood Disorder, or represents Uncomplicated Bereavement.

Types. Symptoms of the disorder are varied. Each specific type presents a predominant clinical picture; many of the types are partial syndromes of specific disorders. For example, Adjustment Disorder with Depressed Mood is an incomplete depressive syndrome that develops in response to a psychosocial stressor.

Age at onset. Adjustment Disorder may begin at any age.

Course. By definition, the disturbance begins within three months of onset of a stressor and lasts no longer than six months. If the stressor is an acute event, such as being fired from a job, the onset of the disturbance is usually within a few days, and its duration is relatively brief—no more than a few months. If the stressor persists (enduring circumstances), as in a chronic physical illness, it may take much longer to achieve a new level of adaptation.

Prevalence. The disorder is apparently common.

Predisposing factors, sex ratio, and familial pattern. No information.

Differential diagnosis. If the symptoms of Adjustment Disorder persist for more than six months, the diagnosis should be changed to some other mental disorder.

In **Conditions Not Attributable to a Mental Disorder That Are a Focus of Attention or Treatment** (V codes), e.g., Other Interpersonal Problem or Phase of Life Problem or Other Life Circumstance Problem, there is neither impairment in social or occupational functioning nor symptoms that are in excess of a normal and expectable reaction to the stressor. No absolute guidelines are available to aid in making this fundamental distinction, so clinical judgment will often be required.

Since **Personality Disorders** are frequently exacerbated by stress, the additional diagnosis of Adjustment Disorder is usually not made. But if new symptoms appear in response to a stressor—such as depressed mood in a person with Paranoid Personality Disorder who has never suffered from depression—then the additional diagnosis of Adjustment Disorder may be appropriate.

In **Psychological Factors Affecting Physical Condition**, the person may be reacting to a psychosocial stressor, but the predominant symptoms are of an actual physical condition or disorder.

Diagnostic criteria for Adjustment Disorder

A. A reaction to an identifiable psychosocial stressor (or multiple stressors) that occurs within three months of onset of the stressor(s).

B. The maladaptive nature of the reaction is indicated by either of the following:

   (1) impairment in occupational (including school) functioning or in usual social activities or relationships with others
   (2) symptoms that are in excess of a normal and expectable reaction to the stressor(s)

C. The disturbance is not merely one instance of a pattern of overreaction to stress or an exacerbation of one of the mental disorders previously described.

D. The maladaptive reaction has persisted for no longer than six months.

E. The disturbance does not meet the criteria for any specific mental disorder and does not represent Uncomplicated Bereavement.

Types of Adjustment Disorder. Code the type according to the predominant symptoms. Specify the stressor(s) and its (their) severity on Axis IV.

309.24   Adjustment Disorder with Anxious Mood
This category should be used when the predominant manifestation is symptoms such as nervousness, worry, and jitteriness.

309.00   Adjustment Disorder with Depressed Mood
This category should be used when the predominant manifestation is symptoms such as depressed mood, tearfulness, and feelings of hopelessness.

309.30   Adjustment Disorder with Disturbance of Conduct
This category should be used when the predominant manifestation is conduct in which there is violation of the rights of others or of major age-appropriate societal norms and rules. *Examples*: truancy, vandalism, reckless driving, fighting, defaulting on legal responsibilities.

309.40   Adjustment Disorder with Mixed Disturbance of Emotions and Conduct
This category should be used when the predominant manifestations are both emotional symptoms (e.g., depression, anxiety) and a disturbance of conduct (see above).

309.28   Adjustment Disorder with Mixed Emotional Features
This category should be used when the predominant manifestation is a combination of depression and anxiety or other emotions. The major differential is with Depressive and Anxiety Disorders. *Example*: an adolescent who, after moving away from home and parental supervision, reacts with ambivalence, depression, anger, and signs of increased dependence.

309.82   Adjustment Disorder with Physical Complaints
This category should be used when the predominant manifestation is physical symptoms, e.g., fatigue, headache, backache, or other aches and pains, that are not diagnosable as a specific Axis III physical disorder or condition.

309.83   Adjustment Disorder with Withdrawal
This category should be used when the predominant manifestation is social withdrawal without significantly depressed or anxious mood.

309.23   Adjustment Disorder with Work (or Academic) Inhibition
This category should be used when the predominant manifestation is an inhibition in work or academic functioning occurring in a person whose previous work or academic performance has been adequate. Frequently there is also a mixture of anxiety and depression. *Example*: inability to study or to write papers or reports.

309.90   Adjustment Disorder Not Otherwise Specified
Disorders involving maladaptive reactions to psychosocial stressors that are not classifiable as specific types of Adjustment Disorder. *Example*: an immediate reaction to a diagnosis of physical illness, e.g., massive denial and noncompliance, that is too maladaptive to be categorized as the V Code V15.81, Noncompliance with Medical Treatment (p. 360).

Psychological Factors Affecting Physical Condition

316.00 Psychological Factors Affecting Physical Condition

A clinician may want to note that psychological factors contribute to the initiation or exacerbation of a physical condition. The physical condition, which should be recorded on Axis III, will usually be a physical disorder, but in some instances may be only a single symptom, such as vomiting.

This manual accepts the tradition of referring to certain factors as "psychological," although it is by no means easy to define what this term means. A limited but useful definition in this context is the meaning the person ascribes to environmental stimuli. Common examples of such stimuli are the sights and sounds arising in interpersonal transactions, such as arguments, or the news that a loved one has died. The person may not be aware of the personal significance of such environmental stimuli or of the relationship between them and the initiation or exacerbation of the physical condition.

The judgment that psychological factors are affecting the physical condition requires evidence of a temporal relationship between the environmental stimuli and the meaning ascribed to them and the initiation or exacerbation of the physical condition. Obviously, this judgment is more certain when there are repeated instances of a temporal relationship.

This category can apply to any physical condition to which psychological factors are judged to be contributory. It can be used to describe disorders that in the past have been referred to as either "psychosomatic" or "psychophysiological."

Common examples of physical conditions for which this category may be appropriate include, but are not limited to: obesity, tension headache, migraine headache, angina pectoris, painful menstruation, sacroiliac pain, neurodermatitis, acne, rheumatoid arthritis, asthma, tachycardia, arrhythmia, gastric ulcer, duodenal ulcer, cardiospasm, pylorospasm, nausea and vomiting, regional enteritis, ulcerative colitis, and frequency of micturition.

This category should not be used in cases of Conversion Disorder or other Somatoform Disorders, which are regarded as disturbances in which the specific pathophysiologic process involved in the disorder is not demonstrable by existing standard laboratory procedures and which are conceptualized by psychological constructs only.

Diagnostic criteria for 316.00 Psychological Factors Affecting Physical Condition

A. Psychologically meaningful environmental stimuli are temporally related to the initiation or exacerbation of a specific physical condition or disorder (recorded on Axis III).

B. The physical condition involves either demonstrable organic pathology (e.g., rheumatoid arthritis) or a known pathophysiologic process (e.g., migraine headache).

C. The condition does not meet the criteria for a Somatoform Disorder.

Personality Disorders

(**Note:** These are coded on Axis II.)

Personality *traits* are enduring patterns of perceiving, relating to, and thinking about the environment and oneself, and are exhibited in a wide range of important social and personal contexts. It is only when *personality traits* are inflexible and maladaptive and cause either significant functional impairment or subjective distress that they constitute *Personality Disorders*. The manifestations of Personality Disorders are often recognizable by adolescence or earlier and continue throughout most of adult life, though they often become less obvious in middle or old age.

The diagnostic criteria for the Personality Disorders refer to behaviors or traits that are characteristic of the person's recent (past year) and long-term functioning since early adulthood. The constellation of behaviors or traits causes either significant impairment in social or occupational functioning or subjective distress.

Many of the features characteristic of the various Personality Disorders, such as Dependent, Paranoid, Schizotypal, or Borderline Personality Disorder, may be seen during an episode of another mental disorder, such as Major Depression. The diagnosis of a Personality Disorder should be made only when the characteristic features are typical of the person's long-term functioning and are not limited to discrete episodes of illness.

DIAGNOSIS OF PERSONALITY DISORDERS IN CHILDREN AND ADOLESCENTS

Certain Personality Disorders are related to corresponding diagnostic categories in the section Disorders Usually First Evident in Infancy, Childhood, or Adolescence. The corresponding disorders are as follows:

Disorders of Childhood or Adolescence	Personality Disorders
Conduct Disorder	Antisocial Personality Disorder
Avoidant Disorder of Childhood or Adolescence	Avoidant Personality Disorder
Identity Disorder	Borderline Personality Disorder

The diagnosis of Conduct Disorder, rather than Antisocial Personality Disorder, should be made if the person is under 18, since studies have indicated that many

335

children with prominent antisocial behavior do not continue to exhibit antisocial behavior in adulthood. (Conduct Disorder may be diagnosed in adults when the full criteria for Antisocial Personality Disorder are not met.)

Avoidant Personality Disorder and Borderline Personality Disorder should be diagnosed in children and adolescents, rather than the corresponding childhood categories, if the Personality Disorder criteria are met, the disturbance is pervasive and persistent, and it is unlikely that it will be limited to a developmental stage.

The other Personality Disorder categories may be applied to children or adolescents in those unusual instances in which the particular maladaptive personality traits appear to be stable. When this is done, there is obviously less certainty that the Personality Disorder will persist unchanged over time into adult life.

Associated features. Frequently the person with a Personality Disorder is dissatisfied with the impact his or her behavior is having on others or with his or her inability to function effectively. This may be the case even when the traits that lead to these difficulties are ego-syntonic, that is, are not regarded by the person as undesirable. In other cases, the traits may be ego-dystonic, but the person may be unable to modify them despite great effort.

Disturbances of mood, frequently involving depression or anxiety, are common, and may even be the person's chief complaint.

Age at onset and course. As noted above, Personality Disorders by definition generally are recognizable by adolescence or early adult life and are characteristic of most of adult life.

Impairment. There may be marked impairment in social and occupational functioning. When occupational functioning is impaired, the impairment is usually sustained, but may be episodic and take the form of recurrent periods of work inhibition (e.g., "writer's block"). With the exception of Antisocial, Schizotypal, and Borderline Personality Disorders, people with Personality Disorders rarely require hospitalization unless there is a superimposed disorder, such as a Psychoactive Substance Use Disorder or Major Depression.

PERSONALITY DISORDERS AND PSYCHOTIC DISORDERS

When a person with a psychotic disorder coded on Axis I, for example, Schizophrenia or Delusional Disorder, has a preexisting Personality Disorder, the Personality Disorder should also be recorded, on Axis II, followed by "Premorbid" in parentheses. For example:

Axis I: 295.32 Schizophrenia, Paranoid Type, Chronic

Axis II: 301.20 Schizoid Personality Disorder (Premorbid)

SPECIFIC PERSONALITY DISORDERS

Traditionally, in diagnosing Personality Disorders, the clinician has been directed to find a single, specific Personality Disorder that adequately describes the person's disturbed personality functioning. Frequently this can be done only with difficulty, since many people exhibit traits that are not limited to a single Personality Disorder. In this manual diagnoses of more than one Personality Disorder should be made if the person meets the criteria for more than one.

The Personality Disorders have been grouped into three clusters. The first cluster, referred to as cluster A, includes Paranoid, Schizoid, and Schizotypal Personality Disorders. People with these disorders often appear odd or eccentric. Cluster B includes Antisocial, Borderline, Histrionic, and Narcissistic Personality Disorders. People with these disorders often appear dramatic, emotional, or erratic. Cluster C includes Avoidant, Dependent, Obsessive Compulsive, and Passive Aggressive Personality Disorders. People with these disorders often appear anxious or fearful. Finally, there is a residual category, Personality Disorder Not Otherwise Specified, that can be used for other specific Personality Disorders or for mixed conditions that do not qualify as any of the specific Personality Disorders described in this manual.

There is great variability in the detail with which various Personality Disorders are described and the specificity of the diagnostic criteria. Disorders studied more extensively and rigorously than others, such as Antisocial Personality Disorder, are described in greater detail.

CLUSTER A

301.00 Paranoid Personality Disorder

The essential feature of this disorder is a pervasive and unwarranted tendency, beginning by early adulthood and present in a variety of contexts, to interpret the actions of people as deliberately demeaning or threatening.

Almost invariably there is a general expectation of being exploited or harmed by others in some way. Frequently a person with this disorder will question, without justification, the loyalty or trustworthiness of friends or associates. Often the person is pathologically jealous, questioning without justification the fidelity of his or her spouse or sexual partner.

Confronted with a new situation, the person may read hidden demeaning or threatening meanings into benign remarks or events, e.g., suspect that a bank has deliberately made a mistake in his account. Often these people are easily slighted and quick to react with anger or counterattack; they may bear grudges for a long time, and never forgive slights, insults, or injuries. They are reluctant to confide in others because of a fear that the information will be used against them. People with this disorder are typically hypervigilant and take precautions against any perceived threat. They tend to avoid blame even when it is warranted. They are often viewed by others as guarded, secretive, devious, and scheming.

When people with this disorder find themselves in a new situation, they intensely and narrowly search for confirmation of their expectations, with no appreciation of the total context. Their final conclusion is usually precisely what they expected in the first place. Often, they have transient ideas of reference, e.g., that others are taking special notice of them, or saying vulgar things about them.

Associated features. People with this disorder are usually argumentative and exaggerate difficulties, "making mountains out of molehills." They often find it difficult to relax, usually appear tense, and have a tendency to counterattack when they perceive any threat. Though they are critical of others, and often litigious, they have great difficulty accepting criticism themselves.

The affectivity of these people is often restricted, and they may appear "cold" to others. They have no true sense of humor and are usually serious. They may pride themselves on always being objective, rational, and unemotional. They usually lack passive, soft, sentimental, and tender feelings.

Occasionally, others see people with this disorder as keen observers who are energetic, ambitious, and capable; but more often they are viewed as hostile, stubborn, and defensive. They tend to be rigid and unwilling to compromise, and may generate uneasiness and fear in others. They often have an inordinate fear of losing their independence or the power to shape events according to their own wishes.

These people usually avoid intimacy except with those in whom they have absolute trust. They display an excessive need to be self-sufficient, to the point of egocentricity and exaggerated self-importance. They avoid participation in group activities unless they are in a dominant position.

People with Paranoid Personality Disorder are often interested in mechanical devices, electronics, and automation. They are generally uninterested in art or aesthetics. They are keenly aware of power and rank and of who is superior or inferior, and are often envious and jealous of those in positions of power. They disdain people they see as weak, soft, sickly, or defective.

During periods of extreme stress, people with this disorder may experience transient psychotic symptoms, but they are usually of insufficient duration to warrant an additional diagnosis.

Impairment. Because people with Paranoid Personality Disorder generally realize that it is prudent to keep their unusual ideas to themselves, impairment tends to be minimal. However, occupational difficulties are common, especially in relating to authority figures or co-workers. In more severe cases, all relationships are grossly impaired.

Complications. The relationship of this disorder to Delusional Disorder and Schizophrenia, Paranoid Type, is unclear. Certain essential features of Paranoid Personality Disorder, such as suspiciousness and hypersensitivity, may predispose to the development of those other disorders, however.

Predisposing factors. No information.

Prevalence. Since people with this disorder rarely seek help for their personality problems or require hospitalization, the disorder seldom comes to clinical attention. Because of a tendency of some of them to be moralistic, grandiose, and extrapunitive, people with this disorder may be overrepresented among leaders of cults and other fringe groups.

Sex ratio. This disorder is more commonly diagnosed in men.

Familial pattern. No information.

Differential diagnosis. In **Delusional Disorder** and **Schizophrenia, Paranoid Type,** there are persistent psychotic symptoms, such as delusions and hallucinations, that are never part of Paranoid Personality Disorder. However, these disorders may be superimposed on Paranoid Personality Disorder. **Antisocial Personality Disorder** shares several features with Paranoid Personality Disorders, e.g., difficulty in forming and sustaining close relationships, and poor occupational performance; but except when the two disorders coexist, a lifelong history of antisocial behavior is not present in Paranoid Personality Disorder. People with **Schizoid Personality Disorder** are often seen as strange and eccentric, cold and aloof, but do not have prominent paranoid ideation.

> **Diagnostic criteria for 301.00 Paranoid Personality Disorder**
>
> A. A pervasive and unwarranted tendency, beginning by early adulthood and present in a variety of contexts, to interpret the actions of people as deliberately demeaning or threatening, as indicated by at least *four* of the following:
>
> (1) expects, without sufficient basis, to be exploited or harmed by others
> (2) questions, without justification, the loyalty or trustworthiness of friends or associates
> (3) reads hidden demeaning or threatening meanings into benign remarks or events, e.g., suspects that a neighbor put out trash early to annoy him
> (4) bears grudges or is unforgiving of insults or slights
> (5) is reluctant to confide in others because of unwarranted fear that the information will be used against him or her
> (6) is easily slighted and quick to react with anger or to counterattack
> (7) questions, without justification, fidelity of spouse or sexual partner
>
> B. Occurrence not exclusively during the course of Schizophrenia or a Delusional Disorder.

301.20 Schizoid Personality Disorder

The essential feature of this disorder is a pervasive pattern of indifference to social relationships and a restricted range of emotional experience and expression, beginning by early adulthood and present in a variety of contexts.

People with this disorder neither desire nor enjoy close relationships, including being part of a family. They prefer to be "loners," and have no close friends or confidants (or only one) other than first-degree relatives. They almost always choose solitary activities and indicate little if any desire to have sexual experiences with another person. Such people are indifferent to the praise and criticism of others. They claim that they rarely experience strong emotions such as anger and joy, and in fact display a constricted affect. They appear cold and aloof.

Associated features. People with this disorder are often unable to express aggressiveness or hostility. They may seem vague about their goals, indecisive in their actions, self-absorbed, and absentminded. Because of a lack of social skills or desire for sexual experiences, males with this disorder are usually incapable of dating and rarely marry. Females may passively accept courtship and marry.

Impairment. Social relations are, by definition, severely restricted. Occupational functioning may be impaired, particularly if interpersonal involvement is required. On the other hand, people with this disorder may, in some instances, be capable of high occupational achievement in situations requiring work performance under conditions of social isolation.

Prevalence. The prevalence in clinical settings is low. However, a significant proportion of people working in jobs that involve little or no contact with others, or living in skid-row sections of cities, may have this disorder.

Predisposing factors, sex ratio, and familial pattern. No information.

Differential diagnosis. In **Schizotypal Personality Disorder** there are eccentricities of communication or behavior. Some people may have both Schizoid and Schizotypal Personality Disorder.

In **Avoidant Personality Disorder,** social isolation is due to hypersensitivity to rejection, and a desire to enter social relationships is present if there are strong guarantees of uncritical acceptance. In contrast, people with Schizoid Personality Disorder have little desire for social relations.

In **Paranoid Personality Disorder,** paranoid ideation is a prominent feature.

Diagnostic criteria for 301.20 Schizoid Personality Disorder

A. A pervasive pattern of indifference to social relationships and a restricted range of emotional experience and expression, beginning by early adulthood and present in a variety of contexts, as indicated by at least *four* of the following:

   (1) neither desires nor enjoys close relationships, including being part of a family

   (2) almost always chooses solitary activities

   (3) rarely, if ever, claims or appears to experience strong emotions, such as anger and joy

   (4) indicates little if any desire to have sexual experiences with another person (age being taken into account)

   (5) is indifferent to the praise and criticism of others

   (6) has no close friends or confidants (or only one) other than first-degree relatives

   (7) displays constricted affect, e.g., is aloof, cold, rarely reciprocates gestures or facial expressions, such as smiles or nods

B. Occurrence not exclusively during the course of Schizophrenia or a Delusional Disorder.

301.22   Schizotypal Personality Disorder

The essential feature of this disorder is a pervasive pattern of peculiarities of ideation, appearance, and behavior and deficits in interpersonal relatedness, beginning by early adulthood and present in a variety of contexts, that are not severe enough to meet the criteria for Schizophrenia.

The disturbance in the content of thought may include paranoid ideation, suspiciousness, ideas of reference, odd beliefs, and magical thinking that is inconsistent with subcultural norms and influences the person's behavior. Examples include superstitiousness, belief in clairvoyance, telepathy, or "sixth sense," or beliefs that "others can feel my feelings" (when it is not a part of a cultural belief system). In children and adolescents, these thoughts may include bizarre fantasies or preoccupations. Unusual perceptual experiences may include illusions and sensing the presence of a force or person not actually present (e.g., "I felt an evil presence in the room"). Often speech shows marked peculiarities, but never to the point of loosening of associations or incoherence. Speech may be impoverished, digressive, vague, or inappropriately abstract. Concepts may be expressed unclearly or oddly, or words may be used in an unusual way. People with this disorder often appear odd and eccentric in behavior and appearance. For example, they are often unkempt, display unusual mannerisms, and talk to themselves.

Interpersonal relatedness is invariably impaired in these people. They display inappropriate or constricted affect, appearing silly and aloof and rarely reciprocating gestures or facial expressions, such as smiling or nodding. They have no close friends or confidants (or only one) other than first-degree relatives, and are extremely anxious in social situations involving unfamiliar people.

Associated features. Varying mixtures of anxiety, depression, and other dysphoric moods are common. Features of Borderline Personality Disorder are often present, and in some cases both diagnoses may be warranted. During periods of extreme stress, people with this disorder may experience transient psychotic symptoms, but they are usually insufficient in duration to warrant an additional diagnosis. Because of peculiarities in thinking, people with Schizotypal Personality Disorder are prone to eccentric convictions.

Impairment. Some interference with social or occupational functioning is common.

Prevalence. Recent studies, using DSM-III criteria, indicate that approximately 3% of the population have this disorder.

Sex ratio. No information.

Familial pattern. There is some evidence that people with Schizotypal Personality Disorder are more common among the first-degree biologic relatives of people with Schizophrenia than among the general population.

Differential diagnosis. In **Schizophrenia, Residual Type,** there is a history of an active phase of Schizophrenia with psychotic symptoms. When psychotic symptoms occur in Schizotypal Personality Disorder, they are transient and not as severe. In **Schizoid Personality Disorder** and **Avoidant Personality Disorder,** there are no oddities of behavior, thinking, perception, and speech, such as are present in Schizotypal Personality Disorder. Frequently, people with **Borderline Personality Disorder** also meet the criteria for Schizotypal Personality Disorder; in such instances, both diagnoses should be recorded. Suspiciousness and paranoid ideation may be present in **Paranoid Personality Disorder,** but other oddities of thought or behavior are not.

Diagnostic criteria for 301.22 Schizotypal Personality Disorder

A. A pervasive pattern of deficits in interpersonal relatedness and peculiarities of ideation, appearance, and behavior, beginning by early adulthood and present in a variety of contexts, as indicated by at least *five* of the following:

   (1) ideas of reference (excluding delusions of reference)
   (2) excessive social anxiety, e.g., extreme discomfort in social situations involving unfamiliar people

(continued)

Diagnostic criteria for 301.22 Schizotypal Personality Disorder continued

   (3) odd beliefs or magical thinking, influencing behavior and inconsistent with subcultural norms, e.g., superstitiousness, belief in clairvoyance, telepathy, or "sixth sense," "others can feel my feelings" (in children and adolescents, bizarre fantasies or preoccupations)

   (4) unusual perceptual experiences, e.g., illusions, sensing the presence of a force or person not actually present (e.g., "I felt as if my dead mother were in the room with me")

   (5) odd or eccentric behavior or appearance, e.g., unkempt, unusual mannerisms, talks to self

   (6) no close friends or confidants (or only one) other than first-degree relatives

   (7) odd speech (without loosening of associations or incoherence), e.g., speech that is impoverished, digressive, vague, or inappropriately abstract

   (8) inappropriate or constricted affect, e.g., silly, aloof, rarely reciprocates gestures or facial expressions, such as smiles or nods

   (9) suspiciousness or paranoid ideation

B.   Occurrence not exclusively during the course of Schizophrenia or a Pervasive Developmental Disorder.

CLUSTER B

301.70   Antisocial Personality Disorder

The essential feature of this disorder is a pattern of irresponsible and antisocial behavior beginning in childhood or early adolescence and continuing into adulthood. For this diagnosis to be given, the person must be at least 18 years of age and have a history of Conduct Disorder before the age of 15.

Lying, stealing, truancy, vandalism, initiating fights, running away from home, and physical cruelty are typical childhood signs. In adulthood the antisocial pattern continues, and may include failure to honor financial obligations, to function as a responsible parent or to plan ahead, and an inability to sustain consistent work behavior. These people fail to conform to social norms and repeatedly perform antisocial acts that are grounds for arrest, such as destroying property, harassing others, stealing, and having an illegal occupation.

People with Antisocial Personality Disorder tend to be irritable and aggressive and to get repeatedly into physical fights and assaults, including spouse- or child-beating. Reckless behavior without regard to personal safety is common, as indicated by frequently driving while intoxicated or getting speeding tickets. Typically, these people are promiscuous (defined as never having sustained a monogamous relationship for more than a year). Finally, they generally have no remorse about the effects of their behavior on others; they may even feel justified in having hurt or mistreated others. After age 30, the more flagrantly antisocial behavior may diminish, particularly sexual promiscuity, fighting, and criminality.

Associated features. In early adolescence these people characteristically use to-bacco, alcohol, and other drugs and engage in voluntary sexual intercourse unusually early for their peer group. Psychoactive Substance Use Disorders are commonly associated diagnoses. Less commonly, Somatization Disorder may be present.

Despite the stereotype of a normal mental status in this disorder, frequently there are signs of personal distress, including complaints of tension, inability to tolerate boredom, depression, and the conviction (often correct) that others are hostile toward them. The interpersonal difficulties and dysphoria tend to persist into late adult life even when the more flagrant antisocial behavior has diminished. Almost invariably there is a markedly impaired capacity to sustain lasting, close, warm, and responsible relationships with family, friends, or sexual partners.

Age at onset. By definition the Conduct Disorder symptoms begin before the age of 15. The first symptoms of Conduct Disorder in females who develop Antisocial Personality Disorder usually appear in puberty, whereas in males the Conduct Disorder is generally obvious in early childhood.

Impairment. The disorder is often extremely incapacitating, resulting in failure to become an independent, self-supporting adult and giving rise to many years of institu-tionalization, more commonly penal than medical. (Some people who have several features of the disorder achieve political and economic success; but these people virtually never present the full picture of the disorder, lacking, in particular, the early onset in childhood that usually interferes with educational achievement and precludes most public careers.)

Complications. People with this disorder are more likely than people in the general population to die prematurely by violent means.

Predisposing factors. Predisposing factors are Attention-deficit Hyperactivity Disorder and Conduct Disorder during prepuberty. The absence of consistent parental discipline apparently increases the likelihood that Conduct Disorder will develop into Antisocial Personality Disorder. Other predisposing factors include abuse as a child, removal from the home, and growing up without parental figures of both sexes.

Prevalence. The estimate of the prevalence of Antisocial Personality Disorder among American males is about 3%, and for American females, less than 1%. The disorder is more common in lower-class populations, partly because it is associated with impaired earning capacity and partly because fathers of those with the disorder frequently have the disorder themselves, and consequently their children often grow up in impoverished homes.

Sex ratio. The disorder is much more common in males than in females.

Familial pattern. Antisocial Personality Disorder is five times more common among first-degree biologic relatives of males with the disorder than among the general popu-lation. The risk to the first-degree biologic relatives of females with the disorder is nearly ten times that of the general population. There is also an increased risk of Somatization Disorder and Psychoactive Substance Use Disorders in the relatives of males and females with the disorder. Within a family that has a member with Antisocial Personality Disorder, males more often have Antisocial Personality Disorder and Psy-choactive Substance Use Disorders, whereas females more often have Somatization

Disorder; but there is an increase in all of these disorders in both males and females compared with the general population. Adoption studies show that both genetic and environmental factors contribute to the risk of this group of disorders, because parents with Antisocial Personality Disorder increase the risk of Antisocial Personality Disorder, Somatization Disorder, and Psychoactive Substance Use Disorders in both their adopted and biologic children.

Differential diagnosis. Conduct Disorder consists of the typical childhood signs of Antisocial Personality Disorder. Since such behavior may terminate spontaneously or evolve into other disorders such as Schizophrenia, a diagnosis of Antisocial Personality Disorder should not be made in children; it is reserved for adults (18 or over), who have had time to show the full longitudinal pattern.

Adult Antisocial Behavior, in the category Conditions Not Attributable to a Mental Disorder, should be considered when criminal or other aggressive or antisocial behavior occurs in people who do not meet the full criteria for Antisocial Personality Disorder and whose antisocial behavior cannot be attributed to any other mental disorder.

When **Psychoactive Substance Abuse** and antisocial behavior begin in childhood and continue into adult life, both Psychoactive Substance Use Disorder and Antisocial Personality Disorder should be diagnosed if the criteria for each disorder are met, regardless of the extent to which some of the antisocial behavior may be a consequence of the Psychoactive Substance Use Disorder, e.g., illegal selling of drugs, or the assaultive behavior associated with Alcohol Intoxication. When antisocial behavior in an adult is associated with a Psychoactive Substance Use Disorder, the diagnosis of Antisocial Personality Disorder is not made unless the childhood signs of Antisocial Personality Disorder were also present and continued into adult life.

Mental Retardation and **Schizophrenia** may present with some of the features of Antisocial Personality Disorder, such as impairment in occupational functioning and parenting; but the additional diagnosis of Antisocial Personality Disorder should be made only if there is a clear pattern of antisocial behavior.

Manic Episodes may be associated with antisocial behavior. However, the absence of Conduct Disorder in childhood and the episodic nature of the antisocial behavior preclude the additional diagnosis of Antisocial Personality Disorder.

Diagnostic criteria for 301.70 Antisocial Personality Disorder

A. Current age at least 18.

B. Evidence of Conduct Disorder with onset before age 15, as indicated by a history of *three* or more of the following:

   (1) was often truant
   (2) ran away from home overnight at least twice while living in parental or parental surrogate home (or once without returning)
   (3) often initiated physical fights
   (4) used a weapon in more than one fight
   (5) forced someone into sexual activity with him or her
   (6) was physically cruel to animals
   (7) was physically cruel to other people
   (8) deliberately destroyed others' property (other than by fire-setting)

Diagnostic criteria for 301.70 Antisocial Personality Disorder continued

   (9) deliberately engaged in fire-setting

  (10) often lied (other than to avoid physical or sexual abuse)

  (11) has stolen without confrontation of a victim on more than one occasion (including forgery)

  (12) has stolen with confrontation of a victim (e.g., mugging, purse-snatching, extortion, armed robbery)

C. A pattern of irresponsible and antisocial behavior since the age of 15, as indicated by at least *four* of the following:

  (1) is unable to sustain consistent work behavior, as indicated by any of the following (including similar behavior in academic settings if the person is a student):

     (a) significant unemployment for six months or more within five years when expected to work and work was available

     (b) repeated absences from work unexplained by illness in self or family

     (c) abandonment of several jobs without realistic plans for others

  (2) fails to conform to social norms with respect to lawful behavior, as indicated by repeatedly performing antisocial acts that are grounds for arrest (whether arrested or not), e.g., destroying property, harassing others, stealing, pursuing an illegal occupation

  (3) is irritable and aggressive, as indicated by repeated physical fights or assaults (not required by one's job or to defend someone or oneself), including spouse- or child-beating

  (4) repeatedly fails to honor financial obligations, as indicated by defaulting on debts or failing to provide child support or support for other dependents on a regular basis

  (5) fails to plan ahead, or is impulsive, as indicated by one or both of the following:

     (a) traveling from place to place without a prearranged job or clear goal for the period of travel or clear idea about when the travel will terminate

     (b) lack of a fixed address for a month or more

  (6) has no regard for the truth, as indicated by repeated lying, use of aliases, or "conning" others for personal profit or pleasure

  (7) is reckless regarding his or her own or others' personal safety, as indicated by driving while intoxicated, or recurrent speeding

  (8) if a parent or guardian, lacks ability to function as a responsible parent, as indicated by one or more of the following:

     (a) malnutrition of child

     (b) child's illness resulting from lack of minimal hygiene

     (c) failure to obtain medical care for a seriously ill child

     (d) child's dependence on neighbors or nonresident relatives for food or shelter

     (e) failure to arrange for a caretaker for young child when parent is away from home

(continued)

Diagnostic criteria for 301.70 Antisocial Personality Disorder continued

        (f) repeated squandering, on personal items, of money required for household necessities

    (9) has never sustained a totally monogamous relationship for more than one year

  (10) lacks remorse (feels justified in having hurt, mistreated, or stolen from another)

D. Occurrence of antisocial behavior not exclusively during the course of Schizophrenia or Manic Episodes.

301.83   Borderline Personality Disorder

The essential feature of this disorder is a pervasive pattern of instability of self-image, interpersonal relationships, and mood, beginning by early adulthood and present in a variety of contexts.

A marked and persistent identity disturbance is almost invariably present. This is often pervasive, and is manifested by uncertainty about several life issues, such as self-image, sexual orientation, long-term goals or career choice, types of friends or lovers to have, or which values to adopt. The person often experiences this instability of self-image as chronic feelings of emptiness or boredom.

Interpersonal relationships are usually unstable and intense, and may be characterized by alternation of the extremes of overidealization and devaluation. These people have difficulty tolerating being alone, and will make frantic efforts to avoid real or imagined abandonment.

Affective instability is common. This may be evidenced by marked mood shifts from baseline mood to depression, irritability, or anxiety, usually lasting a few hours or, only rarely, more than a few days. In addition, these people often have inappropriately intense anger or lack of control of their anger, with frequent displays of temper or recurrent physical fights. They tend to be impulsive, particularly in activities that are potentially self-damaging, such as shopping sprees, psychoactive substance abuse, reckless driving, casual sex, shoplifting, and binge eating.

Recurrent suicidal threats, gestures, or behavior and other self-mutilating behavior (e.g., wrist-scratching) are common in the more severe forms of the disorder. This behavior may serve to manipulate others, may be a result of intense anger, or may counteract feelings of "numbness" and depersonalization that arise during periods of extreme stress.

Some conceptualize this disorder as a level of personality organization rather than as a specific Personality Disorder.

Associated features. Frequently this disorder is accompanied by many features of other Personality Disorders, such as Schizotypal, Histrionic, Narcissistic, and Antisocial Personality Disorders. In many cases more than one diagnosis is warranted. Quite often social contrariness and a generally pessimistic outlook are observed. Alternation between dependency and self-assertion is common. During periods of extreme stress, transient psychotic symptoms may occur, but they are generally of insufficient severity or duration to warrant an additional diagnosis.

Impairment. Often there is considerable interference with social or occupational functioning.

Complications. Possible complications include Dysthymia, Major Depression, Psychoactive Substance Abuse, and psychotic disorders such as Brief Reactive Psychosis. Premature death may result from suicide.

Sex ratio. The disorder is more commonly diagnosed in females.

Prevalence. Borderline Personality Disorder is apparently common.

Predisposing factors and familial pattern. No information.

Differential diagnosis. In **Identity Disorder** there is a similar clinical picture, but Borderline Personality Disorder preempts the diagnosis of Identity Disorder if the criteria for the Personality Disorder are met, the disturbance is sufficiently pervasive and persistent, and it is unlikely that it will be limited to a developmental stage. In **Cyclothymia** there is also affective instability, but in Borderline Personality Disorder (without a coexisting Mood Disorder) there are no Hypomanic Episodes. In some cases, however, both disorders may be present.

Diagnostic criteria for 301.83 Borderline Personality Disorder

A pervasive pattern of instability of mood, interpersonal relationships, and self-image, beginning by early adulthood and present in a variety of contexts, as indicated by at least *five* of the following:

(1) a pattern of unstable and intense interpersonal relationships characterized by alternating between extremes of overidealization and devaluation
(2) impulsiveness in at least two areas that are potentially self-damaging, e.g., spending, sex, substance use, shoplifting, reckless driving, binge eating (Do not include suicidal or self-mutilating behavior covered in [5].)
(3) affective instability: marked shifts from baseline mood to depression, irritability, or anxiety, usually lasting a few hours and only rarely more than a few days
(4) inappropriate, intense anger or lack of control of anger, e.g., frequent displays of temper, constant anger, recurrent physical fights
(5) recurrent suicidal threats, gestures, or behavior, or self-mutilating behavior
(6) marked and persistent identity disturbance manifested by uncertainty about at least two of the following: self-image, sexual orientation, long-term goals or career choice, type of friends desired, preferred values
(7) chronic feelings of emptiness or boredom
(8) frantic efforts to avoid real or imagined abandonment (Do not include suicidal or self-mutilating behavior covered in [5].)

301.50   Histrionic Personality Disorder

The essential feature of this disorder is a pervasive pattern of excessive emotionality and attention-seeking, beginning by early adulthood and present in a variety of contexts. In other classifications this category is termed Hysterical Personality.

People with this disorder constantly seek or demand reassurance, approval, or praise from others and are uncomfortable in situations in which they are not the center of attention. They characteristically display rapidly shifting and shallow expression of emotions. Their behavior is overly reactive and intensely expressed; minor stimuli give rise to emotional excitability. Emotions are often expressed with inappropriate exaggeration, for example, the person may appear much more sad, angry, or delighted than would seem to be warranted. People with this disorder tend to be very self-centered, with little or no tolerance for the frustration of delayed gratification. Their actions are directed to obtaining immediate satisfaction.

These people are typically attractive and seductive, often to the point of looking flamboyant and acting inappropriately. They are typically overly concerned with physical attractiveness. In addition, their style of speech tends to be expressionistic and lacking in detail. For example, a person may describe his vacation as "Just fantastic!" without being able to be more specific.

Associated features. People with this disorder are lively and dramatic and are always drawing attention to themselves. They are prone to exaggeration in their interpersonal relations and often act out a role such as that of "victim" or "princess" without being aware of it. They crave novelty, stimulation, and excitement and quickly become bored with normal routine. Others frequently perceive them as superficially charming and appealing, but lacking genuineness. They are often quick to form friendships, but once a relationship is established, can become egocentric and inconsiderate. They may constantly demand reassurance because of feelings of helplessness and dependency. Their actions are often inconsistent, and may be misinterpreted by others.

In relationships they attempt to control the opposite sex or to enter into a dependent relationship. Flights into romantic fantasy are common. The actual quality of their sexual relationships is variable. Some are promiscuous; others, naive and sexually unresponsive; and still others, apparently normal in their sexual adjustment.

Usually these people show little interest in intellectual achievement and careful, analytic thinking, but they are often creative and imaginative.

People with this disorder tend to be impressionable and easily influenced by others or by fads. They are apt to be overly trusting of others and suggestible, and to show an initially positive response to any strong authority figure who, they think, can provide a magical solution for their problems. Though they adopt convictions strongly and readily, their judgment is not firmly rooted, and they often play hunches.

Frequent complaints of poor health, such as weakness or headaches, or subjective feelings of depersonalization may be present. During periods of extreme stress, people with this disorder may experience transient psychotic symptoms, but they are generally of insufficient severity or duration to warrant an additional diagnosis.

Impairment. Interpersonal relations are usually stormy and ungratifying.

Complications. Complications include Brief Reactive Psychosis, Conversion Disorder, and Somatization Disorder.

Predisposing factors. No information.

Prevalence and sex ratio. The disorder is apparently common, and is diagnosed much more frequently in females than in males.

Familial pattern. The disorder is apparently more common among first-degree biologic relatives of people with this disorder than among the general population.

Differential diagnosis. In **Somatization Disorder,** complaints of physical illness dominate the clinical picture, although histrionic features are common. In many cases Somatization Disorder and Histrionic Personality Disorder coexist. **Borderline Personality Disorder** is also often present; in such cases both diagnoses should be made.

In **Dependent Personality Disorder,** the person similarly is excessively dependent on others for praise and guidance, but is without the flamboyant, exaggerated, emotional features of Histrionic Personality Disorder. People with **Narcissistic Personality Disorder** are similarly excessively self-centered, but are usually preoccupied with a grandiose sense of self and with intense envy.

Diagnostic criteria for 301.50 Histrionic Personality Disorder

A pervasive pattern of excessive emotionality and attention-seeking, beginning by early adulthood and present in a variety of contexts, as indicated by at least *four* of the following:

(1) constantly seeks or demands reassurance, approval, or praise
(2) is inappropriately sexually seductive in appearance or behavior
(3) is overly concerned with physical attractiveness
(4) expresses emotion with inappropriate exaggeration, e.g., embraces casual acquaintances with excessive ardor, uncontrollable sobbing on minor sentimental occasions, has temper tantrums
(5) is uncomfortable in situations in which he or she is not the center of attention
(6) displays rapidly shifting and shallow expression of emotions
(7) is self-centered, actions being directed toward obtaining immediate satisfaction; has no tolerance for the frustration of delayed gratification
(8) has a style of speech that is excessively impressionistic and lacking in detail, e.g., when asked to describe mother, can be no more specific than, "She was a beautiful person."

301.81   Narcissistic Personality Disorder

The essential feature of this disorder is a pervasive pattern of grandiosity (in fantasy or behavior), hypersensitivity to the evaluation of others, and lack of empathy that begins by early adulthood and is present in a variety of contexts.

People with this disorder have a grandiose sense of self-importance. They tend to exaggerate their accomplishments and talents, and expect to be noticed as "special" even without appropriate achievement. They often feel that because of their "specialness," their problems are unique, and can be understood only by other special people. Frequently this sense of self-importance alternates with feelings of special unworthiness. For example, a student who ordinarily expects an A and receives a grade of A minus may, at that moment, express the view that he or she is thus revealed to all as a failure. Conversely, having gotten an A, the student may feel fraudulent, and unable to take genuine pleasure in a real achievement.

These people are preoccupied with fantasies of unlimited success, power, brilliance, beauty, or ideal love, and with chronic feelings of envy for those whom they perceive as being more successful than they are. Although these fantasies frequently substitute for realistic activity, when such goals are actually pursued, it is often with a driven, pleasureless quality and an ambition that cannot be satisfied.

Self-esteem is almost invariably very fragile; the person may be preoccupied with how well he or she is doing and how well he or she is regarded by others. This often takes the form of an almost exhibitionistic need for constant attention and admiration. The person may constantly fish for compliments, often with great charm. In response to criticism, he or she may react with rage, shame, or humiliation, but mask these feelings with an aura of cool indifference.

Interpersonal relationships are invariably disturbed. A lack of empathy (inability to recognize and experience how others feel) is common. For example, the person may be unable to understand why a friend whose father has just died does not want to go to a party. A sense of entitlement, an unreasonable expectation of especially favorable treatment, is usually present. For example, such a person may assume that he or she does not have to wait in line when others must. Interpersonal exploitativeness, in which others are taken advantage of in order to achieve one's ends, or for self-aggrandizement, is common. Friendships are often made only after the person considers how he or she can profit from them. In romantic relationships, the partner is often treated as an object to be used to bolster the person's self-esteem.

Associated features. Frequently, many of the features of Histrionic, Borderline, and Antisocial Personality Disorders are present; in some cases more than one diagnosis may be warranted.

Depressed mood is extremely common. Often the person is painfully self-conscious and preoccupied with grooming and remaining youthful. Personal deficits, defeats, or irresponsible behavior may be justified by rationalization or lying. Feelings may be faked in order to impress others.

Impairment. Some impairment in interpersonal relations is inevitable. Occupational functioning may be impeded by depressed mood, interpersonal difficulties, or the pursuit of unrealistic goals. In other cases, occupational functioning may be enhanced by an unquenchable thirst for success.

Complications. Dysthymia and psychotic disorders such as Brief Reactive Psychosis are possible complications. Major Depression can occur as the person approaches middle age and becomes distressed by awareness of the physical and occupational limitations that become apparent at this stage of life.

Prevalence. This disorder appears to be more common recently than in the past, but this may be due only to more professional interest in it.

Predisposing factors, sex ratio, and familial pattern. No information.

Differential diagnosis. Borderline, Histrionic, and **Antisocial Personality Disorders** are often also present; in such instances, multiple diagnoses should be given. However, in comparison with people with Antisocial Personality Disorder, people with

Narcissistic Personality Disorder tend to be less impulsive, and their exploitation is more for the promotion of feelings of entitlement and power than for material gain. They display less emotional exaggeration than people with Histrionic Personality Disorder, and are less intensely involved with, or dependent on, others. People with Narcissistic Personality Disorder also tend to have a more cohesive identity and to be less impulsive and emotional than people with Borderline Personality Disorder.

Diagnostic criteria for 301.81 Narcissistic Personality Disorder

A pervasive pattern of grandiosity (in fantasy or behavior), lack of empathy, and hypersensitivity to the evaluation of others, beginning by early adulthood and present in a variety of contexts, as indicated by at least *five* of the following:

(1) reacts to criticism with feelings of rage, shame, or humiliation (even if not expressed)

(2) is interpersonally exploitative: takes advantage of others to achieve his or her own ends

(3) has a grandiose sense of self-importance, e.g., exaggerates achievements and talents, expects to be noticed as "special" without appropriate achievement

(4) believes that his or her problems are unique and can be understood only by other special people

(5) is preoccupied with fantasies of unlimited success, power, brilliance, beauty, or ideal love

(6) has a sense of entitlement: unreasonable expectation of especially favorable treatment, e.g., assumes that he or she does not have to wait in line when others must do so

(7) requires constant attention and admiration, e.g., keeps fishing for compliments

(8) lack of empathy: inability to recognize and experience how others feel, e.g., annoyance and surprise when a friend who is seriously ill cancels a date

(9) is preoccupied with feelings of envy

CLUSTER C

301.82 Avoidant Personality Disorder

The essential feature of this disorder is a pervasive pattern of social discomfort, fear of negative evaluation, and timidity, beginning by early adulthood and present in a variety of contexts.

Most people are somewhat concerned about how others assess them, but those with this disorder are easily hurt by criticism and are devastated by the slightest hint of disapproval. They generally are unwilling to enter into relationships unless given an unusually strong guarantee of uncritical acceptance; consequently, they often have no close friends or confidants (or only one) other than first-degree relatives.

Social or occupational activities that involve significant interpersonal contact tend to be avoided. For example, a promotion that will increase social demands may be refused. In social situations, these people are reticent because of a fear of saying something inappropriate or foolish, or of being unable to answer a question. They fear being embarrassed by blushing, crying, or showing signs of anxiety before other people.

Generalized timidity produces resistance to doing anything that will deviate from the person's normal routine. Often the potential difficulties, physical dangers, or risks involved in doing something ordinary, but outside the person's usual activities, are exaggerated. For example, the person may cancel an important trip because of a remote possibility that heavy rain will make driving dangerous.

Unlike people with Schizoid Personality Disorder, who are socially isolated, but have no desire for social relations, those with Avoidant Personality Disorder yearn for affection and acceptance. They are distressed by their lack of ability to relate comfortably to others.

Associated features. Depression, anxiety, and anger at oneself for failing to develop social relations are commonly experienced. Specific phobias may also be present.

Impairment. Social relations are, by definition, severely restricted. Occupational functioning may be impaired, particularly if interpersonal involvement is required.

Complications. Social Phobia may be a complication of this disorder.

Predisposing factors. Avoidant Disorder of Childhood or Adolescence predisposes to the development of this disorder. In addition, disfiguring physical illness may predispose to its development.

Prevalence. Avoidant Personality Disorder is apparently common.

Familial pattern. No information.

Differential diagnosis. In **Schizoid Personality Disorder** there is also social isolation, but little or no desire for social involvement and an indifference to criticism. People with Avoidant Personality Disorder may sometimes appear dependent, since once they have been able to form a relationship, they tend to be very clinging and fearful of losing it.

In **Social Phobias** humiliation is a concern; but usually a specific situation, such as public speaking, is avoided rather than personal relationships. However, as noted in Complications, these disorders may coexist. When **Agoraphobia** is present, avoidant behavior may be relatively pervasive, but is due to a fear of being in places or situations where help may not be available.

In **Avoidant Disorder of Childhood or Adolescence,** there is a similar clinical picture, but Avoidant Personality Disorder preempts this diagnosis if the criteria for the Personality Disorder are met, the disturbance is sufficiently pervasive and persistent, and it is unlikely that it will be limited to a developmental stage.

Diagnostic criteria for 301.82 Avoidant Personality Disorder

A pervasive pattern of social discomfort, fear of negative evaluation, and timidity, beginning by early adulthood and present in a variety of contexts, as indicated by at least *four* of the following:

Diagnostic criteria for 301.82 Avoidant Personality Disorder continued

(1) is easily hurt by criticism or disapproval

(2) has no close friends or confidants (or only one) other than first-degree relatives

(3) is unwilling to get involved with people unless certain of being liked

(4) avoids social or occupational activities that involve significant interpersonal contact, e.g., refuses a promotion that will increase social demands

(5) is reticent in social situations because of a fear of saying something inappropriate or foolish, or of being unable to answer a question

(6) fears being embarrassed by blushing, crying, or showing signs of anxiety in front of other people

(7) exaggerates the potential difficulties, physical dangers, or risks involved in doing something ordinary but outside his or her usual routine, e.g., may cancel social plans because she anticipates being exhausted by the effort of getting there

301.60   Dependent Personality Disorder

The essential feature of this disorder is a pervasive pattern of dependent and submissive behavior beginning by early adulthood and present in a variety of contexts.

People with this disorder are unable to make everyday decisions without an excessive amount of advice and reassurance from others, and will even allow others to make most of their important decisions. For example, an adult with this disorder will typically assume a passive role and allow his or her spouse to decide where they should live, what kind of job he or she should have, and with which neighbors they should be friendly. A child or adolescent with this disorder may allow his or her parent(s) to decide what he or she should wear, with whom to associate, how to spend free time, and what school or college to attend.

This excessive dependence on others leads to difficulty in initiating projects or doing things on one's own. People with this disorder tend to feel uncomfortable or helpless when alone, and will go to great lengths to avoid being alone. They are devastated when close relationships end, and tend to be preoccupied with fears of being abandoned.

These people are easily hurt by criticism and disapproval, and tend to subordinate themselves to others, agreeing with people even when they believe them to be wrong, for fear of being rejected. They will volunteer to do things that are unpleasant or demeaning in order to get others to like them.

Associated features. Frequently another Personality Disorder is present, such as Histrionic, Schizotypal, Narcissistic, or Avoidant Personality Disorder. Anxiety and depression are common.

People with this disorder invariably lack self-confidence. They tend to belittle their abilities and assets. For example, a person with this disorder may constantly refer to himself or herself as "stupid." They may at times seek, or stimulate, overprotection and dominance in others.

Impairment. Occupational functioning may be impaired if the job requires independence. Social relations tend to be limited to those with the few people on whom the person is dependent.

Complications. Dysthymic Disorder and Major Depression are common complications.

Predisposing factors. Chronic physical illness may predispose to the development of this disorder in children and adolescents. Some believe that Separation Anxiety Disorder predisposes to the development of Dependent Personality Disorder.

Prevalence and sex ratio. The disorder is apparently common, and is diagnosed more frequently in females.

Familial pattern. No information.

Differential diagnosis. Dependent behavior is common in **Agoraphobia,** but the person is more likely to actively insist that others assume responsibility, whereas in Dependent Personality Disorder, the person passively maintains a dependent relationship.

Diagnostic criteria for 301.60 Dependent Personality Disorder

A pervasive pattern of dependent and submissive behavior, beginning by early adulthood and present in a variety of contexts, as indicated by at least *five* of the following:

(1) is unable to make everyday decisions without an excessive amount of advice or reassurance from others
(2) allows others to make most of his or her important decisions, e.g., where to live, what job to take
(3) agrees with people even when he or she believes they are wrong, because of fear of being rejected
(4) has difficulty initiating projects or doing things on his or her own
(5) volunteers to do things that are unpleasant or demeaning in order to get other people to like him or her
(6) feels uncomfortable or helpless when alone, or goes to great lengths to avoid being alone
(7) feels devastated or helpless when close relationships end
(8) is frequently preoccupied with fears of being abandoned
(9) is easily hurt by criticism or disapproval

301.40   Obsessive Compulsive Personality Disorder
The essential feature of this disorder is a pervasive pattern of perfectionism and inflexibility, beginning by early adulthood and present in a variety of contexts.

These people constantly strive for perfection, but this adherence to their own overly strict and often unattainable standards frequently interferes with actual completion of tasks and projects. No matter how good an accomplishment, it often does not seem "good enough." Preoccupation with rules, efficiency, trivial details, procedures, or form interferes with the ability to take a broad view of things. For example, such a person, having misplaced a list of things to be done, will spend an inordinate amount of time looking for the list rather than spend a few moments re-creating the list from memory and proceed with accomplishing the tasks. Time is poorly allocated, the most important tasks being left to the last moment.

People with this disorder are always mindful of their relative status in dominance-submission relationships. Although they resist the authority of others, they stubbornly and unreasonably insist that people conform to their way of doing things.

Work and productivity are prized to the exclusion of pleasure and interpersonal relationships. Often there is preoccupation with logic and intellect and intolerance of affective behavior in others. When pleasure is considered, it is something to be planned and worked for. However, the person usually keeps postponing the pleasurable activity, such as a vacation, so that it may never occur.

Decision making is avoided, postponed, or protracted, perhaps because of an inordinate fear of making a mistake. For example, assignments cannot be completed on time because the person is ruminating about priorities. This indecisiveness may cause the person to retain worn or worthless objects even when they have no sentimental value.

People with this disorder tend to be excessively conscientious, moralistic, scrupulous, and judgmental of self and others—for example, considering it "sinful" for a neighbor to leave her child's bicycle out in the rain.

People with this disorder are stingy with their emotions and material possessions. They tend not to express their feelings, and rarely give compliments or gifts. Everyday relationships have a conventional, formal, and serious quality. Others often perceive these people as stilted or "stiff."

Associated features. People with this disorder may complain of difficulty expressing tender feelings. They may experience considerable distress because of their indecisiveness and general ineffectiveness. Their speech may be circumstantial. Depressed mood is common. These people have an unusually strong need to be in control. When they are unable to control others, a situation, or their environment, they often ruminate about the situation and become angry, although the anger is usually not expressed directly. (For example, a man may be angry when service in a restaurant is poor, but instead of complaining to the management, ruminates about how much he will leave as a tip.) Frequently there is extreme sensitivity to social criticism, especially if it comes from someone with considerable status or authority.

Impairment. This disorder frequently is quite incapacitating, particularly in its effect on occupational functioning.

Complications. Obsessive Compulsive Disorder, Hypochondriasis, Major Depression, and Dysthymia may be complications. Many of the features of Obsessive Compulsive Personality Disorder are apparently present in people who develop myocardial infarction, particularly those with overlapping "Type A" personality traits of time urgency, hostility-aggressiveness, and exaggerated competitiveness.

Predisposing factors. No information.

Prevalence and sex ratio. The disorder seems to be common, and is more frequently diagnosed in males.

Familial pattern. The disorder is apparently more common among first-degree biologic relatives of people with this disorder than among the general population.

Differential diagnosis. In **Obsessive Compulsive Disorder** there are, by definition, true obsessions and compulsions, which are not present in Obsessive Compulsive Personality Disorder. However, if the criteria for both disorders are met, both diagnoses should be recorded.

Diagnostic criteria for 301.40 Obsessive Compulsive Personality Disorder

A pervasive pattern of perfectionism and inflexibility, beginning by early adulthood and present in a variety of contexts, as indicated by at least *five* of the following:

(1) perfectionism that interferes with task completion, e.g., inability to complete a project because own overly strict standards are not met
(2) preoccupation with details, rules, lists, order, organization, or schedules to the extent that the major point of the activity is lost
(3) unreasonable insistence that others submit to exactly his or her way of doing things, **or** unreasonable reluctance to allow others to do things because of the conviction that they will not do them correctly
(4) excessive devotion to work and productivity to the exclusion of leisure activities and friendships (not accounted for by obvious economic necessity)
(5) indecisiveness: decision making is either avoided, postponed, or protracted, e.g., the person cannot get assignments done on time because of ruminating about priorities (do not include if indecisiveness is due to excessive need for advice or reassurance from others)
(6) overconscientiousness, scrupulousness, and inflexibility about matters of morality, ethics, or values (not accounted for by cultural or religious identification)
(7) restricted expression of affection
(8) lack of generosity in giving time, money, or gifts when no personal gain is likely to result
(9) inability to discard worn-out or worthless objects even when they have no sentimental value

---

301.84   Passive Aggressive Personality Disorder

The essential feature of this disorder is a pervasive pattern of passive resistance to demands for adequate social and occupational performance, beginning by early adulthood and present in a variety of contexts. The resistance is expressed indirectly rather than directly, and results in pervasive and persistent social and occupational ineffectiveness even when more self-assertive and effective behavior is possible. The name of this disorder is based on the assumption that such people are passively expressing covert aggression.

People with this disorder habitually resent and oppose demands to increase or maintain a given level of functioning. This occurs most clearly in work situations, but is also evident in social functioning. The resistance is expressed indirectly through such maneuvers as procrastination, dawdling, stubbornness, intentional inefficiency, and "forgetfulness." These people obstruct the efforts of others by failing to do their share of the work. For example, when an executive gives a subordinate some material to review for a meeting the next morning, rather than complain that he has no time to do the work, the subordinate may misplace or misfile the material and thus attain his goal by passively resisting the demand on him.

These people become sulky, irritable, or argumentative when asked to do something they do not want to do. They often protest to others about how unreasonable the demands being made on them are, and resent useful suggestions from others concerning how to be more productive. As a result of their resentment of demands, they unreasonably criticize or scorn the people in authority who are making the demands.

Associated features. Often people with this disorder are dependent and lack self-confidence. Typically, they are pessimistic about the future, but have no realization that their behavior is responsible for their difficulties.

Impairment. These people are ineffective both socially and occupationally because of their passive aggressive behavior. For example, because of their intentional inefficiency, job promotions are not offered them. A housewife with the disorder may fail to do the laundry or to stock the kitchen with food because of procrastination and dawdling.

Complications. Frequent complications include Major Depression, Dysthymia, and Alcohol Abuse or Dependence.

Predisposing factors. Oppositional Defiant Disorder in childhood or adolescence apparently predisposes to the development of this disorder.

Prevalence, sex ratio, and familial pattern. No information.

Differential diagnosis. In **Oppositional Defiant Disorder,** the clinical picture may be similar, and this diagnosis preempts the diagnosis of Passive Aggressive Personality Disorder if the person is under 18.

Passive aggressive maneuvers that are used in certain situations in which assertive behavior is discouraged, or actually punished, and that are not part of a pervasive pattern of personality functioning do not warrant this diagnosis.

Diagnostic criteria for 301.84 Passive Aggressive Personality Disorder

A pervasive pattern of passive resistance to demands for adequate social and occupational performance, beginning by early adulthood and present in a variety of contexts, as indicated by at least *five* of the following:

(1) procrastinates, i.e., puts off things that need to be done so that deadlines are not met
(2) becomes sulky, irritable, or argumentative when asked to do something he or she does not want to do
(3) seems to work deliberately slowly or to do a bad job on tasks that he or she really does not want to do
(4) protests, without justification, that others make unreasonable demands on him or her
(5) avoids obligations by claiming to have "forgotten"

(continued)

Diagnostic criteria for 301.84 Passive Aggressive Personality Disorder
continued

   (6) believes that he or she is doing a much better job than others think he or she is doing

   (7) resents useful suggestions from others concerning how he or she could be more productive

   (8) obstructs the efforts of others by failing to do his or her share of the work

   (9) unreasonably criticizes or scorns people in positions of authority

301.90 Personality Disorder Not Otherwise Specified

Disorders of personality functioning that are not classifiable as a specific Personality Disorder. An example is features of more than one specific Personality Disorder that do not meet the full criteria for any one, yet cause significant impairment in social or occupational functioning, or subjective distress. In DSM-III, this was called Mixed Personality Disorder.

    This category can also be used when the clinician judges that a specific Personality Disorder not included in this classification is appropriate, such as Impulsive Personality Disorder, Immature Personality Disorder, Self-defeating Personality Disorder (see p. 371), or Sadistic Personality Disorder (see p. 369). In such instances the clinician should note the specific personality disorder in parentheses, e.g., Personality Disorder NOS (Self-defeating Personality Disorder).

V Codes for Conditions Not Attributable to a Mental Disorder That Are a Focus of Attention or Treatment

The ICD-9-CM includes V Codes for a "Supplementary Classification of Factors Influencing Health Status and Contact with Health Services." A brief list of V Codes adapted from ICD-9-CM is provided here for conditions that are a focus of attention or treatment but are not attributable to any of the mental disorders noted previously. In some instances, a thorough evaluation has failed to uncover any mental disorder; in other instances, the scope of the diagnostic evaluation has not been adequate to determine the presence or absence of a mental disorder, but there is a need to note the reason for contact with the mental health care system. (With further information, the presence of a mental disorder may become apparent.) Finally, a person may have a mental disorder, but the focus of attention or treatment may be on a condition that is not due to the mental disorder. For example, a person with Bipolar Disorder may have marital problems that are not directly related to manifestations of the Mood Disorder but are the principal focus of treatment.

V62.30 Academic Problem
This category can be used when the focus of attention or treatment is an academic problem that is apparently not due to a mental disorder. An example is a pattern of failing grades or of significant underachievement in a person with adequate intellectual capacity in the absence of a Specific Developmental Disorder or any other mental disorder that would account for the problem.

V71.01 Adult Antisocial Behavior
This category can be used when the focus of attention or treatment is adult antisocial behavior that is apparently not due to a mental disorder, such as Conduct Disorder, Antisocial Personality Disorder, or an Impulse Control Disorder. Examples include the behavior of some professional thieves, racketeers, or dealers in illegal psychoactive substances.

V40.00 Borderline Intellectual Functioning
        Note: This is coded on Axis II.

This category can be used when the focus of attention or treatment is associated with Borderline Intellectual Functioning, i.e., an IQ in the 71–84 range. Differential diagnosis between Borderline Intellectual Functioning and Mental Retardation (an IQ of 70 or below) is especially difficult and important when the coexistence of certain mental disorders is involved. For example, when the diagnosis is Schizophrenia, Undifferentiated or Residual Type, and impairment in adaptive functioning is prominent, the existence of Borderline Intellectual Functioning is easily overlooked, and hence the level and quality of potential adaptive functioning may be incorrectly assessed.

V71.02 Childhood or Adolescent Antisocial Behavior
This category can be used when the focus of attention or treatment is antisocial behavior in a child or adolescent that is apparently not due to a mental disorder, such as Conduct Disorder, Antisocial Personality Disorder, or an Impulse Control Disorder. Examples include isolated antisocial acts of children or adolescents (not a pattern of antisocial behavior).

V65.20 Malingering
The essential feature of Malingering is intentional production of false or grossly exaggerated physical or psychological symptoms, motivated by external incentives such as avoiding military conscription or duty, avoiding work, obtaining financial compensation, evading criminal prosecution, obtaining drugs, or securing better living conditions.

Under some circumstances Malingering may represent adaptive behavior, for example, feigning illness while a captive of the enemy during wartime.

Malingering should be strongly suspected if any combination of the following is noted:

(1) medicolegal context of presentation, e.g., the person's being referred by his or her attorney to the physician for examination;
(2) marked discrepancy between the person's claimed stress or disability and the objective findings;
(3) lack of cooperation during the diagnostic evaluation and in complying with the prescribed treatment regimen;
(4) the presence of Antisocial Personality Disorder.

Malingering differs from Factitious Disorder in that the motivation for the symptom production in Malingering is external incentives, whereas in Factitious Disorder there is an absence of external incentives. Evidence of an intrapsychic need to maintain the sick role suggests Factitious Disorder. Thus, a diagnosis of Factitious Disorder excludes a diagnosis of Malingering.

Malingering is differentiated from Conversion and other Somatoform Disorders by the intentional production of symptoms and by the obvious, external incentives. The person who is malingering is much less likely to present his or her symptoms in the context of emotional conflict, and the presenting symptoms are less likely to be symbolically related to an underlying emotional conflict. Symptom relief in Malingering is not often obtained by suggestion, hypnosis, or an amobarbital interview, as it frequently is in Conversion Disorder.

V61.10 Marital Problem
This category can be used when the focus of attention or treatment is a marital problem that is apparently not due to a mental disorder. An example is marital conflict related to estrangement or divorce.

V15.81 Noncompliance with Medical Treatment
This category can be used when the focus of attention or treatment is noncompliance with medical treatment that is apparently not due to a mental disorder. Examples

include: irrationally motivated noncompliance due to denial of illness, noncompliance due to religious beliefs, and decisions based on personal value judgments about the advantages and disadvantages of the proposed treatment. The category should not be used if the noncompliance is due to a mental disorder, such as Schizophrenia or a Psychoactive Substance Use Disorder.

V62.20   Occupational Problem
This category can be used when the focus of attention or treatment is an occupational problem that is apparently not due to a mental disorder. Examples include job dissatisfaction and uncertainty about career choices.

V61.20   Parent–Child Problem
This category can be used for either a parent or a child when the focus of attention or treatment is a parent–child problem that is apparently not due to a mental disorder of the person who is being evaluated. An example is conflict between a mentally healthy adolescent and her parents about her choice of friends.

V62.81   Other Interpersonal Problem
This category can be used when the focus of attention or treatment is an interpersonal problem (other than marital or parent–child) that is apparently not due to a mental disorder of the person who is being evaluated. Examples are difficulties with co-workers or with romantic partners.

V61.80   Other Specified Family Circumstances
This category can be used when the focus of attention or treatment is a family circumstance that is apparently not due to a mental disorder and is not a Parent–Child or a Marital Problem. Examples are interpersonal difficulties with an aged in-law, or sibling rivalry.

V62.89   Phase of Life Problem or Other Life Circumstance Problem
This category can be used when the focus of attention or treatment is a problem associated with a particular developmental phase or some other life circumstance that is apparently not due to a mental disorder. Examples include problems associated with entering school, leaving parental control, starting a new career, and changes involved in marriage, divorce, and retirement.

V62.82   Uncomplicated Bereavement
This category can be used when the focus of attention or treatment is a normal reaction to the death of a loved one (bereavement).

A full depressive syndrome frequently is a normal reaction to such a loss, with feelings of depression and such associated symptoms as poor appetite, weight loss, and insomnia. However, morbid preoccupation with worthlessness, prolonged and marked functional impairment, and marked psychomotor retardation are uncommon and suggest that the bereavement is complicated by the development of a Major Depression.

In Uncomplicated Bereavement, guilt, if present, is chiefly about things done or not done by the survivor at the time of the death; thoughts of death are usually limited to the person's thinking that he or she would be better off dead or that he or she should have died with the deceased person. The person with Uncomplicated Bereavement generally regards the feeling of depressed mood as "normal," although he or she may seek professional help for relief of such associated symptoms as insomnia or anorexia.

The reaction to the loss may not be immediate, but rarely occurs after the first two or three months. The duration of "normal" bereavement varies considerably among different cultural groups.

Additional Codes

Note: Although the terms below distinguish between Axis I and Axis II, in order to maintain compatibility with ICD-9-CM, these Axis I and Axis II codes are the same.

300.90   Unspecified Mental Disorder (Nonpsychotic)
When enough information is available to rule out a psychotic disorder, but further specification is not possible, the residual category Unspecified Mental Disorder (Nonpsychotic) is used. In some cases, with more information the diagnosis can be changed to a specific disorder. This category can also be used for specific mental disorders that are not included in the DSM-III-R classification, for example, Late Luteal Phase Dysphoric Disorder.

V71.09   No Diagnosis or Condition on Axis I
When no Axis I diagnosis or condition (including the V code categories) is present, this should be indicated. There may or may not be an Axis II diagnosis.

799.90   Diagnosis or Condition Deferred on Axis I
When there is insufficient information to make any diagnostic judgment about an Axis I diagnosis or condition, this should be noted as Diagnosis or Condition Deferred on Axis I.

V71.09   No Diagnosis on Axis II
When no Axis II diagnosis (i.e., no Personality Disorder or Specific Developmental Disorder) is present, this should be indicated. There may or may not be an Axis I diagnosis or condition.

799.90   Diagnosis Deferred on Axis II
When there is insufficient information to make any diagnostic judgment about an Axis II diagnosis, this should be noted as Diagnosis Deferred on Axis II.

APPENDIX A

PROPOSED
DIAGNOSTIC CATEGORIES
NEEDING FURTHER STUDY

APPENDIX A: Proposed Diagnostic Categories Needing Further Study

This appendix presents three diagnoses that were proposed for inclusion in DSM-III-R. They are included here to facilitate further systematic clinical study and research.

Late Luteal Phase Dysphoric Disorder

Many females report a variety of physical and emotional changes associated with specific phases of the menstrual cycle. For most of these females, these changes are not severe, cause little distress, and have no effect on social or occupational functioning. In contrast, the essential feature of Late Luteal Phase Dysphoric Disorder is a pattern of clinically significant emotional and behavioral symptoms that occur during the last week of the luteal phase and remit within a few days after the onset of the follicular phase. In most females these symptoms occur in the week before, and remit within a few days after, the onset of menses.

The diagnosis is given only if the symptoms are sufficiently severe to cause marked impairment in social or occupational functioning and have occurred during a majority of menstrual cycles in the past year. The diagnosis should not be made if the symptoms fail to disappear within a few days after onset of the follicular phase. Thus, the diagnosis should not be made in a person who is experiencing only a late luteal phase exacerbation of another disorder, such as Major Depression, Panic Disorder, Dysthymia, or a Personality Disorder.

In menstruating females with this disorder, the timing of the luteal and follicular phases can be ascertained by the onset of menses. However, the disorder has been reported in nonmenstruating females who have had a hysterectomy but retain ovarian function. In such cases the timing of luteal and follicular phases may require measurement of circulating reproductive hormones.

Studies have found that for some females who report severe premenstrual symptoms, daily self-ratings indicate that the symptoms are not as severe as initially reported (perhaps because the monitoring has a therapeutic effect) or that the symptoms do not disappear within a few days after onset of menses, which suggests that the premenstrual disturbance represents an exacerbation of another disorder. Finally, in some cases, daily self-ratings reveal that there is no consistent relationship between the symptoms and the luteal phase. For these reasons the diagnosis of Late Luteal Phase Dysphoric Disorder should be made only provisionally on the basis of retrospective reports; daily self-ratings for at least two symptomatic cycles are required to confirm the diagnosis.

Among the most commonly experienced symptoms are marked affective lability (e.g., sudden episodes of tearfulness, sadness, or irritability); persistent feelings of irritability, anger, or tension (feeling "on edge"); and feelings of depression and self-deprecating thoughts. Also common are decreased interest in usual activities, fatigability and loss of energy, a subjective sense of difficulty in concentrating, changes in appetite, cravings for specific foods (especially carbohydrates), and sleep disturbance. Other physical symptoms, such as breast tenderness or swelling, headaches, joint or muscle pain, a sensation of "bloating," and weight gain, may also be present.

Associated features. Some studies suggest that there may be a higher frequency of Depressive Disorder in females with Late Luteal Phase Dysphoric Disorder.

Age at onset. The age at onset may be any time after menarche. However, females seeking treatment for the disorder are usually over the age of 30.

Course. There is no information about the natural history of the disorder, but females seeking treatment generally report that the condition has worsened with age.

Impairment. Although subthreshold forms of this condition may be characterized only by subjective distress, the disorder as defined here requires that the symptoms seriously interfere with social or occupational functioning.

Complications. Suicidal behavior may be a complication of the disorder.

Predisposing factors. No information.

Prevalence. Although studies have indicated that mild psychological symptoms during the latter part of the luteal phase are common, the prevalence of Late Luteal Phase Dysphoric Disorder is unknown.

Familial pattern. No information.

Differential diagnosis. Dysmenorrhea (painful menses) is characterized by symptoms that occur with menses, whereas in Late Luteal Phase Dysphoric Disorder the onset of the symptoms is premenstrual. The diagnosis of Late Luteal Phase Dysphoric Disorder should not be made if the symptoms preceding the menses are limited to pain and physical discomfort. Other disorders that may be symptomatically similar to Late Luteal Phase Dysphoric Disorder, such as **Depressive Disorders** and **Panic Disorder,** do not remit regularly with the onset of menses.

The diagnosis of Late Luteal Phase Dysphoric Disorder should not be made in a person who is experiencing only a premenstrual exacerbation of one of the above disorders. However, the diagnosis may be made in addition to one of the other diagnoses if the person experiences characteristic Late Luteal Phase Dysphoric Disorder symptoms that are markedly different from those they experience as part of the coexisting disorder.

Diagnostic criteria for Late Luteal Phase Dysphoric Disorder

A. In most menstrual cycles during the past year, symptoms in B occurred during the last week of the luteal phase and remitted within a few days after onset of the follicular phase. In menstruating females, these phases correspond to the week before, and a few days after, the onset of menses. (In nonmenstruating females who have had a hysterectomy, the timing of luteal and follicular phases may require measurement of circulating reproductive hormones.)

B. At least five of the following symptoms have been present for most of the time during each symptomatic late luteal phase, at least one of the symptoms being either (1), (2), (3), or (4):

  (1) marked affective lability, e.g., feeling suddenly sad, tearful, irritable, or angry

  (2) persistent and marked anger or irritability

  (3) marked anxiety, tension, feelings of being "keyed up," or "on edge"

  (4) markedly depressed mood, feelings of hopelessness, or self-deprecating thoughts

  (5) decreased interest in usual activities, e.g., work, friends, hobbies

  (6) easy fatigability or marked lack of energy

  (7) subjective sense of difficulty in concentrating

  (8) marked change in appetite, overeating, or specific food cravings

  (9) hypersomnia or insomnia

 (10) other physical symptoms, such as breast tenderness or swelling, headaches, joint or muscle pain, a sensation of "bloating," weight gain

C. The disturbance seriously interferes with work or with usual social activities or relationships with others.

D. The disturbance is not merely an exacerbation of the symptoms of another disorder, such as Major Depression, Panic Disorder, Dysthymia, or a Personality Disorder (although it may be superimposed on any of these disorders).

E. Criteria A, B, C, and D are confirmed by prospective daily self-ratings during at least two symptomatic cycles. (The diagnosis may be made provisionally prior to this confirmation.)

Note: For coding purposes, record: 300.90 Unspecified Mental Disorder (Late Luteal Phase Dysphoric Disorder).

Sadistic Personality Disorder

The essential feature of this disorder is a pervasive pattern of cruel, demeaning, and aggressive behavior directed toward other people, beginning by early adulthood. The sadistic behavior is often evident both in social relationships (particularly with family members) and at work (with subordinates), but seldom is displayed in contacts with people in positions of authority or higher status.

The diagnosis is not made if the sadistic behavior has been directed toward only one person (e.g., a spouse) or has been only for the purpose of sexual arousal (as in Sexual Sadism).

Many people with this disorder use physical violence or cruelty to establish dominance in interpersonal relationships (not merely to achieve some noninterpersonal goal, such as striking someone in order to rob him or her). This violence is frequently resorted to or escalated when the person perceives that his or her victims are no longer willing to be intimidated or controlled. Other people with this disorder are never physically violent, although in many cases they are fascinated by violence, weapons, martial arts, injury, or torture. For example, a man who has never been violent regularly reads magazines about violent crimes, combat, and weapons and collects guns and knives.

A variety of behaviors reflect a basic lack of respect or empathy for others. For example, a person with Sadistic Personality Disorder may frequently humiliate or demean people in the presence of others or discipline someone under his or her control in an unusually harsh manner: a father may severely punish his child for a minor infraction of table manners; a teacher may force a student to spend many hours in detention at school for breaking a minor rule. The person often restricts the autonomy of people with whom he or she has a close relationship. For example, a husband may not let his wife leave the house without him, or permit his teen-age daughter to attend any social functions. The person with Sadistic Personality Disorder often gets other people to do what he or she wants by frightening them, with tactics ranging from intimidation by hostile glances to terror through threats of violence.

Often people with this disorder seem to be amused or enjoy the psychological or physical suffering of others (including animals). For example, a man enjoys setting cats on fire. The person may inflict pain or suffering by lying; for example, a woman may call her former husband and lie to him about their son's having been seriously hurt.

Associated features. Almost invariably the sadistic behavior is ego-syntonic, and the person rarely comes to clinical attention unless this has been mandated by the courts (usually after apprehension for a crime, or when under investigation for suspected child or spouse abuse). Often these people victimize others who suffer from Self-defeating Personality Disorder.

Frequently many of the features of Narcissistic and Antisocial Personality Disorder are present and, in some instances, diagnoses of two or more personality disorders may be appropriate. People with this disorder rarely experience depression, and their reaction to feeling abandoned is usually anger.

Complications. Psychoactive Substance Use Disorders and marital, occupational, and legal difficulties resulting from the sadistic behavior may complicate this condition.

Predisposing factors. Having been physically, sexually, or psychologically abused as a child or having been reared in a family in which there was abuse of a spouse may predispose to development of this disorder.

Sex ratio. The disorder is far more common in males than in females.

Prevalence. In clinical samples, the disorder is rare; in forensic samples, it is not rare.

Familial pattern. No information.

Differential diagnosis. In **Sexual Sadism** the person engages in sadistic behavior for the purpose of sexual arousal. In rare instances both diagnoses are appropriate. In

Antisocial Personality Disorder there is, by definition, a childhood or adolescent history of conduct problems, which frequently is not present in people with Sadistic Personality Disorder. In some instances, however, both diagnoses are appropriate.

Diagnostic criteria for Sadistic Personality Disorder

A. A pervasive pattern of cruel, demeaning, and aggressive behavior, beginning by early adulthood, as indicated by the repeated occurrence of at least four of the following:

   (1) has used physical cruelty or violence for the purpose of establishing dominance in a relationship (not merely to achieve some noninterpersonal goal, such as striking someone in order to rob him or her)
   (2) humiliates or demeans people in the presence of others
   (3) has treated or disciplined someone under his or her control unusually harshly, e.g., a child, student, prisoner, or patient
   (4) is amused by, or takes pleasure in, the psychological or physical suffering of others (including animals)
   (5) has lied for the purpose of harming or inflicting pain on others (not merely to achieve some other goal)
   (6) gets other people to do what he or she wants by frightening them (through intimidation or even terror)
   (7) restricts the autonomy of people with whom he or she has a close relationship, e.g., will not let spouse leave the house unaccompanied or permit teen-age daughter to attend social functions
   (8) is fascinated by violence, weapons, martial arts, injury, or torture

B. The behavior in A has not been directed toward only one person (e.g., spouse, one child) and has not been solely for the purpose of sexual arousal (as in Sexual Sadism).

Note: For coding purposes, record: 301.90 Personality Disorder NOS (Sadistic Personality Disorder).

Self-defeating Personality Disorder
The essential feature of this disorder is a pervasive pattern of self-defeating behavior, beginning by early adulthood and present in a variety of contexts. The person may often avoid or undermine pleasurable experiences, be drawn to situations or relationships in which he or she will suffer, and prevent others from helping him or her. The diagnosis is not made if the self-defeating behaviors occur only in situations in which the person is responding to or anticipating being physically, sexually, or psychologically abused. Similarly, the diagnosis is not made if the self-defeating behaviors occur only when the person is depressed.

This disorder has been called Masochistic Personality Disorder, but the name of the category has been changed to avoid the historic association of the term *masochistic* with older psychoanalytic views of female sexuality and the implication that a person with the disorder derives unconscious pleasure from suffering. A variety of theories, psychoanalytic, cognitive, and social learning, have been offered to explain the origins of this pattern.

The person repeatedly enters into relationships with persons or places himself or herself in situations that are self-defeating and have painful consequences even when better options are clearly available. For example, a woman repeatedly chooses to enter relationships with men who turn out to have Alcohol Dependence and to be emotionally unavailable; a man with excellent vocational skills persists in entering employment situations in which his work is unrecognized and he is underpaid.

Reasonable offers of assistance from others are rejected. This may vary from repeated polite refusals of offers of favors or gifts from others to sabotage of efforts by others to be helpful or nurturing. For example, the person may often loan money to friends, but refuse to accept loans from others even when badly needed; he may fail to contact his physician when seriously ill. In the treatment situation, the person fails to follow through on an agreed-upon treatment plan.

The person's reaction to positive personal events, such as graduation, a job promotion or raise, or any form of praise or encouragement from others may be depression or feelings of guilt. In some instances, following a positive event the person may do something that produces pain, such as have an accident or lose something valuable.

Characteristically, people with this disorder act in such a way as to cause others to be angry or to reject them. For example, the person may make fun of his or her spouse in public by belittling his or her capabilities only to feel hurt later when the spouse retaliates. In treatment the person may make unreasonable requests for special attention and then feel rejected when the therapist does not comply with them.

Opportunities for pleasure may be repeatedly avoided. For example, the person may not take vacations. Alternatively, he or she may participate in what most people would regard as enjoyable activities, such as going to the movies or to a party, but deny having experienced any pleasure.

The person reports a number of situations in which he or she had the opportunity to accomplish a task crucial to his or her personal success, but despite having the capacity to complete the task, failed to do so. For example, he or she may have contributed excellent ideas to help a colleague complete a proposal, but fail to complete his or her own proposal.

People who consistently treat the person well are often experienced as boring or uninteresting. Relationships with seemingly caring people are rejected or not pursued. These relationships may be personal, e.g., a potential friend or lover, or professional, e.g., a needed potential therapist. The person may describe stimulating sexual relationships with exploitive or insensitive partners, but find caring partners sexually unattractive.

The person frequently attempts to do things for others that require excessive self-sacrifice, even though these sacrifices are unsolicited by the intended recipients. The sacrifice does not make the person feel better (as in the case of altruistic behavior that engenders a sense of pride and enhances the subject's self-esteem). Such sacrifice also has the effect of inducing guilt in others, which often results in others' avoiding or rejecting the person.

Associated features. Other Personality Disorders (or some features of other personality disorders) are common, particularly Borderline, Dependent, Passive Aggressive, Obsessive Compulsive, and Avoidant Personality Disorders.

Complications. Dysthymia and Major Depressive Episodes are common complications of this disorder. Suicidal ideation or behavior may be present.

Predisposing factors. Having been physically, sexually, or psychologically abused as a child or having been reared in a family in which there was abuse of a spouse may predispose to development of this disorder.

Prevalence. Initial studies suggest that the disorder may be one of the more common Personality Disorders in clinical samples.

Sex ratio. In clinical samples, the ratio of females to males ranges from 3:2 to 2:1.

Familial pattern. There is a clinical impression that the disorder is more common among first-degree biologic relatives of people with this disorder than among the general population.

Differential diagnosis. In cases of **physical, sexual, or psychological abuse**, the victim may behave in a way that appears to be "self-defeating." For example, a woman may stay in a relationship with a physically abusive man, or may repeatedly avoid situations, such as seeing friends, that would give her pleasure. However, such behaviors may be only coping strategies to avoid, for example, threats to her life if she terminates the relationship, or further abuse if she spends time with her friends. The diagnosis of Self-defeating Personality Disorder is not made if "self-defeating" behaviors occur only in response to, or in anticipation of, being physically, sexually, or psychologically abused, though there are instances in which the diagnosis of Self-defeating Personality Disorder is appropriate for a person who has been (or is being) physically, sexually, or psychologically abused. In such a case it is necessary to determine that the self-defeating behavior is a persistent pattern that is not limited to situations of actual or anticipated abuse. An example would be a person with a long history of self-defeating behavior who only recently has actually been the victim in a physically abusive relationship.

In **Depressive Disorders**, a person may exhibit self-defeating behavior as a symptom of the Mood Disorder. The diagnosis of Self-defeating Personality Disorder is not made if the self-defeating behavior occurs only when the person is depressed. However, people with Self-defeating Personality Disorder frequently have superimposed Major Depressive Episodes or Dysthymia.

Diagnostic criteria for Self-defeating Personality Disorder

A. A pervasive pattern of self-defeating behavior, beginning by early adulthood and present in a variety of contexts. The person may often avoid or undermine pleasurable experiences, be drawn to situations or relationships in which he or she will suffer, and prevent others from helping him or her, as indicated by at least five of the following:

    (1) chooses people and situations that lead to disappointment, failure, or mistreatment even when better options are clearly available

    (2) rejects or renders ineffective the attempts of others to help him or her

    (3) following positive personal events (e.g., new achievement), responds with depression, guilt, or a behavior that produces pain (e.g., an accident)

(continued)

Diagnostic criteria for Self-defeating Personality Disorder continued

(4) incites angry or rejecting responses from others and then feels hurt, defeated, or humiliated (e.g., makes fun of spouse in public, provoking an angry retort, then feels devastated)

(5) rejects opportunities for pleasure, or is reluctant to acknowledge enjoying himself or herself (despite having adequate social skills and the capacity for pleasure)

(6) fails to accomplish tasks crucial to his or her personal objectives despite demonstrated ability to do so, e.g., helps fellow students write papers, but is unable to write his or her own

(7) is uninterested in or rejects people who consistently treat him or her well, e.g., is unattracted to caring sexual partners

(8) engages in excessive self-sacrifice that is unsolicited by the intended recipients of the sacrifice

B. The behaviors in A do not occur exclusively in response to, or in anticipation of, being physically, sexually, or psychologically abused.

C. The behaviors in A do not occur only when the person is depressed.

Note: For coding purposes, record: 301.90 Personality Disorder NOS (Self-defeating Personality Disorder).

DECISION TREES FOR DIFFERENTIAL DIAGNOSIS

APPENDIX B:
Decision Trees for
Differential Diagnosis[1]

The purpose of these decision trees is to aid the clinician in understanding the organization and hierarchic structure of the classification. Each decision tree starts with a set of clinical features. When one of these features is a prominent part of the presenting clinical picture, either as current or past symptomatology, the clinician can follow the series of questions to rule in or out various disorders. Since the classification may allow several disorders to be diagnosed within a diagnostic area (for example, Social Phobia and Obsessive Compulsive Disorder in Anxiety Disorders), the clinician should proceed down the tree until a leaf (i.e., a point in the tree with no outgoing branches) is found. If features from several different trees are present, each of the appropriate trees should be examined. For example, if a mood disturbance and psychotic symptoms are both present, both the MOOD and the PSYCHOTIC trees should be explored.

Note: Many of the questions only approximate the actual criteria.

I. Psychotic symptoms   p. 378

II. Mood disturbance   p. 380

III. Specific organic factor likely   p. 382

IV. Irrational anxiety, avoidance behavior, and increased arousal   p. 384

V. Physical complaints or anxiety about illness   p. 386

[1]Prepared by Michael B. First, M.D., Janet B. W. Williams, D.S.W., and Robert L. Spitzer, M.D.

Differential Diagnosis of Psychotic Symptoms

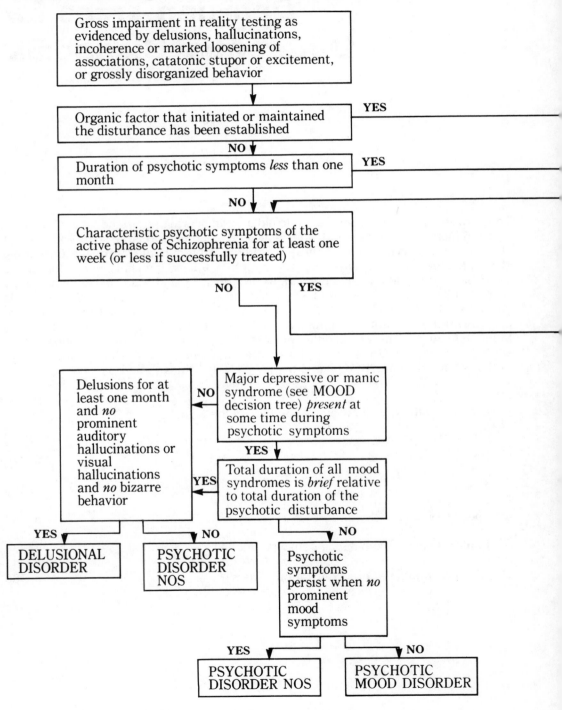

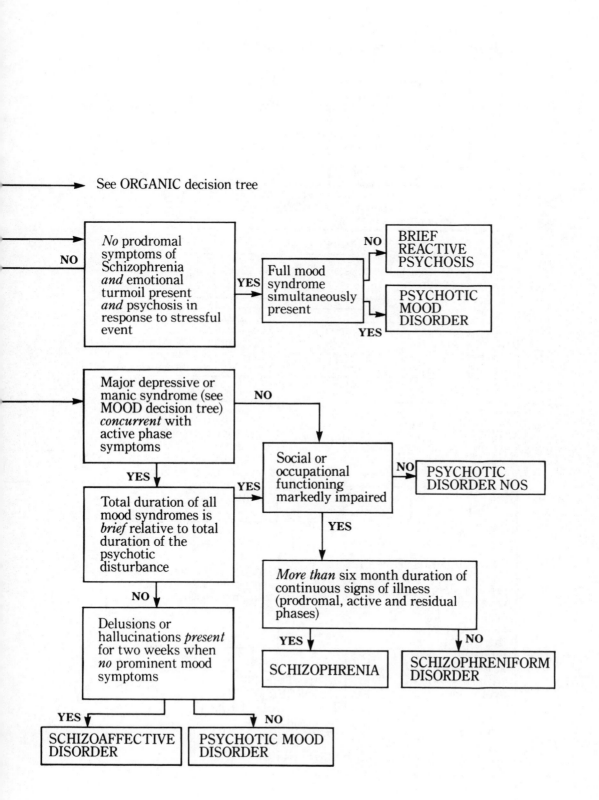

See ORGANIC decision tree

NO → *No* prodromal symptoms of Schizophrenia *and* emotional turmoil present *and* psychosis in response to stressful event

YES → Full mood syndrome simultaneously present

NO → BRIEF REACTIVE PSYCHOSIS

YES → PSYCHOTIC MOOD DISORDER

Major depressive or manic syndrome (see MOOD decision tree) *concurrent* with active phase symptoms

NO → Social or occupational functioning markedly impaired

NO → PSYCHOTIC DISORDER NOS

YES → Total duration of all mood syndromes is *brief* relative to total duration of the psychotic disturbance

YES → (Social or occupational functioning markedly impaired)

YES → *More than* six month duration of continuous signs of illness (prodromal, active and residual phases)

NO → Delusions or hallucinations *present* for two weeks when *no* prominent mood symptoms

YES → SCHIZOPHRENIA

NO → SCHIZOPHRENIFORM DISORDER

YES → SCHIZOAFFECTIVE DISORDER

NO → PSYCHOTIC MOOD DISORDER

Differential Diagnosis of Mood Disturbances

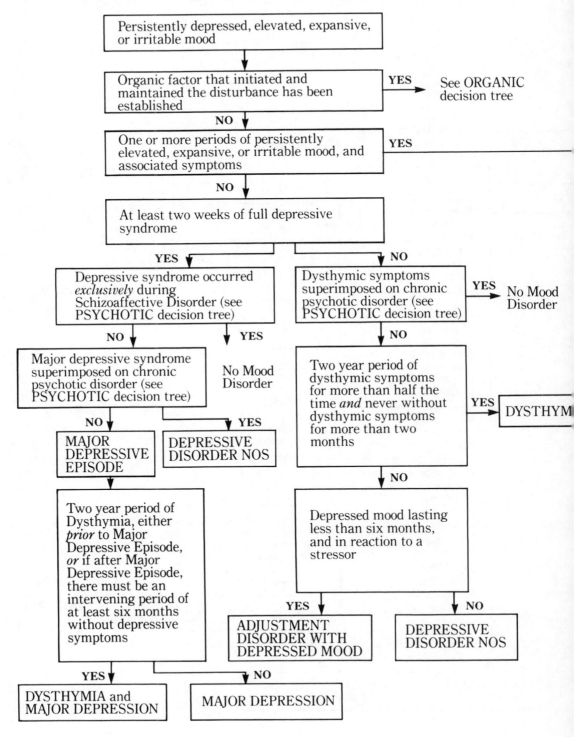

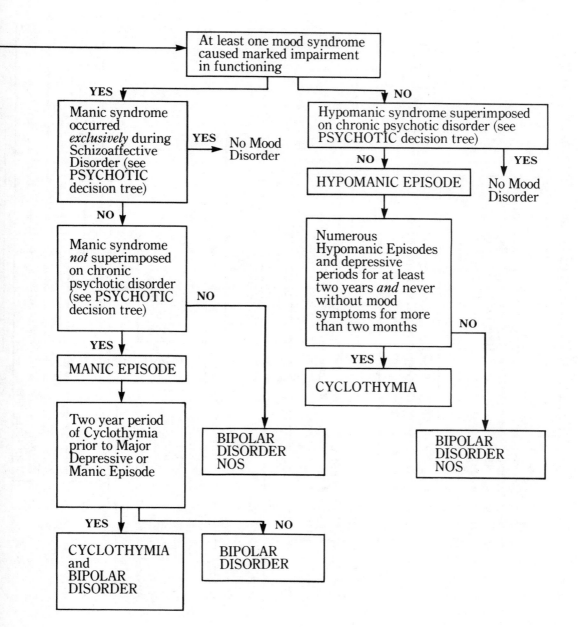

Differential Diagnosis of Organic Mental Disorders

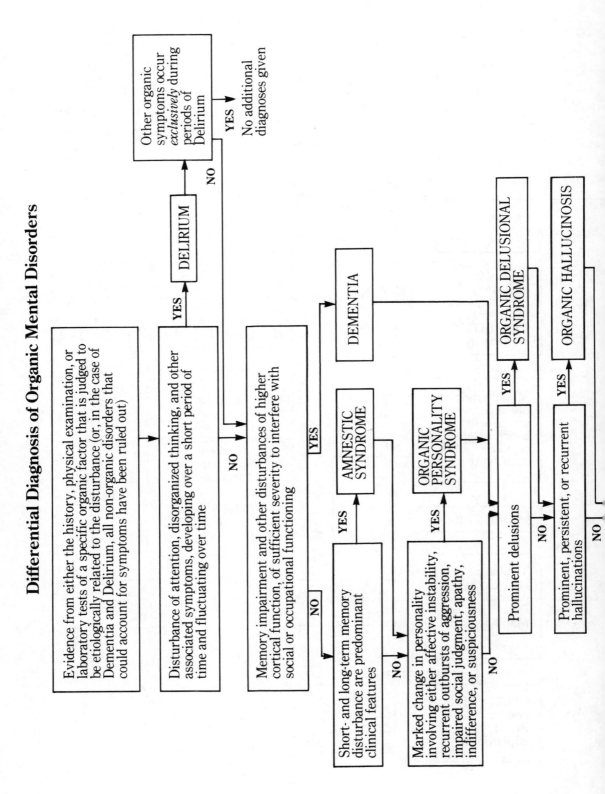

Evidence from either the history, physical examination, or laboratory tests of a specific organic factor that is judged to be etiologically related to the disturbance (or, in the case of Dementia and Delirium, all non-organic disorders that could account for symptoms have been ruled out)

Disturbance of attention, disorganized thinking, and other associated symptoms, developing over a short period of time and fluctuating over time

YES → **DELIRIUM** → Other organic symptoms occur *exclusively* during periods of Delirium

YES → No additional diagnoses given

NO

Memory impairment and other disturbances of higher cortical function, of sufficient severity to interfere with social or occupational functioning

YES →

Short- and long-term memory disturbance are predominant clinical features

YES → **AMNESTIC SYNDROME**

NO → **DEMENTIA**

Marked change in personality involving either affective instability, recurrent outbursts of aggression, impaired social judgment, apathy, indifference, or suspiciousness

YES → **ORGANIC PERSONALITY SYNDROME**

NO

Prominent delusions

YES → **ORGANIC DELUSIONAL SYNDROME**

NO

Prominent, persistent, or recurrent hallucinations

YES → **ORGANIC HALLUCINOSIS**

NO

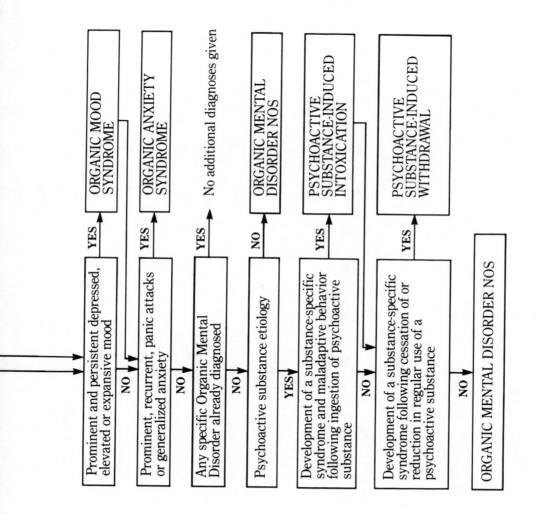

Differential Diagnosis of Anxiety Disorders

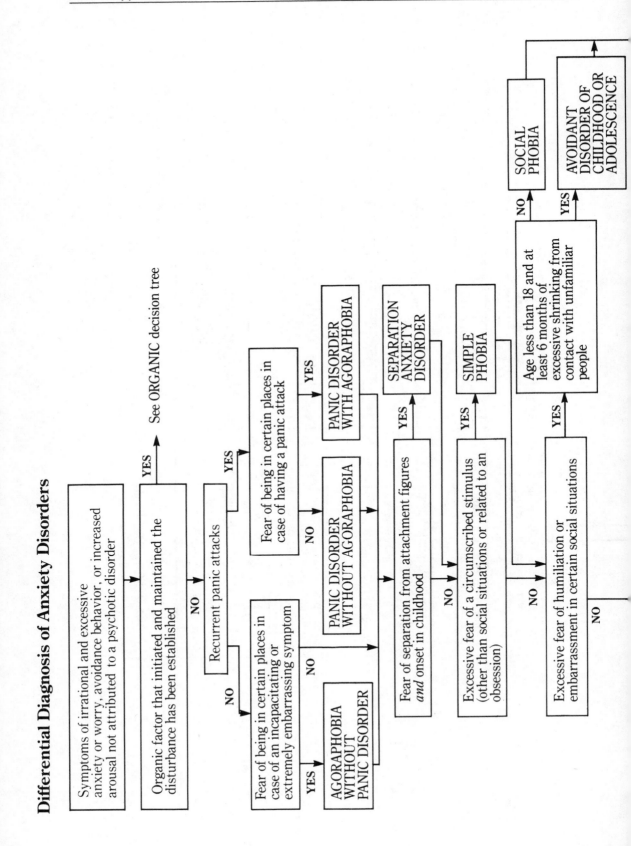

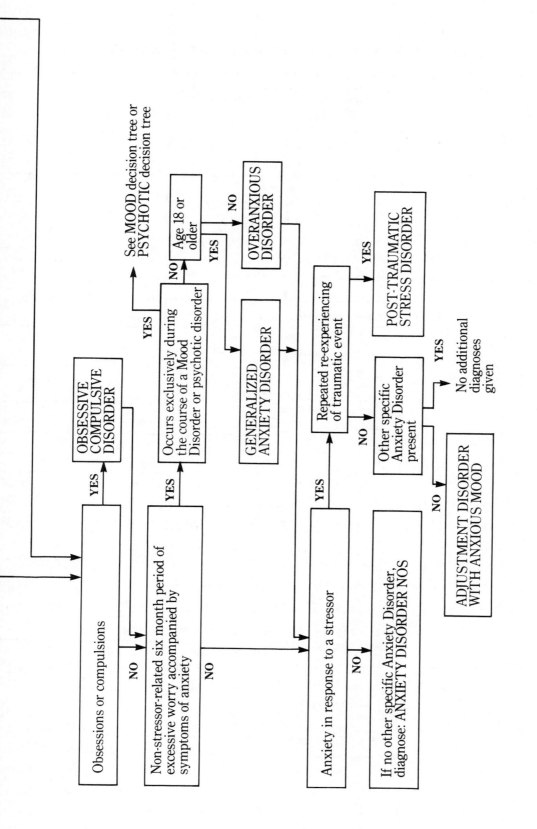

Differential Diagnosis of Somatoform Disorders

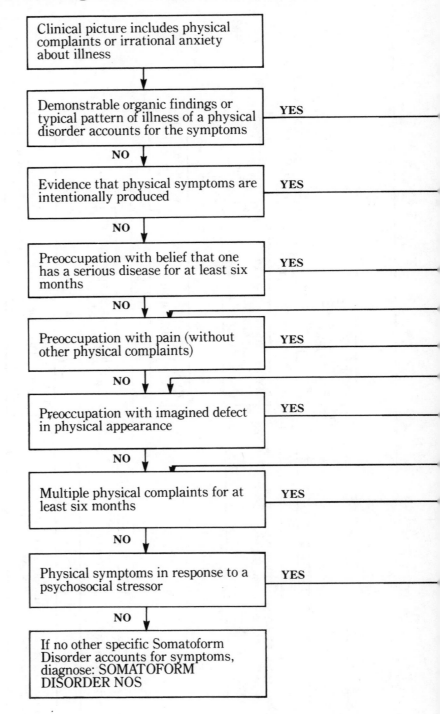

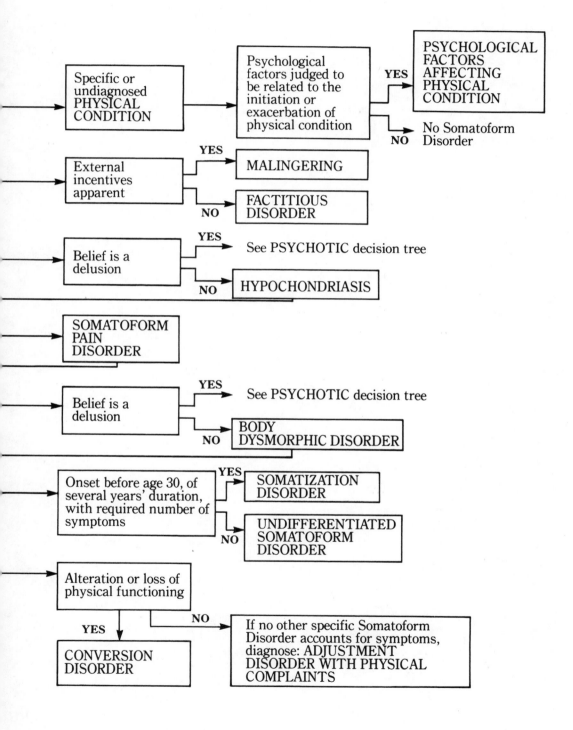

APPENDIX C

GLOSSARY OF
TECHNICAL TERMS

APPENDIX C:
Glossary of Technical Terms

This glossary of technical terms is generally limited to those that are used in either the descriptions and definitions or the diagnostic criteria of DSM-III-R and that are associated with several mental disorders. For example, bulimia is not in this glossary because it is rarely encountered except among Eating Disorders, and the reader wishing to learn about this symptom should refer to the text on those disorders. On the other hand, such symptoms as delusions, phobias, obsessions, and depersonalization are included because they all occur in a number of mental disorders. Also included in this glossary is a list of defense mechanisms, even though they are rarely used in either the descriptions or the diagnostic criteria for the DSM-III-R mental disorders.

Many of the entries list the disorders in which the symptom most frequently occurs; it should be understood, however, that the symptom may also be present in other disorders.

AFFECT. A pattern of observable behaviors that is the expression of a subjectively experienced feeling state (emotion). Common examples of affect are euphoria, anger, and sadness. Affect is variable over time, in response to changing emotional states, whereas mood refers to a pervasive and sustained emotion.

A range of affect may be described as *broad* (normal), *restricted* (constricted), *blunted*, or *flat*. What is considered the normal range of the expression of affect varies considerably, both within and among different cultures. The normal expression of affect involves variability in facial expression, pitch of voice, and hand and body movements. Restricted affect is characterized by a clear reduction in the expressive range and intensity of affects. Blunted affect is marked by a severe reduction in the intensity of affective expression. In flat affect there is virtually no affective expression; generally the voice is monotonous and the face, immobile.

Affect is *inappropriate* when it is clearly discordant with the content of the person's speech or ideation. Example: A patient smiled and laughed while discussing demons who were persecuting him.

Affect is *labile* when it is characterized by repeated, rapid, and abrupt shifts. Examples: An elderly man is tearful one moment and combative the next; a young woman is observed by her friends to be friendly, gregarious, and happy one moment and angry and abusive the next, without apparent reason.

AGITATION. *See* psychomotor agitation.

ANXIETY. Apprehension, tension, or uneasiness that stems from the anticipation of danger, which may be internal or external. Some definitions of anxiety distinguish it from fear by limiting it to anticipation of a danger whose source is largely unknown, whereas fear is the response to a consciously recognized and usually external threat or danger. The manifestations of anxiety and fear are the same and include motor tension, autonomic hyperactivity, apprehensive expectation, and vigilance and scanning.

Anxiety may be focused on an object, situation, or activity, which is avoided (phobia), or may be unfocused (free-floating anxiety). It may be experienced in discrete periods of sudden onset and be accompanied by physical symptoms (panic attacks). When anxiety is focused on physical signs or symptoms and causes preoccupation with the fear or belief of having a disease, it is termed hypochondriasis.

ATTENTION. The ability to focus in a sustained manner on one activity. A disturbance in attention may be manifested by difficulty in finishing tasks that have been started, easy distractibility, or difficulty in concentrating on work.

BLOCKING. Interruption of a train of speech before a thought or idea has been completed. After a period of silence, which may last from a few seconds to minutes, the person indicates that he or she cannot recall what he or she has been saying or meant to say. Blocking should be judged to be present only if the person spontaneously describes losing his or her train of thought or if, upon questioning by an interviewer, gives that as the reason for pausing.

CATATONIC BEHAVIOR. Marked motor anomalies, generally limited to disturbances within the context of a diagnosis of a nonorganic psychotic disorder.

Catatonic excitement. Excited motor activity, apparently purposeless and not influenced by external stimuli.

Catatonic negativism. An apparently motiveless resistance to all instructions or attempts to be moved. When passive, the person may resist any effort to be moved; when active, he or she may do the opposite of what is asked—for example, firmly clench jaws when asked to open mouth.

Catatonic posturing. Voluntary assumption of an inappropriate or bizarre posture, usually held for a long period of time. Example: A patient may stand with arms outstretched as if he were Jesus on the cross.

Catatonic rigidity. Maintenance of a rigid posture against all efforts to be moved.

Catatonic stupor. Marked decrease in reactivity to the environment and reduction in spontaneous movements and activity, sometimes to the point of appearing to be unaware of one's surroundings.

Catatonic waxy flexibility. The person's limbs can be "molded" into any position, which is then maintained. When the limb is being moved, it feels to the examiner as if it were made of pliable wax.

CIRCUMSTANTIALITY. A term used to describe speech that is indirect and delayed in reaching the point because of unnecessary, tedious details and parenthetical remarks. Circumstantial replies or statements may be prolonged for many minutes if the speaker is not interrupted and urged to get to the point. Interviewers often respond to circumstantiality by interrupting the speaker in order to complete the process of history-taking within an allotted time. This may make it difficult to distinguish loosening of associations from circumstantiality. In the former there is a lack of connection between clauses, but in the latter the clauses always retain a meaningful connection. In loosening of associations, the original point is lost, whereas in circumstantiality, the speaker is always aware of the original point, goal, or topic.

Circumstantiality is common in an Obsessive Compulsive Personality Disorder and in many people without mental disorder.

CLANGING. Speech in which sounds, rather than meaningful, conceptual relationships govern word choice; it may include rhyming and punning. The term is generally applied only when it is a manifestation of a pathological condition; thus, it would not be used to describe the rhyming word play of children. Example: "I'm not trying to make noise. I'm trying to make sense. If you can make sense out of nonsense, well, have fun. I'm trying to make sense out of sense. I'm not making sense (cents) anymore. I have to make dollars."

Clanging is observed most commonly in Schizophrenia and Manic Episodes.

COMPULSION. Repetitive and seemingly purposeful behavior that is in response to an obsession, or performed according to certain rules or in a stereotyped fashion. The behavior is not an end in itself, but is designed to produce or prevent some future state of affairs; the activity, however, either is not connected in a realistic way with the state of affairs it is designed to produce or prevent, or may be clearly excessive. The act is performed with a sense of subjective compulsion coupled with a desire to resist it (at least initially); performing the particular act is not pleasurable, although it may afford some relief of tension. Example: A person feels compelled to wash her hands every time she shakes hands because of a fear of contamination, which she recognizes as excessive.

Compulsions are characteristic of Obsessive Compulsive Disorder.

CONFABULATION. Fabrication of facts or events in response to questions about situations or events that are not recalled because of memory impairment. It differs from lying in that the person is not consciously attempting to deceive.

Confabulation is common in Amnestic Disorder.

CONVERSION SYMPTOM. A loss or alteration of physical functioning that suggests a physical disorder, but that is actually a direct expression of a psychological conflict or need. The disturbance is not under voluntary control, and is not explained by any physical disorder (this possibility having been excluded by appropriate examinations).

Conversion symptoms are observed in Conversion Disorder, and may occur in Schizophrenia.

DEFENSE MECHANISMS. Patterns of feelings, thoughts, or behaviors that are relatively involuntary and arise in response to perceptions of psychic danger. They are designed to hide or to alleviate the conflicts or stressors that give rise to anxiety. Some defense mechanisms, such as projection, splitting, and acting-out, are almost invariably maladaptive. Others, such as suppression and denial, may be either maladaptive or adaptive, depending on their severity, their inflexibility, and the context in which they occur. Defense mechanisms that are usually adaptive, such as sublimation and humor, are not included here.

Acting-out. A mechanism in which the person acts without reflection or apparent regard for negative consequences.

Autistic fantasy. A mechanism in which the person substitutes excessive daydreaming for the pursuit of human relationships, more direct and effective action, or problem solving.

Denial. A mechanism in which the person fails to acknowledge some aspect of external reality that would be apparent to others.

Devaluation. A mechanism in which the person attributes exaggeratedly negative qualities to self or others.

Displacement. A mechanism in which the person generalizes or redirects a feeling about an object or a response to an object onto another, usually less threatening, object.

Dissociation. A mechanism in which the person sustains a temporary alteration in the integrative functions of consciousness or identity.

Idealization. A mechanism in which the person attributes exaggeratedly positive qualities to self or others.

Intellectualization. A mechanism in which the person engages in excessive abstract thinking to avoid experiencing disturbing feelings.

Isolation. A mechanism in which the person is unable to experience simultaneously the cognitive and affective components of an experience because the affect is kept from consciousness.

Passive aggression. A mechanism in which the person indirectly and unassertively expresses aggression toward others.

Projection. A mechanism in which the person falsely attributes his or her own unacknowledged feelings, impulses, or thoughts to others.

Rationalization. A mechanism in which the person devises reassuring or self-serving, but incorrect, explanations for his or her own or others' behavior.

Reaction formation. A mechanism in which the person substitutes behavior, thoughts, or feelings that are diametrically opposed to his or her own unacceptable ones.

Repression. A mechanism in which the person is unable to remember or to be cognitively aware of disturbing wishes, feelings, thoughts, or experiences.

Somatization. A mechanism in which the person becomes preoccupied with physical symptoms disproportionate to any actual physical disturbance.

Splitting. A mechanism in which the person views himself or herself or others as all good or all bad, failing to integrate the positive and the negative qualities of self and others into cohesive images; often the person alternately idealizes and devalues the same person.

Suppression. A mechanism in which the person intentionally avoids thinking about disturbing problems, desires, feelings, or experiences.

Undoing. A mechanism in which the person engages in behavior designed to symbolically make amends for or negate previous thoughts, feelings, or actions.

DELUSION. A false personal belief based on incorrect inference about external reality and firmly sustained in spite of what almost everyone else believes and in spite of what constitutes incontrovertible and obvious proof or evidence to the contrary. The belief is not one ordinarily accepted by other members of the person's culture or subculture (i.e., it is not an article of religious faith).

When a false belief involves an extreme value judgment, it is regarded as a delusion only when the judgment is so extreme as to defy credibility. Example: If someone claims he or she is terrible and has disappointed his or her family, this is generally not regarded as a delusion even if an objective assessment of the situation would lead observers to think otherwise; but if someone claims he or she is the worst sinner in the world, this would generally be considered a delusional conviction. Similarly, a person judged by most people to be moderately underweight who asserts that he or she is fat would not be regarded as delusional; but one with Anorexia Nervosa who, at the point of extreme emaciation, insists he or she is fat could rightly be considered delusional.

A delusion should be distinguished from a hallucination, which is a false sensory perception (although a hallucination may give rise to the delusion that the perception is true). A delusion is also to be distinguished from an overvalued idea, in which an unreasonable belief or idea is not as firmly held as is the case with a delusion.

Delusions are subdivided according to their content. Some of the more common types are listed below.

Delusion of being controlled. A delusion in which feelings, impulses, thoughts, or actions are experienced as being not one's own, as being imposed by some external force. This does not include the mere conviction that one is acting as an agent of God, has had a curse placed on him or her, is the victim of fate, or is not sufficiently assertive. The symptom should be judged present only when the subject experiences his or her will, thoughts, or feelings as operating under some external force. Examples: A man claimed that his words were not his own, but those of his father; a student believed that his actions were under the control of a yogi; a housewife believed that sexual feelings were being put into her body from without.

Delusion, bizarre. A false belief that involves a phenomenon that the person's culture would regard as totally implausible. Example: A man believed that when his adenoids had been removed in childhood, a box had been inserted into his head, and that wires had been placed in his head so that the voice he heard was that of the governor.

Delusion, grandiose. A delusion whose content involves an exaggerated sense of one's importance, power, knowledge, or identity. It may have a religious, somatic, or other theme.

Delusion, mood-congruent. *See* mood-congruent psychotic features.

Delusion, mood-incongruent. *See* mood-incongruent psychotic features.

Delusion, nihilistic. A delusion involving the theme of nonexistence of the self or part of the self, others, or the world. Examples: "The world is finished"; "I no longer have a brain"; "There is no need to eat, because I have no insides." A somatic delusion may also be a nihilistic delusion if the emphasis is on nonexistence of the body or a part of the body.

Delusion, persecutory. A delusion in which the central theme is that a person or group is being attacked, harassed, cheated, persecuted, or conspired against. Usually the subject or someone or some group or institution close to him or her is singled out as the object of the persecution.
It is recommended that the term *paranoid delusion* not be used, because its meanings are multiple, confusing, and contradictory. It has often been employed to refer to both persecutory and grandiose delusions because of their presence in the Paranoid Type of Schizophrenia.

Delusion of poverty. A delusion that the person is, or will be, bereft of all, or virtually all, material possessions.

Delusion of reference. A delusion whose theme is that events, objects, or other people in the person's immediate environment have a particular and unusual significance, usually of a negative or pejorative nature. This differs from an idea of reference, in which the false belief is not as firmly held as in a delusion. If the delusion of reference involves a persecutory theme, then a delusion of persecution is present as well. Examples: A woman was convinced that programs on the radio were directed especially to her: when recipes were broadcast, it was to tell her to prepare wholesome food for her child and stop feeding her candy; when dance music was broadcast, it was to tell her to stop what she was doing and start dancing, and perhaps even to resume ballet lessons. A patient noted that the room number of his therapist's office was the same as the number of the hospital room in which his father died and believed that this meant there was a plot to kill him.

Delusion, somatic. A delusion whose main content pertains to the functioning of one's body. Examples: One's brain is rotting; one is pregnant despite being postmenopausal.
Extreme value judgments about the body may, under certain circumstances, also be considered somatic delusions. Example: A person insists that his nose is grossly misshapen despite lack of confirmation of this by observers.
Hypochondriacal delusions are also somatic delusions when they involve specific changes in the functioning or structure of the body rather than merely an insistent belief that one has a disease.

Delusion, systematized. A single delusion with multiple elaborations or a group of delusions that are all related by the person to a single event or theme. Example: A man who failed his bar examination developed the delusion that this occurred because of a conspiracy involving the university and the bar association. He then attributed all other difficulties in his social and occupational life to this continuing conspiracy.

Delusional jealousy. The delusion that one's sexual partner is unfaithful.

DEPERSONALIZATION. An alteration in the perception or experience of the self so that the feeling of one's own reality is temporarily lost. This is manifested in a sense of self-estrangement or unreality, which may include the feeling that one's extremities have changed in size, or a sense of seeming to perceive oneself from a distance (usually from above).

Depersonalization is seen in Depersonalization Disorder, and may also occur in Schizotypal Personality Disorder and Schizophrenia. It is sometimes observed in people without any mental disorder who are experiencing overwhelming anxiety, stress, or fatigue.

DIAGNOSIS. In general usage, and in DSM-III-R, this term refers to the process of identifying specific mental or physical disorders. Some, however, use the term more broadly to refer to a comprehensive evaluation that is not limited to identification of specific disorders. Thus, in the limited sense of the term, only Axis I, II, and III are diagnostic, whereas in the broader sense, Axes IV, V, and other aspects of assessment can also be considered diagnostic.

DISORIENTATION. Confusion about the date or time of day, where one is (place), or who one is (identity). Disorientation is characteristic of some Organic Mental Disorders, such as Delirium and Dementia.

DISTRACTIBILITY. Attention drawn too frequently to unimportant or irrelevant external stimuli. Example: While being interviewed, a subject's attention is repeatedly drawn to noise from an adjoining office, a book that is on a shelf, or the interviewer's school ring.

ECHOLALIA. Repetition (echoing) of the words or phrases of others. Typical echolalia tends to be repetitive and persistent. The echo is often uttered with a mocking, mumbling, or staccato intonation. Echolalia should not be confused with habitual repetition of questions, apparently to clarify the question and formulate its answer, as when a subject is asked, "When did you come to the hospital?" and replies, "Come to the hospital? Yesterday." Example: An interviewer says to a subject, "I'd like to talk with you for a few minutes"; and the subject responds, in a mumbling tone, "Talk with you for a few minutes. Talk with you for a few minutes."

Echolalia is observed in some Pervasive Developmental Disorders, Organic Mental Disorders, and Schizophrenia.

FLIGHT OF IDEAS. A nearly continuous flow of accelerated speech with abrupt changes from topic to topic, usually based on understandable associations, distracting stimuli, or plays on words. When severe, speech may be disorganized and incoherent.

Flight of ideas is most frequently seen in manic episodes, but may also be observed in some cases of Organic Mental Disorders, Schizophrenia, other psychotic disorders, and, occasionally, acute reactions to stress.

FORMAL THOUGHT DISORDER. A disturbance in the form of thought as distinguished from the content of thought. The boundaries of the concept are not clear, and there is no consensus as to which disturbances in speech or thought are included in the concept. For this reason, "formal thought disorder" is not used as a specific descriptive term in DSM-III-R. *See* loosening of associations, incoherence, poverty of content of speech, neologisms, perseveration, blocking, echolalia, clanging.

GRANDIOSITY. An inflated appraisal of one's worth, power, knowledge, importance, or identity. When extreme, grandiosity may be of delusional proportions. Example: A professor who frequently puts his students to sleep with his boring lectures is convinced that he is the most dynamic and exciting teacher at the university.

HALLUCINATION. A sensory perception without external stimulation of the relevant sensory organ. A hallucination has the immediate sense of reality of a true perception, although in some instances the source of the hallucination may be perceived as within the body (e.g., an auditory hallucination may be experienced as coming from within the head rather than through the ears). (Some investigators limit the concept of true hallucinations to sensations whose source is perceived as being external to the body, but the clinical significance of this distinction has yet to be demonstrated, so it is not made in this manual.)

There may or may not be a delusional interpretation of the hallucinatory experience. For example, one person with auditory hallucinations may recognize that he or she is having a false sensory experience whereas another may be convinced that the source of the sensory experience has an independent physical reality. Strictly speaking, hallucinations indicate a psychotic disturbance only when they are associated with gross impairment in reality testing (*see* psychotic). The term *hallucination*, by itself, is not ordinarily applied to the false perceptions that occur during dreaming, while falling asleep (hypnagogic), or when awakening (hypnopompic). Hallucinations occurring in the course of an intensely shared religious experience generally have no pathological significance.

Hallucinations should be distinguished from illusions, in which an external stimulus is misperceived or misinterpreted, and from normal thought processes that are exceptionally vivid. Transient hallucinatory experiences are common in people without mental disorder.

Hallucination, auditory. A hallucination of sound, most commonly of voices, but sometimes of clicks, rushing noises, music, etc.

Hallucination, gustatory. A hallucination of taste, unpleasant tastes being the most common.

Hallucination, mood-congruent. *See* mood-congruent psychotic features.

Hallucination, mood-incongruent. *See* mood-incongruent psychotic features.

Hallucination, olfactory. A hallucination involving smell. Example: A woman complained of a persistent smell of dead bodies. Some people are convinced they have a body odor they themselves cannot smell; this symptom is a delusion, not an olfactory hallucination.

Hallucination, somatic. A hallucination involving the perception of a physical experience localized within the body. Example: A feeling of electricity running through one's body.

Somatic hallucinations are to be distinguished from unexplained physical sensations; a somatic hallucination can be identified with certainty only when a delusional interpretation of a physical illness is present. A somatic hallucination is to be distinguished also from hypochondriacal preoccupation with, or exaggeration of, normal physical sensations and from a tactile hallucination, in which the sensation is usually related to the skin.

Hallucination, tactile. A hallucination involving the sense of touch, often of something on or under the skin. Almost invariably the symptom is associated with a delusional interpretation of the sensation. Examples: A man said he could feel the Devil sticking pins into his flesh; another claimed he could feel himself being penetrated anally; still another complained of experiencing pains, which he attributed to the Devil, throughout his body, although there was no evidence of any physical illness.

A particular tactile hallucination is *formication*, which is the sensation of something creeping or crawling on or under the skin. Often there is a delusional interpretation of the sensation, as when it is attributed to insects or worms. Formication is seen in Alcohol Withdrawal Delirium and the withdrawal phase of Cocaine Intoxication.

Tactile hallucinations of pain are to be distinguished from Somatoform Pain Disorder, in which there is no delusional interpretation.

Hallucination, visual. A hallucination involving sight, which may consist of formed images, such as of people, or of unformed images, such as flashes of light. Visual hallucinations should be distinguished from illusions, which are misperceptions of real external stimuli.

IDEAS OF REFERENCE. An idea, held less firmly than a delusion, that events, objects, or other people in the person's immediate environment have a particular and unusual meaning specifically for him or her. *See also* delusion of reference.

IDENTITY. The sense of self, providing a unity of personality over time. Prominent disturbances in identity or the sense of self are seen in Schizophrenia, Borderline Personality Disorder, and Identity Disorder.

ILLOGICAL THINKING. Thinking that contains obvious internal contradictions or in which conclusions are reached that are clearly erroneous, given the initial premises. It may be seen in people without mental disorder, particularly in situations in which they are distracted or fatigued. Illogical thinking has psychopathological significance only when it is marked, as in the examples noted below, and when it is not due to cultural or religious values or to an intellectual deficit. Markedly illogical thinking may lead to, or result from, a delusional belief, or may be observed in the absence of a delusion.

Examples: A patient explained that she gave her family IBM cards, which she punched, in an effort to improve communication with them. Another patient stated: "Parents are the people that raise you. Parents can be anything—material, vegetable, or mineral—that has taught you something. A person can look at a rock and learn something from it, so a rock is a parent." In response to the question "Why did you go to Kingston?" a patient replied, "Because I believe in the King James Bible and my name is James. I went to Kingston to see the Queen."

ILLUSION. A misperception of a real external stimulus. Examples: The rustling of leaves is heard as the sound of voices; a man claims that when he looks in a mirror, he sees his face distorted and misshapen. *See also* hallucination.

INCOHERENCE. Speech that, for the most part, is not understandable, owing to any of the following: a lack of logical or meaningful connection between words, phrases, or sentences; excessive use of incomplete sentences; excessive irrelevancies or abrupt changes in subject matter; idiosyncratic word usage; distorted grammar. Mildly un-grammatical constructions or idiomatic usages characteristic of particular regional or ethnic backgrounds, lack of education, or low intelligence should not be considered incoherence. The term is generally not applied when there is evidence that the distur-bance in speech is due to an aphasia.

Example: Interviewer: "Why do you think people believe in God?" Subject: "Um, because making a do in life. Isn't none of that stuff about evolution guiding isn't true anymore now. It all happened a long time ago. It happened in eons and eons and stuff they wouldn't believe in Him. The time that Jesus Christ people believe in their thing people believed in, Jehovah God that they didn't believe in Jesus Christ that much."

Incoherence may be seen in some Organic Mental Disorders, Schizophrenia, and other psychotic disorders.

INSOMNIA. Difficulty falling or staying asleep. Initial insomnia is difficulty in falling asleep. Middle insomnia involves an awakening, followed by difficulty returning to sleep, but eventually doing so. Terminal insomnia is awakening at least two hours before one's usual waking time and being unable to return to sleep.

LOOSENING OF ASSOCIATIONS. Thinking characterized by speech in which ideas shift from one subject to another that is completely unrelated or only obliquely related to the first without the speaker's showing any awareness that the topics are uncon-nected. Statements that lack a meaningful relationship may be juxtaposed, or the person may shift idiosyncratically from one frame of reference to another. When loosening of associations is severe, speech may be incoherent. The term is generally not applied when abrupt shifts in topics are associated with a nearly continuous flow of accelerated speech (as in flight of ideas).

Example: Interviewer: "What did you think of the whole Watergate affair?" Sub-ject: "You know I didn't tune in on that, I felt so bad about it. But it seemed to get so murky, and everybody's reports were so negative. Huh, I thought, I don't want any part of this, and I don't care who was in on it, and all I could figure out was Artie had something to do with it. Artie was trying to flush the bathroom toilet of the White House or something. She was trying to do something fairly simple. The tour guests stuck or something. She got blamed because the water overflowed, went down in the basement, down, to the kitchen. They had a, they were going to have to repaint and restore the White House room, the enormous living room. And then it was at this reunion they were having. And it's just such a mess and I just thought, well, I'm just going to pretend like I don't even know what's going on. So I came downstairs and 'cause I pretended like I didn't know what was going on, I slipped on the floor of the kitchen, cracking my toe, when I was teaching some kids how to do some double dives."

Loosening of associations may be seen in Schizophrenia, Manic Episodes, and other psychotic disorders.

MAGICAL THINKING. The person believes that his or her thoughts, words, or actions might, or will in some manner, cause or prevent a specific outcome in some way that defies the normal laws of cause and effect. Example: A man believed that if he said a specific prayer three times each night, his mother's death might be prevented indefinitely; a mother believed that if she had an angry thought, her child would become ill.

Magical thinking may be part of ideas of reference or may reach delusional proportions when the person maintains a firm conviction about the belief despite evidence to the contrary.

Magical thinking is seen in children, in people in primitive cultures, and in Schizotypal Personality Disorder, Schizophrenia, and Obsessive Compulsive Disorder.

MENTAL DISORDER. In DSM-III-R each of the mental disorders is conceptualized as a clinically significant behavioral or psychological syndrome or pattern that occurs in a person and that is associated with present distress (a painful symptom) or disability (impairment in one or more important areas of functioning), or a significantly increased risk of suffering death, pain, disability, or an important loss of freedom. In addition, this syndrome or pattern must not be merely an expectable response to a particular event, e.g., the death of a loved one. Whatever its original cause, it must currently be considered a manifestation of a behavioral, psychological, or biological dysfunction in the person. Neither deviant behavior, e.g., political, religious, or sexual, nor conflicts that are primarily between the individual and society are mental disorders unless the deviance or conflict is a symptom of a dysfunction in the person, as described above.

MOOD. A pervasive and sustained emotion that, in the extreme, markedly colors the person's perception of the world. Common examples of mood include depression, elation, anger, and anxiety.

Mood, dysphoric. An unpleasant mood, such as depression, anxiety, or irritability.

Mood, elevated. A mood that is more cheerful than normal; it does not necessarily imply pathology.

Mood, euphoric. An exaggerated feeling of well-being. As a technical term, *euphoria* implies a pathological mood. Whereas the person with a normally elevated mood may describe himself or herself as being in "good spirits," "very happy," or "cheerful," the euphoric person is likely to exclaim that he or she is "on top of the world," "up in the clouds," or to say, "I feel ecstatic," "I'm flying," or "I am high."

Mood, euthymic. Mood in the "normal" range, which implies the absence of depressed or elevated mood.

Mood, expansive. Lack of restraint in expressing one's feelings, frequently with an overvaluation of one's significance or importance. There may also be elevated or euphoric mood.

Mood, irritable. Internalized feeling of tension associated with being easily annoyed and provoked to anger.

MOOD-CONGRUENT PSYCHOTIC FEATURES. Delusions or hallucinations whose content is entirely consistent with either a depressed or a manic mood. If the mood is depressed, the content of the delusions or hallucinations would involve themes of either personal inadequacy, guilt, disease, death, nihilism, or deserved punishment. If the mood is manic, the content of the delusions or hallucinations would involve themes of inflated worth, power, knowledge, or identity or special relationship to a deity or a famous person.

MOOD-INCONGRUENT PSYCHOTIC FEATURES. Delusions or hallucinations whose content is not consistent with either a depressed or a manic mood: in the case of depression, a delusion or hallucination whose content does not involve themes of either personal inadequacy, guilt, disease, death, nihilism, or deserved punishment; in the case of mania, a delusion or hallucination whose content does not involve themes of either inflated worth, power, knowledge, or identity or special relationship to a deity or a famous person. Examples of such symptoms are persecutory delusions, thought insertion, thought broadcasting, and delusions of being controlled whose content has no apparent relationship to any of the themes listed above. (**Note:** The catatonic symptoms of stupor, mutism, negativism, and posturing in Manic Episodes are also considered mood-incongruent psychotic features.)

NEOLOGISMS. New words invented by the subject, distortions of words, or standard words to which the subject has given new, highly idiosyncratic meaning. The judgment that the subject uses neologisms should be made cautiously and take into account his or her educational and cultural background. Examples: "I was accused of midigation" (meaning the subject was accused of breaking the law). "They had an insinuating machine next door" (person explaining how her neighbors were bothering her).

Neologisms may be observed in Schizophrenia and other psychotic disorders.

OBSESSIONS. Recurrent, persistent, senseless ideas, thoughts, images, or impulses that are ego-dystonic, that is, they are not experienced as voluntarily produced, but rather as ideas that invade consciousness.

Obsessions are characteristic of Obsessive Compulsive Disorder, and may also be seen in Schizophrenia.

ORIENTATION. Awareness of where one is in relation to time, place, and person.

OVERVALUED IDEA. An unreasonable and sustained belief or idea that is maintained with less than delusional intensity. It differs from an obsessional thought in that the person holding the overvalued idea does not recognize its absurdity and thus does not struggle against it. As with a delusion, the idea or belief is not one that is ordinarily accepted by other members of the person's culture or subculture.

Example: A patient with a longstanding hand-washing compulsion thought there might be danger in shaking hands with people, because they might have recently been inoculated against smallpox and be infectious. Although she acknowledged that the danger might not be real, she could not accept reassurances that, medically, there was no danger.

PANIC ATTACKS. Discrete periods of sudden onset of intense apprehension, fearfulness, or terror, often associated with feelings of impending doom. During the attacks there are such symptoms as dyspnea, palpitations, chest pain or discomfort, choking or smothering sensations, and fear of going crazy or losing control.

Panic attacks are characteristic of Panic Disorder, but may also occur in Somatization Disorder, Major Depression, and Schizophrenia.

PARANOID IDEATION. Ideation, of less than delusional proportions, involving suspiciousness or the belief that one is being harassed, persecuted, or unfairly treated. In some instances the term is used when the clinician is unsure of whether the disturbances are actually delusional. Ideas of reference often involve paranoid ideation.

PERSEVERATION. Persistent repetition of words, ideas, or subjects so that, once a person begins speaking about a particular subject or uses a particular word, it continually recurs. Perseveration differs from the repetitive use of "stock words" or interjections such as "you know" or "like."

Examples: "I think I'll put on my hat, my hat, my hat, my hat." Interviewer: "Tell me what you are like, what kind of person you are." Subject: I'm from Marshalltown, Iowa. That's 60 miles northwest, northeast of Des Moines, Iowa. And I'm married at the present time. I'm 36 years old. My wife is 35. She lives in Garwin, Iowa. That's 15 miles southeast of Marshalltown, Iowa. I'm getting a divorce at the present time. And I am at present in a mental institution in Iowa City, Iowa, which is 100 miles southeast of Marshalltown, Iowa."

Perseveration is most commonly seen in Organic Mental Disorders, Schizophrenia, and other psychotic disorders.

PERSONALITY. Deeply ingrained patterns of behavior, which include the way one relates to, perceives, and thinks about the environment and oneself. Personality *traits* are prominent aspects of personality, and do not imply pathology. Personality *disorder* implies inflexible and maladaptive patterns of sufficient severity to cause either significant impairment in adaptive functioning or subjective distress.

PHOBIA. A persistent, irrational fear of a specific object, activity, or situation that results in a compelling desire to avoid the dreaded object, activity, or situation (the phobic stimulus). More commonly, the person does actually avoid the feared situation or object, though he or she recognizes that the fear is unreasonable and unwarranted by the actual dangerousness of the object, activity, or situation. Some people with a phobia claim that their avoidance is rational because they anticipate overwhelming anxiety or some other strong emotion that is out of their control; they do not claim, however, that their anxiety is rationally justified.

POVERTY OF CONTENT OF SPEECH. Speech that is adequate in amount but conveys little information because of vagueness, empty repetitions, or use of stereotyped or obscure phrases. The interviewer may observe that the person has spoken at some length, but has not given adequate information to answer a question. Alternatively, the person may provide enough information to answer the question, but require many words to do so, so that his or her lengthy reply can be summarized in a sentence or two. The expression *poverty of content of speech* is generally not used when the speech is, for the most part, not understandable (incoherence).

Example: Interviewer: "O.K. Why is it, do you think, that people believe in God?" Patient: "Well, first of all because, He is the person that, is their personal savior. He walks with me and talks with me. And uh, the understanding that I have, a lot of peoples, they don't really know their own personal self. Because they ain't, they all, just don't know their own personal self. They don't, know that He uh, seemed like to me, a lot of em don't understand that He walks and talks with them. And uh, show 'em their way to go. I understand also that, every man and every lady, is just not pointed in the same direction. Some are pointed different. They go in their different ways. The way that Jesus Christ wanted 'em to go. Myself, I am pointed in the ways of uh, knowing right from wrong, and doing it. I can't do any more, or not less than that."

POVERTY OF SPEECH. Restriction in the amount of speech, so that spontaneous speech and replies to questions are brief and unelaborated. When the condition is severe, replies may be monosyllabic, and some questions may be unanswered.

Poverty of speech occurs frequently in Schizophrenia, Major Depressive Episodes, and Organic Mental Disorders, such as Dementia.

PRESSURE OF SPEECH. Speech that is increased in amount, accelerated, and difficult or impossible to interrupt. Usually it is also loud and emphatic. Frequently the person talks without any social stimulation, and may continue to talk even though no one is listening.

Pressure of speech is most often seen in manic episodes, but may also occur in some cases of Organic Mental Disorders, Major Depression with psychomotor agitation, Schizophrenia, other psychotic disorders, and, occasionally, acute reactions to stress.

PRODROMAL. Early signs or symptoms of a disorder.

PSEUDODEMENTIA. Clinical features resembling a Dementia that are not due to organic brain dysfunction or disease. Pseudodementia may occur in a Major Depressive Episode or may be seen in Factitious Disorder with Psychological Symptoms.

PSYCHOMOTOR AGITATION. Excessive motor activity associated with a feeling of inner tension; the activity is usually nonproductive and repetitive. When the agitation is severe, it may be accompanied by shouting or loud complaining. The term should be used in a technical sense to refer only to states of tension or restlessness that are accompanied by observable excessive motor activity. Examples: Inability to sit still, pacing, wringing of hands, pulling at clothes.

PSYCHOMOTOR RETARDATION. Visible generalized slowing down of physical reactions, movements, and speech.

PSYCHOTIC. Gross impairment in reality testing and the creation of a new reality. The term may be used to describe a person at a given time, or a mental disorder in which at some time during its course all people with the disorder are psychotic. When a person is psychotic, he or she incorrectly evaluates the accuracy of his or her perceptions and thoughts and makes incorrect inferences about external reality, even in the face of contrary evidence. The term *psychotic* does not apply to minor distortions of reality that involve matters of relative judgment. For example, a depressed person who underestimates his achievements would not be described as psychotic, whereas one who believes he has caused a natural catastrophe would be so described.

Direct evidence of psychotic behavior is the presence of either delusions or hallucinations (without insight into their pathological nature). The term *psychotic* is sometimes appropriate when a person's behavior is so grossly disorganized that a reasonable inference can be made that reality testing is markedly disturbed. Examples include markedly incoherent speech without apparent awareness by the person that the speech is not understandable, and the agitated, inattentive, and disoriented behavior seen in Alcohol Withdrawal Delirium.

In DSM-III-R the psychotic disorders include Schizophrenia, Delusional Disorders, Psychotic Disorders Not Elsewhere Classified, some Organic Mental Disorders, and some Mood Disorders.

RESIDUAL. The phase of an illness that occurs after remission of the florid symptoms or the full syndrome. Examples: The residual states of Autistic Disorder, Attention-deficit Hyperactivity Disorder, and Schizophrenia.

SIGN. An objective manifestation of a pathological condition. Signs are observed by the examiner rather than reported by the individual.

SYMPTOM. A manifestation of a pathological condition. Although in some uses of the term it is limited to subjective complaints, in common use "symptom" includes objective signs of pathological conditions as well.

SYNDROME. A group of symptoms that occur together and that constitute a recognizable condition. "Syndrome" is less specific than "disorder" or "disease." The term *disease* generally implies a specific etiology or pathophysiologic process. In DSM-III-R most of the disorders are, in fact, syndromes.

ANNOTATED COMPARATIVE LISTING OF DSM–III AND DSM–III–R

APPENDIX D: Annotated Comparative Listing of DSM-III and DSM-III-R[1]

The DSM–III categories are listed in the order in which they appear in DSM–III. The corresponding DSM–III–R categories are listed opposite their DSM–III equivalents, and not necessarily in the order in which they appear in DSM–III–R.

When an entry in the following table has no discussion, it indicates that the category is essentially the same in DSM–III as in DSM–III–R except, in some cases, for minor editorial clarifications or the elimination of exclusion criteria.

Conventions

In DSM–III a series of non-ICD-9-CM codes (327.xx) was used to differentiate those DSM–III categories that shared the same ICD-9-CM code. Since the 327 series was rarely used, in DSM–III–R the 327 codes are not used and instead, those categories that share ICD-9-CM codes are marked with a * in the classification.

In DSM–III–R the term ''specify'' following the name of some diagnostic categories indicates qualifying terms that clinicians may wish to add in parentheses after the name of the disorder. In addition, current severity of a disorder may be specified as either: mild, moderate, severe, in partial remission (or residual state), or in complete remission. For some categories, specific criteria are provided for levels of severity.

DSM–III	DSM–III–R
MULTIAXIAL SYSTEM	**MULTIAXIAL SYSTEM**
Axis I: **Clinical Syndromes and V Codes**	Axis I: **Clinical Syndromes and V Codes**
Axis II: **Specific Developmental and Personality Disorders**	Axis II: **Developmental Disorders and Personality Disorders**

---

[1]Prepared by Robert L. Spitzer, M.D., and Janet B.W. Williams, D.S.W.

The lack of a conceptual basis for the Axis I–Axis II distinction in the DSM–III multiaxial system has been noted. In DSM–III–R the distinction has been clarified by adding Mental Retardation, Specific Developmental Disorders and Pervasive Developmental Disorders to Axis II, under the rubric of Developmental Disorders. The Axis II disorders now all share the features of generally having an onset in childhood or adolescence and usually persisting in a stable form (without periods of remission or exacerbation) into adult life. With only a few exceptions, these features are not present for the Axis I disorders.

Axis III: Physical Disorders and Conditions

Axis III: Physical Disorders and Conditions

Axis IV: Severity of Psychosocial Stressors

Axis IV: Severity of Psychosocial Stressors

An important distinction missing in DSM–III's rating of the severity of psychosocial stressors is the distinction between acute events and enduring circumstances. In DSM–III–R it is recommended that clinicians note the stressor(s) as predominantly one or the other (in addition to coding severity). The "minimal" level in the Severity of Psychosocial Stressors Scale has been eliminated, since such a low level of stress cannot be distinguished from baseline normal stress.

Axis V: Highest Level of Adaptive Functioning Past Year

Axis V: Highest Level of Adaptive Functioning

The Axis V rating in DSM–III required the clinician to consider only social and occupational functioning without consideration of psychological functioning. Studies have shown that clinical ratings of overall severity of disturbance are reliable and related to treatment utilization. In DSM–III–R, Axis V is a new scale that assesses psychological, social and occupational functioning on a hypothetical continuum of mental health-illness. The scale is a modification of the Global Assessment Scale and the Children's Global Assessment Scale.

In order to increase the value of Axis V for documenting current need for treatment and assessing prognosis, in DSM–III–R ratings are made for both current functioning (at the time of evaluation) and highest level of functioning (for at least a few months) during the past year.

DISORDERS USUALLY FIRST EVIDENT IN INFANCY, CHILDHOOD, OR ADOLESCENCE

DISORDERS USUALLY FIRST EVIDENT IN INFANCY, CHILDHOOD, OR ADOLESCENCE

Mental retardation

Mental retardation

In DSM–III–R Mental Retardation has been grouped together with Specific and Pervasive Developmental Disorders under the new rubric of Developmental Disorders, all of which are coded on Axis II.

Attention deficit disorder with hyperactivity

Attention-deficit hyperactivity disorder

In DSM–III–R the criteria comprise an index of symptoms so that no single feature is required. The items were selected to better discriminate the disorder from Conduct and Oppositional Defiant Disorder. The index of symptoms and the threshold for diagnosis are based on the results of a field trial of several hundred children. In DSM–III–R Attention-deficit Hyperactivity Disorder is grouped with Conduct Disorder and Oppositional Defiant Disorder under the rubric of Disruptive Behavior Disorders.

| **Attention deficit disorder without hyperactivity** | **Undifferentiated attention-deficit disorder** |

In DSM–III Attention Deficit Disorder included two subtypes: With Hyperactivity and Without Hyperactivity. In a field trial of several hundred children of the DSM–III–R criteria for Attention-deficit Hyperactivity Disorder, Oppositional Defiant Disorder and Conduct Disorder, a clinical diagnosis of the DSM–III category of Attention Deficit Disorder Without Hyperactivity was hardly ever made. This suggests that with the revised and more inclusive criteria for Attention-deficit Hyperactivity Disorder there may be little need for this category. Furthermore, studies have indicated that it is unlikely that the DSM–III categories of Attention Deficit Disorder With and Without Hyperactivity are subtypes of a single disorder. Therefore, in DSM–III–R, Attention-deficit Hyperactivity Disorder (ADHD) now largely corresponds to the DSM–III category of Attention Deficit Disorder with Hyperactivity. Disturbances involving attentional difficulties that are not symptoms of another disorder, such as Mental Retardation or ADHD can be diagnosed in DSM–III–R as Undifferentiated Attention-deficit Disorder. Future research is necessary to indicate whether Undifferentiated Attention-deficit Disorder represents a valid diagnostic category, and if so, how it should be defined.

| **Attention deficit disorder residual type** | **Attention-deficit hyperactivity disorder (residual state)** |

Follow-up studies have indicated that hyperactivity sometimes persists into adulthood, thus indicating that the DSM–III requirement that "signs of hyperactivity are no longer present" is incorrect. With the general convention of specifying "residual state," there is no need for a separate code for the residual form of this disorder.

Conduct disorder
    undersocialized, aggressive
    undersocialized, nonaggressive
    socialized, aggressive
    socialized, nonaggressive
    atypical

Conduct disorder
    isolated aggressive type

    group type
    undifferentiated type

The DSM–III subtyping was judged to lack clinical utility and to be at variance with research findings. The new subtyping attempts to reflect the major distinction that has appeared in the research literature: aggressive antisocial behavior that is not conducted in a group setting (Solitary Aggressive Type) and antisocial behavior that is conducted in a group setting with other children to whom the person feels loyal (Group Type). The Undifferentiated Type acknowledges that the disturbance of many children with the disorder cannot be classified in either of the two specific types.

The revised criteria comprise a single index of symptoms selected to better describe the various manifestations of the disorder and to better identify young children with the disorder. The index of symptoms and the threshold for diagnosis are based on the results of a field trial of several hundred children. In DSM–III–R Conduct Disorder is grouped with Attention-deficit Hyperactivity Disorder and Oppositional Defiant Disorder under the rubric of Disruptive Behavior Disorders.

Anxiety Disorders of Childhood or Adolescence

Anxiety Disorders of Childhood or Adolescence

Separation anxiety disorder

Separation anxiety disorder

Several of the criteria have been revised to raise the threshold for diagnosis.

Avoidant disorder of childhood or adolescence

Avoidant disorder of childhood or adolescence

Overanxious disorder

Overanxious disorder

Other Disorders of Infancy, Childhood or Adolescence

Reactive attachment disorder of infancy

Reactive attachment disorder of infancy or early childhood

The criteria have been extensively revised so as to include older children as well as a broader range of types of grossly inadequate care, such as psychological and physical abuse or neglect.

Schizoid disorder of childhood or adolescence

This category has been eliminated since in clinical settings a defect in the capacity to form social relationships has been observed only in the presence of other signs of psychopathology that suggest a Pervasive Developmental Disorder.

Elective mutism

Elective mutism

Oppositional disorder

Oppositional defiant disorder

The revised criteria comprise a single index of symptoms selected to better describe the various manifestations of the disorder and to better distinguish it from Conduct Disorder. The index of symptoms and the threshold for diagnosis are based on the results of a field trial of several hundred children. In DSM–III–R Oppositional Defiant Disorder (a more descriptive name than the DSM–III name) is grouped with Conduct Disorder and Attention-deficit Hyperactivity Disorder under the rubric of Disruptive Behavior Disorders.

Identity disorder

Identity disorder

Eating Disorders

Eating Disorders

Anorexia nervosa

Anorexia nervosa

The weight loss criterion of at least 25% of original body weight has been found to be too restrictive. Therefore, this criterion has been revised. In addition, in females, a criterion has been added requiring the absence of at least three consecutive menstrual cycles.

Bulimia   **Bulimia nervosa**

The DSM–III–R name is the accepted term among researchers in this area and has the advantage of reflecting the strong relationship of the disorder to Anorexia Nervosa. The revised criteria specify a minimum frequency of binge eating episodes and have eliminated the requirement of depressed mood and self-deprecating thoughts following eating binges, which in DSM–III–R are regarded as common associated features.

Pica   **Pica**
Rumination disorder of infancy   **Rumination disorder of infancy**
Atypical eating disorder   **Eating disorder NOS**

Stereotyped Movement Disorders   **Tic Disorders**

In DSM–III–R the three specific tic disorders are grouped together under the rubric of Tic Disorders, separately from Stereotypy/Habit Disorder. The criteria for each of the Tic Disorders have been extensively revised to reflect recent clinical and research experience that indicates that these conditions reflect varying manifestations of a single underlying disorder.

Transient tic disorder   **Transient tic disorder**
                                               Specify: single episode
                                               recurrent

Chronic motor tic disorder   **Chronic motor or vocal tic disorder**
Tourette's disorder   **Tourette's disorder**
Atypical tic disorder   **Tic disorder NOS**

Atypical stereotyped movement   **Stereotypy/habit disorder**
disorder

This specific category has been added for stereotyped movements, such as head-banging and body-rocking, that are not a symptom of some more pervasive disorder, such as Autistic Disorder.

Other Disorders with Physical
Manifestations

Stuttering   **Stuttering**

In DSM–III–R Stuttering is classified with Cluttering under the rubric of Speech Disorders Not Elsewhere Classified

Functional enuresis   **Functional enuresis**
Functional encopresis   **Functional encopresis**

In DSM–III–R these two disorders are now classified under the rubric of Elimination Disorders.

Sleepwalking disorder **Sleep terror disorder**	**Sleepwalking disorder** **Sleep terror disorder**

In DSM–III–R these two disorders are now classified under the rubric of Sleep Disorders.

Pervasive Developmental Disorders   **Pervasive Developmental Disorders**

Infantile autism ————————┐
                                                           ├———— **Autistic disorder**
Childhood onset pervasive
developmental disorder ————┘

Atypical pervasive developmental   **Pervasive developmental disorder NOS**
disorder

In DSM–III–R, Pervasive Developmental Disorders are grouped together with Mental Retardation and Specific Developmental Disorders under the new rubric of Developmental Disorders. The distinction between the two specific DSM–III categories of Infantile Autism and Childhood Onset Pervasive Developmental Disorder, on the basis of age at onset, was judged to be not valid. Therefore, these two categories have been combined into the single category in DSM–III–R of Autistic Disorder. The criteria have been revised extensively to constitute a richer clinical description of the manifestations of the disorder at different ages.

Specific Developmental Disorders   **Specific Developmental Disorders**

In DSM–III–R, Specific Developmental Disorders are grouped together with Mental Retardation and Pervasive Developmental Disorders under the new rubric of Developmental Disorders. Developmental Language Disorder has been split into Developmental Expressive Language Disorder and Developmental Receptive Language Disorder, a distinction recognized in the DSM–III text.

Developmental reading disorder **Developmental arithmetic disorder**	**Developmental reading disorder** **Developmental arithmetic disorder** **Developmental expressive writing** **disorder**

Expressive writing disorder has been added to DSM–III–R to identify a developmental disturbance in which writing skills are markedly below the expected level, given the person's schooling and intellectual capacity.

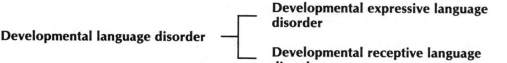

| Developmental language disorder | Developmental expressive language disorder |
| | Developmental receptive language disorder |

| Developmental articulation disorder | Developmental articulation disorder |

Mixed specific developmental disorder

| | Developmental coordination disorder |
| | Cluttering |

These two Specific Developmental Disorders have been added to the DSM–III–R.

| **Atypical specific developmental disorder** | **Specific developmental disorder NOS** |
| | **Developmental disorder NOS** |

Developmental Disorder NOS is a new DSM–III–R category for Developmental Disorders that cannot be classified according to any of the specific DSM–III–R categories.

ORGANIC MENTAL DISORDERS

ORGANIC MENTAL DISORDERS

Dementias Arising in the Senium and Presenium

Dementias Arising in the Senium and Presenium

Substance-Induced Organic Mental Disorders

Psychoactive Substance-Induced Organic Mental Disorders

In DSM–III–R there is a new category of Posthallucinogen Perception Disorder, for diagnosing recurrent "flashbacks" following ingestion of a hallucinogen.

Alcohol
    intoxication
    idiosyncratic intoxication
    withdrawal
    withdrawal delirium
    hallucinosis
    amnestic disorder
    Dementia associated with
      alcoholism

Alcohol
    intoxication
    idiosyncratic intoxication
    Uncomplicated alcohol withdrawal
    withdrawal delirium
    hallucinosis
    amnestic disorder
    Dementia associated with
      alcoholism

Barbiturate or similarly acting sedative or hypnotic
    intoxication
    withdrawal
    withdrawal delirium
    amnestic disorder

Sedative, hypnotic, or anxiolytic

    intoxication
    Uncomplicated withdrawal
    withdrawal delirium
    amnestic disorder

The new name for this group of substances is more accurate.

Opioid
    intoxication
    withdrawal
	Opioid
	    intoxication
	    withdrawal

Cocaine
    intoxication
	Cocaine
	    intoxication
	    withdrawal
	    delirium
	    delusional disorder

Amphetamine or similarly acting
sympathomimetic
    intoxication
 	
    delirium
	Amphetamine or similarly acting
	sympathomimetic
	    intoxication
	    withdrawal
	    delirium
	    delusional disorder

Phencylidine (PCP) or similarly acting
arylcyclohexylamine
    intoxication
    delirium
 	
    mixed organic mental disorder
	Phencyclidine (PCP) or similarly acting
	arylcyclohexylamine
	    intoxication
	    delirium
	    delusional disorder
	    mood disorder
	    organic mental disorder NOS

Hallucinogen
    hallucinosis
 	
    delusional disorder
    affective disorder
	Hallucinogen
	    hallucinosis
	    delirium
	    delusional disorder
	    mood disorder
	    Posthallucinogen perception
	        disorder

Cannabis
    intoxication
    delusional disorder
	Cannabis
	    intoxication
	    delusional disorder

Tobacco
    withdrawal
	Nicotine
	    withdrawal

Caffeine
    intoxication
	Caffeine
	    intoxication

	Inhalant intoxication

Other or unspecified substance

> **intoxication**
> **withdrawal**
> **delirium**
> **dementia**
> **amnestic disorder**
> **delusional disorder**
> **hallucinosis**
> **affective disorder**
>
> **personality disorder**
> **atypical or mixed organic mental**
>   **disorder**

Other drug or unspecified
psychoactive substance
> **intoxication**
> **withdrawal**
> **delirium**
> **dementia**
> **amnestic disorder**
> **delusional disorder**
> **hallucinosis**
> **mood disorder**
> **anxiety disorder**
> **personality disorder**
> **organic mental disorder NOS**

Section 2. Organic brain syndromes
whose etiology or pathophysiologic
process is either noted as an additional
diagnosis from outside the mental
disorders section of ICD-9-CM or is
unknown.

Organic mental disorders associated
with Axis III physical disorders or
conditions, or whose etiology is
unknown.

Delirium
Dementia
Amnestic syndrome
Organic delusional syndrome
Organic hallucinosis
Organic affective syndrome

Delirium
Dementia
Amnestic disorder
Organic delusional disorder
Organic hallucinosis
Organic mood disorder
> **Specify: manic**
>   **depressed**
>   **mixed**
Organic anxiety disorder

Anxiety syndromes caused by physical disorders were recognized in the DSM–III text but are included as a specific category in DSM–III–R.

Organic personality disorder

Organic personality disorder
> **Specify if explosive type**

Atypical or mixed organic brain
disorder

Organic mental disorder NOS

SUBSTANCE USE DISORDERS

PSYCHOACTIVE SUBSTANCE USE DISORDERS

There are many problems with the DSM–III distinction between substance abuse and dependence: problems using social and occupational consequences to define abuse, inadequacy of tolerance or withdrawal as a required criterion for dependence, and inconsistencies in the relationship of abuse to dependence for various substances. In DSM–III–R the definition of dependence is broadened to define a syndrome of clinically significant behaviors, cognitions, and other symptoms that indicate loss of control of substance use and continued use of the substance despite adverse consequences. Most cases of DSM–III abuse will be subsumed under the DSM–III–R category of dependence. The DSM–III–R category of abuse is a residual category for cases in which the disturbance does not meet the criteria for dependence, yet there is a maladaptive pattern of use.

In DSM–III–R the same general criteria for dependence, index of symptoms, and criteria for abuse are used for all of the categories of psychoactive substances.

Alcohol abuse	**Alcohol abuse**
Alcohol dependence	**Alcohol dependence**
Barbiturate or similarly acting sedative or hypnotic abuse	**Sedative, hypnotic, or anxiolytic abuse**
Barbiturate or similarly acting sedative or hypnotic dependence	**Sedative, hypnotic, or anxiolytic dependence**
Opioid abuse	**Opioid abuse**
Opioid dependence	**Opioid dependence**
Cocaine abuse	**Cocaine abuse**
	Cocaine dependence
Amphetamine or similarly acting sympathomimetic abuse	**Amphetamine or similarly acting sympathomimetic abuse**
Amphetamine or similarly acting sympathomimetic dependence	**Amphetamine or similarly acting sympathomimetic dependence**
Phencyclidine (PCP) or similarly acting arylcyclohexylamine abuse	**Phencyclidine (PCP) or similarly acting arylcyclohexylamine abuse**
Phencyclidine (PCP) or similarly acting arylcyclohexylamine dependence	**Phencyclidine (PCP) or similarly acting arylcyclohexylamine dependence**
Hallucinogen abuse	**Hallucinogen abuse**
	Hallucinogen dependence
Cannabis abuse	**Cannabis abuse**
Cannabis dependence	**Cannabis dependence**

Tobacco dependence

Nicotine dependence

Inhalant abuse

Inhalant dependence

Inhalant Abuse and Dependence have been added for psychoactive substances such as paint thinner and glue.

Other, mixed or unspecified substance abuse

Psychoactive substance abuse NOS

Other specified substance dependence ─┐

Unspecified substance dependence ──┘
─ Psychoactive substance dependence NOS

Dependence on combination of opioid and other nonalcoholic substance

Dependence on combination of substances, excluding opioids and alcohol

Polysubstance dependence

SCHIZOPHRENIC DISORDERS

SCHIZOPHRENIA

The A criterion has been reorganized to make it simpler, and slightly modified to take into account changes in the criteria for Delusional (Paranoid) Disorders. Furthermore, to exclude transient psychotic disturbances, the symptoms in A must be present for at least one week (unless the symptoms are successfully treated). The B criterion has been revised to take into account onset in childhood and to avoid the term "deterioration," which suggests that recovery never occurs. The requirement that the illness begin before age 45 has been eliminated since several studies have not supported the validity of this DSM–III criterion. However, to facilitate further study of this issue, a specification is provided for cases with late onset (after 45).

Schizophrenia

Schizophrenia

disorganized
catatonic
paranoid

disorganized
catatonic
paranoid
    Specify if stable type

The criteria for Paranoid Type were revised to increase their predictive validity. In DSM–III–R there is recognition of a Stable Type in which all exacerbations meet the criteria for Paranoid Type.

undifferentiated
residual

undifferentiated
residual
    Specify if late onset

PARANOID DISORDERS	**DELUSIONAL (PARANOID) DISORDER**

DSM–III required either persecutory delusions or delusions of jealousy in making a diagnosis of a Paranoid Disorder. In DSM–III–R the disorder is defined more broadly in terms of delusional themes, but more narrowly in the requirement of a duration of at least one month, both in accordance with traditional concepts of the disorder. Because the ordinary English meaning of the term "paranoid" suggests only suspiciousness, the more nosologically descriptive term "Delusional Disorder" is used for this category.

Paranoia	**Delusional (paranoid) disorder** Specify type: erotomanic grandiose jealous persecutory somatic unspecified

Shared paranoid disorder	**Induced psychotic disorder**

This disorder may involve delusions without a paranoid content, hence the change in terminology. In addition, the term "induced" more accurately describes the essence of the disorder.

Acute paranoid disorder

In DSM–III–R such cases are subsumed under Psychotic Disorders Not Elsewhere Classified.

Atypical paranoid disorder

PSYCHOTIC DISORDERS NOT ELSEWHERE CLASSIFIED	**PSYCHOTIC DISORDERS NOT ELSEWHERE CLASSIFIED**

Schizophreniform disorder	**Schizophreniform disorder** Specify: without good prognostic features or with good prognostic features

The criteria have been revised so that there is no longer a minimal duration. In DSM–III–R it is now possible to note cases with features that are generally associated with good prognosis. Such cases are particularly unlikely to go on to meet the criteria for Schizophrenia.

Schizoaffective disorder	**Schizoaffective disorder** Specify: bipolar type depressive type

In DSM–III–R this category now has specified diagnostic criteria.

Brief reactive psychosis   **Brief reactive psychosis**

In DSM–III–R there is acknowledgment that the stressors may be cumulative and the episode may last as long as one month. Furthermore, the criteria have been clarified to exclude culturally-sanctioned reactions.

Atypical psychosis   **Psychotic disorder NOS (Atypical psychosis)**

AFFECTIVE DISORDERS   ## MOOD DISORDERS

The more descriptive term, "Mood Disorders," has been adopted. The classification has been reorganized so that the Bipolar Disorders (Bipolar Disorder and Cyclothymia) and the Depressive Disorders (Major Depression and Dysthymia) are each grouped together.

Major Affective Disorders

Bipolar disorder   **Bipolar disorder**

    mixed   mixed
    manic   manic
    depressed   depressed

    Specify if seasonal pattern

The threshold for the diagnosis of a Manic Episode has been raised by requiring marked impairment in social or occupational functioning, or the need for hospitalization.

Major depression   **Major depression**

    single episode   single episode
    recurrent episode   recurrent

    Specify if chronic
    Specify if melancholic type
    Specify if seasonal pattern

Criteria A and B have been combined into a single index for simplification and to avoid the redundancy of listing loss of interest or pleasure twice.

Severity levels for Manic and Major Depressive Episodes are now coded in the fifth digit.

The criteria for melancholia have been revised in an effort to increase the validity of this distinction. The criteria are now in the form of an index of symptoms, no one of which is required. Several non-symptom features are included in the revised criteria, such as no significant personality disturbance prior to first Major Depressive Episode and prior good response to specific and adequate somatic antidepressant therapy.

The chronic specification is used when the syndrome has persisted, either in partial remission or at criterion level, for over two years.

The seasonal pattern is used when there has been a regular temporal relationship between a Mood Disorder and a particular 60 day period of the year, such as regularly becoming depressed between the beginning of October and the end of November.

Other Specific Affective Disorders

Cyclothymic disorder   **Cyclothymia**

The criteria have been simplified.

Dysthymic disorder   **Dysthymia**
                                                  Specify primary or secondary
                                                  Specify early or late onset

The criteria have been revised to exclude cases that first begin following a Major Depressive Episode. The primary/secondary specification distinguishes cases of Dysthymia that have developed either before (or in the absence of) another chronic Axis I disorder. The age at onset is specified because of evidence suggesting that early onset characterizes a more homogeneous group.

Atypical bipolar disorder   **Bipolar disorder NOS**
                                                  Specify if seasonal pattern

The concept of "Bipolar II" is now defined in an example of Bipolar Disorder NOS.

Atypical depression   **Depressive disorder NOS**
                                                  Specify if seasonal pattern

ANXIETY DISORDERS   ## ANXIETY DISORDERS

The general DSM–III hierarchic rule that an Anxiety Disorder is preempted by a diagnosis of another mental disorder, such as Major Depression or Schizophrenia, has been eliminated, consistent with the results of several studies.

Phobic Disorders

Agoraphobia with panic attacks   **Panic disorder with agoraphobia**

In the great majority of cases of "agoraphobia" that are seen in clinical settings, the phobic symptoms are a complication of Panic Disorder. This important observation of the typical course of the disorder is reflected in the DSM–III–R classification in which different degrees of phobic avoidance are classified as subtypes of Panic Disorder. The apparently rare cases of agoraphobia that are seen clinically and that do not develop secondary to Panic Disorder are diagnosed as Agoraphobia Without History of Panic Disorder.

Agoraphobia without panic attacks	**Agoraphobia without history of panic disorder** **Specify with or without limited symptom attacks**

DSM–III–R recognizes the concept of a limited symptom attack, i.e., an attack of anxiety that does not meet the symptomatic criteria for a panic attack. This specification distinguishes cases that are associated with sub-panic attacks of anxiety (which may represent mild forms of Panic Disorder), and cases without attacks.

Social phobia	**Social phobia** **Specify if generalized type**

This specification identifies cases in which the phobic situation is most social situations and in which an associated diagnosis of Avoidant Personality Disorder should also be considered.

Simple phobia	**Simple phobia**
Panic disorder	**Panic disorder without agoraphobia**
Generalized anxiety disorder	**Generalized anxiety disorder**

The duration has been extended from one month to six months in order to exclude transient anxiety reactions. The symptom list has been expanded to provide a richer description of the disorder.

Obsessive compulsive disorder	**Obsessive compulsive disorder**

Post-traumatic stress disorder
    acute
    chronic or delayed
	Post-traumatic stress disorder
	    Specify if delayed onset

The nature of the stressor has been clarified, the category of numbing symptoms has been expanded to include symptoms of avoidance and amnesia, and the miscellaneous symptoms category has been replaced with a category of physiologic arousal symptoms. Examples of symptoms specific to children have been included.

Atypical anxiety disorder	**Anxiety disorder NOS**
SOMATOFORM DISORDERS	**SOMATOFORM DISORDERS**
Somatization disorder	**Somatization disorder**

The symptom list was revised so that the number of symptoms required for the disorder is the same for males and females. Seven of the symptoms are highlighted to serve as a screening list since the presence of any two of them suggests a high likelihood of the disorder.

Conversion disorder	**Conversion disorder** Specify: single episode recurrent

Culturally sanctioned response patterns have been excluded. The criterion excluding a diagnosis of Somatization Disorder or Schizophrenia has been eliminated.

Psychogenic pain disorder	**Somatoform pain disorder**

The new term and revised criteria acknowledge that the disorder frequently appears in the absence of clear evidence of the etiologic role of psychological factors.

Hypochondriasis	**Hypochondriasis**

A required duration of six months has been added to exclude transient reactions.

Body dysmorphic disorder

In DSM–III Dysmorphophobia is an example of an Atypical Somatoform Disorder. This often-described condition, which is not a true "phobia," is renamed and included in DSM–III–R as a specific category.

Undifferentiated somatoform disorder

This category recognizes that whereas cases meeting the full criteria for Somatization Disorder are relatively rare, there are many more cases of chronic multiple physical complaints that are apparently of psychological origin and do not meet the criteria for any other Somatoform Disorder.

Atypical somatoform disorder	**Somatoform disorder NOS**
DISSOCIATIVE DISORDERS	**DISSOCIATIVE DISORDERS**
Psychogenic fugue **Psychogenic amnesia** **Multiple personality** **Depersonalization disorder**	**Psychogenic fugue** **Psychogenic amnesia** **Multiple personality disorder** **Depersonalization disorder**
Atypical dissociative disorder	**Dissociative disorder NOS**
PSYCHOSEXUAL DISORDERS	**SEXUAL DISORDERS**
Gender Identity disorders	**Gender Identity Disorders**

Because the symptoms of Gender Identity Disorders almost always begin in childhood, in DSM–III–R this subclass is in Disorders Usually First Evident in Infancy, Childhood, or Adolescence.

Transsexualism	**Transsexualism**

**Gender identity disorder of
adolescence or adulthood,
nontranssexual type**

This category is for rare cases that would otherwise be classified as Transsexualism, but in which there is no preoccupation with getting rid of one's primary and secondary sex characteristics.

Gender identity disorder of childhood	**Gender identity disorder of childhood**
Atypical gender identity disorder	**Gender identity disorder NOS**

The Gender Identity Disorders are now in the childhood section, since these disorders invariably begin in childhood.

Paraphilias   **Paraphilias**

In DSM–III the Paraphilias were inconsistently defined in that for some, deviant acts were required, whereas for others, the behavior could be limited to fantasy. In DSM–III–R, a consistent set of criteria is used for all of the Paraphilias.

Fetishism	**Fetishism**
Transvestism	**Transvestic fetishism**
Pedophilia	**Pedophilia**
Exhibitionism	**Exhibitionism**
Voyeurism	**Voyeurism**
Sexual masochism	**Sexual masochism**
Sexual sadism	**Sexual sadism**

Zoophilia

Because Zoophilia is virtually never a clinically significant problem by itself, in DSM–III–R it is only included as an example of a Paraphilia NOS.

Frotteurism

This category is for cases in which there is a persistent association between intense sexual arousal and acts or fantasies of rubbing against a nonconsenting person.

Atypical paraphilia   **Paraphilia NOS**

Psychosexual Dysfunctions   **Sexual Dysfunctions**
                                                **Specify: psychogenic only
                                                                  psychogenic and biogenic
                                                Specify: lifelong or acquired
                                                Specify: generalized or situational**

The specifications make distinctions that have important treatment implications.

Inhibited sexual desire   **Hypoactive sexual desire disorder**

                                               Sexual aversion disorder

This category is for cases involving persistent or recurrent extreme aversion to, and avoidance of, all or almost all, genital sexual contact with a sexual partner.

Inhibited sexual excitement   **Female sexual arousal disorder**
                                               Male erectile disorder
Inhibited female orgasm   **Inhibited female orgasm**
Inhibited male orgasm   **Inhibited male orgasm**
Premature ejaculation   **Premature ejaculation**
Functional dyspareunia   **Dyspareunia**
Functional vaginismus   **Vaginismus**
Atypical psychosexual dysfunction   **Sexual dysfunction NOS**

Other Psychosexual Disorders   **Other Sexual Disorders**

Ego-dystonic homosexuality

This category has been eliminated for several reasons. It suggested to some that homosexuality itself was considered a disorder. In the United States almost all people who are homosexual first go through a phase in which their homosexuality is ego-dystonic. Furthermore, the diagnosis of Ego-dystonic Homosexuality has rarely been used clinically and there have been only a few articles in the scientific literature that use the concept. Finally, the treatment programs that attempt to help bisexual men become heterosexual have not used this diagnosis. In DSM–III–R, an example of Sexual Disorder NOS are cases that in DSM–III would have met the criteria for Ego-dystonic Homosexuality.

Psychosexual disorder not elsewhere classified   **Sexual disorder NOS**

APPENDIX E: The Diagnostic Classification of Sleep and Arousal Disorders of the Association of Sleep Disorders Centers and the Association for the Psychophysiological Study of Sleep   **Sleep Disorders**

The detailed classification of Sleep and Arousal Disorders that was included in an appendix of DSM–III relied heavily on data from sleep laboratory procedures and included as sleep disorders many disorders that are included in ICD-9-CM as physical disorders. DSM–III–R includes a much simpler classification of Sleep Disorders, and is compatible with the DSM–III–R multiaxial system.

FACTITIOUS DISORDERS

FACTITIOUS DISORDERS

The symptoms of Factitious Disorder are not truly "voluntary," hence the revised criteria more accurately refer to them as "intentionally produced or feigned."

Factitious disorder with psychological symptoms

Factitious disorder with psychological symptoms

Factitious disorder with physical symptoms

Factitious disorder with physical symptoms

Atypical factitious disorder with physical symptoms

Chronic factitious disorder NOS

IMPULSE CONTROL DISORDERS NOT ELSEWHERE CLASSIFIED

IMPULSE CONTROL DISORDERS NOT ELSEWHERE CLASSIFIED

Pathological gambling

Pathological gambling

The criteria have been revised to give a richer description of the disorder and to emphasize the similarity to the essential features of Psychoactive Substance Dependence.

Kleptomania

Kleptomania

Pyromania

Pyromania

Intermittent explosive disorder
Isolated explosive disorder

Intermittent explosive disorder

Intermittent Explosive Disorder has been retained in DSM–III–R although serious questions have been raised about its validity. Isolated Explosive Disorder has not been retained in DSM–III–R because of the high potential for misdiagnosis based on a single episode of aggressive behavior.

Trichotillomania

This well-recognized disorder involving the pulling out of hair fulfills the general criteria for an Impulse Control Disorder.

Atypical impulse control disorder

Impulse control disorder NOS

ADJUSTMENT DISORDER

ADJUSTMENT DISORDER

In DSM–III–R the maximal duration is six months to exclude cases whose chronicity is inconsistent with the construct of a transient reaction to psychosocial stress. The new DSM–III–R subtype, Adjustment Disorder with Physical Complaints, is necessary since the DSM–III–R criteria for nearly all of the Somatoform Disorders require a duration of at least six months.

with depressed mood	with depressed mood
with anxious mood	with anxious mood
with mixed emotional features	with mixed emotional features
with disturbance of conduct	with disturbance of conduct
with mixed disturbance of emotions and conduct	with mixed disturbance of emotions and conduct
with work (or academic) inhibition	with work (or academic) inhibition
with withdrawal	with withdrawal
	with physical complaints
with atypical features	NOS

PSYCHOLOGICAL FACTORS AFFECTING PHYSICAL CONDITION

Psychological factors affecting physical condition

PSYCHOLOGICAL FACTORS AFFECTING PHYSICAL CONDITION

Psychological factors affecting physical condition

PERSONALITY DISORDERS   **PERSONALITY DISORDERS**

The criteria for all of the DSM–III–R Personality Disorders are in the form of a one-sentence general description of the disorder followed by an index of specific behaviors, such that no single behavior is required for the diagnosis. The DSM–III–R criteria for most of the disorders involve more behavioral descriptors than in DSM–III. When the same concept appears in the diagnostic criteria of two disorders (e.g., social isolation in both Avoidant and Schizoid Personality Disorder), it is phrased identically. The DSM–III reference to the behaviors being characteristic of the person's current and long-term functioning is defined more specifically.

Paranoid   **Paranoid**

The DSM–III requirement of "restricted affectivity" has been eliminated and is now one of the features of Schizoid Personality Disorder.

Schizoid   **Schizoid**

The exclusion criterion of features of Schizotypal Personality Disorder has been eliminated so that in some cases, both diagnoses may be given. Since Schizoid Disorder of Childhood has been eliminated from DSM–III–R, this category can now be used with children.

Schizotypal   **Schizotypal**

Depersonalization and derealization have been eliminated as examples of unusual perceptual experiences, since these have not been commonly observed in people with the disorder in recent studies. A new item for odd, eccentric or peculiar behavior or appearance has been added, since such behaviors are commonly seen in people with the disorder.

Histrionic   **Histrionic**

The item referring to suicidal threats, gestures or attempts has been removed to provide better differentiation from Borderline Personality Disorder. An item describing characteristic style of speech has been added.

Narcissistic   **Narcissistic**

An item for preoccupation with feelings of envy has been added.

Antisocial   **Antisocial**

A frequent criticism of the DSM-III criteria for this disorder is the failure to include the concept of absence of guilt or remorse. An item to express this concept has been added.

Borderline   **Borderline**

Avoidant   **Avoidant**

The DSM-III concept of Avoidant Personality Disorder was essentially social withdrawal due to hypersensitivity to interpersonal rejection. It was distinguished from Schizoid Personality Disorder by the presence of a desire for affection and acceptance. The DSM-III-R concept of Avoidant Personality Disorder differs markedly in that it now corresponds to the clinical concept of "phobic character" and is no longer mutually exclusive with Schizoid Personality Disorder.

Dependent   **Dependent**

The item referring to lack of self-confidence has been eliminated since this feature has little diagnostic specificity.

Compulsive   **Obsessive compulsive**

DSM-III dropped the term "obsessive," to avoid confusion with Obsessive Compulsive Disorder. Since important features of the disorder are captured by the term "obsessive," the traditional terminology for the condition is used once again.

Passive-Aggressive   **Passive aggressive**

Doubts about the validity of this category were expressed in DSM-III by the requirement that the disorder could not be diagnosed if the criteria for any other Personality Disorder were met. This exclusion criterion has been eliminated.

Atypical, mixed or other personality   **Personality disorder NOS**
disorder

V CODES FOR CONDITIONS NOT ATTRIBUTABLE TO A MENTAL DISORDER THAT ARE A FOCUS OF ATTENTION OR TREATMENT

The only substantive change is that Borderline Intellectual Functioning is coded on Axis II (with other Developmental Disorders).

ADDITIONAL CODES

V CODES FOR CONDITIONS NOT ATTRIBUTABLE TO A MENTAL DISORDER THAT ARE A FOCUS OF ATTENTION OR TREATMENT

ADDITIONAL CODES

APPENDIX A: PROPOSED DIAGNOSTIC CATEGORIES NEEDING FURTHER STUDY

Late luteal phase dysphoric disorder

Late Luteal Phase Dysphoric Disorder is a narrowly defined version of what is often referred to as "Premenstrual Syndrome." A large body of research has demonstrated the clinical importance of the condition, that the predominant symptoms of the disorder are psychological and behavioral, and that the differential diagnosis primarily involves other mental disorders.

Self-defeating personality disorder

The concept of masochistic personality has a long clinical tradition and the category was included DSM-III as an example of Other Personality Disorder. Many clinicians believe that no other personality disorder is adequate to describe this particular pattern of personality disturbance in which the person is drawn to situations or relationships in which he or she will suffer; undermines pleasurable experiences; and prevents others from helping him or her. The name of the category has been changed to avoid the historical association of the term "masochistic" with psychoanalytic notions about female sexuality and the implication that the "masochist" derives unconscious pleasure from suffering. A field trial of the DSM-III-R criteria with several hundred clinicians indicated that the sensitivity and specificity of the criteria, using the clinician's diagnosis as the criterion, was equal to that obtained in studies of the diagnostic criteria for Schizotypal and Borderline Personality Disorders.

Sadistic personality disorder

Although systematic studies of this category are lacking, it was added to the appendix because of the need to evaluate the personality pattern of people (primarily men) who abuse spouses or children. The disorder is characterized by a pervasive pattern of cruel, demeaning, and aggressive behavior, not directed toward only one person, and not only for the purpose of sexual excitement (as in Sexual Sadism).

HISTORICAL REVIEW, ICD–9 GLOSSARY AND CLASSIFICATION, AND ICD–9–CM CLASSIFICATION

APPENDIX E:
Historical Review, ICD-9 Glossary and Classification, and ICD-9-CM Classification

HISTORICAL REVIEW[1]

This historical review covers the activities of the World Health Organization (WHO) in developing the classification of mental disorders (Section V) of the Ninth Revision of the International Classification of Diseases (ICD-9), and some of the major changes from ICD-8. In addition, the clinical modification of ICD-9 (ICD-9-CM) that was introduced in the United States, and the relationship between it and the DSM-III classification are discussed.

Purposes and Uses of the ICD

The ICD is a statistical classification not only of mental disorders but of diseases and other morbid conditions; complications of pregnancy, childbirth, and the puerperium; congenital abnormalities; causes of perinatal morbidity and mortality; accidents, poisonings, and violence; and symptoms, signs, and ill-defined conditions. Its principal use is in the classification of morbidity and mortality information for statistical purposes, as the unabridged title of the classification makes quite clear: *The International Statistical Classification of Diseases, Injuries, and Causes of Death.*

The ICD has also been adapted for use as a nomenclature of diseases for indexing medical records. The basic purpose of such indexing is to facilitate retrieval of medical records for a variety of purposes (for example, studies of management of patients with specific conditions; follow-up studies of patients with specific diseases who have undergone various operative and therapeutic procedures). Its limitations for these purposes led to the development of the ICD-9-CM in the United States—a subject to be discussed below.

It is essential to keep in mind that the ICD is a statistical classification of diseases, not a nomenclature of diseases. The distinction between these two is important. A nomenclature of diseases is a list or catalogue of approved terms for describing and recording clinical and pathological observations. To serve its full function it must be sufficiently extensive so that any pathological condition can be accurately recorded. As

---

[1]Prepared by Morton Kramer, Sc.D., for DSM-III.

medical science advances, a nomenclature must expand to include the new terms necessary to record new observations. In contrast, a statistical classification indicates the relationship between diagnostic categories and must be confined to a limited number of categories that encompass the entire range of diseases and morbid conditions.

Organizational Arrangement of ICD-9

The ICD is organized into 17 major sections, each of which is devoted to a specific set of conditions (Table 1). Each of these major sections is subdivided into a defined set of categories, each identified by three digits ranging from 001 to 999. To provide greater detail, each such category is further divided into additional subcategories by a fourth digit (.0 to .9). Table 1 shows the number of three-digit categories allotted to each major section. Only 30 are allotted to mental disorders, so that all mental disorders must be classified within these 30 categories and their fourth-digit subdivisions.

Table 1

Distribution of the 3-Digit Categories of the ICD-9 by the Number of Digits Allocated to Each Category

	Major 3-digit categories	Digits allocated to category	Number of 3-digit categories
I	Infectious and Parasitic Diseases	001-139	139
II	Neoplasms	140-239	100
III	Endocrine, Nutritional, and Metabolic Disorders	240-279	40
IV	Diseases of Blood and Blood-forming Organs	280-289	10
V	Mental Disorders	290-319	30
VI	Diseases of the Nervous System and Sense Organs	320-389	70
VII	Diseases of the Circulatory System	390-459	70
VIII	Diseases of the Respiratory System	460-519	60
IX	Diseases of the Digestive System	520-579	60
X	Diseases of the Genito-urinary System	580-629	50
XI	Complications of Pregnancy, Childbirth, and Puerperium	630-679	50
XII	Diseases of the Skin and Subcutaneous Tissue	680-709	30
XIII	Diseases of the Musculoskeletal System and Connective Tissue	710-739	30
XIV	Congenital Abnormalities	740-759	20
XV	Certain Conditions Originating in the Prenatal Period	760-779	20
XVI	Symptoms, Signs, and Ill-defined Conditions	780-799	20
XVII	Injury and Poisoning	800-999	200
		TOTAL	999

The structure of the classification is such that the axes of classification are not consistent within each of the 17 major sections. In some of these categories (e.g., diseases of the respiratory system) the primary axis is topographical; less frequently it is etiological (e.g., infectious diseases) or situational (e.g., complications of pregnancy). In other sections, still other primary axes are used, reflecting the fact that the ICD provides a pragmatic classification that can be used for a variety of purposes.

There are also two supplementary chapters: one for classification of external causes of injury and poisoning (the E codes), and the other for classification of factors influencing health status and contact with health services (the V codes). Both of these classifications contain items of relevance to agencies and facilities that provide mental health services.

Revisions of the ICD

The ICD is revised regularly, at approximately ten-year intervals. This pattern was initiated with the First Revision Conference of the International List of Causes of Death, held in Paris in 1900. The original classification, as indicated by its title, was used solely for coding causes of death, and did not provide a separate section for the mental disorders until the Fifth Revision of that List (1938). In that Revision, mental disorders were assigned only a single three-digit rubric with four subcategories within the section on Diseases of the Nervous System and Sense Organs: (a) mental deficiency; (b) schizophrenia; (c) manic depressive psychosis; and (d) all other mental disorders. The Conference for the Sixth Revision (1948) expanded the classification for use not only for causes of death but also for causes of morbidity. ICD-6 contained the first separate section on mental disorders (Section V). No major revisions were made in that section in ICD-7 (1955).

The international community of psychiatrists expressed considerable dissatisfaction with the classification of mental disorders in ICD-6 and ICD-7; consequently, it was not widely used (Stengel, 1959). As the importance of mental disorders as an international public health problem became more widely recognized, the need for an internationally acceptable classification of mental disorders became increasingly urgent. Accordingly, the World Health Organization developed an active program for revising the content and form of that classification to reflect new knowledge of the differential characteristics of specific mental disorders and their diagnosis and treatment to meet the increasing needs of health and social agencies, research workers, and users of health statistics for more detailed statistical and epidemiological data on mental disorders. The mental disorders chapter of ICD-8, adopted in 1965, reflected these changes (WHO, 1969).

To achieve more uniform usage of the terms in the mental disorders classification of ICD-8, WHO convened a working group of experts from different countries for the purpose of preparing a *Glossary of Mental Disorders and Guide to Their Classification* for use in conjunction with ICD-8 (WHO, 1974). The main aim of this glossary was:

> to ensure as far as possible that those who apply it will arrive at a uniform use of the principal diagnostic terms current in psychiatry. In addition to helping to minimize the discrepancies among the diagnostic concepts used by psychiatrists in different countries for the statistical reporting of mental illness, use of the Glossary in publications dealing with either clinical work or research will also assist psychiatrists from different countries and schools of thought in understanding each other's work and concepts.

The Ninth Revision of ICD

To develop revision proposals for ICD-9, WHO initiated an intensive program to obtain information on problems encountered by psychiatrists in different countries in the use of the mental disorders section of ICD-8 and to formulate recommendations for their solutions (Shepherd et al., 1968). This program resulted in the classification of mental disorders that appears in ICD-9, adopted by the World Health Assembly in 1975 (WHO, 1977).

As stated by WHO (1978):

Changes and new categories in the International Classification of Diseases (ICD-9) have been introduced only for sound reasons and after much consideration. As far as possible, the changes in Chapter V (ICD-9) have been based upon evidence that the new codes function better than the old ones. Some of this evidence, and a large proportion of other changes based upon discussion and consideration of different viewpoints, emanated from the World Health Organization's program on the standardization of psychiatric diagnosis, classification and statistics. A central feature of this program was a series of eight international seminars held annually between 1965 and 1972, each of which focused upon a recognized problem area in psychiatric diagnosis. Psychiatrists from more than 40 countries participated, and the documents and proposals that were used to produce the recommendations for ICD-9 in the eighth and final seminar were seen and commented upon by many more.

The first seven of the seminars focused on the classification of major groups of psychiatric disorders, and the last seminar on program review.

Dr. Jack Ewalt, past President of the American Psychiatric Association, and Dr. Henry Brill, former Chairman of the APA Task Force on Nomenclature and Statistics, played active roles in these seminars and in the development of the final classification of mental disorders of ICD-9. Other members of the Association who participated in and made important contributions to the recommendations developed in several of the seminars included: Dr. Leon Eisenberg (disorders of childhood) and Drs. George Tarjan, Julius Richmond, and J. Wortis (mental retardation) (WHO, 1970, 1971, 1972, 1973).

Place	Year	Subject
London	1965	Functional psychoses, with emphasis on schizophrenia
Oslo	1966	Borderline psychosis, reactive psychosis
Paris	1967	Psychiatric disorders of childhood
Moscow	1968	Mental disorders of old age
Washington, DC	1969	Mental retardation
Basle	1970	Neurotic and psychosomatic disorders
Tokyo	1971	Personality disorders and drug addiction
Geneva	1972	Summary, conclusions, recommendations, and proposals for further research

WHO Glossary of Mental Disorders

A major innovation of the mental disorders section of ICD-9 is the incorporation of a glossary as an integral part of that section. It is the only section of ICD-9 that contains such a glossary. The reason for this, as stated by WHO, is as follows (WHO, 1977a):

> This section of the Classification differs from the others in that it includes a glossary, prepared after consultation with experts from many different countries, defining the contents of the rubrics. This difference is considered to be justified because of the special problems posed for psychiatrists by the relative lack of independent laboratory information upon which to base their diagnoses. The diagnosis of many of the most important mental disorders still relies largely upon descriptions of abnormal experience and behaviour, and without some guidance in the form of a glossary that can serve as a common frame of reference, psychiatric communications easily became unsatisfactory at both clinical and statistical levels.
>
> Many well-known terms have different meanings in current use, and it is important for the user to use the glossary descriptions and not merely the category title when searching for the best fit for the condition he is trying to code. This is particularly important if a separate national glossary also exists.

Differences between the Mental Disorders Sections of ICD-8 and ICD-9

Table 2 provides a comparison of the three-digit categories of mental disorders in ICD-8 and ICD-9.

Table 2
Comparison of ICD-8 and ICD-9 3-Digit Categories of Mental Disorders

ICD-8	ICD-9
PSYCHOSES (290-299)	ORGANIC PSYCHOTIC CONDITIONS (290-294)

ICD-8

PSYCHOSES (290-299)

290   Senile and presenile dementia
291   Alcoholic psychosis
292   Psychosis associated with intracranial infection
293   Psychosis associated with other cerebral condition
294   Psychosis associated with other physical condition
295   Schizophrenia
296   Affective psychoses
297   Paranoid states
298   Other psychoses
299   Unspecified psychosis

NEUROSES, PERSONALITY DISORDERS AND OTHER NONPSYCHOTIC MENTAL DISORDERS (300-309)

300   Neuroses
301   Personality disorders
302   Sexual deviations
303   Alcoholism
304   Drug dependence
305   Physical disorders of presumably psychogenic origin
306   Special symptoms not elsewhere classified
307   Transient situational disturbances
308   Behavior disorders of childhood
309   Mental disorders not specified as psychotic associated with physical conditions

MENTAL RETARDATION (310-315)

310   Borderline mental retardation
311   Mild mental retardation
312   Moderate mental retardation
313   Severe mental retardation
314   Profound mental retardation
315   Unspecified mental retardation

ICD-9

ORGANIC PSYCHOTIC CONDITIONS (290-294)

290   Senile and presenile organic psychotic conditions
291   Alcoholic psychoses
292   Drug psychoses
293   Transient organic psychotic conditions
294   Other organic psychotic conditions (chronic)

OTHER PSYCHOSES (295-299)

295   Schizophrenic psychoses
296   Affective psychoses
297   Paranoid states
298   Other nonorganic psychoses
*299   Psychoses with origin specific to childhood

NEUROTIC DISORDERS, PERSONALITY DISORDERS AND OTHER NONPSYCHOTIC MENTAL DISORDERS (300-316)

300   Neurotic disorders
301   Personality disorders
302   Sexual deviations and disorders
303   Alcohol dependence syndrome
304   Drug dependence
*305   Nondependent abuse of drugs
306   Physiological malfunction arising from mental factors
307   Special symptoms or syndromes not elsewhere classified
*308   Acute reaction to stress
*309   Adjustment reaction
310   Specific nonpsychotic mental disorders following organic brain damage
*311   Depressive disorder, not elsewhere classified
*312   Disturbance of conduct not elsewhere classified
*313   Disturbance of emotions specific to childhood and adolescence
*314   Hyperkinetic syndrome of childhood
*315   Specific delays in development
*316   Psychic factors associated with diseases classified elsewhere

MENTAL RETARDATION (317-319)

317   Mild mental retardation
318   Other specified mental retardation
319   Unspecified mental retardation

Adapted from: World Health Organization (1978) **Mental Disorders: Glossary and Guide to Their Classification in Accordance with the Ninth Revision of the International Classification of Diseases,** Geneva, WHO, 1978.
* New categories in ICD-9 that were not in ICD-8

The classification of the following disorders was thoroughly recast in ICD-9:

Disorder	ICD-9 Codes
Affective psychoses	296
Organic mental disorders	290, 293, 294
Acute reaction to stress	308
Adjustment reaction	309
Specific nonpsychotic mental disorder following organic brain damage	310
Disturbance of conduct, not elsewhere classified	312
Disturbance of emotions specific to childhood and adolescence	313
Hyperkinetic syndrome of childhood	314
Specific delay in development	315
Alcohol disorders	291, 303, 305
Drug disorders	292, 304, 305

Several new three-digit categories were also added:

299   Psychoses with origin specific to childhood
305   Nondependent abuse of drugs
308   Acute reaction to stress
309   Adjustment reaction
311   Depressive disorder, not elsewhere classified
312   Disturbance of conduct, not elsewhere classified
313   Disturbance of emotions specific to childhood and adolescence
314   Hyperkinetic syndrome of childhood
315   Specific delays in development
316   Psychic factors associated with diseases classified elsewhere

Elimination of Combination Categories from ICD-9

ICD-9 also differs from ICD-8 in that it does not include so-called "combination categories," for coding combined mental and physical disorders such as organic mental disorders and mental retardation. To illustrate, in certain instances an ICD-8 category designated a mental disorder associated with a specific physical condition (e.g., psychosis with cerebral arteriosclerosis); in other instances, the category consisted of a specified mental condition and a general class of associated physical disorders (e.g., moderate mental retardation following infections and intoxications). "Combination categories" such as these have been eliminated from ICD-9 and replaced by categories that require coding on two independent axes. Thus, a psychotic condition arising from a physical disorder would be classified by using two code numbers: one for the mental disorder, and one for the underlying physical disorder. The following are categories in which multiple coding is necessary:

Disorder	ICD-9 Codes
Senile and presenile organic psychotic conditions	290
Transient organic psychotic conditions	293
Other organic psychotic conditions (chronic)	294
Specific nonpsychotic mental disorder following organic brain damage	310
Physiological malfunction arising from mental factors	306
Psychic factors associated with diseases classified elsewhere	316
Mental retardation	317–319

The use of the second code will require the clinician to familiarize himself or herself with all of the sections of the ICD and its alphabetical index (WHO, 1977a,b). This index assists in locating the code number for the associated condition.

Multiaxial Classification

The concept of a multiaxial classification system for mental disorders was first proposed at the WHO seminar on the mental disorders of childhood in Paris in 1967 (Rutter et al., 1969). The condition of the child was to be recorded on three axes: clinical syndrome, intellectual level, and etiologic factors. Two years later, during the seminar in Washington on the problems of classification of mental retardation, another axis was suggested for coding associated social and cultural factors (Tarjan et al., 1972).

WHO has initiated a number of international studies to obtain empirical data about the usefulness of the multiaxial classification. In one of these, carried out in the United Kingdom and involving a large number of child psychiatrists, a series of patients were assessed using both the triaxial approach and the ICD. Case histories were also used to assess the agreement between psychiatrists using these two classificatory systems. The results of this study clearly demonstrated that a multiaxial classification system can be used, and that it provides more and better data about the patients seen and assessed (Rutter et al., 1975). This study has now been expanded, and psychiatrists from several European countries are participating. Similar studies are about to begin in other countries. Some of these are concerned with the classification of disorders in old age, and others with the classification of mental disorders in criminals.

Other Details of ICD-9

The interested reader will find more details on the development of the ICD-9 Classification of Mental Disorders and its content in *Mental Disorders: Glossary and Guide to Their Classification in Accordance with the Ninth Revision of the ICD* (WHO, 1978), and a review of other highlights in a paper by Kramer et al. (1979).

International Classification of Diseases, Clinical Modification (ICD-9-CM)

As stated earlier, the ICD is primarily a classification of diseases for use in coding morbidity and mortality data for statistical purposes, and it has been adapted for use in clinical situations for the indexing of hospital records by disease and procedure (H-ICD-A). However, in the United States, clinicians and others responsible for the care of patients found they needed a classification with more specificity than that provided by ICD-9. Accordingly, the National Center for Health Statistics convened during 1977 a steering committee to advise the Council on Clinical Classifications on how to modify ICD-9 to satisfy this need. This Council was sponsored by the following organizations: American Academy of Pediatrics, American College of Obstetricians and Gynecologists, American College of Physicians, American College of Surgeons, American Psychiatric Association, and Commission on Professional and Hospital Activities. The task forces on classification of these organizations provided clinical guidance and technical input to the development of ICD-9-CM, the *Clinical Modification of the World Health Organization's International Classification of Diseases, 9th Revision*. As stated in the introduction to ICD-9-CM (1978):

> The term 'clinical' is used to emphasize the modification's intent: to serve as a useful tool in the area of classification of morbidity data for indexing of medical records, medical care review, and ambulatory and other medical care programs, as well as for basic health statistics. To describe the clinical picture of the patient, the codes must be more precise than those needed only for statistical groupings and trends analysis.

ICD-9-CM is compatible with its parent system, ICD-9, thus meeting the need for comparability of morbidity and mortality statistics at the international level. This was accomplished by: (a) keeping the contents and the sequence of the three-digit rubrics of ICD-9 unchanged; (b) not adding new three-digit rubrics to the main body of the classification; (c) adding a fifth digit to the existing ICD-9 rubrics; and (d) creating a few four-digit codes in existing three-digit rubrics only when the necessary detail could not be accommodated by the use of a fifth-digit subclassification.

As of the time when WHO had essentially completed its work on ICD-9, the American Psychiatric Association's Task Force on Nomenclature and Statistics was still in the midst of preparing the third edition of its Diagnostic and Statistical Manual of Mental Disorders (DSM-III). As a result, it was not possible to have revised diagnostic terms submitted in time for inclusion in ICD-9. However, the Chair of the APA Task Force was invited by the Council on Clinical Classifications to submit for inclusion in ICD-9-CM, those DSM-III terms not included in ICD-9. After ICD-9-CM went into effect on January 1, 1979, further changes were made in the still evolving DSM-III classification. All of the terms in the final DSM-III classification are either included in the ICD-9-CM volume itself or published as addenda to the ICD-9-CM in issues of *Medical Record News* as recommended terms or inclusion terms (acceptable as alternative terms).*

The classification of affective psychoses in ICD-9-CM (code 296) departs considerably from that in ICD-9. It is important for the users of this category to be aware of the fact that, in some instances, the same four-digit code numbers refer to different conditions in ICD-9 and ICD-9-CM. For example, the code 296.2 in ICD-9 is "Manic depressive psychosis, circular type but currently manic," whereas in ICD-9-CM, the same code is used for "Major Depressive Disorder, Single Episode."

It should also be noted that following the practice of ICD-9, "combination codes" are not included in ICD-9-CM. Therefore, it is important for clinicians and others using ICD-9-CM to become acquainted with codes for other diseases and other conditions that are to be entered on Axis III of the DSM-III-R classification (for Physical Disorders and Conditions).

Summary

The International Classification of Diseases (ICD) is an essential tool for the collection and dissemination of comparable mortality and morbidity data throughout the world. Mental disorders have been assigned an increasingly prominent place in the ICD; and the proposals for their classification in the 9th Revision, which became effective as of January 1, 1979, have been formulated on the basis of an extensive

WHO program involving a series of seminars and consultations with leading mental health experts in many countries.

An accompanying glossary and guide to the classification rubrics for the mental disorders were developed for the first time in connection with the 8th Revision. A major innovation in the 9th Revision is the incorporation of the glossary within the text of the section on mental disorders.

The new elements in the ICD-9 section on mental disorders include thoroughly recast rubrics for several categories, including affective disorders and psychiatric conditions specific to childhood. The "combination categories" for coding associations between mental and physical disorders are eliminated and replaced by categories requiring independent coding.

The next revision of the ICD will have to take into account a variety of needs that have emerged since the publication of ICD-9. These include: multiaxial classification methods, classification of disabilities, adaptation of the ICD for use in primary health care, and standardization of medical nomenclature on multilingual bases.

A major development in the United States was the preparation of the ICD-9-CM (Clinical Modification) to provide the additional specificity required by clinicians, research workers, epidemiologists, program planners, medical record librarians, and administrators of inpatient, outpatient, and community programs.

The experiences derived from the use of ICD-9, ICD-9-CM, DSM-III, and DSM-III-R in the United States will be invaluable for those who will participate in the development of ICD-10.

---

* Mr. Robert Seeman, Chief Nosologist, Council on Clinical Classifications, provided invaluable consultation that helped achieve compatibility between the DSM-III and ICD-9-CM classifications.

REFERENCES*

World Health Organization: Manual of the International List of Causes of Death, 5th revision, and Manual of Joint Causes of Death, 4th ed. Geneva, WHO, 1939

World Health Organization: Manual of the International Statistical Classification of Diseases, Injuries, and Causes of Death, 6th revision, Vol 1. Geneva, WHO, 1948

World Health Organization: Manual of the International Statistical Classification of Diseases, Injuries, and Causes of Death, 7th revision, Vol 1. Geneva, WHO, 1955

Stengel, E: Classification of mental disorders. Bull World Health Organization 21:601-603, 1960

World Health Organization: Manual of the International Statistical Classification of Diseases, Injuries, and Causes of Death, 8th revision, Vol 1. Geneva, WHO, 1969

World Health Organization: Glossary of Mental Health Disorders and Guide to Their Classification for Use in Conjunction with the International Classification of Diseases, 8th revision. Geneva, WHO, 1974

Shepherd M, et al: An experimental approach to psychiatric diagnosis: an international study. Acta Psychiat Scand, 44:Suppl 201, 1968

World Health Organization: Manual of the International Statistical Classification of Diseases, Injuries, and Causes of Death, 9th revision, Vol 1. Geneva, WHO, 1977

World Health Organization: Manual of the International Statistical Classification of Diseases, Injuries, and Causes of Death, 9th revision, Vol 2, (Alphabetical Index). Geneva, WHO, 1977

World Health Organization: Fourth Seminar on Standardization of Psychiatric Diagnosis, Classification, and Statistics. Geneva, WHO, 1970

World Health Organization: Report of the Sixth Seminar of Standardization of Psychiatric Diagnosis, Classification, and Statistics. Geneva, WHO, 1971

World Health Organization: Fifth WHO seminar on the standardization of psychiatric diagnosis, classification and statistics. Am J Psychiatry 128(May Suppl):3-14, 1972

World Health Organization: Report of the eighth seminar on the standardization of psychiatric diagnosis, classification, and statistics. Geneva, WHO, 1973

World Health Organization: Mental Disorders: Glossary and Guide to Their Classification in Accordance with the Ninth Revision of the International Classification of Diseases. Geneva, WHO, 1978

Rutter M, et al: A tri-axial classification of mental disorder in childhood. J Child Psychol & Psychiatry 10:41-61, 1969

Tarjan G, Eisenberg L: Some thoughts on the classification of mental retardation in the United States of America. Am J Psychiatry 128(May suppl):14-18, 1972

Rutter M, et al: A Multi-axial Classification of Child Psychiatric Disorders: An Evaluation of a Proposal. Geneva, World Health Organization, 1975

Kramer M, et al: The ICD-9 classification of mental disorders: a review of its development and contents. Acta Psychiat Scand, 59:241-262, 1979

Commission on Professional and Hospital Activities: The International Classification of Diseases, 9th Revision, Clinical Modification. Ann Arbor, Mich., Commission on Professional and Hospital Activities, 1978

American Psychiatric Association: Diagnostic and Statistical Manual of Mental Disorders, 2nd ed. Washington, D.C., APA, 1968

---

* A list of published material and reports is available from the World Health Organization upon request.

OFFPRINT OF MENTAL DISORDERS CHAPTER OF ICD-9
From **Mental Disorders: Glossary and Guide to Their Classification in Accordance with the Ninth Revision of the International Classification of Diseases,** World Health Organization, Geneva, 1978.

This section of the Classification differs from the others in that it includes a glossary, prepared after consultation with experts from many different countries, defining the content of the rubrics. This difference is considered to be justified because of the special problems posed for psychiatrists by the relative lack of independent laboratory information upon which to base their diagnoses. The diagnosis of many of the most important mental disorders still relies largely upon descriptions of abnormal experience and behaviour, and without some guidance in the form of a glossary that can serve as a common frame of reference, psychiatric communications easily become unsatisfactory at both clinical and statistical levels.

Many well-known terms have different meanings in current use, and it is important for the user to use the glossary descriptions and not merely the category titles when searching for the best fit for the condition he is trying to code. This is particularly important if a separate national glossary also exists.

The instructions "Use additional code to identify . . ." are important because of the nature of many psychiatric conditions in which two or more codes are necessary to describe the condition and the associated or casual factors. It should be used whenever possible.

In cases where no other information is available except that a mental disorder is present, the code V40.9 (unspecified mental or behavioural problems) can be used.

Psychoses (290–299)

Mental disorders in which impairment of mental function has developed to a degree that interferes grossly with insight, ability to meet some ordinary demands of life or to maintain adequate contact with reality. It is not an exact or well defined term. Mental retardation is excluded.

Organic psychotic conditions (290–294)

Syndromes in which there is impairment of orientation, memory, comprehension, calculation, learning capacity and judgement. These are the essential features but there may also be shallowness or lability of affect, or a more persistent disturbance of mood, lowering of ethical standards and exaggeration or emergence of personality traits, and diminished capacity for independent decision.

Psychoses of the types classifiable to 295–298 and without the above features are excluded even though they may be associated with organic conditions.

The term *'dementia'* in this glossary includes organic psychoses as just specified, of a chronic or progressive nature, which if untreated are usually irreversible and terminal.

The term *'delirium'* in this glossary includes organic psychoses with a short course in which the above features are overshadowed by clouded consciousness, confusion, disorientation, delusions, illusions and often vivid hallucinations.

Includes: psychotic organic brain sydrome

Excludes: nonpsychotic syndromes of organic aetiology (see 310.–)
psychoses classifiable to 295–298 and without the above features but associated with physical disease, injury or condition affecting the brain
[e.g., following childbirth]; code to 295–298 and use additional code to
identify the associated physical condition

290   Senile and presenile organic psychotic conditions

Excludes: psychoses classifiable to 295–298.8 occurring in the senium without dementia or delirium (295–298)
transient organic psychotic conditions (293.–)
dementia not classified as senile, presenile, or arteriosclerotic (294.1)

290.0 *Senile dementia, simple type*

Dementia occurring usually after the age of 65 in which any cerebral pathology other than that of
senile atrophic change can be reasonably excluded.

Excludes: mild memory disturbances, not amounting to dementia, associated with
senile brain disease (310.1)
senile dementia:
depressed or paranoid type (290.2)
with confusion and/or delirium (290.3)

290.1 *Presenile dementia*

Dementia occurring usually before the age of 65 in patients with the relatively rare forms of diffuse
or lobar cerebral atrophy. Use additional code to identify the associated neurological condition.

Brain syndrome with presenile brain disease
Circumscribed atrophy of the brain
Dementia in:
  Alzheimer's disease
  Pick's disease of the brain

Excludes: arteriosclerotic dementia (290.4)
dementia associated with other cerebral conditions (294.1)

290.2 *Senile dementia, depressed or paranoid type*

A type of senile dementia characterized by development in advanced old age, progressive in
nature, in which a variety of delusions and hallucinations of a persecutory, depressive and somatic
content are also present. Disturbance of the sleep/waking cycle and preoccupation with dead
people are often particularly prominent.

Senile psychosis NOS

Excludes: senile dementia:
with confusion and/or delirium (290.3)
NOS (290.0)

290.3 *Senile dementia with acute confusional state*

Senile dementia with a superimposed reversible episode of acute confusional state

Excludes: senile:
            dementia NOS (290.0)
            psychosis NOS (290.2)

290.4   *Arteriosclerotic dementia*

Dementia attributable, because of physical signs [on examination of the central nervous system] to degenerative arterial disease of the brain. Symptoms suggesting a focal lesion in the brain are common. There may be a fluctuating or patchy intellectual defect with insight, and an intermittent course is common. Clinical differentiation from senile or presenile dementia, which may coexist with it, may be very difficult or impossible. Use additional code to identify cerebral atherosclerosis (437.0).

Excludes: suspected cases with no clear evidence of arteriosclerosis (290.9)

290.8   *Other*

290.9   *Unspecified*

291   Alcoholic psychoses

Organic psychotic states due mainly to excessive consumption of alcohol; defects of nutrition are thought to play an important role. In some of these states, withdrawal of alcohol can be of aetiological significance.

Excludes: alcoholism without psychosis (303)

291.0   *Delirium tremens*

Acute or subacute organic psychotic states in alcoholics, characterized by clouded consciousness, disorientation, fear, illusions, delusions, hallucinations of any kind, notably visual and tactile, and restlessness, tremor and sometimes fever.

Alcoholic delirium

291.1   *Korsakov's psychosis, alcoholic*

A syndrome of prominent and lasting reduction of memory span, including striking loss of recent memory, disordered time appreciation and confabulation, occurring in alcoholics as the sequel to an acute alcoholic psychosis [especially delirium tremens] or, more rarely, in the course of chronic alcoholism. It is usually accompanied by peripheral neuritis and may be associated with Wernicke's encephalopathy.

Alcoholic polyneuritic psychosis

Excludes: Korsakov's psychosis:
            NOS (294.0)
            nonalcoholic (294.0)

291.2   *Other alcoholic dementia*

Nonhallucinatory dementias occurring in association with alcoholism but not characterized by the features of either delirium tremens or Korsakov's psychosis.

Alcoholic dementia NOS
Chronic alcoholic brain syndrome

291.3   *Other alcoholic hallucinosis*

A psychosis usually of less than six months' duration, with slight or no clouding of consciousness and much anxious restlessness in which auditory hallucinations, mostly of voices uttering insults and threats, predominate.

Excludes: schizophrenia (295.–) and paranoid states (297.–) taking the form of
                   chronic hallucinosis with clear consciousness in an alcoholic

291.4   *Pathological drunkenness*

Acute psychotic episodes induced by relatively small amounts of alcohol. These are regarded as individual idiosyncratic reactions to alcohol, not due to excessive consumption and without conspicuous neurological signs of intoxication.

Excludes: simple drunkenness (305.0)

291.5   *Alcoholic jealousy*

Chronic paranoid psychosis characterized by delusional jealousy and associated with alcoholism.

Alcoholic paranoia

Excludes: nonalcoholic paranoid states (297.–)
                   schizophrenia, paranoid type (295.3)

291.8   *Other*

Alcoholic withdrawal syndrome

Excludes: delirium tremens (291.0)

291.9   *Unspecified*

Alcoholic:
   mania NOS
   psychosis NOS
Alcoholism (chronic) with psychosis

292   Drug psychoses

Syndromes that do not fit the descriptions given in 295–298 (nonorganic psychoses) and which are due to consumption of drugs [notably amphetamines, barbiturates and the opiate and LSD groups] and solvents. Some of the syndromes in this group are not as severe as most conditions labelled "psychotic" but they are included here for practical reasons. Use additional E Code to identify the drug and also code drug dependence (304.–) if present.

292.0   *Drug withdrawal syndrome*

States associated with drug withdrawal ranging from severe, as specified for alcohol under 291.0 (delirium tremens) to less severe characterized by one or more symptoms such as convulsions, tremor, anxiety, restlessness, gastrointestinal and muscular complaints, and mild disorientation and memory disturbance.

292.1   *Paranoid and/or hallucinatory states induced by drugs*

States of more than a few days but not usually of more than a few months duration, associated with large or prolonged intake of drugs, notably of the amphetamine and LSD groups. Auditory hallucinations usually predominate, and there may be anxiety and restlessness.

Excludes: the described conditions with confusion or delirium (293.–)
states following LSD or other hallucinogens, lasting only a few days or
less ["bad trips"] (305.3)

292.2 *Pathological drug intoxication*

Individual idiosyncratic reactions to comparatively small quantities of a drug, which take the form of acute, brief psychotic states of any type.

Excludes: physiological side-effects of drugs [e.g., dystonias]
expected brief psychotic reactions to hallucinogens ["bad trips"] (305.3)

292.8 *Other*

292.9 *Unspecified*

293   Transient organic psychotic conditions

States characterized by clouded consciousness, confusion, disorientation, illusions and often vivid hallucinations. They are usually due to some intra- or extracerebral toxic, infectious, metabolic or other systemic disturbance and are generally reversible. Depressive and paranoid symptoms may also be present but are not the main feature. Use additional code to identify the associated physical or neurological condition.

Excludes: confusional state of delirium superimposed on senile dementia (290.3)
dementia due to:
alcohol (291.–)
arteriosclerosis (290.4)
senility (290.0)

293.0 *Acute confusional state*

Short-lived states, lasting hours or days, of the above type.

Acute:
  delirium
  infective psychosis
  organic reaction
  post-traumatic organic psychosis

Acute:
  psycho-organic syndrome
  psychosis associated with endocrine,
    metabolic or cerebrovascular
    disorder
Epileptic:
  confusional state
  twilight state

293.1 *Subacute confusional state*

States of the above type in which the symptoms, usually less florid, last for several weeks or longer, during which they may show marked fluctuations in intensity.

Subacute:
  delirium
  infective psychosis
  organic reaction
  post-traumatic organic psychosis

Subacute:
  psycho-organic syndrome
  psychosis associated with endocrine
    or metabolic disorder

293.8   *Other*

293.9   *Unspecified*

294   Other organic psychotic conditions (chronic)

294.0   *Korsakov's psychosis or syndrome (nonalcoholic)*
Syndromes as described under 291.1 but not due to alcohol.

294.1   *Dementia in conditions classified elsewhere*
Dementia not classifiable as senile, presenile or arteriosclerotic (290.–) but associated with other underlying conditions.

Dementia in:
  cerebral lipidoses
  epilepsy
  general paralysis of the insane
  hepatolenticular degeneration
  Huntington's chorea
  multiple sclerosis
  polyarteritis nodosa
Use additional code to identify the underlying physical condition

294.8   *Other*
States that fulfill the criteria of an organic psychosis but do not take the form of a confusional state (293.–), a nonalcoholic Korsakov's psychosis (294.0) or a dementia (294.1).

Mixed paranoid and affective organic   Epileptic psychosis NOS (code also
    psychotic states   345.–)

Excludes: mild memory disturbances, not amounting to dementia (310.1)

294.9   *Unspecified*

OTHER PSYCHOSES (295–299)

295   Schizophrenic psychoses

A group of psychoses in which there is a fundamental disturbance of personality, a characteristic distortion of thinking, often a sense of being controlled by alien forces, delusions which may be bizarre, disturbed perception, abnormal affect out of keeping with the real situation, and autism. Nevertheless, clear consciousness and intellectual capacity are usually maintained. The disturbance of personality involves its most basic functions which give the normal person his feeling of individuality, uniqueness and self-direction. The most intimate thoughts, feelings and acts are often felt to be known to or shared by others and explanatory delusions may develop, to the effect that natural or supernatural forces are at work to influence the schizophrenic person's thoughts and actions in ways that are often bizarre. He may see himself as the pivot of all that happens. Hallucinations, especially of hearing, are common and may comment on the patient or address him. Perception is frequently disturbed in other ways; there may be perplexity, irrelevant features may become all-important and, accompanied by passivity feelings, may lead the patient to believe that everyday objects and situations possess a special, usually sinister, meaning intended for him. In the characteristic schizophrenic disturbance of thinking, peripheral and irrelevant features of a total concept, which are inhibited in normal directed mental activity, are brought to the forefront and utilized in place of the elements relevant and appropriate to the situation. Thus thinking becomes vague, elliptical and obscure, and its expression in speech sometimes incomprehensible. Breaks and interpolations in the flow of consecutive thought are frequent, and the patient may be convinced that his thoughts are being withdrawn by some outside agency. Mood may be shallow, capricious or incongruous. Ambivalence and disturbance of volition may appear as inertia, negativism or stupor. Catatonia may be present. The diagnosis "schizophrenia" should not be made unless there is, or has been evident during the same illness, characteristic disturbance of thought, perception, mood, conduct, or personality—preferably in at least two of these areas. The diagnosis should not be restricted to conditions running a protracted, deteriorating, or chronic course. In addition to making the diagnosis on the criteria just given, effort should be made to specify one of the following subdivisions of schizophrenia, according to the predominant symptoms.

Includes: schizophrenia of the types described in 295.0–295.9 occurring in
                children

Excludes: childhood type schizophrenia (299.9)
                infantile autism

295.0   *Simple type*

A psychosis in which there is insidious development of oddities of conduct, inability to meet the demands of society, and decline in total performance. Delusions and hallucinations are not in evidence and the condition is less obviously psychotic than are the hebephrenic, catatonic and paranoid types of schizophrenia. With increasing social impoverishment vagrancy may ensue and the patient becomes self-absorbed, idle and aimless. Because the schizophrenic symptoms are not clear-cut, diagnosis of this form should be made sparingly, if at all.

Schizophrenia simplex

Excludes: latent schizophrenia (295.5)

295.1   *Hebephrenic type*

A form of schizophrenia in which affective changes are prominent, delusions and hallucinations fleeting and fragmentary, behaviour irresponsible and unpredictable and mannerisms common. The mood is shallow and inappropriate, accompanied by giggling or self-satisfied, self-absorbed smiling, or by a lofty manner, grimaces, mannerisms, pranks, hypochondriacal complaints and reiterated phrases. Thought is disorganized. There is a tendency to remain solitary, and behaviour seems empty of purpose and feeling. This form of schizophrenia usually starts between the ages of 15 and 25 years.

Hebephrenia

295.2   *Catatonic type*

Includes as an essential feature prominent psychomotor disturbances often alternating between extremes such as hyperkinesis and stupor, or automatic obedience and negativism. Constrained attitudes may be maintained for long periods: if the patient's limbs are put in some unnatural position they may be held there for some time after the external force has been removed. Severe excitement may be a striking feature of the condition. Depressive or hypomanic concomitants may be present.

Catatonic:
  agitation
  excitation
  stupor

Schizophrenic:
  catalepsy
  catatonia
  flexibilitas cerea

295.3   *Paranoid type*

The form of schizophrenia in which relatively stable delusions, which may be accompanied by hallucinations, dominate the clinical picture. The delusions are frequently of persecution but may take other forms [for example of jealousy, exalted birth, Messianic mission, or bodily change]. Hallucinations and erratic behaviour may occur; in some cases conduct is seriously disturbed from the outset, thought disorder may be gross, and affective flattening with fragmentary delusions and hallucinations may develop.

Paraphrenic schizophrenia

Excludes: paraphrenia, involutional paranoid state (297.2)
        paranoia (297.1)

295.4   *Acute schizophrenic episode*

Schizophrenic disorders, other than those listed above, in which there is a dream-like state with slight clouding of consciousness and perplexity. External things, people and events may become charged with personal significance for the patient. There may be ideas of reference and emotional turmoil. In many such cases remission occurs within a few weeks or months, even without treatment.

Oneirophrenia

Schizophreniform:
  attack
  psychosis, confusional type

Excludes: acute forms of schizophrenia of:
        catatonic type (295.2)
        hebephrenic type (295.1)
        paranoid type (295.3)
        simple type (295.0)

295.5   *Latent schizophrenia*

It has not been possible to produce a generally acceptable description for this condition. It is not recommended for general use, but a description is provided for those who believe it to be useful: a condition of eccentric or inconsequent behaviour and anomalies of affect which give the impression of schizophrenia though no definite and characteristic schizophrenic anomalies, present or past, have been manifest.

The inclusion terms indicate that this is the best place to classify some other poorly defined varieties of schizophrenia.

Latent schizophrenic reaction
Schizophrenia:
  borderline
  prepsychotic
  prodromal

Schizophrenia:
  pseudoneurotic
  pseudopsychopathic

Excludes: schizoid personality (301.2)

295.6   *Residual schizophrenia*

A chronic form of schizophrenia in which the symptoms that persist from the acute phase have mostly lost their sharpness. Emotional response is blunted and thought disorder, even when gross, does not prevent the accomplishment of routine work.

Chronic undifferentiated schizophrenia
Restzustand (schizophrenic)
Schizophrenic residual state

295.7   *Schizoaffective type*

A psychosis in which pronounced manic or depressive features are intermingled with schizophrenic features and which tends towards remission without permanent defect, but which is prone to recur. The diagnosis should be made only when both the affective and schizophrenic symptoms are pronounced.

Cyclic schizophrenia
Mixed schizophrenic and affective psychosis
Schizoaffective psychosis
Schizophreniform psychosis, affective type

295.8   *Other*

Schizophrenia of specified type not classifiable under 295.0–295.7.

Acute (undifferentiated) schizophrenia   Atypical schizophrenia
                                                 Coenesthopathic schizophrenia

Excludes: infantile autism (299.0)

295.9   *Unspecified*

To be used only as a last resort.

Schizophrenia NOS
Schizophrenic reaction NOS
Schizophreniform psychosis NOS

296   **Affective psychoses**

Mental disorders, usually recurrent, in which there is a severe disturbance of mood [mostly compounded of depression and anxiety but also manifested as elation and excitement] which is accompanied by one or more of the following: delusions, perplexity, disturbed attitude to self, disorder of perception and behaviour; these are all in keeping with the patient's prevailing mood [as are hallucinations when they occur]. There is a strong tendency to suicide. For practical reasons, mild disorders of mood may also be included here if the symptoms match closely the descriptions given; this applies particularly to mild hypomania.

Excludes: reactive depressive psychosis (298.0)
            reactive excitation (298.1)
            neurotic depression (300.4)

296.0   *Manic-depressive psychosis, manic type*

Mental disorders characterized by states of elation or excitement out of keeping with the patient's circumstances and varying from enhanced liveliness [hypomania] to violent, almost uncontrollable excitement. Aggression and anger, flight of ideas, distractibility, impaired judgement, and grandiose ideas are common.

Hypomania NOS
Hypomanic psychosis
Mania (monopolar) NOS
Manic disorder

Manic psychosis
Manic-depressive psychosis or reaction:
  hypomanic
  manic

Excludes: circular type if there was a previous attack of depression (296.2)

296.1 *Manic-depressive psychosis, depressed type*

An affective psychosis in which there is a widespread depressed mood of gloom and wretchedness with some degree of anxiety. There is often reduced activity but there may be restlessness and agitation. There is a marked tendency to recurrence; in a few cases this may be at regular intervals.

Depressive psychosis
Endogenous depression
Involutional melancholia

Manic-depressive reaction, depressed
Monopolar depression
Psychotic depression

Excludes: circular type if previous attack was of manic type (296.3)
        depression NOS (311)

296.2 *Manic-depressive psychosis, circular type but currently manic*

An affective psychosis which has appeared in both the depressive and the manic form, either alternating or separated by an interval of normality, but in which the manic form is currently present. [The manic phase is far less frequent than the depressive.]

Bipolar disorder, now manic

Excludes: brief compensatory or rebound mood swings (296.8)

296.5 *Manic-depressive psychosis, circular type but currently depressed*

Circular type (see 296.2) in which the depressive form is currently present.

Bipolar disorder, now depressed

Excludes: brief compensatory or rebound mood swings (296.8)

296.4 *Manic-depressive psychosis, circular type, mixed*

An affective psychosis in which both manic and depressive symptoms are present at the same time.

296.5 *Manic-depressive psychosis, circular type, current condition not specified*

Circular type (see 296.2) in which the current condition is not specified as either manic or depressive.

296.6 *Manic-depressive psychosis, other and unspecified*

Use this code for cases where no other information is available, except the unspecified term, manic-depressive psychosis, or for syndromes corresponding to the descriptions of depressed (296.1) or manic (296.0) types but which for other reasons cannot be classified under 296.0–296.5.

Manic-depressive psychosis:
  NOS
  mixed type

Manic-depressive:
  reaction NOS
  syndrome NOS

296.8 *Other*

Excludes: psychogenic affective psychoses (298.–)

296.9   *Unspecified*

Affective psychosis NOS   Melancholia NOS

297   **Paranoid states**

Excludes: acute paranoid reaction (298.3)
            alcoholic jealousy (291.5)
            paranoid schizophrenia (295.3)

297.0   *Paranoid state, simple*

A psychosis, acute or chronic, not classifiable as schizophrenia or affective psychosis, in which delusions, especially of being influenced, persecuted or treated in some special way, are the main symptoms. The delusions are of a fairly fixed, elaborate and systematized kind.

297.1   *Paranoia*

A rare chronic psychosis in which logically constructed systematized delusions have developed gradually without concomitant hallucinations or the schizophrenic type of disordered thinking. The delusions are mostly of grandeur [the paranoiac prophet or inventor], persecution or somatic abnormality.

Excludes: paranoid personality disorder (301.0)

297.2   *Paraphrenia*

Paranoid psychosis in which there are conspicuous hallucinations, often in several modalities. Affective symptoms and disordered thinking, if present, do not dominate the clinical picture and the personality is well preserved.

Involutional paranoid state   Late paraphrenia

297.3   *Induced psychosis*

Mainly delusional psychosis, usually chronic and often without florid features, which appears to have developed as a result of a close, if not dependent, relationship with another person who already has an established similar psychosis. The delusions are at least partly shared. The rare cases in which several persons are affected should also be included here.

Folie à deux   Induced paranoid disorder

297.8   *Other*

Paranoid states which, though in many ways akin to schizophrenic or affective states, cannot readily be classified under any of the preceding rubrics, nor under 298.4.

Paranoia querulans   Sensitiver Beziehungswahn

Excludes: senile paranoid state (297.2)

297.9   *Unspecified*

Paranoid:
  psychosis NOS
  reaction NOS
  state NOS

298   Other nonorganic psychoses

Categories 298.0–298.8 should be restricted to the small group of psychotic conditions that are largely or entirely attributable to a recent life experience. They should not be used for the wider range of psychoses in which environmental factors play some [but not the *major*] part in aetiology.

298.0   *Depressive type*

A depressive psychosis which can be similar in its symptoms to manic-depressive psychosis, depressed type (296.1) but is apparently provoked by saddening stress such as a bereavement, or a severe disappointment or frustration. There may be less diurnal variation of symptoms than in 296.1, and the delusions are more often understandable in the context of the life experiences. There is usually a serious disturbance of behaviour, e.g., major suicidal attempt.

Reactive depressive psychosis
Psychogenic depressive psychosis

Excludes: manic-depressive psychosis, depressed type (296.1)
      neurotic depression (300.4)

298.1   *Excitative type*

An affective psychosis similar in its symptoms to manic-depressive psychosis, manic type, but apparently provoked by emotional stress.

Excludes: manic-depressive psychosis, manic type (296.0)

298.2   *Reactive confusion*

Mental disorders with clouded consciousness, disorientation [though less marked than in organic confusion] and diminished accessibility often accompanied by excessive activity and apparently provoked by emotional stress.

Psychogenic confusion
Psychogenic twilight state

Excludes: acute confusional state (293.0)

298.3   *Acute paranoid reaction*

Paranoid states apparently provoked by some emotional stress. The stress is often misconstrued as an attack or threat. Such states are particularly prone to occur in prisoners or as acute reactions to a strange and threatening environment, e.g., in immigrants.

Bouffée délirante

Excludes: paranoid states (297.–)

298.4   *Psychogenic paranoid psychosis*

Psychogenic or reactive paranoid psychosis of any type which is more protracted than the acute reactions covered in 298.3. Where there is a diagnosis of psychogenic paranoid psychosis which does not specify "acute" this coding should be made.

Protracted reactive paranoid psychosis

298.8   *Other and unspecified reactive psychosis*

Hysterical psychosis   Psychogenic stupor
Psychogenic psychosis NOS

298.9   *Unspecified psychosis*

To be used only as a last resort, when no other term can be used.

Psychosis NOS

299   Psychoses with origin specific to childhood

This category should be used only for psychoses which always begin before puberty. Adult-type psychoses such as schizophrenia or manic-depressive psychoses when occurring in childhood should be coded elsewhere under the appropriate heading—i.e., 295 and 296 for the examples given.

299.0   *Infantile autism*

A syndrome present from birth or beginning almost invariably in the first 30 months. Responses to auditory and sometimes to visual stimuli are abnormal and there are usually severe problems in the understanding of spoken language. Speech is delayed and, if it develops, is characterized by echolalia, the reversal of pronouns, immature grammatical structure and inability to use abstract terms. There is generally an impairment in the social use of both verbal and gestural language. Problems in social relationships are most severe before the age of five years and include an impairment in the development of eye-to-eye gaze, social attachments, and cooperative play. Ritualistic behaviour is usual and may include abnormal routines, resistance to change, attachment to odd objects and stereotyped patterns of play. The capacity for abstract or symbolic thought and for imaginative play is diminished. Intelligence ranges from severely subnormal to normal or above. Performance is usually better on tasks involving rote memory or visuospatial skills than on those requiring symbolic or linguistic skills.

Childhood autism   Kanner's syndrome
Infantile psychosis

Excludes: disintegrative psychosis (299.1)
             Heller's syndrome (299.1)
             schizophrenic syndrome of childhood (299.9)

299.1   *Disintegrative psychosis*

A disorder in which normal or near-normal development for the first few years is followed by a loss of social skills and of speech, together with a severe disorder of emotions, behaviour and relation-ships. Usually this loss of speech and of social competence takes place over a period of a few months and is accompanied by the emergence of over-activity and of stereotypies. In most cases there is intellectual impairment, but this is not a necessary part of the disorder. The condition may follow overt brain disease—such as measles encephalitis—but it may also occur in the absence of any known organic brain disease or damage. Use additional code to identify any associated neurological disorder.

Heller's syndrome

Excludes: infantile autism (299.0)
             schizophrenic syndrome of childhood (299.9)

299.8   *Other*

A variety of atypical psychoses which may show some, but not all, of the features of infantile autism. Symptoms may include stereotyped repetitive movements, hyperkinesis, self-injury, retarded speech development, echolalia and impaired social relationships. Such disorders may occur in children of any level of intelligence but are particularly common in those with mental retardation.

Atypical childhood psychosis

Excludes: simple stereotypies without psychotic disturbance (307.3)

299.9   *Unspecified*

Child psychosis NOS
Schizophrenia, childhood type NOS
Schizophrenic syndrome of childhood NOS

Excludes: schizophrenia of adult type occurring in childhood (295.0–295.8)

NEUROTIC DISORDERS, PERSONALITY DISORDERS AND OTHER
NONPSYCHOTIC MENTAL DISORDERS (300–316)

300   Neurotic disorders

The distinction between neurosis and psychosis is difficult and remains subject to debate. However, it has been retained in view of its wide use.

Neurotic disorders are mental disorders without any demonstrable organic basis in which the patient may have considerable insight and has unimpaired reality testing, in that he usually does not confuse his morbid subjective experiences and fantasies with external reality. Behavior may be greatly affected although usually remaining within socially acceptable limits, but personality is not disorganized. The principal manifestations include excessive anxiety, hysterical symptoms, phobias, obsessional and compulsive symptoms, and depression.

300.0   *Anxiety states*

Various combinations of physical and mental manifestations of anxiety, not attributable to real danger and occurring either in attacks or as a persisting state. The anxiety is usually diffuse and may extend to panic. Other neurotic features such as obsessional or hysterical symptoms may be present but do not dominate the clinical pictures.

Anxiety:
  neurosis
  reaction
  state (neurotic)

Panic:
  attack
  disorder
  state

Excludes: neurasthenia (300.5)
            psychophysiological disorders (306.–)

300.1   *Hysteria*

Mental disorders in which motives, of which the patient seems unaware, produce either a restriction of the field of consciousness or disturbances of motor or sensory function which may seem to have psychological advantage or symbolic value. It may be characterized by conversion phenomena or dissociative phenomena. In the conversion form the chief or only symptoms consist of psychogenic disturbance of function in some part of the body, e.g., paralysis, tremor, blindness, deafness, seizures. In the dissociative variety, the most prominent feature is a narrowing of the field of consciousness which seems to serve an unconscious purpose and is commonly accompanied or followed by a selective amnesia. There may be dramatic but essentially superficial changes of personality sometimes taking the form of a fugue [wandering state]. Behaviour may mimic psychosis or, rather, the patient's idea of psychosis.

Astasia-abasia, hysterical
Compensation neurosis
Conversion hysteria
Conversion reaction

Dissociative reaction or state
Ganser's syndrome, hysterical
Hysteria NOS
Multiple personality

Excludes: adjustment reaction (309.–)
anorexia nervosa (307.1)
gross stress reaction (308.–)
hysterical personality (301.5)
psychophysiological disorders (306.–)

300.2   Phobic state

Neurotic states with abnormally intense dread of certain objects or specific situations which would not normally have that affect. If the anxiety tends to spread from a specified situation or object to a wider range of circumstances, it becomes akin to or identical with anxiety state, and should be classified as such (300.0).

Agoraphobia
Animal phobias
Anxiety-hysteria

Claustrophobia
Phobia NOS

Excludes: anxiety state (300.0)
obsessional phobias (300.3)

300.3   Obsessive-compulsive disorders

States in which the outstanding symptom is a feeling of subjective compulsion—which must be resisted—to carry out some action, to dwell on an idea, to recall an experience, or to ruminate on an abstract topic. Unwanted thoughts which intrude, the insistency of words or ideas, ruminations or trains of thought are perceived by the patient to be inappropriate or nonsensical. The obsessional urge or idea is recognized as alien to the personality but as coming from within the self. Obsessional actions may be quasi-ritual performances designed to relieve anxiety, e.g., washing the hands to cope with contamination. Attempts to dispel the unwelcome thoughts or urges may lead to a severe struggle, with intense anxiety.

Anankastic neurosis
Compulsive neurosis

Excludes: obsessive-compulsive symptoms occurring in:
endogenous depression (296.1)
schizophrenia (295.–)
organic states, e.g., encephalitis

300.4   Neurotic depression

A neurotic disorder characterized by disproportionate depression which has usually recognizably ensued on a distressing experience; it does not include among its features delusions or hallucinations, and there is often preoccupation with the psychic trauma which preceded the illness, e.g., loss of a cherished person or possession. Anxiety is also frequently present and mixed states of anxiety and depression should be included here. The distinction between depressive neurosis and psychosis should be made not only upon the degree of depression but also on the presence or absence of other neurotic and psychotic characteristics and upon the degree of disturbance of the patient's behaviour.

Anxiety depression   Neurotic depressive state
Depressive reaction   Reactive depression

Excludes: adjustment reaction with depressive symptoms (309.0)
           depression NOS (311)
           manic-depressive psychosis, depressed type (296.1)
           reactive depressive psychosis (298.0)

300.5   *Neurasthenia*

A neurotic disorder characterized by fatigue, irritability, headache, depression, insomnia, difficulty in concentration, and lack of capacity for enjoyment [anhedonia]. It may follow or accompany an infection or exhaustion, or arise from continued emotional stress. If neurasthenia is associated with a physical disorder, the latter should also be coded.

Nervous debility

Excludes: anxiety state (300.0)
           neurotic depression (300.4)
           psychophysiological disorders (306.–)
           specific nonpsychotic mental disorders following organic brain damage
               (310.–)

300.6   *Depersonalization syndrome*

A neurotic disorder with an unpleasant state of disturbed perception in which external objects or parts of one's own body are experienced as changed in their quality, unreal, remote or automa- tized. The patient is aware of the subjective nature of the change he experiences. Depersonaliza- tion may occur as a feature of several mental disorders including depression, obsessional neurosis, anxiety and schizophrenia; in that case the condition should not be classified here but in the corresponding major category.

Derealization (neurotic)

300.7   *Hypochondriasis*

A neurotic disorder in which the conspicuous features are excessive concern with one's health in general or the integrity and functioning of some part of one's body, or, less frequently, one's mind. It is usually associated with anxiety and depression. It may occur as a feature of severe mental disorder and in that case should not be classified here but in the corresponding major category.

Excludes: hysteria (300.1)
           manic-depressive psychosis, depressed type (296.1)
           neurasthenia (300.5)
           obsessional disorder (300.3)
           schizophrenia (295.–)

300.8   *Other neurotic disorders*

Neurotic disorders not classified elsewhere, e.g., occupational neurosis. Patients with mixed neu- roses should not be classified in this category but according to the most prominent symptoms they display.

Briquet's disorder
Occupational neurosis, including writer's cramp
Psychasthenia
Psychasthenic neurosis

300.9   *Unspecified*

To be used only as a last resort.

Neurosis NOS   Psychoneurosis NOS

301   Personality disorders

Deeply ingrained maladaptive patterns of behaviour generally recognizable by the time of adolescence or earlier and continuing throughout most of adult life, although often becoming less
obvious in middle or old age. The personality is abnormal either in the balance of its components,
their quality and expression or in its total aspect. Because of this deviation or psychopathy the
patient suffers or others have to suffer and there is an adverse effect upon the individual or on
society. It includes what is sometimes called psychopathic personality, but if this is determined
primarily by malfunctioning of the brain, it should not be classified here but as one of the
nonpsychotic organic brain syndromes (310). When the patient exhibits an anomaly of personality
directly related to his neurosis or psychosis, e.g., schizoid personality and schizophrenia or
anankastic personality and obsessive compulsive neurosis, the relevant neurosis or psychosis
which is in evidence should be diagnosed in addition.

Character neurosis

301.0   *Paranoid personality disorder*

Personality disorder in which there is excessive sensitiveness to setbacks or to what are taken to be
humiliations and rebuffs, a tendency to distort experience by misconstruing the neutral or friendly
actions of others as hostile or contemptuous, and a combative and tenacious sense of personal
rights. There may be a proneness to jealousy or excessive self-importance. Such persons may feel
helplessly humiliated and put upon; others, likewise excessively sensitive, are aggressive and
insistent. In all cases there is excessive self-reference.

Fanatic personality   Paranoid personality (disorder)
Paranoid traits

Excludes: acute paranoid reaction (298.3)
            alcoholic paranoia (291.5)
            paranoid schizophrenia (295.3)
            paranoid states (297.–)

301.1   *Affective personality disorder*

Personality disorder characterized by lifelong predominance of a pronounced mood which may be
persistently depressive, persistently elated, or alternately one then the other. During periods of
elation there is unshakeable optimism and an enhanced zest for life and activity, whereas periods
of depression are marked by worry, pessimism, low output of energy and a sense of futility.

Cycloid personality   Depressive personality
Cyclothymic personality

Excludes: affective psychoses (296.–)
            cyclothymia (296.2–296.5)
            neurasthenia (300.5)
            neurotic depression (300.4)

301.2   *Schizoid personality disorder*

Personality disorder in which there is withdrawal from affectional, social and other contacts with autistic preference for fantasy and introspective reserve. Behaviour may be slightly eccentric or indicate avoidance of competitive situations. Apparent coolness and detachment may mask an incapacity to express feeling.

Excludes: schizophrenia (295.–)

301.3   *Explosive personality disorder*

Personality disorder characterized by instability of mood with liability to intemperate outbursts of anger, hate, violence or affection. Aggression may be expressed in words or in physical violence. The outbursts cannot readily be controlled by the affected persons, who are not otherwise prone to antisocial behaviour.

Aggressive: Emotional instability (excessive)
   personality   Pathological emotionality
   reaction   Quarrelsomeness
Aggressiveness

Excludes: dyssocial personality (301.7)
            hysterical neurosis (300.1)

301.4   *Anankastic personality disorder*

Personality disorder characterized by feelings of personal insecurity, doubt and incompleteness leading to excessive conscientiousness, checking, stubbornness and caution. There may be insistent and unwelcome thoughts or impulses which do not attain the severity of an obsessional neurosis. There is perfectionism and meticulous accuracy and a need to check repeatedly in an attempt to ensure this. Rigidity and excessive doubt may be conspicuous.

Compulsive personality   Obsessional personality

Excludes: obsessive-compulsive disorder (300.3)
            phobic state (300.2)

301.5   *Hysterical personality disorder*

Personality disorder characterized by shallow, labile affectivity, dependence on others, craving for appreciation and attention, suggestibility and theatricality. There is often sexual immaturity, e.g., frigidity and over-responsiveness to stimuli. Under stress hysterical symptoms [neurosis] may develop.

Histrionic personality   Psychoinfantile personality

Excludes: hysterical neurosis (300.1)

301.6   *Asthenic personality disorder*

Personality disorder characterized by passive compliance with the wishes of elders and others and a weak inadequate response to the demands of daily life. Lack of vigour may show itself in the intellectual or emotional spheres; there is little capacity for enjoyment.

Dependent personality   Passive personality
Inadequate personality

Excludes: neurasthenia (300.5)

301.7   *Personality disorder with predominantly sociopathic or asocial manifestation*

Personality disorder characterized by disregard for social obligations, lack of feeling for others, and impetuous violence or callous unconcern. There is a gross disparity between behaviour and the prevailing social norms. Behaviour is not readily modifiable by experience, including punishment. People with this personality are often affectively cold and may be abnormally aggressive or irresponsible. Their tolerance to frustration is low; they blame others or offer plausible rationalizations for the behaviour which brings them into conflict with society.

Amoral personality   Asocial personality
Antisocial personality

Excludes: disturbance of conduct without specifiable personality disorder (312.–)
            explosive personality (301.3)

301.8   *Other personality disorders*

Personality: Personality:
  eccentric   immature
  "haltlose" type   passive-aggressive
                                                  psychoneurotic

Excludes: psychoinfantile personality (301.5)

301.9   *Unspecified*

Pathological personality NOS   Psychopathic:
Personality disorder NOS   constitutional state
                                                   personality (disorder)

302   Sexual deviations and disorders

Abnormal sexual inclinations or behaviour which are part of a referral problem. The limits and features of normal sexual inclination and behaviour have not been stated absolutely in different societies and cultures but are broadly such as serve approved social and biological purposes. The sexual activity of affected persons is directed primarily either towards people not of the opposite sex, or towards sexual acts not associated with coitus normally or towards coitus performed under abnormal circumstances. If the anomalous behaviour becomes manifest only during psychosis or other mental illness the condition should be classified under the major illness. It is common for more than one anomaly to occur together in the same individual; in that case the predominant deviation is classified. It is preferable not to include in this category individuals who perform deviant sexual acts when normal sexual outlets are not available to them.

302.0   *Homosexuality*

Exclusive or predominant sexual attraction for persons of the same sex with or without physical relationship. Code homosexuality here whether or not it is considered as a mental disorder.

Lesbianism

Excludes: homosexual paedophilia (302.2)

302.1   *Bestiality*

Sexual or anal intercourse with animals.

302.2   *Paedophilia*

Sexual deviations in which an adult engages in sexual activity with a child of the same or opposite sex.

302.3   *Transvestism*

Sexual deviation in which sexual pleasure is derived from dressing in clothes of the opposite sex. There is no consistent attempt to take on the identity or behaviour of the opposite sex.

Excludes: trans-sexualism (302.5)

302.4   *Exhibitionism*

Sexual deviation in which the main sexual pleasure and gratification is derived from exposure of the genitals to a person of the opposite sex.

302.5   *Trans-sexualism*

Sexual deviation centered around fixed beliefs that the overt bodily sex is wrong. The resulting behaviour is directed towards either changing the sexual organs by operation, or completely concealing the bodily sex by adopting both the dress and behaviour of the opposite sex.

Excludes: transvestism (302.3)

302.6   *Disorders of psychosexual identity*

Behaviour occurring in preadolescents of immature psychosexuality which is similar to that shown in the sexual deviations described under transvestism (302.3) and trans-sexualism (302.5). Cross-dressing is intermittent, although it may be frequent, and identification with the behaviour and appearance of the opposite sex is not yet fixed. The commonest form is feminism in boys.

Gender-role disorder

Excludes: homosexuality (302.0)
           trans-sexualism (302.5)
           transvestism (302.3)

302.7   *Frigidity and impotence*

Frigidity—dislike of or aversion to sexual intercourse, of psychological origin, of sufficient intensity to lead, if not to active avoidance, to marked anxiety, discomfort or pain when normal sexual intercourse takes place. Less severe degrees of this disorder that also give rise to consultation should also be coded here.

Impotence—sustained inability, due to psychological causes, to maintain an erection which will allow normal heterosexual penetration and ejaculation to take place.

Dyspareunia, psychogenic

Excludes: impotence of organic origin
           normal transient symptoms from ruptured hymen
           transient or occasional failures of erection due to fatigue, anxiety, alcohol
               or drugs

302.8   *Other*

Fetishism   Sadism
Masochism

302.9   *Unspecified*

303 Alcohol dependence syndrome

A state, psychic and usually also physical, resulting from taking alcohol, characterized by behavioural and other responses that always include a compulsion to take alcohol on a continuous or periodic basis in order to experience its psychic effects, and sometimes to avoid the discomfort of its absence; tolerance may or may not be present. A person may be dependent on alcohol and other drugs; if so also make the appropriate 304 coding. If dependence is associated with alcoholic psychosis or with physical complications, *both* should be coded.

Acute drunkenness in alcoholism   Dipsomania
Chronic alcoholism

Excludes: alcoholic psychoses (291.–)
         drunkenness NOS (305.0)
         physical complications of alcohol, such as:
           cirrhosis of liver (571.2)
           epilepsy (345.–)
           gastritis (535.3)

304 Drug dependence

A state, psychic and sometimes also physical, resulting from taking a drug, characterized by behavioural and other responses that always include a compulsion to take a drug on a continuous or periodic basis in order to experience its psychic effects, and sometimes to avoid the discomfort of its absence. Tolerance may or may not be present. A person may be dependent on more than one drug.

Excludes: nondependent abuse of drugs (305.–)

304.0   *Morphine type*

Heroin   Opium alkaloids and their derivatives
Methadone   Synthetics with morphine-like effects
Opium

304.1   *Barbiturate type*

Barbiturates
Nonbarbiturate sedatives and tranquillizers with a similar effect:
   chlordiazepoxide
   diazepam
   glutethimide
   meprobamate

304.2   *Cocaine*

Coca leaves and derivatives

304.3   *Cannabis*

Hemp   Marijuana
Hashish

304.4 *Amphetamine type and other psychostimulants*

Phenmetrazine   Methylphenidate

304.5 *Hallucinogens*

LSD and derivatives   Mescaline
Psilocybin

304.6 *Other*

Absinthe addiction   Glue sniffing

Excludes: tobacco dependence (305.1)

304.7 *Combinations of morphine type drug with any other*

304.8 *Combinations excluding morphine type drug*

304.9 *Unspecified*

Drug addiction NOS   Drug dependence NOS

305   Nondependent abuse of drugs

Includes cases where a person, for whom no other diagnosis is possible, has come under medical care because of the maladaptive effect of a drug on which he is not dependent (as defined in 304.–) and that he has taken on his own initiative to the detriment of his health or social functioning. When drug abuse is secondary to a psychiatric disorder, code the disorder.

Excludes: alcohol dependence syndrome (303)
            drug dependence (304.–)
            drug withdrawal syndrome (292.0)
            poisoning by drugs or medicaments (960–979)

305.0 *Alcohol*

Cases of acute intoxication or "hangover" effects.

Drunkenness NOS   "Hangover" (alcohol)
Excessive drinking of alcohol NOS   Inebriety NOS

Excludes: alcoholic psychoses (291.–)
            physical complications of alcohol, such as:
                cirrhosis of liver (571.2)
                epilepsy (345.–)
                gastritis (535.3)

305.1 *Tobacco*

Cases in which tobacco is used to the detriment of a person's health or social functioning or in which there is tobacco dependence. Dependence is included here rather than under 304.– because tobacco differs from other drugs of dependence in its psychotoxic effects.

Tobacco dependence

305.2   *Cannabis*

305.3   *Hallucinogens*

Cases of acute intoxication or "bad trips."

LSD reaction

305.4   *Barbiturates and tranquilizers*

Cases where a person has taken the drug to the detriment of his health or social functioning, in doses above or for periods beyond those normally regarded as therapeutic.

305.5   *Morphine type*

305.6   *Cocaine type*

305.7   *Amphetamine type*

305.8   *Antidepressants*

305.9   *Other, mixed or unspecified*

"Laxative habit"
Misuse of drugs NOS

Nonprescribed use of drugs or patent
medicinals

306   Physiological malfunction arising from mental factors

A variety of physical symptoms or types of physiological malfunction of mental origin, not involving tissue damage and usually mediated through the autonomic nervous system. The disorders are grouped according to body system. Codes 306.0–306.9 should not be used if the physical symptom is secondary to a psychiatric disorder classifiable elsewhere. If tissue damage is involved, code under 316.

Excludes: hysteria (300.1)
    psychic factors associated with physical conditions involving tissue
        damage classified elsewhere (316)
    specific nonpsychotic mental disorders following organic brain damage
        (310.–)

306.0   *Musculoskeletal*

Psychogenic torticollis

Excludes: Gilles de la Tourette's syndrome (307.2)
    tics (307.2)

306.1   *Respiratory*

Air hunger
Hiccough (psychogenic)
Hyperventilation

Psychogenic cough
Yawning

Excludes: psychogenic asthma (316 and 493.9)

306.2   *Cardiovascular*

Cardiac neurosis   Neurocirculatory asthenia
Cardiovascular neurosis   Psychogenic cardiovascular disorder

Excludes: psychogenic paroxysmal tachycardia (316 and 427.9)

306.3   *Skin*

Psychogenic pruritus

Excludes: psychogenic:
                alopecia (316 and 704.0)
                dermatitis (316 and 692.–)
                eczema (316 and 691.9 or 692.–)
                urticaria (316 and 708.–)

306.4   *Gastrointestinal*

Aerophagy   Cyclical vomiting, psychogenic

Excludes: cyclical vomiting NOS (536.2)
                mucous colitis (316 and 564.1)
                psychogenic:
                    cardiospasm (316 and 530.0)
                    duodenal ulcer (316 and 532.–)
                    gastric ulcer (316 and 531.–)
                    peptic ulcer (316 and 533.–)

306.5   *Genitourinary*

Psychogenic dysmenorrhoea

Excludes: dyspareunia (302.7)
                enuresis (307.6)
                frigidity (302.7)
                impotence (302.7)

306.6   *Endocrine*

306.7   *Organs of special sense*

Excludes: hysterical blindness or deafness (300.1)

306.8   *Other*

Teeth-grinding

306.9   *Unspecified*

Psychophysiologic disorder NOS   Psychosomatic disorder NOS

307   Special symptoms or syndromes not elsewhere classified

Conditions in which an outstanding symptom or group of symptoms is not manifestly part of a more
fundamental classifiable condition.

Excludes: when due to mental disorders classified elsewhere
when of organic origin

307.0   *Stammering and stuttering*

Disorders in the rhythm of speech, in which the individual knows precisely what he wishes to say, but at the time is unable to say it because of an involuntary, repetitive prolongation or cessation of a sound.

Excludes: dysphasia (784.5)
lisping or lalling (307.9)
retarded development of speech (315.3)

307.1   *Anorexia nervosa*

A disorder in which the main features are persistent active refusal to eat and marked loss of weight. The level of activity and alertness is characteristically high in relation to the degree of emaciation. Typically the disorder begins in teenage girls but it may sometimes begin before puberty and rarely it occurs in males. Amenorrhoea is usual and there may be a variety of other physiological changes including slow pulse and respiration, low body temperature and dependent oedema. Unusual eating habits and attitudes toward food are typical and sometimes starvation follows or alternates with periods of overeating. The accompanying psychiatric symptoms are diverse.

Excludes: eating disturbance NOS (307.5)
loss of appetite (783.0)
of nonorganic origin (307.5)

307.2   *Tics*

Disorders of no known organic origin in which the outstanding feature consists of quick, involuntary, apparently purposeless, and frequently repeated movements which are not due to any neurological condition. Any part of the body may be involved but the face is most frequently affected. Only one form of tic may be present, or there may be a combination of tics which are carried out simultaneously, alternatively or consecutively. Gilles de la Tourette's syndrome refers to a rare disorder occurring in individuals of any level of intelligence in which facial tics and tic-like throat noises become more marked and more generalized and in which later, whole words or short sentences [often with an obscene content] are ejaculated spasmodically and involuntarily. There is some overlay with other varieties of tic.

Excludes: nail-biting or thumb-sucking (307.9)
stereotypies occurring in isolation (307.3)
tics of organic origin (333.3)

307.3   *Stereotyped repetitive movements*

Disorders in which voluntary repetitive stereotyped movements, which are not due to any psychiatric or neurological condition, constitute the main feature. Includes headbanging, spasmus nutans, rocking, twirling, finger-flicking mannerisms and eye poking. Such movements are particularly common in cases of mental retardation with sensory impairment or with environmental monotony.

Stereotypies NOS

Excludes: tics:
NOS (307.2)
of organic origin (333.3)

307.4   *Specific disorders of sleep*

This category should only be used when a more precise medical or psychiatric diagnosis cannot be made.

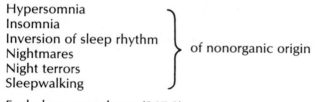

Hypersomnia
Insomnia
Inversion of sleep rhythm
Nightmares   } of nonorganic origin
Night terrors
Sleepwalking

Excludes: narcolepsy (347.0)
          when of unspecified cause (780.5)

307.5   *Other and unspecified disorders of eating*

This category should only be used when a more precise medical or psychiatric diagnosis cannot be made.

Infantile feeding disturbances
Loss of appetite
Overeating   } of nonorganic origin
Pica
Psychogenic vomiting

Excludes: anorexia:
          nervosa (307.1)
          of unspecified cause (783.0)
        overeating of unspecified cause (783.6)
        vomiting:
          NOS (787.0)
          cyclical (536.2)
            psychogenic (306.4)

307.6   *Enuresis*

A disorder in which the main manifestation is a persistent involuntary voiding of urine by day or night which is considered abnormal for the age of the individual. Sometimes the child will have failed to gain bladder control and in other cases he will have gained control and then lost it. Episodic or fluctuating enuresis should be included. The disorder would not usually be diagnosed under the age of four years.

Enuresis (primary) (secondary) of nonorganic origin

Excludes: enuresis of unspecified cause (788.3)

307.7   *Encopresis*

A disorder in which the main manifestation is the persistent voluntary or involuntary passage of formed motions of normal or near-normal consistency into places not intended for that purpose in the individual's own sociocultural setting. Sometimes the child has failed to gain bowel control, and sometimes he has gained control but then later again become encopretic. There may be a variety of associated psychiatric symptoms and there may be smearing of faeces. The condition would not usually be diagnosed under the age of four years.

Encopresis (continuous) (discontinuous) of nonorganic origin

Excludes: encopresis of unspecified cause (787.6)

307.8 *Psychalgia*

Cases in which there are pains of mental origin, e.g., headache or backache, when a more precise medical or psychiatric diagnosis cannot be made.

Tension headache   Psychogenic backache

Excludes: migraine (346.–)
                    pains not specifically attributable to a psychological cause (in):
                        back (784.5)
                        headache (784.0)
                        joint (719.4)
                        limb (729.5)
                        lumbago (724.2)
                        rheumatic (729.0)

307.9 *Other and unspecified*

The use of this category should be discouraged. Most of the items listed in the inclusion terms are not indicative of psychiatric disorder and are included only because such terms may sometimes still appear as diagnoses.

Hair plucking   Masturbation
Lalling   Nail-biting
Lisping   Thumb-sucking

308   Acute reaction to stress

Very transient disorders of any severity and nature which occur in individuals without any apparent mental disorder in response to exceptional physical or mental stress, such as natural catastrophe or battle, and which usually subside within hours or days.

Catastrophic stress   Exhaustion delirium
Combat fatigue

Excludes: adjustment reaction (309.–)

308.0 *Predominant disturbance of emotions*

Panic states, excitability, fear, depressions and anxiety fulfilling the above criteria.

308.1 *Predominant disturbance of consciousness*

Fugues fulfilling the above criteria.

308.2 *Predominant psychomotor disturbance*

Agitation states, stupor fulfilling the above criteria.

308.3 *Other*

Acute situational disturbance

308.4 *Mixed*

Many gross stress reactions include several elements but whenever possible a specific coding under .0, .1, .2 or .3 should be made according to the *preponderant* type of disturbance. The category of mixed disorders should only be used when there is such an admixture that this cannot be done.

308.9 *Unspecified*

309   Adjustment reaction

Mild or transient disorders lasting longer than acute stress reactions (308.–) which occur in individuals of any age without any apparent pre-existing mental disorder. Such disorders are often relatively circumscribed or situation-specific, are generally reversible, and usually last only a few months. They are usually closely related in time and content to stresses such as bereavement, migration or separation experiences. Reactions to major stress that last longer than a few days are also included here. In children such disorders are associated with no significant distortion of development.

Excludes: acute reaction to major stress (308.–)
             neurotic disorders (300.–)

309.0   *Brief depressive reaction*

States of depression, not specifiable as manic-depressive, psychotic or neurotic, generally transient, in which the depressive symptoms are usually closely related in time and content to some stressful event.

Grief reaction

Excludes: affective psychoses (296.–)
             neurotic depression (300.4)
             prolonged depressive reaction (309.1)
             psychogenic depressive psychosis (298.0)

309.1   *Prolonged depressive reaction*

States of depression, not specifiable as manic-depressive, psychotic or neurotic, generally long-lasting; usually developing in association with prolonged exposure to a stressful situation.

Excludes: affective psychoses (296.–)
             brief depressive reaction (309.0)
             neurotic depression (300.4)
             psychogenic depressive psychosis (298.0)

309.2   *With predominant disturbance of other emotions*

States, fulfilling the general criteria for adjustment reaction, in which the main symptoms are emotional in type [anxiety, fear, worry, etc.] but not specifically depressive.

Abnormal separation anxiety   Culture shock

309.3   *With predominant disturbance of conduct*

Mild or transient disorders, fulfilling the general criteria for adjustment reaction, in which the main disturbance predominantly involves a disturbance of conduct. For example, an adolescent grief reaction resulting in aggressive or antisocial disorder would be included here.

Excludes: disturbance of conduct NOS (312.–)
disssocial behaviour without manifest psychiatric disorder (V71.0)
personality disorder with predominantly sociopathic or asocial
manifestations (301.7)

309.4   *With mixed disturbance of emotions and conduct*

Disorders fulfilling the general definition in which both emotional disturbance and disturbance of conduct are prominent features.

309.8   *Other*

Adjustment reaction with elective mutism
Hospitalism in children NOS

309.9   *Unspecified*

Adjustment reaction NOS   Adaptation reaction NOS

310   Specific nonpsychotic mental disorders following organic brain damage

Note: This category should be used only for conditions where the *form* of the disorder is determined by the brain pathology.

Excludes: neuroses, personality disorders or other nonpsychotic conditions occurring in a form similar to that seen with functional disorders but in association with a physical condition; code to 300.–, 301.–, etc., and use additional code to identify the physical condition

310.0   *Frontal lobe syndrome*

Changes in behaviour following damage to the frontal areas of the brain or following interference with the connections of those areas. There is a general diminution of self-control, foresight, creativity and spontaneity, which may be manifest as increased irritability, selfishness, restlessness and lack of concern for others. Conscientiousness and powers of concentration are often diminished, but measurable deterioration of intellect or memory is not necessarily present. The overall picture is often one of emotional dullness, lack of drive and slowness; but, particularly in persons previously with energetic, restless or aggressive characteristics, there may be a change towards impulsiveness, boastfulness, temper outbursts, silly fatuous humour, and the development of unrealistic ambitions; the direction of change usually depends upon the previous personality. A considerable degree of recovery is possible and may continue over the course of several years.

Lobotomy syndrome
Postleucotomy syndrome (state)

Excludes: postcontusional syndrome (310.2)

310.1   *Cognitive or personality change of other type*

Chronic, mild states of memory disturbance and intellectual deterioration, often accompanied by increased irritability, querulousness, lassitude and complaints of physical weakness. These states are often associated with old age, and may precede more severe states due to brain damage classifiable under dementia of any type (290.–, and 294.–) or any condition in 293.– (Transient organic psychotic conditions).

Mild memory disturbance
Organic psychosyndrome of nonpsychotic severity

310.2   *Postconcussional syndrome*

States occurring after generalized contusion of the brain, in which the symptom picture may resemble that of the frontal lobe syndrome (310.0) or that of any of the neurotic disorders (300.0–300.9), but in which in addition, headache, giddiness, fatigue, insomnia and a subjective feeling of impaired intellectual ability are usually prominent. Mood may fluctuate, and quite ordinary stress may produce exaggerated fear and apprehension. There may be marked intolerance of mental and physical exertion, undue sensitivity to noise, and hypochondriacal preoccupation. The symptoms are more common in persons who have previously suffered from neurotic or personality disorders, or when there is a possibility of compensation. This syndrome is particularly associated with the closed type of head injury where signs of localized brain damage are slight or absent, but it may also occur in other conditions.

Postcontusional syndrome (encephalopathy)
Status post commotio cerebri
Post-traumatic brain syndrome, nonpsychotic

Excludes: frontal lobe syndrome (310.0)
              postencephalitic syndrome (310.8)
              any organic psychotic conditions following head injury (290.– to 294.0)

310.8   *Other*

Include here disorders resembling the postcontusional syndrome (310.2), associated with infective or other diseases of the brain or surrounding tissues.

Other focal (partial) organic psychosyndromes

310.9   *Unspecified*

311   Depressive disorders, not elsewhere classified

States of depression, usually of moderate but occasionally of marked intensity, which have no specifically manic-depressive or other psychotic depressive features and which do not appear to be associated with stressful events or other features specified under neurotic depression.

Depressive disorder NOS   Depression NOS
Depressive state NOS

Excludes: acute reaction to major stress with depressive symptoms (308.0)
              affective personality disorder (301.1)
              affective psychoses (296.–)
              brief depressive reaction (309.0)
              disturbance of emotions specific to childhood and adolescence, with
                  misery and unhappiness (313.1)
              mixed adjustment reaction with depressive symptoms (309.4)
              neurotic depression (300.4)
              prolonged depressive adjustment reaction (309.1)
              psychogenic depressive psychosis (298.0)

312   Disturbance of conduct not elsewhere classified

Disorders mainly involving aggressive and destructive behaviour and disorders involving delinquency. It should be used for abnormal behaviour, in individuals of any age, which gives rise to social disapproval but which is not part of any other psychiatric condition. Minor emotional disturbances may also be present. To be included, the behaviour—as judged by its frequency, severity and type of associations with other symptoms—must be abnormal in its context. Disturbances of conduct are distinguished from an adjustment reaction by a longer duration and by a lack of close relationship in time and content to some stress. They differ from a personality disorder by the absence of deeply ingrained maladaptive patterns of behaviour present from adolescence or earlier.

Excludes: adjustment reaction with disturbance of conduct (309.3)
            drug dependence (304.–)
            dyssocial behaviour without manifest psychiatric disorder (V71.0)
            personality disorder with predominantly sociopathic or asocial
                manifestations (301.7)
            sexual deviations (302.–)

312.0   *Unsocialized disturbance of conduct*

Disorders characterized by behaviours such as defiance, disobedience, quarrelsomeness, aggression, destructive behaviour, tantrums, solitary stealing, lying, teasing, bullying and disturbed relationships with others. The defiance may sometimes take the form of sexual misconduct.

Unsocialized aggressive disorder.

312.1   *Socialized disturbance of conduct*

Disorders in individuals who have acquired the values or behaviours of a delinquent peer group to whom they are loyal and with whom they characteristically steal, play truant, and stay out late at night. There may also be promiscuity.

Group delinquency

Excludes: gang activity without manifest psychiatric disorder (V71.0)

312.2   *Compulsive conduct disorder*

Disorder of conduct or delinquent act which is specifically compulsive in origin.

Kleptomania

312.3   *Mixed disturbance of conduct and emotions*

Disorders involving behaviours listed for 312.0 and 312.1 but in which there is also *considerable* emotional disturbance as shown for example by anxiety, misery or obsessive manifestations.

Neurotic delinquency

Excludes: compulsive conduct disorder (312.2)

312.8   *Other*

312.9   *Unspecified*

313   Disturbance of emotions specific to childhood and adolescence

Less well differentiated emotional disorders characteristic of the childhood period. Where the emotional disorder takes the form of a neurotic disorder under 300.–, the appropriate 300.– coding should be made. This category differs from category 308.– in terms of longer duration and by the lack of close relationship in time and content to some stress.

Excludes: adjustment reaction (309.–)
            masturbation, nail-biting, thumb-sucking and other isolated symptoms
                (307.–)

313.0   *With anxiety and fearfulness*

Ill-defined, emotional disorders characteristic of childhood in which the main symptoms involve anxiety and fearfulness. Many cases of school refusal or elective mutism might be included here.

Overanxious reaction of childhood or adolescence

Excludes: abnormal separation anxiety (309.2)
            anxiety states (300.0)
            hospitalism in children (309.8)
            phobic state (300.2)

313.1   *With misery and unhappiness*

Emotional disorders characteristic of childhood in which the main symptoms involve misery and unhappiness. There may also be eating and sleep disturbances.

Excludes: depressive neurosis (300.4)

313.2   *With sensitivity, shyness and social withdrawal*

Emotional disorders characteristic of childhood in which the main symptoms involve sensitivity, shyness, or social withdrawal. Some cases of elective mutism might be included here.

Withdrawing reaction of childhood or adolescence

Excludes: infantile autism (299.0)
            schizoid personality (301.2)
            schizophrenia (295.–)

313.3   *Relationship problems*

Emotional disorders characteristic of childhood in which the main symptoms involve relationship problems.

Sibling jealousy

Excludes: relationship problems associated with aggression, destruction or other
                forms of conduct disturbance (312.–)

313.8   *Other or mixed*

Many emotional disorders of childhood include several elements but whenever possible a specific coding under .0, .1, .2 or .3 should be made according to the *preponderant* type of disturbance. The category of mixed disorders should only be used when there is such an admixture that this cannot be done.

313.9   *Unspecified*

314   Hyperkinetic syndrome of childhood

Disorders in which the essential features are short attention span and distractibility. In early childhood the most striking symptom is disinhibited, poorly organized and poorly regulated extreme overactivity but in adolescence this may be replaced by underactivity. Impulsiveness, marked mood fluctuations and aggression are also common symptoms. Delays in the development of specific skills are often present and disturbed, poor relationships are common. If the hyperkinesis is symptomatic of an underlying disorder, code the underlying disorder instead.

314.0   *Simple disturbance of activity and attention*

Cases in which short attention span, distractibility, and overactivity are the main manifestations without significant disturbance of conduct or delay in specific skills.

Overactivity NOS

314.1   *Hyperkinesis with developmental delay*

Cases in which the hyperkinetic syndrome is associated with speech delay, clumsiness, reading difficulties or other delays in specific skills.

Developmental disorder of hyperkinesis

Use additional code to identify any associated neurological disorder

314.2   *Hyperkinetic conduct disorder*

Cases in which the hyperkinetic syndrome is associated with marked conduct disturbance but not developmental delay.

Hyperkinetic conduct disorder

Excludes: hyperkinesis with significant delays in specific skills (314.1)

314.8   *Other*

314.9   *Unspecified*

Hyperkinetic reaction of childhood or   Hyperkinetic syndrome NOS
    adolescence NOS

315   Specific delays in development

A group of disorders in which a specific delay in development is the main feature. In each case development is related to biological maturation but it is also influenced by nonbiological factors and the coding carries no aetiological implications.

Excludes: when due to a neurological disorder (320–389)

315.0   *Specific reading retardation*

Disorders in which the main feature is a serious impairment in the development of reading or spelling skills which is not explicable in terms of general intellectual retardation or of inadequate schooling. Speech or language difficulties, impaired right-left differentiation, perceptuo-motor problems, and coding difficulties are frequently associated. Similar problems are often present in other members of the family. Adverse psychosocial factors may be present.

Developmental dyslexia   Specific spelling difficulty

315.1   Specific arithmetical retardation

Disorders in which the main feature is a serious impairment in the development of arithmetical skills which is not explicable in terms of general intellectual retardation or of inadequate schooling.

Dyscalculia

315.2   Other specific learning difficulties

Disorders in which the main feature is a serious impairment in the development of other learning skills which are not explicable in terms of general intellectual retardation or of inadequate schooling.

Excludes: specific arithmetical retardation (315.1)
            specific reading retardation (315.0)

315.3   Developmental speech or language disorder

Disorders in which the main feature is a serious impairment in the development of speech or language [syntax or semantics] which is not explicable in terms of general intellectual retardation. Most commonly there is a delay in the development of normal word-sound production resulting in defects of articulation. Omissions or substitutions of consonants are most frequent. There may also be a delay in the production of spoken language. Rarely, there is also a developmental delay in the comprehension of sounds. Includes cases in which delay is largely due to environmental privation.

Developmental aphasia   Dyslalia

Excludes: acquired aphasia (784.3)
            elective mutism (309.8, 313.0 or 313.2)
            lisping and lalling (307.9)
            stammering and stuttering (307.0)

315.4   Specific motor retardation

Disorders in which the main feature is a serious impairment in the development of motor coordination which is not explicable in terms of general intellectual retardation. The clumsiness is commonly associated with perceptual difficulties.

Clumsiness syndrome   Dyspraxia syndrome

315.5   Mixed development disorder

A delay in the development of one specific skill [e.g., reading, arithmetic, speech or coordination] is frequently associated with lesser delays in other skills. When this occurs the coding should be made according to the skill most seriously impaired. The mixed category should be used only where the mixture of delayed skills is such that no one skill is preponderantly affected.

315.8   Other

315.9   Unspecified

Developmental disorder NOS

316   Psychic factors associated with diseases classified elsewhere

Mental disturbances or psychic factors of any type thought to have played a major part in the aetiology of physical conditions, usually involving tissue damage, classified elsewhere. The mental disturbance is usually mild and nonspecific and psychic factors [worry, fear, conflict, etc.] may be present without any overt psychiatric disorder. Use an additional code to identify the physical condition. In the rare instance that an overt psychiatric disorder is thought to have caused a physical condition, use a second additional code to record the psychiatric diagnosis.

Examples of the use of this category are:
    psychogenic:
        asthma 316 and 493.9
        dermatitis 316 and 692.–
        eczema 316 and 691.– or 692.–
        gastric ulcer 316 and 531.–
        mucous colitis 316 and 564.1
        ulcerative colitis 316 and 556
        urticaria 316 and 708.–
    psychosocial dwarfism 316 and 259.4

Excludes: physical symptoms and physiological malfunctions, not involving tissue
                damage, of mental origin (306.–)

MENTAL RETARDATION (317–319)

A condition of arrested or incomplete development of mind which is especially characterized by subnormality of intelligence. The coding should be made on the individual's *current* level of functioning *without regard to its nature* or causation—such as psychosis, cultural deprivation, Down's syndrome, etc. Where there is a specific cognitive handicap—such as in speech—the four-digit coding should be based on assessments of cognition *outside the area of specific handicap*. The assessment of intellectual level should be based on whatever information is available, including clinical evidence, adaptive behaviour and psychometric findings. The IQ levels given are based on a test with a mean of 100 and a standard deviation of 15—such as the Wechsler scales. They are provided only as a guide and should not be applied rigidly. Mental retardation often involves psychiatric disturbances and may often develop as a result of some physical disease or injury. In these cases, an additional code or codes should be used to identify any associated condition, psychiatric or physical. The Impairment and Handicap codes should also be consulted.

317   Mild mental retardation

Feeble-minded   Moron
High-grade defect   IQ 50–70
Mild mental subnormality

318   Other specific mental retardation

318.0   *Moderate mental retardation*

Imbecile   Moderate mental subnormality
IQ 35–49

318.1   *Severe mental retardation*

IQ 20–34   Severe mental subnormality

318.2   *Profound mental retardation*

Idiocy   Profound mental subnormality
IQ under 20

319   Unspecified mental retardation

Mental deficiency NOS   Mental subnormality NOS

ICD-9-CM CLASSIFICATION OF MENTAL DISORDERS
(without inclusion and exclusion terms)

From **The International Classification of Diseases, Clinical Modification, Ninth Revision (ICD-9-CM)**, Commission on Professional and Hospital Activities, Edwards Bros., Ann Arbor, MI, 1979.

Italics indicate specific ICD-9-CM codes and their categories not included in DSM-III-R. The lozenge symbol (⬠) printed in the left margin preceding the disease code denotes a four-digit rubric unique to ICD-9-CM. The contents of these rubrics in ICD-9-CM are not the same as those in ICD-9.

MENTAL DISORDERS (290–319)

PSYCHOSES (290–299)

ORGANIC PSYCHOTIC CONDITIONS (290–294)

290   Senile and presenile organic psychotic conditions

   290.0   Senile dementia, uncomplicated

   290.1   Presenile dementia

      290.10   Presenile dementia, uncomplicated

      290.11   Presenile dementia with delirium

      290.12   Presenile dementia with delusional features

      290.13   Presenile dementia with depressive features

   290.2   Senile dementia with delusional or depressive features

      290.20   Senile dementia with delusional features

      290.21   Senile dementia with depressive features

   290.3   Senile dementia with delirium

   290.4   Arteriosclerotic dementia

290.40   Arteriosclerotic dementia, uncomplicated

290.41   Arteriosclerotic dementia with delirium

290.42   Arteriosclerotic dementia with delusional features

290.43   Arteriosclerotic dementia with depressive features

290.8   Other specified senile psychotic conditions

290.9   Unspecified senile psychotic condition

291   Alcohol psychoses

291.0   Alcohol withdrawal delirium

291.1   Alcohol amnestic syndrome

291.2   Other alcoholic dementia

291.3   Alcohol withdrawal hallucinosis

291.4   Idiosyncratic alcohol intoxication

291.5   Alcoholic jealousy

291.8   Other specified alcoholic psychosis

291.9   Unspecified alcoholic psychosis

292   Drug psychoses

292.0   Drug withdrawal syndrome

292.1   Paranoid and/or hallucinatory states induced by drugs

292.11   Drug-induced organic delusional syndrome

292.12   Drug-induced hallucinosis

292.2   Pathological drug intoxication

292.8   Other specified drug-induced mental disorders

292.81   Drug-induced delirium

292.82   Drug-induced dementia

292.83   Drug-induced amnestic syndrome

292.84   Drug-induced organic affective syndrome

292.89   Other

292.9   Unspecified drug-induced mental disorder

293   Transient organic psychotic conditions

293.0   Acute delirium

293.1   Subacute delirium

293.8   Other specified transient organic mental disorders

293.81   Organic delusional syndrome

293.82   Organic hallucinosis syndrome

293.83   Organic affective syndrome

293.89   Other

293.9   Unspecified transient organic mental disorder

294   Other organic psychotic conditions (chronic)

294.0   Amnestic syndrome

294.1   Dementia in conditions classified elsewhere

294.8   Other specified organic brain syndromes (chronic)

294.9   Unspecified organic brain syndrome (chronic)

OTHER PSYCHOSES (295–299)

295   Schizophrenic disorders

295.0   *Simple type*

295.1   Disorganized type

295.2   Catatonic type

295.3   Paranoid type

295.4   Acute schizophrenic episode

295.5   *Latent schizophrenia*

295.6   Residual schizophrenia

295.7   Schizo-affective type

295.8   Other specified types of schizophrenia

295.9   Unspecified schizophrenia

296   Affective psychoses

□296.0   *Manic disorder, single episode*

□296.1   *Manic disorder, recurrent episode*

□296.2   Major depressive disorder, single episode

□296.3   Major depressive disorder, recurrent episode

□296.4   Bipolar affective disorder, manic

□296.5   Bipolar affective disorder, depressed

□296.6   Bipolar affective disorder, mixed

□296.7   Bipolar affective disorder, unspecified

□296.8   Manic-depressive psychosis, other and unspecified

    296.80   Manic-depressive psychosis, unspecified

    296.81   Atypical manic disorder

    296.82   Atypical depressive disorder

    296.89   Other

□296.9   Other and unspecified affective psychoses

    296.90   Unspecified affective psychosis

    296.99   Other specified affective psychoses

297   Paranoid states

    297.0   Paranoid state, simple

    297.1   Paranoia

    297.2   Paraphrenia

    297.3   Shared paranoid disorder

    297.8   Other specified paranoid states

    297.9   Unspecified paranoid state

298   Other nonorganic psychoses

    298.0   Depressive type psychosis

    298.1   Excitative type psychosis

    298.2   Reactive confusion

    298.3   Acute paranoid reaction

    298.4   Psychogenic paranoid psychosis

    298.8   Other and unspecified reactive psychosis

    298.9   Unspecified psychosis

299   Psychoses with origin specific to childhood

    299.0   Infantile autism

    299.1   Disintegrative psychosis

    299.8   Other specified early childhood psychoses

    299.9   Unspecified

NEUROTIC DISORDERS, PERSONALITY DISORDERS, AND OTHER NONPSYCHOTIC MENTAL DISORDERS (300–316)

300   Neurotic disorders

300.0   Anxiety states

    300.00   Anxiety state, unspecified

    300.01   Panic disorder

    300.02   Generalized anxiety disorder

    300.09   Other

300.1   Hysteria

    300.10   Hysteria, unspecified

    300.11   Conversion disorder

    300.12   Psychogenic amnesia

    300.13   Psychogenic fugue

    300.14   Multiple personality

    300.15   Dissociative disorder or reaction, unspecified

    300.16   Factitious illness with psychological symptoms

    300.19   Other and unspecified factitious illness

300.2   Phobic disorders

    300.20   Phobia, unspecified

    300.21   Agoraphobia with panic attacks

    300.22   Agoraphobia without mention of panic attacks

    300.23   Social phobia

    300.29   Other isolated or simple phobias

300.3   Obsessive-compulsive disorders

300.4   Neurotic depression

300.5   Neurasthenia

300.6   Depersonalization syndrome

300.7   Hypochondriasis

300.8   Other neurotic disorders

    300.81   Somatization disorder

    300.89   Other

300.9   Unspecified neurotic disorder

301   Personality disorders

301.0   Paranoid personality disorder

301.1   Affective personality disorder

    301.10   Affective personality disorder, unspecified

301.11   Chronic hypomanic personality disorder

301.12   Chronic depressive personality disorder

301.13   Cyclothymic disorder

301.2   Schizoid personality disorder

301.20   Schizoid personality disorder, unspecified

301.21   Introverted personality

301.22   Schizotypal personality

301.3   Explosive personality disorder

301.4   Compulsive personality disorder

301.5   Histrionic personality disorder

301.50   Histrionic personality disorder, unspecified

301.51   Chronic factitious illness with physical symptoms

301.59   Other histrionic personality disorder

301.6   Dependent personality disorder

301.7   Antisocial personality disorder

301.8   Other personality disorder

301.81   Narcissistic personality

301.82   Avoidant personality

301.83   Borderline personality

301.84   Passive-aggressive personality

301.89   Other

301.9   Unspecified personality disorder

302   Sexual deviations and disorders

302.0   Homosexuality

302.1   Zoophilia

302.2   Pedophilia

302.3   Transvestism

302.4   Exhibitionism

302.5   Trans-sexualism

302.6   Disorders of psychosexual identity

302.7   Psychosexual dysfunction

302.70   Psychosexual dysfunction, unspecified

302.71   With inhibited sexual desire

302.72   With inhibited sexual excitement

302.73   With inhibited female orgasm

302.74   With inhibited male orgasm

302.75   With premature ejaculation

302.76   With functional dyspareunia

302.79   With other specified psychosexual dysfunctions

302.8   Other specified psychosexual disorders

302.81   Fetishism

302.82   Voyeurism

302.83   Sexual masochism

302.84   Sexual sadism

302.85   Gender identity disorder of adolescent or adult life

302.89   Other

302.9   Unspecified psychosexual disorder

303   Alcohol dependence syndrome

303.0   Acute alcoholic intoxication

303.9   Other and unspecified alcohol dependence

304   Drug dependence

304.0   Opioid type dependence

304.1   Barbiturate and similarly acting sedative or hypnotic dependence

304.2   Cocaine dependence

304.3   Cannabis dependence

304.4   Amphetamine and other psychostimulant dependence

304.5   Hallucinogen dependence

304.6   Other specified drug dependence

304.7   Combinations of opioid type drug with any other

304.8   Combinations of drug dependence excluding opioid type drug

304.9   Unspecified drug dependence

305   Nondependent abuse of drugs

305.0   Alcohol abuse

305.1   Tobacco use disorder

305.2   Cannabis abuse

305.3   Hallucinogen abuse

305.4   Barbiturate and similarly acting sedative or hypnotic abuse

305.5   Opioid abuse

305.6   Cocaine abuse

305.7   Amphetamine or related acting sympathomimetic abuse

305.8   Antidepressant type abuse

305.9   Other, mixed, or unspecified drug abuse

306   Physiological malfunction arising from mental factors

306.0   Musculoskeletal

306.1   Respiratory

306.2   Cardiovascular

306.3   Skin

306.4   Gastrointestinal

306.5   Genitourinary

306.50   Psychogenic genitourinary malfunction, unspecified

306.51   Psychogenic vaginismus

306.52   Psychogenic dysmenorrhea

306.53   Psychogenic dysuria

306.59   Other

306.6   Endocrine

306.7   Organs of special sense

306.8   Other specified psychophysiological malfunction

306.9   Unspecified psychophysiological malfunction

307   Special symptoms or syndromes, not elsewhere classified

307.0   Stammering and stuttering

307.1   Anorexia nervosa

307.2   Tics

307.20   Tic disorder, unspecified

307.21   Transient tic disorder of childhood

307.22   Chronic motor tic disorder

307.23   Gilles de la Tourette's disorder

307.3   Stereotyped repetitive movements

307.4   Specific disorders of sleep of nonorganic origin

    307.40   Nonorganic sleep disorder, unspecified

    307.41   Transient disorder of initiating or maintaining sleep

    307.42   Persistent disorder of initiating or maintaining sleep

    307.43   Transient disorder of initiating or maintaining wakefulness

    307.44   Persistent disorder of initiating or maintaining wakefulness

    307.45   Phase-shift disruption of 24-hour sleep-wake cycle

    307.46   Somnambulism or night terrors

    307.47   Other dysfunctions of sleep stages or arousal from sleep

    307.48   Repetitive intrusions of sleep

    307.49   Other

307.5   Other and unspecified disorders of eating

    307.50   Eating disorder, unspecified

    307.51   Bulimia

    307.52   Pica

    307.53   Psychogenic rumination

    307.54   Psychogenic vomiting

    307.59   Other

307.6   Enuresis

307.7   Encopresis

307.8   Psychalgia

    307.80   Psychogenic pain, site unspecified

    307.81   Tension headache

    307.89   Other

307.9   Other and unspecified special symptoms or syndromes, not elsewhere classified

308   Acute reaction to stress

    308.0   Predominant disturbance of emotions

    308.1   Predominant disturbance of consciousness

    308.2   Predominant psychomotor disturbance

    308.3   Other acute reactions to stress

    308.4   Mixed disorders as reaction to stress

    308.9   Unspecified acute reaction to stress

309 Adjustment reaction

    309.0 Brief depressive reaction

    309.1 Prolonged depressive reaction

    309.2 With predominant disturbance of other emotions

        309.21 Separation anxiety disorder

        309.22 Emancipation disorder of adolescence and early adult life

        309.23 Specific academic or work inhibition

        309.24 Adjustment reaction with anxious mood

        309.28 Adjustment reaction with mixed emotional features

        309.29 Other

    309.3 With predominant disturbance of conduct

    309.4 With mixed disturbance of emotions and conduct

    309.8 Other specified adjustment reactions

        309.81 Prolonged posttraumatic stress disorder

        309.82 Adjustment reaction with physical symptoms

        309.83 Adjustment reaction with withdrawal

        309.89 Other

    309.9 Unspecified adjustment reaction

310 Specific nonpsychotic mental disorders due to organic brain damage

    310.0 Frontal lobe syndrome

    310.1 Organic personality syndrome

    310.2 Postconcussion syndrome

    310.8 Other specified nonpsychotic mental disorders following organic brain damage

    310.9 Unspecified nonpsychotic mental disorder following organic brain damage

311 Depressive disorder, not elsewhere classified

312 Disturbance of conduct, not elsewhere classified

    □312.0 Undersocialized conduct disorder, aggressive type

    □*312.1 Undersocialized conduct disorder, unaggressive type*

    □312.2 Socialized conduct disorder

    □312.3 Disorders of impulse control, not elsewhere classified

        312.30 Impulse control disorder, unspecified

312.31   Pathological gambling

312.32   Kleptomania

312.33   Pyromania

312.34   Intermittent explosive disorder

312.35   Isolated explosive disorder

312.39   Other

□*312.4   Mixed disturbance of conduct and emotions*

312.8   Other specified disturbances of conduct, not elsewhere classified

312.9   Unspecified disturbance of conduct

313   Disturbance of emotions specific to childhood and adolescence

313.0   Overanxious disorder

313.1   Misery and unhappiness disorder

313.2   Sensitivity, shyness, and social withdrawal disorder

313.21   Shyness disorder of childhood

313.22   Introverted disorder of childhood

313.23   Elective mutism

313.3   Relationship problems

313.8   Other or mixed emotional disturbances of childhood or adolescence

313.81   Oppositional disorder

313.82   Identity disorder

313.83   Academic underachievement disorder

313.89   Other

313.9   Unspecified emotional disturbance of childhood or adolescence

314   Hyperkinetic syndrome of childhood

314.0   Attention deficit disorder

314.00   Without mention of hyperactivity

314.01   With hyperactivity

314.1   Hyperkinesis with developmental delay

314.2   Hyperkinetic conduct disorder

314.8   Other specified manifestations of hyperkinetic syndrome

314.9   Unspecified hyperkinetic syndrome

315   Specific delays in development

315.0   Specific reading disorder

   315.00   Reading disorder, unspecified

   315.01   Alexia

   315.02   Developmental dyslexia

   315.09   Other

315.1   Specific arithmetical disorder

315.2   Other specific learning difficulties

315.3   Developmental speech or language disorder

   315.31   Developmental language disorder

   315.39   Other

315.4   Coordination disorder

315.5   Mixed development disorder

315.8   Other specified delays in development

315.9   Unspecified delay in development

316   Psychic factors associated with diseases classified elsewhere

MENTAL RETARDATION (317–319)

317   Mild mental retardation

318   Other specified mental retardation

   318.0   Moderate mental retardation

   318.1   Severe mental retardation

   318.2   Profound mental retardation

319   Unspecified mental retardation

APPENDIX F

DSM–III–R FIELD TRIAL PARTICIPANTS

Appendix F:
DSM-III-R Field Trial
Participants

FIELD TRIAL OF DIAGNOSTIC CRITERIA FOR DISRUPTIVE BEHAVIOR DISORDERS

The purpose of this field trial was to examine the feasibility of proposed criteria for the Disruptive Behavior Disorders and to determine the optimal number of items to require for maximizing sensitivity and specificity, using the clinicians' diagnoses as the criterion. The clinicians assessed 550 children in four diagnostic groups (many with multiple diagnoses):

Attention-deficit Hyperactivity Disorder N = 311
Oppositional Defiant Disorder N = 140
Conduct Disorder N = 130
Other and No Mental Disorder N = 134

Participants (coordinators listed first):

Center for Children, Youth, & Families, Dept. of Psychiatry, University of Vermont, Burlington, VT
Thomas M. Achenbach, Ph.D.
Stephanie H. McConaughy, Ph.D.

Child Study Center Summer Treatment Program, Dept. of Psychology, Florida State University, Tallahassee, FL
William E. Pelham, Jr., Ph.D.

Child Psychiatry Branch, National Institute of Mental Health, Bethesda, MD
Maureen Donnelly, M.D.
Judith L. Rapoport, M.D.

Division of Child Psychiatry, Washington University School of Medicine, St. Louis, MO
Felton Earls, M.D.
David Goldmeier, M.D.
Haruo Kusama, M.D.
Dean Smith, M.D.
Jean Thomas, M.D.
Richard Todd, M.D.

Division of Child and Adolescent Psychiatry, Columbia Presbyterian Medical Center and New York State Psychiatric Institute, New York, NY
William J. Chambers, M.D.
Laurence L. Greenhill, M.D.
Sherry Barron-Seabrook, M.D.
Margaret Anderson, M.D.
Doris R. Borden, M.D.
Lee Cohen, M.D.
Sara Fox, M.D.
Ansar Haroun, M.D.

Long Island Jewish Medical Center, Hillside Division, Dept. of Research, Glen Oaks, NY
Harold Koplewicz, M.D.
Rachel G. Klein, Ph.D.

University of Massachusetts Medical Center, Dept. of Psychiatry, Worcester, MA
Russell A. Barkley, Ph.D.

Western Psychiatric Institute and Clinic, University of Pittsburgh School of Medicine, Pittsburgh, PA
Anthony Costello, M.D.
Ann Bowes, Ph.D.
Judy Cohen, M.D.
Mina Dulcan, M.D.
Arthur Dworetz, M.D.
Virginia Fargione, M.S.W.
Sharon Fishman, M.S.W.
Elizabeth Forbes, M.S.W.
Jackie Griffith, M.S.W.
Robert Groman, M.S.W.
Bob Kalas, A.C.S.W.
Alexanndra Kreps, M.D.

Anthony Mannarino, Ph.D.
Esther Marine, Ph.D.
Patty Metosky, P.N.P.
Pat Piercy, Ph.D.
Elaine Portner, Ph.D.
Barbara Ripley, M.S.W.
Chris Thomas, M.D.

Yale University School of Medicine and Yale Child Study Center, New Haven, CT
Bennett A. Shaywitz, M.D.
Donald J. Cohen, M.D.
Sheila M. Gillespie, R.N., M.S.N.
John E. Schowalter, M.D.
Sally E. Shaywitz, M.D.

FIELD TRIAL OF DIAGNOSTIC CRITERIA FOR PERVASIVE DEVELOPMENTAL DISORDERS

The purpose of this field trial was to examine the feasibility of proposed criteria for Autistic Disorder and to determine the optimal number of items to require for maximizing sensitivity and specificity, using the clinicians' diagnoses as the criterion. The clinicians assessed 506 children in three diagnostic groups:

Autistic Disorder N = 223
Pervasive Developmental Disorder NOS N = 109
Other N = 174

Participants (coordinators listed first):

Bellevue Hospital and New York University Medical Center, New York, NY
Magda Campbell, M.D.
Karen Meiselas, M.D.
Mae S. Sokol, M.D.

Boston University School of Medicine, Boston, MA
Deborah Fein, Ph.D.
Morris Stambler, M.D.

Chedoke-McMaster Hospitals, Child and Family Centre, Chedoke Division, Hamilton, Ontario, Canada
Peter Szatmari, M.D.
Joan Canby, M.D.

Child Behavior Study, Trenton State College, Trenton, NJ
Lynn H. Waterhouse, Ph.D.

Child Study Center, Yale University, New Haven, CT
Fred R. Volkmar, M.D.
Joel Bregman, M.D.
Donald J. Cohen, M.D.
Wendy Marans, M.S.
Nancy Moss, Ph.D.

Children's Evaluation & Rehabilitation Center, Albert Einstein College of Medicine, Yeshiva University, Bronx, NY
Howard B. Demb, M.D.

Cornell University Medical College, New York, NY
Theodore Shapiro, M.D.
Margaret Hertzig, M.D.

Dept. of Psychiatry, Queen's University, Kingston, Ontario; The Clarke Institute, Toronto, Canada
M. Konstantereas, Ph.D.
K. Minde, M.D.

Dept. of Psychiatry, University of North Carolina at Chapel Hill; The Piedmont TEACCH Center, Chapel Hill, NC
Eric Schopler, Ph.D.
Lee M. Marcus, Ph.D.

Division of Child Psychiatry and Child Development, Dept. of Psychiatry and Behavioral Sciences, Stanford University School of Medicine, Stanford, CA
Bryna Siegel, Ph.D.
Glen R. Elliott, Ph.D., M.D.

The Emma Pendleton Bradley Hospital, East Providence, RI
Carl Feinstein, M.D.
Rowland Barrett, Ph.D.

Medical Research Council Social Psychiatry Unit, London, England
Lorna Wing, M.D.

University of Manitoba, Winnipeg, Manitoba, Canada
Sheila Cantor, M.D.

FIELD TRIAL OF DIAGNOSTIC CRITERIA FOR AGORAPHOBIA WITHOUT HISTORY OF PANIC DISORDER, AND GENERALIZED ANXIETY DISORDER

The purpose of this field trial was to examine the feasibility of proposed criteria for Agoraphobia Without History of Panic Disorder and Generalized Anxiety Disorder and to collect information about these categories that would be useful in preparing the text, such as sex ratio and usual age at onset. The clinicians assessed 53 cases of Generalized Anxiety Disorder and 16 cases of Agoraphobia Without History of Panic Disorder.

Participants (coordinators listed first):

Center for Stress and Anxiety Disorders, State University of New York at Albany, Albany, NY
David H. Barlow, Ph.D.
William C. Sanderson, B.A.

Dept. of Psychiatry, University of Texas Health Sciences Center, Dallas, TX
Rege S. Stewart, M.D.
A. John Rush, Jr., M.D.

Dept. of Psychiatry, University of Barcelona, Hospital Clinic, Barcelona, Spain
Joan Massana, M.D.
Jordi Buiges, M.D.
Aurora Otero, M.D

Dept. of Psychiatry, University of Melbourne, Austin Hospital, Victoria, Australia
Graham D. Burrows, M.D.
Fiona K. Judd, Ph.D.
Trevor Norman, Ph.D.

Dept. of Psychiatry, University of Munich, Munich, Germany
Professor Peter Buchheim
Professor G. Scheibe

Hôpital de la Salpêtrière, Unit. INSERM 302, Paris, France
Daniel Widlöcher, M.D.
Yves Lecrubier, M.D.
Daniel Manceaux, M.D.

Institute of Clinical Psychiatry, University of Pisa, Pisa, Italy
Professor Giovanni B. Cassano
Joseph A. Deltito, M.D.
Laura Musetti, M.D.
Christiana Nisita, M.D.
Giulio Perugi, M.D.
Alberto Petracca, M.D.

Institute of Psychiatry, London, England
Paul Lelliott, M.B.B.S., MRC Psych.
Metin Basoglu, M.D.
Isaac Marks, M.D., FRC Psych.

McLean Hospital, Belmont, MA
Alan F. Schatzberg, M.D.
Adrienne Bentman, M.D.
Thomas C. Bond, M.D.
Daniel R. Wilson, M.D.

Medical University of South Carolina, Dept. of Psychiatry and Behavioral Services, Charleston, SC
R. Bruce Lydiard, Ph.D., M.D.
James C. Ballenger, M.D.

Mexican Institute of Psychiatry, Division of Clinical Research, Mexico City, Mexico
Juan Ramon de la Fuente, M.D.
Ana Louisa Sosa, M.D.

Phobia Clinic, Hillside Hospital, Division of Long Island Jewish Medical Center, Glen Oaks, NY
Charlotte Zitrin, M.D.
Michael Kahan, M.D.

Psychiatric Research Unit, University of Cambridge Clinical School, Cambridge, England
Nicholas Argyle, M.D.

Psychiatry Service, Hospital of Santa Cruz and San Pablo, Barcelona, Spain
Claudi Udina, M.D.

Toronto General Hospital, Toronto, Ontario, Canada
Richard P. Swinson, M.D.
Klaus Kuch, M.D.

Tufts University, School of Medicine, Division of Adult Psychiatry, Boston, MA
David A. Adler, M.D.
Domenic Ciraulo, M.D.
Richard I. Shader, M.D.

Universidad del Pais Vasco, Dept. of Psychiatry, Lejona (Vazcayo), Spain
Jose Guimon, M.D.

APPENDIX G

ALPHABETIC LISTING OF DSM–III–R DIAGNOSES AND CODES

APPENDIX G:
Alphabetic Listing
of DSM-III-R Diagnoses
and Codes

V62.30	Academic problem
309.90	Adjustment disorder NOS
	Adjustment disorder
309.24	with anxious mood
309.00	with depressed mood
309.30	with disturbance of conduct
309.40	with mixed disturbance of emotions and conduct
309.28	with mixed emotional features
309.82	with physical complaints
309.83	with withdrawal
309.23	with work (or academic) inhibition
V71.01	Adult antisocial behavior
300.22	Agoraphobia without history of panic disorder
	Alcohol
305.00	abuse
291.10	amnestic disorder
303.90	dependence
291.30	hallucinosis
291.40	idiosyncratic intoxication
303.00	intoxication
291.00	withdrawal delirium
294.00	Amnestic disorder (etiology noted on Axis III or is unknown)
	Amphetamine or similarly acting sympathomimetic
305.70	abuse
292.81	delirium
292.11	delusional disorder
304.40	dependence
305.70	intoxication
292.00	withdrawal
307.10	Anorexia nervosa
301.70	Antisocial personality disorder
300.00	Anxiety disorder NOS

314.01	Attention-deficit hyperactivity disorder
299.00	Autistic disorder
313.21	Avoidant disorder of childhood or adolescence
301.82	Avoidant personality disorder
296.70	Bipolar disorder NOS
	Bipolar disorder, depressed,
296.56	in full remission
296.55	in partial remission
296.51	mild
296.52	moderate
296.53	severe, without psychotic features
296.50	unspecified
296.54	with psychotic features
	Bipolar disorder, manic,
296.46	in full remission
296.45	in partial remission
296.41	mild
296.42	moderate
296.43	severe, without psychotic features
296.40	unspecified
296.44	with psychotic features
	Bipolar disorder, mixed,
296.66	in full remission
296.65	in partial remission
296.61	mild
296.62	moderate
296.63	severe, without psychotic features
296.60	unspecified
296.64	with psychotic features
300.70	Body dysmorphic disorder
V40.00	Borderline intellectual functioning
301.83	Borderline personality disorder
298.80	Brief reactive psychosis
307.51	Bulimia nervosa
305.90	Caffeine intoxication
	Cannabis
305.20	abuse
292.11	delusional disorder
304.30	dependence
305.20	intoxication
V71.02	Childhood or adolescent antisocial behavior
307.22	Chronic motor or vocal tic disorder
307.00	Cluttering
	Cocaine
305.60	abuse
292.81	delirium
292.11	delusional disorder
304.20	dependence
305.60	intoxication
292.00	withdrawal

	Conduct disorder,
312.20	group type
312.00	solitary aggressive type
312.90	undifferentiated type
300.11	Conversion disorder
301.13	Cyclothymia
293.00	Delirium (etiology noted on Axis III or is unknown)
297.10	Delusional disorder
294.10	Dementia (etiology noted on Axis III or is unknown)
291.20	Dementia associated with alcoholism
301.60	Dependent personality disorder
300.60	Depersonalization disorder
311.00	Depressive disorder NOS
	Developmental
315.10	arithmetic disorder
315.39	articulation disorder
315.40	coordination disorder
315.90	disorder NOS
315.31	expressive language disorder
315.80	expressive writing disorder
315.00	reading disorder
315.31	receptive language disorder
799.90	Diagnosis or condition deferred on Axis I
799.90	Diagnosis or condition deferred on Axis II
300.15	Dissociative disorder NOS
307.47	Dream anxiety disorder (Nightmare disorder)
302.76	Dyspareunia
307.40	Dyssomnia NOS
300.40	Dysthymia
307.50	Eating Disorder NOS
313.23	Elective mutism
302.40	Exhibitionism
300.19	Factitious disorder NOS
	Factitious disorder
301.51	with physical symptoms
300.16	with psychological symptoms
302.72	Female sexual arousal disorder
302.81	Fetishism
302.89	Frotteurism
307.70	Functional encopresis
307.60	Functional enuresis
	Gender identity disorder
302.85	NOS
302.85	of adolescence or adulthood, nontranssexual type
302.60	of childhood
300.02	Generalized anxiety disorder
	Hallucinogen
305.30	abuse
292.11	delusional disorder
304.50	dependence
305.30	hallucinosis

292.84   mood disorder
301.50   Histrionic personality disorder
780.50   Hypersomnia related to a known organic factor
307.44   Hypersomnia related to another mental disorder (nonorganic)
302.71   Hypoactive sexual desire disorder
300.70   Hypochondriasis
313.82   Identity disorder
312.39   Impulse control disorder NOS
297.30   Induced psychotic disorder
          Inhalant
305.90   abuse
304.60   dependence
305.90   intoxication
302.73   Inhibited female orgasm
302.74   Inhibited male orgasm
780.50   Insomnia related to a known organic factor
307.42   Insomnia related to another mental disorder (nonorganic)
312.34   Intermittent explosive disorder
312.32   Kleptomania
307.90   Late luteal phase dysphoric disorder
          Major depression, recurrent,
296.36   in full remission
296.35   in partial remission
296.31   mild
296.32   moderate
296.33   severe, without psychotic features
296.30   unspecified
296.34   with psychotic features
          Major depression, single episode,
296.26   in full remission
296.25   in partial remission
296.21   mild
296,22   moderate
296.23   severe, without psychotic features
296.20   unspecified
296.24   with psychotic features
302.72   Male erectile disorder
V65.20   Malingering
V61.10   Marital problem
317.00   Mild mental retardation
318.00   Moderate mental retardation
          Multi-infarct dementia,
290.40   uncomplicated
290.41   with delirium
290.42   with delusions
290.43   with depression
300.14   Multiple personality disorder
301.81   Narcissistic personality disorder
          Nicotine
305.10   dependence
292.00   withdrawal

V71.09	No diagnosis or condition on Axis I
V71.09	No diagnosis or condition on Axis II
V15.81	Noncompliance with medical treatment
300.30	Obsessive compulsive disorder
301.40	Obsessive compulsive personality disorder
V62.20	Occupational problem
	Opioid
305.50	abuse
304.00	dependence
305.50	intoxication
292.00	withdrawal
313.81	Oppositional defiant disorder
294.80	Organic anxiety disorder (etiology noted on Axis III or is unknown)
293.81	Organic delusional disorder (etiology noted on Axis III or is unknown)
293.82	Organic hallucinosis (etiology noted on Axis III or is unknown)
294.80	Organic mental disorder NOS (etiology noted on Axis III or is unknown)
293.83	Organic mood disorder (etiology noted on Axis III or is unknown)
310.10	Organic personality disorder (etiology noted on Axis III or is unknown)
	Other or unspecified psychoactive substance
292.83	amnestic disorder
292.89	anxiety disorder
292.81	delirium
292.11	delusional disorder
292.82	dementia
292.12	hallucinosis
305.90	intoxication
292.84	mood disorder
292.90	organic mental disorder NOS
292.89	personality disorder
292.00	withdrawal
V62.81	Other interpersonal problem
V61.80	Other specified family circumstances
313.00	Overanxious disorder
	Panic disorder,
300.21	with agoraphobia
300.01	without agoraphobia
301.00	Paranoid personality disorder
302.90	Paraphilia NOS
307.40	Parasomnia NOS
V61.20	Parent-child problem
301.84	Passive aggressive personality disorder
312.31	Pathological gambling
302.20	Pedophilia
301.90	Personality disorder NOS
299.80	Pervasive developmental disorder NOS
V62.89	Phase of life problem or other life circumstance problem
	Phencyclidine (PCP) or similarly acting arylcyclohexylamine
305.90	abuse
292.81	delirium
292.11	delusional disorder
304.50	dependence

305.90	intoxication
292.84	mood disorder
292.90	organic mental disorder NOS
307.52	Pica
304.90	Polysubstance dependence
292.89	Posthallucinogen perception disorder
309.89	Post-traumatic stress disorder
302.75	Premature ejaculation
290.10	Presenile dementia NOS
	Primary degenerative dementia of the Alzheimer type,
290.10	presenile onset, uncomplicated
290.11	presenile onset, with delirium
290.12	presenile onset, with delusions
290.13	presenile onset, with depression
	Primary degenerative dementia of the Alzheimer type,
290.00	senile onset, uncomplicated
290.30	senile onset, with delirium
290.20	senile onset, with delusions
290.21	senile onset, with depression
780.54	Primary hypersomnia
307.42	Primary insomnia
318.20	Profound mental retardation
305.90	Psychoactive substance abuse NOS
304.90	Psychoactive substance dependence NOS
300.12	Psychogenic amnesia
300.13	Psychogenic fugue
316.00	Psychological factors affecting physical condition
298.90	Psychotic disorder NOS
312.33	Pyromania
313.89	Reactive attachment disorder of infancy or early childhood
307.53	Rumination disorder of infancy
295.70	Schizoaffective disorder
301.20	Schizoid personality disorder
	Schizophrenia, catatonic type,
295.22	chronic
295.24	chronic with acute exacerbation
295.25	in remission
295.21	subchronic
295.23	subchronic with acute exacerbation
295.20	unspecified
	Schizophrenia, disorganized type,
295.12	chronic
295.14	chronic with acute exacerbation
295.15	in remission
295.11	subchronic
295.13	subchronic with acute exacerbation
295.10	unspecified
	Schizophrenia, paranoid type,
295.32	chronic
295.34	chronic with acute exacerbation

295.35	in remission
295.31	subchronic
295.33	subchronic with acute exacerbation
295.30	unspecified
	Schizophrenia, residual type,
295.62	chronic
295.61	subchronic
295.60	unspecified
	Schizophrenia, undifferentiated type,
295.92	chronic
295.94	chronic with acute exacerbation
295.95	in remission
295.91	subchronic
295.93	subchronic with acute exacerbation
295.90	unspecified
295.40	Schizophreniform disorder
301.22	Schizotypal personality disorder
	Sedative, hypnotic, or anxiolytic
305.40	abuse
292.83	amnestic disorder
304.10	dependence
305.40	intoxication
292.00	withdrawal delirium
290.00	Senile dementia NOS
309.21	Separation anxiety disorder
318.10	Severe mental retardation
302.79	Sexual aversion disorder
302.90	Sexual disorder NOS
302.70	Sexual dysfunction NOS
302.83	Sexual masochism
302.84	Sexual sadism
300.29	Simple phobia
307.46	Sleep terror disorder
307.45	Sleep-wake schedule disorder
307.46	Sleepwalking disorder
300.23	Social phobia
300.81	Somatization disorder
300.70	Somatoform disorder NOS
307.80	Somatoform pain disorder
315.90	Specific developmental disorder NOS
307.30	Stereotypy/habit disorder
307.00	Stuttering
307.20	Tic disorder NOS
307.23	Tourette's disorder
307.21	Transient tic disorder
302.50	Transsexualism
302.30	Transvestic fetishism
312.39	Trichotillomania
291.80	Uncomplicated alcohol withdrawal
V62.82	Uncomplicated bereavement
292.00	Uncomplicated sedative, hypnotic, or anxiolytic withdrawal

314.00   Undifferentiated attention-deficit disorder
300.70   Undifferentiated somatoform disorder
300.90   Unspecified mental disorder (nonpsychotic)
319.00   Unspecified mental retardation
306.51   Vaginismus
302.82   Voyeurism

APPENDIX H

NUMERIC LISTING OF DSM−III−R DIAGNOSES AND CODES

APPENDIX H: Numeric Listing of DSM-III-R Diagnoses and Codes

In order to maintain compatibility with ICD-9-CM, some DSM-III-R diagnoses share the same code numbers. These are indicated in this list by a bracket.

290.00 Primary degenerative dementia of the Alzheimer type, senile onset, uncomplicated
290.00 Senile dementia NOS
290.10 Presenile dementia NOS
290.10 Primary degenerative dementia of the Alzheimer type, presenile onset, uncomplicated
290.11 Primary degenerative dementia of the Alzheimer type, presenile onset, with delirium
290.12 Primary degenerative dementia of the Alzheimer type, presenile onset, with delusions
290.13 Primary degenerative dementia of the Alzheimer type, presenile onset, with depression
290.20 Primary degenerative dementia of the Alzheimer type, senile onset, with delusions
290.21 Primary degenerative dementia of the Alzheimer type, senile onset, with depression
290.30 Primary degenerative dementia of the Alzheimer type, senile onset, with delirium
290.40 Multi-infarct dementia, uncomplicated
290.41 Multi-infarct dementia, with delirium
290.42 Multi-infarct dementia, with delusions
290.43 Multi-infarct dementia, with depression
291.00 Alcohol withdrawal delirium
291.10 Alcohol amnestic disorder
291.20 Dementia associated with alcoholism
291.30 Alcohol hallucinosis
291.40 Alcohol idiosyncratic intoxication
291.80 Uncomplicated alcohol withdrawal
292.00 Amphetamine or similarly acting sympathomimetic withdrawal
292.00 Cocaine withdrawal
292.00 Nicotine withdrawal

292.00   Opioid withdrawal
292.00   Other or unspecified psychoactive substance withdrawal
292.00   Sedative, hypnotic, or anxiolytic withdrawal delirium
292.00   Uncomplicated sedative, hypnotic, or anxiolytic withdrawal
292.11   Amphetamine or similarly acting sympathomimetic delusional disorder
292.11   Cannabis delusional disorder
292.11   Cocaine delusional disorder
292.11   Hallucinogen delusional disorder
292.11   Other or unspecified psychoactive substance delusional disorder
292.11   Phencyclidine (PCP) or similarly acting arylcyclohexylamine delusional
           disorder
292.12   Other or unspecified psychoactive substance hallucinosis
292.81   Amphetamine or similarly acting sympathomimetic delirium
292.81   Cocaine delirium
292.81   Other or unspecified psychoactive substance delirium
292.81   Phencyclidine (PCP) or similarly acting arylcyclohexylamine delirium
292.82   Other or unspecified psychoactive substance dementia
292.83   Other or unspecified psychoactive substance amnestic disorder
292.83   Sedative, hypnotic, or anxiolytic amnestic disorder
292.84   Hallucinogen mood disorder
292.84   Other or unspecified psychoactive substance mood disorder
292.84   Phencyclidine (PCP) or similarly acting arylcyclohexylamine mood disorder
292.89   Other or unspecified psychoactive substance anxiety disorder
292.89   Other or unspecified psychoactive substance personality disorder
292.89   Posthallucinogen perception disorder
292.90   Other or unspecified psychoactive substance organic mental disorder NOS
292.90   Phencyclidine (PCP) or similarly acting arylcyclohexylamine organic mental
           disorder NOS
293.00   Delirium (etiology noted on Axis III or is unknown)
293.81   Organic delusional disorder (etiology noted on Axis III or is unknown)
293.82   Organic hallucinosis (etiology noted on Axis III or is unknown)
293.83   Organic mood disorder (etiology noted on Axis III or is unknown)
294.00   Amnestic disorder (etiology noted on Axis III or is unknown)
294.10   Dementia (etiology noted on Axis III or is unknown)
294.80   Organic anxiety disorder (etiology noted on Axis III or is unknown)
294.80   Organic mental disorder NOS (etiology noted on Axis III or is unknown)
295.10   Schizophrenia, disorganized type, unspecified
295.11   Schizophrenia, disorganized type, subchronic
295.12   Schizophrenia, disorganized type, chronic
295.13   Schizophrenia, disorganized type, subchronic with acute exacerbation
295.14   Schizophrenia, disorganized type, chronic with acute exacerbation
295.15   Schizophrenia, disorganized type, in remission
295.20   Schizophrenia, catatonic type, unspecified
295.21   Schizophrenia, catatonic type, subchronic
295.22   Schizophrenia, catatonic type, chronic
295.23   Schizophrenia, catatonic type, subchronic with acute exacerbation
295.24   Schizophrenia, catatonic type, chronic with acute exacerbation
295.25   Schizophrenia, catatonic type, in remission
295.30   Schizophrenia, paranoid type, unspecified
295.31   Schizophrenia, paranoid type, subchronic
295.32   Schizophrenia, paranoid type, chronic

295.33   Schizophrenia, paranoid type, subchronic with acute exacerbation
295.34   Schizophrenia, paranoid type, chronic with acute exacerbation
295.35   Schizophrenia, paranoid type, in remission
295.40   Schizophreniform disorder
295.60   Schizophrenia, residual type, unspecified
295.61   Schizophrenia, residual type, subchronic
295.62   Schizophrenia, residual type, chronic
295.70   Schizoaffective disorder
295.90   Schizophrenia, undifferentiated type, unspecified
295.91   Schizophrenia, undifferentiated type, subchronic
295.92   Schizophrenia, undifferentiated type, chronic
295.93   Schizophrenia, undifferentiated type, subchronic with acute exacerbation
295.94   Schizophrenia, undifferentiated type, chronic with acute exacerbation
295.95   Schizophrenia, undifferentiated type, in remission
296.20   Major depression, single episode, unspecified
296.21   Major depression, single episode, mild
296.22   Major depression, single episode, moderate
296.23   Major depression, single episode, severe, without psychotic features
296.24   Major depression, single episode, with psychotic features
296.25   Major depression, single episode, in partial remission
296.26   Major depression, single episode, in full remission
296.30   Major depression, recurrent, unspecified
296.31   Major depression, recurrent, mild
296.32   Major depression, recurrent, moderate
296.33   Major depression, recurrent, severe, without psychotic features
296.34   Major depression, recurrent, with psychotic features
296.35   Major depression, recurrent, in partial remission
296.36   Major depression, recurrent, in full remission
296.40   Bipolar disorder, manic, unspecified
296.41   Bipolar disorder, manic, mild
296.42   Bipolar disorder, manic, moderate
296.43   Bipolar disorder, manic, severe, without psychotic features
296.44   Bipolar disorder, manic, with psychotic features
296.45   Bipolar disorder, manic, in partial remission
296.46   Bipolar disorder, manic, in full remission
296.50   Bipolar disorder, depressed, unspecified
296.51   Bipolar disorder, depressed, mild
296.52   Bipolar disorder, depressed, moderate
296.53   Bipolar disorder, depressed, severe, without psychotic features
296.54   Bipolar disorder, depressed, with psychotic features
296.55   Bipolar disorder, depressed, in partial remission
296.56   Bipolar disorder, depressed, in full remission
296.60   Bipolar disorder, mixed, unspecified
296.61   Bipolar disorder, mixed, mild
296.62   Bipolar disorder, mixed, moderate
296.63   Bipolar disorder, mixed, severe, without psychotic features
296.64   Bipolar disorder, mixed, with psychotic features
296.65   Bipolar disorder, mixed, in partial remission
296.66   Bipolar disorder, mixed, in full remission
296.70   Bipolar disorder NOS
297.10   Delusional disorder

297.30 Induced psychotic disorder
298.80 Brief reactive psychosis
298.90 Psychotic disorder NOS
299.00 Autistic disorder
299.80 Pervasive developmental disorder NOS
300.00 Anxiety disorder NOS
300.01 Panic disorder, without agoraphobia
300.02 Generalized anxiety disorder
300.11 Conversion disorder
300.12 Psychogenic amnesia
300.13 Psychogenic fugue
300.14 Multiple personality disorder
300.15 Dissociative disorder NOS
300.16 Factitious disorder with psychological symptoms
300.19 Factitious disorder NOS
300.21 Panic disorder, with agoraphobia
300.22 Agoraphobia without history of panic disorder
300.23 Social phobia
300.29 Simple phobia
300.30 Obsessive compulsive disorder
300.40 Dysthymia
300.60 Depersonalization disorder
⌈300.70 Body dysmorphic disorder
│300.70 Hypochondriasis
│300.70 Somatoform disorder NOS
⌊300.70 Undifferentiated somatoform disorder
300.81 Somatization disorder
300.90 Unspecified mental disorder (nonpsychotic)
301.00 Paranoid personality disorder
301.13 Cyclothymia
301.20 Schizoid personality disorder
301.22 Schizotypal personality disorder
301.40 Obsessive compulsive personality disorder
301.50 Histrionic personality disorder
301.51 Factitious disorder with physical symptoms
301.60 Dependent personality disorder
301.70 Antisocial personality disorder
301.81 Narcissistic personality disorder
301.82 Avoidant personality disorder
301.83 Borderline personality disorder
301.84 Passive aggressive personality disorder
301.90 Personality disorder NOS
302.20 Pedophilia
302.30 Transvestic fetishism
302.40 Exhibitionism
302.50 Transsexualism
302.60 Gender identity disorder of childhood
302.70 Sexual dysfunction NOS
302.71 Hypoactive sexual desire disorder
⌈302.72 Female sexual arousal disorder
⌊302.72 Male erectile disorder

302.73   Inhibited female orgasm
302.74   Inhibited male orgasm
302.75   Premature ejaculation
302.76   Dyspareunia
302.79   Sexual aversion disorder
302.81   Fetishism
302.82   Voyeurism
302.83   Sexual masochism
302.84   Sexual sadism
⌈302.85   Gender identity disorder NOS
⌊302.85   Gender identity disorder of adolescence or adulthood, nontranssexual type
302.89   Frotteurism
⌈302.90   Sexual disorder NOS
⌊302.90   Paraphilia NOS
303.00   Alcohol intoxication
303.90   Alcohol dependence
304.00   Opioid dependence
304.10   Sedative, hypnotic, or anxiolytic dependence
304.20   Cocaine dependence
304.30   Cannabis dependence
304.40   Amphetamine or similarly acting sympathomimetic dependence
⌈304.50   Hallucinogen dependence
⌊304.50   Phencyclidine (PCP) or similarly acting arylcyclohexylamine dependence
304.60   Inhalant dependence
⌈304.90   Polysubstance dependence
⌊304.90   Psychoactive substance dependence NOS
305.00   Alcohol abuse
305.10   Nicotine dependence
⌈305.20   Cannabis abuse
⌊305.20   Cannabis intoxication
⌈305.30   Hallucinogen abuse
⌊305.30   Hallucinogen hallucinosis
⌈305.40   Sedative, hypnotic, or anxiolytic abuse
⌊305.40   Sedative, hypnotic, or anxiolytic intoxication
⌈305.50   Opioid abuse
⌊305.50   Opioid intoxication
⌈305.60   Cocaine abuse
⌊305.60   Cocaine intoxication
⌈305.70   Amphetamine or similarly acting sympathomimetic abuse
⌊305.70   Amphetamine or similarly acting sympathomimetic intoxication
⌈305.90   Caffeine intoxication
305.90   Inhalant abuse
305.90   Inhalant intoxication
305.90   Other or unspecified psychoactive substance intoxication
305.90   Phencyclidine (PCP) or similarly acting arylcyclohexylamine abuse
305.90   Phencyclidine (PCP) or similarly acting arylcyclohexylamine intoxication
⌊305.90   Psychoactive substance abuse NOS
306.51   Vaginismus
⌈307.00   Cluttering
⌊307.00   Stuttering

307.10   Anorexia nervosa
307.20   Tic disorder NOS
307.21   Transient tic disorder
307.22   Chronic motor or vocal tic disorder
307.23   Tourette's disorder
307.30   Stereotypy/habit disorder
⌈307.40   Dyssomnia NOS
⌊307.40   Parasomnia NOS
⌈307.42   Insomnia related to another mental disorder (nonorganic)
⌊307.42   Primary insomnia
307.44   Hypersomnia related to another mental disorder (nonorganic)
307.45   Sleep-wake schedule disorder
⌈307.46   Sleep terror disorder
⌊307.46   Sleepwalking disorder
307.47   Dream anxiety disorder (Nightmare disorder)
307.50   Eating Disorder NOS
307.51   Bulimia nervosa
307.52   Pica
307.53   Rumination disorder of infancy
307.60   Functional enuresis
307.70   Functional encopresis
307.80   Somatoform pain disorder
307.90   Late luteal phase dysphoric disorder
309.00   Adjustment disorder with depressed mood
309.21   Separation anxiety disorder
309.23   Adjustment disorder with work (or academic) inhibition
309.24   Adjustment disorder with anxious mood
309.28   Adjustment disorder with mixed emotional features
309.30   Adjustment disorder with disturbance of conduct
309.40   Adjustment disorder with mixed disturbance of emotions and conduct
309.82   Adjustment disorder with physical complaints
309.83   Adjustment disorder with withdrawal
309.89   Post-traumatic stress disorder
309.90   Adjustment disorder NOS
310.10   Organic personality disorder (etiology noted on Axis III or is unknown)
311.00   Depressive disorder NOS
312.00   Conduct disorder, solitary aggressive type
312.20   Conduct disorder, group type
312.31   Pathological gambling
312.32   Kleptomania
312.33   Pyromania
312.34   Intermittent explosive disorder
⌈312.39   Impulse control disorder NOS
⌊312.39   Trichotillomania
312.90   Conduct disorder, undifferentiated type
313.00   Overanxious disorder
313.21   Avoidant disorder of childhood or adolescence
313.23   Elective mutism
313.81   Oppositional defiant disorder
313.82   Identity disorder
313.89   Reactive attachment disorder of infancy or early childhood

314.00   Undifferentiated attention-deficit disorder
314.01   Attention-deficit hyperactivity disorder
315.00   Developmental reading disorder
315.10   Developmental arithmetic disorder
⌈315.31   Developmental expressive language disorder
⌊315.31   Developmental receptive language disorder
315.39   Developmental articulation disorder
315.40   Developmental coordination disorder
315.80   Developmental expressive writing disorder
⌈315.90   Developmental disorder NOS
⌊315.90   Specific developmental disorder NOS
316.00   Psychological factors affecting physical condition
317.00   Mild mental retardation
318.00   Moderate mental retardation
318.10   Severe mental retardation
318.20   Profound mental retardation
319.00   Unspecified mental retardation
⌈780.50   Hypersomnia related to a known organic factor
⌊780.50   Insomnia related to a known organic factor
780.54   Primary hypersomnia
⌈799.90   Diagnosis or condition deferred on Axis I
⌊799.90   Diagnosis or condition deferred on Axis II
V15.81   Noncompliance with medical treatment
V40.00   Borderline intellectual functioning
V61.10   Marital problem
V61.20   Parent-child problem
V61.80   Other specified family circumstances
V62.20   Occupational problem
V62.30   Academic problem
V62.81   Other interpersonal problem
V62.82   Uncomplicated bereavement
V62.89   Phase of life problem or other life circumstance problem
V65.20   Malingering
V71.01   Adult antisocial behavior
V71.02   Childhood or adolescent antisocial behavior
⌈V71.09   No diagnosis or condition on Axis I
⌊V71.09   No diagnosis or condition on Axis II

INDEX OF SELECTED SYMPTOMS INCLUDED IN THE DIAGNOSTIC CRITERIA

Symptom Index: Index of Selected Symptoms Included in the Diagnostic Criteria[1]

The purpose of this index is to identify those diagnostic criteria in the various disorders that refer, either precisely or in a more general way, to a particular symptom. For example, this index lists 21 disorders that have a criterion that refers in some way to *decreased energy*. In the index, the name of each disorder is followed by the letter or number of the criterion that refers to the symptom. For example, among the disorders listed under *decreased energy* is "Dysthymia: B(3)," which indicates that criterion B(3) in the diagnostic criteria for Dysthymia refers to decreased energy.

Since the significance of any given clinical finding has to be weighed within the total context of the person's history and presentation, this index should not be the basis for making a differential diagnosis. In the above example, although 21 disorders include the symptom *decreased energy*, the importance of this symptom is quite variable from one disorder to another.

Often a disorder is listed whose criteria do not directly mention the indexing symptom. For example, Schizoaffective Disorder is listed under *psychomotor retardation*, although this symptom is not directly mentioned in the criteria for this disorder. However, *psychomotor retardation* is referred to in criterion A(5) for Major Depressive Episode, which is mentioned in Criterion A for Schizoaffective Disorder, and is therefore *indirectly* referred to in the criteria for Schizoaffective Disorder. When the criterion for a disorder refers to a symptom only indirectly, the direct reference to the symptom is included in brackets. In the above example, the index entry "Schizoaffective disorder: A [see Major depressive episode: A(5)]" indicates that *psychomotor retardation* is indirectly referred to in criterion A of Schizoaffective Disorder, but is directly referred to in criterion A(5) of Major Depressive Episode.

It should be noted that this index deals only with symptoms that appear in the DSM-III-R diagnostic criteria; it does not index associated features. The list for a particular symptom is therefore limited to diagnoses in which the symptom is (directly or indirectly) part of the defining criteria for the disorder. For example, although *depressed mood* is often associated with Schizophrenia, Schizophrenia is not listed under *depressed mood* because this symptom does not appear in the diagnostic criteria for Schizophrenia. In addition, the residual disorders within each major diagnostic class (for example, Eating Disorder Not Otherwise Specified) are not listed in the index.

---

[1]Prepared by Michael B. First, M.D., and Robert L. Spitzer, M.D.

Use of the Index. The symptoms are organized into the following symptom groups:

I.   ACTIVITY
II.   ANXIETY SYMPTOMS
III.   APPEARANCE
IV.   BEHAVIOR
V.   COGNITION/MEMORY/ATTENTION
VI.   EATING DISTURBANCE
VII.   ENERGY
VIII.   FORM AND AMOUNT OF THOUGHT/SPEECH
IX.   MOOD/AFFECT DISTURBANCE
X.   OCCUPATIONAL AND SOCIAL IMPAIRMENT
XI.   PERCEPTUAL DISTURBANCE (INCLUDING HALLUCINATIONS)
XII.   PERSONALITY TRAITS
XIII.   PHYSICAL SIGNS AND SYMPTOMS
XIV.   SLEEP DISTURBANCE
XV.   THOUGHT CONTENT (INCLUDING DELUSIONS)

The clinician should first consult these symptom groups to select the one most likely to include the symptom under consideration. Usually, the choice of symptom group will be clear. Symptoms that cannot be clearly categorized by a single group are listed in several groups. For example, *grandiosity* is listed under MOOD/AFFECT DISTURBANCE, THOUGHT CONTENT, and PERSONALITY TRAITS. Listed after each symptom is a page number that indicates where in this appendix the list of indexed diagnoses can be found.

An example of how to use this appendix follows:

1. The clinician is interested in determining all of the disorders that have as one of their defining features the symptom "repeated awakening in the middle of the night."

2. The clinician consults the list of symptom groups above and decides that "repeated awakening in the middle of the night" will most likely be listed under SLEEP DISTURBANCE.

3. The clinician looks up SLEEP DISTURBANCE and finds that the most likely listed sleep symptom that corresponds to "repeated awakening in the middle of the night" is *insomnia*. The clinician then turns to the page number following the word *insomnia* and finds the list of disorders whose diagnostic criteria refer to *insomnia*.

4. The clinician then turns to the Index of Diagnostic Terms to locate the page on which the diagnosis is described or on which the criteria for that diagnosis appear.

LIST OF SELECTED SYMPTOMS

I.   ACTIVITY
     catatonia p. 526
     incoordination p. 539
     increase in social, occupational,
        or sexual activity p. 539
     psychomotor agitation p. 546
     psychomotor retardation p. 547

II.   ANXIETY SYMPTOMS
     avoidance behavior p. 525
     compulsions p. 527
     depersonalization or derealiza-
        tion p. 530
     fear of embarrassment due to a
        physical symptom p. 533
     fear of situations where escape is
        difficult p. 533
     fear of social situations p. 533
     obsessions p. 548
     panic attacks p. 544
     travel away from home restricted
        p. 551
     worrying p. 532

III. APPEARANCE
     sad or tearful appearance p. 548
     sexually seductive appearance
        p. 548
     untidy appearance p. 551

IV.   BEHAVIOR
     aggression or rage p. 544
     antisocial behavior p. 524
     apathy p. 524
     assumption of a new identity
        p. 525
     avoidance behavior p. 525
     catatonia p. 526
     compulsions p. 527
     cross-dressing p. 527
     disorganized behavior p. 534
     feigning of symptoms p. 534
     reckless activity p. 541
     self-induced vomiting p. 548
     self-mutilating behavior p. 548
     substance use when hazardous
        p. 550
     suicide attempt p. 550
     travel away from home restricted
        p. 551

V.   COGNITION/MEMORY/
     ATTENTION
     aphasia p. 525
     distractibility p. 530
     impaired abstract thinking p. 536
     impaired judgment p. 536
     inability to maintain attention or
        poor concentration p. 538
     indecisiveness p. 539
     memory impairment p. 543

VI.   EATING DISTURBANCE
     binge eating p. 525
     decreased appetite p. 527
     increased appetite p. 539
     refusal to maintain normal body
        weight p. 548
     self-induced vomiting p. 548
     weight gain p. 549
     weight loss p. 549

VII. ENERGY
     decrease in energy or fatigue
        p. 527

VIII. FORM AND AMOUNT OF
     THOUGHT/SPEECH
     abnormalities in the production
        of speech p. 543
     circumstantiality p. 527
     flight of ideas p. 534
     incoherence or loosening of asso-
        ciations p. 538
     impressionistic speech p. 544
     pressured speech p. 545
     racing thoughts p. 547
     slurred speech p. 549
     tangentiality p. 551

IX.   MOOD/AFFECT DISTURBANCE
     anger p. 545
     apathy p. 524
     blunted affect p. 526
     depressed mood p. 530
     elevated mood p. 531
     flat affect p. 534
     grandiosity p. 534
     hopelessness p. 533
     irritable mood or irritability (in
        adults) p. 541

irritable mood or irritability (in children and adolescents) p. 542

loss of interest in activities p. 542

marked mood shifts p. 543

X.   OCCUPATIONAL AND SOCIAL IMPAIRMENT

absent or abnormal social play p. 524

impairment grossly in excess than expected from physical findings p. 537

impairment in occupational (or academic) functioning p. 537

indiscriminate socializing p. 540

XI.   PERCEPTUAL DISTURBANCE

depersonalization or derealization p. 530

disturbance in perception of body (nondelusional) p. 531

hallucinations p. 534

illusions or perceptual distortions p. 536

XII.   PERSONALITY TRAITS

interpersonal

avoids significant interpersonal contact p. 525

chooses relationships that lead to disappointment p. 527

devastated when close relationships end p. 530

expects to be exploited or harmed by others p. 533

extreme reticence in social situations p. 533

indifferent to feelings of others p. 540

interpersonal exploitativeness p. 541

no close friends or confidants p. 543

unstable and intense relationships p. 551

occupational

avoids obligations by claiming to have forgotten p. 525

excessive devotion to work p. 532

inability to sustain consistent work behavior p. 538

indecisiveness p. 539

perfectionism p. 544

procrastination p. 548

self

chronic emptiness and boredom p. 527

constantly seeking praise or admiration p. 527

entitlement p. 532

exaggerated expression of emotions p. 532

excessively self-centered p. 533

feels uncomfortable when alone p. 533

grandiosity p. 534

need for excessive advice from others p. 543

persistent identity disturbance p. 545

repeated lying p. 548

responds to success with depression and guilt p. 548

restricted expression of emotion p. 548

volunteers to do demeaning things p. 552

XIII.   PHYSICAL SIGNS AND SYMPTOMS

autonomic

dizziness or lightheadedness p. 531

dry mouth p. 531

elevated blood pressure p. 531

flushes or chills p. 534

pupillary constriction p. 547

pupillary dilation p. 547

sweating p. 546

tachycardia p. 551

cardiovascular

chest pain p. 526

dizziness or lightheadedness p. 531

elevated blood pressure p. 531

tachycardia p. 551

gastrointenstinal

abdominal pain p. 524

diarrhea p. 530

nausea p. 543
vomiting p. 552
neurologic
    blurred vision p. 526
    gait abnormalities p. 534
    headache p. 535
    numbness p. 543
    nystagmus p. 544
    paralysis p. 544
    tremor or trembling p. 551
pain
    chest pain p. 526
    headache p. 535
    other pain p. 544
unspecified
    disturbance in perception of body (nondelusional) p. 531
    impairment grossly in excess than expected from physicial findings p. 537
    physical complaint without organic pathology p. 545

XIV. SLEEP DISTURBANCE
hypersomnia p. 535
insomnia p. 540

XV. THOUGHT CONTENT (INCLUDING DELUSIONS)
delusions
    bizarre delusions p. 525
    delusions concerning appearance p. 528
    delusions of grandeur p. 528
    delusions of guilt p. 529
    erotomanic delusions p. 532
    persecutory delusions p. 544
    somatic delusions p. 549
distress about assigned gender p. 545
disturbance in perception of body (nondelusional) p. 531
grandiosity p. 534
hopelessness p. 533
ideas of reference p. 536
obsessions p. 548
paranoid ideation (nondelusional) p. 544
recurrent recollection of distressing events p. 548
suicidal ideation p. 550

SYMPTOM INDEX

abdominal pain
    Adjustment disorder with physical complaints
    Caffeine intoxication: B(7)
    Generalized anxiety disorder: D(10)
    Hypochondriasis: A
    Late luteal phase dysphoric disorder: B(10)
    Organic anxiety syndrome: A [see Generalized anxiety disorder: D(10) or Panic disorder: C(7)]
    Overanxious disorder: A(4)
    Panic disorder: C(7)
    Panic disorder with agoraphobia: A [see Panic disorder: C(7)]
    Separation anxiety disorder: A(7)
    Somatization disorder: B(2)
    Undifferentiated somatoform disorder: A

absent or abnormal social play
    Autistic disorder: A(4)
    Reactive attachment disorder of infancy or early childhood: A(1)

antisocial behavior
    Adjustment disorder with disturbance of conduct
    Adjustment disorder with mixed disturbance of emotions and conduct
    Adult antisocial behavior
    Antisocial personality disorder: C(2)
    Bipolar disorder, manic: A [see Manic episode: B(7)]
    Bipolar disorder, mixed: A [see Manic episode: B(7)]
    Borderline personality disorder: (2)
    Childhood or adolescent antisocial behavior
    Conduct disorder: A
    Cyclothymia: A [see Hypomanic/Manic episode: B(7)]
    Hallucinogen mood disorder: A [see Manic episode: B(7)]
    Intermittent explosive disorder: A
    Kleptomania: A
    Organic mood syndrome: A [see Manic episode: B(7)]
    Phencyclidine (PCP) or similarly acting arylcyclohexylamine mood disorder: A [see Manic episode: B(7)]
    Pyromania: A
    Schizoaffective disorder: A [see Manic episode: B(7)]

apathy
    Bipolar disorder, depressed: B [see Major depressive episode: A(2)]
    Bipolar disorder, mixed: A [see Major depressive episode: A(2)]
    Dementia: B(4)
    Dementia associated with alcoholism: A [see Dementia: B(4)]
    Hallucinogen mood disorder: A [see Major depressive episode: A(2)]
    Inhalant intoxication: B
    Major depression, single or recurrent episode: A [see Major depressive episode: A(2)]
    Major depressive episode, melancholic type: (1)
    Multi-infarct dementia with depression [see Dementia: B(4) or Major depressive episode: A(2)]
    Opioid intoxication: B
    Organic mood syndrome: A [see Major depressive episode: A(2)]
    Organic personality syndrome: A(4)
    Phencyclidine (PCP) or similarly acting arylcyclohexylamine mood disorder: A [see Major depressive episode: A(2)]
    Post-traumatic stress disorder: C(4)
    Primary degenerative dementia of the Alzheimer type with depression [see Dementia: B(4) or Major depressive episode: A(2)]
    Schizoaffective disorder: A [see Major depressive episode: A(2)]
    Schizophrenia: D(9)

Uncomplicated bereavement

aphasia
Conversion disorder: A
Dementia: B(3)
Dementia associated with alcoholism: A [see Dementia: B(3)]
Multi-infarct dementia: A [see Dementia: B(3)]
Primary degenerative dementia of the Alzheimer type: A [see Dementia: B(3)]

assumption of a new identity
Psychogenic fugue: B

avoidance behavior
Agoraphobia without history of panic disorder: A
Avoidant disorder of childhood or adolescence: A
Avoidant personality disorder: (4)
Borderline personality disorder: (8)
Dependent personality disorder: (6)
Panic disorder with agoraphobia: B
Post-traumatic stress disorder: C(2)
Separation anxiety disorder: A(5)
Sexual aversion disorder: A
Simple phobia: C
Social phobia: D

avoids activities that involve significant interpersonal contact
Adjustment disorder with withdrawal
Avoidant disorder of childhood or adolescence: A
Avoidant personality disorder: (4)
Schizoid personality disorder: A(2)
Schizophrenia: D(1)
Schizotypal personality disorder: A(2)
Social phobia: A

avoids obligations by claiming to have forgotten
Passive aggressive personality disorder: (5)

binge eating
Borderline personality disorder: (2)
Bulimia nervosa: A

bizarre delusions
Bipolar disorder, depressed: B [see Major depressive episode with psychotic features]
Bipolar disorder, manic: A [see Manic episode with psychotic features]
Bipolar disorder, mixed: A [see Manic episode with psychotic features]
Brief reactive psychosis: A(2)
Cannabis delusional disorder: A
Hallucinogen delusional disorder: A
Hallucinogen mood disorder: A [see Major depressive episode with psychotic features or Manic episode with psychotic features]
Induced psychotic disorder: A
Major depression, single or recurrent episode: A [see Major depressive episode with psychotic features]
Multi-infarct dementia with delusions
Multi-infarct dementia with depression [see Major depressive episode with psychotic features]
Organic delusional syndrome: A
Organic mood syndrome: A [see Major depressive episode with psychotic features or Manic episode with psychotic features]
Phencyclidine (PCP) or similarly acting arylcyclohexylamine delusional disorder: A
Phencyclidine (PCP) or similarly acting arylcyclohexylamine mood disorder: A [see Major depressive episode with psychotic features or Manic episode with psychotic features]
Primary degenerative dementia of the Alzheimer type with delusions

Primary degenerative dementia of the Alzheimer type with depression [see Major depressive episode with psychotic features]

Schizoaffective disorder: A [see Major depressive episode with psychotic features or Manic episode with psychotic features or Schizophrenia: A(2)]

Schizophrenia: A(2)

Schizophrenia, undifferentiated type: A

Schizophreniform disorder: A [see Schizophrenia: A(2)]

blunted affect

Post-traumatic stress disorder: C(6)

Schizoid personality disorder: A(7)

Schizophrenia: D(5)

Schizotypal personality disorder: A(8)

blurred vision

Adjustment disorder with physical complaints

Conversion disorder: A

Hallucinogen hallucinosis: D(5)

Inhalant intoxication: C(11)

Multi-infarct dementia: C

Somatization disorder: B(21)

Undifferentiated somatoform disorder: A

catatonia

Bipolar disorder, depressed: B [see Major depressive episode with psychotic features]

Bipolar disorder, manic: A [see Manic episode with mood-incongruent psychotic features: (b)]

Bipolar disorder, mixed: A [see Major depressive episode with psychotic features or Manic episode, with mood-incongruent psychotic features: (b)]

Brief reactive psychosis: A(4)

Hallucinogen mood disorder: A [see Major depressive episode with psychotic features or Manic

episode with mood-incongruent psychotic features: (b)]

Major depression, single or recurrent episode: A [see Major depressive episode with psychotic features]

Multi-infarct dementia with depression [see Major depressive episode with psychotic features]

Organic mood syndrome: A [see Major depressive episode with psychotic features or Manic episode with mood-incongruent psychotic features: (b)]

Phencyclidine (PCP) or similarly acting arylcyclohexylamine mood disorder: A [see Major depressive episode with psychotic features or Manic episode with mood-incongruent psychotic features: (b)]

Primary degenerative dementia of the Alzheimer type with depression [see Major depressive episode with psychotic features]

Schizoaffective disorder: A [see Major depressive episode with psychotic features or Manic episode with mood-incongruent psychotic features: (b) or Schizophrenia: A(1)(d)]

Schizophrenia: A(1)(d)

Schizophreniform disorder: A [see Schizophrenia: A(1)(d)]

chest pain

Adjustment disorder with physical complaints

Hypochondriasis: A

Late luteal phase dysphoric disorder: B(10)

Organic anxiety syndrome: A [see Panic disorder: C(11)]

Overanxious disorder: A(4)

Panic disorder: C(11)

Panic disorder with agoraphobia: A [see Panic disorder: C(11)]

Separation anxiety disorder: A(7)

Somatization disorder: B(14)

Somatoform pain disorder: A
Undifferentiated somatoform disorder: A

chooses situations and relationships that
lead to disappointment
Self-defeating personality disorder:
A(1)

chronic emptiness and boredom
Borderline personality disorder: (7)

circumstantiality
Schizophrenia: D(6)
Schizotypal personality disorder:
A(7)

compulsions
Obsessive compulsive disorder,
definition of compulsion: (1)

constantly seeking praise or admiration
Histrionic personality disorder: (1)
Narcissistic personality disorder: (7)

cross-dressing
Gender identity disorder of adolescence or adulthood, nontranssexual type (GIDAANT): B
Gender identity disorder of childhood: B(1)
Transvestic fetishism: A

decrease in energy or fatigue
Adjustment disorder with depressed
mood
Amphetamine or similarly acting
sympathomimetic withdrawal:
A(1)
Bipolar disorder, depressed: B [see
Major depressive episode:
A(6)]
Bipolar disorder, mixed: A [see Ma-
jor depressive episode: A(6)]
Cocaine withdrawal: A(1)
Dysthymia: B(3)
Hallucinogen mood disorder: A [see
Major depressive episode:
A(6)]
Inhalant intoxication: C(6)

Insomnia disorder: B
Late luteal phase dysphoric disorder: B(6)
Major depression, single or recurrent episode: A [see Major depressive episode: A(6)]
Multi-infarct dementia with depression [see Major depressive epi-
sode: A(6)]
Organic mood syndrome: A [see
Major depressive episode:
A(6)]
Phencyclidine (PCP) or similarly act-
ing arylcyclohexylamine mood
disorder: A [see Major depres-
sive episode: A(6)]
Primary degenerative dementia of
the Alzheimer type with de-
pression [see Major depressive
episode: A(6)]
Schizoaffective disorder: A [see Ma-
jor depressive episode: A(6)]
Schizophrenia: D(9)
Sleep-Wake schedule disorder: A
[see Insomnia disorder: B]
Uncomplicated alcohol withdrawal:
A(2)
Uncomplicated bereavement
Uncomplicated sedative, hypnotic,
or anxiolytic withdrawal: A(2)

decreased appetite
Adjustment disorder with depressed
mood
Bipolar disorder, depressed: B [see
Major depressive episode:
A(3)]
Bipolar disorder, mixed: A [see Ma-
jor depressive episode: A(3)]
Dysthymia: B(1)
Hallucinogen mood disorder: A [see
Major depressive episode:
A(3)]
Major depression, single or recur-
rent episode: A [see Major de-
pressive episode: A(3)]
Multi-infarct dementia with depres-
sion [see Major depressive epi-
sode: A(3)]

Organic mood syndrome: A [see Major depressive episode: A(3)]

Phencyclidine (PCP) or similarly acting arylcyclohexylamine mood disorder: A [see Major depressive episode: A(3)]

Primary degenerative dementia of the Alzheimer type with depression [see Major depressive episode: A(3)]

Schizoaffective disorder: A [see Major depressive episode: A(3)]

Uncomplicated bereavement

delusions concerning appearance

Bipolar disorder, depressed: B [see Major depressive episode with psychotic features]

Bipolar disorder, manic: A [see Manic episode with psychotic features]

Bipolar disorder, mixed: A [see Manic episode with psychotic features]

Brief reactive psychosis: A(2)

Cannabis delusional disorder: A

Delusional disorder, somatic type: A

Hallucinogen delusional disorder: A

Hallucinogen mood disorder: A [see Major depressive episode with psychotic features or Manic episode with psychotic features]

Induced psychotic disorder: A

Major depression, single or recurrent episode: A [see Major depressive episode with psychotic features]

Multi-infarct dementia with delusions

Multi-infarct dementia with depression [see Major depressive episode with psychotic features]

Organic delusional syndrome: A

Organic mood syndrome: A [see Major depressive episode with psychotic features or Manic episode with psychotic features]

Phencyclidine (PCP) or similarly acting arylcyclohexylamine delusional disorder: A

Phencyclidine (PCP) or similarly acting arylcyclohexylamine mood disorder: A [see Major depressive episode with psychotic features or Manic episode with psychotic features]

Primary degenerative dementia of the Alzheimer type, with delusions

Primary degenerative dementia of the Alzheimer type with depression [see Major depressive episode with psychotic features]

Schizoaffective disorder: A [see Major depressive episode with psychotic features or Manic episode with psychotic features or Schizophrenia: A(1)(a)]

Schizophrenia: A(1)(a)

Schizophrenia, undifferentiated type: A

Schizophreniform disorder: A [see Schizophrenia: A(1)(a)]

delusions of grandeur

Bipolar disorder, depressed: B [see Major depressive episode with psychotic features]

Bipolar disorder, manic: A [see Manic episode with mood-congruent psychotic features]

Bipolar disorder, mixed: A [see Manic episode with mood-congruent psychotic features]

Brief reactive psychosis: A(2)

Cannabis delusional disorder: A

Delusional disorder, grandiose type: A

Hallucinogen delusional disorder: A

Hallucinogen mood disorder: A [see Major depressive episode with psychotic features or Manic episode with mood-congruent psychotic features]

Induced psychotic disorder: A

Major depression, single or recurrent episode: A [see Major depressive episode with psychotic features]

Multi-infarct dementia with delusions

Multi-infarct dementia with depression [see Major depressive episode with psychotic features]

Organic delusional syndrome: A

Organic mood syndrome: A [see Major depressive episode with psychotic features or Manic episode with mood-congruent psychotic features]

Phencyclidine (PCP) or similarly acting arylcyclohexylamine delusional disorder: A

Phencyclidine (PCP) or similarly acting arylcyclohexylamine mood disorder: A [see Major depressive episode with psychotic features or Manic episode with mood-congruent psychotic features]

Primary degenerative dementia of the Alzheimer type with delusions

Primary degenerative dementia of the Alzheimer type with depression [see Major depressive episode with psychotic features]

Schizoaffective disorder: A [see Major depressive episode with psychotic features or Manic episode, with mood-congruent psychotic features or Schizophrenia: A(1)(a)]

Schizophrenia: A(1)(a)

Schizophrenia, undifferentiated type: A

Schizophreniform disorder: A [see Schizophrenia: A(1)(a)]

delusions of guilt

Bipolar disorder, depressed: B [see Major depressive episode with mood-congruent psychotic features]

Bipolar disorder, manic: A [see Manic episode with psychotic features]

Bipolar disorder, mixed: A [see Manic episode with psychotic features]

Brief reactive psychosis: A(2)

Cannabis delusional disorder: A

Delusional disorder: A

Hallucinogen delusional disorder: A

Hallucinogen mood disorder: A [see Major depressive episode with mood-congruent psychotic features or Manic episode with psychotic features]

Induced psychotic disorder: A

Major depression, single or recurrent episode: A [see Major depressive episode with mood-congruent psychotic features]

Multi-infarct dementia with delusions

Multi-infarct dementia with depression [see Major depressive episode, with mood-congruent psychotic features]

Organic delusional syndrome: A

Organic mood syndrome: A [see Major depressive episode with mood-congruent psychotic features or Manic episode with psychotic features]

Phencyclidine (PCP) or similarly acting arylcyclohexylamine delusional disorder: A

Phencyclidine (PCP) or similarly acting arylcyclohexylamine mood disorder: A [see Major depressive episode with mood-congruent psychotic features or Manic episode with psychotic features]

Primary degenerative dementia of the Alzheimer type with delusions

Primary degenerative dementia of the Alzheimer type with depression [see Major depressive episode with mood-congruent psychotic features]

Schizoaffective disorder: A [see Major depressive episode with mood-congruent psychotic features or Manic episode with

psychotic features or Schizo-
phrenia A(1)(a)]
Schizophrenia: A(1)(a)
Schizophrenia, undifferentiated
type: A
Schizophreniform disorder: A [see
Schizophrenia: A(1)(a)]

depersonalization or derealization
Depersonalization disorder: A
Hallucinogen hallucinosis: C
Organic anxiety syndrome: A [see
Panic disorder: C(8)]
Panic disorder: C(8)
Panic disorder with agoraphobia: A
[see Panic disorder: C(8)]
Posthallucinogen perception disor-
der: A

depressed mood
Adjustment disorder with depressed
mood
Adjustment disorder with mixed
disturbance of emotions and
conduct
Adjustment disorder with mixed
emotional features
Amphetamine or similarly acting
sympathomimetic withdrawal:
A
Bipolar disorder, depressed: B [see
Major depressive episode:
A(1)]
Bipolar disorder, mixed: A [see Ma-
jor depressive episode: A(1)]
Cocaine withdrawal: A
Cyclothymia: A
Dysthymia: A
Hallucinogen hallucinosis: B
Hallucinogen mood disorder: A [see
Major depressive episode:
A(1)]
Late luteal phase dysphoric disor-
der: B(4)
Major depression, single or recur-
rent episode: A [see Major de-
pressive episode: A(1)]
Multi-infarct dementia with depres-
sion [see Major depressive epi-
sode: A(1)]

Opioid intoxication: B
Organic mood syndrome: A [see
Major depressive episode:
A(1)]
Phencyclidine (PCP) or similarly act-
ing arylcyclohexylamine mood
disorder: A [see Major depres-
sive episode: A(1)]
Primary degenerative dementia of
the Alzheimer type with de-
pression [see Major depressive
episode: A(1)]
Schizoaffective disorder: A [see Ma-
jor depressive episode: A(1)]
Uncomplicated alcohol withdrawal:
A(5)
Uncomplicated bereavement

devastated when close relationships end
Borderline personality disorder: (8)
Dependent personality disorder: (7)

diarrhea
Adjustment disorder with physical
complaints
Caffeine intoxication: B(7)
Generalized anxiety disorder: D(10)
Hypochondriasis: A
Late luteal phase dysphoric disor-
der: B(10)
Opioid withdrawal: A(6)
Organic anxiety syndrome: A [see
Generalized anxiety disorder:
D(10) or Panic disorder: C(7)]
Overanxious disorder: A(4)
Panic disorder: C(7)
Panic disorder with agoraphobia: A
[see Panic disorder: C(7)]
Separation anxiety disorder: A(7)
Somatization disorder: B(5)
Undifferentiated somatoform disor-
der: A

distractibility
Alcohol withdrawal delirium: A [see
Delirium: A]
Amphetamine or similarly acting
sympathomimetic delirium: A
[see Delirium: A]
Attention-deficit hyperactivity dis-
order: A(3)

Bipolar disorder, manic: A [see Manic episode: B(5)]

Bipolar disorder, mixed: A [see Manic episode: B(5)]

Cocaine delirium: A [see Delirium: A]

Cyclothymia: A [see Hypomanic/ Manic episode: B(5)]

Delirium: A

Hallucinogen mood disorder: A [see Manic episode: B(5)]

Multi-infarct dementia with delirium [see Delirium: A]

Opioid intoxication: C(3)

Organic mood syndrome: A [see Manic episode: B(5)]

Phencyclidine (PCP) or similarly acting arylcyclohexylamine delirium: A [see Delirium: A]

Phencyclidine (PCP) or similarly acting arylcyclohexylamine mood disorder: A [see Manic episode: B(5)]

Primary degenerative dementia of the Alzheimer type with delirium [see Delirium: A]

Schizoaffective disorder: A [see Manic episode: B(5)]

Sedative, hypnotic, or anxiolytic intoxication: C(4)

Sedative, hypnotic, or anxiolytic withdrawal delirium: A [see Delirium: A]

Undifferentiated attention-deficit disorder

disturbance in perception of body (non-delusional)

Anorexia nervosa: C

Body dysmorphic disorder: A

Bulimia nervosa: E

dizziness or lightheadedness

Adjustment disorder with physical complaints

Generalized anxiety disorder: D(9)

Hypochondriasis: A

Inhalant intoxication: C(1)

Organic anxiety syndrome: A [see Panic disorder: C(2)]

Overanxious disorder: A(4)

Panic disorder: C(2)

Panic disorder with agoraphobia: A [see Panic disorder: C(2)]

Separation anxiety disorder: A(7)

Somatization disorder: B(15)

Undifferentiated somatoform disorder: A

dry mouth

Adjustment disorder with physical complaints

Alcohol withdrawal delirium: B

Cannabis intoxication: C(3)

Generalized anxiety disorder: D(8)

Hypochondriasis: A

Organic anxiety syndrome: A [see Generalized anxiety disorder: D(8)]

Overanxious disorder: A(4)

Sedative, hypnotic, or anxiolytic withdrawal delirium: B

Uncomplicated alcohol withdrawal: A(3)

Uncomplicated sedative, hypnotic, or anxiolytic withdrawal: A(3)

Undifferentiated somatoform disorder: A

elevated blood pressure

Alcohol withdrawal delirium: B

Amphetamine or similarly acting sympathomimetic intoxication: C(3)

Cocaine intoxication: C(3)

Phencyclidine (PCP) or similarly acting arylcyclohexylamine intoxication: C(2)

Sedative, hypnotic, or anxiolytic withdrawal delirium: B

Uncomplicated alcohol withdrawal: A(3)

Uncomplicated sedative, hypnotic, or anxiolytic withdrawal: A(3)

elevated mood

Bipolar disorder, manic: A [see Manic episode: A]

Bipolar disorder, mixed: A [see Manic episode: A]

Cannabis intoxication: B
Cocaine intoxication: B
Cyclothymia: A [see Hypomanic/
    Manic episode: A]
Hallucinogen mood disorder: A [see
    Manic episode: A]
Inhalant intoxication: C(13)
Opioid intoxication: B
Organic mood syndrome: A [see
    Manic episode: A]
Phencyclidine (PCP) or similarly act-
    ing arylcyclohexylamine mood
    disorder: A [see Manic episode:
    A]
Schizoaffective disorder: A [see
    Manic episode: A]

entitlement
    Narcissistic personality disorder: (6)

erotomanic delusions
    Bipolar disorder, depressed: B [see
        Major depressive episode with
        psychotic features]
    Bipolar disorder, manic: A [see
        Manic episode with psychotic
        features]
    Bipolar disorder, mixed: A [see
        Manic episode with psychotic
        features]
    Brief reactive psychosis: A(2)
    Cannabis delusional disorder: A
    Delusional disorder, erotomanic
        type: A
    Hallucinogen delusional disorder: A
    Hallucinogen mood disorder: A [see
        Major depressive episode with
        psychotic features or Manic
        episode with psychotic fea-
        tures]
    Induced psychotic disorder: A
    Major depression, single or recur-
        rent episode: A [see Major de-
        pressive episode with psy-
        chotic features]
    Multi-infarct dementia with delu-
        sions
    Multi-infarct dementia with depres-
        sion [see Major depressive epi-
        sode with psychotic features]

Organic delusional syndrome: A
Organic mood syndrome: A [see
    Major depressive episode with
    psychotic features or Manic
    episode with psychotic fea-
    tures]
Phencyclidine (PCP) or similarly act-
    ing arylcyclohexylamine delu-
    sional disorder: A
Phencyclidine (PCP) or similarly act-
    ing arylcyclohexylamine mood
    disorder: A [see Major depres-
    sive episode with psychotic
    features or Manic episode with
    psychotic features]
Primary degenerative dementia of
    the Alzheimer type with delu-
    sions
Primary degenerative dementia of
    the Alzheimer type with de-
    pression [see Major depressive
    episode with psychotic fea-
    tures]
Schizoaffective disorder: A [see Ma-
    jor depressive episode with
    psychotic features or Manic
    episode with psychotic features
    or Schizophrenia: A(1)(a)]
Schizophrenia: A(1)(a)
Schizophrenia, undifferentiated
    type: A
Schizophreniform disorder: A [see
    Schizophrenia: A(1)(a)]

exaggerated expression of emotions
    Histrionic personality disorder: (4)

excessive devotion to work
    Obsessive compulsive personality
        disorder: (4)

excessive worrying
    Adjustment disorder with anxious
        mood
    Adjustment disorder with mixed
        disturbance of emotions and
        conduct
    Adjustment disorder with mixed
        emotional features
    Generalized anxiety disorder: A

Organic anxiety syndrome: A [see Generalized anxiety disorder: A]
Overanxious disorder: A
Separation anxiety disorder: A(1)

excessively self-centered
Histrionic personality disorder: (7)
Narcissistic personality disorder: (8)

expects to be exploited or harmed by others
Organic personality syndrome: A(5)
Paranoid personality disorder: A(1)
Schizotypal personality disorder: A(9)

extreme reticence in social situations
Avoidant disorder of childhood or adolescence: A
Avoidant personality disorder: (5)
Schizotypal personality disorder: A(2)
Social phobia: A

fear of embarrassment due to physical symptoms
Agoraphobia without history of panic disorder: A
Body dysmorphic disorder: A
Panic disorder with agoraphobia: B
Social phobia: A

fear of situations where escape is difficult
Agoraphobia without history of panic disorder: A
Panic disorder with agoraphobia: B

fear of social situations
Avoidant disorder of childhood or adolescence: A
Avoidant personality disorder: (5)
Schizotypal personality disorder: A(2)
Social phobia: A

feelings of hopelessness
Adjustment disorder with depressed mood

Adjustment disorder with mixed disturbance of emotions and conduct
Adjustment disorder with mixed emotional features
Amphetamine or similarly acting sympathomimetic withdrawal: A
Bipolar disorder, depressed: B [see Major depressive episode: A(1)]
Bipolar disorder, mixed: A [see Major depressive episode: A(1)]
Cocaine withdrawal: A
Cyclothymia: A
Dysthymia: B(6)
Hallucinogen hallucinosis: B
Hallucinogen mood disorder: A [see Major depressive episode: A(1)]
Late luteal phase dysphoric disorder: B(4)
Major depression, single or recurrent episode: A [see Major depressive episode: A(1)]
Multi-infarct dementia with depression [see Major depressive episode: A(1)]
Opioid intoxication: B
Organic mood syndrome: A [see Major depressive episode: A(1)]
Phencyclidine (PCP) or similarly acting arylcyclohexylamine mood disorder: A [see Major depressive episode: A(1)]
Primary degenerative dementia of the Alzheimer type with depression [see Major depressive episode: A(1)]
Schizoaffective disorder: A [see Major depressive episode: A(1)]
Uncomplicated alcohol withdrawal: A(5)
Uncomplicated bereavement

feels uncomfortable when alone
Dependent personality disorder: (6)
Separation anxiety disorder: A(5)

feigning of symptoms
 Factitious disorder: A
 Malingering

flat affect
 Schizoaffective disorder: A [see Schizophrenia: A(1)(e)]
 Schizophrenia: A(1)(e)
 Schizophrenia, disorganized type: B
 Schizophreniform disorder: A [see Schizophrenia: A(1)(e)]

flight of ideas
 Bipolar disorder, manic: A [see Manic episode: B(4)]
 Bipolar disorder, mixed: A [see Manic episode: B(4)]
 Cyclothymia: A [see Hypomanic/ Manic episode: B(4)]
 Hallucinogen mood disorder: A [see Manic episode: B(4)]
 Organic mood syndrome: A [see Manic episode: B(4)]
 Phencyclidine (PCP) or similarly acting arylcyclohexylamine mood disorder: A [see Manic episode: B(4)]
 Schizoaffective disorder: A [see Manic episode: B(4)]

flushes or chills
 Alcohol withdrawal delirium: B
 Amphetamine or similarly acting sympathomimetic intoxication: C(4)
 Cocaine intoxication: C(4)
 Generalized anxiety disorder: D(11)
 Hypochondriasis: A
 Organic anxiety syndrome: A [see Generalized anxiety disorder: D(11) or Panic disorder: C(10)]
 Panic disorder: C(10)
 Panic disorder with agoraphobia: A [see Panic disorder: C(10)]
 Sedative, hypnotic, or anxiolytic withdrawal delirium: B
 Uncomplicated alcohol withdrawal: A(3)
 Uncomplicated sedative, hypnotic, or anxiolytic withdrawal: A(3)

gait abnormalities
 Adjustment disorder with physical complaints
 Alcohol intoxication: C(3)
 Conversion disorder: A
 Inhalant intoxication: C(5)
 Multi-infarct dementia: C
 Phencyclidine (PCP) or similarly acting arylcyclohexylamine intoxication: C(4)
 Sedative, hypnotic, or anxiolytic intoxication: C(3)
 Somatization disorder: B(25)
 Undifferentiated somatoform disorder: A

grandiosity
 Amphetamine or similarly acting sympathomimetic intoxication: B
 Bipolar disorder, manic: A [see Manic episode: B(1)]
 Bipolar disorder, mixed: A [see Manic episode: B(1)]
 Cocaine intoxication: B
 Cyclothymia: A [see Hypomanic/ Manic episode: B(1)]
 Hallucinogen mood disorder: A [see Manic episode: B(1)]
 Narcissistic personality disorder: (3)
 Organic mood syndrome: A [see Manic episode: B(1)]
 Phencyclidine (PCP) or similarly acting arylcyclohexylamine mood disorder: A [see Manic episode: B(1)]
 Schizoaffective disorder: A [see Manic episode: B(1)]

grossly disorganized behavior
 Brief reactive psychosis: A(4)
 Schizophrenia, disorganized type: A
 Schizophrenia, undifferentiated type: A

hallucinations
 Alcohol hallucinosis: A
 Alcohol withdrawal delirium: A [see Delirium: C(2)]

Amphetamine or similarly acting sympathomimetic delirium: A [see Delirium: C(2)]

Bipolar disorder, depressed: B [see Major depressive episode with psychotic features]

Bipolar disorder, manic: A [see Manic episode with psychotic features]

Bipolar disorder, mixed: A [see Manic episode with psychotic features]

Brief reactive psychosis: A(3)

Cocaine delirium: A [see Delirium: C(2)]

Cocaine intoxication: C(6)

Delirium: C(2)

Hallucinogen hallucinosis: C

Hallucinogen mood disorder: A [see Major depressive episode with psychotic features or Manic episode with psychotic features]

Major depression, single or recurrent episode: A [see Major depressive episode with psychotic features]

Multi-infarct dementia with delirium [see Delirium: C(2)]

Multi-infarct dementia with depression [see Major depressive episode with psychotic features]

Organic hallucinosis: A

Organic mood syndrome: A [see Major depressive episode with psychotic features or Manic episode with psychotic features]

Phencyclidine (PCP) or similarly acting arylcyclohexylamine delirium: A [see Delirium: C(2)]

Phencyclidine (PCP) or similarly acting arylcyclohexylamine mood disorder: A [see Major depressive episode with psychotic features or Manic episode with psychotic features]

Posthallucinogen perception disorder: A

Primary degenerative dementia of the Alzheimer type with delirium [see Delirium: C(2)]

Primary degenerative dementia of the Alzheimer type with depression [see Major depressive episode with psychotic features]

Schizoaffective disorder: A [see Major depressive episode with psychotic features or Manic episode with psychotic features or Schizophrenia: A(1)(b)]

Schizophrenia: A(1)(b)

Schizophrenia, undifferentiated type: A

Schizophreniform disorder: A [see Schizophrenia: A(1)(b)]

Sedative, hypnotic, or anxiolytic withdrawal delirium: A [see Delirium: C(2)]

headache
Adjustment disorder with physical complaints

Hypochondriasis: A

Late luteal phase dysphoric disorder: B(10)

Overanxious disorder: A(4)

Separation anxiety disorder: A(7)

Somatoform pain disorder: A

Uncomplicated alcohol withdrawal: A(7)

Undifferentiated somatoform disorder: A

hypersomnia
Adjustment disorder with depressed mood

Alcohol withdrawal delirium: A [see Delirium: C(3)]

Amphetamine or similarly acting sympathomimetic delirium: A [see Delirium: C(3)]

Amphetamine or similarly acting sympathomimetic withdrawal: A(2)

Bipolar disorder, depressed: B [see Major depressive episode: A(4)]

Bipolar disorder, mixed: A [see Major depressive episode: A(4)]
Cocaine delirium: A [see Delirium: C(3)]
Cocaine withdrawal: A(2)
Delirium: C(3)
Dysthymia: B(2)
Hallucinogen mood disorder: A [see Major depressive episode: A(4)]
Hypersomnia disorder: A(1)
Late luteal phase dysphoric disorder: B(9)
Major depression, single or recurrent episode: A [see Major depressive episode: A(4)]
Multi-infarct dementia with delirium [see Delirium: C(3)]
Multi-infarct dementia with depression [see Major depressive episode: A(4)]
Organic mood syndrome: A [see Major depressive episode: A(4)]
Phencyclidine (PCP) or similarly acting arylcyclohexylamine delirium: A [see Delirium: C(3)]
Phencyclidine (PCP) or similarly acting arylcyclohexylamine mood disorder: A [see Major depressive episode: A(4)]
Primary degenerative dementia of the Alzheimer type with delirium [see Delirium: C(3)]
Primary degenerative dementia of the Alzheimer type with depression [see Major depressive episode: A(4)]
Schizoaffective disorder: A [see Major depressive episode: A(4)]
Sedative, hypnotic, or anxiolytic withdrawal delirium: A [see Delirium: C(3)]
Sleep-wake schedule disorder: A [see Hypersomnia disorder: A(1)]
Uncomplicated bereavement

ideas of reference
Hallucinogen hallucinosis: B

Schizophrenia: D(7)
Schizotypal personality disorder: A(1)

illusions or perceptual distortions
Alcohol withdrawal delirium: A [see Delirium: C(2)]
Amphetamine or similarly acting sympathomimetic delirium: A [see Delirium: C(2)]
Cocaine delirium: A [see Delirium: C(2)]
Delirium: C(2)
Hallucinogen hallucinosis: C
Multi-infarct dementia with delirium [see Delirium: C(2)]
Phencyclidine (PCP) or similarly acting arylcyclohexylamine delirium: A [see Delirium: C(2)]
Posthallucinogen perception disorder: A
Primary degenerative dementia of the Alzheimer type with delirium [see Delirium: C(2)]
Schizophrenia: D(8)
Schizotypal personality disorder: A(4)
Sedative, hypnotic, or anxiolytic withdrawal delirium: A [see Delirium: C(2)]

impaired abstract thinking
Dementia: B(1)
Dementia associated with alcoholism: A [see Dementia: B(1)]
Mental retardation: A
Multi-infarct dementia: A [see Dementia: B(1)]
Primary degenerative dementia of the Alzheimer type: A [see Dementia: B(1)]

impaired judgment
Alcohol intoxication: B
Amphetamine or similarly acting sympathomimetic intoxication: B
Attention-deficit hyperactivity disorder: A(14)
Bipolar disorder, manic: A [see Manic episode: B(7)]

Bipolar disorder, mixed: A [see Manic episode: B(7)]
Borderline personality disorder: (2)
Cannabis intoxication: B
Cocaine intoxication: B
Cyclothymia: A [see Hypomanic/ Manic episode: B(7)]
Dementia: B(2)
Dementia associated with alcoholism: A [see Dementia: B(2)]
Hallucinogen hallucinosis: B
Hallucinogen mood disorder: A [see Manic episode: B(7)]
Inhalant intoxication: B
Mental retardation: B
Multi-infarct dementia: A [see Dementia: B(2)]
Opioid intoxication: B
Organic mood syndrome: A [see Manic episode: B(7)]
Organic personality syndrome: A(3)
Phencyclidine (PCP) or similarly acting arylcyclohexylamine intoxication: B
Phencyclidine (PCP) or similarly acting arylcyclohexylamine mood disorder: A [see Manic episode: B(7)]
Primary degenerative dementia of the Alzheimer type: A [see Dementia: B(2)]
Schizoaffective disorder: A [see Manic episode: B(7)]
Sedative, hypnotic, or anxiolytic intoxication: B

impairment grossly in excess than expected from physical finding
Adjustment disorder with physical complaints
Hypochondriasis: A
Late luteal phase dysphoric disorder: B(10)
Overanxious disorder: A(4)
Separation anxiety disorder: A(7)
Somatization disorder, significance list: (1)
Somatoform pain disorder: B(2)
Undifferentiated somatoform disorder: B(2)

impairment in occupational (or academic) functioning
Adjustment disorder: B(1)
Adjustment disorder with work (or academic) inhibition
Alcohol intoxication: B
Amphetamine or similarly acting sympathomimetic intoxication: B
Bipolar disorder, manic: A [see Manic episode: C]
Bipolar disorder, mixed: A [see Manic episode: C]
Cocaine intoxication: B
Dementia: C
Dementia associated with alcoholism: A [see Dementia: C]
Developmental arithmetic disorder: B
Developmental coordination disorder: B
Developmental expressive language disorder: B
Developmental expressive writing disorder: B
Developmental reading disorder: B
Developmental receptive language disorder: B
Hallucinogen hallucinosis: B
Hallucinogen mood disorder: A [see Manic episode: C]
Hypersomnia disorder: B
Identity disorder: B
Inhalant intoxication: B
Late luteal phase dysphoric disorder: C
Mental retardation: B
Multi-infarct dementia: A [see Dementia: C]
Obsessive compulsive disorder: B
Opioid intoxication: B
Organic mood syndrome: A [see Manic episode: C]
Phencyclidine (PCP) or similarly acting arylcyclohexylamine intoxication: B
Phencyclidine (PCP) or similarly acting arylcyclohexylamine mood disorder: A [see Manic episode: C]

Primary degenerative dementia of the Alzheimer type: A [see Dementia: C]

Schizoaffective disorder: A [see Manic episode: C]

Schizophrenia: B and D(2)

Sedative, hypnotic, or anxiolytic intoxication: B

Simple phobia: D

Social phobia: E

inability to maintain attention or poor concentration

Adjustment disorder with depressed mood

Adjustment disorder with mixed disturbance of emotions and conduct

Adjustment disorder with mixed emotional features

Alcohol withdrawal delirium: A [see Delirium: A]

Amphetamine or similarly acting sympathomimetic delirium: A [see Delirium: A]

Attention-deficit hyperactivity disorder: A(7)

Bipolar disorder, depressed: B [see Major depressive episode: A(8)]

Bipolar disorder, manic: A [see Manic episode: B(5)]

Bipolar disorder, mixed: A [see Major depressive episode: A(8) or Manic episode: B(5)]

Cocaine delirium: A [see Delirium: A]

Cyclothymia: A [see Hypomanic/Manic episode: B(5)]

Delirium: A

Dysthymia: B(5)

Generalized anxiety disorder: D(16)

Hallucinogen mood disorder: A [see Major depressive episode: A(8) or Manic episode: B(5)]

Late luteal phase dysphoric disorder: B(7)

Major depression, single or recurrent episode: A [see Major depressive episode: A(8)]

Multi-infarct dementia with delirium [see Delirium: A]

Multi-infarct dementia with depression [see Major depressive episode: A(8)]

Nicotine withdrawal: B(4)

Opioid intoxication: C(3)

Organic anxiety syndrome: A [see Generalized anxiety disorder: D(16)]

Organic mood syndrome: A [see Major depressive episode: A(8) or Manic episode: B(5)]

Phencyclidine (PCP) or similarly acting arylcyclohexylamine delirium: A [see Delirium: A]

Phencyclidine (PCP) or similarly acting arylcyclohexylamine mood disorder: A [see Major depressive episode: A(8) or Manic episode: B(5)]

Post-traumatic stress disorder: D(3)

Primary degenerative dementia of the Alzheimer type with delirium [see Delirium: A]

Primary degenerative dementia of the Alzheimer type with depression [see Major depressive episode: A(8)]

Schizoaffective disorder: A [see Major depressive episode: A(8) or Manic episode: B(5)]

Sedative, hypnotic, or anxiolytic intoxication: C(4)

Sedative, hypnotic, or anxiolytic withdrawal delirium: A [see Delirium: A]

Uncomplicated bereavement

Undifferentiated attention-deficit disorder

inability to sustain consistent work behavior

Antisocial personality disorder: C(1)

incoherence or loosening of associations

Alcohol withdrawal delirium: A [see Delirium: B]

Amphetamine or similarly acting sympathomimetic delirium: A [see Delirium: B]

Brief reactive psychosis: A(1)
Cocaine delirium: A [see Delirium: B]
Delirium: B
Multi-infarct dementia with delirium [see Delirium: B]
Phencyclidine (PCP) or similarly acting arylcyclohexylamine delirium: A [see Delirium: B]
Primary degenerative dementia of the Alzheimer type with delirium [see Delirium: B]
Schizoaffective disorder: A [see Schizophrenia: A(1)(c)]
Schizophrenia: A(1)(c)
Schizophrenia, disorganized type: A
Schizophrenia, undifferentiated type: A
Schizophreniform disorder: A [see Schizophrenia: A(1)(c)]
Sedative, hypnotic, or anxiolytic withdrawal delirium: A [see Delirium: B]

incoordination
Alcohol intoxication: C(2)
Developmental coordination disorder: A
Hallucinogen hallucinosis: D(7)
Inhalant intoxication: C(3)
Sedative, hypnotic, or anxiolytic intoxication: C(2)

increase in social, occupational, or sexual activity
Bipolar disorder, manic: A [see Manic episode: B(6)]
Bipolar disorder, mixed: A [see Manic episode: B(6)]
Cyclothymia: A [see Hypomanic/ Manic episode: B(6)]
Hallucinogen mood disorder: A [see Manic episode: B(6)]
Organic mood syndrome: A [see Manic episode: B(6)]
Phencyclidine (PCP) or similarly acting arylcyclohexylamine mood disorder: A [see Manic episode: B(6)]
Schizoaffective disorder: A [see Manic episode: B(6)]

increased appetite
Adjustment disorder with depressed mood
Bipolar disorder, depressed: B [see Major depressive episode: A(3)]
Bipolar disorder, mixed: A [see Major depressive episode: A(3)]
Cannabis intoxication: C(2)
Dysthymia: B(1)
Hallucinogen mood disorder: A [see Major depressive episode: A(3)]
Late luteal phase dysphoric disorder: B(8)
Major depression, single or recurrent episode: A [see Major depressive episode: A(3)]
Multi-infarct dementia with depression [see Major depressive episode: A(3)]
Nicotine withdrawal: B(7)
Organic mood syndrome: A [see Major depressive episode: A(3)]
Phencyclidine (PCP) or similarly acting arylcyclohexylamine mood disorder: A [see Major depressive episode: A(3)]
Primary degenerative dementia of the Alzheimer type with depression [see Major depressive episode: A(3)]
Schizoaffective disorder: A [see Major depressive episode: A(3)]
Uncomplicated bereavement

indecisiveness
Adjustment disorder with depressed mood
Adjustment disorder with mixed disturbance of emotions and conduct
Adjustment disorder with mixed emotional features
Bipolar disorder, depressed: B [see Major depressive episode: A(8)]
Bipolar disorder, mixed: A [see Major depressive episode: A(8)]

Dependent personality disorder: (1)
Dysthymia: B(5)
Hallucinogen mood disorder: A [see Major depressive episode: A(8)]
Major depression, single or recurrent episode: A [see Major depressive episode: A(8)]
Multi-infarct dementia with depression [see Major depressive episode: A(8)]
Obsessive compulsive personality disorder: (5)
Organic mood syndrome: A [see Major depressive episode: A(8)]
Phencyclidine (PCP) or similarly acting arylcyclohexylamine mood disorder: A [see Major depressive episode: A(8)]
Primary degenerative dementia of the Alzheimer type with depression [see Major depressive episode: A(8)]
Schizoaffective disorder: A [see Major depressive episode: A(8)]
Uncomplicated bereavement

indifferent to feelings of others
Autistic disorder: A(1)
Narcissistic personality disorder: (8)

indiscriminate socializing
Bipolar disorder, manic: A [see Manic episode: B(6)]
Bipolar disorder, mixed: A [see Manic episode: B(6)]
Cyclothymia: A [see Hypomanic/Manic episode: B(6)]
Hallucinogen mood disorder: A [see Manic episode: B(6)]
Organic mood syndrome: A [see Manic episode: B(6)]
Organic personality syndrome: A(3)
Phencyclidine (PCP) or similarly acting arylcyclohexylamine mood disorder: A [see Manic episode: B(6)]
Reactive attachment disorder of infancy or early childhood: A(2)

Schizoaffective disorder: A [see Manic episode: B(6)]

insomnia
Adjustment disorder with depressed mood
Alcohol withdrawal delirium: A [see Delirium: C(3)]
Amphetamine or similarly acting sympathomimetic delirium: A [see Delirium: C(3)]
Amphetamine or similarly acting sympathomimetic withdrawal: A(2)
Bipolar disorder, depressed: B [see Major depressive episode: A(4)]
Bipolar disorder, manic: A [see Manic episode: B(2)]
Bipolar disorder, mixed: A [see Manic episode: B(2)]
Caffeine intoxication: B(4)
Cocaine delirium: A [see Delirium: C(3)]
Cocaine withdrawal: A(2)
Cyclothymia: A [see Hypomanic/Manic episode: B(2)]
Delirium: C(3)
Dysthymia: B(2)
Generalized anxiety disorder: D(17)
Hallucinogen mood disorder: A [see Major depressive episode: A(4) or Manic episode: B(2)]
Insomnia disorder: A
Late luteal phase dysphoric disorder: B(9)
Major depression, single or recurrent episode: A [see Major depressive episode: A(4)]
Multi-infarct dementia with delirium [see Delirium: C(3)]
Multi-infarct dementia with depression [see Major depressive episode: A(4)]
Opioid withdrawal: A(9)
Organic anxiety syndrome: A [see Generalized anxiety disorder: D(17)]
Organic mood syndrome: A [see Major depressive episode: A(4) or Manic episode: B(2)]

Phencyclidine (PCP) or similarly acting arylcyclohexylamine delirium: A [see Delirium: C(3)]
Phencyclidine (PCP) or similarly acting arylcyclohexylamine mood disorder: A [see Major depressive episode: A(4) or Manic episode: B(2)]
Post-traumatic stress disorder: D(1)
Primary degenerative dementia of the Alzheimer type with delirium [see Delirium: C(3)]
Primary degenerative dementia of the Alzheimer type with depression [see Major depressive episode: A(4)]
Schizoaffective disorder: A [see Major depressive episode: A(4) or Manic episode: B(2)]
Sedative, hypnotic, or anxiolytic withdrawal delirium: A [see Delirium: C(3)]
Sleep-wake schedule disorder: A [see Insomnia disorder: A]
Uncomplicated bereavement
Uncomplicated sedative, hypnotic, or anxiolytic withdrawal: A(7)

interpersonal exploitativeness
Narcissistic personality disorder: (2)

involvement in reckless activities
Adjustment disorder with disturbance of conduct
Adjustment disorder with mixed disturbance of emotions and conduct
Adult antisocial behavior
Antisocial personality disorder: C(7)
Attention-deficit hyperactivity disorder: A(14)
Bipolar disorder, manic: A [see Manic episode: B(7)]
Bipolar disorder, mixed: A [see Manic episode: B(7)]
Borderline personality disorder: (2)
Cyclothymia: A [see Hypomanic/Manic episode: B(7)]
Hallucinogen mood disorder: A [see Manic episode: B(7)]

Organic mood syndrome: A [see Manic episode: B(7)]
Phencyclidine (PCP) or similarly acting arylcyclohexylamine mood disorder: A [see Manic episode: B(7)]
Schizoaffective disorder: A [see Manic episode: B(7)]

irritable mood or irritability (in adults)
Alcohol intoxication: B
Amphetamine or similarly acting sympathomimetic withdrawal: A
Antisocial personality disorder: C(3)
Bipolar disorder, manic: A [see Manic episode: A]
Bipolar disorder, mixed: A [see Manic episode: A]
Borderline personality disorder: (4)
Cocaine intoxication: B
Cocaine withdrawal: A
Cyclothymia: A [see Hypomanic/Manic episode: A]
Generalized anxiety disorder: D(18)
Hallucinogen mood disorder: A [see Manic episode: A]
Insomnia disorder: B
Late luteal phase dysphoric disorder: B(2)
Nicotine withdrawal: B(2)
Opioid intoxication: B
Organic anxiety syndrome: A [see Generalized anxiety disorder: D(18)]
Organic mood syndrome: A [see Manic episode: A]
Pathological gambling: (4)
Phencyclidine (PCP) or similarly acting arylcyclohexylamine mood disorder: A [see Manic episode: A]
Post-traumatic stress disorder: D(2)
Schizoaffective disorder: A [see Manic episode: A]
Sleep-wake schedule disorder: A [see Insomnia disorder: B]
Uncomplicated alcohol withdrawal: A(5)
Uncomplicated sedative, hypnotic, or anxiolytic withdrawal: A(4)

irritable mood or irritability (in children and adolescents)

Adjustment disorder with depressed mood

Adjustment disorder with mixed disturbance of emotions and conduct

Adjustment disorder with mixed emotional features

Alcohol intoxication: B

Amphetamine or similarly acting sympathomimetic withdrawal: A

Bipolar disorder, depressed: B [see Major depressive episode: A(1)]

Bipolar disorder, manic: A [see Manic episode: A]

Bipolar disorder, mixed: A [see Manic episode: A]

Cocaine intoxication: B

Cocaine withdrawal: A

Cyclothymia: A [see Hypomanic/ Manic episode: A]

Dysthymia: A

Generalized anxiety disorder: D(18)

Hallucinogen hallucinosis: B

Hallucinogen mood disorder: A [see Major depressive episode: A(1) or Manic episode: A]

Insomnia disorder: B

Late luteal phase dysphoric disorder: B(2)

Major depression, single or recurrent episode: A [see Major depressive episode: A(1)]

Nicotine withdrawal: B(2)

Opioid intoxication: B

Oppositional defiant disorder: A(6)

Organic anxiety syndrome: A [see Generalized anxiety disorder: D(18)]

Organic mood syndrome: A [see Major depressive episode: A(1) or Manic episode: A]

Pathological gambling: (4)

Phencyclidine (PCP) or similarly acting arylcyclohexylamine mood disorder: A [see Major depressive episode: A(1) or Manic episode: A]

Post-traumatic stress disorder: D(2)

Schizoaffective disorder: A [see Major depressive episode: A(1) or Manic episode: A]

Sleep-wake schedule disorder: A [see Insomnia disorder: B]

Uncomplicated alcohol withdrawal: A(5)

Uncomplicated bereavement

Uncomplicated sedative, hypnotic, or anxiolytic withdrawal: A(4)

loss of interest in activities

Bipolar disorder, depressed: B [see Major depressive episode: A(2)]

Bipolar disorder, mixed: A [see Major depressive episode: A(2)]

Hallucinogen mood disorder: A [see Major depressive episode: A(2)]

Late luteal phase dysphoric disorder: B(5)

Major depression, single or recurrent episode: A [see Major depressive episode: A(2)]

Major depressive episode, melancholic type: (1)

Multi-infarct dementia with depression [see Major depressive episode: A(2)]

Organic mood syndrome: A [see Major depressive episode: A(2)]

Phencyclidine (PCP) or similarly acting arylcyclohexylamine mood disorder: A [see Major depressive episode: A(2)]

Post-traumatic stress disorder: C(4)

Primary degenerative dementia of the Alzheimer type with depression [see Major depressive episode: A(2)]

Schizoaffective disorder: A [see Major depressive episode: A(2)]

Schizophrenia: D(9)

Uncomplicated bereavement

marked abnormalities in the production
of speech
    Autistic disorder: B(4)
    Cluttering
    Stuttering

marked mood shifts
    Alcohol intoxication: B
    Borderline personality disorder: (3)
    Brief reactive psychosis: B
    Histrionic personality disorder: (6)
    Late luteal phase dysphoric disor-
        der: B(1)
    Organic personality syndrome: A(1)
    Sedative, hypnotic, or anxiolytic
        intoxication: B

memory impairment
    Alcohol amnestic disorder: A [see
        Amnestic syndrome: A]
    Alcohol withdrawal delirium: A [see
        Delirium: C(6)]
    Amnestic syndrome: A
    Amphetamine or similarly acting
        sympathomimetic delirium: A
        [see Delirium: C(6)]
    Cocaine delirium: A [see Delirium:
        C(6)]
    Conversion disorder: A
    Delirium: C(6)
    Dementia: A
    Dementia associated with alco-
        holism: A [see Dementia: A]
    Multi-infarct dementia with delir-
        ium [see Delirium: C(6) or De-
        mentia: A]
    Opioid intoxication: C(3)
    Phencyclidine (PCP) or similarly act-
        ing arylcyclohexylamine delir-
        ium: A [see Delirium: C(6)]
    Post-traumatic stress disorder: C(3)
    Primary degenerative dementia of
        the Alzheimer type with delir-
        ium [see Delirium: C(6) or De-
        mentia: A]
    Psychogenic amnesia: A
    Psychogenic fugue: A
    Sedative, hypnotic, or anxiolytic
        amnestic disorder: A [see Am-
        nestic syndrome: A]

Sedative, hypnotic, or anxiolytic
    intoxication: C(4)
Sedative, hypnotic, or anxiolytic
    withdrawal delirium: A [see
    Delirium: C(6)]
Somatization disorder: B(16)

nausea
    Adjustment disorder with physical
        complaints
    Amphetamine or similarly acting
        sympathomimetic intoxication:
        C(5)
    Caffeine intoxication: B(7)
    Cocaine intoxication: C(5)
    Generalized anxiety disorder: D(10)
    Hypochondriasis: A
    Late luteal phase dysphoric disor-
        der: B(10)
    Opioid withdrawal: A(2)
    Organic anxiety syndrome: A [see
        Generalized anxiety disorder:
        D(10) or Panic disorder: C(7)]
    Overanxious disorder: A(4)
    Panic disorder: C(7)
    Panic disorder with agoraphobia: A
        [see Panic disorder: C(7)]
    Separation anxiety disorder: A(7)
    Somatization disorder: B(3)
    Uncomplicated alcohol withdrawal:
        A(1)
    Uncomplicated sedative, hypnotic,
        or anxiolytic withdrawal: A(1)
    Undifferentiated somatoform disor-
        der: A

need for excessive advice from others
    Dependent personality disorder: (1)

no close friends or confidants
    Avoidant personality disorder: (2)
    Schizoid personality disorder: A(6)
    Schizotypal personality disorder:
        A(6)

numbness
    Adjustment disorder with physical
        complaints
    Conversion disorder: A
    Multi-infarct dementia: C

Organic anxiety syndrome: A [see Panic disorder: C(9)]
Panic disorder: C(9)
Panic disorder with agoraphobia: A [see Panic disorder: C(9)]
Phencyclidine (PCP) or similarly acting arylcyclohexylamine intoxication: C(3)
Undifferentiated somatoform disorder: A

nystagmus
Alcohol intoxication: C(4)
Inhalant intoxication: C(2)
Multi-infarct dementia: C
Phencyclidine (PCP) or similarly acting arylcyclohexylamine intoxication: C(1)

other pain
Adjustment disorder with physical complaints
Hypochondriasis: A
Late luteal phase dysphoric disorder: B(10)
Overanxious disorder: A(4)
Separation anxiety disorder: A(7)
Somatization disorder: B(7)
Somatoform pain disorder: A
Undifferentiated somatoform disorder: A

outbursts of aggression or rage
Alcohol idiosyncratic intoxication: A
Alcohol intoxication: B
Amphetamine or similarly acting sympathomimetic intoxication: B
Antisocial personality disorder: C(3)
Borderline personality disorder: (4)
Cocaine intoxication: B
Dementia: B(4)
Dementia associated with alcoholism: A [see Dementia: B(4)]
Inhalant intoxication: B
Intermittent explosive disorder: A
Late luteal phase dysphoric disorder: B(2)
Mental retardation: B
Multi-infarct dementia: A [see Dementia: B(4)]

Nicotine withdrawal: B(2)
Oppositional defiant disorder: A(7)
Organic personality syndrome: A(2)
Post-traumatic stress disorder: D(2)
Primary degenerative dementia of the Alzheimer type: A [see Dementia: B(4)]
Sedative, hypnotic, or anxiolytic intoxication: B

overly impressionistic speech
Histrionic personality disorder: (8)
Schizophrenia: D(6)
Schizotypal personality disorder: A(7)

panic attacks
Organic anxiety syndrome: A [see Panic disorder: A]
Panic disorder: A
Panic disorder with agoraphobia: A

paralysis
Adjustment disorder with physical complaints
Conversion disorder: A
Multi-infarct dementia: C
Somatization disorder: B(26)
Undifferentiated somatoform disorder: A

paranoid ideation (non-delusional)
Amphetamine or similarly acting sympathomimetic intoxication: B
Cannabis intoxication: B
Cocaine intoxication: B
Hallucinogen hallucinosis: B
Organic personality syndrome: A(5)
Paranoid personality disorder: A(3)
Schizotypal personality disorder: A(9)

perfectionism
Obsessive compulsive personality disorder: (1)

persecutory delusions
Amphetamine or similarly acting sympathomimetic delusional disorder: B

Bipolar disorder, depressed: B [see Major depressive episode with psychotic features]

Bipolar disorder, manic: A [see Manic episode with psychotic features]

Bipolar disorder, mixed: A [see Manic episode with psychotic features]

Brief reactive psychosis: A(2)

Cannabis delusional disorder: A

Cocaine delusional disorder: B

Delusional disorder, persecutory type: A

Hallucinogen delusional disorder: A

Hallucinogen mood disorder: A [see Major depressive episode with psychotic features or Manic episode with psychotic features]

Induced psychotic disorder: A

Major depression, single or recurrent episode: A [see Major depressive episode with psychotic features]

Multi-infarct dementia with delusions

Multi-infarct dementia with depression [see Major depressive episode with psychotic features]

Organic delusional syndrome: A

Organic mood syndrome: A [see Major depressive episode with psychotic features or Manic episode with psychotic features]

Phencyclidine (PCP) or similarly acting arylcyclohexylamine delusional disorder: A

Phencyclidine (PCP) or similarly acting arylcyclohexylamine mood disorder: A [see Major depressive episode with psychotic features or Manic episode with psychotic features]

Primary degenerative dementia of the Alzheimer type with delusions

Primary degenerative dementia of the Alzheimer type with depression [see Major depressive episode with psychotic features]

Schizoaffective disorder: A [see Major depressive episode with psychotic features or Manic episode, with psychotic features or Schizophrenia: A(1)(a)]

Schizophrenia: A(1)(a)

Schizophrenia, undifferentiated type: A

Schizophreniform disorder: A [see Schizophrenia: A(1)(a)]

persistent anger
    Borderline personality disorder: (4)
    Late luteal phase dysphoric disorder: B(2)
    Nicotine withdrawal: B(2)
    Oppositional defiant disorder: A(7)

persistent distress about assigned gender
    Gender identity disorder of adolescence or adulthood, nontranssexual type (GIDAANT): A
    Gender identity disorder of childhood: A
    Transsexualism: A

persistent identity disturbance
    Borderline personality disorder: (6)
    Identity disorder: A

physical complaint without organic pathology
    Adjustment disorder with physical complaints
    Conversion disorder: D
    Hypochondriasis: B
    Late luteal phase dysphoric disorder: B(10)
    Overanxious disorder: A(4)
    Separation anxiety disorder: A(7)
    Somatization disorder, significance list: (1)
    Somatoform pain disorder: B(1)
    Undifferentiated somatoform disorder: B(1)

pressured speech
    Bipolar disorder, manic: A [see Manic episode: B(3)]

Bipolar disorder, mixed: A [see Manic episode: B(3)]

Cyclothymia: A [see Hypomanic/ Manic episode: B(3)]

Hallucinogen mood disorder: A [see Manic episode: B(3)]

Organic mood syndrome: A [see Manic episode: B(3)]

Phencyclidine (PCP) or similarly acting arylcyclohexylamine mood disorder: A [see Manic episode: B(3)]

Schizoaffective disorder: A [see Manic episode: B(3)]

profuse sweating

Adjustment disorder with physical complaints

Alcohol withdrawal delirium: B

Amphetamine or similarly acting sympathomimetic intoxication: C(4)

Cocaine intoxication: C(4)

Generalized anxiety disorder: D(7)

Hallucinogen hallucinosis: D(3)

Hypochondriasis: A

Late luteal phase dysphoric disorder: B(10)

Opioid withdrawal: A(5)

Organic anxiety syndrome: A [see Generalized anxiety disorder: D(7) or Panic disorder: C(5)]

Overanxious disorder: A(4)

Panic disorder: C(5)

Panic disorder with agoraphobia: A [see Panic disorder: C(5)]

Sedative, hypnotic, or anxiolytic withdrawal delirium: B

Separation anxiety disorder: A(7)

Uncomplicated alcohol withdrawal: A(3)

Uncomplicated sedative, hypnotic, or anxiolytic withdrawal: A(3)

Undifferentiated somatoform disorder: A

psychomotor agitation

Alcohol withdrawal delirium: A [see Delirium: C(4)]

Amphetamine or similarly acting sympathomimetic delirium: A [see Delirium: C(4)]

Amphetamine or similarly acting sympathomimetic intoxication: B

Amphetamine or similarly acting sympathomimetic withdrawal: A(3)

Bipolar disorder, depressed: B [see Major depressive episode: A(5)]

Bipolar disorder, manic: A [see Manic episode: B(6)]

Bipolar disorder, mixed: A [see Major depressive episode: A(5) or Manic episode: B(6)]

Caffeine intoxication: B(12)

Cocaine delirium: A [see Delirium: C(4)]

Cocaine intoxication: B

Cocaine withdrawal: A(3)

Cyclothymia: A [see Hypomanic/ Manic episode: B(6)]

Delirium: C(4)

Hallucinogen mood disorder: A [see Major depressive episode: A(5) or Manic episode: B(6)]

Inhalant intoxication: B

Major depression, single or recurrent episode: A [see Major depressive episode: A(5)]

Major depressive episode, melancholic type: (5)

Multi-infarct dementia with delirium [see Delirium: C(4)]

Multi-infarct dementia with depression [see Major depressive episode: A(5)]

Organic mood syndrome: A [see Major depressive episode: A(5) or Manic episode: B(6)]

Phencyclidine (PCP) or similarly acting arylcyclohexylamine delirium: A [see Delirium: C(4)]

Phencyclidine (PCP) or similarly acting arylcyclohexylamine intoxication: B

Phencyclidine (PCP) or similarly acting arylcyclohexylamine mood disorder: A [see Major depres-

sive episode: A(5) or Manic episode: B(6)]
Primary degenerative dementia of
the Alzheimer type with delirium [see Delirium: C(4)]
Primary degenerative dementia of
the Alzheimer type with depression [see Major depressive
episode: A(5)]
Schizoaffective disorder: A [see Major depressive episode: A(5) or
Manic episode: B(6)]
Sedative, hypnotic, or anxiolytic
withdrawal delirium: A [see
Delirium: C(4)]

psychomotor retardation
Alcohol withdrawal delirium: A [see
Delirium: C(4)]
Amphetamine or similarly acting
sympathomimetic delirium: A
[see Delirium: C(4)]
Bipolar disorder, depressed: B [see
Major depressive episode:
A(5)]
Bipolar disorder, mixed: A [see Ma-
jor depressive episode: A(5)]
Cocaine delirium: A [see Delirium:
C(4)]
Delirium: C(4)
Hallucinogen mood disorder: A [see
Major depressive episode:
A(5)]
Inhalant intoxication: C(8)
Major depression, single or recur-
rent episode: A [see Major de-
pressive episode: A(5)]
Major depressive episode, melan-
cholic type: (5)
Multi-infarct dementia with delir-
ium [see Delirium: C(4)]
Multi-infarct dementia with depres-
sion [see Major depressive epi-
sode: A(5)]
Opioid intoxication: B
Organic mood syndrome: A [see
Major depressive episode:
A(5)]

Phencyclidine (PCP) or similarly acting arylcyclohexylamine delirium: A [see Delirium: C(4)]
Phencyclidine (PCP) or similarly acting arylcyclohexylamine mood
disorder: A [see Major depressive episode: A(5)]
Primary degenerative dementia of
the Alzheimer type with delirium [see Delirium: C(4)]
Primary degenerative dementia of
the Alzheimer type with depression [see Major depressive
episode: A(5)]
Schizoaffective disorder: A [see Major depressive episode: A(5)]
Sedative, hypnotic, or anxiolytic
withdrawal delirium: A [see
Delirium: C(4)]

pupillary constriction
Opioid intoxication: C

pupillary dilation
Amphetamine or similarly acting
sympathomimetic intoxication:
C(2)
Cocaine intoxication: C(2)
Hallucinogen hallucinosis: D(1)
Opioid intoxication: C
Opioid withdrawal: A(5)

racing thoughts
Bipolar disorder, manic: A [see
Manic episode: B(4)]
Bipolar disorder, mixed: A [see
Manic episode: B(4)]
Cyclothymia: A [see Hypomanic/
Manic episode: B(4)]
Hallucinogen mood disorder: A [see
Manic episode: B(4)]
Organic mood syndrome: A [see
Manic episode: B(4)]
Phencyclidine (PCP) or similarly act-
ing arylcyclohexylamine mood
disorder: A [see Manic episode:
B(4)]
Schizoaffective disorder: A [see
Manic episode: B(4)]

recurrent recollection of distressing events
    Post-traumatic stress disorder: B(1)

refusal to maintain normal body weight
    Anorexia nervosa: A

repeated lying
    Antisocial personality disorder: B(10) and C(6)
    Conduct disorder: A(3)

repeated procrastination
    Obsessive compulsive personality disorder: (5)
    Passive aggressive personality disorder: (1)

responds to success with depression and guilt
    Self-defeating personality disorder: A(3)

restricted expression of emotions
    Obsessive compulsive personality disorder: (7)
    Post-traumatic stress disorder: C(6)
    Schizoid personality disorder: A(3) or A(7)
    Schizophrenia: D(5)
    Schizotypal personality disorder: A(8)

sad or tearful appearance
    Adjustment disorder with depressed mood
    Adjustment disorder with mixed disturbance of emotions and conduct
    Adjustment disorder with mixed emotional features
    Bipolar disorder, depressed: B [see Major depressive episode: A(1)]
    Bipolar disorder, mixed: A [see Major depressive episode: A(1)]
    Cyclothymia: A
    Dysthymia: A
    Hallucinogen hallucinosis: B

Hallucinogen mood disorder: A [see Major depressive episode: A(1)]
Late luteal phase dysphoric disorder: B(4)
Major depression, single or recurrent episode: A [see Major depressive episode: A(1)]
Multi-infarct dementia with depression [see Major depressive episode: A(1)]
Organic mood syndrome: A [see Major depressive episode: A(1)]
Phencyclidine (PCP) or similarly acting arylcyclohexylamine mood disorder: A [see Major depressive episode: A(1)]
Primary degenerative dementia of the Alzheimer type with depression [see Major depressive episode: A(1)]
Schizoaffective disorder: A [see Major depressive episode: A(1)]
Uncomplicated bereavement

self-induced vomiting
    Bulimia nervosa: C
    Factitious disorder with physical symptoms
    Malingering

self-mutilating behavior
    Borderline personality disorder: (5)
    Factitious disorder with physical symptoms
    Malingering
    Sexual masochism: A
    Stereotypy/habit disorder: B

senseless thoughts and ideas (obsessions)
    Obsessive compulsive disorder, definition of obsession: (1)

sexually seductive appearance
    Bipolar disorder, manic: A [see Manic episode: B(6)]
    Bipolar disorder, mixed: A [see Manic episode: B(6)]

Cyclothymia: A [see Hypomanic/
Manic episode: B(6)]
Hallucinogen mood disorder: A [see
Manic episode: B(6)]
Histrionic personality disorder: (2)
Organic mood syndrome: A [see
Manic episode: B(6)]
Phencyclidine (PCP) or similarly act-
ing arylcyclohexylamine mood
disorder: A [see Manic episode:
B(6)]
Schizoaffective disorder: A [see
Manic episode: B(6)]

significant weight gain
Bipolar disorder, depressed: B [see
Major depressive episode:
A(3)]
Bipolar disorder, mixed: A [see Ma-
jor depressive episode: A(3)]
Hallucinogen mood disorder: A [see
Major depressive episode:
A(3)]
Late luteal phase dysphoric disor-
der: B(10)
Major depression, single or recur-
rent episode: A [see Major de-
pressive episode: A(3)]
Multi-infarct dementia with depres-
sion [see Major depressive epi-
sode: A(3)]
Nicotine withdrawal: B(7)
Organic mood syndrome: A [see
Major depressive episode:
A(3)]
Phencyclidine (PCP) or similarly act-
ing arylcyclohexylamine mood
disorder: A [see Major depres-
sive episode: A(3)]
Primary degenerative dementia of
the Alzheimer type with depression [see Major depressive
episode: A(3)]
Schizoaffective disorder: A [see Major depressive episode: A(3)]
Uncomplicated bereavement

significant weight loss
Anorexia nervosa: A

Bipolar disorder, depressed: B [see
Major depressive episode:
A(3)]
Bipolar disorder, mixed: A [see Ma-
jor depressive episode: A(3)]
Hallucinogen mood disorder: A [see
Major depressive episode:
A(3)]
Major depression, single or recur-
rent episode: A [see Major de-
pressive episode: A(3)]
Major depressive episode, melan-
cholic type: (6)
Multi-infarct dementia with depres-
sion [see Major depressive epi-
sode: A(3)]
Organic mood syndrome: A [see
Major depressive episode:
A(3)]
Phencyclidine (PCP) or similarly act-
ing arylcyclohexylamine mood
disorder: A [see Major depressive episode: A(3)]
Primary degenerative dementia of
the Alzheimer type with depression [see Major depressive
episode: A(3)]
Schizoaffective disorder: A [see Major depressive episode: A(3)]
Uncomplicated bereavement

slurred speech
Alcohol intoxication: C(1)
Inhalant intoxication: C(4)
Opioid intoxication: C(2)

somatic delusions
Bipolar disorder, depressed: B [see
Major depressive episode with
psychotic features]
Bipolar disorder, manic: A [see
Manic episode with psychotic
features]
Bipolar disorder, mixed: A [see
Manic episode with psychotic
features]
Brief reactive psychosis: A(2)
Cannabis delusional disorder: A
Delusional disorder, somatic type

Hallucinogen delusional disorder: A

Hallucinogen mood disorder: A [see Major depressive episode with psychotic features or Manic episode, with psychotic features]

Induced psychotic disorder: A

Major depression, single or recurrent episode: A [see Major depressive episode with psychotic features]

Multi-infarct dementia with delusions

Multi-infarct dementia with depression [see Major depressive episode with psychotic features]

Organic delusional syndrome: A

Organic mood syndrome: A [see Major depressive episode with psychotic features or Manic episode with psychotic features]

Phencyclidine (PCP) or similarly acting arylcyclohexylamine delusional disorder: A

Phencyclidine (PCP) or similarly acting arylcyclohexylamine mood disorder: A [see Major depressive episode with psychotic features or Manic episode with psychotic features]

Primary degenerative dementia of the Alzheimer type with delusions

Primary degenerative dementia of the Alzheimer type with depression [see Major depressive episode with psychotic features]

Schizoaffective disorder: A [see Major depressive episode with psychotic features or Manic episode, with psychotic features or Schizophrenia: A(1)(a)]

Schizophrenia: A(1)(a)

Schizophrenia, undifferentiated type: A

Schizophreniform disorder: A [see Schizophrenia: A(1)(a)]

substance use when hazardous
Borderline personality disorder: (2)
Psychoactive substance abuse: A(2)
Psychoactive substance dependence: A(4)

suicidal ideation
Bipolar disorder, depressed: B [see Major depressive episode: A(9)]
Bipolar disorder, mixed: A [see Major depressive episode: A(9)]
Borderline personality disorder: (5)
Hallucinogen mood disorder: A [see Major depressive episode: A(9)]
Major depression, single or recurrent episode: A [see Major depressive episode: A(9)]
Multi-infarct dementia with depression [see Major depressive episode: A(9)]
Organic mood syndrome: A [see Major depressive episode: A(9)]
Phencyclidine (PCP) or similarly acting arylcyclohexylamine mood disorder: A [see Major depressive episode: A(9)]
Primary degenerative dementia of the Alzheimer type with depression [see Major depressive episode: A(9)]
Schizoaffective disorder: A [see Major depressive episode: A(9)]

suicide attempt
Bipolar disorder, depressed: B [see Major depressive episode: A(9)]
Bipolar disorder, mixed: A [see Major depressive episode: A(9)]
Borderline personality disorder: (5)
Hallucinogen mood disorder: A [see Major depressive episode: A(9)]
Major depression, single or recurrent episode: A [see Major depressive episode: A(9)]

Multi-infarct dementia with depression [see Major depressive episode: A(9)]

Organic mood syndrome: A [see Major depressive episode: A(9)]

Phencyclidine (PCP) or similarly acting arylcyclohexylamine mood disorder: A [see Major depressive episode: A(9)]

Primary degenerative dementia of the Alzheimer type with depression [see Major depressive episode: A(9)]

Schizoaffective disorder: A [see Major depressive episode: A(9)]

tachycardia

Adjustment disorder with physical complaints

Alcohol withdrawal delirium: B

Amphetamine or similarly acting sympathomimetic intoxication: C(1)

Caffeine intoxication: B(10)

Cannabis intoxication: C(4)

Cocaine intoxication: C(1)

Generalized anxiety disorder: D(6)

Hallucinogen hallucinosis: D(2)

Hypochondriasis: A

Late luteal phase dysphoric disorder: B(10)

Organic anxiety syndrome: A [see Generalized anxiety disorder: D(6) or Panic disorder: C(3)]

Panic disorder: C(3)

Panic disorder with agoraphobia: A [see Panic disorder: C(3)]

Phencyclidine (PCP) or similarly acting arylcyclohexylamine intoxication: C(2)

Sedative, hypnotic, or anxiolytic withdrawal delirium: B

Somatization disorder: B(13)

Uncomplicated alcohol withdrawal: A(3)

Uncomplicated sedative, hypnotic, or anxiolytic withdrawal: A(3)

Undifferentiated somatoform disorder: A

tangentiality

Schizophrenia: D(6)

Schizotypal personality disorder: A(7)

travel away from home restricted

agoraphobia without history of panic disorder: A

Panic disorder with agoraphobia: B

tremor or trembling

Adjustment disorder with physical complaints

Conversion disorder: A

Generalized anxiety disorder: D(1)

Hallucinogen hallucinosis: D(6)

Inhalant intoxication: C(9)

Organic anxiety syndrome: A [see Generalized anxiety disorder: D(1) or Panic disorder: C(4)]

Panic disorder: C(4)

Panic disorder with agoraphobia: A [see Panic disorder: C(4)]

Uncomplicated alcohol withdrawal: A

Uncomplicated sedative, hypnotic, or anxiolytic withdrawal: B(6)

Undifferentiated somatoform disorder: A

unstable and intense relationships

Borderline personality disorder: (1)

untidy appearance

Bipolar disorder, manic: A [see Manic episode: C]

Bipolar disorder, mixed: A [see Manic episode: C]

Dementia: C

Dementia associated with alcoholism: A [see Dementia: C]

Multi-infarct dementia: A [see Dementia: C]

Primary degenerative dementia of the Alzheimer type: A [see Dementia: C]

Schizophrenia: B or D(4)

Schizotypal personality disorder: A(5)

volunteers to do demeaning things
  Dependent personality disorder: (5)
  Self-defeating personality disorder:
    A(8)

vomiting
  Adjustment disorder with physical
    complaints
  Amphetamine or similarly acting
    sympathomimetic intoxication:
    C(5)
  Bulimia nervosa: C
  Caffeine intoxication: B(7)
  Cocaine intoxication: C(5)
  Conversion disorder: A
  Generalized anxiety disorder: D(10)
  Hypochondriasis: A

Late luteal phase dysphoric disor-
    der: B(10)
Opioid withdrawal: A(2)
Organic anxiety syndrome: A [see
    Generalized anxiety disorder:
    D(10) or Panic disorder: C(7)]
Overanxious disorder: A(4)
Panic disorder: C(7)
Panic disorder with agoraphobia: A
    [see Panic disorder: C(7)]
Separation anxiety disorder: A(7)
Somatization disorder: B(1)
Uncomplicated alcohol withdrawal:
    A(1)
Uncomplicated sedative, hypnotic,
    or anxiolytic withdrawal: A(1)
Undifferentiated somatoform disor-
    der: A

INDEX OF DSM–III–R DIAGNOSES AND SELECTED DIAGNOSTIC TERMS

Diagnostic Index:
Index of DSM-III-R Diagnoses and Selected Diagnostic Terms

This index includes names of diagnostic categories in DSM-III-R and DSM-III, as well as some other widely used diagnostic terms. Descriptive terms included in Appendix B: Glossary of Technical Terms are not included.

Page numbers for diagnostic criteria are in parenthesis.

Abuse   169(169)
   Alcohol   173
   Amphetamine or similarly acting
      sympathomimetic   175
   Cannabis   176
   Cocaine   177
   Hallucinogen   179
   Inhalant   180
   Opioid   182
   Phencyclidine (PCP) or similarly acting
      arylcyclohexylamine   183
   Psychoactive substance   169(169)
   Psychoactive substance, not otherwise
      specified   185
   Sedative, hypnotic, or anxiolytic   184
Academic or work inhibition. See
      Adjustment disorder with work (or
      academic) inhibition   331
Academic problem   359
Academic skills disorders   41
   Developmental arithmetic disorder
      41(42)
   Developmental expressive writing
      disorder   42(43)
   Developmental reading disorder   43(44)
Acrophobia. See Simple phobia   243(244)
Acute
   confusional state. See Delirium   100(103)
   paranoid disorder. See Psychotic disorder
      not otherwise specified   211
   schizophrenic episode. See Brief reactive
      psychosis   205(206) or
      Schizophreniform disorder   207(208)

Additional codes   363
   Diagnosis or condition deferred on
      Axis I   363
   Diagnosis deferred on Axis II   363
   No diagnosis or condition on Axis I   363
   No diagnosis on Axis II   363
   Unspecified mental disorder
      (nonpsychotic)   363
Adjustment disorder   329(330)
   not otherwise specified   331
   with anxious mood   331
   with atypical features. See Adjustment
      disorder not otherwise specified
      331
   with depressed mood   331
   with disturbance of conduct   331
   with mixed disturbance of emotions and
      conduct   331
   with mixed emotional features   331
   with physical complaints   331
   with withdrawal   331
   with work (or academic) inhibition   331
Adjustment reaction. See Adjustment
      disorder   329(330)
Adolescence
   Avoidant disorder of childhood or
      61(62)
   Disorders usually first evident in infancy,
      childhood, or   27
   Gender identity disorder of, or
      adulthood   76(77)

Adolescent antisocial behavior. *See*
    Childhood or adolescent antisocial
    behavior 360
Adult antisocial behavior 359
Affective disorders. *See* Mood disorders
    213
Agoraphobia
    with panic attacks. *See* Panic Disorder
        with agoraphobia 235(238)
    without history of panic disorder
        240(241)
    without panic attacks. *See* Agoraphobia
        without history of panic disorder
        240(241)
Alcohol use disorders, abuse/
    dependence 173
Alcohol-induced organic mental disorders
    127
    amnestic disorder 133(133)
    dementia. *See* Dementia associated with
        alcoholism 133(134)
    hallucinosis 131(132)
    idiosyncratic intoxication 128(129)
    intoxication 127(128)
    jealousy. *See* Delusional (paranoid)
        disorder, jealous type 200(203)
    withdrawal delirium 131(131)
    withdrawal, Uncomplicated 129(130)
Alzheimer's disease. *See* Primary
    degenerative dementia of the
    Alzheimer type 119(121)
Amnesia
    anterograde. *See* Amnestic syndrome
        108(109) or Psychogenic amnesia
        273(275)
    Psychogenic 273(275)
    retrograde. *See* Amnestic syndrome
        108(109) or Psychogenic amnesia
        273(275)
Amnestic disorder
    Alcohol 133(133)
    associated with Axis III physical disorders
        or conditions or is unknown 162
    Other or unspecified psychoactive
        substance 162
    Sedative, hypnotic, or anxiolytic
        161(161)
Amnestic syndrome 108(109)
Amphetamine or similarly acting
    sympathomimetic use disorders,
    abuse/dependence 175
Amphetamine or similarly acting
    sympathomimetic-induced organic
    mental disorders 134
    delirium 136(137)
    delusional disorder 137(138)
    intoxication 134(135)
    withdrawal 136(136)

Anankastic personality. *See* Obsessive
    compulsive personality disorder
    354(356)
Anorexia nervosa 65(67)
Antisocial
    behavior, adult 359
    behavior, childhood and adolescent 360
    personality disorder 342(344)
Anxiety disorders (or anxiety and phobic
        neuroses) 235
    Agoraphobia without history of panic
        disorder 240(241)
    Generalized anxiety disorder 251(252)
    not otherwise specified 253
    Obsessive compulsive disorder
        245(247)
    Panic disorder 235(237)
    Panic disorder with agoraphobia
        235(238)
    Panic disorder without agoraphobia
        235(239)
    Post-traumatic stress disorder 247(250)
    Simple phobia 243(244)
    Social phobia 241(243)
Anxiety disorders of childhood or
        adolescence 58
    Avoidant disorder of childhood or
        adolescence 61(62)
    Overanxious disorder 63(64)
    Separation anxiety disorder 58(60)
Anxiety neuroses. *See* Panic disorder
    235(237) or Generalized anxiety
    disorder 251(252)
Anxious mood. *See* Adjustment disorder
    with anxious mood 331
Arithmetic disorder. *See* Developmental
    arithmetic disorder 41(42)
Arousal, sexual. *See* Female sexual arousal
    disorder (294) or Male erectile
    disorder (294)
Arteriosclerotic dementia. *See* Multi-infarct
    dementia 121(123)
Articulation disorder. *See* Developmental
    articulation disorder 44(45)
Arylcyclohexylamine. *See* Phencyclidine
    (PCP) or similarly acting
    arylcyclohexylamine
Asthenic personality. *See* Dependent
    personality disorder 353(354)
Attention-deficit disorder
    with hyperactivity. *See* Attention-deficit
        hyperactivity disorder 50(52)
    without hyperactivity. *See*
        Undifferentiated attention-deficit
        disorder 95
Attention-deficit
    hyperactivity disorder 50(52)
    Undifferentiated, disorder 95

Atypical
  affective disorder. *See* Bipolar disorder
    not otherwise specified   228   or
    Depressive disorder not otherwise
    specified   233
  anxiety disorder. *See* Anxiety disorder not
    otherwise specified   253
  bipolar disorder. *See* Bipolar disorder not
    otherwise specified   228
  depression. *See* Depressive disorder not
    otherwise specified   233
  development. *See* Pervasive
    developmental disorders   33
  dissociative disorder. *See* Dissociative
    disorder not otherwise specified
    277
  eating disorder. *See* Eating disorder not
    otherwise specified   71
  factitious disorder with physical
    symptoms. *See* Factitious disorder
    not otherwise specified   320
  features, Adjustment disorder with. *See*
    Adjustment disorder not otherwise
    specified   331
  gender identity disorder. *See* Gender
    identity disorder not otherwise
    specified   77
  impulse control disorder. *See* Impulse
    control disorders not elsewhere
    specified   321
  mixed or other personality disorder. *See*
    Personality disorder not otherwise
    specified   358
  or mixed organic brain syndrome. *See*
    Organic mental syndrome not
    otherwise specified   119
  paranoid disorder. *See* Psychotic disorder
    not otherwise specified   211
  paraphilia. *See* Paraphilia not otherwise
    specified   290
  pervasive developmental disorder. *See*
    Pervasive developmental disorder
    not otherwise specified   39
  psychosexual dysfunction. *See* Sexual
    dysfunction not otherwise
    specified   295
  psychosis. *See* Psychotic disorder not
    otherwise specified   211
  somatoform disorder. *See*
    Undifferentiated somatoform
    disorder   266(267) or Somatoform
    disorder not otherwise specified
    267
  specific developmental disorder. *See*
    Specific developmental disorder not
    otherwise specified   49

  stereotyped movement disorder. *See* Tic
    disorder not otherwise specified   82
    or Stereotypy/habit disorder   93(95)
  tic disorder. *See* Tic disorder not
    otherwise specified   82
Autism, Infantile. *See* Autistic disorder
  38(38)
Autistic disorder   38(38)
Avoidant
  disorder of childhood or adolescence
    61(62)
  personality disorder   351(352)

Barbiturate. *See* Sedative, hypnotic, or
  anxiolytic
Behavior disorders. *See* Disruptive behavior
  disorders   49
Bereavement, Uncomplicated   361
Bipolar II. *See* Bipolar disorder not
  otherwise specified   228
Bipolar disorder
  depressed   225(226)
  manic   225(226)
  mixed   225(225)
  not otherwise specified   228
Blood-injury phobia. *See* Simple phobia
  243(244)
Body dysmorphic disorder   255(256)
Borderline
  intellectual functioning   359
  mental retardation. *See* Borderline
    intellectual functioning   359
  personality disorder   346(347)
  schizophrenia. *See* Schizotypal
    personality disorder   340(341)
Brief reactive psychosis   205(206)
Briquet's syndrome. *See* Somatization
  disorder   261(263)
Bulimia nervosa   67(68)

Caffeine-induced organic mental disorder
  138
Caffeine intoxication   138(139)
Caffeinism. *See* Caffeine intoxication
  138(139)
Cannabis use disorders, abuse/
  dependence   176
Cannabis-induced organic mental
  disorders   139
  delusional disorder   140(141)
  hallucinosis. *See* Cannabis intoxication
    139
  intoxication   139(140)
Cardiac neurosis. *See* Hypochondriasis
  259(261)
Catatonic type, Schizophrenia   196(196)
Child abuse. *See* Parent-child problem
  361

Childhood, Gender identity disorder of 71(73)
Childhood or adolescence
 Anxiety disorders of 58
 Avoidant disorder of 61(62)
 Disorders usually first evident in infancy 27
Childhood onset pervasive developmental disorder. See Autistic disorder 38(38)
Childhood or adolescent antisocial behavior 360
Childhood psychosis. See Pervasive developmental disorders 33
Childhood, Reactive attachment disorder. See Reactive attachment disorder of infancy or early childhood 91(93)
Childhood schizophrenia. See Pervasive developmental disorders 33
Chronic mood disorders
 Cyclothymia 226(227)
 Dysthymia 230(232)
Chronic motor or vocal tic disorder 81(81)
Claustrophobia. See Simple phobia 243(244)
Cluttering 85(86)
Cocaine use disorders, abuse/ dependence 177
Cocaine-induced organic mental disorders 141
 delirium 143(143)
 delusional disorder 143(144)
 intoxication 141(142)
 withdrawal 142(142)
Compensation neurosis. See Psychological factors affecting physical condition 333(334)
Compulsions. See Obsessive compulsive disorder 245(247)
Compulsive personality. See Obsessive compulsive personality disorder 354(356)
Concentration camp syndrome. See Post-traumatic stress disorder 247(250)
Conduct disorder 53(55)
 atypical. See Conduct disorder, undifferentiated type 56
 group type 56
 socialized, nonaggressive. See Conduct disorder, group type 56
 solitary aggressive type 56
 undersocialized, aggressive. See Conduct disorder, solitary aggressive type 56
 undersocialized, nonagressive. See Conduct disorder, undifferentiated type 56
 undifferentiated type 56

Conduct disturbance. See Adjustment disorder with disturbance of conduct 331
Conjugal paranoia. See Delusional (paranoid) disorder, jealous type 200(203)
Conversion disorder 257(259)
Coordination disorder. See Developmental coordination disorder 48(49)
Coprophilia. See Paraphilia not otherwise specified 290
Crack. See Cocaine
Cyclothymia 226(227)
Cyclothymic disorder. See Cyclothymia 226(227)
Cyclothymic personality. See Cyclothymia 226(227)

Deferred diagnoses 363
 Diagnosis or condition deferred on Axis I 363
 Diagnosis or condition deferred on Axis II 363
Delirium 100(103)
 Alcohol withdrawal 131(131)
 Amphetamine or similarly acting sympathomimetic 136(137)
 associated with Axis III physical disorders or conditions, or whose etiology is unknown 162
 Cocaine 143(143)
 Multi-infarct dementia, with 123
 Other or unspecified psychoactive substance 162
 Phencyclidine (PCP) or similarly acting arylcyclohexylamine 155(156)
 Primary degenerative dementia of the Alzheimer type, presenile onset, with 121
 Primary degenerative dementia of the Alzheimer type, senile onset, with 121
 Sedative, hypnotic, or anxiolytic withdrawal 160(161)
 tremens. See Alcohol withdrawal delirium 131(131)
Delusional (paranoid) disorder 199(202)
 erotomanic type 199(202)
 grandiose type 200(203)
 jealous type 200(203)
 persecutory type 200(203)
 somatic type 200(203)
 unspecified type 203
Delusional disorder
 Amphetamine or similarly acting sympathomimetic 137(138)
 Cocaine 143(144)
 Hallucinogen 146(146)

Organic, associated with Axis III physical
  disorders or conditions, or whose
  etiology is unknown   162
Other or unspecified psychoactive
  substance   162
Phencyclidine (PCP) or similarly acting
  arylcyclohexylamine   156(156)
Delusions
  Multi-infarct dementia, with   123
  Primary degenerative dementia of the
    Alzheimer type, presenile onset,
    with   121
  Primary degenerative dementia of the
    Alzheimer type, senile onset, with
    121
Dementia   103(107)
  associated with alcoholism   133(134)
  associated with Axis III physical disorders
    or conditions, or whose etiology is
    unknown   162
  Multi-infarct   121(123)
  Other or unspecified psychoactive
    substance   162
  Presenile, not otherwise specified   123
  Primary degenerative, of the Alzheimer
    type   119(121)
  Senile, not otherwise specified   123
Dementias arising in the senium and
    presenium   119
  Multi-infarct dementia   121(123)
  Presenile dementia not otherwise
    specified   123
  Primary degenerative dementia of the
    Alzheimer type, presenile onset   121
  Primary degenerative dementia of the
    Alzheimer type, senile onset   121
  Senile dementia not otherwise
    specified   123
Dependence   166(167)
  Alcohol   173
  Amphetamine or similarly acting
    sympathomimetic   175
  Cannabis   176
  Cocaine   177
  Hallucinogen   179
  Inhalant   180
  Nicotine   181
  on combination of opioid and other
    nonalcoholic substances. See
    Polysubstance dependence   185
  on combination of substances, excluding
    opioids and alcohol. See
    Polysubstance dependence   185
  Opioid   182
  Phencyclidine (PCP) or similarly acting
    arylcyclohexylamine   183
  Polysubstance   185
  Psychoactive substance   166(167)

Psychoactive substance, not otherwise
    specified   185
  Sedative, hypnotic, or anxiolytic   184
Dependent personality disorder   353(354)
Depersonalization disorder   275(276)
Depersonalization neurosis. See
    Depersonalization disorder
    275(276)
Depressed mood. See Adjustment disorder
    with depressed mood   331
Depressive disorders   228
  Depressive neurosis. See Dysthymia
    230(232)
  Dysthymia   230(232)
  Major depression, single episode or
    recurrent   228(229)
  not otherwise specified   233
Depressive episode, Major   218(222)
Derealization. See Depersonalization
    disorder   275(276)
Developmental disorders   28
  Autistic disorder   38(38)
  Developmental arithmetic disorder
    41(42)
  Developmental articulation disorder
    44(45)
  Developmental coordination disorder
    48(49)
  Developmental expressive language
    disorder   45(47)
  Developmental expressive writing
    disorder   42(43)
  Developmental language disorder. See
    Developmental expressive language
    disorder   45(47) or Developmental
    receptive language disorder   47(48)
  Developmental reading disorder   43(44)
  Developmental receptive language
    disorder   47(48)
  Language and speech disorders   44
  Mental retardation   28(31)
  Motor skills disorder   48
  not otherwise specified   49
  Pervasive developmental disorder not
    otherwise specified   39
  Pervasive developmental disorders   33
  Specific developmental disorder not
    otherwise specified   49
  Specific developmental disorders   39
Deviation, Sexual. See Paraphilias
    279(281)
Diagnosis or condition deferred on Axis I
    363
Diagnosis deferred on Axis II   363
Disintegrative psychosis. See Pervasive
    developmental disorders   33
Disorganized type, Schizophrenia
    196(197)

Disruptive behavior disorders 49
  Attention-deficit hyperactivity disorder
    50(52)
  Conduct disorder 53(55)
  Oppositional defiant disorder 56(57)
Dissociative disorders 269
  Depersonalization disorder 275(276)
  Depersonalization neurosis. See
    Depersonalization disorder
    275(276)
  Multiple personality disorder 269(272)
  not otherwise specified 277
  Psychogenic amnesia 273(275)
  Psychogenic fugue 272(273)
Dream anxiety disorder (Nightmare
  disorder) 308(310)
Dyslexia. See Developmental reading
  disorder 43(44)
Dysmorphophobia. See Body dysmorphic
  disorder 255(256)
Dyspareunia (295)
Dyssomnias 298
  Hypersomnia disorders 302(303)
  Insomnia disorders 298(299)
  not otherwise specified 308
  Sleep-wake schedule disorder 305(307)
Dysthymia 230(232)
Dysthymic disorder. See Dysthymia
  230(232)

Eating Disorders 65
  Anorexia nervosa 65(67)
  Bulimia nervosa 67(68)
  not otherwise specified 71
  Pica 69(69)
  Rumination disorder of infancy 70(70)
Ego-dystonic homosexuality. See Sexual
  disorder not otherwise specified
  296
Ejaculation, Premature (295)
Elective mutism 88(89)
Elimination disorders 82
  Functional encopresis 82(83)
  Functional enuresis 84(85)
Encopresis, Functional 82(83)
Enuresis, Functional 84(85)
Erectile dysfunction. See Male erectile
  disorder (294)
Erotomanic type, Delusional (paranoid)
  disorder 199(202)
Exhibitionism 282(282)
Explosive disorder, Intermittent 321(322)
Expressive
  language disorder. See Developmental
    expressive language disorder 45(47)
  writing disorder. See Developmental
    expressive writing disorder 42(43)

Factitious disorders 315
  not otherwise specified 320
  with physical symptoms 316(318)
  with psychological symptoms 318(319)
Failure to thrive. See Reactive attachment
  disorder of infancy or early
  childhood 91(93)
Family circumstances, Other specified 361
Female sexual arousal disorder (294)
Fetishism 282(283)
Flashbacks. See Posthallucinogen
  perception disorder 147(148)
Folie à deux. See Induced psychotic
  disorder 210(211)
Frigidity. See Hypoactive sexual desire
  disorder (293), Female sexual arousal
  disorder (294), or Inhibited female
  orgasm (294)
Frotteurism 283(284)
Fugue state. See Psychogenic fugue
  272(273)
Functional
  dyspareunia. See Dyspareunia (295)
  encopresis 82(83)
  enuresis 84(85)
  vaginismus. See Vaginismus (295)

Gambling. See Pathological gambling
  324(325)
Ganser's syndrome. See Dissociative
  disorder not otherwise specified
  277
Gender identity disorders 71
  not otherwise specified 77
  of adolescence or adulthood,
    nontranssexual type (GIDAANT)
    76(77)
  of childhood 71(73)
  Transsexualism 74(76)
Generalized anxiety disorder 251(252)
Gilles de la Tourette's syndrome. See
  Tourette's disorder 79(80)
Grandiose type, Delusional (paranoid)
  disorder 200(203)
Group type, Conduct disorder 56

Hallucinogen use disorders, abuse/
  dependence 179
Hallucinogen-induced organic mental
  disorders 144
  affective disorder. See Hallucinogen
    mood disorder 146(147)
  delusional disorder 146(146)
  hallucinosis 144(145)
  mood disorder 146(147)
  Posthallucinogen perception disorder
    147(148)

Hallucinosis
  Alcohol   131(132)
  Hallucinogen   144(145)
  Organic, associated with Axis III disorders
    or conditions, or whose etiology is
    unknown   162
  Other or unspecified psychoactive
    substance   162
Hebephrenic schizophrenia. *See*
    Schizophrenia, disorganized type
    196(197)
Heller's syndrome. *See* Pervasive
    developmental disorders   33
Histrionic personality disorder   348(349)
Homosexuality, Ego-dystonic. *See* Sexual
    disorder not otherwise specified
    296
Hospitalism. *See* Reactive attachment
    disorder of infancy or early
    childhood   91(93)
Hyperactive child syndrome. *See* Attention-
    deficit hyperactivity disorder   50(52)
Hyperactivity, Attention-deficit, disorder
    50(52)
Hyperkinesis with developmental delay. *See*
    Attention-deficit hyperactivity
    disorder   50(52)
Hypersomnia disorders   302(303)
  Primary   305(305)
  related to a known organic factor
    303(304)
  related to another mental disorder
    (nonorganic)   303(303)
Hypnotic. *See* Sedative, hypnotic, or
    anxiolytic
Hypoactive sexual desire disorder (293)
Hypochondriacal neurosis. *See*
    Hypochondriasis   259(261)
Hypochondriasis   259(261)
Hypomanic disorder. *See* Bipolar disorder
    not otherwise specified   228
Hypomanic episode   218
Hypoxyphilia. *See* Sexual masochism
    286(287)
Hysterical neurosis
  conversion type. *See* Conversion
    disorder   257(259)
  dissociative type. *See* Dissociative
    disorders   269
Hysterical personality. *See* Histrionic
    personality disorder   348(349)
Hysterical psychosis. *See* Brief reactive
    psychosis   205(206) or Factitious
    disorder with psychological
    symptoms   318(319)

Identity disorder   89(90)
Identity disorders, Gender   71

Immature personality. *See* Personality
    disorder not otherwise specified
    358
Impulse control disorders not elsewhere
    classified   321
  Intermittent explosive disorder   321(322)
  Kleptomania   322(323)
  Pathological gambling   324(325)
  Pyromania   325(326)
  Trichotillomania   326(328)
Impulse control disorder not otherwise
    specified   328
Impulsive personality. *See* Personality
    disorder not otherwise specified
    358
Induced psychotic disorder   210(211)
Infancy, childhood, or adolescence,
    Disorders of. *See* Disorders usually
    first evident in infancy, childhood, or
    adolescence   27
Infancy, Reactive attachment disorder. *See*
    Reactive attachment disorder of
    infancy or early childhood   91(93)
Infancy, Rumination disorder of   70(70)
Infantile autism. *See* Autistic disorder
    38(38)
Inhalant use disorders, abuse/
    dependence   180
Inhalant-induced organic mental disorder
    148
  intoxication   148(149)
Inhibited
  female orgasm   (294)
  male orgasm   (295)
  sexual desire. *See* Hypoactive sexual
    desire disorder (293) or Sexual
    aversion disorder (293)
  sexual excitement. *See* Female sexual
    arousal disorder (294) or Male
    erectile disorder (294)
Insomnia disorders   298(299)
  Primary   301(301)
  related to a known organic factor
    300(301)
  related to another mental disorder
    (nonorganic)   300(300)
Interpersonal problem, Other   361
Intermittent explosive disorder   321(322)
Intoxication   116(117)
  Alcohol   127(128)
  Alcohol idiosyncratic   128(129)
  Amphetamine or similarly acting
    sympathomimetic   134(135)
  Caffeine   138(139)
  Cocaine   141(142)
  Hallucinogen. *See* Hallucinogen
    hallucinosis   144(145)
  Inhalant   148(149)

Intoxication, continued
Opioid 151(152)
Other or unspecified substance 162
Phencyclidine (PCP) or similarly acting arylcyclohexylamine 154(155)
Sedative, hypnotic, or anxiolytic 158(159)
Involutional melancholia. *See* Major depressive episode, melancholic type 218(224)
Isolated explosive disorder. *See* Impulse control disorder not otherwise specified 328

Jealous type, Delusional (paranoid) disorder 200(203)

Kanner's syndrome. *See* Autistic disorder 38(38)
Kleptomania 322(323)
Klismaphilia. *See* Paraphilia not otherwise specified 290
Korsakoff's syndrome. *See* Alcohol amnestic disorder 133(133)

LSD. *See* Hallucinogen
Labile personality disorder. *See* Cyclothymia 226(227)
Language and speech disorders (developmental) 44
Developmental articulation disorder 44(45)
Developmental expressive language disorder 45(47)
Developmental receptive language disorder 47(48)
Late luteal phase dysphoric disorder 367(369)
Latent schizophrenia. *See* Schizotypal personality disorder 340(341)

Major affective disorders. *See* Bipolar disorder 225(225) or Major depression 228(229)
Major depression, single episode or recurrent 228(229)
Major depressive episode 218(222)
Male erectile disorder (294)
Malingering 360
Manic-depression. *See* Bipolar disorder 225(225)
Manic episode 214(217)
Marijuana. *See* Cannabis
Marital problem 360
Masochism, Sexual 286(287)
Masochistic personality. *See* Self-defeating personality disorder 371(373)

Melancholia. *See* Major depressive episode, melancholic type 218(224)
Mental retardation 28(31)
Mild 32
Moderate 32
Profound 33
Severe 33
Unspecified 33
Mild mental retardation 32
Minimal brain dysfunction. *See* Attention-deficit hyperactivity disorder 50(52)
Mixed, Bipolar disorder 225(225)
Mixed disturbance of emotions and conduct. *See* Adjustment disorder with mixed disturbance of emotions and conduct 331
Mixed emotional features. *See* Adjustment disorder with mixed emotional features 331
Mixed or other personality disorder, Atypical. *See* Personality disorder not otherwise specified 358
Mixed or unspecified substance abuse, Other. *See* Psychoactive substance abuse not otherwise specified 185
Mixed or unspecified substance-induced mental disorder. *See* Other or unspecified psychoactive substance organic mental disorder not otherwise specified 162
Mixed specific developmental disorder. *See* Specific developmental disorders 39
Moderate mental retardation 32
Mood disorders 213
Bipolar disorder 225(225)
Bipolar disorder not otherwise specified 228
Cyclothymia 226(227)
Depressive disorder not otherwise specified 233
Dysthymia 230(232)
Major depression, single episode or recurrent 228(229)
Seasonal pattern (224)
Motor, chronic, or vocal tic disorder. *See* Chronic motor or vocal tic disorder 81(81)
Motor skills disorder 48
Developmental coordination disorder 48(49)
Movement disorders. *See* Tic disorders 78 or Stereotypy/habit disorder 93(95)
Multi-infarct dementia 121(123)
Multiple personality disorder 269(272)
Munchausen syndrome. *See* Factitious disorder with physical symptoms 316(318)

Mutism, Elective   88(89)

Narcissistic personality disorder   349(351)
Necrophilia. *See* Paraphilia not otherwise
    specified   290
Neurasthenia. *See* Dysthymia   230(232)
Neurosis
    Anxiety. *See* Panic disorder   235(237) or
        Generalized anxiety disorder
        251(252)
    Depersonalization. *See* Depersonalization
        disorder   275(276)
    Depressive. *See* Dysthymia   230(232),
        Major depression   228(229) or
        Adjustment disorder with depressed
        mood   331
    Hypochondriacal. *See* Hypochondriasis
        259(261)
    Hysterical, conversion type. *See*
        Conversion disorder   257(259) or
        Somatoform pain disorder   264(266)
    Hysterical, dissociative type. *See*
        Dissociative disorders   269 or
        Sleepwalking disorder   311(313)
    Neurasthenic. *See* Dysthymia   230(232)
    Obsessive compulsive. *See* Obsessive
        compulsive disorder   245(247)
    Phobic. *See* Simple phobia   243(244),
        Social phobia   241(243), or
        Separation anxiety disorder   58(60)
Nicotine dependence   181
Nicotine-induced organic mental disorder
    150
    withdrawal   150(151)
Nightmare disorder. *See* Dream anxiety
        disorder   308(310)
No diagnosis or condition on Axis I   363
No diagnosis on Axis II   363
Noncompliance with medical treatment
    360
Nonpsychotic mental disorder. *See*
        Unspecified mental disorder
        (nonpsychotic)   363

Obsessive compulsive disorder   245(247)
Obsessive compulsive personality
        disorder   354(356)
Occupational problem   361
Opioid use disorders, abuse/dependence
    182
Opioid-induced organic mental disorders
    151
    intoxication   151(152)
    withdrawal   152(153)
Oppositional defiant disorder   56(57)
Organic affective syndrome. *See* Organic
        mood syndrome   111(112)
Organic anxiety

    disorder   163
    syndrome   113(114)
Organic brain syndromes. *See* Organic
        mental syndromes   100
Organic delusional
    disorder   162
    syndrome   109(110)
Organic hallucinosis   110(111)
    associated with Axis III disorders or
        conditions, or whose etiology is
        unknown   162
Organic mental disorders   119
    associated with Axis III physical disorders
        or conditions, or whose etiology in
        unknown   162
    Dementias arising in the senium and
        presenium   119
    not otherwise specified   163
    Psychoactive substance-induced   123
Organic mental syndromes   100
    Amnestic syndrome   108(109)
    Delirium   100(103)
    Dementia   103(107)
    Intoxication   116(117)
    Organic affective syndrome. *See* Organic
        mood syndrome   111(112)
    Organic anxiety syndrome   113(114)
    Organic delusional syndrome   109(110)
    Organic hallucinosis   110(111)
    Organic mood syndrome   111(112)
    Organic personality syndrome   114(115)
    not otherwise specified   119
    Withdrawal   118(118)
Organic mood
    disorder   162
    syndrome   111(112)
Organic personality
    disorder   163
    syndrome   114(115)
Orgasm disorders   294
    Inhibited female orgasm   (294)
    Inhibited male orgasm   (295)
    Premature ejaculation   (295)
Other developmental disorders   49
    Developmental disorder not otherwise
        specified   49
Other disorders of infancy, childhood, or
        adolescence   88
    Elective mutism   88(89)
    Identity disorder   89(90)
    Reactive attachment disorder of infancy
        or early childhood   91(93)
    Stereotypy/habit disorder   93(95)
    Undifferentiated attention-deficit
        disorder   95
Other or unspecified psychoactive
        substance-induced organic mental
        disorders   162

Other interpersonal problem   361
Other, mixed or unspecified substance abuse. *See* Psychoactive substance abuse not otherwise specified   185
Other psychosexual disorders. *See* Sexual disorder not otherwise specified   296
Other sexual disorders   296
  Sexual disorder not otherwise specified   296
Other specified family circumstances   361
Other specified substance dependence. *See* Psychoactive substance dependence not otherwise specified   185
Overanxious disorder   63(64)

Pain, Somatoform. *See* Somatoform pain disorder   264(266)
Panic disorder   235(237)
    with agoraphobia   235(238)
    without agoraphobia   235(239)
Paranoia. *See* Delusional (paranoid) disorder   199(202)
Paranoid disorder. *See* Delusional (paranoid) disorder   199(202)
  Acute. *See* Psychotic disorder not otherwise specified   211
  Atypical. *See* Psychotic disorder not otherwise specified   211
  Shared. *See* Induced psychotic disorder   210(211)
Paranoid personality disorder   337(339)
Paranoid type, Schizophrenia   197(197)
Paraphilias   279(281)
  Exhibitionism   282(282)
  Fetishism   282(283)
  Frotteurism   283(284)
  not otherwise specified   290
  Pedophilia   284(285)
  Sexual masochism   286(287)
  Sexual sadism   287(288)
  Transvestic fetishism   288(289)
  Voyeurism   289(290)
Parasomnias   308
  Dream anxiety disorder (Nightmare disorder)   308(310)
  not otherwise specified   313
  Sleep terror disorder   310(311)
  Sleepwalking disorder   311(313)
Partialism. *See* Paraphilia not otherwise specified   290
Parent-child problem   361
Passive aggressive personality disorder   356(357)
Pathologic intoxication. *See* Idiosyncratic alcohol intoxication   128(129)
Pathological gambling   324(325)

Pavor Nocturnus. *See* Sleep terror disorder   310(311)
Pedophilia   284(285)
Persecutory type, Delusional (paranoid) disorder   200(202)
Personality disorders   335
  Antisocial   342(344)
  Avoidant   351(352)
  Borderline   346(347)
  Dependent   353(354)
  Histrionic   348(349)
  Multiple   269(272)
  Narcissistic   349(351)
  not otherwise specified   358
  Obsessive compulsive   354(356)
  Organic   163
  Paranoid   337(339)
  Passive aggressive   356(357)
  Sadistic   369(371)
  Schizoid   339(340)
  Schizotypal   340(341)
  Self-defeating   371(373)
Pervasive developmental disorders   33
  Autistic disorder   38(38)
  not otherwise specified   39
Phase of life problem or other life circumstance problem   361
Phencyclidine (PCP) or similarly acting arylcyclohexylamine use disorders, abuse/dependence   183
Phencyclidine (PCP) or similarly acting arylcyclohexylamine-induced organic mental disorders   154
  delirium   155(156)
  delusional disorder   156(156)
  intoxication   154(155)
  mixed organic mental disorder. *See* Phencyclidine (PCP) or similarly acting arlycyclohexylamine-induced organic mental disorder not otherwise specified   157(158)
  mood disorder   156(157)
  organic mental disorder not otherwise specified   157(158)
Phobia
  Simple   243(244)
  Social   241(243)
Physical complaints. *See* Adjustment disorder with physical complaints   331
Physical condition, Psychological factors affecting   333(334)
Pica   69(69)
Pick's disease. *See* Presenile dementia not otherwise specified   123
Polysubstance dependence   185
Post-traumatic stress disorder   247(250)

Posthallucinogen perception disorder 147(148)

Premature ejaculation   (295)

Premenstrual syndrome. See Late luteal phase dysphoric disorder   367(369)

Presenile dementia. See Primary degenerative dementia of the Alzheimer type, presenile onset 121 or Presenile dementia not otherwise specified   123

Primary degenerative dementia of the Alzheimer type   119(121)

Primary hypersomnia   305(305)

Primary insomnia   301(301)

Profound mental retardation   33

Pseudocyesis. See Conversion disorder 257(259)

Pseudodementia. See Major depressive episode   218(222) or Dementia 103(107)

Pseudoneurotic schizophrenia. See Schizotypal personality disorder 340(341)

Pseudopsychosis. See Factitious disorder with psychological symptoms 318(319)

Psychoactive substance abuse   169(169)

Psychoactive substance abuse not otherwise specified   185

Psychoactive substance dependence 166(167)

Psychoactive substance dependence not otherwise specified   185

Psychoactive substance use disorders (by substance)   165
Alcohol   173
Amphetamine or similarly acting sympathomimetic   175
Cannabis   176
Cocaine   177
Hallucinogen   179
Inhalant   180
Nicotine   181
Opioid   182
Phencyclidine (PCP) or similarly acting arylcyclohexylamine   183
Sedative, hypnotic, or anxiolytic   184

Psychoactive substance-induced organic mental disorders (by substance)   123
Alcohol   127
Amphetamine or similarly acting sympathomimetic   134
Caffeine   138
Cannabis   139
Cocaine   141
Hallucinogen   144
Inhalant   148
Nicotine   150

Opioid   151
Other or unspecific psychoactive substance   162
Phencyclidine (PCP) or similarly acting arylcyclohexylamine   154
Sedative, hypnotic, or anxiolytic   158

Psychogenic
amnesia   273(275)
fugue   272(273)
pain disorder. See Somatoform pain disorder   264(266)

Psychological factors affecting physical condition   333(334)

Psychosexual dysfunctions. See Sexual dysfunctions   290

Psychosexual disorder not elsewhere classified. See Sexual disorder not elsewhere specified   296

Psychosis with Cerebral Arteriosclerosis. See Multi-infarct dementia   121(123)

Psychotic depressive reaction. See Major depression   228(229)

Psychotic disorders
Brief reactive psychosis   205(206)
Delusional (paranoid) disorder   199(202)
Induced psychotic disorder   210(211)
Major depressive episode with psychotic features   (223)
Manic episode with psychotic features (218)
not otherwise specified   211
Organic delusional disorder   162
Organic hallucinosis   162
Schizoaffecive disorder   208(210)
Schizophrenia   187(194)
Schizophreniform disorder   207(208)

Psychotic disorders not elsewhere classified   205
Brief reactive psychosis   205(206)
Induced psychotic disorder   210(211)
Psychotic disorder not otherwise specified   211
Schizoaffective disorder   208(210)
Schizophreniform disorder   207(208)

Pyromania   325(326)

Rapid cycling. See Bipolar disorder, mixed 225(225)

Reactive attachment disorder of infancy or early childhood   91(93)

Reading disorder. See Developmental reading disorder   43(44)

Receptive language disorder. See Developmental receptive language disorder   47(48)

Residual type, Schizophrenia   198(198)

Retardation, Mental   28(31)

Rum fits. *See* Alcohol withdrawal delirium 131(131) or Uncomplicated alcohol withdrawal   129(130)
Rumination disorder of infancy   70(70)

Sadistic personality disorder   369(371)
Scatalogia, Telephone. *See* Paraphilia not otherwise specified   290
Schizoaffective disorder   208(210)
Schizoid disorder of childhood or adolescence. *See* Pervasive development disorders   33
Schizoid personality disorder   339(340)
Schizophrenia   187(194)
   catatonic type   196(196)
   disorganized type   196(197)
   paranoid type   197(197)
   residual type   198(198)
   undifferentiated type   198(198)
Schizophrenic disorders. *See* Schizophrenia   187(194)
Schizophreniform disorder   207(208)
Schizotypal personality disorder   340(341)
School phobia. *See* Separation anxiety disorder   58(60)
Seasonal depression. *See* Major depression, seasonal pattern   (224)
Seasonal mood disorders. *See* Mood disorders, seasonal pattern   (224)
Sedative, hypnotic, or anxiolytic use disorders, abuse/dependence   184
Sedative, hypnotic, or anxiolytic-induced organic mental disorders   158
   amnestic disorder   161(161)
   intoxication   158(159)
   Uncomplicated, withdrawal   159(160)
   withdrawal delirium   160(161)
Senile dementia. *See* Primary degenerative dementia of the Alzheimer type, senile onset   121 or Senile dementia not otherwise specified   123
Separation anxiety disorder   58(60)
Severe mental retardation   33
Sexual arousal disorders   294
   Female sexual arousal disorder (294)
   Male sexual arousal disorder. *See* Male erectile disorder   (294)
Sexual aversion disorder   (293)
Sexual desire disorders   293
   Hypoactive sexual desire disorder   (293)
   Sexual aversion disorder   (293)
Sexual deviations. *See* Paraphilias   279(281)
Sexual disorders   279
   not otherwise specified   296
   Paraphilias   279(281)
   Sexual dysfunctions   290
Sexual dysfunctions   290

not otherwise specified   295
Orgasm disorders   294
Sexual arousal disorders   294
Sexual desire disorders   293
Sexual pain disorders   295
Sexual masochism   286(287)
Sexual pain disorders   295
   Dyspareunia   (295)
   Vaginismus   (295)
Sexual sadism   287(288)
Shared paranoid disorder. *See* Induced psychotic disorder   210(211)
Simple phobia   243(244)
Simple schizophrenia. *See* Schizotypal personality disorder   340(341)
Sleep disorders   297
   Dyssomnias   298
   Parasomnias   308
Sleep terror disorder   310(311)
Sleep-wake schedule disorder   305(307)
Sleepwalking disorder   311(313)
Social phobia   241(243)
Socialized conduct disorder, Aggressive/ Nonaggressive. *See* Conduct disorder, group type   56
Sociopathic personality. *See* Antisocial personality disorder   342(344)
Solitary aggressive type, conduct disorder. *See* Conduct disorder, solitary aggressive type   56
Somatic type, Delusional (paranoid) disorder   200(203)
Somatization disorder   261(263)
Somatoform disorders   255
   Body dysmorphic disorder   255(256)
   Conversion disorder   257(259)
   Hypochondriasis   259(261)
   not otherwise specified   267
   Somatization disorder   261(263)
   Somatoform pain disorder   264(266)
   Undifferentiated somatoform disorder   266(267)
Somatoform pain disorder   264(266)
Somnambulism. *See* Sleepwalking disorder   311(313)
Specific developmental disorders   39
   Academic skills disorder   41
   Language and speech disorders   44
   Motor skills disorder   48
   not otherwise specified   49
Specific phobias. *See* Simple phobia   243(244)
Speech disorders, developmental. *See* Language and speech disorders (developmental)   44
Speech disorders not elsewhere classified   85
   Cluttering   85(86)
   Stuttering   86(88)

Speed. *See* Amphetamine or other similarly acting sympathomimetic
Stereotyped movement disorders. *See* Stereotypy/habit disorder   93(95) or Tic disorders   78
Stereotypy/habit disorder   93(95)
Stress disorder, Post-traumatic. *See* Post-traumatic stress disorder   247(250)
Stuttering   86(88)
Substance use. *See* Psychoactive substance use
Substance-induced organic mental disorders. *See* Psychoactive substance-induced organic mental disorders   123
Symbiotic psychosis. *See* Pervasive developmental disorders   33
Sympathomimetic. *See* Amphetamine or similarly acting sympathomimetic

THC. *See* Cannabis
Tic disorders   78
    Chronic motor or vocal tic disorder   81(81)
    not otherwise specified   82
    Tourette's disorder   79(80)
    Transient tic disorder   81(82)
Tobacco. *See* Nicotine
Tourette's disorder   79(80)
Transient tic disorder   81(82)
Transsexualism   74(76)
Transvestic fetishism   288(289)
Transvestism. *See* Transvestic fetishism   288(289)
Traumatic neurosis. *See* Post-traumatic stress disorder   247(250)
Trichotillomania   326(328)

Uncomplicated alcohol withdrawal   129(130)
Uncomplicated bereavement   361
Uncomplicated sedative, hypnotic, or anxiolytic withdrawal   159(160)
Undersocialized conduct disorder. *See* Conduct disorder   53(55)
    Aggressive type. *See* Conduct disorder, solitary aggressive type   56

Nonaggressive type. *See* Conduct disorder, undifferentiated type   56
Undifferentiated attention-deficit disorder   95
Undifferentiated somatoform disorder   266(267)
Undifferentiated type, Schizophrenia   198(198)
Unspecified mental disorder (nonpsychotic)   363
Unspecified mental retardation   33
Unspecified substance dependence. *See* Psychoactive substance dependence not otherwise specified   185
Urophilia. *See* Paraphilia not otherwise specified   290

Vaginismus   (295)
Vocal, Chronic motor or, tic disorder. *See* Chronic motor or vocal tic disorder   81(81)
Voyeurism   289(290)

Withdrawal. *See* Adjustment disorder with withdrawal   331
Withdrawal   118(118)
    Alcohol, Uncomplicated   129(130)
    Amphetamine or similarly acting sympathomimetic   136(136)
    Cocaine   142(142)
    Nicotine   150(151)
    Opioid   152(153)
    Other or unspecified psychoactive substance   162
    Sedative, hypnotic, or anxiolytic, Uncomplicated   159(160)
Withdrawal delirum
    Alcohol   131(131)
    Sedative, hypnotic, or anxiolytic   160(161)
Work inhibition. *See* Adjustment disorder with work (or academic) inhibition   331
Writing disorder. *See* Developmental expressive writing disorder   42(43)

Zoophilia. *See* Paraphilia not otherwise specified   290